KARL MARX
FREDERICK ENGELS
COLLECTED WORKS
VOLUME
18

KARL MARX
FREDERICK ENGELS

COLLECTED
WORKS

INTERNATIONAL PUBLISHERS

NEW YORK

KARL MARX
FREDERICK ENGELS

Volume
18

MARX AND ENGELS: 1857-62

INTERNATIONAL PUBLISHERS

NEW YORK

This volume has been prepared jointly by Lawrence & Wishart Ltd., London, International Publishers Co. Inc., New York, and Progress Publishers, Moscow, in collaboration with the Institute of Marxism-Leninism, Moscow.

Editorial commissions:

GREAT BRITAIN: Jack Cohen, Maurice Cornforth, E. J. Hobsbawm, Nicholas Jacobs, Martin Milligan, Ernst Wangermann.
USA: James S. Allen, Louis Diskin, Philip S. Foner, Dirk J. Struik, William W. Weinstone.
USSR: for Progress Publishers—N. P. Karmanova, V. I. Neznanov, V. N. Sedikh, M. K. Shcheglova; for the Institute of Marxism-Leninism— P. N. Fedoseyev, L. I. Golman, A. I. Malysh, M. P. Mchedlov, A. G. Yegorov.

Library of Congress Cataloging in Publication Data

Marx, Karl, 1818-1883.

Karl Marx, Frederick Engels: collected works.

1. Socialism—Collected works. 2. Economics— Collected works. I. Engels, Friedrich, 1820-1895. Works. English. 1975. II. Title.
HX 39.5. A 16 1975   335.4   73-84671
ISBN 0-7178-0518-2 (v. 18)

Printed in the Union of Soviet Socialist Republics

Contents

FROM THE PREPARATORY MATERIALS
FOR THE ARTICLES
IN *THE NEW AMERICAN CYCLOPAEDIA*

FREDERICK ENGELS
ARTICLES FOR THE *ALLGEMEINE MILITÄR-ZEITUNG* AND *THE VOLUNTEER JOURNAL, FOR LANCASHIRE AND CHESHIRE*

NOTES AND INDEXES

ILLUSTRATIONS

TRANSLATORS:

HENRY MINS: An Inspection of English Volunteers
PETER and BETTY ROSS: To the Editor of the
    Allgemeine Militär-Zeitung
BARRIE SELMAN: Summary of John W. Kaye's *History of
    the War in Afghanistan;* Excerpts from the Article
    "Blum" Published in *Meyer's Conversations-Lexicon;*
    Excerpts Made for the Article "Bourrienne"; Ex-
    cerpts from the Article "Bülow" Published in
    Meyer's Conversations-Lexicon

Preface

Volume 18 of the *Collected Works* of Karl Marx and Frederick Engels contains mainly military and military-historical works written between 1857 and 1862. It includes a series of articles written by Marx and Engels between July 1857 and November 1860 for *The New American Cyclopaedia,* and the preparatory materials for some of them. A separate section is devoted to articles by Engels for military periodicals, namely the British weekly *The Volunteer Journal, for Lancashire and Cheshire* and the German weekly *Allgemeine Militär-Zeitung* (August 1860 to August 1862).

Marx's and Engels' contributions to *The New American Cyclopaedia* form a notable page in the history of their literary output. From their letters, notebooks and from the preparatory materials for some of the articles it is clear that they took their work for this publication very seriously. As required by such works of reference, their essays, articles and shorter items are concise, factual and clear. Despite the demand of the editors that the contributors refrain from political judgments, Marx and Engels managed even in these articles to express their opinion on social development and historical events, to expound dialectical-materialist views on them, and to evaluate the subjects of their contributions from a revolutionary socialist position.

Most of the articles for the *Cyclopaedia* were written by Engels, although Marx was the official contributor. Engels undertook the bulk of the work in order to leave Marx free for his studies in political economy, the elaboration of which they both regarded at the time as the paramount theoretical task for the working-class movement. By helping to write these articles Engels also sought to alleviate the financial difficulties his friend's family continued to experience. However, many articles were the fruit of close collaboration between Marx and Engels, which often amounted to co-authorship.

It should be remembered that the work of Marx and Engels for the *Cyclopaedia* and of Engels for the military periodicals ran parallel with their other theoretical and practical activities, and with their efforts to unite the proletarian revolutionaries, which became particularly intense at the end of the 1850s, at the time of the revival of the democratic and proletarian movements in Europe and the United States. The essays and articles for the *Cyclopaedia* and the military periodicals were written concurrently with Marx's economic manuscripts and other works (*A Contribution to the Critique of Political Economy* and *Herr Vogt*), with Engels' pamphlets (*Po and Rhine* and *Savoy, Nice and the Rhine*), and with their articles on topical questions for the European and American press (the London newspaper *Das Volk*, the Viennese *Die Presse* and the *New-York Daily Tribune*). A complete picture of the work of Marx and Engels during this period can therefore only be obtained by collating the contents of this volume with those of volumes 16, 17, 19, 29 and 30, and also with the relevant volumes of their correspondence (40 and 41).

* * *

A central place in the volume is held by the writings of Engels on military subjects, like "Army", "Artillery", "Cavalry," "Fortification", "Infantry", "Navy" and "The History of the Rifle". These works, particularly the articles for *The New American Cyclopaedia*, deal with a wide range of military problems and analyse many important events in military history, from the campaigns of ancient times to the wars of Engels' own day. They consider, mainly from the historical standpoint, the problems of the formation, structure and equipping of armies, their recruitment and training, the control of the armed forces, strategy and tactics, the organisation and use of the different fighting services, the various aspects of military engineering, permanent and field fortifications, methods of siege and defence of fortresses, logistical problems and encamping.

The major works are supplemented and illustrated in concrete terms by shorter articles. Some of these, like "Actium", "Albuera", "Alma", "Aspern", "Borodino" and "Bidassoa", analyse specific battles. Others, like "Amusette", "Ammunition", "Bonnet", "Case Shot" and "Bridge-Head", were written by Engels to explain specific military and military-technical terms. The articles "Attack", "Battle" and "Campaign" contain important theoretical statements on the forms and methods of conducting battle, the use of various battle formations and the employment of reserves.

The volume reflects an important stage in the elaboration of the Marxist theory of war and the army. Particularly after the revolution of 1848-49, Engels had always shown a lively interest in military affairs. He had responded in the press to all the key military events, and in the early 1850s began a systematic study of the various military sciences, creatively absorbing the legacy of the military theorists of the past, and contemporary writings. Marx wrote to Ferdinand Lassalle on February 25, 1859 that, after being in action with the Baden-Palatinate insurgent army in 1849, Engels had "made military matters his special study" (see present edition, Vol. 40). And Lenin called Engels "the great expert on this subject" (*Collected Works*, Vol. 8, p. 565).

In his earlier works Engels used specific examples to show how the condition of the army and the outcome of military operations are influenced by the level of socio-economic development and the political system of the country in question, how strategy depends on the policy of the ruling classes and on the aims which they pursue in war. He also set down his thoughts about various types of war, defined what he meant by revolutionary, liberation wars, and pointed out many specific features of the tactics of armed uprising and revolutionary armies. The works included in the present volume, particularly the more general *New American Cyclopaedia* articles, systematise and concretise Engels' views on armed struggle and war, and back them up with new conclusions and generalisations. For the first time he applied dialectical-materialist analysis not only to separate periods or episodes in military history but to the evolution of warfare as a whole, on land and sea, including the history of the different fighting services.

In these works Engels cast light on the historical conditions giving rise to wars, and especially to organised armed forces, which he associated with the epoch of the formation of class society and the state. On the basis of a vast amount of factual material he traced the main stages and specific features of the development of armies and noted the changes in their organisation, strategy and tactics through various historical periods. He showed the determining influence of the economic basis and class structure of society on the organisation, equipping and composition of armies, on the methods of conducting armed struggle and on the development of the art of war. His work in this field was based not on isolated examples but on copious factual material covering the main stages of world history. "More graphically than anything else," Marx wrote to Engels on September 25, 1857, after reading his article "Army", "the history of the *army* demonstrates the rightness of our views as to the connection between the productive forces and social relations" (see present edition, Vol. 40).

The impact of the productive forces on warfare, as Engels showed, manifested itself primarily in the role played in its evolution by changes in the technical means of armed struggle. Engels attached exceptional importance to the technical aspect of warfare. Besides the many pages devoted to the history of military technology in the above-mentioned works, he wrote several shorter items on specific types of weapons ("Arquebuse", "Bayonet", "Carabine", "Carronade", "Catapult", etc.), and on various offensive, defensive and accessory means of armed struggle ("Bastion", "Battery", "Blindage", "Bomb-Proof", "Bomb Vessel", "Bridge, Military", etc.). His numerous examples revealed the revolutionising effect of the major technical discoveries—the invention of gunpowder, the use and improvement of fire-arms, the introduction of the bayonet, which made it possible to combine thrust weapons with the fire-arms, the progress in artillery and military engineering, the use of steam power in navies, etc.—on the development of armed forces and the art of war. The dependence of military tactics on military technology, the emergence of new tactical forms of military operations as a result of the spread of new types of mass weapons, Engels argued in his articles, reflects the determining influence of social production on social life, including the military sphere.

However, Engels did not reduce the cause of the evolution of warfare and the art of war exclusively to technological progress. He pointed to other, primarily social and political, factors that influenced this evolution. Engels overcame the tendency in the military historical writings of his day to isolate military history from that of civil life and to underrate the impact of social conditions on military organisation. He was thus virtually the first to examine the history of warfare on the basis of the Marxist theory of socio-economic formations. He demonstrated that the armed forces of every society were the product of a certain social system, that every social formation tended to have a corresponding type of army and, to some degree, a corresponding way of waging war. Engels established the fact that ever since the army—"the organised body of armed men which a state maintains for purposes of offensive or defensive war" (p. 85)—arose in slave-owning society, its organisation, condition and fighting qualities, as well as its armaments, had been determined by the socio-political system that engendered it, by the class environment from which it was recruited. The specific features of every social formation had left their mark on the social composition of the army, its level of training, and the psychology and morale of its soldiers.

Nor did the conduct of warfare remain static within the framework of a given social formation. Within these historical limits, Engels noted, armies and the art of war evolved in a way that reflected the internal dynamic of the given social system. The armies of ancient Greece and Macedonia with their phalanx tactics were superseded by the Roman army with its more advanced system of legions. This in turn fell into decline owing to the growing contradictions in slave society, its profound crisis, causing a deterioration of the elements composing the army, which "very soon reacted upon its armament and tactics" (pp. 102-03). The decay of the feudal social system led to the disintegration of the feudal military system, to the disappearance of the no longer battleworthy mounted knights in armour. As capitalism arose, Engels noted, the armed forces underwent a significant evolution, from mercenary troops to mass armies recruited on the basis of universal conscription, an evolution ultimately conditioned by the needs of bourgeois society.

Engels held that a key role in the development of warfare was played by revolutionary periods, which gave a fresh impetus to progress in the military sphere. Moreover, the initiators and carriers of these progressive changes were, he pointed out, the revolutionary classes fighting the decaying forces of society. Engels illustrated this law by the history of the bourgeois revolutions of the sixteenth and seventeenth centuries, and particularly by the French Revolution of 1789-94. "The war consequent upon the rebellion of the Netherlands," he wrote about the Netherlands revolution of the late sixteenth century, "was of great influence on the formation of armies" (p. 107). In his article "Cavalry" he noted the substantial improvement in this service and in its tactics during the revolution and civil war in England in the mid-seventeenth century (p. 300). He linked the emergence of the new, more complex battle formation (extended order combined with columns as opposed to the linear tactics of the armies of the feudal-absolutist states of the eighteenth century), and other important changes in warfare (more effective use of artillery, the bivouac system of stationing troops, who were thus freed of unwieldy baggage trains, camp equipment, etc.), with the French Revolution of the eighteenth century and partly with the war of England's North-American colonies for independence. When the war of the coalition of counter-revolutionary states against the French Republic began, he wrote, a new tactical system was called for. "The American revolution had shown the advantage to be gained, with undisciplined troops, from extended order and skirmishing fire. The French adopted it, and supported the skirmishers by deep columns, in which a little disorder was less objectionable, so long as the mass remained well together. In this formation, they launched their superior numbers against the enemy, and were generally successful" (pp. 113-14).

Engels stressed the point that revolutionary wars brought out the military creativity of the masses, the direct participants in the armed struggle. To cope with the new conditions they sought, and found, new forms of combat and tactical formation, which were later formalised in the organisation and regulations of armies and reduced to a system by military leaders, generals, and so on.

Engels attached great importance to the struggle of oppressed peoples against foreign invaders and pointed out that it was often interwoven with action by the working masses against their own exploiting classes. Ever since the Middle Ages this struggle had greatly influenced the conduct of warfare, bringing about progressive changes in it. For example, the revival of infantry in the fourteenth and fifteenth centuries, after its long decline, when the battlefields were dominated by mounted knights in armour, was the work of the freedom-loving Swiss peasants, who defended their country's independence against incursions by Austrian and Burgundian feudal forces, and also of the urban artisans of Flanders, who resisted the encroachments of the French nobility upon the Flemish lands. "The French chivalry succumbed as much to the weavers and fullers, the goldsmiths and tanners of the Belgian cities, as the Burgundian and Austrian nobility to the peasants and cowherds of Switzerland" (p. 350). In modern times, too, wars of national liberation played an extremely important role in military history, as seen in the resistance of some of the peoples of Europe to the domination of Napoleonic France, the war of the Hungarians against Austrian oppression in 1848-49, and so on. Engels touched upon these wars not only in his major works but also in a number of short articles for the *Cyclopaedia* ("Albuera", "Buda" and others).

Besides giving a Marxist interpretation of the role of the masses in history with reference to the military sphere, Engels set forth scientific principles for assessing the activities of outstanding generals, military reformers, engineers and inventors, and acknowledged their contribution to the development of the art of war. He showed, however, that their activities were also determined by material factors and by social demands operating independently of their will. In analysing the generalship of many military leaders from ancient times to his own day, and the innovations they made in warfare, he shows how their role lies in the skilful application of the forms and methods of warfare, produced by the objective development of the armed forces resulting from social change and revolution. The service rendered by Napoleon, for example, was that he made the new mode of warfare generated by the French Revolution into a regular system (p. 114).

At the same time Engels criticised the cult of generals and the exaggeration of their role characteristic of idealist military history, and found class limitations and contradictions in the activities of even outstanding military leaders. Frederick II of Prussia, he wrote, though successful in military operations and organising the army, had, "beside laying the foundation for that pedantry and martinetism which have since distinguished the Prussians, actually prepared them for the unparalleled disgrace of Jena and Auerstädt" (p. 359). In Napoleon's strategy and tactics Engels stressed the elements of adventurism and schematicism, such as the use of huge divisional columns, which "lost him many a battle" (p. 313).

Engels exploded the conception cherished by some bourgeois military theoreticians that the basic rules of the art of war are eternal and immutable. His works argue vigorously in favour of the principle of historicism in military science and of the dialectical approach to the various aspects of warfare. Thus, he pointed out that the tactical rules that could be applied in one set of historical circumstances often proved inapplicable in another. In his article "Blenheim", for instance, analysing one of the major battles of the early eighteenth century, he drew attention to the fact that the very circumstances which, with the linear tactics of those days, caused the defeat of the French army would, in the nineteenth century, in the age of extended order supported by columns, have been regarded as "one of the greatest advantages of a defensive position" (p. 250).

*   *   *

The series of articles which Engels wrote for *The Volunteer Journal, for Lancashire and Cheshire,* published in Manchester, was an important contribution to the Marxist elaboration of the problems of military history and theory. Engels was prompted to write for this journal by his desire to support the democratic volunteer movement against the annexationist policies of the Bonapartist circles of the Second Empire, which were seen as a threat to the British Isles. This movement gained a wide response among the democratic sections of the population, including the workers. Many trade unions demanded that workers should be allowed to join the volunteer units. The progressive forces counted on using the volunteer organisations to promote military reform, reorganise the extremely conservative military system, and get rid of the aristocratic caste practices prevailing in the British army and its still surviving traditions of mercenary service and annexationist colonial wars. Engels took a keen interest in the campaign to organise volunteer units. In addition to his series of articles for *The Volunteer Journal* (the most important of them were also published as a separate book), he popularised the volunteer movement in the columns of the German *Allgemeine Militär-Zeitung* (pp. 409-16, 535-41). At the same time he openly criticised the defects in the organisation and system of military training of the volunteer units and suggested ways of remedying them. He believed that the volunteers could play an important role in national defence and in reorganising the British armed forces if they acquired real professional skill and learned from the experience of past wars. This was what he sought to promote in his articles.

Engels' articles for *The Volunteer Journal* ("The History of the Rifle", "Volunteer Artillery", "Volunteer Engineers: Their Value and Sphere of Action", "The French Light Infantry", "On the Moral Element in Fighting. By Marshal Bugeaud", "Company Drill", and others) illustrate how the development of military technology and the improvement of weapons lead to changes in the tactics of armed struggle, and show the various methods of raising the morale and fighting capacity of troops. In his articles for the *Cyclopaedia* Engels stressed the importance of bravery and moral and psychological preparedness in armed struggle. In discussing cavalry battles, for instance, Engels observed that at the decisive moment of the clash of cavalry "the moral element, bravery, is here at once transformed into material force" (p. 310). He also emphasised the importance of developing moral and psychological qualities in soldiers and officers.

In his articles for *The Volunteer Journal* Engels focussed attention on the methods and forms of military and physical training, drilling and shooting practice. He spoke of the importance of approximating the conditions of training to those of actual battle and the need to develop the men's initiative, as well as the fostering of a spirit of solidarity and military discipline. Engels was exacting in his demands on officers. He held that in the volunteer units both officers and men should strive to broaden and perfect their military knowledge, to assimilate the military experience of other countries besides their own, and to know not only how to use their weapons but how those weapons function. "No intelligent soldier ought to be ignorant of the principles on which his arms are constructed, and are expected to act" (p. 459).

Engels urged the readers of *The Volunteer Journal* to keep track of military developments in all countries. Significant in this respect were his articles on the American Civil War ("Lessons of the American War" and "The War in America"). They summed up the results of the military operations in the initial period of this crucial military conflict and touched upon the prospects of the struggle between the Northern states and the slave-owning South (pp. 525-34).

The military works by Engels included in this volume analyse the history of war in various epochs, particularly that of capitalism. Engels discussed the achievements of military theory, from the writers of antiquity to the bourgeois theorists and historians of his own day. He traced the development of the armies of many nations, attempting to show the contribution made by each nation to military science and the art of war in general. His coverage of the military experience of Oriental countries and of Russia was less complete, the military history of the latter being discussed mainly in the biographies of Russian military leaders, written in collaboration with Marx ("Barclay de Tolly" and "Bennigsen"). This may be attributed to the inadequate presentation of the military history of these countries in the writings available to Engels, which moreover often suffered from preconceived notions about the military past of the Russian people. While not claiming to cover the whole military history of mankind, Engels none the less laid the foundation for the dialectical-materialist interpretation and elaboration of military theory and history. His generalisations and conclusions, and also his method of investigating the various spheres of the art of war and military events, have become an integral part of Marxist theory.

The predictions concerning certain trends in the development of the armed forces which Engels made in some of his articles and which have been confirmed by history are significant examples of scientific foresight. They include, for example, his forecast of changes in infantry tactics under the influence of increasingly effective fire-arms ("Infantry"), and also in naval tactics and types of vessels in view of the growing firepower of warships ("Navy").

At the same time it should be remembered that Engels was generalising the experience of wars that preceded the period of the mass employment of machinery and automatic weapons. His propositions and judgments reflecting the peculiarities of warfare in the pre-imperialist epoch should not therefore be automatically applied to contemporary conditions and accepted unconditionally in modern strategy and tactics. To do this would conflict with the creative spirit of the legacy of military theory left to us by Engels, who firmly opposed any such absolutising of the rules of military art and consistently advocated an historical approach in this as in other spheres.

* * *

The essays on Asian and African countries written by Engels for the *Cyclopaedia*—"Afghanistan", "Algeria" and "Burmah"—make a group of their own in the volume. These are reference articles supplying geographical and ethnographical data and descriptions of the economy, political organisation and the main stages in the historical development of these countries. An important feature, however, is a sharp condemnation of the colonial policies of capitalist powers, the system of enslavement and exploitation of the peoples of Asia and Africa by the West European bourgeoisie, and its colonial annexations and adventures, to which one country after another of these continents fell victim. In this respect these essays rank among the series of denunciations of colonialism that constituted an outstanding page in the journalistic writings of Marx and Engels of that period. They testify to the concern they felt for the destinies of the peoples of the East and their national liberation movements.

In his essay "Burmah" Engels shows how the country's natural resources aroused the annexationist appetites of the British ruling classes and their desire to expand Britain's colonial empire at Burma's expense. As in the case of other countries in Asia and Africa, the colonisers took advantage of Burma's economic backwardness and semi-patriarchal system to turn it into an arena of plunder. Engels noted that as a result of the first and second Anglo-Burmese wars (1824-26 and 1852) "Burmah has been robbed of its most fertile territory" and deprived of its access to the sea (p. 280). This was the prologue to Britain's annexation of the whole country, which occurred in 1885.

The essay on Afghanistan centres on the failure of Britain's ruling circles to subdue the country at the close of the 1830s and in the early 1840s. This attempt was to be followed by further encroachments on the independence of the Afghan people. Engels exposed the machinations of the British agents in Afghanistan, their blatant interference in the country's internal affairs, and the provocatory methods used to unleash the Anglo-Afghan war of 1838-42, the purpose of which was the annexation of Afghanistan. The invasion of Afghanistan was to be seen as an integral part of Britain's colonial expansion in Central Asia.

The essay on Afghanistan is supplemented by the summary of John W. Kaye's *History of the War in Afghanistan* which Engels made while working on the essay. In contrast to the author's apologetics, Engels found facts in the documents cited in the book that showed what had really been going on. These facts exposed the expansionist aims and ambitions of the organisers of the Afghan expedition that lay behind the fabrications about the threat to British possessions in India from Tsarist Russia, and the cynicism and guile of the British aggressors who, to get what they wanted, had no scruples about using such means as inflaming tribal enmity, bribing venal elements among the feudal-tribal nobility and hiring assassins to dispose of anyone considered dangerous to British domination (pp. 380, 382, 387 and elsewhere).

Engels recorded the collapse of the British adventure in Afghanistan and dwelt in detail on the uprisings of the local population against the aggressors in 1840-41, by which the Afghans, this "brave, hardy, and independent race", resolutely opposed the colonisers and succeeded in driving them from the country.

Engels' description of the French conquest of Algeria vividly illustrated the harsh methods of colonial rule and the grievous consequences of colonial enslavement. "From the first occupation of Algeria by the French to the present time," he wrote, "the unhappy country has been the arena of unceasing bloodshed, rapine, and violence. Each town, large and small, has been conquered in detail at an immense sacrifice of life. The Arab and Kabyle tribes, to whom independence is precious, and hatred of foreign domination a principle dearer than life itself, have been crushed and broken by the terrible razzias in which dwellings and property are burnt and destroyed, standing crops cut down, and the miserable wretches who remain massacred, or subjected to all the horrors of lust and brutality" (p. 67).

Stressing the instability of the colonial regime, Engels noted the continual uprisings of the Algerian people against French rule. He wrote that despite three decades of bloody wars (beginning from 1830), despite the large forces sent to subdue Algeria, and the vast sums expended, "the French supremacy is perfectly illusory, except on the coast and near the towns. The tribes still assert their independence and detestation of the French regime" (p. 69).

Engels' articles on colonial topics are inspired with faith in the mounting strength and invincibility of the anti-colonial liberation movement which, as he showed, had deep roots in the people, who hated colonial oppression and longed for freedom. Although written for a bourgeois publication, these articles reflect the common interest of the proletariat throughout the world, the solidarity of proletarian revolutionaries with participants in the anti-colonial struggle, and the desire to foster feelings of sympathy for the peoples of colonial and dependent countries among the working people of the metropolitan countries.

* * *

In addition to works by Engels *The New American Cyclopaedia* published a number of articles by Marx. They are mostly biographies of military leaders and politicians of the late eighteenth and first half of the nineteenth centuries. Many of them—"Barclay de Tolly", "Bennigsen", "Bem", "Bosquet", "Blücher" and "Beresford"— were actually written in collaboration with Engels, as were the articles "Armada" and "Ayacucho" (the latter dealt with the decisive battle in the liberation war of the peoples of Latin America against Spanish domination).

The biographical essays included in this volume are graphic character sketches of leading figures in various military and political events. They demonstrate clearly that schematicism is alien to the Marxist approach to history, that Marx and Engels saw the task of historical science not only in revealing the trends that determine social development but also in tracing their concrete embodiment in the varied panorama of historical reality itself, in the actions of real people. In many of their works Marx and Engels portrayed various historical figures and achieved considerable mastery in doing so. In the case of the biographies written for the *Cyclopaedia* they also showed their ability to single out not only individual peculiarities but features that reflected the epoch, and the class attributes of the individuals represented.

Marx's articles "Berthier", "Bourrienne", "Bessières", "Bernadotte" and "Brune" provide us with a gallery of military leaders and statesmen of Napoleonic France. As Marx showed, the careers of many of them reflected the evolution of the sections of the French bourgeoisie who took part in the revolutionary events of 1789-94 and later became pillars of the Bonapartist regime. Most of them owed their military or diplomatic careers solely to the revolution, which "opened a field for military talents" (p. 56). In the conditions of the supremacy of the counter-revolutionary big bourgeoisie they grew into ruthless money-grubbers and knights of profit (Bourrienne and Brune), ambitious men hungering for rank, title and vacant thrones (Bernadotte), and careerists prepared to serve any regime (Berthier). The biographies of Napoleon's marshals written by Marx offer a striking picture of the morals of the bourgeois coterie of Napoleon I's empire.

In his article "Bugeaud" Marx graphically portrayed a cruel and unscrupulous reactionary, a faithful servant of the July monarchy, whose political and military career was marked by bloody reprisals against French workers, by the treacherous and ferocious methods used to subdue Algeria, and by the colonial adventure in Morocco. Another typical figure of the time was the British General Beresford, who led several colonial expeditions and participated in the suppression of the revolutionary movement in Brazil and Portugal.

The biography of Field Marshal Blücher written by Marx and Engels forms a broad historical canvas. The activities of this outstanding German general and patriot are shown against the backdrop of the war of liberation fought by the German and other peoples against Napoleonic domination. Noting the major role played by Blücher in the campaigns of 1813-15 against Napoleonic France and emphasising that he participated "to the highest degree in the popular hatred against Napoleon" and was "popular with the multitude for his plebeian passions", Marx and Engels maintained that Blücher "was the true general for the military operations of 1813-15, which bore the character half of regular and half of insurrectionary warfare" (p. 187). Linked with the biography of Blücher is a brief biographical note by Marx on Bülow, also a participant in the wars against Napoleonic France.

The articles "Blum" and "Bem" recount the lives of these revolutionaries. The former was composed on the basis of Blum's own autobiographical material, as indicated by the excerpts made by Marx from German encyclopaedias of the 1840s and early 1850s, where it was first reproduced. The character sketch of Robert Blum, a prominent figure in the revolution of 1848 and a victim of the counter-revolutionary terror that followed, shows that Marx, while clearly aware of the limitations and moderation of the German petty-bourgeois democrats as a whole, had a high opinion of those who remained loyal to the interests of the people. The article devoted to Józef Bem described this Polish general, who came to the fore in the revolutionary war of 1849 in

Hungary, as "a first-rate general for the partisan and small mountain warfare" (p. 132).

In his article "Bolivar y Ponte" Marx showed the role of the masses in the struggle of the Latin American countries against Spanish colonial rule (1810-26), stressing the revolutionary, emancipatory nature of this struggle. He was misled, however, by the numerous memoirs and writings of the time, whose authors were hostile to Simon Bolivar, the leader of the national liberation movement, and therefore his assessment of Bolivar's activities and personality is one-sided. To some extent this was due to Marx's and Engels' anti-Bonapartist orientation in those years, and their desire to explode the mystique of Napoleon and his imitators, among whom Marx, on the basis of the sources he was using (he could not have discovered their lack of objectivity at the time), counted Bolivar.

Marx's method of writing the biographical essays for *The New American Cyclopaedia* is illustrated by the preparatory materials for some of them (besides the already mentioned excerpts for the article "Blum", this volume includes excerpts for the articles "Bourrienne" and "Bülow" and the rough draft of the article "Brune"). A comparison of these materials with the text of the articles will introduce the reader to the methods Marx used to deal with the original sources, the notes he made in the course of this work, and also certain facts that he had gathered but that did not appear in the final versions.

* * *

In all, this volume contains 107 works by Marx and Engels, seven of which (including the works comprising the section "From the Preparatory Materials for the Articles in *The New American Cyclopaedia*") are published in English for the first time. Of the remaining works, all of which were written in English, the majority have not been reprinted in that language since their publication during the authors' lifetime.

The works in this volume, including the articles for *The New American Cyclopaedia*, appear in chronological order, according to the date of writing, as distinct from the alphabetical order in which they were printed in the *Cyclopaedia* itself (see the list on page 2 of this volume). The dating of the articles for the *Cyclopaedia* was verified on the basis of references in the Marx-Engels correspondence and entries in Marx's notebooks concerning their dispatch to New York. Overlong paragraphs in the articles for the *Cyclopaedia* have been divided into paragraphs of more convenient length.

The texts of the articles by Engels that have come down to us in several versions owing to their parallel publication in the *Allgemeine Militär-Zeitung* and *The Volunteer Journal*, or their republication from the latter in the collection *Essays Addressed to Volunteers*, have been collated. Changes in headings and in the form of publication are mentioned in the editorial notes at the end of the volume, and variant readings that alter the meaning are reproduced in footnotes.

The specific features of the publication of the preparatory materials are also noted.

Misprints in quotations, proper and geographical names, numerical data, dates, and so on, have been corrected with reference to the sources used by Marx and Engels. The known literary and documentary sources are referred to in footnotes and in the index of quoted and mentioned literature.

The compilation of the volume, its preface and notes, the subject index, the index of quoted and mentioned literature and the glossary of geographical names, is the work of Tatyana Vasilyeva, under the editorship of Lev Golman (CC CPSU Institute of Marxism-Leninism). The name index and the index of periodicals were prepared by Yelizaveta Ovsyannikova (CC CPSU Institute of Marxism-Leninism).

The translations were made by Henry Mins, Peter and Betty Ross and Barrie Selman, and edited by J. S. Allen (International Publishers), Nicholas Jacobs (Lawrence and Wishart), Richard Dixon, Lydia Belyakova and Victor Schnittke (Progress Publishers), and Vladimir Mosolov, scientific editor (CC CPSU Institute of Marxism-Leninism).

The volume was prepared for the press by the editors Lydia Belyakova, Yelena Chistyakova, Mzia Pitskhelauri and Lyudgarda Zubrilova and the assistant editors Natalia Kim and Lyudmila Mikhailova (Progress Publishers).

KARL MARX
and
FREDERICK ENGELS

ARTICLES
FOR *THE NEW AMERICAN CYCLOPAEDIA* [1]

THE NEW

AMERICAN CYCLOPÆDIA:

A

Popular Dictionary

OF

GENERAL KNOWLEDGE.

EDITED BY

GEORGE RIPLEY AND CHARLES A. DANA.

VOLUME I.

A–ARAGUAY.

NEW YORK:

D. APPLETON AND COMPANY,

846 & 348 BROADWAY.

LONDON: 16 LITTLE BRITAIN.

M.DCCC.LVIII.

Title page of Volume I of *The New American Cyclopaedia*

In *The New American Cyclopaedia* the articles by Marx and Engels were printed as follows:

Frederick Engels

ABENSBERG[2]

Abensberg, a small town with 1,200 inhabitants, in the circle of Regen, kingdom of Bavaria. It is believed to have been the Abasinum of the Romans. There is a thermal spring in the neighborhood, with the ruins of a fine castle. On April 20, 1809, Bonaparte fought and defeated the Austrians near Abensberg, who lost twelve guns and 13,000 men. This victory was the precursor of the victories of Landshut and Eckmühl,[3] and opened the road to Vienna.

Written between July 11 and 24, 1857

First published in *The New American Cyclopaedia*, Vol. 1, 1858

Reproduced from *The New American Cyclopaedia*

Frederick Engels

ACRE

Acre, St. Jean d', Acca, Ptolemais, or *Acco,* a harbor of Syria, at the foot of Mt. Carmel, lat. 32° 54' N. long. 35° 4' E., population about 15,000. It is the best bay on that part of the coast, although very shallow. The place is renowned for its desperate sieges and defences. In 1104 it was taken by the Genoese, from whom Saladin retook it in 1187. The assault upon it by Richard Cœur de Lion in 1191 was one of the most daring feats in the Crusades. It remained until 1292 in the custody of the Knights of St. John,[4] who fortified it strongly, but were compelled to evacuate it by the Turks. It was here that the Turks, supported by the chivalric Sydney Smith and a handful of British sailors, kept Napoleon and the French army at bay for sixty days, when he raised the siege and retreated.[5] In 1832 Ibrahim Pasha, after a six months' siege, took it by storm when Mehemet Ali revolted from the Porte, and seized upon Syria. In 1839, however, Syria was restored to Turkey, and Acre again felt the bitterness of war, Ibrahim refusing to evacuate until after a bombardment by the combined British, Austrian, and Turkish fleets, Nov. 4, 1840.[6]

Written between July 11 and 24, 1857

First published in *The New American Cyclopaedia,* Vol I, 1858

Reproduced from *The New American Cyclopaedia*

Frederick Engels

ACTIUM

Actium (Ακτιου, now La Punta), a promontory and village in Acarnania, at the entrance of the Ambracian gulf, near which Caesar Octavius, afterwards the Emperor Augustus, and Mark Antony, had a naval engagement, in which the former was completely victorious, Sept. 2, B.C. 31. This battle decided the question of universal dominion. Octavius had been master of the West, Antony of the East.[7] Both armies were encamped on opposite sides of the Ambracian bay. Octavius had 80,000 men on foot, 12,000 horsemen, and 260 ships of war. Antony had 100,000 foot soldiers, 12,000 horsemen, and 220 ships. Antony's ships were armed with catapults, but were cumbersome. Those of Octavius were small, but had more speed. Cleopatra reinforced Antony with 60 ships, and at her instigation, and against the advice of his own most experienced captains, he offered a naval battle to Octavius. It was accepted. Agrippa, the admiral of Octavius, after the battle had lasted several hours without decisive effect, made a rapid manoeuvre, and Cleopatra took flight with her galleys. The voluptuous Antony could not refrain from following her with a few ships. His fleet, on being deserted by its leader, surrendered, and his army did the like after waiting seven days for his return. The miserable man had fled with his mistress into Egypt. The conqueror, to commemorate his victory, beautified the temple of Apollo which stood at Actium, and erected Nicopolis (city of victory) on the northern side of the gulf.

Written between July 11 and 24, 1857

First published in *The New American Cyclopaedia*, Vol. I, 1858

Reproduced from *The New American Cyclopaedia*

Frederick Engels

ADJUTANT

Adjutant, an assistant officer or *aide-de-camp* attached to commanders of larger or smaller bodies of troops. Generally every commander of a battalion of infantry, or of a regiment of cavalry, has an adjutant; the chiefs of brigades, divisions, *corps d'armée,* and the commander-in-chief, have one or more as the importance of the command may require. The adjutant has to make known the commands of his chief, and to see to their execution, as well as to receive or collect the reports intended for his chief. He has, therefore, in his charge, to a great extent, the internal economy of his body of troops. He regulates the rotation of duty among its component parts, and gives out the daily orders; at the same time, he is a sort of clerk to his chief, carries on the correspondence with detachments and with the superior authorities, arranges the daily reports and returns into tabular form, and keeps the journal and statistical books of his body of troops. Larger bodies of troops now generally have a regular staff attached—taken from the general staff of the army, and under a "chief of the staff," who takes to himself the higher functions of adjutant, and leaves him merely the transmission of orders and the regulation of the internal routine duty of the corps. The arrangements in such cases, however, are so different in different armies, that it is impossible to give even a general view of them. In no two armies, for instance, are the functions of an adjutant to a general commanding a *corps d'armée* exactly alike. Beside these real adjutants, the requirements of monarchical institutions have created in almost all European states hosts of titular adjutants-general to the monarch, whose functions are imaginary, except when called upon to do duty with their master; and even then, these functions are of a purely formal kind.

Written between July 11 and 24, 1857

First published in *The New American Cyclopaedia,* Vol. I, 1858

Reproduced from *The New American Cyclopaedia*

Frederick Engels

AIREY[8]

Airey, Sir Richard, K.C.B.,[a] major-general, and, at present, quartermaster-general of the British army, entered the service in 1821 as ensign, was made a captain 1825, a lieutenant-colonel 1851,[b] and as such took the command of a brigade in the army of the east in 1854. When the Crimean expedition was about to sail from Varna, he was made, Sept. 1854, quartermaster-general of the expeditionary force, and, as such, became one of the 6 or 8 officers who, under the command of Lord Raglan, have been charged with destroying the English army by dint of routine, ostensible fulfilment of duty, and want of common sense and energy. To Airey's share, fell the fixing of the proportions in which the different articles of camp-equipage, tents, great-coats, blankets, boots, should be dealt out to the various regiments. According to his own admission (before the Chelsea commission of inquiry),

"there never was a period after the first week in Dec. 1854, when there was not at Balaklava a considerable supply of warm clothing, and [...] at that very time there were regiments engaged at the front [...] in the trenches, which were suffering acutely from the want of these very articles, which [...] lay in readiness for them at a distance of 7 or 8 miles."[c]

This, he says, was not his fault; there never having been the slightest difficulty in getting his signature of approval to a requisition for such articles. On the contrary, he gives himself

---

[a] Knight Commander of the Order of the Bath.— *Ed.*

[b] Sir Richard Airey was made lieutenant-colonel in 1838; in 1851 he was promoted to the rank of colonel.— *Ed.*

[c] *Opening Address of Major-General Sir Richard Airey, K.C.B.*, p. 149.— *Ed.*

credit for having, as much as possible, abridged and simplified the routine process of approving, reducing, or disapproving the requisition sent to him by divisional and regimental officers.

Written before July 24, 1857

First published in *The New American Cyclopaedia*, Vol. I, 1858

Reproduced from *The New American Cyclopaedia*

Frederick Engels

ÅLAND ISLANDS

Åland Islands, a group of about 200 rocky islets, of which 80 are inhabited, situated at the entrance of the Bothnian gulf, between lat. 59° and 60° 32″ N. and long. 19° and 21° E. They belong to Russia, having been ceded by Sweden in 1809, and form a part of the government of Abo, in Finland.[9] The population, about 15,000 in number, are of Swedish descent, and are excellent sailors and fishermen. The rocks, covered with a thin soil, produce pines and birches, rye, barley, potatoes, hops, flax, and the inhabitants keep great numbers of cattle, and export cheese, butter, and hides; they also manufacture cloth for home use and for sails. The chief island is named Åland; its area is 28 square miles, its population 10,000; it has a good harbor on the W. side. All the harbors are more or less fortified; foremost among these was the island and harbor of Bomarsund, taken and blown up in 1854 by the allied fleets of England and France during their war against Russia.[10] In 1714, the Russian admiral Apraxin won a decisive naval victory against the Swedes near the cliffs of Signilskar.[11]

Written between July 11 and 24, 1857

First published in *The New American Cyclopaedia*, Vol. I, 1858

Reproduced from *The New American Cyclopaedia*

Frederick Engels

ALBUERA

Albuera, a village and rivulet in the Spanish province of
Estremadura, about 12 miles S. E. of Badajos. In the spring of
1811, the British laid siege to Badajos, then in the hands of the
French, and were pressing the fortress very hard.[12] Beresford,
with about 10,000 British and Germans, and 20,000 Portuguese
and Spanish troops, covered the siege at Albuera. Soult advanced
with the disposable portion of the army of Andalusia, and attacked
him May 16. The English right was posted on a rounded hill,
from which a saddle-shaped prolongation extended along the
centre and left. In front the position was covered by the Albuera
river. Soult at once recognized this round hill as the commanding
point and key of the position; he therefore merely occupied the
centre and left, and prepared an attack *en masse* upon the English
right. In spite of the protestation of his officers, Beresford had
posted nearly all the English and German troops on the centre
and left, so that the defence of the hill devolved almost exclusively
upon Spanish levies. Accordingly, when Soult's infantry advanced
in dense concentric columns up this hill, the Spaniards very soon
gave way, and the whole British position was at once turned. At
this decisive moment, after Beresford had several times refused to
send British or German troops to the right, a subordinate staff
officer,[a] on his own responsibility, ordered the advance of some
7,000 English troops. They deployed on the back of the
saddle-shaped height, crushed the first French battalions by their
fire, and on arriving at the hill, found it occupied by a not very
orderly mass of deep columns, without space to deploy. Upon

---

[a] Henry Hardinge.— *Ed.*

these they advanced. The fire of their deployed line told with murderous effect on the dense masses; and when the British, finally, charged with the bayonet, the French fled in disorder down the hill. This supreme effort cost the British line four-fifths of their number very near in killed and wounded; but the battle was decided, and Soult retreated, though the siege of Badajos was raised a few days afterward.

Written between July 11 and 24, 1857

First published in *The New American Cyclopaedia*, Vol. I, 1858

Reproduced from *The New American Cyclopaedia*

Frederick Engels

ALDENHOVEN

Aldenhoven, a small town in Rhenish Prussia, on the road from Jülich to Aix-la-Chapelle, has given its name to a victory of the Austrians, under Coburg, over a part of the French army of Dumouriez, March 1, 1793. After the conquest of Belgium, in 1792, Dumouriez, meditating an invasion of Holland, left 70,000 men between the Maes and the Roer, to besiege Maestricht and Venloö and to cover these sieges, while, with the remainder of the army, he advanced from Antwerp into Holland. The troops on the Maes were necessarily much dispersed; the divisions covering the sieges were cantoned near Aix-la-Chapelle, Aldenhoven, and Eschweiler. Coburg collected 40,000 men, and marched in 2 columns on the 2 latter places, turned the position of Eschweiler, took that of Aldenhoven by a front attack, and threw the French in disorder on Aix-la-Chapelle, which place was taken on the next day. Maestricht was delivered, and the Austrian advanced guard followed the French even across the Maes, and beat them at Tongres. The dispersed French divisions did not rally before arriving at Tirlemont, where they waited for Dumouriez. Thus the road into Belgium was open to the allies, and the conquest of the country completed, a few days afterward, by the further victory of Neerwinden.[13] The loss of the French during the battle of Aldenhoven, and the pursuit, cannot have been less than 10,000 in killed, wounded, and prisoners, besides 10,000 who deserted immediately afterward; a great amount of *materiel,* too, fell into the hands of the Austrians.[14]

Written between July 11 and 24, 1857

First published in *The New American Cyclopaedia,* Vol. I, 1858

Reproduced from *The New American Cyclopaedia*

Frederick Engels

ALESSANDRIA [15]

A fortified city in Piedmont, situated on the confluence of the Bormida and Tanaro, a few miles from the Po. It was founded in 1178 by the Milanese, as a bulwark against the invasions of the German emperors, and has in modern times again received significance as a national Italian fortress against Austria, since the campaigns of 1848 and '49. Though up to the beginning of this century its fortifications were but old-fashioned and indifferent, the French in vain besieged it in 1657, and Prince Eugene of Savoy, in 1706, only took it after a protracted defence. [16] The principal strength of the fortifications as they at present exist, consists in the additions made by Napoleon after the annexation of Piedmont to France. [17] It is the only fortress Napoleon built, and in its works Montalembert's new system of casemated batteries for the defence of the ditch, was applied for the first time, though only partly. Napoleon especially strengthened the citadel, a six-fronted bastioned work, with many outworks, and constructed a bridge-head on the opposite side of the Bormida. The Piedmontese government has recently resolved to add more works to the fortress, which, if the passage of the Po at Valenza were properly fortified, might become the nucleus of a vast entrenched camp in a commanding position. The city has a college, theological seminary, 13 churches, including a cathedral, and manufactories of linen, silks, cloths, and wax candles. Population, with the suburbs, 36,000.

Written between July 11 and 24, 1857

First published in *The New American Cyclopaedia*, Vol. I, 1858

Reproduced from *The New American Cyclopaedia*

Frederick Engels

ALMA [18]

Alma, a small river in the Crimea, running from the high ground in the neighborhood of Bakhtchisarai in a westerly direction, and emptying its waters into Kalamita bay, between Eupatoria and Sebastopol. The southern bank of this river, which rises very steep toward its mouth, and everywhere commands the opposite shore, was selected during the late Russo-Turkish war [a] by Prince Mentchikoff as a defensive position in which to receive the onset of the allied armies just landed in the Crimea.

The forces under his command comprised 42 battalions, 16 squadrons, 1,100 [b] Cossacks, and 96 guns, in all 35,000 men. The allies landed on Sept. 14, 1854, a little north of the Alma, 28,000 French (4 divisions), 28,000 English (five infantry and one cavalry division), and 6,000 Turks. Their artillery was exactly as numerous as that of the Russians, viz.: 72 French and 24 English guns. The Russian position was of considerable apparent strength, but in reality offered many weak points. Its front extended nearly 5 miles, far too great a distance for the small number of troops at Mentchikoff's disposal. The right wing was completely unsupported, while the left (on account of the allied fleets, the fire from which commanded the coast) could not occupy the position as far as the sea, and therefore labored under the same defect. The plan of the allies was founded on these facts. The front of the Russians was to be occupied by false attacks, while the French, under the cover of the 5 fleets, were to turn the Russian left, and the English, under the cover of their cavalry, to turn their right.

---

[a] A reference to the Crimean war of 1853-56 between Russia and the coalition of Britain, France, Turkey and Piedmont.—*Ed.*

[b] Incorrectly given as 100 in *The New American Cyclopaedia.*—*Ed.*

BATTLE OF THE ALMA, SEPTEMBER 20, 1854

ST. ARNAUD

RAGLAN

Cardigan
Cathcart
RESERVE
Duke of Cambridge
Brown
Evans
England

RESERVE
Ahmed Pasha
Forey
Napoleon
Canrobert
Bosquet

Tarkhanlar
Uglich
Suzdal
Vladimir
Kazan
Burlyuk
Borodino
Belostok
Tarutino
Alma Tamak
Brest

Cossacks
GORCHAKOV
KIRYAKOV
MOSCOW
Volhynia
Minsk
RESERVE

Adshi-Bulat
Orta-Kissjok
Aklijas
2nd Battalion, Minsk Rgt.

Alma

RUSSIAN ARMY

ALLIED ARMIES

Divisions
Infantry — English, French, Turks
Cavalry

Skirmishing lines
English
French
Turks
Artillery
Movement

Regiments
Infantry
Cavalry

Battalions, squadrons, hundreds
Skirmishing lines
Artillery
Movement

Eupatoria
Bulganak
Alma
Kacha
Belbek
Sebastopol
BLACK SEA

18.IX
19-IX
20.IX
XI-18.I-IV

0   1   2 km

On the 20th the attack took place. It was to be made at daybreak, but owing to the slow movements of the English, the French could not venture to advance across the river before that time. On the French extreme right, Bosquet's division passed the river, which was almost everywhere fordable, and climbed the steep banks of the southern shore without finding any resistance. Means were also found, by vigorous effort, to bring 12 guns up to the plateau. To the left of Bosquet, Canrobert brought his division across the river, and began to deploy on the high ground, while Prince Napoleon's division was engaged in clearing the gardens, vineyards, and houses of the village of Alma from the Russian skirmishers. To all these attacks, made with 29 battalions, Mentchikoff opposed in his first and second lines only 9 battalions, in support of which 7 more soon arrived. These 16 battalions, supported by 40 guns and 4 squadrons of hussars, had to bear the brunt of the immensely superior attack of the French, who were soon supported by the remaining 9 battalions of Forey's division. Thus all St. Arnaud's troops were engaged, with the exception of the Turks, who remained in reserve. The result could not long be doubtful. The Russians slowly gave way, and retired in as good order as could be expected. In the mean time the English had commenced their attack. About 4 o'clock the fire of Bosquet's guns from the height of the plateau at the left of the Russian position had shown the battle to be seriously engaged; in about an hour the English skirmishing line engaged that of the Russians. The English had given up the plan of turning the Russian right, since the Russian cavalry, twice as strong, without Cossacks, as that of the British, covered that wing so as even to menace the English left. Accordingly, Lord Raglan determined to attack the Russians straight before him. He fell upon their centre, having in his first line Brown's light division and Evans' division; the two divisions of the duke of Cambridge and Gen. England formed the second line, while the reserve (Cathcart's division), supported by the cavalry, followed behind the left wing. The first line deployed and charged two villages before its front, and after dislodging the Russians, passed the Alma. Here the reports vary. The English distinctly maintain that their light division reached the breastwork behind which the Russians had placed their heavy artillery, but were then repulsed. The Russians declare that the light division never got well across the river, much less up the steep on which this breastwork was placed. At all events, the second line marched close behind, deployed, had to fall into column again to pass the Alma and to climb up the heights; deployed again, and after several volleys, charged. It was the duke of Cambridge's division (guards and Highlanders) especially, which came to the rescue of the light division. Evans, though slow in his advance, was not repelled, so that England's division in his rear could scarcely give him any support. The breastwork was taken by the guards and Highlanders, and the position was, after a short but violent struggle, abandoned by the Russians. Eighteen Russian battalions were here engaged against the same number of English battalions; and if the English battalions were stronger than the Russian by some 50 men each, the Russians amply made up for this by their superiority in artillery and the strength of the position. The English infantry fire, however, which is generally reputed as very murderous, was especially so on this occasion. Most of the troops engaged were armed with the Minié rifle, and the impact of their bullets, killing whole files at once, was most destructive to the deep Russian columns. The Russians, having all their infantry, except 6 battalions, engaged, and no hope to stem the advancing tide, broke off the battle, the cavalry and light artillery, together with the small infantry reserve, covering the retreat, which was not molested. The English fought decidedly better than any other troops in this battle, but in their habitual clumsy way of manoeuvring, deploying, forming columns, and deploying again, unnecessarily, under the enemy's fire, by which both time and lives were lost. The consequence of this battle was to the allies the undisputed possession of the open country of the Crimea as long as the Russians remained without reinforcements, and the opening of the road to Sebastopol. By the first advantage they did not profit, but of the second they availed themselves without delay.

Written between July 11 and 24, 1857

First published in *The New American Cyclopaedia*, Vol. I, 1858

Reproduced from *The New American Cyclopaedia*

Frederick Engels

ALMEIDA [19]

A town of Portugal, in the province of Beira, between the rivers Coa and Duas Casa. Population, 6,200. It is strongly fortified, and was the scene of the defeat of the French, under Masséna, by the duke of Wellington, Aug. 5, 1811.

Written between July 11 and 24, 1857

First published in *The New American Cyclopaedia*, Vol. I, 1858

Reproduced from *The New American Cyclopaedia*

Frederick Engels

AMUSETTE

Amusette, a small light cannon carrying a ball of one pound weight, and formerly used for service in mountainous countries. This gun was highly esteemed by Marshal Saxe, but has now gone entirely out of use.

Written between July 11 and 24, 1857

First published in *The New American Cyclopaedia*, Vol. I, 1858

Reproduced from *The New American Cyclopaedia*

Frederick Engels

ANTWERP

Antwerp, a maritime city of Belgium, the capital of a province bearing the same name. It is situated on the N. bank of the Scheldt, 26 miles N. of Brussels, and 32 miles E. N. E. from Ghent. Population (1855), 79,000. The city has the shape of a bow, the walls forming the semicircle, and the river the cord. The fortifications, which are very complete, have a length, including the citadel, of about 2 ³/₄ miles. The strong pentagonal citadel was built by the duke of Alva, in 1567. Antwerp is a very ancient city. It was at the height of its prosperity in the 15th and 16th centuries, at which time it was the commercial centre of Europe, had a widely extended foreign commerce, was frequented by ships of all nations (as many as 2,500 vessels lying in port at one time), and is said to have had a population of 200,000. In 1576 it was sacked and burned by the Spaniards. In 1585 it was taken, after a protracted siege,[20] by Alexander, prince of Parma.[a] Thereafter its trade was removed to Amsterdam, and other towns of the United Provinces. In 1794 it fell into the hands of the French. In 1832, after the revolt of the Belgian provinces, it was retaken, after a memorable siege, by the French Marshal Gérard.[21] Although not so important a city now as in the middle ages, the commerce and manufactures of Antwerp, at the present day, are far from inconsiderable. The river admits vessels of the largest size. The basins erected by Napoleon, and which have been turned into spacious commercial docks, are capable of containing 1,000 vessels. Extensive communication by canal gives to Antwerp an extended inland commerce; 1,970 vessels, of a tonnage of 286,474 tons,

---

[a] Alexander Farnese.— *Ed.*

arrived here in 1846. It is the point of a regular and much frequented steam communication with England, and has lately become a point of departure for numerous emigrants to the United States. It is one of the most important hide markets in Europe. Its chief manufactures are black silks and velvets. It has also manufactories of cotton, linen, laces, carpets, hats, and cutlery, as well as sugar refineries, and ship-yards. The city retains to the present day much of its ancient splendor. Most of the houses are ancient, and solidly built. It has many fine public buildings, the chief of which is its cathedral, a superb Gothic structure, begun early in the 15th century, and completed in not less than 84 years. There are 3 other churches of note, the exchange, built 1583, the hotel de ville, a palace for the king when he chooses to reside in Antwerp, and the hall of the Hanse towns. It has, beside, an academy of painting, sculpture, and the sciences, a public library containing 15,000 volumes, a picture gallery with 200 very valuable pictures, many of them masterpieces of the old Flemish masters, a botanical garden, and diverse schools, hospitals, and asylums.

Written between July 11 and 24, 1857

First published in *The New American Cyclopaedia*, Vol. I, 1858

Reproduced from *The New American Cyclopaedia*

Frederick Engels

ARBELA [22]

Arbela, now Arbil or Erbil, a small village in Koordistan, which lies on the usual route between Bagdad and Mosul in 36° 11' N. lat. according to Niebuhr's observations.[a] The houses are built of sun-dried bricks. Arbela was the name of the third and last of the great battles fought between Alexander and Darius 331 B.C.[23] The battle was not actually fought at Arbela, but at a little place 36 miles west by north, called Gaugamela, now Karmeles. After the battle Alexander crossed the Lycus and rested at Arbela.

Written between July 14 and 24, 1857

First published in *The New American Cyclopaedia,* Vol. II, 1858

Reproduced from *The New American Cyclopaedia*

---

[a] *C. Niebuhrs Reisebeschreibung nach Arabien und andern umliegenden Ländern,* Bd. 2, S. 343.— *Ed.*

Frederick Engels

ARQUEBUSE

Arquebuse, sometimes, but incorrectly, written harquebuse, from the French *arquebuse*, and corrupted in English, particularly on the Scottish borders, into hagbut, or hackbut—the earliest form of the musket, which became really serviceable in the field for military purposes. So long ago as the battle of Bosworth, A.D. 1485,[24] it was introduced under the name of a hand-gun, which was nothing more than a short iron cylinder closed with a *quasi*-breech at one end, and provided with a touch-hole, fastened to the end of a stout wooden pole, like the handle of a spear or halberd. This hand-gun or miniature cannon was loaded with slugs or small bullets upon a charge of coarse powder, and was discharged by means of a match applied to the vent, the instrument being supported on the shoulder of the front rank man, who was a pikeman or halberdier, and directed by means of the handle, and fired, though of course without any aim, by the rear rank. Even earlier than this, at the battle of Agincourt,[25] according to Hall's chronicle, the Britons were armed "with fiery hand-guns."[a] So clumsy, however, and slow of operation were these antique firearms, that, in spite of their formidable sound and unaccustomed appearance, they produced little or no effect. In the reign of Henry VIII, although during its earlier years, the battle of Pavia[26] was won by the fire of the Spanish arquebusiers, the longbow still held its own as the superior weapon, in virtue of its

---

[a] E. Halle, *The Union of the Two Noble and Illustrate Families of Lancastre & Yorke.—Ed.*

accuracy of aim, its range, and penetration; and even in the reign of Elizabeth, the longbow is spoken of as "the queen of weapons," although she had musketeers in her army, and assisted Henry IV, of France, with a body of horse arquebusiers, commanded by Col. James, an ancestor of the well-known novelist.[a] During her reign, this arm was greatly improved, although it was still so long and cumbersome that it could only be fired from a forked rest planted in the earth before the marksman, that indispensable instrument being sometimes furnished with a pike or halberd-head, so as, when set obliquely in the ground, to serve as a palisade.

The barrels of these old pieces are extremely long, of very thick metal, usually small-bored, and sometimes, already, rifled; as is the case with the piece still preserved at Hamilton palace, in Scotland, with which the regent Murray was shot by Hamilton of Bothwell-haugh, in the year 1570. They were fired by means of a coil of match, or wick, of prepared hemp, passed through a hammer, like that of a modern firelock, which, being released by the pulling of the trigger, threw down the lighted match into the pan, and discharged the piece. In due time the matchlock gave way to the wheel-lock, in which the flint was fixed so as to be stationary, over the pan, and a toothed wheel, by means of a spring, was set in rapid motion against its edge, so as to project a shower of sparks into the powder below. To the wheel-lock succeeded the snaphance, as it was called. This was the first uncouth rudiment of the flint and steel lock, which was brought to such perfection by Joseph Manton, and which has only, within a few years, been entirely superseded by the percussion cap, than which it is not easy to imagine a quicker and more infallible instrument of ignition. The snaphance came into use for fine pistols, fowling-pieces, and choice musquetoons, during the English civil wars[27]; but their rarity and high price kept them out of general use, except as the arms of gentlemen and officers of rank, while the matchlock still continued the weapon of the rank and file. It is remarkable that there has been far less advancement than one would have imagined, from the first invention of the improved arquebuse until very recent days, in the mere workmanship of the barrel and the accurate flight of the ball. The difficulty of aiming truly seems to have arisen solely from the defective method of firing, the clumsiness of the piece, and the extreme slowness of

---

[a] George Payne Rainsford James.— *Ed.*

the ignition; for many arquebuse barrels of great antiquity, especially those of Spanish manufacture, having been altered to the percussion principle, new-stocked, and properly balanced, are found to shoot with great accuracy and even unusual penetration, at long ranges.

Written between July 14 and 24, 1857

First published in *The New American Cyclopaedia*, Vol. II, 1858

Reproduced from *The New American Cyclopaedia*

Frederick Engels

ASPERN

Aspern and *Essling*, a town and village on the north side of the Danube, the former about half a league, the latter about 2 leagues below Vienna, situated on the great meadowy plain of the Marchfield, extending from the river to the wooded mountain heights of the Bisamberg, celebrated for the 2 days' terrible fighting between the French and Austrians, on May 21 and 22, 1809, and the first defeat of the emperor Napoleon, who was here beaten and forced to retreat by the archduke Charles.

In the early part of the campaign, Napoleon, with the grand army,[28] had made his way through the Tyrol, up the rivers Inn and Isar; had defeated the archduke at Eckmühl; forced him across the Danube, into the mountains of Bohemia, at Ratisbon,[a] which he took by assault, thus interposing between the Austrian army and capital[29] and then, detaching Davout with 40,000 men to amuse the imperial general, had descended the Danube, and made himself master of Vienna; while from the Italian side his lieutenants, Eugène Beauharnais, and Macdonald, were advancing victoriously through Dalmatia, Carniola, and up the valley of the Muhr, in which Jellachich was severely defeated, to join their commander. In the mean time, the archduke Charles, who since his defeat at Eckmühl had been moving slowly down the river, on the northern side, hoping for an opportunity to fight at advantage and rescue the empire under the walls of the capital itself, took post with his army on the Bisamberg, over against the island of Lobau, and another smaller islet, which here divide the Danube into 4 channels.

---

[a] Regensburg.— *Ed.*

The archduke was at the head of 100,000 men, and was in hourly expectation of being joined by his brother, the archduke John, with 40,000 more, which would have been raised to 60,000, had that prince effected his junction, as he was explicitly ordered to do, with Kolowrat at Lintz, and which would have occupied a most commanding position in the rear of Napoleon, and on the principal line of his communications.

It was Napoleon's object, who had concentrated under his own orders 80,000 admirable soldiers ready to take the field, including the imperial guard and the reserve cavalry of Bessières, to cross the Danube and give battle to the archduke, in the hope of crushing him before the arrival of his reinforcements. To this intent, he bridged the river from the right bank to the island of Lobau, with a structure of most solid materials, supported on 68 large boats and 9 huge rafts, and from Lobau to the Marchfield, midway between the villages of Aspern and Essling, with a slighter fabric of pontoons; and on the morning of the 21st began to pass his troops across, with the utmost alacrity and diligence. The Austrian commander, from his mountain position, perceived the rashness of the manoeuvre, by which the emperor was pushing his vast host across a wide and rapid river, by means of a single bridge, which could only admit of a slow and gradual defiling of the men of all arms, over its long and narrow causeway, difficult to cavalry, yet more difficult to artillery; and which, in case of his being forced to retreat, scarcely offered a possibility of saving the army; and perceiving it, resolved at once to avail himself of the opportunity of crushing half the French host on the northern bank, while the rest of the army was either in the act of passing, or on the southern side. Sending orders to Kolowrat, Nordmann, and the other officers in command up the river, to prepare boats laden with heavy materials and combustibles for the destruction of the bridges, when the time should arrive, the archduke kept his great army out of sight, ordering his cavalry and outposts only to make a nominal resistance, and then to fall back before the advance of the French, which was led by Masséna; until at 12 o'clock the movement of the enemy was sufficiently developed, above 40,000 French being already on the northern shore—to justify his assuming the initiative.

At that hour, descending from the wooded heights of the Bisamberg, with 80,000 men, of whom 14,000 were splendid cavalry, and 288 cannons, he precipitated himself upon the enemy, making the 2 villages of Aspern and Essling, on Napoleon's flanks, the principal points of his attack; the central

BATTLE OF ASPERN, MAY 21-22, 1809

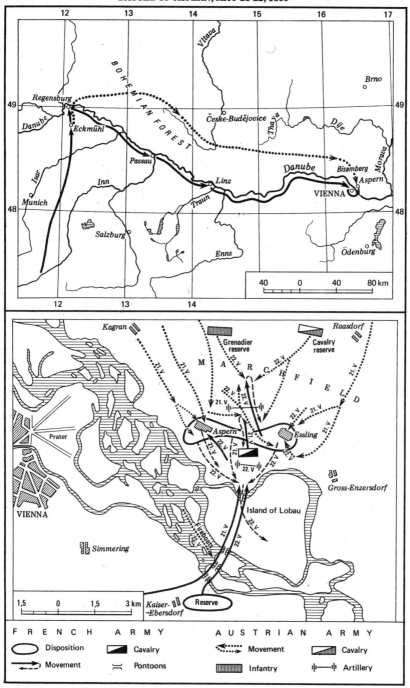

FRENCH ARMY

- ⬭ Disposition
- ➡ Movement
- ⇥ Pontoons

- ◣ Cavalry

AUSTRIAN ARMY

- ⬳••• Movement
- ▥▥ Infantry

- ▨ Cavalry
- ⊩—⊩ Artillery

space between these 2 strong places, which were built of stone, with garden walls and many enclosures, was occupied by the tremendous Austrian batteries, guarded chiefly by cavalry, with Hohenzollern's infantry in reserve in the rear. The fighting on both the flank attacks was terrific, and the fury of the assaults and obstinacy of the defence almost unparalleled in the history of war. Both villages were taken and retaken several times, and so terribly did the Austrian artillery devastate the French lines, that Napoleon ordered a grand charge of cavalry to take the batteries, if possible. The superb French cuirassiers of the guard charged with their usual impetuous valor, routed the Austrian horse, and would have carried the guns, but that they were hastily withdrawn, and the infantry formed in squares, which, as at Waterloo[30] afterward, defied all attempts to break their impenetrable formation, and at last defeated the horse, and compelled them to retire, shattered and decimated, into their own lines. In the mean time, Aspern was taken by the imperialists, their centre was gradually but irresistibly gaining ground, in spite of the gallant devotion of the cuirassiers, who charged again and again with constantly diminishing numbers, and who alone prevented the French lines from being broken through.

Night brought a brief cessation of the strife; but the French had suffered a decided defeat in a pitched battle; their left flank was turned, their centre forced back almost to the bridges; and although Essling, on their right, had been defended by the gallantry of Lannes, it was surrounded by the Austrians, who slept on their arms among the French dead, waiting only the return of light to renew their offensive operations.

During the whole night, however, fresh forces were defiling across the bridges, and debouching upon the Marchfield, and at daybreak, after all the losses of the preceding day, Napoleon had full 70,000 men in line, while Davout was beginning to cross over at the head of 30,000 more. The battle began by renewed attacks on the two disputed villages; Essling was carried by the imperialists, and Aspern retaken by the French. Both villages were the scene of desperate fighting all day long, and both were taken and retaken several times with the bayonet, but at last remained in the hands of the Austrians, who, in the evening, advanced their artillery beyond both places, and actually crossed their fire upon the rear of the French. But during these bloody conflicts, Napoleon, who was relieved by his vast accession of forces from the necessity of acting on the defensive, had recourse to his favorite manoeuvre of an overwhelming attack on the centre. At the head of a huge column of above 20,000 infantry, with 200 cannon preceding them, and a tremendous cavalry force in their rear, he launched Lannes and Oudinot directly on the Austrian centre, where the lines appeared the weakest, between the left of Hohenzollern and the right of Rosenberg. At first, this tremendous attack seemed to be perfectly successful; the Austrian lines were forced; a huge gap made between Rosenberg and Hohenzollern, into which the cavalry burst with appalling fury, and cut their way clear through to the reserves of the prince of Reuss, far in the rear; and already the cry went abroad, that the battle was lost; but the archduke Charles was equal to the emergency; the reserve grenadiers were brought up at double quick time, and formed in a checker of squares; the numerous dragoons of Prince Liechtenstein came galloping up behind them, and, with the colors of Zach's corps in his own hand, the gallant prince restored the battle.

The terrific column of Lannes could advance no further, but halting, began to exchange volleys with the squares, and, unable to deploy, was crushed by the concentrated fire of the batteries, playing on it at half musket shot. In vain the cavalry charged home on the bayonets of the squares, for not a square wavered or was broken; and, at length, the Austrian dragoons of the reserve, coming up with loud shouts, charged the cuirassiers in their turn, routed them, and drove them in confusion back upon their infantry, and completed the disorder. Immediately after this repulse, Hohenzollern broke through the French lines on the right of the centre with 6 Hungarian regiments of grenadiers, and carried all before him, even to the rear of Essling, which, with Aspern, were both carried finally by the imperialists. From these villages, as the Austrian centre was now driving all before it, in spite of the unparalleled exertions of the French army, which was now in full retreat to the island of Lobau, the Austrian batteries crossed their fire, with fatal effect, on the bridges, every shot telling on the crowded masses of men and horses.

Meanwhile, to augment the perils of the French, the bridge connecting the island with the southern shore was broken by the Austrian fireboats and rafts, and all escape from the island was rendered, for the moment, impossible. Still, with unexampled firmness the rear-guard of the French held the Austrians in check, until, at midnight, the last of the enemy having withdrawn from the field of battle into the island, the thunder of the Austrian batteries ceased, and the exhausted artillerists fell asleep beside their guns, worn out by the fatigues of that unparalleled and glorious day.

Seven thousand French were buried on the field of battle by the victors; 29,793 were carried, wounded and prisoners, into Vienna. Lannes and St. Hilaire were mortally wounded, and died a few days afterward. On the side of the imperialists, 87 superior officers, and 4,200 privates, were killed; beside 16,300 wounded. But the victory, gained under the very walls, and almost within sight of the capital, was complete; the enemy, broken, defeated, and dispirited, were cooped up in the narrow limits of the island of Lobau, and, had the archduke John, in obedience to his orders, made his appearance in the rear of the French with 60,000 fresh men, on the morning following the defeat of Aspern, it were difficult to say what might not have been the result.

But Napoleon's time had not yet arrived, and the nations were yet doomed to suffer 4 years longer, before the final downfall of the military colossus should restore them to their lost freedom, by the fields of Leipsic[31] and Waterloo.

Written between July 14 and 24, 1857

First published in *The New American Cyclopaedia*, Vol. II, 1858

Frederick Engels

ATTACK

Attack, in its general, strategetical meaning, is held to signify the taking of the initiative in any particular skirmish, combat, engagement, or pitched battle; in all of which one party must necessarily commence with offensive, the other with defensive, operations. The attack is generally considered the more successful, and consequently, armies acting on the defensive, that is to say, in wars of a strictly defensive nature, often initiate offensive campaigns, and even in defensive campaigns deliver offensive actions. In the former case, the object to be gained is that the defending army, by shifting the place and scene of operation, disturbs the calculations of the enemy, takes him away from his base of operations, and compels him to fight at times and places different from those which he expected, and for which he was prepared; and perhaps, positively disadvantageous to him.

The two most remarkable instances of offensive operations and direct attacks, used in strictly defensive campaigns, occurred in the two wonderful campaigns of Napoleon: that of 1814, which resulted in his banishment to Elba; and that of 1815, which was terminated by the rout of Waterloo and the surrender of Paris.[32] In both these extraordinary campaigns, the leader, who was acting strictly in the defence of an invaded country, attacked his enemies on all sides, and on every occasion; and, being always vastly inferior, on the whole, to the invaders, contrived always to be superior, and generally victorious, on the point of attack. The unfortunate result of both these campaigns detracts nothing from the conception or the details of either. They were both lost from causes entirely independent of their plan or execution, causes both political and strategical, the principal of which were the vast

superiority of the allied means, and the impossibility that any one
nation, exhausted by wars of a quarter of a century, should resist
the attack of a world in arms against it.

It has been said that when two armies are set face to face in the
field, that army which takes the initiative, or in other words,
attacks, has the decided advantage. It would appear, however, that
those who have adopted this view, have been dazzled by the
splendid achievements of a few great generals, and of one or two
great military nations, which have owed their successes to attacks
on the grandest scale; and that the opinion requires much
modification. Epaminondas, Alexander, Hannibal, Caesar, and,
last not least, Napoleon I, were, emphatically, attacking generals,
and won all their great victories, as, in the main, they endured all
their great reverses, in actions wherein [they] themselves assumed
the initiative. The French owe every thing to the impetuosity of
their almost irresistible onset, and to their rapid intelligence in following up successes and converting disasters, on the part of their
enemy, into irretrievable ruin. They are by no means equal in the
defensive. The history of the greatest battles in the world seems to
show that, where the attacked army has solid and obstinate
endurance sufficient to make it to resist, unbroken, until the fire
of the assailants begins to die out, and exhaustion and reaction to
succeed, and can then assume the offensive and attack in its turn,
the defensive action is the safest. But there are few armies, or,
indeed, races of men, who can be intrusted to fight such battles.
Even the Romans, though magnificent in the defence of walled
towns, and wonderful in offensive field operations, were never
celebrated in the defensive; and their history shows no battle in
which, after fighting all day under reverse and on the defensive,
they in the end attacked and won. The same is generally
characteristic of the French armies and leaders. The Greeks, on
the contrary, fought many of their best battles, as those of
Marathon, Thermopylae, Plataea,[33] and many others, but the latter
especially, on the plan of receiving the assault until it slackens, and
then attacking the half-exhausted and surprised assailants. The
same has been the English, and, to a great extent, the Swiss and
German system for many ages, and generally successful with those
troops, as it has been in later days with the Americans. The battles
of Crécy, Poitiers, Agincourt,[34] Waterloo, Aspern and Essling[a] and
many others, too numerous to be recorded, were fought exactly
on the same principle; and it may be added that in the war of

---

[a] On the battle of Aspern and Essling see this volume, pp. 27-33.—*Ed.*

1812-'14,[35] the Americans successfully retorted on the English, who almost invariably attacked them, and that too—contrary to their usual mode—in column, the plan which they had proved to be so valuable against the French, and which they have still more recently proved against the Russians.[a]

The ordinary modes of attack are the following, when two armies are opposed face to face, in the field, and when both intend to fight. First, and simplest, the direct parallel attack, when the assailing force joins battle, at once, along the whole front, from wing to wing, and fights it out by sheer force. Second, the attack by the wings, either on both simultaneously, or on one first and then on the other, successively, keeping the centre retired. This was Napoleon's favorite battle, by which, having caused the enemy to weaken his centre in order to strengthen his wings, while he kept his own centre retired and fortified by immense reserves of cavalry, he finally rushed into the central gap and finished the action with an exterminating blow. Third, the attack by the centre, keeping the wings retired and in reserve. This is the most faulty of all attacks, and has rarely been adopted, and, it is believed, never successfully. If an army be forced into this position, it is generally surrounded and annihilated, as was the Roman attacking army at Cannae.[36] It is, on the contrary, an admirable position of defence. Fourth, the oblique attack, invented by Epaminondas, and practised by him, with splendid success, at Leuctra and Mantinea.[37] It consists in attacking one wing of the enemy, with one wing secretly and successively reinforced, while the centre and other wing are retired, but are so manoeuvred as to threaten a constant attack, and prevent the defending party from strengthening its own weak point, until it is too late. This was the favorite method of the Austrian Clerfayt, by which he constantly defeated the Turks; and of Frederick the Great, who was wont to say that "he was only fighting Epaminondas his battles over again," in his own finest victories.

It is worthy of remark that the Greeks, the French generally, as well as the Russians and the Austrians, have gained all their best battles by attack of columns; which, when they are not effectually checked and brought to a stand, break through the centre and carry all before them. The Romans, the English, and the Americans, almost invariably, have fought and still fight, whether in attack or on defence, in line; in which formation they have

---

[a] A reference to the Crimean war of 1853-56.— Ed.

always proved able to resist and hold in check the assaulting column with their centre, until by the advance of their wings they can overlap the enemy's flanks and crush him. It is worthy of remark, that wherever the English have varied from what may be called their national order of attack, in line two deep, and have assailed in column, as at Fontenoy and Chippewa,[38] they have suffered disaster. The inference is nearly irresistible, that the central attack by column is radically faulty against firm and steady troops, although it is sure of success against an enemy of inferior physique and discipline, especially if he be demoralized in spirit.

In attacking a redoubt or field fortification, if it be defended only by infantry, the assailants may march immediately to the attack; if it be defended also by cannon, it is necessary first to silence cannon by cannon. The cannonade is conducted in such a way as to break the palisades, dismount the pieces, and plough up the parapet, and thus to oblige the defending cannon to be withdrawn into the interior. After the attacking artillery has thus produced its effect, the light infantry, principally riflemen, envelop a part of the work, directing their fire upon the crest of the parapet, so as to oblige the defenders either not to show themselves at all, or at least to fire hurriedly. Gradually the riflemen approach, and converge their aim, and the columns of attack are formed, preceded by men armed with axes and carrying ladders. The men in the front rank may also be furnished with fascines which both serve as bucklers and will assist in filling up the ditch. The guns of the work are now brought back and directed against the assailing columns, and the attacking riflemen redouble their fire, aiming particularly upon the artillery men of the defence who may attempt to reload their pieces. If the assailants succeed in reaching the ditch, it is essential that they should in the assault act together, and leap into the work from all sides at once. They therefore wait a moment upon the brim for a concerted signal; and in mounting upon the parapet they are met by howitzer shells, rolling stones, and trunks of trees, and at the top are received by the defenders at the point of the bayonet or with the butt of the musket. The advantage of position is still with the defenders, but the spirit of attack gives to the assailants great moral superiority; and if the work be not defended by other works upon its flanks, it will be difficult, though not quite unprecedented, to repel even at this point a valiant assault. Temporary works may be attacked by surprise or by open force, and in either case it is the first duty of the commander to obtain, by spies or reconnoissance, the fullest possible information concerning the

3*

character of the work, its garrison, defences, and resources. The infantry are often thrown in an attack upon their own resources, when they must rely upon their own fertile invention, firing the abatis by lighted fagots, filling up small ditches with bundles of hay, escalading palisades with ladders under the protection of a firing party, bursting barricaded doors or windows by a bag of powder; and by such measures decisively and boldly used, they will generally be able to overcome any of the ordinary obstructions.

Written between July 14 and 24, 1857

First published in *The New American Cyclopaedia*, Vol. II, 1858

Reproduced from *The New American Cyclopaedia*

Frederick Engels

ABATIS[39]

Abatis, or *abattis,* in military strategy, a bulwark made of felled trees, in frequent use in rude mountain warfare. On emergency, the trees are laid lengthwise, with the branches pointed outwards to repel the invaders, while the trunks serve as a breastwork for the defendants. When the abatis is deliberately employed as the means of defending a mountain pass, for instance, the boughs of the tree are stripped of their leaves and pointed, the trunks are embedded in the ground, and the branches interwoven, so as to form a sort of *chevaux de frise.*

Written between July 30 and August 11, 1857

First published in *The New American Cyclopaedia,* Vol. I, 1858

Reproduced from *The New American Cyclopaedia*

Frederick Engels

AFGHANISTAN [40]

Afghanistan, an extensive country of Asia, north-west of India. It lies between Persia and the Indies, and in the other direction between the Hindoo Koosh and the Indian Ocean. It formerly included the Persian provinces of Khorassan and Kohistan, together with Herat, Beloochistan, Cashmere, and Sinde, and a considerable part of the Punjaub. In its present limits there are probably not more than 4,000,000 inhabitants. The surface of Afghanistan is very irregular,—lofty table lands, vast mountains, deep valleys, and ravines. Like all mountainous tropical countries it presents every variety of climate. In the Hindoo Koosh, the snow lies all the year on the lofty summits, while in the valleys the thermometer ranges up to 130°. The heat is greater in the eastern than in the western parts, but the climate is generally cooler than that of India; and although the alternations of temperature between summer and winter, or day and night, are very great, the country is generally healthy. The principal diseases are fevers, catarrhs, and ophthalmia. Occasionally the small-pox is destructive. The soil is of exuberant fertility. Date palms flourish in the oases of the sandy wastes; the sugar cane and cotton in the warm valleys; and European fruits and vegetables grow luxuriantly on the hill-side terraces up to a level of 6,000 or 7,000 feet. The mountains are clothed with noble forests, which are frequented by bears, wolves, and foxes, while the lion, the leopard, and the tiger, are found in districts congenial to their habits. The animals useful to mankind are not wanting. There is a fine variety of sheep of the Persian or large-tailed breed. The horses are of good size and blood. The camel and ass are used as beasts of burthen, and goats, dogs, and cats, are to be found in great numbers. Beside the

Hindoo Koosh, which is a continuation of the Himalayas, there is a mountain chain called the Solyman mountain, on the south-west; and between Afghanistan and Balkh, there is a chain known as the Paropamisan range, very little information concerning which has, however, reached Europe. The rivers are few in number; the Helmund and the Cabool are the most important. These take their rise in the Hindoo Koosh, the Cabool flowing east and falling into the Indus near Attock; the Helmund flowing west through the district of Seiestan and falling into the lake of Zurrah. The Helmund has the peculiarity of overflowing its banks annually like the Nile, bringing fertility to the soil, which, beyond the limit of the inundation, is sandy desert. The principal cities of Afghanistan are Cabool, the capital, Ghuznee, Peshawer, and Candahar. Cabool is a fine town, lat. 34° 10′ N. long. 60° 43′ E., on the river of the same name. The buildings are of wood, neat and commodious, and the town being surrounded with fine gardens, has a very pleasing aspect. It is environed with villages, and is in the midst of a large plain encircled with low hills. The tomb of the emperor Baber is its chief monument. Peshawer is a large city, with a population estimated at 100,000. Ghuznee, a city of ancient renown, once the capital of the great sultan Mahmoud, has fallen from its great estate and is now a poor place. Near it is Mahmoud's tomb. Candahar was founded as recently as 1754. It is on the site of an ancient city. It was for a few years the capital; but in 1774 the seat of government was removed to Cabool. It is believed to contain 100,000 inhabitants. Near the city is the tomb of Shah Ahmed, the founder of the city, an asylum so sacred that even the king may not remove a criminal who has taken refuge within its walls.

The geographical position of Afghanistan, and the peculiar character of the people, invest the country with a political importance that can scarcely be over-estimated in the affairs of Central Asia. The government is a monarchy, but the king's authority over his high-spirited and turbulent subjects, is personal and very uncertain. The kingdom is divided into provinces, each superintended by a representative of the sovereign, who collects the revenue and remits it to the capital. The Afghans are a brave, hardy, and independent race; they follow pastoral or agricultural occupations only, eschewing trade and commerce, which they contemptuously resign to Hindoos, and to other inhabitants of towns. With them, war is an excitement and relief from the monotonous occupation of industrial pursuits. The Afghans are divided into clans,[41] over which the various chiefs exercise a sort of feudal supremacy. Their indomitable hatred of rule, and their love of individual independence, alone prevents their becoming a powerful nation; but this very irregularity and uncertainty of action makes them dangerous neighbors, liable to be blown about by the wind of caprice, or to be stirred up by political intriguers, who artfully excite their passions. The two principal tribes are the Dooranees and Ghilgies, who are always at feud with each other. The Dooranee is the more powerful; and in virtue of their supremacy their ameer or khan made himself king of Afghanistan. He has a revenue of about $10,000,000. His authority is supreme only in his tribe. The military contingents are chiefly furnished by the Dooranees; the rest of the army is supplied either by the other clans, or by military adventurers who enlist into the service in hopes of pay or plunder. Justice in the towns is administered by cadis, but the Afghans rarely resort to law. Their khans have the right of punishment even to the extent of life or death. Avenging of blood is a family duty; nevertheless, they are said to be a liberal and generous people when unprovoked, and the rights of hospitality are so sacred that a deadly enemy who eats bread and salt, obtained even by stratagem, is sacred from revenge, and may even claim the protection of his host against all other danger. In religion they are Mohammedans, and of the Soonee sect; but they are not bigoted, and alliances between Sheeahs and Soonees[42] are by no means uncommon.

Afghanistan has been subjected alternately to Mogul[43] and Persian dominion. Previous to the advent of the British on the shores of India the foreign invasions which swept the plains of Hindostan always proceeded from Afghanistan. Sultan Mahmoud the Great, Genghis Khan, Tamerlane, and Nadir Shah, all took this road. In 1747 after the death of Nadir, Shah Ahmed, who had learned the art of war under that military adventurer, determined to shake off the Persian yoke. Under him Afghanistan reached its highest point of greatness and prosperity in modern times. He belonged to the family of the Suddosis, and his first act was to seize upon the booty which his late chief had gathered in India. In 1748 he succeeded in expelling the Mogul governor from Cabool and Peshawer, and crossing the Indus he rapidly overran the Punjaub. His kingdom extended from Khorassan to Delhi, and he even measured swords with the Mahratta powers.[44] These great enterprises did not, however, prevent him from cultivating some of the arts of peace, and he was favorably known as a poet and historian. He died in 1772, and left his crown to his son Timour, who, however, was unequal to the weighty charge.

He abandoned the city of Candahar, which had been founded by his father, and had, in a few years, become a wealthy and populous town, and removed the seat of government back to Cabool. During his reign the internal dissensions of the tribes, which had been repressed by the firm hand of Shah Ahmed, were revived. In 1793 Timour died, and Siman succeeded him. This prince conceived the idea of consolidating the Mohammedan power of India, and this plan, which might have seriously endangered the British possessions, was thought so important that Sir John Malcolm was sent to the frontier to keep the Afghans in check, in case of their making any movement, and at the same time negotiations were opened with Persia, by whose assistance the Afghans might be placed between two fires. These precautions were, however, unnecessary; Siman Shah was more than sufficiently occupied by conspiracies, and disturbances at home, and his great plans were nipped in the bud. The king's brother, Mahmud, threw himself into Herat with the design of erecting an independent principality, but failing in his attempt he fled into Persia. Siman Shah had been assisted in attaining the throne by the Bairukshee family, at the head of which was Sheir Afras Khan. Siman's appointment of an unpopular vizier excited the hatred of his old supporters, who organized a conspiracy which was discovered, and Sheir Afras was put to death. Mahmud was now recalled by the conspirators, Siman was taken prisoner and his eyes put out. In opposition to Mahmud, who was supported by the Dooranees, Shah Soojah was put forward by the Ghilgies, and held the throne for some time; but he was at last defeated, chiefly through the treachery of his own supporters, and was forced to take refuge amongst the Sikhs.[45]

In 1809 Napoleon had sent Gen. Gardane to Persia in the hope of inducing the shah[a] to invade India, and the Indian government sent a representative[b] to the court of Shah Soojah to create an opposition to Persia. At this epoch, Runjeet Singh rose into power and fame. He was a Sikh chieftain, and by his genius made his country independent of the Afghans, and erected a kingdom in the Punjaub, earning for himself the title of Maharajah (chief rajah), and the respect of the Anglo-Indian government. The usurper Mahmud was, however, not destined to enjoy his triumph long. Futteh Khan, his vizier, who had alternately fluctuated between Mahmud and Shah Soojah, as ambition or temporary

---

[a] Fath Ali.— *Ed.*
[b] Mountstuart Elphinstone.— *Ed.*

interest prompted, was seized by the king's son Kamran, his eyes
put out, and afterward cruelly put to death. The powerful family
of the murdered vizier swore to avenge his death. The puppet
Shah Soojah was again brought forward and Mahmud expelled.
Shah Soojah having given offence, however, was presently
deposed, and another brother crowned in his stead. Mahmud fled
to Herat, of which he continued in possession, and in 1829 on his
death his son Kamran succeeded him in the government of that
district. The Bairukshee family, having now attained chief power,
divided the territory among themselves, but following the national
usage quarrelled, and were only united in presence of a common
enemy. One of the brothers, Mohammed Khan, held the city of
Peshawer, for which he paid tribute to Runjeet Singh; another
held Ghuznee; a third Candahar; while in Cabool, Dost Mohammed, the most powerful of the family, held sway.

To this prince, Capt. Alexander Burnes was sent as ambassador
in 1835, when Russia and England were intriguing against each
other in Persia and Central Asia. He offered an alliance which the
Dost was but too eager to accept; but the Anglo-Indian government demanded every thing from him, while it offered absolutely
nothing in return. In the mean time, in 1838, the Persians, with
Russian aid and advice, laid siege to Herat, the key of Afghanistan
and India[46]; a Persian and a Russian agent arrived at Cabool, and
the Dost, by the constant refusal of any positive engagement on
the part of the British, was, at last, actually compelled to receive
overtures from the other parties. Burnes left, and Lord Auckland,
then governor-general of India, influenced by his secretary
W. McNaghten, determined to punish Dost Mohammed, for what
he himself had compelled him to do. He resolved to dethrone
him, and to set up Shah Soojah, now a pensioner of the Indian
government. A treaty was concluded with Shah Soojah, and with
the Sikhs; the shah began collecting an army, paid and officered
by the British, and an Anglo-Indian force was concentrated on the
Sutlej. McNaghten, seconded by Burnes, was to accompany the
expedition in the quality of envoy in Afghanistan. In the mean
time the Persians had raised the siege of Herat, and thus the only
valid reason for interference in Afghanistan was removed, but,
nevertheless, in December 1838, the army marched toward Sinde,
which country was coerced into submission, and the payment of a
contribution for the benefit of the Sikhs and Shah Soojah.[47] Feb.
20, 1839, the British army passed the Indus. It consisted of about
12,000 men, with above 40,000 camp-followers, beside the new
levies of the shah. The Bolan pass was traversed in March; want of

provisions and forage began to be felt; the camels dropped by hundreds, and a great part of the baggage was lost. April 7, the army entered the Khojak pass, traversed it without resistance, and on April 25 entered Candahar, which the Afghan princes, brothers of Dost Mohammed, had abandoned. After a rest of two months, Sir John Keane, the commander, advanced with the main body of the army toward the north, leaving a brigade, under Nott, in Candahar. Ghuznee, the impregnable stronghold of Afghanistan, was taken, July 22, a deserter having brought information that the Cabool gate was the only one which had not been walled up; it was accordingly blown down, and the place was then stormed. After this disaster, the army which Dost Mohammed had collected, at once disbanded, and Cabool too opened its gates, Aug. 6. Shah Soojah was installed in due form, but the real direction of government remained in the hands of McNaghten, who also paid all Shah Soojah's expenses out of the Indian treasury.

The conquest of Afghanistan seemed accomplished, and a considerable portion of the troops was sent back. But the Afghans were noways content to be ruled by the *Feringhee Kaffirs* (European infidels), and during the whole of 1840 and '41, insurrection followed on insurrection in every part of the country. The Anglo-Indian troops had to be constantly on the move. Yet, McNaghten declared this to be the normal state of Afghan society, and wrote home that every thing went on well, and Shah Soojah's power was taking root. In vain were the warnings of the military officers and the other political agents. Dost Mohammed had surrendered to the British in October, 1840, and was sent to India; every insurrection during the summer of '41 was successfully repressed, and toward October, McNaghten, nominated governor of Bombay, intended leaving with another body of troops for India. But then the storm broke out. The occupation of Afghanistan cost the Indian treasury £1,250,000 per annum: 16,000 troops, Anglo-Indian, and Shah Soojah's, had to be paid in Afghanistan; 3,000 more lay in Sinde, and the Bolan pass; Shah Soojah's regal splendors, the salaries of his functionaries, and all expenses of his court and government, were paid by the Indian treasury, and finally, the Afghan chiefs were subsidized, or rather bribed, from the same source, in order to keep them out of mischief. McNaghten was informed of the impossibility of going on at this rate of spending money. He attempted retrenchment, but the only possible way to enforce it was to cut down the allowances of the chiefs. The very day he attempted this, the chiefs formed a conspiracy for the extermination of the British, and thus McNaghten himself was the means of bringing about the concentration of those insurrectionary forces, which hitherto had struggled against the invaders singly, and without unity or concert; though it is certain, too, that by this time the hatred of British dominion among the Afghans had reached the highest point. The English in Cabool were commanded by Gen. Elphinstone, a gouty, irresolute, completely helpless old man, whose orders constantly contradicted each other. The troops occupied a sort of fortified camp, which was so extensive that the garrison was scarcely sufficient to man the ramparts, much less to detach bodies to act in the field. The works were so imperfect that ditch and parapet could be ridden over on horseback. As if this was not enough, the camp was commanded almost within musket range by the neighboring heights, and to crown the absurdity of the arrangements, all provisions, and medical stores, were in two detached forts at some distance from camp, separated from it, moreover, by walled gardens and another small fort not occupied by the English. The citadel or Bala Hissar of Cabool would have offered strong and splendid winter quarters for the whole army, but to please Shah Soojah, it was not occupied. Nov. 2, 1841, the insurrection broke out. The house of Alexander Burnes, in the city, was attacked and he himself murdered. The British general did nothing, and the insurrection grew strong by impunity. Elphinstone, utterly helpless, at the mercy of all sorts of contradictory advice, very soon got every thing into that confusion which Napoleon described by the three words, *ordre, contreordre, désordre.* The Bala Hissar was, even now, not occupied. A few companies were sent against the thousands of insurgents, and of course were beaten. This still more emboldened the Afghans. Nov. 3, the forts close to the camp were occupied. On the 9th, the commissariat fort (garrisoned by only 80 men) was taken by the Afghans, and the British were thus reduced to starvation. On the 5th, Elphinstone already talked of buying a free passage out of the country. In fact, by the middle of November, his irresolution and incapacity had so demoralized the troops that neither Europeans nor Sepoys[48] were any longer fit to meet the Afghans in the open field. Then the negotiations began. During these, McNaghten was murdered in a conference with Afghan chiefs. Snow began to cover the ground, provisions were scarce. At last, Jan. 1, a capitulation was concluded. All the money, £190,000, was to be handed over to the Afghans, and bills signed for £140,000 more. All the artillery and ammunition, except 6 six-pounders and 3 mountain guns, were to remain. All Afghanistan was to be evacuated. The chiefs, on the other hand, promised a safe conduct, provisions, and baggage cattle. Jan. 5, the British marched out, 4,500 combatants and 12,000 camp-followers. One march sufficed to dissolve the last remnant of order, and to mix up soldiers and camp-followers in one hopeless confusion, rendering all resistance impossible. The cold and snow and the want of provisions acted as in Napoleon's retreat from Moscow.[a] But instead of Cossacks keeping a respectful distance, the British were harassed by infuriated Afghan marksmen, armed with long-range matchlocks, occupying every height. The chiefs who signed the capitulation neither could nor would restrain the mountain tribes. The Koord-Cabool pass became the grave of nearly all the army, and the small remnant, less than 200 Europeans, fell at the entrance of the Jugduluk pass. Only one man, Dr. Brydon, reached Jelalabad to tell the tale. Many officers, however, had been seized by the Afghans, and kept in captivity, Jelalabad was held by Sale's brigade. Capitulation was demanded of him, but he refused to evacuate the town, so did Nott at Candahar. Ghuznee had fallen; there was not a single man in the place that understood any thing about artillery, and the Sepoys of the garrison had succumbed to the climate.

In the mean time, the British authorities on the frontier, at the first news of the disaster of Cabool, had concentrated at Peshawer the troops destined for the relief of the regiments in Afghanistan. But transportation was wanting and the Sepoys fell sick in great numbers. Gen. Pollock, in February, took the command, and by the end of March, 1842, received further reinforcements. He then forced the Khyber pass, and advanced to the relief of Sale at Jelalabad; here Sale had a few days before completely defeated the investing Afghan army. Lord Ellenborough, now governor-general of India, ordered the troops to fall back; but both Nott and Pollock found a welcome excuse in the want of transportation. At last, by the beginning of July, public opinion in India forced Lord Ellenborough to do something for the recovery of the national honor and the prestige of the British army; accordingly, he authorized an advance on Cabool, both from Candahar and Jelalabad. By the middle of August, Pollock and Nott had come to an understanding respecting their movements, and Aug. 20, Pollock moved towards Cabool, reached Gundamuck, and beat a body of Afghans on the 23d, carried the Jugduluk pass Sept. 8,

---

[a] In 1812.— *Ed.*

defeated the assembled strength of the enemy on the 13th at Tezeen, and encamped on the 15th under the walls of Cabool. Nott, in the mean time, had, Aug. 7, evacuated Candahar, and marched with all his forces toward Ghuznee. After some minor engagements, he defeated a large body of Afghans, Aug. 30, took possession of Ghuznee, which had been abandoned by the enemy, Sept. 6, destroyed the works and town, again defeated the Afghans in the strong position of Alydan, and, Sept. 17, arrived near Cabool, where Pollock at once established his communication with him. Shah Soojah had, long before, been murdered by some of the chiefs, and since then no regular government had existed in Afghanistan; nominally, Futteh Jung, his son, was king. Pollock despatched a body of cavalry after the Cabool prisoners, but these had succeeded in bribing their guard, and met him on the road. As a mark of vengeance, the bazaar of Cabool was destroyed, on which occasion the soldiers plundered part of the town and massacred many inhabitants. Oct. 12, the British left Cabool and marched by Jelalabad and Peshawer to India. Futteh Jung, despairing of his position, followed them. Dost Mohammed was now dismissed from captivity, and returned to his kingdom. Thus ended the attempt of the British to set up a prince of their own making in Afghanistan.

Written in July and the first decade of August 1857

First published in *The New American Cyclopaedia*, Vol. I, 1858

Reproduced from *The New American Cyclopaedia*

Frederick Engels

BARBETTE [49]

In a battery, guns are said to be placed *en barbette* when they stand high enough to fire over the crest of the parapet instead of, as usual, through embrasures. To raise the guns to this height, various means are adopted. In field fortifications, an earthwork platform behind the parapet forms the station for the gun. In a permanent fortification, the common high sliding carriage or the traversing platform raises the gun to the required level. Guns placed *en barbette* have not the same cover from the enemy's fire as those firing through embrasures; they are, therefore, disposed in this manner where the parapet cannot afford to be weakened by the cutting of embrasures, or where it is desirable to extend their range more to the right and left than would be possible with embrasures. On this account, guns are placed *en barbette* in field fortifications; in the salient angles of works; and in strand batteries destined to act against ships, especially if the parapet is of masonry. To protect them from enfilading fire, traverses and bonnets are constructed when necessary.

Written between the end of August and September 15, 1857

First published in *The New American Cyclopaedia*, Vol. II, 1858

Reproduced from *The New American Cyclopaedia*

Karl Marx and Frederick Engels

BARCLAY DE TOLLY[50]

Barclay de Tolly, Michel, Russian prince and field-marshal, born in Livonia in 1759,[a] died at Insterburg, in East Prussia, May 25, 1818. In 1769, when not yet 11, he entered the Russian army, and served during 29 years in its different campaigns against the Turks, Swedes, and Poles, but did not emerge from the inferior ranks before 1798. He distinguished himself in the campaign of 1806. His military reputation dates from the year 1807, when, at the head of the Russian vanguard, he most gallantly defended Prussian Eylau, making a prolonged stand in the streets, the church, and the churchyard of that town.[51] In 1808 he forced the Swedes back into Carelia, and, in 1809, as general of infantry, imitated, on a much larger scale, the celebrated march of Charles Gustavus over the frozen waters of the Little Belt, by marching 12,000 Russians with artillery, ammunition, provisions, and baggage, over the ice which covered the gulf of Bothnia. He took Umea, accelerated by his appearance the revolution preparing against Gustavus IV, and compelled the Swedes to sue for peace.[52] After 1810 he was intrusted with the direction of the Russian war ministry.

In 1812 he assumed the command of the 1st army of the west. Its principal corps, at the head of which he placed himself, and which official reports had swollen to 550,000 men, proved, in fact, to consist of 104,000 only, while the aggregate of the troops, stationed from the coasts of the Baltic to the banks of the Pruth, did not muster beyond 200,000. Thus the retreat of the Russian army, the original design of which Napoleon, in his memorials of

---

[a] Barclay de Tolly was born in 1761.—*Ed.*

St. Helena,[a] falsely attributed to Barclay de Tolly, and which, long
before the rupture between Russia and France, had been
elaborated by the Prussian general, Phull,[53] and after the
declaration of war, was again pressed upon Alexander by
Bernadotte, had now become not a thing of choice, but of dire
necessity. While Barclay de Tolly had the great merit of resisting
the ignorant clamors for battle which arose from the Russian rank
and file, as well as from headquarters, he executed the retreat
with remarkable ability, incessantly engaging some part of his
troops in order to afford to Prince Bagration the means of
effecting a junction with him, and to Admiral Tschitschagoff the
facilities for falling in the rear of the enemy. When forced to a
battle, as at Smolensk,[54] he took a position which prevented the
battle from becoming decisive. When, not far from Moscow, a
decisive battle was no longer to be avoided, he selected the strong
position of Gzhatsk, hardly to be assailed in the front, and to be
turned only by very extended roundabout ways.[55] He had already
posted his army when Kutusoff arrived, in whose hands the
intrigues of the Russian generals, and the murmurs of the
Muscovite army against the foreigner heading the holy war, had
placed the supreme command. Out of spite against Barclay de
Tolly, Kutusoff abandoned the lines of Gzhatsk, in consequence of
which the Russian army had to accept battle in the unfavorable
position of the Borodino. During that battle, Aug. 26,[b] Barclay,
commanding the right wing, was the only general who held his
post, not retiring until the 27th, thus covering the retreat of the
Russian army, which, but for him, would have been completely
destroyed. After the retreat from the Borodino, beyond Moscow,
it was Barclay de Tolly again who prevented any useless attempt at
a defence of the holy city.

During the campaign of 1813, Barclay took the fortress of
Thorn,[c] April 4,[d] 1813, vanquished Lauriston at Königswartha,
covered, after the defeat of Bautzen, May 8,[e] the retreat of the
allied army, won the battle of Görlitz, contributed to Vandamme's

---

[a] *Mémoires pour servir à l'histoire de France, sous Napoléon, écrits à Sainte-Hélène.—*
Ed.

[b] The date of this battle, as well as the dates of the military events mentioned
below, is given according to the Old Style adopted in Russia at that time. According
to the New Style the battle took place on September 7, 1812 (see this volume,
pp. 251-55).—Ed.

[c] Polish name: Toruń.—Ed.

[d] April 16.—Ed.

[e] May 20.—Ed.

capitulation, and distinguished himself in the battle of Leipsic.[56] During the campaign of 1814 he commanded no independent corps, and acted in an administrative and diplomatical, rather than in a military character. By the stern discipline he imposed upon the troops under his immediate control, he won the good opinions of the French people. On Napoleon's return from Elba, he arrived too late from Poland to assist at the battle of Waterloo,[57] but partook in the second invasion of France. He died on a journey to the bath of Carlsbad. The last years of his life were darkened by calumny. He was, beyond question, the best of Alexander's generals, unpretending, persevering, resolute, and full of common sense.

Written between the end of August and September 15, 1857

First published in *The New American Cyclopaedia*, Vol. II, 1858

Reproduced from *The New American Cyclopaedia*

Frederick Engels

BASTION

In ancient fortification, the walls of towns were flanked by round or square towers, from which archers and war machines could direct their projectiles on the storming enemy while he was held in check by the ditch. On the introduction of artillery into Europe, these towers were made considerably larger, and ultimately, in the beginning of the 16th century, the Italian engineers made them polygonal instead of round or square, thus forming a bastion. This is an irregular pentagon, one side of which is turned inward toward the tower, so that the opposite salient angle faces the open field. The 2 longer sides, enclosing the salient angle, are called the faces; the 2 shorter ones, connecting them with the town wall or rampart, are called the flanks. The faces are destined to reply to the distant fire of the enemy, the flanks to protect the ditch by their fire. The first Italian bastions still showed their descent from the ancient towers. They kept close to the main walls; the salient angle was very obtuse, the faces short, and the parapet revetted with masonry to the very top. With such small bastions, the main office of the flank was the defence of the ditch in front of the curtain connecting 2 bastions; consequently, the flanks were placed perpendicular to the curtain. These bastions were distributed either on the angles of the polygon forming the whole *enceinte* of the fortress, or where one side of the polygon was so long that a part was not within effective musket range of the 2 projecting flanks, an intermediate bastion, called *piatta forma,* was erected on its middle.

With the improving siege artillery of the 17th century, larger bastions became necessary, and very soon the curtain lost its importance, the bastions being now the principal points to be attacked. The office of the flanks was also changed: they now had to enfilade, chiefly, the ditch in front of the face of the opposite bastion, and instead of being erected perpendicular to the curtain, they were made perpendicular to the prolongation of that face, called the line of defence. The height of the masonry revetement was reduced so as to be covered from direct fire by the glacis or the parapet of the lower outworks. Thus bastions, in the hands of the old French and German school, and subsequently in those of Vauban and Coehorn, underwent many changes of form and size, until about 1740, Cormontaigne published a system of bastionary fortification[a] which is generally considered as the most perfect of its kind. His bastions are as large as they can well be made; his flanks are nearly, but not quite, perpendicular to the lines of defence, and great improvements are made in the outworks.

Bastions are either full or empty. In the first case, the whole of the interior is raised to the height of the rampart; in the latter, the rampart goes round the interior side of the bastion with a sufficient breadth for serving the guns, and leaves a hollow in the middle of the work. In full bastions, cavaliers are sometimes erected: works, the sides of which run parallel with those of the bastion, and are elevated high enough to allow of the guns being fired over its parapet. From the commanding height of such cavaliers, guns of the greatest range are generally placed in them in order to annoy the enemy at a distance.

The system of fortification based upon bastions was the only one known from the 16th to the end of the 18th century, when Montalembert put forward several new methods without bastions, among which the polygonal or *caponnière* system for inland fortresses, and the system of casemated forts with several tiers of guns, have found most favor.

Written between the end of August and
September 15, 1857

First published in *The New American
Cyclopaedia*, Vol. II, 1858

Reproduced from *The New American
Cyclopaedia*

---

[a] *Architecture militaire, ou l'art de fortifier.—Ed.*

Frederick Engels

BAYONET

This weapon, now generally introduced for all line infantry, is usually stated to have been invented in France (apparently at Bayonne, whence the name) about the year 1640. According to other accounts, it was adopted by the Dutch from the Malays, who attached their *kris,* or dagger, to a musket, and introduced into France about the year 1679. Up to that time, the musketeers had no effective weapon for close combat, and consequently had to be mixed with pikemen to protect them from a closing enemy. The bayonet enabled musketeers to withstand cavalry or pikemen, and thus gradually superseded the latter arm. Originally, it was fastened to a stick for insertion into the barrel of the musket, but as it thus prevented the soldier from firing with bayonet fixed, the tube passing round the barrel was afterward invented. Still, the pike maintained itself for above half a century as an infantry weapon. The Austrians were the first to exchange it, for all their line infantry, for the musket and bayonet; the Prussians followed in 1689; the French did not do away entirely with the pike until 1703, nor the Russians till 1721. The battle of Spire, in 1703, was the first in which charges of infantry were made with fixed bayonets.[58] For light infantry, the bayonet is now generally replaced by a short, straight and sharp-pointed sword, which can be fixed in a slide on one side of the muzzle of the rifle. It is thus certainly less firmly fixed, but as such infantry are expected to charge in line in exceptional cases only, this drawback is considered to be balanced by the manifold uses in which such an instrument can be employed.

Written between the end of August and September 15, 1857

First published in *The New American Cyclopaedia,* Vol. II, 1858

Reproduced from *The New American Cyclopaedia*

Karl Marx

BERTHIER [59]

Berthier, Louis Alexandre, marshal of France, prince and duke
of Neufchâtel and Valengin, prince of Wagram, born at Versailles,
Nov. 20, 1753, murdered at Bamberg, June 1, 1815. He was
educated as a soldier by his father,[a] the chief of the corps of
topographical engineers under Louis XVI. From the topographical
bureau of the king, he passed to active service, first as lieutenant
in the general staff, and subsequently as a captain of dragoons. In
the American war of independence[60] he served under Lafayette.
In 1789, Louis XVI appointed him major-general of the national
guard of Versailles, and on Oct. 5 and 6, 1789, as well as Feb. 19,
1791, he did good service to the royal family.[61] He perceived,
however, that the revolution opened a field for military talents,
and we find him, in turn, the chief of the general staff, under
Lafayette, Luckner, and Custine. During the reign of terror he
avoided suspicion by exhibiting zeal in the Vendean war. His
personal bravery at the defence of Saumur, June 12, 1793,
secured an honorable mention in the reports of the commissaries
of the convention.[62] After the 9th Thermidor,[63] he was appointed
chief of the general staff of Kellermann,[64] and by causing the
French army to take up the lines of Borghetto, contributed to
arrest the advance of the enemy. Thus his reputation as a chief of
the general staff was established before Bonaparte singled him out
for that post. During the campaign of 1796-'7, he also proved
himself a good general of division in the battles of Mondovi (April
22, 1796), Lodi (May 10, 1796), Codogno (May 9, 1796), and
Rivoli (Jan. 14, 1797).[65]

---

[a] Jean Baptiste Berthier.— *Ed.*

Of a weak character, of a tenacious activity, of a herculean strength of constitution, which allowed him to work during 8 consecutive nights, of a stupendous memory for every thing respecting the details of military operations, such as movements of corps, number of forces, cantonments, chiefs; of a promptitude always to be relied upon, orderly and exact, well versed in the use of maps, with an acute appreciation of the peculiarities of the ground, schooled to report in simple and lucid terms on the most complicated military movements, sufficiently experienced and quick-sighted to know on the day of action where to deliver the orders received, and himself attending to their execution, the living telegraph of his chief on the field of battle, and his indefatigable writing machine at the desk, he was the paragon of a staff officer for a general who reserved to himself all the superior staff functions. Despite his remonstrances, Bonaparte placed him, in 1798, at the head of the army destined to occupy Rome, there to proclaim the republic, and to take the pope prisoner.[66] Equally unable to prevent the robberies committed at Rome by French generals, commissaries and purveyors, and to arrest the mutiny in the French ranks, he resigned his command to the hands of Masséna, and repaired to Milan, where he fell in love with the beautiful Madame Visconti; his eccentric and lasting passion for whom caused him during the expedition to Egypt[67] to be nicknamed the chief of the *faction des amoureux*,[a] and cost him the best part of the 40,000,000 francs successively bestowed upon him by his imperial master.

After his return from Egypt, he seconded Bonaparte's intrigues on the 18th and 19th Brumaire,[68] and was appointed minister of war, a post he occupied till April 2, 1800. Acting again as chief of the general staff during the second Italian campaign, he contributed somewhat to the apparently false position in which Bonaparte had placed himself at Marengo, by crediting false reports as to the route and position of the Austrian army.[69] After the victory, having concluded an armistice with Gen. Melas, he was employed on several diplomatic errands, and then reinstated in the war ministry, which he held till the proclamation of the empire. He then became completely attached to the person of the emperor, whom, with the title of major-general of the grand army,[70] he accompanied as chief of the general staff during all his campaigns. Napoleon showered titles, dignities, emoluments, pensions, and donations upon him. May 19, 1804, he was created

---

[a] Party of lovers.— *Ed.*

marshal of the empire, grand cordon of the legion of honor,
grand huntsman of France. Oct. 17, 1805, he had the honor of
stipulating with Mack the terms of the capitulation of Ulm.[71] From
the Prussian campaign of 1806, he carried home the dignity of
sovereign prince of Neufchâtel and Valengin. In 1808 he was
ordered to marry the princess Elizabeth Maria of Bavaria-
Birkenfeld, the king of Bavaria's[a] niece, and was made vice-
constable of France. In 1809, Napoleon placed him as general-in-
chief at the head of the grand army destined to operate from
Bavaria against Austria. On April 6 he declared war, and on the
15th had already contrived to compromise the campaign. He
divided the army into 3 parts, posting Davout with half of the
French forces at Regensburg, Masséna with the other half at
Augsburg, and between them, at Abensberg, the Bavarians, so that
by quickly advancing, the archduke Charles might have vanquished these corps singly. The slowness of the Austrians and the
arrival of Napoleon saved the French army. In his more congenial
functions, however, and under the eyes of his master, he rendered
excellent service in this same campaign, and added to his long list
of titles that of prince of Wagram.[72]

During the Russian campaign[b] he broke down even as chief of
the general staff. After the conflagration of Moscow he proved
unable even to interpret the orders of his master; but in spite of
his urgent request to be allowed to return with Napoleon to
France, the latter ordered him to stay with the army in Russia.
The narrowness of his mind and his devotion to routine were now
fully illustrated in the midst of the fearful odds against which the
French had to struggle. True to his traditions, he gave to a
battalion, sometimes to a company of the rear-guard, the same
orders as if that rear-guard was still composed of 30,000 men;
assigned posts to regiments and divisions which had long ceased to
exist, and, to make up for his own want of activity, multiplied
couriers and formulas. During the years 1813-'14 we find him
again at his usual post.[c] After the deposition of Napoleon had
been proclaimed by the senate,[d] Berthier, under false pretences,
slunk away from his patron, sent in his own adhesion to the senate
and the provisional government,[73] even before Napoleon's abdication, and proceeded, at the head of the marshals of the empire, to

---

a Maximilian I Joseph.— *Ed.*
b Of 1812.— *Ed.*
c Chief of the General Staff.— *Ed.*
d The Senate's decision of April 3, 1814 was made public the next day.— *Ed.*

Compiègne, there to address Louis XVIII in the most servile language. On June 4, 1814, Louis XVIII created him peer of France, and captain of a company of the newly established royal guard. His principality of Neufchâtel he resigned to the king of Prussia[a] in exchange for a pension of 34,000 florins. On Napoleon's return from Elba, he followed Louis XVIII to Ghent. However, having fallen into disgrace with the king in consequence of the concealment of a letter received from Napoleon, he withdrew to Bamberg, where, June 1, 1815, he was killed by 6 men in masks, who threw him out of one of the windows of his father-in-law's[b] palace. His memoirs were published in Paris in 1826.[c]

Written between the end of August and September 15, 1857

First published in *The New American Cyclopaedia*, Vol. III, 1858

Reproduced from *The New American Cyclopaedia*

---

[a] Frederick William III.— *Ed.*
[b] Prince of Birkenfeld.— *Ed.*
[c] *Mémoires du Maréchal Berthier.*— *Ed.*

Frederick Engels

ALGERIA [74]

Algeria, a division of northern Africa, formerly the Turkish pashalic of Algiers, but since 1830 included in the foreign dominions of France. It is bounded N. by the Mediterranean, E. by Tunis, W. by Morocco, S. by the Great Sahara. The extreme length is 500 miles from E. to W.; the extreme breadth 200 miles from N. to S. The Atlas ridge constitutes an important physical feature in the country, and divides the arable land of the sea-board from the desert. It also constitutes the northern and southern watershed of the province. The main ridge runs from east to west, but the whole province is intersected in all directions with spurs from the central range. The loftiest of the western mountains is Mount Wanashrees, the Mons Zalacus of Ptolemy; of the eastern the Jurjura and Aurès. These attain a height of nearly 7,000 feet. The principal river is the Sheliff. There are rivers of considerable size also, which flow from the south side of the Atlas, and lose themselves in the desert. None of these rivers are navigable. They are nearly dried up in the summer, but overflow a considerable extent of country in the spring and fertilize the soil.

The climate is not considered unhealthy by some travellers. Ophthalmia and cutaneous diseases are common. It is said there are no endemic fevers, but the great loss of the French troops by disease may perhaps lead to a different conclusion. The atmosphere is pure and bright, the summer very hot; and in the winter severe weather is occasionally experienced, especially in the hill country. On the limits of the desert the soil is arid and sandy, but between the mountain districts it is fertile, and especially so in the neighborhood of the streams. Grain crops of all kinds, fruits, European and tropical; flowers, and particularly roses, of remarkable beauty; and a species of sugar-cane, said to be the largest and most productive of any known species, grow in Algeria. The domestic animals of every variety are numerous. Horses, of course, are excellent; asses are of fine growth and much used for riding. The camel and dromedary of Algeria are very superior. The merino sheep is indigenous, and Spain was first supplied from Algeria. The Numidian lion, the panther and leopard, ostriches, serpents, scorpions, and other venomous reptiles, are abundant.

The Berbers, Kabyles, or Mazidh, for they are known by the three names, are believed to have been the aboriginal inhabitants. Of their history as a race little is known, further than that they once occupied the whole of north-western Africa, and are to be found also on the eastern coast. The Kabyles live in the mountain district. The other inhabitants are Arabs, the descendants of the Mussulman invaders. Moors, Turks, Kouloughs,[a] Jews, and negroes, and lastly the French, are found in the country. The population in 1852 was 2,078,035, of which 134,115 were Europeans of all nations, beside a military force of 100,000 men. The Kabyles are an industrious race, living in regular villages, excellent cultivators, and working in mines, in metals, and in coarse woollen and cotton factories. They make gunpowder and soap, gather honey and wax, and supply the towns with poultry, fruit, and other provisions. The Arabs follow the habits of their ancestors, leading a nomadic life, and shifting their camps from place to place according as the necessities of pasturage or other circumstances compel them. The Moors are probably the least respectable of the inhabitants. Living in the towns, and more luxurious than either the Arabs or Kabyles, they are, from the constant oppression of their Turkish rulers, a timid race, reserving nevertheless their cruelty and vindictiveness, while in moral character they stand very low.

The chief towns of Algeria are Algiers the capital, Constantine, population about 20,000, and Bona, a fortified town on the sea-coast, population about 10,000 in 1847. Near this are the coral fisheries, frequented by the fishers from France and Italy. Bougiah is on the gulf of the same name. The capture of this place was hastened by the outrages of the Kabyles in the

---

[a] *Kouloughs*—the offspring of Turks and Algerian women.— *Ed.*

neighborhood, who wrecked a French brig by cutting her cable and then plundered her and massacred the crew.

There are some remains of antiquity in the interior, especially in the province of Constantine, among others those of the ancient city of Lambessa; with remains of the city gates, parts of an amphitheatre, and a mausoleum supported by Corinthian pillars. On the coast is Coleah [and] Cherchell, the ancient Julia Caesarea, a place of some importance to the French. It was the residence of Juba, and in its neighborhood are ancient remains. Oran is a fortified town. It remained in possession of the Spaniards until 1792. Tlemcen, once the residence of Abd-el-Kader, is situated in a fertile country; the ancient city was destroyed by fire in 1670, and the modern town was almost destroyed by the French. It has manufactures of carpets and blankets. South of the Atlas is the Zaab, the ancient Gaetulia. The chief place is Biscara; the Biscareens are a peaceful race, much liked in the northern ports as servants and porters.

Algeria has been successively conquered by the Roman, the Vandal, and the Arab. When the Moors were driven from Spain in 1492, Ferdinand sent an expedition against Algiers, and seizing on Oran, Bougiah, and Algiers, he threatened the subjugation of the country. Unable to cope with the powerful invader, Selim Cutemi, the emir of the Metidjah, a fertile plain in the neighborhood of Algiers, asked assistance from the Turks, and the celebrated corsair, Barbarossa Horush, was sent to his assistance. Horush appeared in 1516, and having first made himself master of the country and slain Selim Cutemi with his own hand, he attacked the Spaniards, and after a war of varying fortunes, was obliged to throw himself into Tlemcen, where a Spanish army besieged him, and having succeeded in capturing him, put him to death in 1518. His brother, Khair-ed-Deen, succeeded him, sought assistance from the sultan, Selim I, and acknowledged that prince as his sovereign. Selim accordingly appointed him pasha of Algiers, and sent him a body of troops with which he was able to repulse the Spaniards, and eventually to make himself master of the country. His exploits against the Christians in the Mediterranean gained him the dignity of capudan pasha from Solyman I. Charles V made an attempt to reinstate the Spanish authority, and a powerful expedition of 370 vessels and 30,000 men crossed the Mediterranean in 1541. But a terrible storm and earthquake dispersed the fleet, and cut off all communication between it and the army. Without shelter, and exposed to the harassing attacks of a daring enemy, the troops were compelled to reembark, and make their escape with a loss of 8,000 men, 15 vessels of war, and 140 transports. From this time forward there were unceasing hostilities between the Barbary powers and the knights of Malta; thence sprang that system of piracy which made the Algerine corsairs so terrible in the Mediterranean, and which was so long submitted to by the Christian powers.[75] The English under Blake, the French under Duquesne, the Dutch, and other powers, at various times attacked Algiers; and Duquesne having twice bombarded it, the dey sent for the French consul of Louis XIV, and having learned from him the cost of the bombardment, jeeringly told him that he would himself have burnt down the city for half the money.

The system of privateering was continued in spite of the constant opposition of the European powers; and even the shores of Spain and Italy were sometimes invaded by the desperadoes who carried on this terrible trade of war and plunder. Thousands of Christian slaves constantly languished in captivity in Algiers; and societies of pious men were formed, whose express object was to pass to and from Algiers annually for the purpose of ransoming the prisoners with the funds remitted to their care by relatives. Meanwhile, the authority of the Turkish government had been reduced to a name. The deys were elected by the janizaries,[76] and had declared their independence of the Porte. The last Turkish pasha had been expelled by Dey Ibrahim in 1705; and the janizaries by tumultuous elections appointed new chiefs, whom in their mutinies they often murdered. The janizaries were recruited from the immigrants from Turkey, no native, though the son of a janizary by a woman of the country, being admitted into their ranks. The dey sent occasional presents to Constantinople as a token of his nominal allegiance; but all regular tribute was withdrawn, and the Turks, hampered by their constant struggles with Russia, were too weak to chastise the rebels of a distant province. It was reserved to the young republic of the United States to point the way to an abolition of the monstrous tyranny. During the wars of the French revolution and of Napoleon, the powerful fleets in the Mediterranean had protected commerce, and the Algerines had been compelled to a respite of their lawless exactions. On the renewal of peace, the Algerines commenced their depredations; and the Americans, who in 1795 had been compelled to follow the example of European nations, and to subsidize the dey for peace, now refused the tribute. In 1815, Commodore Decatur encountered an Algerine squadron, took a frigate and a brig, and sailed into the bay of Algiers, where he forced the dey to surrender all American prisoners, and to abandon all future claims for tribute. This bold example was followed by the English, who, under Lord Exmouth, bombarded the city in 1816, and reduced it to ashes, compelling the dey to surrender his prisoners. This was, however, only a punishment; for piracy was not suppressed, and in 1826 the Algerines openly seized Italian vessels in the Mediterranean, and even carried their incursions into the North sea. In 1818, Hussein dey succeeded to the government; in 1823, the dwelling of the French consul[a] having been plundered, and various outrages having been committed on vessels under the French flag, reparation was demanded without success. At last the dey of Algiers personally insulted the consul of France, and used expressions disrespectful to the king of France, who had not replied to a letter which the dey had written, in respect of a debt due by the French government to Jew merchants who were indebted to Hussein.[77] To enforce an apology, a French squadron was sent, which blockaded Algiers. Negotiations were opened between France, Mehemet Ali, and the Porte, by which Mehemet Ali, with the assistance of France, undertook to conquer Algiers, and to pay a regular tribute to the sultan,[b] from whom he would hold the government. This was broken off partly from the opposition of England, and partly because Mehemet Ali and France could not agree as to the precise arrangements by which the scheme was to be carried into effect. The government of Charles X now undertook an expedition against Algiers single-handed, and on June 13, 1830, an army of 38,000 men, and 4,000 horses, disembarked before Algiers, under command of Gen. Bourmont. Hussein dey had levied an army of 60,000 to oppose them, but having allowed them to land, he could make no effective resistance; and Algiers capitulated July 4, on condition that persons' private property and the religion of the country should be respected, and that the dey and his Turks should retire. The French took possession of the city. Among the spoil, they took 12 ships of war, 1,500 bronze cannon, and nearly $10,000,000 in specie. They immediately garrisoned Algiers, and established a military regency. The government of Charles X had intended to surrender Algiers to the sultan, and instructions to that effect were actually on their way to Constantinople, when the events of July, 1830, deposed Charles X.[78] One of the first acts of

---

a Deval.— *Ed.*
b Mahmud II.— *Ed.*

NATIONAL LIBERATION MOVEMENT IN ALGERIA IN THE 1st HALF OF THE 19th CENTURY

Legend:
- ┤├ State boundaries (1857)
- ⋯⋯ Boundaries of the Algerian provinces
- ✦ Main centres of national resistance
- V. 1841 Dates of major battles

Scale: 60 — 0 — 60 — 120 km

his successor [a] was to decide on retaining the conquest, and Clausel was sent over as general-in-chief in place of Bourmont. From the first occupation of Algeria by the French to the present time, the unhappy country has been the arena of unceasing bloodshed, rapine, and violence. Each town, large and small, has been conquered in detail at an immense sacrifice of life. The Arab and Kabyle tribes, to whom independence is precious, and hatred of foreign domination a principle dearer than life itself, have been crushed and broken by the terrible razzias in which dwellings and property are burnt and destroyed, standing crops cut down, and the miserable wretches who remain massacred, or subjected to all the horrors of lust and brutality. This barbarous system of warfare has been persisted in by the French against all the dictates of humanity, civilization, and Christianity. It is alleged in extenuation, that the Kabyles are ferocious, addicted to murder, torturing their prisoners, and that with savages lenity is a mistake. The policy of a civilized government resorting to the *lex talionis* [b] may well be doubted. And judging of the tree by its fruits, after an expenditure of probably $100,000,000, and a sacrifice of hundreds of thousands of lives, all that can be said of Algeria is that it is a school of war for French generals and soldiers, in which all the French officers who won laurels in the Crimean war received their military training and education. As an attempt at colonization, the numbers of Europeans compared with the natives show its present almost total failure; and this in one of the most fertile countries of the world, the ancient granary of Italy, within 20 hours of France, where security of life and property alike from military friends and savage enemies alone are wanted. Whether the failure is attributable to an inherent defect in the French character, which unfits them for emigration, or to injudicious local administration, it is not within our province to discuss. Every important town, Constantine, Bona, Bougiah, Arzew, Mostaganem, Tlemcen, was carried by storm with all the accompanying horrors. The natives submitted with an ill grace to their Turkish rulers, who had at least the merit of being co-religionists; but they found no advantage in the so-called civilization of the new government, against which, beside, they had all the repugnance of religious fanaticism. Each governor came but to renew the severities of his predecessor; proclamations

---

[a] Louis Philippe.— *Ed.*

[b] The law of retaliation, based on the Old Testament precept of "an eye for an eye, a tooth for a tooth".— *Ed.*

announced the most gracious intentions, but the army of occupation, the military movements, the terrible cruelties practised on both sides, all refuted the professions of peace and good-will.

In 1831, Baron Pichon had been appointed civil intendant, and he endeavored to organize a system of civil administration which should move with the military government, but the check which his measures would have placed on the governor-in-chief offended Savary, duc de Rovigo, Napoleon's ancient minister of police, and on his representation Pichon was recalled. Under Savary, Algeria was made the exile of all those whose political or social misconduct had brought them under the lash of the law; and a foreign legion, the soldiers of which were forbidden to enter the cities, was introduced into Algeria. In 1833, a petition was presented to the chamber of deputies, stating,

"for 3 years we have suffered every possible act of injustice. Whenever complaints are preferred to the authorities, they are only answered by new atrocities, particularly directed against those by whom the complaints were brought forward. On that account no one dares to move, for which reason there are no signatures to this petition. O my lords, we beseech you in the name of humanity, to relieve us from this crushing tyranny: to ransom us from the bonds of slavery. If the land is to be under martial law, if there is to be no civil power, we are undone; there will never be peace for us." [a]

This petition led to a commission of inquiry, the consequence of which was the establishment of a civil administration. After the death of Savary, under the *ad interim* rule of Gen. Voirol, some measures had been commenced calculated to allay the irritation; the draining of swamps, the improvement of the roads, the organization of a native militia. This, however, was abandoned on the return of Marshal Clausel, under whom a first and most unfortunate expedition against Constantine was undertaken.[79] His government was so unsatisfactory, that a petition praying inquiry into its abuses, signed by 54 leading persons connected with the province, was forwarded to Paris in 1836. This led eventually to Clausel's resignation. The whole of Louis Philippe's reign was occupied in attempts at colonization, which only resulted in land-jobbing operations; in military colonization, which was useless, as the cultivators were not safe away from the guns of their own block-houses; in attempts to settle the eastern part of Algeria, and to drive out Abd-el-Kader from Oran and the west.[80] The fall of that restless and intrepid chieftain so far pacified the

---

[a] Presumably quoted from *Wigand's Conversations-Lexikon*, Bd. 1, S. 253-54.— *Ed.*

country, that the great tribe of the Hamianes Garabas sent in their submission at once.

On the revolution of 1848, Gen. Cavaignac was appointed to supersede the Duke d'Aumale in the governorship of the province, and he and the Prince de Joinville, who was also in Algeria, then retired. But the republic did not seem more fortunate than the monarchy in the administration of this province. Several governors succeeded each other during its brief existence. Colonists were sent out to till the lands, but they died off, or quitted in disgust. In 1849, Gen. Pélissier marched against several tribes, and the villages of the Beni Sillem; their crops and all accessible property were burnt and destroyed as usual, because they refused tribute. In Zaab, a fertile district on the edge of the desert, great excitement having arisen in consequence of the preaching of a marabout,[81] an expedition was despatched against them 1,200 strong, which they succeeded in defeating; and it was found that the revolt was wide-spread, and fomented by secret associations called the Sidi Abderrahman, whose principal object was the extirpation of the French. The rebels were not put down until an expedition under Generals Canrobert and Herbillion had been sent against them; and the siege of Zoatcha, an Arab town, proved that the natives had neither lost courage nor contracted affection for their invaders. The town resisted the efforts of the besiegers for 51 days, and was taken by storm at last. Little Kabylia did not give in its surrender till 1851, when Gen. St. Arnaud subdued it, and thereby established a line of communication between Philippeville and Constantine.

The French bulletins and French papers abound in statements of the peace and prosperity of Algeria. These are, however, a tribute to national vanity. The country is even now as unsettled in the interior as ever. The French supremacy is perfectly illusory, except on the coast and near the towns. The tribes still assert their independence and detestation of the French regime, and the atrocious system of razzias has not been abandoned; for in the year 1857 a successful razzia was made by Marshal Randon on the villages and dwelling-places of the hitherto unsubdued Kabyles, in order to add their territory to the French dominions. The natives are still ruled with a rod of iron, and continual outbreaks show the uncertain tenure of the French occupation, and the hollowness of peace maintained by such means. Indeed, a trial which took place at Oran in August, 1857, in which Captain Doineau, the head of the *Bureau Arabe,*[82] was proved guilty of murdering a prominent and wealthy native, revealed a habitual exercise of the most cruel

4*

and despotic power on the part of the French officials, even of subordinate rank, which justly attracted the attention of the world.

At present, the government is divided into the three provinces of Constantine on the east, Algiers in the centre, and Oran in the west. The country is under the control of a governor-general, who is also commander-in-chief, assisted by a secretary and civil intendant, and a council composed of the director of the interior, the naval commandant, the military intendant, and attorney-general, whose business is to confirm the acts of the governor. The *conseil des contentieux* at Algiers takes cognizance of civil and criminal offences. The provinces where a civil administration has been organized have mayors, justices, and commissioners of police. The native tribes living under the Mohammedan religion still have their cadis; but between them a system of arbitration has been established, which they are said to prefer, and an officer (*l'avocat des Arabes*) is specially charged with the duty of defending Arab interests before the French tribunals.

Since the French occupation, it is stated that commerce has considerably increased. The imports are valued at about $22,000,000, the exports, $3,000,000. The imports are cotton, woollen, and silk goods, grain and flour, lime, and refined sugar; the exports are rough coral, skins, wheat, oil, and wool, with other small matters.

Written between July and September 18, 1857

First published in *The New American Cyclopaedia*, Vol. I, 1858

Reproduced from *The New American Cyclopaedia*

Frederick Engels

AMMUNITION [83]

Ammunition, comprises the projectiles, charges, and articles used for priming, required for the use of fire-arms, and, as the word is generally understood, supposes these articles to be made up ready for use. Thus, small-arm ammunition comprises cartridges and percussion caps (the latter, of course, are unnecessary where flint-locks or the needle-gun are in use); field-artillery ammunition is composed of shot, loaded shell, case shot, shrapnell, cartridges, priming tubes, matches, portfires, &c., with rockets for rocket-batteries. In fortresses and for sieges, the powder is generally kept in barrels, and made up in cartridges when required for use; so are the various compositions required during a siege; the hollow shot are also filled on the spot. The proportion of ammunition accompanying an army in the field varies according to circumstances. Generally an infantry soldier carries 60 rounds, seldom more; and a similar quantity per man accompanies the army in wagons, while a further supply follows with the park columns a march or two to the rear. For field-artillery, between 150 and 200 rounds per gun are always with the battery, partly in the gun-limber boxes, partly in separate wagons; another 200 rounds are generally with the ammunition-reserve of the army, and a third supply follows with the park columns. This is the rule in most civilized armies, and applies, of course, to the beginning of a campaign only; after a few months of campaigning, the ammunition-reserves are generally very severely drawn upon, perhaps lost after a disastrous battle, and their replacing is often difficult and slow.

Written between September 15 and 18, 1857

First published in *The New American Cyclopaedia,* Vol. I, 1858

Reproduced from *The New American Cyclopaedia*

Frederick Engels

BATTLE[84]

The encounter of two hostile bodies of troops is called a battle, when these bodies form the main armies of either party, or at least, are acting independently on their own separate seat of war. Before the introduction of gunpowder, all battles were decided by actual hand-to-hand fight. With the Greeks and Macedonians, the charge of the close phalanx bristling with spears, followed up by a short engagement with the sword, brought about the decision. With the Romans, the attack of the legion disposed in three lines, admitted of a renewal of the charge by the second line, and of decisive manoeuvring with the third. The Roman line advanced up to within 10 or 15 yards of the enemy, darted their *pila,* very heavy' javelins, into him, and then closed sword in hand. If the first line was checked, the second advanced through the intervals of the first, and if still the resistance was not overcome, the third line, or reserve, broke in upon the enemy's centre, or fell upon one of his wings. During the middle ages, charges of steel-clad cavalry of the knights had to decide general actions, until the introduction of artillery and small fire-arms restored the preponderance of infantry. From that time the superior number and construction of fire-arms with an army was the chief element in battle, until, in the 18th century, the whole of the armies of Europe had provided their infantry with muskets, and were about on a par as to the quality of their fire-arms. It was then the number of shots fired in a given time, with average precision, which became the decisive element. The infantry was drawn up in long lines, three deep; it was drilled with the minutest care, to insure steadiness and rapid firing, up to 5 times in a minute; the long lines advanced slowly against each other, firing all the while, and supported by artillery firing grape; finally, the losses incurred by one party caused the troops to waver, and this moment was seized by the other party for an advance with the bayonet, which generally proved decisive. If one of the two armies, before the beginning of the battle, had already taken up its position, the other attempted generally to attack it under an acute angle, so as to outflank, and there to envelop, one of his wings; that wing, and the nearest portion of the centre, were thus thrown into disorder by superior forces, and crowded together in deep masses, upon which the attacking party played with his heavy artillery. This was the favorite manoeuvre of Frederick the Great, especially success- ful at Leuthen.[85] Sometimes, too, the cavalry was let loose upon the wavering infantry of the enemy, and in many instances with signal success; but upon the whole, the quick fire of the infantry lines gave the decision—and this fire was so effective, that it has rendered the battles of this period the bloodiest of modern times. Frederick the Great lost, at Kolin, 12,000 men out of 18,000, and at Kunersdorf, 17,000 out of 30,000,[86] while in the bloodiest battle of all Napoleon's campaigns, at Borodino,[a] the Russians lost not quite one-half of their troops in killed and wounded.

The French revolution and Napoleon completely changed the aspect of battles. The army was organized in divisions of about 10,000 men, infantry, cavalry, and artillery mixed; it fought no longer in line exclusively, but in column and in skirmishing order also. In this formation it was no longer necessary to select open plains alone for battle-fields; woods, villages, farm-yards, any intersected ground was rather welcome than otherwise. Since this new formation has been adopted by all armies, a battle has become a very different thing from what it was in the 18th century. Then, although the army was generally disposed in three lines, one attack, or at most two or three attacks, in rapid succession, decided its fate; now, the engagement may last a whole day, and even two or three days, attacks, counter-attacks, and manoeuvres succeeding each other, with varying success, all the time through. A battle, at the present day, is generally engaged by the advanced guard of the attacking party sending skirmishers out with their supports. As soon as they find serious resistance, which generally happens at some ground favorable for defence, the light artillery, covered by skirmishers and small bodies of cavalry, advances, and the main body of the advanced guard takes position. A cannonade generally follows, and a deal of ammunition is wasted, in order to facilitate

---

[a] See this volume, pp. 251-55.— Ed.

reconnoitring, and to induce the enemy to show his strength. In the mean time, division after division arrives, and is shown into its fighting position, according to the knowledge so far obtained of the measures of the enemy. On the points favoring an attack, skirmishers are sent forward, and supported where necessary by lines and artillery; flank attacks are prepared, troops are concentrated for the attack of important posts in front of the main position of the enemy, who makes his arrangements accordingly. Some manoeuvring takes place, in order to threaten defensive positions, or to menace a threatening attack with a counter-charge. Gradually the army draws nearer to the enemy, the points of attack are finally fixed, and the masses advance from the covered positions they hitherto occupied. The fire of infantry in line, and of artillery, now prevails, directed upon the points to be attacked; the advance of the troops destined for the charge follows, a cavalry charge on a small scale occasionally intervening. The struggle for important posts has now set in; they are taken and retaken, fresh troops being sent forward in turns by either party. The intervals between such posts now become the battle-field for deployed lines of infantry, and for occasional bayonet charges, which, however, scarcely at any time result in actual hand-to-hand fight, while in villages, farm-yards, intrenchments, &c., the bayonet is often enough actually used. In this open ground, too, the cavalry darts forward whenever opportunities offer themselves, while the artillery continues to play and to advance to new positions. While thus the battle is oscillating, the intentions, the dispositions, and, above all, the strength of the two contending armies are becoming more apparent; more and more troops are engaged, and it soon is shown which party has the strongest body of intact forces in reserve for the final and decisive attack. Either the attacking party has so far been successful, and may now venture to launch his reserve upon the centre or flank of the defending party, or the attack has been so far repulsed and cannot be sustained by fresh troops, in which case the defending party may bring his reserves forward, and by a powerful charge, convert the repulse into a defeat. In most cases, the decisive attack is directed against some part of the enemy's front, in order to break through his line. As much artillery as possible is concentrated upon the chosen point; infantry advances in close masses, and as soon as its charge has proved successful, cavalry dashes into the opening thus made, deploying right and left, taking in flank and rear the enemy's line, and, as the expression is, rolling it up toward its two wings. Such an attack, to be actually decisive, must, however, be undertaken with a large force, and not before the enemy has engaged his last reserves; otherwise, the losses incurred would be out of all proportion to the very meagre results to be obtained, and might even cause the loss of the battle. In most cases, a commander will rather break off a battle taking a decidedly unfavorable turn, than engage his last reserves, and wait for the decisive charge of his opponent; and with the present organization and tactics, this may in most cases be done with a comparatively moderate loss, as the enemy after a well-contested battle, is generally in a shattered condition also. The reserves and artillery take a fresh position to the rear, under cover of which the troops are gradually disengaged and retire. It then depends upon the vivacity of the pursuit, whether the retreat be made in good order or not. The enemy will send his cavalry against the troops trying to disengage themselves; and cavalry must, therefore, be at hand to assist them. But if the cavalry of the retiring party be routed and his infantry attained before it is out of reach, then the rout becomes general, and the rear-guard, in its new defensive position, will have hard work before it unless night is approaching, which is generally the case.

Such is the average routine of a modern battle, supposing the parties to be pretty equal in strength and leadership; with a decided superiority on one side, the affair is much abridged, and combinations take place, the variations of which are innumerable; but under all circumstances, modern battles between civilized armies will, on the whole, bear the character above described.

Written between September 18 and 22, 1857

First published in *The New American Cyclopaedia*, Vol. II, 1858

Reproduced from *The New American Cyclopaedia*

Karl Marx and Frederick Engels

BENNIGSEN [87]

Bennigsen, Levin August Theophile, count, a Russian general, born in Brunswick, Feb. 10, 1745, where his father served as colonel in the guards, died Oct. 3, 1826. As a page, he spent 5 years at the Hanoverian court of George II; entered the Hanoverian army, and having advanced to the rank of captain in the foot guards, participated in the last campaign of the 7 years' war.[88] His excessive passion for the fair sex at that time made more noise than his warlike exploits. In order to marry the daughter of the baron of Steinberg, the Hanoverian minister at the court of Vienna, he left the army, retired to his Hanoverian estate of Banteln, by dint of lavish expenditure got hopelessly in debt, and, on the death of his wife, resolved to restore his fortune by entering the Russian military service. Made a lieutenant-colonel by Catherine II, he served first under Romanzoff, against the Turks, and then under Suwaroff, against the rebel Pugatcheff. During a furlough granted to him he went to Hanover to carry off Mlle. von Schwiehelt, a lady renowned for her beauty. On his return to Russia, the protection of Romanzoff and Potemkin procured for him the command of a regiment. Having distinguished himself at the siege of Otchakov,[89] in 1788, he was appointed brigadier-general. In the Polish campaign of 1793-'94, he commanded a corps of light troops; was created general after the affairs of Oszmiana and Solli; decided the victory of Vilna,[90] by breaking up, at the head of the horse, the centre of the Polish army, and, in consequence of some bold surprises, successfully executed on the banks of the lower Niemen, was rewarded by Catherine II with the order of St. Vladimir, a sabre of honor, and 200 serfs. During his Polish campaign he exhibited the qualities of a good cavalry officer—fire, audacity, and quickness—but not the higher attainments indispensable for the chief of an army. After the Polish campaign, he was despatched to the army in Persia, where, by means of a bombardment, lasting 10 days, he compelled Derbent, on the Caspian sea, to surrender.[91] The cross of the order of St . George of the third class, was the last gift he received from Catherine II, after whose death he was recalled and disgraced by her successor.[a]

Count Pahlen, military governor of St. Petersburg, was organizing at that time the conspiracy by which Paul lost his life. Pahlen, knowing the reckless character of Bennigsen, let him into the secret, and gave him the post of honor—that of leading the conspirators in the emperor's bedchamber. It was Bennigsen who dragged Paul from the chimney, where he had secreted himself; and when the other conspirators hesitated, on Paul's refusal to abdicate, Bennigsen exclaimed, "Enough talk," untied his own sash, rushed on Paul, and after a struggle, in which he was aided by the others, succeeded in strangling the victim. To shorten the process, Bennigsen struck him on the head with a heavy silver snuff box. Immediately on the accession of Alexander I, Bennigsen received a military command in Lithuania.

At the commencement of the campaign of 1806-'7,[92] he commanded a corps in the first army under Kamenski—the second being commanded by Buxhövden—he tried in vain to cover Warsaw against the French, was forced to retreat to Pultusk on the Narev, and there, Dec. 26, 1806, proved able to repulse an attack of Lannes and Bernadotte, his forces being greatly superior, since Napoleon, with his main force, had marched upon the second Russian army. Bennigsen forwarded vain-glorious reports to the emperor Alexander, and, by dint of intrigues against Kamenski and Buxhövden, soon gained the supreme command of the army destined to operate against Napoleon. At the end of January, 1807, he made an offensive movement against Napoleon's winter quarters, and escaped by mere chance the snare Napoleon had laid for him, and then fought the battle of Eylau. Eylau having fallen on the 7th, the main battle, which, in order to break Napoleon's violent pursuit, Bennigsen was forced to accept, occurred on Feb. 8. The tenacity of the Russian troops, the arrival of the Prussians under L'Estocq, and the slowness with which the single French corps appeared on the scene of action, made the victory doubtful. Both parties claimed it, and at any rate, the field

---

[a] Paul I.—Ed.

of Eylau—as Napoleon himself said—was the bloodiest among all his battles.[a] Bennigsen had *Te Deums* sung, and received from the czar a Russian order, a pension of 12,000 rubles, and a letter of congratulation, praising him as "the vanquisher of the never vanquished captain."

In the spring, he intrenched himself at Heilsberg, and neglected to attack Napoleon, while part of the French army was still occupied with the siege of Dantzic[93]; but, after the fall of Dantzic, and the junction of the French army, thought the time for attack had arrived. First delayed by Napoleon's vanguard, which mustered the third part only of his own numerical force, he was soon manoeuvred back by Napoleon into his intrenched camp. There Napoleon attacked him in vain June 10, with but two corps and some battalions of the guard, but on the next day induced him to abandon his camp and beat a retreat. Suddenly, however, and without waiting for a corps of 28,000 men, which had already reached Tilsit, he returned to the offensive, occupied Friedland, and there drew up his army, with the river Alle in his rear, and the bridge of Friedland as his only line of retreat. Instead of quickly advancing, before Napoleon was able to concentrate his troops, he allowed himself to be amused for 5 or 6 hours by Lannes and Mortier, until, toward 5 o'clock, Napoleon had his forces ready, and then commanded the attack. The Russians were thrown on the river, Friedland was taken, and the bridge destroyed by the Russians themselves, although their whole right wing stood still on the opposite side. Thus the battle of Friedland, June 14, costing the Russian army above 20,000 men, was lost. It was said that Bennigsen was at that time influenced by his wife, a Polish woman. During this whole campaign Bennigsen committed fault upon fault, his whole conduct exhibiting a strange compound of rash imprudence and weak irresolution.

During the campaign of 1812, his principal activity was displayed at the head-quarters of the emperor Alexander, where he intrigued against Barclay de Tolly, with a view to get his place. In the campaign of 1813, he commanded a Russian army of reserve, and was created count by Alexander, on the battle-field of Leipsic.[94] Receiving afterward the order to dislodge Davout from Hamburg, he beleaguered it until Napoleon's abdication of April, 1814, put an end to hostilities. For the peaceful occupation of Hamburg, then effected by him, he claimed and received new

---

[a] A reference to Napoleon's *Mémoires pour servir à l'histoire de France, sous Napoléon, écrits à Sainte-Hélène*, t. 2, p. 67.— *Ed.*

honors and emoluments. After having held the command of the army of the south, in Bessarabia, from 1814 to 1818, he finally retired to his Hanoverian estate, where he died, having squandered most of his fortune, and leaving his children poor in the Russian service.

Written in September (not later than the 22nd), 1857

First published in *The New American Cyclopaedia*, Vol. III, 1858

Reproduced from *The New American Cyclopaedia*

Karl Marx

BLUM [95]

Blum, Robert, one of the martyrs of the German revolution, born at Cologne, Nov. 10, 1807, executed in Vienna, Nov. 9, 1848. He was the son of a poor journeyman cooper, who died in 1815, leaving 3 children and a distressed widow, who, in 1816, again married a common lighterman. This second marriage proved unhappy, and the family misery rose to a climax in the famine of 1816-'17. In 1819 young Robert, belonging to the Catholic confession, obtained an employment as mass-servant; then became apprentice to a gilder, then to a girdler, and, according to the German custom, became a travelling journeyman, but was not up to the requirements of his handicraft, and, after a short absence, had to return to Cologne. Here he found occupation in a lantern manufactory, ingratiated himself with his employer,[a] was by him promoted to a place in the counting-house, had to accompany his patron on his journeys through the southern states of Germany, and, in the year 1829-'30, resided with him at Berlin. During this period he endeavored, by assiduous exertion, to procure a sort of encyclopaedic knowledge, without however betraying a marked predilection or a signal endowment for any particular science. Summoned, in 1830, to the military service, to which every Prussian subject is bound, his relations with his protector were broken off. Dismissed from the army after a six weeks' service, and finding his employment gone, he returned again to Cologne, in almost the same circumstances in which he had twice left it. There the misery of his parents, and his own helplessness, induced him to accept, at the hands of Mr. Ringelhardt, the manager of

---

[a] Schmitz.— *Ed.*

the Cologne theatre, the office of man of all work of the theatre. His connection with the stage, although of a subaltern character, drew his attention to dramatic literature, while the political excitement which the French revolution of July had caused throughout Rhenish Prussia, allowed him to mingle in certain political circles, and to insert poetry in the local papers.

In 1831, Ringelhardt, who had meanwhile removed to Leipsic, appointed Blum cashier and secretary of the Leipsic theatre, a post he held until 1847. From 1831 to 1837 he made contributions to the Leipsic family papers, such as the *Comet*, the *Abend-Zeitung*, &c., and published a "Theatrical Cyclopaedia,"[a] the "Friend of the Constitution,"[b] an almanac entitled *Vorwärts*, &c. His writings are impressed with the stamp of a certain household mediocrity. His later productions were, moreover, spoiled by a superfluity of bad taste. His political activity dates from 1837, when, as the spokesman of a deputation of Leipsic citizens, he handed over a present of honor to 2 opposition members of the Saxon estates.[c] In 1840 he became one of the founders, and in 1841 one of the directors of the Schiller associations, and of the association of German authors.[96] His contributions to the *Sächsische Vaterlands-Blätter*, a political journal, made him the most popular journalist of Saxony, and the particular object of government persecution. German catholicism,[97] as it was called, found a warm partisan in him. He founded the German Catholic church at Leipsic, and became its spiritual director in 1845. On Aug. 13, 1845, when an immense meeting of armed citizens and students, assembling before the riflemen's barracks at Leipsic, threatened to storm it in order to revenge the murderous onslaught committed the day before by a company of the riflemen,[98] Blum, by his popular eloquence, persuaded the excited masses not to deviate from legal modes of resistance, and himself took the lead in the proceedings for legal redress. In reward for his exertions, the Saxon government renewed its persecutions against him, which, in 1848, ended in the suppression of the *Vaterlands-Blätter.*

On the outbreak of the revolution of February, 1848, he became the centre of the liberal party of Saxony, founded the "Father-land's Association,"[99] which soon mustered above 40,000 members, and generally proved an indefatigable agitator. Sent by the city of

---

[a] A reference to the *Allgemeines Theater-Lexikon oder Encyklopädie alles Wissenswerthen für Bühnenkünstler, Dilettanten und Theaterfreunde*, published in Leipzig from 1839 by Robert Blum and others.— *Ed.*

[b] *Verfassungsfreund.—Ed.*

[c] Karl Gotthold Todt and Julius Dieskau.— *Ed.*

Leipsic to the "preliminary parliament," [100] he there acted as vice-chairman, and by preventing the secession *en masse* of the opposition, contributed to sustain that body. After its dissolution, he became a member of the committee it left behind, and afterward of the Frankfort parliament, in which he was the leader of the moderate opposition.[101] His political theory aimed at a republic as the summit of Germany, but as its base the different traditionary kingdoms, dukedoms, &c.; since, in his opinion, the latter alone were able to preserve, intact, what he considered a peculiar beauty of German society, the independent development of its different orders. As a speaker he was plausible, rather theatrical, and very popular.

When the news of the Vienna insurrection [102] reached Frankfort, he was charged, in company with some other members of the German parliament, to carry to Vienna an address drawn up by the parliamentary opposition. As the spokesman of the deputation, he handed the address to the municipal council of Vienna, Oct. 17, 1848.[a] Having enrolled himself in the ranks of the students' corps, and commanded a barricade during the fight, he sat, after the capture of Vienna by Windischgrätz, quietly conversing in a hotel, when the hotel was surrounded by soldiers, and he himself made prisoner. Placed before a court-martial, and not condescending to deny any of his speeches or acts, he was sentenced to the gallows, a punishment commuted to that of being shot. This execution took place at daybreak, in the Brigittenau.

Written in September (not later than the 22nd), 1857

First published in *The New American Cyclopaedia*, Vol. III, 1858

Reproduced from *The New American Cyclopaedia*

---

[a] "An die Wiener", *Wiener Zeitung*, No. 290, October 22, 1848.— *Ed.*

Karl Marx

BOURRIENNE [103]

Bourrienne, Louis Antoine Fauvelet de, private secretary of Napoleon, born at Sens, July 9, 1769, died near Caen, Feb. 7, 1834. He entered the military school of Brienne in 1778, and was there some 6 years as Napoleon's school-fellow. From 1789 to 1792, he spent his time as attaché to the French embassy at Vienna, as a student of international law and northern languages at Leipsic, and at the court of Poniatowski, at Warsaw. After his return to Paris, he renewed his intimacy with Napoleon, then a poor and friendless officer; but the decisive turn taken by the revolutionary movement after June 20, 1792,[104] drove him back to Germany. In 1795 he again returned to Paris, and there again met Napoleon, who however treated him coldly; but toward the end of 1796, he applied again to him, and was summoned to headquarters, and installed at once as his private secretary. After the second Italian campaign,[105] Bourrienne received the title of councillor of state, was lodged at the Tuileries, and admitted to the first consul's family circle. In 1802 the house of Coulon, army contractors, whose partner Bourrienne had secretly become, and for which he had procured the lucrative business of supplying the whole cavalry equipment, failed with a deficit of 3 millions; the chief of the house disappeared, and Bourrienne was banished to Hamburg. In 1806 he was appointed to oversee at Hamburg the strict execution of Napoleon's continental system.[106] Accusations of peculation rising against him from the Hamburg senate, from which he had obtained 2,000,000 francs, and from the emperor Alexander, whose relative, the duke of Mecklenburg, he had also mulcted, Napoleon sent a commission to inquire into his conduct, and ordered him to refund 1,000,000 francs to the imperial treasury.

Thus, a disgraced and ruined man, he lived at Paris until Napoleon's downfall, in 1814, when he stepped forward, had his million paid back by the French provisional government,[107] was installed its postmaster-general, deposed from this post by Louis XVIII, and at the first rumor of Napoleon's return from Elba, made, by the same prince, prefect of the Paris police, a post he held for 8 days. As Napoleon, in his decree dated Lyons, March 13, had exempted him from the general amnesty, he followed Louis XVIII to Belgium, was thence despatched to Hamburg, and created, on his return to Paris, state councillor, subsequently minister of state. His pecuniary embarrassments forced him in 1828 to seek a refuge in Belgium, on an estate of the duchess of Brancas at Fontaine l'Evêque, not far from Charleroy. Here, with the assistance of M. de Villemarest and others, he drew up his "Memoirs" (10 vols. 8vo), which appeared in 1829, at Paris, and caused a great deal of excitement.[108] He died in a lunatic hospital.

Written in September (not later than the 22nd), 1857

First published in *The New American Cyclopaedia*, Vol. III, 1858

Reproduced from *The New American Cyclopaedia*

Frederick Engels

ARMY [109]

Army, the organized body of armed men which a state maintains for purposes of offensive or defensive war. Of the armies of ancient history the first of which we know any thing positive is that of Egypt. Its grand epoch of glory coincides with the reign of Rhamses II (Sesostris), and the paintings and inscriptions relating to his exploits on the numerous monuments of his reign, form the principal source of our knowledge on Egyptian military matters. The warrior caste of Egypt was divided into two classes, *hermotybii* and *calasirii,* the first 160,000, the other 250,000 strong, in their best times. It appears that these two classes were distinguished from each other merely by age or length of service, so that the calasirii, after a certain number of years, passed into the hermotybii or reserve. The whole army was settled in a sort of military colonies, an ample extent of land being set apart for each man as an equivalent for his services. These colonies were mostly situated in the lower part of the country, where attacks from the neighboring Asiatic states were to be anticipated; a few colonies only were established on the upper Nile, the Ethiopians not being very formidable opponents. The strength of the army lay in its infantry, and particularly in its archers. Beside these latter there were bodies of foot soldiers, variously armed and distributed into battalions,[a] according to their arms; spearmen, swordsmen, clubmen, slingers, &c. The infantry was supported by numerous war-chariots, each manned by 2 men, one to drive and the other to use the bow. Cavalry does not figure on the monuments. One

---

[a] Engels uses this term to designate tactical units of the ancient Egyptian infantry.— *Ed.*

solitary drawing of a man on horseback is considered to belong to
the Roman epoch, and it appears certain that the use of the horse
for riding and of cavalry became known to the Egyptians through
their Asiatic neighbors only. That at a later period they had a
numerous cavalry, acting, like all cavalry in ancient times, on the
wings of the infantry, is certain from the unanimity of the ancient
historians on this point. The defensive armor of the Egyptians
consisted of shields, helmets, and breastplates, or coats-of-mail, of
various materials. Their mode of attacking a fortified position
shows many of the means and artifices known to the Greeks and
Romans. They had the *testudo*, or battering-ram, the *vinea*,[110] and
scaling-ladder; that they, however, also knew the use of movable
towers, and that they undermined walls, as Sir G. Wilkinson
maintains,[a] is a mere supposition. From the time of Psammetichus
a corps of Grecian mercenaries was maintained; they were also
colonized in lower Egypt.

Assyria furnishes us with the earliest specimen of those Asiatic
armies which, for above 1,000 years, struggled for the possession
of the countries between the Mediterranean and the Indus. There,
as in Egypt, the monuments are our principal source of
information. The infantry appear armed similar to the Egyptian,
though the bow seems less prominent, and the arms offensive and
defensive are generally of better make and more tasteful
appearance. There is, beside, more variety of armament, on
account of the greater extent of the empire. Spear, bow, sword,
and dagger, are the principal weapons. Assyrians in the army of
Xerxes are also represented with iron-mounted clubs. The
defensive armament consisted of a helmet (often very tastefully
worked), a coat-of-mail of felt or leather, and a shield. The
war-chariots still formed an important portion of the army; it had
2 occupants, and the driver had to shelter the bowman with his
shield. Many of those who fight in chariots are represented in long
coats-of-mail. Then there was the cavalry, which here we meet
with for the first time. In the earliest sculptures the rider mounts
the bare back of his horse; later on, a sort of pad is introduced,
and in one sculpture a high saddle is depicted, similar to that now
in use in the East. The cavalry can scarcely have been very
different from that of the Persians and later eastern nations—
light, irregular horse, attacking in disorderly swarms, easily
repelled by a well-armed, solid infantry, but formidable to a

---

[a] J. G. Wilkinson, *Manners and Customs of the Ancient Egyptians*, Vol. I,
pp. 67-68.— *Ed.*

disordered or beaten army. Accordingly, it figured in rank behind the charioteers, who appear to have formed the aristocratic arm of the service. In infantry tactics some progress toward regular movements and formations in ranks and files appears to have been made. The bowmen either fought in advance, where they were always covered, each of them, by a shield-bearer, or they formed the rear rank, the first and second ranks, armed with spears, stooping or kneeling to enable them to shoot. In sieges they certainly knew the use of movable towers and mining; and, from a passage in Ezekiel,[a] it would almost appear that they made some sort of mound or artificial hill to command the walls of the town—a rude beginning of the Roman *agger*.[b] Their movable and fixed towers, too, were elevated to the height of the besieged wall, and higher, so as to command it. The ram and vinea they used also; and, numerous as their armies were, they turned off whole arms of rivers into new beds in order to gain access to a weak front of the attacked place, or to use the dry bed of the river as a road into the fortress. The Babylonians seem to have had armies similar to those of the Assyrians, but special details are wanting.

The Persian empire owed its greatness to its founders, the warlike nomads of the present Farsistan, a nation of horsemen, with whom cavalry took at once that predominant rank which it has since held in all eastern armies, up to the recent introduction of modern European drill. Darius Hystaspes established a standing army, in order to keep the conquered provinces in subjection, as well as to prevent the frequent revolts of the satraps, or civil governors. Every province thus had its garrison, under a separate commander; fortified towns, beside, were occupied by detachments. The provinces had to bear the expense of maintaining these troops. To this standing army also belonged the guards of the king, 10,000 chosen infantry (the Immortals, *Athanatoi*), resplendent with gold, followed on the march by long trains of carriages, with their harems and servants, and of camels with provisions, beside 1,000 halberdiers, 1,000 horse guards, and numerous war-chariots, some of them armed with scythes. For expeditions of magnitude this armament was considered insufficient, and a general levy from all the provinces of the empire took place. The mass of these various contingents formed a truly oriental army, composed of the most heterogeneous parts, varying among themselves in armament and mode of fighting, and

---

[a] Ezekiel 21:22 and 26:8.— *Ed.*
[b] Rampart.— *Ed.*

accompanied by immense trains of baggage and innumerable camp-followers. It is to the presence of these latter that we must ascribe the enormous numbers of the Persian armies as estimated by the Greeks. The soldiers, according to their respective nationality, were armed with bows, javelins, spears, swords, clubs, daggers, slings, &c. The contingent of every province had its separate commander; they appear, from Herodotus, to have been divided by tens, hundreds, thousands, &c., with officers to command each decimal subdivision.[a] The commands of large corps or of the wings of the army were generally given to members of the royal family. Among the infantry the Persian and the other Aryan nations (Medes and Bactrians) formed the *élite*. They were armed with bows, spears of moderate size, and a short sword; the head was protected by a sort of turban, the body by a coat covered with iron scales; the shield was mostly of wicker-work. Yet this *élite*, as well as the rest of the Persian infantry, was miserably beaten whenever it was opposed to even the smallest bodies of Greeks, and its unwieldy and disorderly crowds appear quite incapable of any but passive resistance against the incipient phalanx of Sparta and Athens; witness Marathon, Plataea, Mycale, and Thermopylae.[111] The war-chariots, which in the Persian army appear for the last time in history, might be useful on quite level ground against such a motley crowd as the Persian infantry themselves were, but against a solid mass of pikemen, such as the Greeks formed, or against light troops taking advantage of inequalities of ground, they were worse than useless. The least obstacle stopped them. In battle the horses got frightened, and, no longer under command, ran down their own infantry. As to the cavalry, the earlier periods of the empire give us little proof of its excellence. There were 10,000 horse on the plain of Marathon—a good cavalry country—yet they could not break the Athenian ranks. In later times it distinguished itself at the Granicus,[112] where, formed in one line, it fell on the heads of the Macedonian columns as they emerged from the fords of the river, and upset them before they could deploy. It thus successfully opposed Alexander's advanced guard, under Ptolemy, for a long while, until the main body arrived and the light troops manoeuvred on its flanks, when, having no second line or reserve, it had to retire. But at this period the Persian army had been strengthened by the infusion of a Greek element, imported by the Greek mercenaries, who, soon after Xerxes, were taken into pay by the king; and the

---

[a] Herodotus, *History*, Book VII, Ch. 81.—*Ed.*

cavalry tactics displayed by Memnon on the Granicus are so thoroughly un-Asiatic that we may, in the absence of positive information, at once ascribe them to Greek influence. The armies of Greece are the first of the detailed organization of which we have ample and certain information. With them the history of tactics, especially infantry tactics, may be said to begin. Without stopping to give an account of the warlike system of the heroic age of Greece, as described in Homer,[a] when cavalry was unknown, when the nobility and chiefs fought in war-chariots, or descended from them for a duel with an equally prominent enemy, and when the infantry appears to have been little better than that of the Asiatics, we at once pass to the military force of Athens in the time of her greatness. In Athens every free born man was liable to military service. The holders of certain public offices alone, and, in the earlier times, the fourth or poorest class of freemen, were exempt.[113] It was a militia system based upon slavery. Every youth on attaining his 18th year was obliged to do duty for 2 years, especially in watching the frontiers. During this time his military education was completed; afterward he remained liable to service up to his 60th year. In case of war the assembled citizens fixed the number of men to be called out; in extreme cases only the *levées en masse (panstratia)* were resorted to. The *strategi*, 10 of whom were annually elected by the people, had to levy these troops and to organize them, so that the men of each tribe, or *phyle*, formed a body under a separate *phylarch*. These officers, as well as the *taxiarchs*, or captains of companies, were equally elected by the people. The whole of this levy formed the heavy infantry (*hoplitae*) destined for the phalanx or deep line formation of spearmen, which originally formed the whole of the armed force, and subsequently, after the addition of light troops and cavalry, remained its mainstay—the corps which decided the battle. The phalanx was formed in various degrees of depth; we find mentioned phalanxes of 8, 12, 25 deep. The armature of the hoplitae consisted of a breastplate or corslet, helmet, oval target, spear, and short sword. The *forte* of the Athenian phalanx was attack; its charge was renowned for its furious impetus, especially after Miltiades, at Marathon, had introduced the quickening of the pace during the charge, so that they came down on the enemy with a run. On the defensive, the more solid and closer phalanx of Sparta was its superior. While at Marathon the whole force of the Athenians consisted of a heavy armed phalanx of 10,000 hoplitae,

---

[a] In the *Iliad.— Ed.*

at Plataea they had, beside 8,000 hoplitae, an equal number of light infantry. The tremendous pressure of the Persian invasions necessitated an extension of the liability to service; the poorest class, that of the thetes, was enrolled. They were formed into light troops (*gymnetae, psili*); they had no defensive armor at all, or a target only, and were supplied with a spear and javelins. With the extension of the Athenian power, their light troops were reinforced by the contingents of their allies,[114] and even by mercenary troops. Acarnanians, Ætolians, and Cretans, celebrated as archers and slingers, were added. An intermediate class of troops, between them and the hoplitae, was formed, the *peltastae*, armed similar to the light infantry, but capable of occupying and maintaining a position. They were, however, of but little importance until after the Peloponnesian war,[115] when Iphicrates reorganized them. The light troops of the Athenians enjoyed a high reputation for intelligence and quickness both in resolution and in execution. On several occasions, probably in difficult ground, they even successfully opposed the Spartan phalanx. The Athenian cavalry was introduced at a time when the republic was already rich and powerful. The mountainous ground of Attica was unfavorable to this arm, but the neighborhood of Thessaly and Boeotia, countries rich in horses, and consequently the first to form cavalry, soon caused its introduction in the other states of Greece. The Athenian cavalry, first 300, then 600, and even 1,000 strong, was composed of the richest citizens, and formed a standing corps even in time of peace. They were a very effective body, extremely watchful, intelligent, and enterprising. Their position in battle, as well as that of the light troops, was generally on the wings of the phalanx. In later times, the Athenians also maintained a corps of 200 mercenary mounted archers (*hippotoxotae*). The Athenian soldier, up to the time of Pericles, received no pay. Afterward 2 oboli (beside 2 more for provisions, which the soldier had to find) were given, and sometimes even the hoplitae received as much as 2 drachms. Officers received double pay, cavalry soldiers three-fold, generals four-fold. The corps of heavy cavalry alone cost 40 talents ($40,000) per annum in time of peace, during war considerably more. The order of battle and mode of fighting were extremely simple; the phalanx formed the centre, the men locking their spears, and covering the whole front with their row of shields. They attacked the hostile phalanx in a parallel front. When the first onset was not sufficient to break the enemy's order, the struggle hand to hand with the sword decided the battle. In the mean time the light troops and cavalry either attacked the corresponding troops of the enemy, or attempted to operate on the flank and rear of the phalanx, and to take advantage of any disorder manifesting itself in it. In case of a victory they undertook the pursuit, in case of defeat they covered the retreat as much as possible. They were also used for reconnoitring expeditions and forays, they harassed the enemy on the march, especially when he had to pass a defile, and they tried to capture his convoys and stragglers. Thus the order of battle was extremely simple; the phalanx always operated as a whole; its subdivisions into smaller bodies had no tactical[a] significance; their commanders had no other task than to see that the order of the phalanx was not broken, or at least quickly restored. What the strength of Athenian armies was during the Persian wars, we have shown above by a few examples. At the beginning of the Peloponnesian war, the force mustered 13,000 hoplitae for field service, 16,000[b] (the youngest and the oldest soldiers) for garrison duty, 1,200 horsemen, and 1,600 archers. According to Boeckh's calculations the force sent against Syracuse numbered 38,560 men; reinforcements despatched afterward, 26,000 men; in all nearly 65,000 men.[c] After the complete ruin of this expedition,[116] indeed, Athens was as much exhausted as France after the Russian campaign of 1812.

Sparta was the military state, *par excellence*, of Greece. If the general gymnastic education of the Athenians developed the agility as much as the strength of the body, the Spartans directed their attention mostly to strength, endurance, and hardiness. They valued steadiness in the ranks, and military point of honor, more than intelligence. The Athenian was educated as if he was to fight among light troops, yet in war he was fitted into his fixed place in the heavy phalanx; the Spartan, on the contrary, was brought up for service in the phalanx, and nothing else. It is evident that as long as the phalanx decided the battle, the Spartan, in the long run, had the best of it. In Sparta, every freeman was enrolled in the army lists from his 20th to his 60th year. The *ephori*[117] determined the number to be called out, which was generally chosen among the middle-aged men, from 30 to 40. As in Athens, the men belonging to the same tribe or locality were enrolled in the same body of troops. The organization of the army was based upon the confraternities (*enomotiae*) introduced by Lycurgus, 2 of which formed a pentecostys; 2 of these were united into a lochos,

---

[a] *The New American Cyclopaedia* has "technical" here.— *Ed.*

[b] *The New American Cyclopaedia* has 61,000 here.— *Ed.*

[c] A. Böckh, *Die Staatshaushaltung der Athener*, Bd. 1, S. 287.— *Ed.*

and 8, or 4 lochi, into a mora. This was the organization in
Xenophon's time; in former periods it appears to have varied. The
strength of a mora is variously stated at from 400 to 900 men, and
their number at one time was said to be 600. These various bodies
of free Spartans formed the phalanx; the hoplitae forming it were
armed with a spear, a short sword, and a shield fastened round
the neck. Later on, Cleomenes introduced the large Carian shield,
fastened by a string on the left arm, and leaving both hands of the
soldier free. The Spartans considered it disgraceful for their men
to return, after a defeat, without their shields; the preservation of
the shield proved the retreat to have been made in good order
and a compact phalanx, while single fugitives, running for their
lives, of course had to throw away the clumsy shield. The Spartan
phalanx was generally 8 deep, but sometimes the depth was
doubled by placing one wing behind the other. The men appear
to have marched in step; some elementary evolutions were also in
use, such as changing front to the rear by the half-turn of each
man, advancing or retiring a wing by wheeling, &c., but they
would seem to have been introduced at a later period only. In
their best times, the Spartan phalanx, like that of Athens, knew
the parallel front attack only. The ranks, on the march, were
distant from each other 6 feet, in the charge 3 feet, and in a
position receiving the charge, only $1\,^1/_2$ foot, from rank to rank.
The army was commanded by one of the kings, who, with his suite
(*damosia*), occupied a position in the centre of the phalanx.
Afterward, the number of the free Spartans having considerably
decreased, the strength of the phalanx was kept up by a selection
from the subjected *Periaeci*.[118] The cavalry was never stronger
than about 600 men, divided into troops (*ulami*) of 50 men. It
merely covered the wings. There was, beside, a body of 300
mounted men, the *élite* of the Spartan youth, but they dismounted
in battle, and formed a sort of body-guard of hoplitae around the
king. Of light troops, there were the *skiritae*, inhabitants of the
mountains near Arcadia, who generally covered the left wing; the
hoplitae of the phalanx, beside, had Helot servants,[119] who were
expected in battle to do duty as skirmishers; thus, the 5,000
hoplitae at Plataea brought 35,000 Helot light troops with them,
but of the exploits of these latter we find nothing stated in history.

The simple tactics of the Greeks underwent considerable
changes after the Peloponnesian war. At the battle of Leuctra,[120]
Epaminondas had to oppose, with a small force of Thebans, the
far more numerous, and hitherto invincible Spartan phalanx. The
plain, parallel front attack, here, would have been equivalent to

certain defeat, both wings being outflanked by the longer front of the enemy. Epaminondas, instead of advancing in line, formed his army into a deep column, and advanced against one wing of the Spartan phalanx, where the king[a] had taken his station. He succeeded in breaking through the Spartan line at this, the decisive point; he then wheeled his troops round, and moving on either hand, he himself outflanked the broken line, which could not form a new front without losing its tactical order. At the battle of Mantinea,[121] the Spartans formed their phalanx with a greater depth, but, nevertheless, the Theban column again broke through it. Agesilaus in Sparta, Timotheus, Iphicrates, Chabrias in Athens, also introduced changes in infantry tactics. Iphicrates improved the *peltastae*, a sort of light infantry, capable, however, in case of need, to fight in line. They were armed with a small round target, strong linen corslet, and long spear of wood. Chabrias made the first ranks of the phalanx, when on the defensive, kneel down to receive the enemy's charge. Full squares, and other columns, &c., were introduced, and accordingly deployments formed part of the elementary tactics. At the same time, greater attention was paid to light infantry of all kinds; several species of arms were borrowed from the barbarous and semi-barbarous neighbors of the Greeks, such as archers, mounted and on foot, slingers, &c. The majority of the soldiers of this period consisted of mercenaries. The wealthy citizens, instead of doing duty themselves, found it more convenient to pay for a substitute. The character of the phalanx, as the preeminently national portion of the army, in which the free citizens of the state only were admitted, thus suffered from this admixture of mercenaries, who had no right of citizenship. Toward the approach of the Macedonian epoch, Greece and her colonies were as much a mart for soldiers of fortune, and mercenaries, as Switzerland in the 18th and 19th centuries. The Egyptian kings had at an early time formed a corps of Greek troops. Afterward, the Persian king gave his army some steadiness by the admission of a body of Greek mercenaries. The chiefs of these bodies were regular condottieri, as much as those of Italy in the 16th century. During this period, warlike engines for throwing stones, darts, and incendiary projectiles, were introduced, especially by the Athenians. Pericles already used some similar machines at the siege of Samos.[122] Sieges were carried on by forming a line of contravallation, with ditch, or parapet, round the place, investing it, and by the attempt to place the war-engines in a

---

[a] Cleombrotus I.— *Ed.*

commanding position near the walls. Mining was regularly made use of, to bring the walls down. At the assault, the column formed the *synaspismus*, the outer ranks holding their shields before them, and the inner ranks holding them over their heads, so as to form a roof (called by the Romans, *testudo*), against the projectiles of the enemy.

While Greek skill was thus mainly directed toward shaping the flexible material of the mercenary bands into all sorts of novel and artificial formations, and in adopting or inventing new species of light troops, to the detriment of the ancient Doric heavy phalanx, which at that time alone could decide battles, a monarchy grew up, which, adopting all real improvements, formed a body of heavy infantry of such colossal dimensions, that no army with which it came in contact could resist its shock. Philip of Macedon formed a standing army of about 30,000 infantry, and 3,000 cavalry. The main body of the army was an immense phalanx of some 16,000 or 18,000 men, formed upon the principle of the Spartan phalanx, but improved in armament. The small Grecian shield was replaced by the large oblong Carian buckler, and the moderately sized spear by the Macedonian pike (*sarissa*) of 24 feet in length. The depth of this phalanx varied, under Philip, from 8, to 10, 12, 24 men. With the tremendous length of the pikes, each of the 6 front ranks could, on levelling them, make the points project in front of the first rank. The regular advance of such a long front of from 1,000 to 2,000 men, presupposes a great perfection of elementary drill, which in consequence was continually practised. Alexander completed this organization. His phalanx was, normally, 16,384 men strong, or 1,024 in front by 16 deep. The file of 16 (*lochos*) was conducted by a lochagos, who stood in the front rank. Two files formed a dilochy, 2 of which made a tetrarchy, 2 of which a taxiarchy, 2 of which a xenagy or syntagma, 16 men in front by 16 deep. This was the evolutionary unit, the march being made in columns of xenagies, 16 in front. Sixteen xenagies (equal to 8 pentecosiarchies, or 4 chiliarchies, or 2 telarchies) formed a small phalanx, 2 of which a diphalangarchy, and 4 a tetraphalangarchy or phalanx properly so called. Every one of these subdivisions had its corresponding officer. The diphalangarchy of the right wing was called head, that of the left wing, tail, or rear. Whenever extraordinary solidity was required, the left wing took station behind the right, forming 512 men in front by 32 in depth. On the other hand, by deploying the 8 rear ranks on the left of the front ranks, the extent of front could be doubled, and the depth reduced to 8. The distances of ranks and files were similar to those of the Spartans, but the close order was so compact that the single soldier in the middle of the phalanx could not turn. Intervals between the subdivisions of the phalanx were not allowed in battle; the whole formed one continuous line, charging *en muraille*. The phalanx was formed by Macedonian volunteers exclusively; though, after the conquest of Greece, Greeks also could enter it.[123] The soldiers were all heavy armed hoplitae. Beside shield and pike, they carried a helmet and sword, although the hand-to-hand fight with the latter weapon cannot very often have been required after the charge of that forest of pikes. When the phalanx had to meet the Roman legion, the case indeed was different. The whole phalangite system, from the earliest Doric times down to the breaking up of the Macedonian empire, suffered from one great inconvenience; it wanted flexibility. Unless on a level and open plain, these long, deep lines, could not move with order and regularity. Every obstacle in front forced it to form column, in which shape it was not prepared to act. Moreover, it had no second line or reserve. As soon, therefore, as it was met by an army, formed in smaller bodies and adapted to turn obstacles of ground without breaking line, and disposed in several lines seconding each other, the phalanx could not help going into broken ground, where its new opponent completely cut it up. But to such opponents as Alexander had at Arbela,[a] his 2 large phalanxes must have appeared invincible. Beside this heavy infantry of the line, Alexander had a guard of 6,000 hyraspistae, still more heavily armed, with even larger bucklers and longer pikes. His light infantry consisted of argyraspides, with small silver-plated shields, and of numerous peltastae, both of which troops were organized in demi-phalanxes of normally 8,192 men, being able to fight either in extended order or in line, like the hoplitae; and their phalanx often had the same success. The Macedonian cavalry was composed of young Macedonian and Thessalian noblemen, with the addition, subsequently, of a body of horsemen from Greece proper. They were divided into squadrons (*ilae*), of which the Macedonian nobility alone formed 8. They belonged to what we should call heavy cavalry; they wore a helmet, cuirass with cuissarts of iron scales to protect the leg, and were armed with a long sword and pike. The horse, too, wore a frontlet of iron. This class of cavalry, the cataphracti, received great attention both from Philip and Alexander; the latter used it for his decisive manoeuvre at Arbela, when

---

[a] See this volume, p. 23.— *Ed.*

he first beat and pursued one wing of the Persians, and then, passing behind their centre, fell upon the rear of the other wing. They charged in various formations: in line, in common rectangular column, in rhomboid or wedge-shaped column. The light cavalry had no defensive armor; it carried javelins and light short lances; there was also a corps of acrobalistae, or mounted archers. These troops served for outpost duty, patrols, reconnoitring, and irregular warfare generally. They were the contingents of Thracian and Illyrian tribes, which, beside, furnished some few thousands of irregular infantry. A new arm, invented by Alexander, claims our attention from the circumstance that it has been imitated in modern times, the dimachae, mounted troops, expected to fight either as cavalry or as infantry. The dragoons of the 16th and following centuries are a complete counterpart to these, as we shall see hereafter. We have, however, no information as to whether these hybrid troops of antiquity were more successful in their double task than the modern dragoons.

Thus was composed the army with which Alexander conquered the country between the Mediterranean, the Oxus, and the Sutledj. As to its strength, at Arbela, it consisted of 2 large phalanxes of hoplitae (say 30,000 men), 2 semi-phalanxes of peltastae (16,000), 4,000 cavalry, and 6,000 irregular troops, in all about 56,000 men. At the Granicus, his force of all arms was 35,000 men, of whom 5,000 were cavalry.

Of the Carthaginian army we know no details; even the strength of the force with which Hannibal passed the Alps, is disputed. The armies of the successors of Alexander show no improvements on his formations; the introduction of elephants was but of short duration; when terrified by fire, these animals were more formidable to their own troops than to the enemy. The later Greek armies (under the Achaean league [124]) were formed partly on the Macedonian, partly on the Roman system.

The Roman army presents us with the most perfect system of infantry tactics invented during the time when the use of gunpowder was unknown. It maintains the predominance of heavy infantry and compact bodies, but adds to it mobility of the separate smaller bodies, the possibility of fighting in broken ground, the disposition of several lines one behind the other, partly as supports and reliefs, partly as a powerful reserve, and finally a system of training the single soldier which was even more to the purpose than that of Sparta. The Romans, accordingly, overthrew every armament opposed to them, the Macedonian phalanx as well as the Numidian horse.

In Rome every citizen, from his 17th to his 45th or 50th year, was liable to serve, unless he belonged to the lowest class, or had served in 20 campaigns on foot, or 10 campaigns as a horseman. Generally the younger men only were selected. The drill of the soldier was very severe, and calculated to develop his bodily powers in every imaginable way. Running, jumping, vaulting, climbing, wrestling, swimming, first naked, then in full armament, were largely practised, beside the regular drill in the use of the arms and the various movements. Long marches in heavy marching order, every soldier carrying from 40 to 60 lbs., were kept up at the rate of 4 miles an hour. The use of the intrenching tools, and the throwing up of intrenched camps in a short time, also formed part of the military education; and not only the recruits, but even the legions of veterans, had to undergo all these exercises in order to keep their bodies fresh and supple, and to remain inured to fatigue and want. Such soldiers were, indeed, fit to conquer the world.

In the best times of the republic there were generally 2 consular armies, each consisting of 2 legions and the contingents of the allies (in infantry of equal strength, cavalry double the strength of the Romans). The levy of the troops was made in a general assembly of the citizens on the capitol or Campus Martius; an equal number of men was taken from every tribe,[125] which was again equally subdivided among the 4 legions, until the number was completed. Very often citizens, freed from service by age or their numerous campaigns, entered again as volunteers. The recruits were then sworn in and dismissed until required. When called in, the youngest and poorest were taken for the velites, the next in age and means for the hastati and principes, the oldest and wealthiest for the triarii. Every legion counted 1,200 velites, 1,200 hastati, 1,200 principes, 600 triarii, and 300 horsemen (knights),[126] in all 4,500. The hastati, principes, and triarii, were each divided into 10 manipuli or companies, and an equal number of velites attached to each. The velites (*rorarii, accensi, ferentarii*[a]) formed the light infantry of the legion, and stood on its wings along with the cavalry. The hastati formed the 1st, the principes the 2d line; they were originally armed with spears. The triarii formed the reserve, and were armed with the pilum, a short but extremely heavy and dangerous spear, which they threw into the front ranks of the enemy immediately before engaging him sword in hand. Every manipulus was commanded by a centurion, having

---

[a] Soldiers placed behind the triarii; auxiliaries; skirmishers.— *Ed.*

a 2d centurion for his lieutenant. The centurions ranked through
the whole of the legion, from the 2d centurion of the last or 10th
manipulus of the hastati to the 1st centurion of the 1st manipulus
of the triarii (*primus pilus*), who, in the absence of a superior
officer, even took the command of the whole legion. Commonly,
the primus pilus commanded all the triarii, the same as the *primus
princeps* (1st centurion of 1st manipulus of principes), all the
principes, and the *primus hastatus*, and all the hastati of the legion.
The legion was commanded in the earlier times in turns by its 6
military tribunes; each of them held the command for 2 months.
After the 1st civil war,[127] legates were placed as standing chiefs at
the head of every legion; the tribunes now were mostly officers
intrusted with the staff or administrative business. The difference
of armament of the 3 lines had disappeared before the time of
Marius. The pilum had been given to all 3 lines of the legion; it
now was the national arm of the Romans. The qualitative
distinction between the 3 lines, as far as it was based upon age and
length of service, soon disappeared too. In the battle of Metellus
against Jugurtha,[128] there appeared, according to Sallust,[a] for the
last time hastati, principes, triarii. Marius now formed out of the
30 manipuli of the legion 10 cohorts, and disposed them in 2 lines
of 5 cohorts each. At the same time, the normal strength of the
cohort was raised to 600 men; the 1st cohort, under the primus
pilus, carried the legionary eagle.[129] The cavalry remained formed
in turmae of 30 rank and file and 3 decurions, the 1st of whom
commanded the turma. The armature of the Roman infantry
consisted of a shield of demi-cylindric shape, 4 feet by $2\,^1/_2$, made
of wood, covered with leather and strengthened with iron
fastenings; in the middle it had a boss (*umbo*) to parry off
spear-thrusts. The helmet was of brass, generally with a prolongation behind to protect the neck, and fastened on with leather
bands covered with brass scales. The breastplate, about a foot
square, was fastened on a leather corslet with scaled straps passing
over the shoulder; for the centurions, in consisted of a coat-of-
mail covered with brass scales. The right leg, exposed when
advanced for the sword-thrust, was protected by a brass plate.
Beside the short sword, which was used for thrusting more
than for cutting, the soldiers carried the pilum, a heavy spear $4\,^1/_2$
feet wood, with a projecting iron point of $1\,^1/_2$ foot, or nearly 6
feet in all long, but $2\,^1/_2$ inches square in the wood, and weighing
about 10 or 11 lbs. When thrown at 10 or 15 paces distance, it

---

[a] Sallust, *Jugurthine War*, XLVIII-LIII.— *Ed.*

often penetrated shields and breastplates, and almost every time threw down its man. The velites, lightly equipped, carried light short javelins. In the later periods of the republic, when barbaric auxiliaries undertook the light service, this class of troops disappears entirely. The cavalry were provided with defensive armor similar to that of the infantry, a lance and a longer sword. But the Roman national cavalry was not very good, and preferred to fight dismounted. In later periods it was entirely done away with, and Numidian, Spanish, Gallic, and German horsemen, supplanted it.

The tactical disposition of the troops admitted of great mobility. The manipuli were formed with intervals equal to their extent of front; the depth varied from 5 or 6 to 10 men. The manipuli of the 2d line were placed behind the intervals of the lst; the triarii still further to the rear, but in one unbroken line. According to circumstances, the manipuli of each line could close up or form line without intervals, or those of the 2d line could march up to fill the intervals of the 1st; or else, where greater depth was required, the manipuli of the principes closed up each in rear of the corresponding manipulus of the hastati, doubling its depth. When opposed to the elephants of Pyrrhus,[130] the 3 lines all formed with intervals, each manipulus covering the one in its front, so as to leave room for the animals to pass straight through the order of battle. In this formation the clumsiness of the phalanx was in every way successfully overcome. The legion could move and manoeuvre, without breaking its order of battle, in ground where the phalanx durst not venture without the utmost risk. One or two manipuli at most would have to shorten their front to defile past an obstacle; in a few moments, the front was restored. The legion could cover the whole of its front by light troops, as they could retire, on the advance of the line, through the intervals. But the principal advantage was the disposition in a plurality of lines, brought into action successively, according to the requirements of the moment. With the phalanx, one shock had to decide. No fresh troops were in reserve to take up the fight in case of a reverse—in fact that case was never provided for. The legion could engage the enemy with its light troops and cavalry on the whole of his front—could oppose to the advance of his phalanx its first line of hastati, which was not so easily beaten, as at least 6 of the 10 manipuli had first to be broken singly—could wear out the strength of the enemy by the advance of the principes, and finally decide the victory by the triarii. Thus the troops and the progress of the battle remained in the hand of the general, while the phalanx, once engaged, was irretrievably engaged with all its strength, and had to see the battle out. If the Roman general desired to break off the combat, the legionary organization permitted him to take up a position with his reserves, while the troops engaged before retired through the intervals, and took up a position in their turn. Under all circumstances, there was always a portion of the troops in good order, for even if the triarii were repulsed, the 2 first lines had re-formed behind them. When the legions of Flamininus met Philip's phalanx in the plains of Thessaly,[131] their first attack was at once repulsed; but charge following charge, the Macedonians got tired and lost part of their compactness of formation; and wherever a sign of disorder manifested itself, there was a Roman manipulus to attempt an inroad into the clumsy mass. At last, 20 manipuli attacking the flanks and rear of the phalanx, tactical continuity could no longer be maintained; the deep line dissolved into a swarm of fugitives, and the battle was lost. Against cavalry, the legion formed the *orbis,* a sort of square with baggage in the centre. On the march, when an attack was to be apprehended, it formed the *legio quadrata,* a sort of lengthened column with a wide front, baggage in the centre. This was of course possible in the open plain, only where the line of march could go across the country.

In Caesar's time the legions were mostly recruited by voluntary enlistment in Italy. Since the Social war,[132] the right of citizenship, and with it liability for service, was extended to all Italy, and consequently there were far more men available than required. The pay was about equal to the earnings of a laborer; recruits, therefore, were plentiful, even without having recourse to the conscription. In exceptional cases only were legions recruited in the provinces; thus Caesar had his fifth legion recruited in Roman Gallia,[133] but afterward it received the Roman naturalization *en masse.* The legions were far from having the nominal strength of 4,500 men; those of Caesar were seldom much above 3,000. Levies of recruits were formed into new legions (*legiones tironum*), rather than mixed with the veterans in the old legions; these new legions were at first excluded from battles in the open field, and principally used for guarding the camp. The legion was divided into 10 cohorts of 3 manipuli each. The names of hastati, principes, triarii, were maintained as far as necessary to denote the rank of officers according to the system indicated above; as to the soldiers, these names had lost all significance. The 6 centurions of the first cohort of each legion were, by right, present at councils of war. The centurions rose from the ranks, and seldom attained

higher command; the school for superior officers was in the
personal staff of the general, consisting of young men of
education, who soon advanced to the rank of *tribuni militum,* and
later on to that of *legati.* The armament of the soldier remained
the same: pilum and sword. Beside his accoutrements, the soldier
carried his personal baggage, weighing from 35 to 60 pounds. The
contrivance for carrying it was so clumsy that the baggage had
first to be deposited before the soldier was ready for battle. The
camp-utensils of the army were carried on the back of horses and
mules, of which a legion required about 500. Every legion had its
eagle, and every cohort its colors. For light infantry, Caesar drew
from his legions a certain number of men (*antesignani*), men
equally fit for light service and for close fight in line. Beside these,
he had his provincial auxiliaries, Cretan archers, Balearic slingers,
Gallic and Numidian contingents, and German mercenaries. His
cavalry consisted partly of Gallic, partly of German troops. The
Roman velites and cavalry had disappeared some time ago.

The staff of the army consisted of the *legati,* appointed by the
senate, the lieutenants of the general, whom he employed to
command detached corps, or portions of the order of battle.
Caesar, for the first time, gave to every legion a legate as standing
commander. If there were not legati enough, the *quaestor,* too, had
to take the command of a legion. He was properly the paymaster
of the army, and chief of the commissariat, and was assisted in this
office by numerous clerks and orderlies. Attached to the staff were
the *tribuni militum,* and the young volunteers above mentioned
(*contubernales, comites praetorii*), doing duty as adjutants, orderly
officers; but in battle they fought in line, the same as private
soldiers, in the ranks of the *cohors praetoria,* consisting of the
lictors, clerks, servants, guides (*speculatores*), and orderlies (*appari-
tores*) of the head-quarters. The general, beside, had a sort of
personal guard, consisting of veterans who voluntarily had
reënlisted on the call of their former chief. This troop, mounted
on the march, but fighting on foot, was considered the *élite* of the
army; it carried and guarded the *vexillum,* the signal-banner for
the whole army. In battle, Caesar generally fought in 3 lines, 4
cohorts per legion in the first, and 3 in the second and third lines
each; the cohorts of the second line dressed on the intervals of the
first. The second line had to relieve the first; the third line formed
a general reserve for decisive manoeuvres against the front or
flank of the enemy, or for parrying his decisive thrusts. Wherever
the enemy so far outflanked the line that its prolongation became
necessary, the army was disposed in two lines only. One single line

(*acies simplex*) was made use of in an extreme case of need only, and then without intervals between the cohorts; in the defence of a camp, however, it was the rule, as the line was still 8 to 10 deep, and could form a reserve from the men who had no room on the parapet.

Augustus completed the work of making the Roman troops a regular standing army. He had 25 legions distributed all over the empire, of which 8 were on the Rhine (considered the main strength, *praecipium robur*, of the army), 3 in Spain, 2 in Africa, 2 in Egypt, 4 in Syria and Asia Minor, 6 in the Danubian countries. Italy was garrisoned by chosen troops recruited exclusively in that country, and forming the imperial guard; this consisted of 12, later on, of 14 cohorts; beside these the city of Rome had 7 cohorts of municipal guards (*vigiles*), formed, originally, from emancipated slaves. Beside this regular army, the provinces had to furnish, as formerly, their light auxiliary troops, now mostly reduced to a sort of militia for garrison and police duty. On menaced frontiers, however, not only these auxiliary troops, but foreign mercenaries, too, were employed in active service. The number of legions increased under Trajan to 30, under Septimius Severus to 33. The legions, beside their numbers, had names, taken from their stations (*L. Germanica, L. Italica*), from emperors (*L. Augusta*), from gods (*L. Primigenia, L. Apollinaris*[a]), or conferred as honorary distinctions (*L. fidelis, L. pia, L. invicta*[b]). The organization of the legion underwent some changes. The commander was now called praefectus. The first cohort was doubled in strength (*cohors milliaria*), and the normal strength of the legion raised to 6,100 infantry and 726 cavalry; this was to be the minimum, and in case of need one or more *cohortes milliariae* were to be added. The *cohors milliaria* was commanded by a military tribune, the others by tribunes or *praepositi;* the rank of *centurio* was thus confined to subalterns. The admission of liberated, or non-liberated slaves, natives of the provinces, and all sorts of people into the legions, became the rule; Roman citizenship being required for the praetorians in Italy only, and even there this was abandoned in later times. The Roman nationality of the army was thus very soon drowned in the influx of barbaric and semi-barbaric, Romanized and non-Romanized elements; the officers alone maintained the Roman character. This deterioration of the elements composing the army very soon

---

[a] Jupiter's Legion, Apollo's Legion.— *Ed.*
[b] Loyal Legion, Pious Legion, Invincible Legion.— *Ed.*

reacted upon its armament and tactics. The heavy breastplate and pilum were thrown overboard; the toilsome system of drill, which had formed the conquerors of the world, was neglected; camp-followers and luxuries became necessary to the army, and the *impedimenta* (train of baggage) increased as strength and endurance decreased. As had been the case in Greece, the decline was marked by neglect of the heavy line infantry, by a foolish fancy for all sorts of light armament, and by the adoption of barbaric equipments and tactics. Thus we find innumerable classifications of light troops (*auxiliatores, exculcatores, jaculatores, excursatores, praecursatores, scutati, funditores, balistarii, tragularii*[a]), armed with all sorts of projectiles, and we are told by Vegetius that the cavalry had been improved in imitation of the Goths, Alani, and Huns.[b] Finally, all distinction of equipment and armament between Romans and barbarians ceased, and the Germans, physically and morally superior, marched over the bodies of the un-Romanized legions.

The conquest of the Occident by the Germans thus was opposed by but a small remnant, a dim tradition of the ancient Roman tactics; but even this small remnant was now destroyed. The whole of the middle ages is as barren a period for the development of tactics as for that of any other science. The feudal system, though in its very origin a military organization, was essentially opposed to discipline. Rebellions and secessions of large vassals, with their contingents, were of regular occurrence. The distribution of orders to the chiefs turned generally into a tumultuous council of war, which rendered all extensive operations impossible. Wars, therefore, were seldom directed on decisive points; struggles for the possession of a single locality filled up entire campaigns. The only operations of magnitude occurring in all this period (passing over the confused times from the 6th to the 12th century), are the expeditions of the German emperors against Italy, and the crusades,[134] the one as resultless as the other.

The infantry of the middle ages, composed of the feudal retainers and part of the peasantry, was chiefly composed of pikemen, and mostly contemptible. It was great sport for the knights, covered as they were with iron all over, to ride singly into this unprotected rabble, and lay about them with a will. A portion of the infantry was armed, on the continent of Europe, with the

---

[a] Auxiliaries, advanced detachments, throwers (of pikes, javelins), reconnoiterers, skirmishers, shield bearers, slingers, ballista men, pikemen.— *Ed.*

[b] Vegetius, *Epitome Institutorum Rei militaris.*— *Ed.*

crossbow, while in England the longbow became the national weapon of the peasantry. This longbow was a very formidable weapon, and secured the superiority of the English over the French at Crécy, Poitiers, and Agincourt.[135] Easily protected against rain, which rendered the crossbow unserviceable at times, it projected its arrow to distances above 200 yards, or not much less than the effective range of the old smooth-bored musket. The arrow penetrated a one-inch board, and would even pass through breastplates. Thus it long maintained its place even against the first small fire-arms, especially as six arrows could be shot off while the musket of that epoch could be loaded and fired once; and even as late as the end of the 16th century Queen Elizabeth attempted to reintroduce the national longbow as a weapon of war. It was especially effective against cavalry; the arrows, even if the armor of the men-at-arms was proof against them, wounded or killed the horses, and the unhorsed knights were thereby disabled, and generally made prisoners. The archers acted either in skirmishing order or in line.

Cavalry was the decisive arm of the middle ages. The knights in full armor formed the first effective body of heavy cavalry, charging in regular formation, which we meet with in history; for Alexander's cataphracti, though they decided the day at Arbela,[a] were so much an exception that we hear nothing more of them after that day, and during the whole sequel of ancient history, infantry maintains its preeminent rank in battle. The only progress, then, which the middle ages have bequeathed to us, is the creation of a cavalry, from which our modern mounted service descends in a direct line. And yet, what a clumsy thing this cavalry was, is proved by the one fact, that during the whole middle ages the cavalry was the heavy, slow-moving arm, while all light service and quick movements were executed by infantry. The knights, however, did not always fight in close order. They preferred fighting duels with single opponents, or spurring their horses into the midst of the hostile infantry; thus the mode of fighting out a battle was carried back to the Homeric times. When they did act in close order, they charged either in line (one deep, the more lightly-armed esquires forming the second rank) or in deep column. Such a charge was undertaken, as a rule, against the knights (men-at-arms) only of the opposing army; upon its infantry it would have been wasted. The horses, heavily laden with their own as well as their rider's armor, could run but slowly and

---

[a] See this volume, p. 23.—*Ed.*

for short distances. During the crusades, therefore, and in the wars with the Mongolians in Poland and Silesia,[136] this immovable cavalry was constantly tired out, and, finally, worsted by the active light horsemen of the East. In the Austrian and Burgundian wars against Switzerland,[137] the men-at-arms, entangled in difficult ground, had to dismount and form a phalanx even more immovable than that of Macedon; in mountain defiles, rocks and stumps of trees were hurled down upon them, in consequence of which the phalanx lost its tactical order, and was scattered by a resolute attack.

Toward the 14th century a kind of lighter cavalry was introduced, and a portion of the archers were mounted to facilitate their manoeuvring; but these and other changes were soon rendered useless, abandoned, or turned to different account by the introduction of that new element, which was destined to change the whole system of warfare—gunpowder.

From the Arabs in Spain the knowledge of the composition and the use of gunpowder spread to France and the rest of Europe; the Arabs themselves had received it from nations further east, who again had it from the original inventors, the Chinese. In the first half of the 14th century cannon first was introduced into European armies; heavy, unwieldy pieces of ordnance, throwing stone balls, and unfit for any thing but the war of sieges. Small arms were, however, soon invented. The city of Perugia in Italy supplied itself in 1364, with 500 hand-guns, the barrels not more than eight inches long; they subsequently gave rise to the manufacture of pistols (so called from Pistoja in Tuscany). Not long afterward longer and heavier hand-guns (*arquebuses*) were manufactured, corresponding to our present musket; but short and heavy in the barrel, they had but a restricted range, and the matchlock was an almost absolute hindrance to correct aim, beside having nearly every other possible disadvantage. Toward the close of the 14th century there was no military force in western Europe without its artillery and arquebusiers. But the influence of the new arm on general tactics was very little perceptible. Both large and small fire-arms took a very long time in loading, and what with their clumsiness and costliness, they had not even superseded the crossbow by 1450.

In the mean time the general breaking up of the feudal system, and the rise of cities, contributed to change the composition of armies. The larger vassals were either subdued by central authority, as in France, or had become quasi-independent sovereigns, as in Germany and Italy. The power of the lesser nobility was broken by the central authority in conjunction with the cities. The feudal armies no longer existed; new armies were formed from the numerous mercenaries whom the ruin of feudalism had set free to serve those who would pay them. Thus, something approaching standing armies arose; but these mercenaries, men of all nations, difficult to keep in order, and not very regularly paid, committed very great excesses. In France, King Charles VII therefore formed a permanent force from native elements. In 1445 he levied 15 *compagnies d'ordonnance* of 600 men each; in all, 9,000 cavalry garrisoned in the towns of the kingdom, and paid with regularity. Every company was divided into 100 lances; a lance consisted of one man-at-arms, 3 archers, an esquire, and a page. Thus they formed a mixture of heavy cavalry with mounted archers, the 2 arms, in battle, acting of course separately. In 1448 he added 16,000 francs-archers, under 4 captains-general, each commanding 8 companies of 500 men. The whole of the archers had the crossbow. They were recruited and armed by the parishes, and free from all taxes. This may be considered the first standing army of modern times.

At the close of this first period of modern tactics, as they emerged from mediaeval confusion, the state of things may be summed up as follows: The main body of the infantry, consisting of mercenaries, was armed with pike and sword, breastplate and helmet. It fought in deep, close masses, but, better armed and drilled than the feudal infantry, it showed greater tenacity and order in combat. The standing levies and the mercenaries, soldiers by profession, were of course superior to the casual levies and disconnected bands of feudal retainers. The heavy cavalry now found it sometimes necessary to charge in close array against infantry. The light infantry was still principally composed of archers, but the use of the hand-gun for skirmishers gained ground. The cavalry remained, as yet, the principal arm; heavy cavalry, men-at-arms encased in iron, but no longer composed, in every case, of the nobility, and reduced from its former chivalrous and Homeric mode of fighting to the more prosaic necessity of charging in close order. But the unwieldiness of such cavalry was now generally felt, and many devices were planned to find a lighter kind of horse. Mounted archers, as has been stated, had in part to supply this want; in Italy and the neighboring countries the *stradioti,* light cavalry on the Turkish plan, composed of Bosnians and Albanian mercenaries, a sort of Bashi-Bozuks,[138] found ready employment, and were much feared, especially in pursuits. Poland and Hungary had, beside the heavy cavalry adopted from the West, retained their own national light cavalry. The artillery was in its infancy. The heavy guns of the time were, indeed, taken into the field, but could not leave their position after it was once taken up; the powder was bad, the loading difficult and slow, and the range of the stone-balls short.

The close of the 15th and the beginning of the 16th century are marked by a double progress; the French improved the artillery, and the Spaniards gave a new character to the infantry. Charles VIII of France so far made his guns movable that, not only could he take them into the field, but make them change their position during battle and follow the other troops in their movements, which, however, were not very quick. He thereby became the founder of field artillery. His guns, mounted on wheeled carriages and plentifully horsed, proved immensely superior to the old-fashioned clumsy artillery of the Italians (drawn by bullocks), and did such execution in the deep columns of the Italian infantry, that Machiavelli wrote his "Art of War"[a] principally in order to propose formations, by which the effect of such artillery on infantry could be counteracted. In the battle of Marignano,[139] Francis I of France defeated the Swiss pikemen by the effective fire and the mobility of this artillery, which, from flanking positions, enfiladed the Swiss order of battle. But the reign of the pike, for infantry, was on the decline. The Spaniards improved the common hand-gun (arquebuse) and introduced it into the regular heavy infantry. Their musket (hacquebutte) was a heavy, long-barrelled arm, bored for 2-ounce bullets, and fired from a rest formed by a forked pole. It sent its bullet through the strongest breastplate, and was therefore decisive against the heavy cavalry, which got into disorder as soon as the men began falling. Ten or 15 musketeers were placed with every company of pikemen, and the effect of their fire, at Pavia,[140] astonished both allies and enemies. Frundsberg relates that, in that battle a single shot from such a musket used to bring down several men and horses. From that time dates the superiority of the Spanish infantry, which lasted for above 100 years.

The war consequent upon the rebellion of the Netherlands[141] was of great influence on the formation of armies. Both Spaniards and Dutch improved all arms considerably. Hitherto, in the armies of mercenaries, every man offering for enlistment had to come fully equipped, armed, and acquainted with the use of his arms. But in this long war, carried on during 40 years on a small extent

---

[a] A reference to Niccolò Machiavelli's *I sette libri dell' arte della guerra.—Ed.*

of country, the available recruits of this class soon became scarce. The Dutch had to put up with such able-bodied volunteers as they could get, and the government now was under the necessity of seeing them drilled. Maurice of Nassau composed the first drill-regulations of modern times, and thereby laid the foundation for the uniform instruction of a whole army. The infantry began again to march in step; it gained much in homogeneity and solidity. It was now formed into smaller bodies; the companies, hitherto 400 to 500, were reduced to 150 and 200 men, 10 companies forming a regiment. The improved musket gained ground upon the pike; one-third of the whole infantry consisted of musketeers, mixed in each company with the pikemen. These latter, being required for hand-to-hand fight only, retained their helmet, breastplate, and steel gauntlets; the musketeers threw away all defensive armor. The formation was generally 2 deep for the pikemen, and from 5 to 8 deep for the musketeers; as soon as the first rank had fired, it retired to load again. Still greater changes took place in cavalry, and here, too, Maurice of Nassau took the lead. In the impossibility of forming a heavy cavalry of men-at-arms, he organized a body of light-horse recruited in Germany, armed them with a helmet, cuirass, brassarts for the arms, steel gauntlets, and long boots, and as with the lance they would not have been a match for the heavy-armed Spanish cavalry, he gave them a sword and long pistols. This new class of horsemen, approaching our modern cuirassiers, soon proved superior to the far less numerous and less movable Spanish men-at-arms, whose horses they shot down before the slow mass broke in upon them. Maurice of Nassau had his cuirassiers drilled as well as his infantry; he so far succeeded, that he could venture to execute in battle, changes of front and other evolutions, with large and small bodies of them. Alva, too, soon found the necessity of improving his light horse; hitherto they had been fit for skirmishing and single combat only, but under his direction they soon learned to charge in a body, the same as the heavy cavalry. The formation of cavalry remained still 5 to 8 deep. About this time Henry IV of France introduced a new kind of mounted service, the dragoons, originally infantry, mounted on horses for quicker locomotion only; but very few years after their introduction, they were used as cavalry as well, and equipped for this double service. They had neither defensive armor nor high boots, but a cavalry sword, and sometimes a lance; beside, they carried the infantry musket, or a shorter carbine. These troops did not, however, come up to the expectations which had led to their formation; they soon became a portion of the regular cavalry, and ceased to fight as infantry. (The emperor Nicholas of Russia attempted to revive the original dragoons by forming a body of 16,000 men strong, fit for dismounted as well as mounted service; they never found occasion to dismount in battle, always fought as cavalry, and are now broken up and incorporated, as cavalry dragoons, with the remaining Russian cavalry.) In artillery the French maintained the superiority they had gained. The prolonge was invented by them about this time, and case-shot introduced by Henry IV. The Spaniards and Dutch, too, lightened and simplified their artillery, but still it remained a clumsy concern, and light, movable pieces of effective calibre and range were still unknown.

With the 30 years' war [142] opens the period of Gustavus Adolphus, the great military reformer of the 17th century. His infantry regiments were composed of two-thirds musketeers, and one-third pikemen. Some regiments consisted of musketeers alone. The muskets were so much lightened, that the rest for firing them became unnecessary. He also introduced paper cartridges, by which loading was much facilitated. The deep formation was done away with; his pikemen stood 6, his musketeers only 3 deep. These latter were drilled in firing by platoons and ranks. The unwieldy regiments of 2,000 or 3,000 men were reduced to 1,300 or 1,400, in 8 companies, and 2 regiments formed into a brigade. With this formation he defeated the deep masses of his opponents, often disposed, like a column or full square, 30 deep, upon which his artillery played with terrible effect. The cavalry was reorganized upon similar principles. The men-at-arms were completely done away with. The cuirassiers lost the brassarts, and some other useless pieces of defensive armor; they were thus made considerably lighter and more movable. His dragoons fought nearly always as cavalry. Both cuirassiers and dragoons were formed only 3 deep, and had strict orders not to lose time with firing, but to charge at once sword in hand. They were divided into squadrons of 125 men. The artillery was improved by the addition of light guns. The leather guns of Gustavus Adolphus are celebrated, but were not long retained. They were replaced by cast-iron 4-pounders, so light that they could be drawn by 2 horses; they could be fired 6 times while a musketeer fired twice; 2 of these were attached to every regiment of infantry. Thus, the division of light and heavy field artillery was established; the light guns accompanied the infantry while the heavy ones remained in reserve, or took up a position for the whole of the battle. The armies of this time begin to show the increasing preponderance of infantry over cavalry. At Leipsic, in 1631, Gustavus Adolphus had 19,000 infantry and 11,000 cavalry; Tilly had 31,000 infantry and 13,000 cavalry. At Lützen, 1632, Wallenstein had 24,000 infantry and 16,000 cavalry (in 170 squadrons). The number of guns, too, increased with the introduction of light pieces; the Swedes often had from 5 to 12 guns for every 1,000 men; and at the battle of the Lech, Gustavus Adolphus forced the passage of that river under cover of the fire of 72 heavy guns.[143]

During the latter half of the 17th and the first half of the 18th century, the pike, and all defensive armor for infantry, was finally done away with by the general introduction of the bayonet. This weapon, invented in France about 1640, had to struggle 80 years against the pike. The Austrians first adopted it for all their infantry, the Prussians next; the French retained the pike till 1703, the Russians till 1721. The flint-lock, invented in France about the same time as the bayonet, was also gradually introduced, before the year 1700, into most armies. It materially abridged the operation of loading, protected, to some degree, the powder in the pan from rain, and thus contributed very much to the abolition of the pike. Yet firing was still so slow that a man was not expected to use more than from 24 to 36 cartridges in a battle; until in the latter half of this period improved regulations, better drill, and further improvement in the construction of small arms (especially the iron ramrod, first introduced in Prussia), enabled the soldier to fire with considerable rapidity. This necessitated a still further reduction of the depth of formation, and infantry was now formed only 4 deep. A species of *élite* infantry was created in the companies of grenadiers, originally intended to throw hand-grenades before coming to close quarters, but soon reduced to fight with the musket only. In some German armies riflemen had been formed as early as the 30 years' war; the rifle itself had been invented at Leipsic in 1498. This arm was now mixed with the musket, the best shots in each company being armed with it; but, out of Germany, the rifle found but little favor. The Austrians had also a sort of light infantry, called *pandours:* Croatian and Servian irregulars from the military frontier[144] against Turkey, useful in roving expeditions and pursuit, but, from the tactics of the day and their absolute want of drill, useless in battle. The French and Dutch created, for similar purposes, irregular infantry called *compagnies franches.* Cavalry, too, was lightened in all armies. There were no longer any men-at-arms; the cuirassiers maintained the breastplate and helmet only; in France and Sweden, the breastplate was done away with too. The increasing efficiency and rapidity of infantry fire told very much against cavalry. It was soon considered perfectly useless for this latter arm to charge infantry sword in hand; and the opinion of the irresistibility of a firing line became so prevalent that cavalry, too, was taught to rely more on its carbines than on the sword. Thus, during this period, it often occurs that 2 lines of cavalry maintain a firing fight against each other the same as if they were infantry; and it was considered very daring, to ride up to 20 yards from the enemy, fire a volley, and charge at a trot. Charles XII, however, stuck to the rule of his great predecessor.[a] His cavalry never stopped to fire; it always charged, sword in hand, against any thing opposing it, cavalry, infantry, batteries, and intrenchments; and always with success. The French, too, broke through the new system and recommenced relying on the sword only. The depth of cavalry was still further reduced from 4 to 3. In artillery, the lightening of the guns, the use of cartridges and case-shot, became, now, general. Another great change was that of the incorporation of this arm with the army. Hitherto, though the guns belonged to the state, the men serving them were no proper soldiers, but formed a sort of guild, and artillery was considered not an arm but a handicraft. The officers had no rank in the army, and were considered more related to master-tailors and carpenters than to gentlemen with a commission in their pockets. About this time, however, artillery was made a component part of the army, and divided into companies and battalions; the men were converted into permanent soldiers, and the officers ranked with the infantry and cavalry. The centralization and permanence of the armed contingent upon this change, paved the way for the science of artillery, which, under the old system, could not develop itself.

The passage from deep formation to line, from the pike to the musket, from the supremacy of cavalry to that of infantry, had thus been gradually accomplished when Frederick the Great opened his campaigns, and, with them, the classical era of line tactics. He formed his infantry 3 deep, and got it to fire 5 times in 1 minute. In his very first battles at Mollwitz,[145] this infantry deployed in line, and repelled, by its rapid fire, all charges of the Austrian cavalry, which had just totally routed the Prussian horse; after finishing with the cavalry, the Prussian infantry attacked the Austrian infantry, defeated it, and thus won the battle. Formation of squares against cavalry was never attempted in great battles, but

---

only when infantry, on the march, was surprised by hostile cavalry. In a battle, the extreme wings of the infantry stretched round *en potence*,[a] when menaced by cavalry, and this was generally found sufficient. To oppose the Austrian pandours, Frederick formed similar irregular troops, infantry and cavalry, but never relied on them in battle, where they seldom were engaged. The slow advance of the firing-line decided his battles. Cavalry, neglected under his predecessor,[b] was now made to undergo a complete revolution. It was formed only 2 deep, and firing, except on pursuit, was strictly prohibited. Horsemanship, considered, hitherto, of minor importance, was now cultivated with the greatest attention. All evolutions had to be practised at full speed, and the men were required to remain well closed up. By the exertions of Seydlitz, the cavalry of Frederick was made superior to any other then existing or ever existing before it; and its bold riding, close order, dashing charge, and quick rallying, have never yet been equalled by any that succeeded it. The artillery was considerably lightened, and, indeed, so much that some of the heavy-calibred guns were not able to stand full charges, and had, therefore, to be abolished afterward. Yet the heavy artillery was still very slow and clumsy in its movements, owing to inferior and heavy carriages and imperfect organization. In battle, it took up its position from the first, and sometimes changed it for a second position, more in advance, but manoeuvring, there was none. The light artillery, the regimental guns attached to the infantry, were placed in front of the infantry-line, 50 paces in advance of the intervals of the battalions; they advanced with the infantry, the guns dragged by the men, and opened fire with canister at 300 yards. The number of guns was very large, from 3 to 6 guns per 1,000 men. The infantry, as well as the cavalry, were divided into brigades and divisions, but as there was scarcely any manoeuvring after the battle had once begun, and every battalion had to remain in its proper place in the line, these subdivisions had no tactical influence; with the cavalry, a general of brigade might, during a charge, now and then, have to act upon his own responsibility; but with the infantry, such a case could never occur. This line-formation, infantry in 2 lines in the centre, cavalry in 2 or 3 lines on the wings, was a considerable progress upon the deep formation of former days; it developed the full effect of infantry fire, as well as of the charge of cavalry, by allowing as many men as possible to act simultaneously; but its very perfection in this

---

[a] In T-shaped formation.— *Ed.*
[b] Frederick William I.— *Ed.*

point confined the whole army, as it were, in a strait-waistcoat. Every squadron, battalion, or gun, had its regulated place in the order of battle, which could not be inverted or in any way disturbed without affecting the efficiency of the whole. On the march, therefore, every thing had to be so arranged that when the army formed front again for encampment or battle, every subdivision got exactly into its correct place. Thus, any manoeuvres to be executed, had to be executed with the whole army; to detach a single portion of it for a flank attack, to form a particular reserve for the attack, with superior forces, of a weak point, would have been impracticable and faulty with such slow troops, fit, only, to fight in line, and with an order of battle of such stiffness. Then, the advance in battle of such long lines was executed with considerable slowness, in order to keep up with the alignment. Tents followed the army constantly, and were pitched every night; the camp was slightly intrenched. The troops were fed from magazines, the baking establishments accompanying the army as much as possible. In short, the baggage and other train of the army were enormous, and hampered its movements to a degree unknown nowadays. Yet, with all these drawbacks, the military organization of Frederick the Great was by far the best of its day, and was eagerly adopted by all other European governments. The recruiting of the forces was almost everywhere carried on by voluntary enlistments, assisted by kidnapping; and it was only after very severe losses that Frederick had recourse to forced levies from his provinces.

When the war of the coalition against the French republic[146] began, the French army was disorganized by the loss of its officers, and numbered less than 150,000 men. The numbers of the enemy were far superior; new levies became necessary and were made, to an immense extent, in the shape of national volunteers, of which, in 1793, there must have been at least 500 battalions in existence. These troops were not drilled, nor was there time to drill them according to the complicated system of line-tactics, and to the degree of perfection required by movements in line. Every attempt to meet the enemy in line was followed by a signal defeat, though the French had far superior numbers. A new system of tactics became necessary. The American revolution[147] had shown the advantage to be gained, with undisciplined troops, from extended order and skirmishing fire. The French adopted it, and supported the skirmishers by deep columns, in which a little disorder was less objectionable, so long as the mass remained well together. In this formation, they launched their superior numbers against the enemy, and were generally successful. This new formation and the want of experience of their troops led them to fight in broken ground, in villages and woods, where they found shelter from the enemy's fire, and where his line was invariably disordered; their want of tents, field-bakeries, &c., compelled them to bivouac without shelter, and to live upon what the country afforded them. Thus they gained a mobility unknown to their enemies, who were encumbered with tents and all sorts of baggage. When the revolutionary war had produced, in Napoleon, the man who reduced this new mode of warfare to a regular system, combined it with what was still useful in the old system, and brought the new method at once to that degree of perfection which Frederick had given to line-tactics—then the French were almost invincible, until their opponents had learnt from them, and organized their armies upon the new model. The principal features of this new system are: the restoration of the old principle that every citizen is liable, in case of need, to be called out for the defence of the country, and the consequent formation of the army, by compulsory levies, of greater or less extent, from the whole of the inhabitants; a change by which the numeric force of armies was at once raised to three-fold the average of Frederick's time, and might, in case of need, be increased to larger proportions still. Then, the discarding of camp utensils, and of depending for provisions upon magazines, the introduction of the bivouac and of the rule that war feeds war; the celerity and independence of an army was hereby increased as much as its numeric force by the rule of general liability to serve. In tactical organization, the principle of mixing infantry, cavalry, and artillery in the smaller portions of an army, in corps and divisions, became the rule. Every division thus became a complete army on a reduced scale, fit to act independently, and capable of considerable power of resistance even against superior numbers. The order of battle, now, was based upon the column; it served as the reservoir, from which sallied and to which returned the swarms of skirmishers; as the wedgelike compact mass to be launched against a particular point of the enemy's line; as the form to approach the enemy and then to deploy, if the ground and the state of the engagement made it desirable to oppose firing-lines to the enemy. The mutual supporting of the 3 arms developed to its full extent by their combination in small bodies, and the combination of the 3 forms of fighting; skirmishers, line, and column, composed the great tactical superiority of modern armies. Any kind of ground, thereby, became fit for fighting in it; and the ability of rapidly judging the advantages and disadvantages of ground, and of at once disposing troops accordingly, became one of the chief requirements of a captain. And not only ·in the commander-in-. chief, but in the subordinate officers, these qualities, and general aptness for independent command, were now a necessity. Corps, divisions, brigades, and detachments, were constantly placed in situations where their commanders had to act on their own responsibility; the battle-field no longer presented its long unbroken lines of infantry disposed in a vast plain with cavalry on the wings; but the single corps and divisions, massed in columns, stood hidden behind villages, roads, or hills, separated from each other by seemingly large intervals, while but a small portion of the troops appeared actually engaged in skirmishing and firing artillery, until the decisive moment approached. Lines of battle extended with the numbers and with this formation; it was not necessary actually to fill up every interval with a line visible to the enemy, so long as troops were at hand to come up when required. Turning of flanks now became generally a strategical operation, the stronger army placing itself completely between the weaker one and its communications, so that a single defeat could annihilate an army and decide a campaign. The favorite tactical manoeuvre was the breaking through the enemy's centre, with fresh troops, as soon as the state of affairs showed that his last reserves were engaged. Reserves, which in line-tactics would have been out of place and would have deducted from the efficiency of the army in the decisive moment, now became the chief means to decide an action. The order of battle, extending as it did in front, extended also in depth; from the skirmishing line to the position of the reserves the depth was very often 2 miles and more. In short, if the new system required less drill and parade-precision, it required far greater rapidity, exertions, and intelligence from every one, from the highest commander as well as the lowest skirmisher; and every fresh improvement made since Napoleon, tends in that direction.

The changes in the *matériel* of armies were but trifling during this period; constant wars left little time for such improvements the introduction of which requires time. Two very important innovations took place in the French army shortly before the revolution; the adoption of a new model of musket of reduced calibre and windage, and with a curved stock instead of the straight one hitherto in use. This weapon, more accurately worked, contributed a great deal toward the superiority of the French skirmishers, and remained the model upon which with trifling alterations the muskets in use in all armies up to the introduction of percussion locks, were constructed. The second was the simplification and improvement of the artillery by Gribeauval. The French artillery under Louis XV was completely neglected; the guns were of all sorts of calibres, the carriages were old-fashioned, and the models upon which they were constructed not even uniform. Gribeauval, who had served during the 7 years' war[148] with the Austrians, and there seen better models, succeeded in reducing the number of calibres, equalizing and improving the models, and greatly simplifying the whole system. It was with his guns and carriages that Napoleon fought his wars. The English artillery, which was in the worst possible state when the war with France broke out, was gradually, but slowly, considerably improved; with it originated the block-trail carriage, which has since been adopted by many continental armies, and the arrangement for mounting the foot artillerymen on the limbers and ammunition wagons. Horse-artillery, invented by Frederick the Great, was much cultivated during Napoleon's period, especially by himself, and its proper tactics were first developed. When the war was over, it was found that the British were the most efficient in this arm. Of all large European armies, the Austrian is the only one which supplies the place of horse-artillery by batteries in which the men are mounted on wagons provided for the purpose.

The German armies still kept up the especial class of infantry armed with rifles, and the new system of fighting in extended order gave a fresh importance to this arm. It was especially cultivated, and in 1838 taken up by the French, who felt the want of a long range musket for Algiers. The *tirailleurs de Vincennes,* afterward *chasseurs à pied,* were formed, and brought to a state of efficiency without parallel. This formation gave rise to great improvements in rifles, and by which both range and precision were increased to a wonderful degree. The names of Delvigne, Thouvenin, Minié, became celebrated thereby. For the totality of the infantry, the percussion lock was introduced between 1830 and 1840 in most armies; as usual, the English and the Russians were the last. In the mean time, great efforts were made in various quarters still further to improve small arms, and to produce a musket of superior range which could be given to the whole of the infantry. The Prussians introduced the needle gun, a rifle arm loaded at the breech, and capable of very rapid firing, and having a long range; the invention, originated in Belgium, was considerably improved by them. This gun has been given to all their light battalions; the remainder of the infantry have recently got their old muskets, by a very simple process, turned into Minié rifles. The English were the first this time to arm the whole of their infantry with a superior musket, viz., the Enfield rifle, a slight alteration of the Minié; its superiority was fully proved in the Crimea, and saved them at Inkermann.[149]

In tactical arrangements, no changes of importance have taken place for infantry and cavalry, if we except the great improvement of light infantry tactics by the French *chasseurs,* and the new Prussian system of columns of companies, which latter formation, with perhaps some variations, will no doubt soon become general from its great tactical advantages. The formation is still 3 deep with the Russians and Austrians, the English have formed 2 deep ever since Napoleon's time; the Prussians march 3 deep, but mostly fight 2 deep, the 3d rank forming the skirmishers and their supports; and the French, hitherto formed 3 deep, have fought 2 deep in the Crimea, and are introducing this formation in the whole army. As to cavalry, the Russian experiment of restoring the dragoons of the 17th century and its failure have been mentioned.

In artillery, considerable improvements of detail and simplification of calibres, and models for wheels, carriages, &c., have taken place in every army. The science of artillery has been greatly improved. Yet no considerable changes have taken place. Most continental armies carry 6 and 12-pounders; the Piedmontese 8 and 16-pounders; the Spanish 8 and 12-pounders; the French, who hitherto had 8 and 12-pounders, are now introducing Louis Napoleon's so-called howitzer gun, a simple light 12-pounder, from which small shells are also fired, and which is to replace every other kind of field gun. The British have 3 and 6-pounders in the colonies, but in their armies sent out from England, now only use 9-pounders, 12-pounders, and 18-pounders. In the Crimea they even had a field battery of 32-pounders, but it always stuck fast.

The general organization of modern armies is very much alike. With the exception of the British and American, they are recruited by compulsory levy, based either upon conscription, in which case the men, after serving their time, are dismissed for life, or upon the reserve system, in which the time of actual service is short, but the men remain liable to be called out again for a certain time afterward. France is the most striking example of the first, Prussia of the second system. Even in England, where both line and militia are generally recruited by voluntary enlistment, the conscription (or ballot) is by law established for the militia should volunteers be wanting. In Switzerland, no standing army exists; the whole force consists of militia drilled for a short time only. The enlistment of foreign mercenaries is still the rule in some countries; Naples and the Pope still have their Swiss regiments; the French their foreign legion; and England, in case of serious war, is regularly compelled to resort to this expedient. The time of actual service varies very much; from a couple of weeks with the Swiss, 18 months to 2 years with the smaller German states, and 3 years with the Prussians, to 5 or 6 years in France, 12 years in England, and 15 to 25 in Russia. The officers are recruited in various ways. In most armies there are now no legal impediments to advancement from the ranks, but the practical impediments vary very much. In France and Austria a portion of the officers must be taken from the sergeants; in Russia the insufficient number of educated candidates makes this a necessity. In Prussia the examination for officers' commissions, in peace, is a bar to uneducated men; in England advancement from the ranks is a rare exception. For the remainder of the officers, there are in most countries military schools, though with the exception of France, it is not necessary to pass through them. In military education the French, in general education the Prussian officers are ahead; the English and the Russians stand lowest in both. As to the horses required, we believe Prussia is the only country in which the equine population too is subject to compulsory levies, the owners being bought off at fixed rates. With the exceptions named above, the equipment and armament of modern armies is now everywhere nearly the same. There is, of course, a great difference in the quality and workmanship of the material. In this respect, the Russians stand lowest, the English, where the industrial advantages at their command are really made use of, stand highest.

The infantry of all armies is divided into line and light infantry. The 1st is the rule, and composes the mass of all infantry; real light infantry is everywhere the exception. Of this latter, the French have at present decidedly the best in quality and a considerable number: 21 battalions of chasseurs, 9 of Zouaves, and 6 of native Algerian tirailleurs. The Austrian light infantry, especially the rifles, are very good, too; there are 32 battalions of them. The Prussians have 9 battalions of rifles and 40 of light infantry; the latter, however, not sufficiently up in their special duty. The English have no real light infantry, except their 6 battalions of rifles, and are, next to the Russians, decidedly the least fit for that kind of duty. The Russians may be said to be without any real light infantry, for their 6 rifle battalions vanish in their enormous army.

Cavalry, too, is everywhere divided into heavy and light. Cuirassiers are always heavy, hussars, chasseurs, chevaux-legers, always light horse. Dragoons and lancers are in some armies light, in others heavy cavalry; and the Russians would also be without light cavalry were it not for the Cossacks. The best light cavalry is undoubtedly that of the Austrians, the national Hungarian hussars and Polish hussars. The same division holds good with artillery, with the exception of the French, who as stated now have only one calibre. In other armies there are still light and heavy batteries, according to the calibres attached to them. Light artillery is still subdivided in horse and foot, the lst especially intended to act in company with cavalry. The Austrians, as stated, have no horse-artillery; the English and French have no proper foot-artillery, the men being carried on the limbers and ammunition wagons.

The infantry is formed into companies, battalions, and regiments. The battalion is the tactical unity; it is the form in which the troops fight, a few exceptional cases left aside. A battalion, therefore, must not be too strong to be commanded by the voice and eye of its chief, nor too weak to act as an independent body in battle, even after the losses of a campaign. The strength, therefore, varies from 600 to 1,400 men; 800 to 1,000 forms the average. The division of a battalion into companies has for its object the fixing of its evolutionary subdivisions, the efficiency of the men in the details of the drill, and the more commodious, economical administration. Practically, companies appear as separate bodies in skirmishing only, and with the Prussians, in the formation in columns of companies, where each of the 4 companies forms columns in 3 platoons; this formation presupposes strong companies, and they are in Prussia 250 strong. The number of companies in a battalion varies as much as their strength. The English have 10, of from 90 to 120 men, the Russians and Prussians 4 of 250 men, the French and Austrians 6 of varying strength. Battalions are formed into regiments, more for administrative and disciplinarian purposes and to insure uniformity of drill, than for any tactical object; in formations for war, therefore, the battalions of one regiment are often separated. In Russia and Austria there are 4, in Prussia 3, in France 2 service battalions, beside depots to every regiment; in England, most regiments are formed, in peace, of but 1 battalion. Cavalry is divided into squadrons and regiments. The squadron, from 100 to

200 men, forms the tactical and administrative unity; the English alone subdivide the squadron, for administrative purposes, into 2 troops. There are from 3 to 10 service squadrons to a regiment; the British have, in peace, but 3 squadrons, of about 120 horse; the Prussians 4 of 150 horse; the French 5 of 180 to 200 horse; the Austrians 6 or 8 of 200 horse; the Russians 6 to 10 of 150 to 170 horse. With cavalry the regiment is a body of tactical significance, as a regiment offers the means to make an independent charge, the squadrons mutually supporting each other, and is for this purpose formed of sufficient strength, viz., between 500 and 1,600 horse. The British alone have such weak regiments that they are obliged to put 4 or 5 of them to 1 brigade; on the other hand, the Austrian and Russian regiments in many cases are as strong as an average brigade. The French have nominally very strong regiments, but have hitherto appeared in the field in considerably reduced numbers, owing to their poverty in horses. Artillery is formed in batteries; the formation in regiments or brigades in this arm is only for peace purposes, as almost in every case of actual service the batteries are sure to become separated, and are always used so. Four guns is the least number, and the Austrians have 8; the French and English 6 guns per battery. Riflemen or other real light infantry are generally organized in battalions and companies only, not in regiments; the nature of the arm is repugnant to its reunion in large masses. The same is the case with sappers and miners, they being, beside, but a very small portion of the army. The French alone make an exception in this latter case; but their 3 regiments, sappers and miners, count only 6 battalions in all. With the regiment the formation of most armies in time of peace is generally considered complete. The larger bodies, brigades, divisions, army-corps, are mostly formed when war breaks out. The Russians and Prussians alone have their army fully organized and the higher commands filled up, as if for actual war. But in Prussia this is completely illusory, unless at least a whole army-corps be mobilized, which supposes the calling in of the Landwehr [150] of a whole province; and if in Russia the troops are actually with the regiments, yet the late war [a] has shown that the original divisions and corps very soon got mixed, so that the advantage gained from such a formation is more for peace than for war.

In war, several battalions or squadrons are formed into a brigade; from 4 to 8 battalions for infantry, or from 6 to 20

---

[a] The Crimean war of 1853-56.— *Ed.*

squadrons for cavalry. With large cavalry regiments these latter may very well stand in lieu of brigade; but they are very generally reduced to smaller strength by the detachments they have to send to the divisions. Light and line infantry may with advantage be mixed in a brigade, but not light and heavy cavalry. The Austrians very generally add a battery to each brigade. A combination of brigades forms the division. In most armies, it is composed of all the 3 arms, say 2 brigades of infantry, 4 to 6 squadrons, and 1 to 3 batteries. The French and Russians have no cavalry to their divisions, the English form them of infantry exclusively. Unless, therefore, these nations wish to fight at a disadvantage, they are obliged to attach cavalry (and artillery respectively) to the divisions whenever the case occurs; which is easily overlooked or often inconvenient or impossible. The proportion of divisionary cavalry, however, is everywhere but small, and therefore the remainder of this arm is formed into cavalry divisions of 2 brigades each, for the purpose of reserve cavalry. Two or 3 divisions, sometimes 4, are, for larger armies, formed into an army-corps. Such a corps has everywhere its own cavalry and artillery, even where the divisions have none; and, where these latter are mixed bodies, there is still a reserve of cavalry and artillery placed at the disposal of the commander of the corps. Napoleon was the first to form these, and, not satisfied therewith, he organized the whole of the remaining cavalry into reserve cavalry-corps of 2 or 5 divisions of cavalry with horse-artillery attached. The Russians have retained this formation of their reserve cavalry, and the other armies are likely to take it up again in a war of importance, though the effect obtained has never yet been in proportion to the immense mass of horsemen thus concentrated on one point. Such is the modern organization of the fighting part of an army. But, in spite of the abolition of tents, magazines, field-bakeries, and bread-wagons, there is still a large train of non-combatants and of vehicles necessary to insure the efficiency of the army in a campaign. To give an idea of this, we will only state the train required, according to the existing regulations, for 1 army-corps of the Prussian service:—

Artillery train: 6 park columns of 30 wagons, 1 laboratory do., 6 wagons.
Pontoon train: 34 pontoon wagons, 5 tool wagons, 1 forge.
Infantry train: 116 wagons, 108 team horses.
Medical train: 50 wagons (for 1,600 or 2,000 sick).
Reserve commissariat train: 159 wagons.
Reserve train: 1 wagon, 75 reserve horses.
In all, 402 wagons, 1,791 horses, 3,000 men.

To enable the commanders of armies, army-corps and divisions to conduct, each in his sphere, the troops intrusted to him, a separate corps is formed in every army except the British, composed of officers exclusively, and called the staff. The functions of these officers are to reconnoitre and sketch the ground on which the army moves or may move; to assist in making out plans for operations, and to arrange them in detail so that no time is lost, no confusion arises, no useless fatigue is incurred by the troops. They are, therefore, in highly important positions, and ought to have a thoroughly finished military education, with a full knowledge of the capabilities of each arm on the march and in battle. They are accordingly taken in all countries from the most able subjects, and carefully trained in the highest military schools. The English alone imagine any subaltern or field-officer selected from the army at large is fit for such a position, and the consequence is that their staffs are inferior, and the army incapable of any but the slowest and simplest ma-noeuvres, while the commander, if at all conscientious, has to do all the staff work himself. A division can seldom have more than one staff-officer attached, an army-corps has a staff of its own under the direction of a superior or a staff-officer, and an army has a full staff, with several generals, under a chief who, in urgent cases, gives his orders in the name of the commander. The chief of the staff, in the British army, has an adjutant-general and a quartermaster-general under his orders; in other armies the adjutant-general is at the same time chief of the staff; in France the chief of the staff unites both capacities in himself, and has a different department for each under his orders. The adjutant-general is the chief of the *personnel* of the army, receives the reports of all subordinate departments and bodies of the army, and arranges all matters relative to discipline, instruction, forma-tion, equipment, armament, &c. All subordinates correspond through him with the commander-in-chief. If chief of the staff at the same time, he cooperates with the commander in the formation and working out of plans of operation and movements for the army. The proper arrangement of these in detail is the department of the quartermaster-general; the details of marches, cantonments, encampments, are prepared by him. A sufficient number of staff-officers are attached to head-quarters for recon-noitring the ground, preparing projects as to the defence or attack of positions, &c. There is, beside, a commander-in-chief of the artillery, and a superior engineer-officer for their respective departments; a few deputies to represent the chief of the staff on

Pages of Marx's notebook with entries on the dispatch of articles to *The New American Cyclopaedia*

particular points of the battle-field, and a number of orderly officers and orderlies to carry orders and despatches. To the head-quarters are further attached the chief of the commissariat, with his clerks, the paymaster of the army, the chief of the medical department, and the judge-advocate, or director of the department of military justice. The staffs of the army-corps and divisions are regulated on the same model, but with greater simplicity and a reduced *personnel;* the staffs of brigades and regiments are still less numerous, and the staff of a battalion may consist merely of the commander, his adjutant, an officer as paymaster, a sergeant as clerk, and a drummer or bugleman.

To regulate and keep up the military force of a great nation, numerous establishments, beside those hitherto named, are required. There are recruiting and remounting commissioners, the latter often connected with the administration of national establishments for the breeding of horses, military schools for officers and non-commissioned officers, model battalions, squadrons, and batteries, normal riding schools, and schools for veterinary surgeons. There are in most countries national founderies and manufactories for small arms and gunpowder; there are the various barracks, arsenals, stores, the fortresses with their equipments and the staff of officers commanding them; finally, there are the commissariat and general staff of the army, which, for the whole of the armed force, are even more numerous and have more extensive duties to perform than the staff and commissariat of a single active army. The staff especially has very important duties. It is generally divided into a historical section (collecting materials relative to the history of war, the formation of armies, &c., past and present), a topographical section (intrusted with the collection of maps and the trigonometrical survey of the whole country), a statistical section, &c. At the head of all these establishments, as well as of the army, stands the ministry of war, organized differently in different countries, but comprising, as must be evident from the preceding observations, a vast variety of subjects. As an example we give the organization of the French ministry of war. It comprises 7 directions or divisions: 1, of the *personnel;* 2, of the artillery; 3, of the engineers and fortresses; 4, of administrative affairs; 5, of Algeria; 6, war depôt (historical, topographical, &c., and sections of the staff); 7, finances of the war department. Immediately attached to the ministry are the following consultative commissions, composed of generals and field-officers and professional men, viz.: the committees of the staff of infantry, of cavalry, of artillery, of fortification, of medical affairs, and the commissions for veterinary science and for public works. Such is the vast machinery devoted to recruiting, remounting, feeding, directing, and always reproducing a modern first class army. The masses brought together correspond to such an organization. Though Napoleon's grand army of 1812, when he had 200,000 men in Spain, 200,000 in France, Italy, Germany, and Poland, and invaded Russia with 450,000 men and 1,300 guns, has never yet been equalled; though we shall most likely never see such an army again united for one operation as these 450,000 men, yet the large continental states of Europe, Prussia included, can each of them raise an armed and disciplined force of 500,000 men, and more; and their armies, though not more than from $1\,^1/_2$ to 3 per ct. of their population, have never yet been reached at any former period of history.

The system of the United States bases the defence of the country substantially on the militia of the different states, and on volunteer armies raised as occasion demands; the standing military force, employed mainly in preserving order among the Indian tribes of the West, consisting, according to the report of the secretary of war[a] for 1857, of only about 18,000 men.[151]

Written between July and September 25, 1857

First published in *The New American Cyclopaedia*, Vol. II, 1858

Reproduced from *The New American Cyclopaedia*

---

[a] John Buchanan Floyd.— *Ed.*

Frederick Engels

BATTERY[152]

In field artillery, this expression means a number of guns, from 4 to 12, with the necessary horses, gunners, and equipments, and destined generally to act together in battle. The British and French have 6, the Prussians and Austrians 8, the Russians 8 or 12, guns to a battery. Field batteries are divided into light, heavy, and howitzer batteries; in some countries, there are, beside, mountain batteries. In describing a position for battle, the word battery is also used to indicate any spot where guns are placed. In siege artillery, battery means either any one of the lines of the fortress which is armed with guns, or else, and especially, a number of guns placed in line for the attack of a fortress, and covered by a parapet. The construction of this parapet, and the emplacements for the guns, are what is understood by the construction of a battery. With respect to their profiles, batteries are either elevated, half sunken, or sunken; with respect to their armament, guns, howitzer, mortar batteries; with respect to the shelter afforded, batteries with embrasures, barbette batteries (without embrasures), casemated batteries (covered in bomb proof). With respect to the purpose aimed at, there are dismounting batteries, to dismount the guns in one of the lines of the fortress, parallel to which they are constructed; ricochetting batteries, constructed in the prolongation of a line, and destined to enfilade it, the balls and shells just passing over the parapet and hopping along the line in low jumps; mortar batteries, to bombard the interior of the bastions and the buildings in the fortress; breaching batteries, to bring down the revetement walls of the scarp of the rampart; counter batteries, erected on the crown of the glacis opposite the flanks, to silence the fire of a flank which protects the ditch in front of the breach. Strand batteries are intrenchments thrown up on particular points of a sea shore to act against hostile men-of-war; they are either permanent, in which case they are generally constructed of masonry, and often casemated, with several tiers of guns, or temporary earthworks, mostly barbette batteries to insure a wider sweep; in either case they are generally closed to the rear against a sudden attack by landed infantry.

To construct an earthwork battery, the principal dimensions are traced, and the earth procured from a ditch in front or rear of the intended parapet. The outer slope of the parapet is left without revetement, but the interior slope and the cheeks or interior sides of the embrasures are revetted with fascines, gabions, hurdles, casks filled with earth, sandbags, or sods of turf, so as to retain the earth in its position, even with a steep slope. A *berme,* or level space, is generally left standing between the outer slope of the parapet and the ditch in front, to strengthen the parapet. A banquette is constructed inside the battery, between the embrasures, high enough for a man to stand on and look over the parapet. An epaulment of parapet forming an obtuse angle with that of the battery is often constructed on one or both flanks, to protect it against flanking fire. Where the battery can be enfiladed, traverses or epaulments between the guns become necessary. In barbette batteries, this protection is strengthened by a further elevation of the traverses several feet above the height of the parapet, which elevation is continued across the parapet to its outer crest, and called a bonnet. The guns are placed on platforms constructed of planks and sleepers, or other timbers, to insure permanency of emplacement. The ammunition is kept partly in recesses under the parapet, partly in a sunken building of timber covered in bomb proof with earth. To shelter the gunners from rifle firing, the embrasures are often closed by blindages of strong planks, to open to either side when the gun is run out, or provided with a hole for the muzzle to pass through. The fire of the enemy is rendered innocuous by blindages of timbers laid with one end on the inner crest of the parapet, and sloping to the ground behind. In batteries where howitzers are used, the soles of the embrasures slope upward instead of downward; in mortar batteries, there are no embrasures at all, the high elevation taken insuring the passage of the shell over the crest of the parapet. To give effective protection against the fire of heavy guns, the parapet should be at least 17 or 18 feet thick; but if the calibre of the enemy is very heavy, and the ground bad, a thickness of 24 feet may be required. A height of 7 or 8 feet gives sufficient protection. The guns should have a clear distance of from 10 to 14 feet; if traverses are necessary, the parapet will have to be lengthened accordingly.

Written between September 18 and 29, 1857

First published in *The New American Cyclopaedia*, Vol. II, 1858

Reproduced from *The New American Cyclopaedia*

Karl Marx and Frederick Engels

BEM [153]

Bem, Józef, a Polish general, born at Tarnow, in Galicia, in 1795,[a] died Dec. 10, 1850. The passion of his life was hatred of Russia. At the epoch when Napoleon, by victories and proclamations, was exciting a belief in the resurrection of Poland, Bem entered the corps of cadets at Warsaw, and received his military training at the artillery-school directed by Gen. Pelletier. On leaving this school, he was appointed lieutenant of the horse-artillery; served in that capacity under Davout and Macdonald in the campaign of 1812; won the cross of the legion of honor by his cooperation in the defence of Dantzic [154]; and, after the surrender of that fortress, returned to Poland. As the czar Alexander, affecting a great predilection for the Polish nation, now reorganized the Polish army, Bem entered the latter in 1815, as an officer of artillery, but was soon dismissed for fighting a duel with his superior. However, he was subsequently appointed military teacher at the artillery-school of Warsaw and promoted to the rank of captain. He now introduced the use of the Congreve rocket into the Polish army, recording the experiments made on this occasion in a volume originally published in French and then translated into German.[b] He was querulous and insubordinate, and, from 1820 to 1825, was several times arraigned before courts-martial, punished with imprisonment, released, imprisoned again, and at last sent to Kock, a remote Polish village, there to

---

[a] Józef Bem was born in 1794 but because of his ill health was not registered until 1795.— *Ed.*

[b] J. Bem, *Erfahrungen über die Congrevschen Brand-Raketen bis zum Jahre 1819 in der Königl. Polnischen Artillerie gesammelt.— Ed.*

vegetate under strict police surveillance. He did not obtain his discharge from the Polish army until the death of Alexander, and the Petersburg insurrection [155] made Constantine lose sight of him. Leaving Russian Poland, Bem now retired to Lemberg, where he became an overseer in a large distillery, and elaborated a book on steam applied to the distillation of alcohol.[a]

When the Warsaw insurrection of 1830 broke out he joined it, after a few months was made a major of artillery, and fought, in May,[b] 1831, at the battle of Ostrolenka, where he was noticed for the skill and perseverance with which he fought against the superior Russian batteries.[156] When the Polish army had been finally repulsed in its attacks against the Russians who had passed the Narev, he covered the retreat by a bold advance with the whole of his guns. He was now created colonel, soon after general, and called to the command-in-chief of the Polish artillery. At the storming of Warsaw by the Russians he fought bravely, but, as a commander, committed the fault of not using his 40 guns, and allowing the Russians to take Vola, the principal point of defence. After the fall of Warsaw he emigrated to Prussia with the rest of the army, urged the men not to lay down their arms before the Prussians, and thus provoked a bloody and unnecessary struggle, called at that time the battle of Fischau. He then abandoned the army and organized in Germany committees for the support of Polish emigrants, after which he went to Paris.

His extraordinary character, in which a laborious fondness for the exact sciences was blended with restless impulses for action, caused him to readily embark in adventurous enterprises, whose failure gave an advantage to his enemies. Thus having in 1833, on his own responsibility, undertaken without success to raise a Polish legion for Don Pedro,[157] he was denounced as a traitor, and was fired at by one of his disappointed countrymen, in Bourges, where he came to engage the Poles for his legion. Travels through Portugal, Spain, Holland, Belgium, and France, absorbed his time during the period from 1834 to 1848.

In 1848, on the first appearance of revolutionary symptoms in Austrian Poland, he hastened to Lemberg and thence, Oct. 14, to Vienna, where all that was done to strengthen the works of defence and organize the revolutionary forces, was due to his personal exertions. The disorderly flight in which, Oct. 25, a sally of the Viennese mobile guard,[158] headed by himself, had resulted,

----

[a] J. Bem, *O machinach parowych*, Vol. I.— *Ed.*
[b] *The New American Cyclopaedia* has "June" here.— *Ed.*

wrung from him stern expressions of reproof, replied to by noisy accusations of treason, which, in spite of their absurdity, gained such influence that, but for fear of an insurrection on the part of the Polish legion, he would have been dragged before a court-martial. After his remarkable defence, Oct. 28, of the great barricade erected in the Jägernzeile, and after the opening of negotiations between the Vienna magistrates and Prince Windischgrätz, he disappeared. Suspicion, heightened by his mysterious escape, dogged him from Vienna to Pesth, where, on account of his prudent advice to the Hungarian government, not to allow the establishment of a special Polish legion, a Pole named Kolodjecki fired a pistol on the pretended traitor and severely wounded him.

The war in Transylvania, with the command of which the Hungarian government intrusted Bem, leaving it, however, to his own ingenuity to find the armies with which to carry it on, forms the most important portion of his military life, and throws a great light upon the peculiar character of his generalship. Opening the first campaign toward the end of Dec. 1848, with a force of about 8,000 men, badly armed, hastily collected, and consisting of most heterogeneous elements—raw Magyar levies, Honveds,[159] Viennese refugees, and a small knot of Poles, a motley crew reenforced in his progress through Transylvania by successive drafts from Szeklers,[a] Saxons, Slavs and Roumanians—Bem had about 2 months later ended his campaign, vanquished Puchner with an Austrian army of 20,000 men, Engelhardt with the auxiliary force of 6,000 Russians, and Urban with his freebooters. Compelling the latter to take refuge in the Bukovina, and the two former to withdraw to Wallachia, he kept the whole of Transylvania save the small fortress of Karlsburg. Bold surprises, audacious manoeuvres, forced marches, and the great confidence he knew how to inspire in his troops by his own example, by the skilful selection of covered localities, and by always affording artillery support at the decisive moment, proved him to be a first-rate general for the partisan and small mountain warfare of this first campaign. He also showed himself a master in the art of suddenly creating and disciplining an army; but being content with the first rough sketch of organization, and neglecting to form a nucleus of choice troops, which was a matter of prime necessity, his extemporized army was sure to vanish like a dream on the first serious disasters.

During his hold of Transylvania he did himself honor by preventing the useless and impolitic cruelties contemplated by the

---

[a] The Magyar inhabitants of Transylvania.— *Ed.*

Magyar commissioners. The policy of conciliation between the antagonist nationalities aided him in swelling his force, in a few months, to 40,000 or 50,000 men, well provided with cavalry and artillery. If, notwithstanding, some admirable manoeuvres, the expedition to the Banat,[160] which he engaged in with this numerically strong army, produced no lasting effect, the circumstance of his hands being tied by the cooperation of the incapable Hungarian general,[a] must be taken into account.

The irruption into Transylvania of large Russian forces, and the defeats consequently sustained by the Magyars, called Bem back to the theatre of his first campaign. After a vain attempt to create a diversion in the rear of the enemy, by the invasion of Moldavia, he returned to Transylvania, there to be completely routed, July 31,[b] at Schässburg, by the 3 times stronger Russian forces under Lüders, escaping captivity himself only by a plunge into a morass from which some dispersed Magyar hussars happened to pick him up. Having collected the remainder of his forces, he stormed Hermannstadt for the second time, Aug. 5, but for want of reenforcements soon had to leave it, and after an unfortunate fight, Aug. 7, he retraced his steps to Hungary, where he arrived in time to witness the loss of the decisive battle at Temesvár.[161] After a vain attempt to make a last stand at Lugos with what remained of the Magyar forces, he reentered Transylvania, kept his ground there against overwhelming forces, until Aug. 19, when he was compelled to take refuge in the Turkish territory.

With the purpose of opening to himself a new field of activity against Russia, Bem embraced the Mussulman faith, and was raised by the sultan[c] to the dignity of a pasha, under the name of Amurath, with a command in the Turkish army; but, on the remonstrances of the European powers, he was relegated to Aleppo. Having there succeeded in repressing some sanguinary excesses committed during Nov. 1850, on the Christian residents by the Mussulman populace,[162] he died about a month later, of a violent fever, for which he would allow no medical aid.

Written in September (not later than the 29th), 1857

First published in *The New American Cyclopaedia*, Vol. III, 1858

Reproduced from *The New American Cyclopaedia*

---

[a] Károly Vécsey.— *Ed.*
[b] *The New American Cyclopaedia* has "July 29" here.— *Ed.*
[c] Abdul Mejid.— *Ed.*

6*

Karl Marx

BESSIÈRES [163]

Bessières, Jean Baptiste, marshal of the French empire, born at Praissac, in the department of Lot, Aug. 6, 1768, killed at Lützen, May 1, 1813. He entered the constitutional guard [164] of Louis XVI, in 1791, served as a non-commissioned officer in the mounted chasseurs of the Pyrénées, and soon after became a captain of chasseurs. After the victory of Roveredo, Sept. 4, 1796, Bonaparte promoted him on the battle-field to the rank of colonel. Commander of the guides [165] of the general-in-chief during the Italian campaign of 1796-'97, colonel of the same corps in Egypt, he remained attached to it for the greater part of his life. In 1802, the rank of general of division was conferred upon him, and, in 1804, that of marshal of the empire. He fought at the battles of Roveredo, Rivoli, St. Jean d'Acre, Aboukir, Marengo—where he commanded the last decisive cavalry charge—Austerlitz, Jena, Eylau, and Friedland. [166] Despatched in 1808 to assume the command of a division of 18,000 men stationed in the Spanish province of Salamanca, he found on his arrival that Gen. Cuesta had taken up a position between Valladolid and Burgos, thus threatening to intersect the line of communication of Madrid with France. Bessières attacked him and won the victory of Medina del Rio Secco. After the failure of the English Walcheren expedition, [167] Napoleon substituted Bessières for Bernadotte, in command of the Belgian army. In the same year (1809), he was created duke of Istria. At the head of a cavalry division he routed the Austrian general, Hohenzollern, at the battle of Essling.[a] During the Russian expedition he acted as chief commander of

---

[a] See this volume, pp. 27-33.—*Ed.*

the mounted guard, and on the opening of the German campaign of 1813, as the commander of the French cavalry. He died on the battle-field while attacking the defile of Rippach, in Saxony, on the eve of the battle of Lützen.[168] His popularity with the common soldiers may be inferred from the circumstance that it was thought prudent to withhold the news of his death for some time from the army.

Written in September (not later than the 29th), 1857

First published in *The New American Cyclopaedia*, Vol. III, 1858

Reproduced from *The New American Cyclopaedia*

Frederick Engels

BIVOUAC

Bivouac (Fr., probably from Ger. *bei* and *Wache*[a]), an encampment of troops by night in the open air, without tents, each soldier sleeping in his clothes, with his arms by his side. In the warfare of the ancients, the troops were protected by tents, as by movable cities. In mediaeval times, castles and abbeys were opened to feudal and princely armies as they marched by. The popular masses who, impelled by religious enthusiasm, precipitated themselves in the crusades into Asia, formed rather a mob than an army, and all but the leading knights and princes and their immediate followers bivouacked upon the ground, like the wild nomadic tribes who roam the plains of Asia. With the return of regular warfare tented camps again reappeared, and were common in Europe during the last 2 centuries. But in the gigantic Napoleonic wars it was found that rapid movements were of more importance than the health of soldiers, and the luxury of tents disappeared from the fields of Europe, excepting sometimes in the case of the English armies. Entire armies bivouacked around fires, or, if the neighborhood of the enemy rendered it necessary, without fires, sleeping upon straw, or perhaps upon the naked ground, a part of the soldiers keeping guard. Among historical bivouacs none has been more celebrated by poetry and painting than that of the eve of the battle of Austerlitz.[169]

Written before September 29, 1857

First published in *The New American Cyclopaedia*, Vol. III, 1858

Reproduced from *The New American Cyclopaedia*

---

a *Bei Wache* means "on guard", "on the alert".—*Ed.*

Frederick Engels

BLINDAGE

Blindage, in fortification, any fixture for preventing the enemy from seeing what is going on in a particular spot. Such are, for instance, the fascines placed on the inner crest of a battery, and continued over the top of the embrasures; they make it more difficult, from a distance, to perceive any thing through the embrasures. More complete blindages are sometimes fixed to the embrasures, consisting of 2 stout boards, moving in slides from either side, so that the embrasure can be completely closed by them. If the line of fire is always directed to the same spot, they need not be opened out when the gun is run out, a hole being cut through them for the muzzle to pass. A movable lid closes the hole, when necessary. Other blindages are used to cover the gunners in a battery from vertical fire; they consist of plain strong timbers, one end of which is laid on the inner crest of the parapet, the other on the ground. Unless the shells are very heavy, and come down nearly in a vertical direction, they do not pass through such a blindage, but merely graze it, and go off at an angle. In trenching, some kinds of blindages are used to protect the sappers from fire; they are movable on trucks, and pushed forward as the work advances. Against musket fire, a wall of strong boards, lined on the outside with sheet iron, supported by strong timbers, is sufficient. Against cannon fire, large square boxes, or frames, filled with earth, sandbags, or fascines, are necessary. The most common kind of sappers' blindage consists of a very large gabion, or cylinder of wicker work, filled with fascines, which is rolled before them by the workmen. Wherever the sap has to be covered in from above, the blindage is constructed by laying square balks across the top, and covering them with fascines, and finally with earth, which renders them sufficiently bomb and shot proof.

Written before September 29, 1857

First published in *The New American Cyclopaedia,* Vol. III, 1858

Reproduced from *The New American Cyclopaedia*

Frederick Engels

BONNET [170]

Bonnet, in fortification, a transverse elevation of the parapet, or traverse and parapet, used either to prevent the enemy from seeing the interior of a work from some elevated point, or, in barbette batteries, to protect men and guns from flanking fire. In these latter batteries, the guns firing over the crest of the parapet have to be placed on high traversing platforms, on which the gun-carriage rests, recoils, and is run forward. The men are, therefore, partly exposed to the fire of the enemy while they serve the gun; and flanking or ricocheting fire is especially dangerous, the object to be hit being nearly twice as high as in batteries with embrasures and low gun-carriages. To prevent this, traverses or cross parapets are placed between the guns, and have to be constructed so much higher than the parapet, that they fully cover the gunners while mounted on the platform. This superstructure is continued from the traverse across the whole thickness of the parapet. It confines the sweep of the guns to an angle of from 90° to 120°, if a gun has a bonnet on either side.

Bonnet-à-Prêtre, or *Queue d'Hirondelle* (swallow tail), in field fortification, is an intrenchment having 2 salient angles, and a reentering angle between them. The latter is always 90°, the 2 salient angles mostly 60°, so that the 2 outer faces, which are longer than the inner ones, diverge to the rear. This work is sometimes used for small bridge heads, or in other situations where the entrance to a defile has to be defended.

Written between September 16 and 29, 1857

First published in *The New American Cyclopaedia*, Vol. III, 1858

Reproduced from *The New American Cyclopaedia*

Karl Marx and Frederick Engels

BOSQUET [171]

Bosquet, Marie Joseph, a marshal of France, born in 1810, at Pau, in the department of Basses Pyrénées. He entered the polytechnic school of Paris in 1829, the military school at Metz in 1831, became lieutenant of artillery in 1833, and in that capacity went to Algeria with the 10th regiment of artillery, in 1834. There on one occasion, when a small French detachment found itself in a very critical position, the commanding officer being at a loss how to disengage his troops, young Bosquet stepped forward and proposed a plan which led to the total discomfiture of the enemy. He was appointed lieutenant in 1836, captain in 1839, major in 1842, lieut.-colonel in 1845, colonel, and soon after, under the auspices of the republican government, general of brigade, in 1848. During the campaign of Kabylia in 1851,[a] he was wounded, at the head of his brigade, while storming the defile of Monagal. His promotion to the rank of general of division was put off in consequence of his reserve toward Louis Napoleon, but when troops were sent to the war in Turkey[b] he obtained the command of the second division.

At the battle of the Alma[c] he executed the flanking attack of the French right wing upon the Russian left, with a speed and energy praised by the Russians themselves, and even succeeded in bringing his artillery through pathless and apparently impracticable ravines up to the plateau. It must, however, be added that on this occasion his own numerical force greatly surpassed that of the

---

[a] See this volume, p. 69.— *Ed.*

[b] A reference to the Crimean war of 1853-56.— *Ed.*

[c] See this volume, pp. 14-18.— *Ed.*

enemy. At Balaklava he hastened to disengage the English right wing, so that the remainder of the English light cavalry was enabled to retreat under the cover of his troops, while the Russians were compelled to stop their pursuit.[172] At Inkermann [173] he was ready early in the morning to support the English with 3 battalions and 2 batteries. This offer being declined, he posted as reserves, in the rear of the English right wing, 3 French brigades, with 2 of which, at 11 o'clock, he advanced to the line of battle, thus forcing the Russians to fall back. But for this succor, the English would have been completely destroyed, since they had all their troops engaged and no more reserves to draw upon, while the Russians had 16 battalions not yet touched. As chief of the corps destined to cover the allied forces on the slope of the Tchernaya, Bosquet constantly distinguished himself by quickness, vigilance, and activity. He took part in the storming of the Malakoff,[174] and after that event was made a marshal, and in 1856 a senator.

Written between September 15 and 29, 1857

First published in *The New American Cyclopaedia*, Vol. III, 1858

Reproduced from *The New American Cyclopaedia*

Frederick Engels

BOMB [175]

Bomb, or Shell, a hollow iron shot for heavy guns and mortars, filled with powder, and thrown at a considerable elevation, and intended to act by the force of its fall and explosion. They are generally the largest of all projectiles used, as a mortar, being shorter than any other class of ordnance, can be made so much larger in diameter and bore. Bombs of 10, 11, and 13 inches are now of common use; the French, at the siege of Antwerp [176] in 1832, used a mortar and shells cast in Belgium, of 24 inches calibre. The powder contained in a bomb is exploded by a fuze or hollow tube filled with a slow-burning composition, which takes fire by the discharge of the mortar. These fuzes are so timed that the bomb bursts as short a time as possible after it has reached its destination, sometimes just before it reaches the ground. Beside the powder, there are sometimes a few pieces of Valenciennes composition [177] put into the shell, to set fire to combustible objects, but it is maintained that these pieces are useless, the explosion shattering them to atoms, and that the incendiary effects of shells without such composition are equally great. Bombs are thrown at angles varying from 15° to 45°, but generally from 30° to 45°; the larger shells and smaller charges having the greatest proportional ranges at about 45°, while smaller shells with greater charges range furthest at about 30°. The charges are in all instances proportionally small: a 13-inch bomb weighing 200 lbs., thrown out of a mortar at the elevation of 45°, with a charge of $3\frac{1}{2}$ lbs. powder, ranges 1,000 yards, and with 20 lbs. or $\frac{1}{10}$ of its weight, 4,200 yards. The effects of such a bomb, coming down from a tremendous height, are very great if it falls on any thing destructible. It will go through all the floors in a house, and penetrate vaulted arches of considerable strength; and, though a 13-inch shell only contains about 7 lbs. of powder, yet its bursting acts like the explosion of a mine, and the fragments will fly to a distance of 800 or 1,000 yards if unobstructed. On the contrary, if it falls on soft soil, it will imbed itself in the earth to a depth of from 8 to 12 feet, and either be extinguished or explode without doing any harm. Bombs are therefore often used as small mines, or *fougasses*, being imbedded in the earth about a foot deep in such places where the enemy must pass; to fire them, a slow match or train is prepared. This is the first shape in which they occur in history: the Chinese, according to their chronicles, several centuries before our era used metal balls filled with bursting composition and small pieces of metal, and fired by a slow match. They were employed in the defence of defiles, being deposited there on the approach of the enemy. In 1232, at the siege of Kaï-fong-fu, the Chinese used, against an assault, to roll bombs down the parapet among the assailant Mongols. Mahmood, Shah of Guzerat, in the siege of Champaneer, in 1484, threw bombs into the town. In Europe, not to mention earlier instances of a more doubtful character, the Arabs in Spain, and the Spaniards after them, threw shells and carcasses from ordnance after the beginning of the 14th century, but the costliness and difficulties of manufacturing hollow shot long prevented their general introduction. They have become an important ingredient of siege artillery since the middle of the 17th century only.

Written between September 29 and October 6, 1857

First published in *The New American Cyclopaedia*, Vol. III, 1858

Reproduced from *The New American Cyclopaedia*

Frederick Engels

BOMB KETCH

Bomb ketch is now generally used to designate the more old-fashioned sort of mortar vessels (*galiotes à bombes*). They were built strong enough to resist the shock caused by the recoil of the mortar, 60 to 70 feet long, 100 to 150 tons burden; they drew from 8 to 9 feet water, and were rigged usually with 2 masts. They used to carry 2 mortars and some guns. The sailing qualities of these vessels were naturally very inferior. A tender, generally a brig, was attached to them, which carried the artillerymen and the greater part of the ammunition, until the action commenced.

Written between September 29 and October 6, 1857

First published in *The New American Cyclopaedia*, Vol. III, 1858

Reproduced from *The New American Cyclopaedia*

Frederick Engels

BOMB-PROOF

Bomb-proof, the state of a roof strong enough to resist the shock of bombs falling upon it. With the enormous calibres now in use, it is almost impossible, and certainly as yet not worth while, to aim at absolute security from vertical fire for most buildings covered in bomb-proof. A circular vault $3\,^1/_2$ feet thick at the keystone, will resist most shells, and even a single 13-inch shell might not break through; but a second one could in most cases do so. Absolutely bomb-proof buildings are therefore confined to powder magazines, laboratories, &c., where a single shell would cause an immense explosion. Strong vaults covered over with 3 or 4 feet of earth, will give the greatest security. For common casemates the vaults need not be so very strong, as the chance of shells falling repeatedly into the same place is very remote. For temporary shelter against shells, buildings are covered in with strong balks laid close together and overlaid with fascines, on which some dung and finally earth is spread. The introduction of casemated batteries and forts, and of casemated defensive barracks, placed mostly along the inner slope of the rampart, at a short distance from it, has considerably increased the number of bomb-proof buildings in fortresses; and with the present mode of combining violent bombardments, continued night and day, with the regular attack of a fortress, the garrison cannot be expected to hold out unless effective shelter is provided in which those off duty can recover their strength by rest. This sort of buildings is therefore likely to be still more extensively applied in the construction of modern fortresses.

Written between September 29 and October 6, 1857

First published in *The New American Cyclopaedia*, Vol. III, 1858

Reproduced from *The New American Cyclopaedia*

Frederick Engels

BOMB VESSEL

Bomb Vessel, or *Mortar Boat*, is the expression in use for the more modern class of ships constructed to carry mortars. Up to the Russian war,[a] those built for the British service drew 8 or 9 feet water, and carried, beside their 2 10-inch mortars, 4 68-pounders, and 6 18 lb. carronades. When the Russian war made naval warfare in shallow waters and intricate channels a necessity, and mortar boats were required on account of the strong sea-fronts of the Russian fortresses, which defied any direct attack by ships, a new class of bomb vessels had to be devised. The new boats thus built are about 60 feet long, with great breadth of beam, round bows like a Dutch galliot, flat bottoms, drawing 6 or 7 feet water, and propelled by steam. They carry 2 mortars, 10 or 13-inch calibre, and a few field-guns or carronades to repel boarding parties by grape, but no heavy guns. They were used with great effect at Sveaborg, which place they bombarded from a distance of 4,000 yards.[178]

Written between September 29 and October 6, 1857

First published in *The New American Cyclopaedia*, Vol. III, 1858

---

[a] The Crimean war of 1853-56.— *Ed.*

Frederick Engels

BOMBARDIER

Bombardier, originally the man having charge of a mortar in a mortar battery, but now retained in some armies to designate a non-commissioned rank in the artillery, somewhat below a sergeant. The bombardier generally has the pointing of the gun for his principal duty. In Austria, a bombardier corps is formed as a training school for non-commissioned officers of the artillery, an institution which has contributed much to the effective and scientific mode of serving their guns, for which that branch of the Austrian service is distinguished.

Written between September 29 and October 6, 1857

First published in *The New American Cyclopaedia*, Vol. III, 1858

Reproduced from *The New American Cyclopaedia*

Frederick Engels

BOMBARDMENT

Bombardment, the act of throwing bombs or shells into a town or fortress for incendiary purposes. A bombardment is either desultory, when ships, field batteries, or a proportionally small number of siege batteries, throw shells into a place in order to intimidate the inhabitants and garrison into a hasty surrender, or for some other purpose; or it is regular, and then forms one of the methods of conducting the attack of a fortified place. The attack by regular bombardment was first introduced by the Prussians in their sieges in 1815, after Waterloo,[179] of the fortresses in the north of France. The army and the Bonapartist party being then much dispirited, and the remainder of the inhabitants anxiously wishing for peace, it was thought that the formalities of the old methodical attack in this case might be dispensed with, and a short and heavy bombardment substituted, which would create fires and explosions of magazines, prevent every soul in the place from getting a night's rest, and thus in a short time compel a surrender, either by the moral pressure of the inhabitants on the commander, or by the actual amount of devastation caused, and by out-fatiguing the garrison. The regular attack by direct fire against the defences, though proceeded with, became secondary to vertical fire and shelling from heavy howitzers. In some cases a desultory bombardment was sufficient, in others a regular bombardment had to be resorted to; but in every instance the plan was successful; and it is now a maxim in the theory of sieges, that to destroy the resources, and to render unsafe the interior of a fortress by vertical fire, is as important (if not more so) as the destruction of its outer defences by direct and ricochet firing. A bombardment will be most effective against a fortress of middling size, with numerous non-military inhabitants, the moral effect upon them being one of the means applied to force the commander into surrender. For the bombardment of a large fortress, an immense *matériel* is required. The best example of this is the siege of Sebastopol, in which quantities of shells formerly unheard of were used.[180] The same war furnishes the most important example of a desultory bombardment, in the attack upon Sweaborg by the Anglo-French mortar boats, in which above 5,000 shells and the same number of solid shot were thrown into the place.[181]

Written between September 29 and October 6, 1857

First published in *The New American Cyclopaedia*, Vol. III, 1858

Reproduced from *The New American Cyclopaedia*

Karl Marx

BERNADOTTE[182]

Bernadotte, Jean Baptiste Jules, marshal of the French empire, prince of Ponte Corvo, and, under the name of Charles XIV John, king of Sweden and Norway, was born Jan. 26, 1764, at Pau, in the department of Basses Pyrénées, died March 8, 1844, in the royal palace at Stockholm. He was the son of a lawyer, and was educated for that profession, but his military impulses induced him to enlist secretly, in 1780, in the royal marines, where he had advanced to the grade of sergeant, when the French revolution broke out. Thence his advancement became rapid. In 1792 he served as colonel in Custine's army; commanded a demi-brigade in 1793; was in the same year, through Kléber's patronage, promoted to the rank of brigadier-general, and contributed, as general of division in the army of the Sambre and Meuse, under Kléber and Jourdan, to the victory of Fleurus, June 26, 1794, the success of Jülich, and the capitulation of Maestricht.[183] He also did good service in the campaign of 1795-'96 against the Austrian generals Clerfayt, Kray, and the archduke Charles. Ordered by the directory,[184] at the beginning of 1797, to march 20,000 men as reenforcements to the Italian army, his first interview in Italy with Bonaparte decided their future relations. In spite of his natural greatness, Bonaparte entertained a petty and suspicious jealousy of the army of the Rhine and its generals. He understood at once that Bernadotte aspired to an independent career. The latter, on his part, was too much of a Gascon to justly appreciate the distance between a genius like Bonaparte and a man of abilities like himself. Hence their mutual dislike. During the invasion of Istria[185] Bernadotte distinguished himself at the passage of the Tagliamento, where he led the vanguard, and at the capture of the fortress of Gradisca, March 19, 1797.

After the so-called revolution of the 18th Fructidor,[186] Bonaparte ordered his generals to collect from their respective divisions addresses in favor of that *coup d'état;* but Bernadotte first protested, then affected great reluctance in obeying, and at last sent an address to the directory,[a] but quite the reverse of that asked for, and without conveying it through Bonaparte's hands. The latter on his journey to Paris, whither he repaired to lay before the directory the treaty of Campo Formio,[187] visited and cajoled Bernadotte at his head-quarters at Udine, but the following day, through an order from Milan, deprived him of half his division of the army of the Rhine, and commanded him to march the other half back to France. After many remonstrances, compromises, and new quarrels, Bernadotte was at last prevailed upon to accept the embassy to Vienna. There, acting up to the instructions of Talleyrand, he assumed a conciliatory attitude which the Paris journals, inspired by Bonaparte and his brothers, declared to be full of royalist tendencies; expatiating, in proof of these charges, on the suppression of the tricolored flag at the entrance of his hotel, and of the republican cockade on the hats of his suite. Being reprimanded for this by the directory, Bernadotte, on April 13, 1798, the anniversary of a Viennese anti-Jacobin demonstration, hoisted the tricolored flag with the inscription, "Liberty, equality, fraternity," and had his hotel stormed by a Viennese mob, his flag burnt, and his own life endangered. The Austrian government declining to give the satisfaction demanded, Bernadotte withdrew to Rastadt with all his legation; but the directory, on the advice of Bonaparte, who had himself been instrumental in provoking the scandal, hushed up the affair and dropped their representative.

Bernadotte's relationship to the Bonaparte family consequent upon his marriage, in Aug. 1798, with Mlle. Désirée Clary, the daughter of a Marseilles merchant, and Joseph Bonaparte's sister-in-law, seemed but to confirm his opposition to Napoleon. As commander of the army of observation on the upper Rhine, in 1799, he proved incompetent for the charge, and thus verified beforehand Napoleon's judgment at St. Helena, that he was a better lieutenant than general-in-chief.[b] At the head of the war ministry, after the directorial émeute of the 30th Prairial,[188] his plans

---

[a] According to the publication in the *Gazette nationale ou le moniteur universel,* No. 325, August 12, 1797, this address was sent before the coup d'état of the 18th Fructidor and not after it.— *Ed.*

[b] A. H. Jomini, *Vie politique et militaire de Napoléon,* t. 2, p. 60.— *Ed.*

of operation were less remarkable than his intrigues with the Jacobins, through whose reviving influence he tried to create for himself a personal following in the ranks of the army. Yet one morning, Sept. 15, 1799, he found his resignation announced in the *Moniteur* before he was aware that he had tendered it.[a] This trick was played upon him by Sieyès and Roger Ducos, the directors allied to Bonaparte.

While commanding the army of the west, he extinguished the last sparks of the Vendean war.[189] After the proclamation of the empire[b] which made him a marshal, he was intrusted with the command of the army of Hanover. In this capacity as well as during his later command of the army of northern Germany, he took care to create for himself, among the northern people, a reputation for independence, moderation, and administrative ability. At the head of the corps stationed in Hanover, which formed the first corps of the grand army,[190] he participated in the campaign of 1805 against the Austrians and Russians. He was sent by Napoleon to Iglau, to observe the movements of Archduke Ferdinand in Bohemia; then, called back to Brünn, he, with his corps, was posted at the battle of Austerlitz[191] in the centre between Soult and Lannes, and contributed to baffle the attempt of the allied right wing at outflanking the French army. On June 5, 1806, he was created prince of Ponte Corvo. During the campaign of 1806-'7 against Prussia, he commanded the first *corps d'armée.* He received from Napoleon the order to march from Naumburg upon Dornburg, while Davout, also stationed at Naumburg, was to march upon Apolda; the order held by Davout adding that, if Bernadotte had already effected his junction with him, they might conjointly march upon Apolda. Having reconnoitred the movements of the Prussians, and made sure that no enemy was to be encountered in the direction of Dornburg, Davout proposed to Bernadotte a combined march upon Apolda, and even offered to place himself under his command. The latter, however, sticking to the literal interpretation of Napoleon's order, marched off in the direction of Dornburg without meeting an enemy during the whole day; while Davout had alone to bear the brunt of the battle of Auerstädt, which, through Bernadotte's absence, ended in an indecisive victory. It was only the meeting of the fugitives of Auerstädt with the fugitives from Jena,[192] and the

---

[a] *Gazette nationale ou le moniteur universel*, No. 359, 29 Fructidor an. 7 (1799), p. 1458.— *Ed.*

[b] In 1804.— *Ed.*

strategetical combinations of Napoleon, that counteracted the consequences of the deliberate blunder committed by Bernadotte. Napoleon signed an order to bring Bernadotte before a court-martial, but on further consideration rescinded it. After the battle of Jena, Bernadotte defeated the Prussians at Halle, Oct. 17, conjointly with Soult and Murat, pursued the Prussian general Blücher to Lübeck, and contributed to his capitulation at Ratekau, Nov. 7, 1806. He also defeated the Russians in the plains of Mohrungen, not far from Thorn, Jan. 25, 1807.

After the peace of Tilsit, according to the alliance concluded between Denmark and Napoleon, French troops were to occupy the Danish islands, thence to act against Sweden.[193] Accordingly, March 23, 1808, the very day when Russia invaded Finland, Bernadotte was commanded to move upon Seeland in order to penetrate with the Danes into Sweden, to dethrone its king,[a] and to partition the country between Denmark and Russia; a strange mission for a man destined soon after to reign at Stockholm. He passed the Belt and arrived in Seeland at the head of 32,000 Frenchmen, Dutch, and Spaniards; 10,000 of the latter, however, contriving, by the assistance of an English fleet, to decamp under Gen. de la Romana. Bernadotte undertook nothing and effected nothing during his stay in Seeland. Being recalled to Germany, there to assist in the new war between France and Austria, he received the command of the 9th corps, mainly composed of Saxons.

The battle of Wagram, July 5 and 6, 1809,[194] added new fuel to his misunderstandings with Napoleon. On the first day, Eugène Beauharnais, having debouched in the vicinity of Wagram, and dashed into the centre of the hostile reserves, was not sufficiently supported by Bernadotte, who engaged his troops too late, and too weakly. Attacked in front and flank, Eugène was roughly thrown back upon Napoleon's guard, and the first shock of the French attack was thus broken by Bernadotte's lukewarmness, who, meanwhile, had occupied the village of Adlerklaa, in the centre of the French army, but somewhat in advance of the French line. On the following day, at 6 o'clock in the morning, when the Austrians advanced for a concentric attack, Bernadotte deployed before Adlerklaa, instead of placing that village, strongly occupied, in his front. Judging, on the arrival of the Austrians, that this position was too hazardous, he fell back upon a plateau in the rear of Adlerklaa, leaving the village unoccupied, so that it was

---

[a] Gustavus IV Adolphus.— Ed.

immediately taken by Bellegarde's Austrians. The French centre being thus endangered, Masséna, its commander, sent forward a division to retake Adlerklaa, which division, however, was again dislodged by D'Aspre's grenadiers. At that moment, Napoleon himself arrived, took the supreme command, formed a new plan of battle, and baffled the manoeuvres of the Austrians. Thus Bernadotte had again, as at Auerstädt, endangered the success of the day. On his part, he complained of Napoleon's having, in violation of all military rules, ordered Gen. Dupas, whose French division formed part of Bernadotte's corps, to act independently of his command. His resignation, which he tendered, was accepted, after Napoleon had become aware of an order of the day addressed by Bernadotte to his Saxons, in discord with the imperial bulletin.

Shortly after his arrival at Paris, where he entered into intrigues with Fouché, the Walcheren expedition (July 30, 1809) caused the French ministry, in the absence of the emperor, to intrust Bernadotte with the defence of Antwerp.[195] The blunders of the English rendered action on his part unnecessary; but he took the occasion to slip into a proclamation, issued to his troops, the charge against Napoleon of having neglected to prepare the proper means of defence for the Belgian coast. He was deprived of his command; ordered, on his return to Paris, to leave it for his princedom of Ponte Corvo, and, refusing to comply with that order, he was summoned to Vienna. After some lively altercations with Napoleon, at Schönbrunn,[196] he accepted the general government of the Roman states, a sort of honorable exile.

The circumstances which brought about his election as crown prince of Sweden, were not fully elucidated until long after his death. Charles XIII, after the adoption of Charles August, duke of Augustenburg, as his son, and as heir to the Swedish throne, sent Count Wrede to Paris, to ask for the duke the hand of the princess Charlotte, daughter of Lucien Bonaparte. On the sudden death of the duke of Augustenburg, May 18, 1810, Russia pressed upon Charles XIII the adoption of the duke of Oldenburg, while Napoleon supported the claims of Frederick VI, king of Denmark. The old king himself offered the succession to the brother[a] of the late duke of Augustenburg, and despatched Baron Moerner to Gen. Wrede, with instructions enjoining the latter to bring Napoleon over to the king's choice. Moerner, however, a young man belonging to the very large party in Sweden which then

---

[a] Frederick Christian.—Ed.

expected the recovery of their country only from an intimate alliance with France, on his arrival at Paris, took upon himself, in connection with Lapie, a young French officer in the engineers, with Seigneul, the Swedish consul-general, and with Count Wrede himself, to present Bernadotte as candidate for the Swedish throne, all of them taking care to conceal their proceedings from Count Lagerbjelke, the Swedish minister at the Tuileries, and all firmly convinced by a series of misunderstandings, artfully kept up by Bernadotte, that the latter was really the candidate of Napoleon. On June 29, accordingly, Wrede and Seigneul sent despatches to the Swedish minister of foreign affairs, both announcing that Napoleon would, with great pleasure, see the royal succession offered to his lieutenant and relative. In spite of the opposition of Charles XIII, the diet of the States, at Örebro, elected Bernadotte crown prince of Sweden, Aug. 21, 1810. The king was also compelled to adopt him as his son, under the name of Charles John. Napoleon reluctantly, and with bad grace, ordered Bernadotte to accept the offered dignity. Leaving Paris, Sept. 28, 1810, he landed at Helsingborg, Oct. 21, there abjured the Catholic profession, entered Stockholm Nov. 1, attended the assembly of the States, Nov. 5, and from that moment grasped the reins of the state. Since the disastrous peace of Frederikshamm,[197] the idea prevailing in Sweden was the reconquest of Finland, without which, it was thought, as Napoleon wrote to Alexander, Feb. 28, 1811, "Sweden had ceased to exist," at least as a power independent of Russia.[a] It was but by an intimate alliance with Napoleon that the Swedes could hope to recover that province. To this conviction Bernadotte owed his election. During the king's sickness, from March 17, 1811, to January 7, 1812, Charles John was appointed regent; but this was a question of etiquette only, since from the day of his arrival, he conducted all affairs.

Napoleon, too much of a parvenu himself to spare the susceptibilities of his ex-lieutenant, compelled him, Nov. 17, 1810, in spite of a prior engagement, to accede to the continental system,[198] and declare war against England. He suppressed his revenues as a French prince; declined to receive his despatches directly addressed to him, because he was not "a sovereign his equal"[b]; and sent back the order of the Seraphim, bestowed upon the new-born king of Rome[c] by Charles John. This petty

---

    [a] Marx may have used G. Lallerstedt's book *La Scandinavie*, Paris, 1856, pp. 89-90.— *Ed.*

    [b] ibid., p. 97.— *Ed.*

    [c] Duke of Reichstadt, son of Napoleon I.— *Ed.*

chicanery afforded to the latter the pretext only for a course of action long decided upon. Hardly was he installed at Stockholm, when he admitted to a public audience the Russian general, Suchtelen, who was detested by the Swedes for having suborned the commander of Sweaborg, and even allowed that personage to be accredited as ambassador to the Swedish court. On Dec. 18, 1810, he held a conference with Czernicheff, in which he declared himself "to be anxious to win the good opinion of the czar," and to resign Finland forever, on the condition of Norway being detached from Denmark, and annexed to Sweden.[a] By the same Czernicheff, he sent a most flattering letter to the czar Alexander. As he thus drew nearer to Russia, the Swedish generals who had overthrown Gustavus IV, and favored his own election, retired from him. Their opposition, reechoed by the army and the people, threatened to become dangerous, when the invasion of Swedish Pomerania by a French division, Jan. 17, 1812—a measure executed by Napoleon on secret advice from Stockholm—afforded at last to Charles John a plausible pretext for officially declaring the neutrality of Sweden. Secretly, however, and behind the back of the diet, he concluded with Alexander an offensive alliance against France, signed March 24,[b] 1812, at St. Petersburg, in which the annexation of Norway to Sweden was also stipulated.

Napoleon's declaration of war against Russia made Bernadotte for a time the arbiter of the destinies of Europe. Napoleon offered him, on the condition of his attacking Russia with 40,000 Swedes, Finland, Mecklenburg, Stettin, and all the territory between Stettin and Volgast. Bernadotte might have decided the campaign and occupied St. Petersburg before Napoleon arrived at Moscow. He preferred acting as the Lepidus of a triumvirate formed with England and Russia. Inducing the sultan[c] to ratify the peace of Bucharest,[199] he enabled the Russian admiral Tchitchakoff to withdraw his forces from the banks of the Danube and to operate on the flank of the French army. He also mediated the peace of Örebro, concluded July 18, 1812, between England on the one side, and Russia and Sweden on the other.[200] Frightened at Napoleon's first successes, Alexander invited Charles John to an interview, at the same time offering him the command-in-chief of the Russian armies. Prudent enough to decline the latter offer, he

---

[a] Lallerstedt, op. cit., p. 95.— Ed.
[b] April 5 (New Style).— Ed.
[c] Mahmud II.— Ed.

accepted the invitation. On Aug. 27 he arrived at Abo, where he found Alexander very low-spirited and rather inclined to sue for peace. Having himself gone too far to recede, he steeled the wavering czar by showing that Napoleon's apparent successes must lead to his ruin. The conference resulted in the so-called treaty of Abo,[201] to which a secret article was appended, giving the alliance the character of a family compact. In fact, Charles John received nothing but promises, while Russia, without the slightest sacrifice, secured the then invaluable alliance of Sweden. By authentic documents it has been recently proved that it depended at that time on Bernadotte alone to have Finland restored to Sweden; but the Gascon ruler, deluded by Alexander's flattery, that "one day the imperial crown of France, when fallen from Napoleon's brow, might rest upon his," already considered Sweden as a mere *pis-aller.*[a]

After the French retreat from Moscow, he formally broke off diplomatic relations with France, and when England guaranteed him Norway by treaty of March 3, 1813,[202] he entered the coalition. Furnished with English subsidies, he landed in May, 1813, at Stralsund with about 25,000 Swedes and advanced toward the Elbe. During the armistice of June 5, 1813,[203] he played an important part at the meeting in Trachenberg, where the emperor Alexander presented him to the king of Prussia,[b] and where the general plan of the campaign was decided upon. As commander-in-chief of the army of the north, composed of Swedes, Russians, Prussians, English, Hanseatic, and north German troops, he kept up very equivocal connections with the French army, managed by an individual who frequented his head-quarters as a friend, and grounded on his presumption that the French would gladly exchange Napoleon's rule for Bernadotte's, if he only gave them proofs of forbearance and clemency. Consequently, he prevented the generals placed under his command from taking the offensive, and when Bülow twice, at Grossbeeren and Dennewitz, had vanquished the French despite his orders, stopped the pursuit of the beaten army. When Blücher, in order to force him to action, had marched upon the Elbe, and effected his junction with him, it was only the threat held out by Sir Charles Stewart, the English commissary in his camp, of stopping the supplies, that induced

---

[a] Expedient. The account of the talks between Charles John and Alexander I is given according to Lallerstedt's *La Scandinavie,* p. 122 et seq. Alexander I's words are to be found on p. 130 of this book.— *Ed.*

[b] Frederick William III.— *Ed.*

him to move on. Still the Swedes appeared on the battle field of Leipsic[204] for appearance' sake only, and during the whole campaign lost not 200 men before the enemy. When the allies entered France, he retained the army of Sweden on her frontiers. After Napoleon's abdication, he repaired personally to Paris to remind Alexander of the promises held out to him at Abo. Talleyrand cut short his puerile hopes by telling the council of the allied kings, that "there was no alternative but Bonaparte or the Bourbons,—every thing else being a mere intrigue."[a]

Charles John having, after the battle of Leipsic, invaded the duchies of Holstein and Schleswig, at the head of an army composed of Swedes, Germans, and Russians, Frederick VI, king of Denmark, in the presence of vastly superior forces, was forced to sign, Jan. 14, 1814, the peace of Kiel, by which Norway was ceded to Sweden. The Norwegians, however, demurring to being so unceremoniously disposed of, proclaimed the independence of Norway under the auspices of Christian Frederick, crown prince of Denmark. The representatives of the nation assembling at Edisvold, adopted, May 17, 1814, a constitution still in force, and the most democratic of modern Europe. Having put in motion a Swedish army and fleet, and seized upon the fortress of Frederickstadt, which commands the access to Christiania, Charles John entered into negotiation, agreed to consider Norway as an independent state and to accept the constitution of Edisvold, carried the assent of the assembled storthing Oct. 7, and Nov. 10, 1814, repaired to Christiania, there, in his own and the king's name, to take the oath upon the constitution.

Charles XIII expiring Feb. 5, 1818, Bernadotte, under the name of Charles XIV John, was acknowledged by Europe as king both of Sweden and Norway. He now attempted to change the Norwegian constitution, to restore the abolished nobility, to secure to himself an absolute veto and the right of dismissing all officers, civil and military. This attempt gave rise to serious conflicts, and led, May 18, 1828, even to a cavalry charge upon the inhabitants of Christiania, who were celebrating the anniversary of their constitution. A violent outbreak seemed imminent, when the French revolution of 1830 caused the king to resort for the moment to conciliatory steps. Still Norway, for the acquisition of which he had sacrificed every thing, remained the constant source of embarrassments throughout his whole reign. After the first days of the French revolution of 1830, there existed a single man

---

a *Mémoires de M. de Bourrienne*, t. X, p. 42.—*Ed.*

in Europe who thought the king of Sweden a fit pretender for the French throne, and that man was Bernadotte himself. More than once he repeated to the French diplomatic agents at Stockholm, "How does it happen that Laffitte has not thought of me?"[a] The changed aspect of Europe, and, above all, the Polish insurrection,[205] inspired him for a moment with the idea of making front against Russia. His offers in this sense to Lord Palmerston meeting with a flat refusal, he had to expiate his transitory idea of independence by concluding, June 23, 1834, a convention of alliance with the emperor Nicholas, which rendered him a vassal of Russia. From that moment his policy in Sweden was distinguished by encroachments on the liberty of the press, persecution of the crime of *lèse-majesté,* and resistance to improvements, even such as the emancipation of industry from the old laws of guilds and corporations. By playing upon the jealousies of the different orders constituting the Swedish diet, he long succeeded in paralyzing all movement, but the liberal resolutions of the diet of 1844,[206] which were to be converted, according to the constitution, into laws by the diet of 1845, threatened his policy with final discomfiture, when his death occurred.

If Sweden, during the reign of Charles XIV, partly recovered from a century and a half of miseries and misfortunes, this was due not to Bernadotte, but exclusively to the native energies of the nation, and the agencies of a long peace.

Written between September and October 15, 1857

First published in *The New American Cyclopaedia,* Vol. III, 1858

Reproduced from *The New American Cyclopaedia*

---

[a] Lallerstedt, *La Scandinavie,* p. 201.— *Ed.*

Frederick Engels

BRIDGE, MILITARY[207]

The art of constructing temporary bridges for the passage, by troops, of large rivers and narrow arms of the sea, was well known to the ancients, whose works in this respect are sometimes of surprising magnitude. Darius passed the Bosporus and Danube, and Xerxes the Hellespont, by bridges of boats, the description of which we find in Herodotus.[a] The army of Xerxes constructed 2 bridges across the Dardanelles, the first of 360 vessels, anchored head and stern alongside each other, their keels in the direction of the current, the vessels connected with each other by strong cables, over which planks were laid, fastened by a rail on either side, and covered in by a bed of earth. The 2d bridge had 314 vessels, and was similarly constructed. According to Arrian, Alexander had a regular pontoon-train of light boats attached to his army.[b] The Romans had wicker-work vessels, covered with the skins of animals, destined to support the timber platform of a bridge; these formed a part of the train of their armies until the end of the empire. They, however, also knew how to construct a more solid kind of military bridge, whenever a rapid river had to be crossed; witness the famous bridges on piles, on which Caesar passed the Rhine.[208]

During the middle ages we find no notice of bridge equipages, but during the 30 years' war[209] the various armies engaged carried materials with them to form bridges across the large rivers of Germany. The boats used were very heavy, and generally made of oak. The platform of the bridge was laid on trestles standing in

---

[a] Herodotus, *History,* Book IV, Ch. 83; Book VII, Ch. 36.— *Ed.*
[b] Flavius Arrianus, *The Anabasis, or Ascent of Alexander.—Ed.*

the bottoms of these boats. The Dutch first adopted a smaller kind of vessel, flat-bottomed, with nearly vertical sides, pointed head and stern, and both ends projecting, in an inclined plane, above the surface of the water. They consisted of a framework of wood, covered with sheets of tin, and were called pontoons. The French, too, according to Folard,[a] claim the invention of pontoons made of copper, and are said to have had, about 1672, a complete pontoon train. By the beginning of the 18th century all European armies had provided themselves with this kind of vessels, mostly wooden frames, covered in with tin, copper, leather, or tarred canvas. The latter material was used by the Russians. The boats were small, and had to be placed close together, with not more than 4 or 5 feet clear space between them, if the bridge was to have any buoyancy; the current of the water was thereby greatly obstructed, the safety of the bridge endangered, and a chance given to the enemy to destroy it by sending floating bodies against it.

The pontoons now employed by the continental armies of Europe are of a larger kind, but similar in principle to those 100 years ago. The French have used, since 1829, a flat-bottomed vessel with nearly vertical sides, diminishing in breadth toward the stem, and also, but a little less, toward the stern; the 2 ends rise above the gunwales and are curved like those of a canoe. The dimensions are: length, 31 ft.; breadth, at top, 5 ft. 7 in.; at bottom, 4 ft. 4 in. The framework is of oak, covered with fir planking. Every pontoon weighs 1,658 lbs. and has a buoyancy (weight of cargo which would sink the vessel to the top of the gunwales) of 18,675 lbs. When formed into a bridge, they are placed at intervals of 14 ft. clear space from gunwale to gunwale, and the road of the bridge is 11 ft. wide. For the advanced guard of an army a smaller kind of pontoon is used, for bridging over rivers of less importance. The Austrian pontoons are similar to the larger French pontoon, but divided transversely in the middle, for more convenient carriage, and put together in the water. Two vessels placed close alongside each other, and connected by short timbers, a longitudinal timber supporting the balks of the platform, constitute a floating pier of a bridge. These pontoons, invented by Birago, were introduced in 1825. The Russians have a framework of wood for their pontoons, so constructed that the centre pieces, or thwarts, may be unshipped; over this frame is stretched sail-cloth, covered with tar or a solution of India rubber. They are in length, 21 ft. 9 in.; breadth, 4 ft. 11 in.; depth, 2 ft. 4

---

[a] *Abregé des commentaires de M. de Folard, sur l'Histoire de Polybe*, t. 3, p. 82.— *Ed.*

in., and weigh 718 lbs. each. Breadth of road of bridge, 10 ft.; distance from pontoon to pontoon, 8 ft. The Russians also have pontoons with a similar framework, covered over with leather. The Prussians are said to have been the first to divide their pontoons transversely into compartments, so as to prevent one leak from sinking them. Their pontoons are of wood and flat-bottomed. The span or clear distance between the pontoons, in their bridges, varies from 8 to 16 ft., according to circumstances. The Dutch, since 1832, and the Piedmontese, have pontoon trains similar to those in the Austrian service. The Belgian pontoon has a pointed head, but is not contracted at the stern. In all continental armies small boats to carry out the anchors accompany the pontoon train.

The British and the U.S. armies have entirely abandoned the use of boats for the formation of their pontoon trains, and adopted hollow cylinders of light material, closed on all sides, to support their bridges. In England the cylindrical pontoons, with conical, hemispherical or paraboloidal ends, as constructed in 1828 by Col. Blanchard, were adopted in 1836 to the exclusion of all other kinds. The larger British pontoon is $24^1/_2$ ft. long and 2 ft. 8 in. in diameter. It is formed of sheet tin, framed round a series of wheels constructed of tin, having hollow cylinders of tin for their spokes; a larger tin cylinder, $1^3/_4$ in. in diameter, forms their common axis, and runs through the entire length of the pontoon.

Experiments have been made in the United States with India rubber cylindrical pontoons. In 1836 Capt. (afterward Col.) Lane constructed bridges over a deep and rapid river in Alabama with such pontoons, and in 1839 Mr. Armstrong submitted similar floats, 18 ft. long, 18 in. in diameter when inflated, and weighing 39 lbs. each, 3 to form 1 link of the bridge. Pontoons of inflated India rubber were, in 1846, introduced in the U.S. army, and used in the war against Mexico.[210] They are very easily carried, from their lightness and the small space they take up when folded; but, beside being liable to be damaged and rendered useless by friction on gravel, &c., they partake the common faults of all cylindrical pontoons. These are, that when once sunk in the water to $^1/_2$ of their depth, their immersion becomes greater and greater with every equal addition of load, the reverse of what should be; their ends, moreover, easily catch and lodge floating matter; and finally, 2 of them must be joined to a raft by a platform before they can be moved in the water, whereas boat pontoons are as capable of independent motion in the water as common boats, and may serve for rowing rapidly across the river a detachment of troops. To compare the buoyant power of the cylindrical pontoon with that of the boat pontoon, the following may suffice: The French pontoon supports about 20 ft. of bridge, and has a buoyancy (the weight of the superstructure deducted) of more than 150 cwt. A British raft of 2 pontoons, supporting about the same length of bridge, has a buoyancy, superstructure deducted, of only 77 cwt., $1/2$ of which is a safe load.

A pontoon train contains, beside the pontoons, the oars, boat-hooks, anchors, cables, &c., necessary to move them about in the water, and to fix them in their position, and the balks and planks (chesses) to form the platform of the bridge. With boat pontoons, every pontoon is generally secured in its place, and then the balks and chesses stretched across; with cylindrical pontoons, 2 are connected to a raft, which is anchored at the proper distance from the end of the bridge, and connected with it by balks and chesses. Where circumstances admit of it, whole links, consisting of 3, 4, or 5 pontoons bridged over, are constructed in sheltered situations above the site fixed on for the bridge, and floated down successively into their positions. In some cases, with very experienced pontoniers, the whole bridge has been constructed on one bank of the river and swung round by the current when the passage was attempted. This was done by Napoleon when crossing the Danube, the day before the battle of Wagram.[211] The whole of this campaign is highly instructive with regard to the passing of large rivers in the face of the enemy by military bridges.

Pontoon trains are, however, not always at hand, and the military engineer must be prepared to bridge over a river, in case of need, without them. For this purpose a variety of materials and modes of construction are employed. The larger kind of boats generally found on navigable rivers are made use of for bridges of boats. If no boats are to be found, and the depth or configuration of bottom of the river renders the use of floating supports necessary, rafts of timber, floats of casks, and other buoyant bodies may be used. If the river is shallow, and has a hard and tolerably level bottom, standing supports are constructed, consisting either of piles, which form the most durable and the safest kind of bridge, but require a great deal of time and labor, or of trestles, which may be easily and quickly constructed. Sometimes wagons loaded with fascines, &c., and sunk in the deeper places of the river, will form convenient supports for the platform of a bridge. Inundations, marshes, &c., are bridged over by means of gabions. For narrow rivers and ravines, where infantry only have to pass, various kinds of suspension bridges are adopted; they are generally suspended by strong cables.

The construction of a military bridge under the actual fire of the enemy is now a matter of but rare occurrence; yet the possibility of resistance must always be provided for. On this account the bridge is generally constructed in a reentering bend of the river, so that the artillery placed right and left sweeps the ground on the opposite bank close to where the bridge is to land, and thus protects its construction. The concave bank, moreover, is generally higher than the convex one, and thus, in most cases, the advantage of command is added to that of a cross fire. Infantry are rowed across in boats or pontoons, and established immediately in front of the bridge. A floating bridge may be constructed to carry some cavalry and a few light guns across. The division of the river into several branches by islands, or a spot immediately below the junction of some smaller river, also offers advantages. In the latter, and sometimes in the former case, the several links of the bridge may be composed in sheltered water, and then floated down. The attacking party, having commonly to choose between many favorable points on a long line of river, may easily mislead his opponent by false attacks, and then effect the real passage at a distant point; and the danger of scattering the defending forces over that long line is so great, that it is nowadays preferred to keep them concentrated at some distance from the river, and march them in a body against the real point of passage as soon as it has once been ascertained, and before the enemy can have brought over all his army. It is from these causes that in none of the wars since the French revolution has the construction of a bridge on any of the large rivers of Europe been seriously contested.

Written between September 16 and October 15, 1857

First published in *The New American Cyclopaedia*, Vol. III, 1858

Reproduced from *The New American Cyclopaedia*

Karl Marx

BROWN [212]

Brown, Sir George, a British general, was born in August, 1790, at Linkwood, near Elgin, Scotland. He entered the army Jan. 23, 1806, as ensign in the 43d regiment of foot, and, as lieutenant in the same regiment, was present at the bombardment of Copenhagen [213]; served in the peninsular war, from its beginning in 1808 to its close in 1814; was severely wounded at the battle of Talavera, and one of the forlorn hope at the storming of Badajos.[214] He was appointed captain in the 85th regiment, June 20, 1811; in Sept. 1814, he was a lieutenant-colonel in Major-General Ross's expedition to the United States, and took part in the battle of Bladensburg, and the capture of Washington.[215] He was appointed commander of a battalion of the rifle brigade, Feb. 6, 1824; colonel, May 6, 1831; major-general, Nov. 23, 1841; deputy adjutant-general in 1842; adjutant-general of the forces in April, 1850, and lieut.-general in 1851. During the Crimean campaign, he led the English light division at the battle of Alma [a] and the battle of Inkermann, and took the command-in-chief of the storming party in the first unsuccessful attack on the Redan.[216] Among the allied armies he became distinguished as a martinet; but, by his personal prowess, and the strict impartiality with which he held the young aristocratic officers to all the duties of field discipline, he became popular among the common

---

[a] See this volume, pp. 14-18.— Ed.

soldiers. In 1855 he was created a knight commander of the Bath, and April 4, 1856, gazetted "General in the army for distinguished service in the field."[a]

Written between September 21 and October 15, 1857

First published in *The New American Cyclopaedia*, Vol. III, 1858

Reproduced from *The New American Cyclopaedia*

---

[a] "War Department, Pall-Mall, April 4. General Order, No. 665", *The Times*, No. 22334, April 5, 1856.— *Ed.*

Karl Marx and Frederick Engels

ARMADA[217]

Armada, Spanish, the great naval armament sent by King Philip II of Spain, in 1588, for the conquest of England, in order thereby

"to serve God, and to returne unto his church a great many contrite souls that are oppressed by the heretics, enemies to our holy Catholic faith, which have them subject to their sects, and unhappiness." *(Expedit. Hispan. in Angl. Vera Descriptio, A. D. 1588.)*

The fullest account of this armament is given in a book published, about the time it set sail, by order of Philip, under the title *La Felicisima Armada que el Rey Don Felipe nuestro Señor mando juntar en el Puerto de Lisboa 1588. Hecha por Pedro de Pax Salas.* A copy of this work was procured for Lord Burleigh, so that the English government was beforehand acquainted with every detail of the expedition. (This copy, containing notes up to March, 1588, is now in the British museum.) The fleet is therein stated to have consisted of 65 galleons and large ships, 25 *urcas* of 300 to 700 tons, 19 tenders of 70 to 100 tons, 13 small frigates, 4 galeasses and 4 galleys, in all 130 vessels, with a total tonnage of 57,868 tons. They were armed with 2,431 guns, of which 1,497 were of bronze, mostly full cannon (48 pdrs.), culverines (long 30 and 20 pdrs.), &c.; the ammunition consisted of 123,790 round shot and 5,175 cwt. of powder, giving about 50 rounds per gun, at an average charge of $4^1/_2$ lbs. The ships were manned with 8,052 sailors, and carried 19,295 soldiers and 180 priests and monks. Mules, carts, &c., were on board to move the field artillery when landed. The whole was provisioned, according to the above authority, for 6 months. This fleet, unequalled in its time, was to proceed to the Flemish coast, where another army of 30,000 foot and 4,000 horse, under the duke of Parma, was to embark, under its protection, in flat-bottomed vessels constructed for the purpose, and manned by sailors brought from the Baltic. The whole were then to proceed to England.

In that country Queen Elizabeth had, by vigorous exertions, increased her fleet of originally 30 ships, to some 180 vessels of various sizes, but generally inferior in that respect to those of the Spaniards. They were, however, manned by 17,500 sailors, and therefore possessed far more numerous crews than the Spanish fleet. The English military force was divided into two armies, one, of 18,500 men, under the earl of Leicester, for immediately opposing the enemy; the other, 45,000, for the defence of the queen's person. According to a MS. in the British museum, entitled "Details of the English Force Assembled to Oppose the Spanish Armada," (MS. Reg. 18th c. xxi.), 2,000 infantry were also expected from the Low Countries.

The armada was to leave Lisbon in the beginning of May, but, owing to the death of the admiral Santa Cruz, and his vice-admiral, the departure was delayed. The duke of Medina Sidonia, a man totally unacquainted with naval matters, was now made captain-general of the fleet; his vice-admiral, Martinez de Ricalde, however, was an expert seaman. Having left Lisbon for Corunna for stores, May 29, 1588, the fleet was dispersed by a violent storm, and, though all the ships joined at Corunna with the exception of four, they were considerably shattered, and had to be repaired. Reports having reached England that the armament was completely disabled, the government ordered its own ships to be laid up; but Lord Howard, the admiral, opposed this order, set sail for Corunna, learned the truth, and, on his return, continued warlike preparations. Soon after, being informed that the armada had hove in sight, he weighed anchor and accompanied it on its way up the channel, harassing the Spanish ships whenever an opportunity presented itself. The Spaniards, in the mean time, proceeded to the coast of Flanders, keeping as close together as possible. In the various minor engagements which took place, the handier ships, more numerous crews, and better seamanship of the English, always gave them the victory over the clumsy and undermanned Spanish galleons, crowded as they were with soldiers. The Spanish artillery, too, was very badly served, and almost always planted too high. Off Calais the armada cast anchor, waiting for the duke of Parma's fleet to come out of the Flemish harbors; but it soon received word that his ships, being unfit for fighting, could not come out until the armada had passed the straits and driven off the Anglo-Dutch blockading squadron. It accordingly weighed again, but, when in sight of Dunkirk, was becalmed between the English fleet on one side and the Dutch on the other. Lord Howard prepared fire-ships, and when, during the night of Aug. 7, the breeze sprang up again, he sent 8 of them among the enemy. They produced a perfect panic in the Spanish fleet. Some ships weighed anchor, some cut their cables, drifting before the wind; the whole fleet got into confusion, several ships ran foul of each other and were disabled. By morning order was far from being restored, and the several divisions were scattered far and wide. Then Lord Howard, reinforced as he was by the ships equipped by the nobility and gentry, as also by the blockading squadron under Lord Byron, and ably seconded by Sir Francis Drake, engaged the enemy at 4 A.M. The battle, or rather chase (for the English were evidently superior on every point of attack), lasted till dark. The Spaniards fought bravely, but their unwieldy ships were unfit for the navigation of narrow waters, and for a moving fight. They were completely defeated, and suffered severe loss.

The junction with the duke of Parma's transports having thus been foiled, a landing in England by the armada alone was out of the question. It was found that the greater part of the provisions on board had been consumed, and as access to Spanish Flanders was now impossible, nothing remained but to return to Spain to lay in fresh stores. (See "Certain Advertisements out of Ireland Concerning the Losses and Distresses Happened to the Spanish Navie on the Coast of Ireland," London, 1588—Examination of Emanuel Fremosa, who served in the *San Juan,* 1,100 tons, flag-ship of Admiral Ricalde.[a]) The passage through the channel being also closed by the English fleet, nothing remained but to round Scotland on their way home. The armada was but little harassed by the fleet of Lord Seymour sent in pursuit, as that fleet was badly supplied with ammunition and could not venture on an attack. But after the Spaniards had rounded the Orkneys dreadful storms arose and dispersed the whole fleet. Some ships were driven back as far as the coast of Norway, where they fell on the rocks; others foundered in the North sea, or struck on the rocks on the coast of Scotland or the Hebrides. Soon after, fresh storms overtook them on the west coast of Ireland, where above 30

---

[a] For quoting this source Marx and Engels used, apparently, *The Harleian Miscellany: A Collection of Scarce, Curious, and Entertaining Pamphlets and Tracts, etc.,* Vol. I, London, 1808, p. 129.—*Ed.*

vessels were lost. Those of the crews who escaped on shore were mostly killed; about 200 were executed by command of the lord deputy.[a] Of the whole fleet not more than 60 vessels, and those in the most shattered condition, and with famine on board, reached Santander about the middle of September, when the plan of invading England was definitively given up.

Written in September-October, not later than October 23, 1857

Reproduced from *The New American Cyclopaedia*

First published in *The New American Cyclopaedia*, Vol. II, 1858

---

[a] Sir William Fitzwilliam.— *Ed.*

Karl Marx and Frederick Engels

AYACUCHO [218]

Ayacucho, a department in the republic of Peru; pop. 131,921. Near its chief town, also named Ayacucho, the battle was fought which finally secured the independence of Spanish South America. After the battle of Junin (Aug. 6, 1824),[219] the Spanish viceroy, Gen. La Serna, attempted by manoeuvring to cut off the communications of the insurgent army, under Gen. Sucre. Unsuccessful in this, he at last drew his opponent to the plain of Ayacucho, where the Spaniards took up a defensive position on a height. They numbered 13 battalions of infantry, with artillery and cavalry, in all 9,310 men. On Dec. 8, 1824, the advanced guards of both armies became engaged, and on the following day Sucre advanced with 5,780 men to the attack. The 2d Colombian division, under Gen. Córdova, attacked the Spanish left, and at once threw it into disorder. The Peruvian division on the left, under Gen. Lamar, met with a more obstinate resistance, and could make no progress until the reserve, under Gen. Lara, came up. The enemy's retreat now becoming general, the cavalry was launched in pursuit, dispersing the Spanish horse and completing the defeat of the infantry. The Spaniards lost 6 generals killed and 2,600 killed, wounded, and prisoners, among the latter the viceroy. The South American loss was 1 general and 308 officers and men killed, 520 wounded, among them 6 generals. The next day Gen. Canterac, who now commanded the Spanish army, concluded a capitulation, by which not only he and all his troops surrendered prisoners of war, but also all the Spanish troops in Peru, all military posts, artillery, and magazines, and the whole of Peru, as far as they still held it (Cuzco, Arequipa, Puno, Quillca, &c.), were delivered up to the insurgents. The troops thus delivered up as prisoners of war amounted in all to nearly 12,000. Thus the Spanish dominion was definitively destroyed, and on Aug. 26, 1825, the congress of Chuquisaca proclaimed the independence of the republic of Bolivia.

The name *Ayacuchos* has in Spain been given to Espartero and his military partisans. A portion of the military camarilla grouped around him had served with him in the war against the South American insurrection, where, beside by military comradeship, they were bound together by their common habits of gambling, and mutually pledged themselves to support each other politically when returned to Spain. This pledge they have honestly kept, much to their mutual interests. The nickname of Ayacuchos was conferred on them in order to imply that Espartero and his party had materially contributed to the unfortunate issue of that battle. This, however, is false, though the report has been so assiduously spread that even now it is generally credited in Spain. Espartero not only was not present at the battle of Ayacucho, but he was not even in America when it happened, being on his passage to Spain, whither Viceroy La Serna had sent him with despatches for Ferdinand VII. He had embarked at Quillca, June 5, 1824, in the British brig *Tiber,* arriving in Cadiz Sept. 28, and at Madrid Oct. 12, and again sailed for America from Bordeaux on that very same Dec. 9, 1824, on which the battle of Ayacucho was fought. (See Don José Segundo Flórez, *Espartero,* Madrid, 1844 [-5], 4 vols., and Principe, *Espartero,* Madrid, 1848.)

Written between September 21 and October 23, 1857

First published in *The New American Cyclopaedia,* Vol. II, 1858

Reproduced from *The New American Cyclopaedia*

Karl Marx and Frederick Engels

BLÜCHER[220]

Blücher, Gebhard Leberecht von, prince of Wahlstadt, Prussian field-marshal, born Dec. 16, 1742, at Rostock, in Mecklenburg-Schwerin, died at Krieblowitz, in Silesia, Sept. 12, 1819. He was sent in 1754, while a boy, to the island of Rügen, and there secretly enlisted in a regiment of Swedish hussars as ensign, to serve against Frederick II of Prussia. Made prisoner in the campaign of 1758, he was, after a year's captivity, and after he had obtained his dismissal from the Swedish service, prevailed upon to enter the Prussian army. March 3, 1771, he was appointed senior captain of cavalry. In 1778, Capt. von Jägersfeld, a natural son of the margrave of Schwedt, being appointed in his stead to the vacant post of major, he wrote to Frederick II:

"Sire, Jägersfeld, who possesses no merit but that of being the son of the margrave of Schwedt, has been preferred to me. I beg your majesty to grant my dismissal." [a]

In reply Frederick II ordered him to be shut up in prison, but when, notwithstanding a somewhat protracted confinement, he refused to retract his letter, the king complied with his petition in a note to this effect: "Capt. von Blücher may go to the devil." He now retired to Polish Silesia, married soon after, became a farmer, acquired a small estate in Pomerania, and, after the death of Frederick II, reentered his former regiment as major, on the express condition of his appointment being dated back to 1779. Some months later his wife died. Having participated in the bloodless invasion of Holland,[221] he was appointed lieutenant-

---

[a] Quoted from *Meyer's Conversations-Lexicon,* Bd. 4, 1845, S. 1210.— *Ed.*

colonel, June 3, 1788. Aug. 20, 1790, he became colonel and commander of the 1st battalion of the regiment of hussars he had entered in 1760.

In 1794 he distinguished himself during the campaign in the Palatinate against republican France as a leader of the light cavalry. Being promoted, May 28, 1794, after the victorious affair of Kirrweiler, to the rank of major-general, the actions of Luxemburg, Kaiserslautern, Morschheim, Weidenthal, Edesheim, Edenkoben, secured him a rising reputation. While incessantly alarming the French by bold *coups de main* and successful enterprises, he never neglected keeping the head-quarters supplied with the best information as to the hostile movements. His diary, written during this campaign, and published in 1796, by Count Goltz, his adjutant, is considered, despite its illiterate style, as a classical work on vanguard service.[a] After the peace of Basel[222] he married again. Frederick William III, on his accession to the throne, appointed him lieutenant-general, in which quality he occupied, and administered as governor, Erfurt, Mühlhausen, and Münster. In 1805 a small corps was collected under him at Bayreuth to watch the immediate consequences for Prussia of the battle of Austerlitz,[223] viz., the occupation of the principality of Anspach by Bernadotte's corps.

In 1806 he led the Prussian vanguard at the battle of Auerstädt.[224] His charge was, however, broken by the terrible fire of Davout's artillery, and his proposal to renew it with fresh forces and the whole of the cavalry, was rejected by the king of Prussia. After the double defeat at Auerstädt and Jena, he retired down the Elbe, while Napoleon drove the main body of the Prussian army in one wild chase from Jena to Stettin. On his retrograde movement, Blücher took up the remnants of different corps, which swelled his army to about 25,000 men. His retreat to Lübeck, before the united forces of Soult, Bernadotte, and Murat, forms one of the few honorable episodes in that epoch of German degradation. Since Lübeck was a neutral territory, his making the streets of that open town the theatre of a desperate fight, which exposed it to a 3 days' sack on the part of the French soldiery, afforded the subject of passionate censure; but under existing circumstances the important thing was to give the German people one example, at least, of stanch resistance. Thrown out of Lübeck, he had to capitulate in the plain of Ratekau, Nov. 7, 1806, on the express condition that the cause of his surrender should be stated

---

[a] G. L. Blücher, *Kampagne-Journal der Jahre 1793 und 1794.—Ed.*

in writing to be "want of ammunition and provisions." [a] Liberated on his word of honor, he repaired to Hamburg, there, in company with his sons, to kill time by card-playing, smoking, and drinking. Being exchanged for Gen. Victor, he was appointed governor-general of Pomerania; but one of the secret articles of the alliance concluded, Feb. 24, 1812, by Prussia with Napoleon, stipulated for Blücher's discharge from service, like that of Scharnhorst, and other distinguished Prussian patriots. To soothe this official disgrace, the king secretly bestowed upon him the handsome estate of Kunzendorf, in Silesia.

During the years that marked the period of transition between the peace of Tilsit and the German war of independence, Scharnhorst and Gneisenau, the chiefs of the Tugendbund,[225] desiring to extemporize a popular hero, chose Blücher. In propagating his fame among the masses, they succeeded so well, that when Frederick William III called the Prussians to arms by the proclamation of March 17, 1813, they were strong enough to impose him upon the king as the general-in-chief of the Prussian army. In the well-contested, but for the allies unfortunate, battles of Lützen and Bautzen,[226] he acted under the command of Wittgenstein. During the retreat of the allied armies from Bautzen to Schweidnitz, he lay in ambush at Haynau, from which he fell,[b] with his cavalry, on the French advanced guard under Maison, who, in this affair, lost 1,500 men and 11 guns. Through this surprise Blücher raised the spirit of the Prussian army, and made Napoleon very cautious in pursuit.

Blücher's command of an independent army dates from the expiration of the truce of Trachenberg, Aug. 10, 1813.[227] The allied sovereigns had then divided their forces into 3 armies: the army of the north under Bernadotte, stationed along the lower Elbe; the grand army advancing through Bohemia, and the Silesian army, with Blücher as its commander-in-chief, supported by Gneisenau as the chief of his staff, and Müffling as his quartermaster-general. These 2 men, attached to him in the same quality until the peace of 1815, supplied all his strategetical plans. Blücher himself, as Müffling says,

"understood nothing of the strategetical conduct of a war; so little indeed, that when a plan was laid before him for approval, even relating to some unimportant operation, he could not form any clear idea of it, or judge whether it was good or bad." [c]

---

[a] *Meyer's Conversations-Lexicon*, Bd. 4, 1845, S. 1211.— *Ed.*

[b] On May 26, 1813.— *Ed.*

[c] Müffling, *Passages from My Life; together with Memoirs of the Campaign of 1813 and 1814*, p. 225 (the word "strategetical" at the beginning of the quotation, added

Like many of Napoleon's marshals, he was unable to read the maps. The Silesian army was composed of 3 *corps d'armée:* 40,000 Russians, under Count Langeron; 16,000 men under Baron von Sacken; and a Prussian corps of 40,000 men under Gen. York. Blücher's position was extremely difficult at the head of this heterogeneous army. Langeron, who had already held independent commands, and demurred to serving under a foreign general, was, moreover, aware that Blücher had received secret orders to limit himself to the defensive, but was altogether ignorant that the latter, in an interview, on Aug. 11, with Barclay de Tolly, at Reichenbach, had extorted the permission to act according to circumstances. Hence Langeron thought himself justified in disobeying orders, whenever the general-in-chief seemed to him to swerve from the preconcerted plan, and in this mutinous conduct he was strongly supported by Gen. York.

The danger arising from this state of things became more and more threatening, when the battle on the Katzbach secured Blücher that hold on his army which guided it to the gates of Paris. Marshal Macdonald, charged by Napoleon to drive the Silesian army back into the interior of Silesia, began the battle by attacking, Aug. 26, Blücher's outposts, stationed from Prausnitz to Kraitsch, where the Neisse flows into the Katzbach. The so-called battle on the Katzbach consisted, in fact, of 4 different actions, the first of which, the dislodging by a bayonet attack from a plateau behind a ridge on the right bank of the Neisse of about 8 French battalions, which constituted hardly one-tenth of the hostile force, led to results quite out of proportion to its original importance, in consequence of the fugitives from the plateau not being collected at Niedercrayn, and left behind the Katzbach at Kraitsch, in which case their flight would have had no influence whatever on the rest of the French army; in consequence of different defeats inflicted at nightfall upon the enemy by Sacken's and Langeron's corps stationed on the left bank of the Neisse; in consequence of Marshal Macdonald, who commanded in person on the left bank, and had defended himself weakly till 7 o'clock in the evening against Langeron's attack, marching his troops at once after sunset to Goldberg, in such a state of exhaustion that they could no longer fight, and must fall into the enemy's hand; and, lastly, in consequence of the state of the season, violent rains swelling the otherwise insignificant streams the fugitive French had to

_____

by Engels in his letter to Marx of September 22, was preserved in the final version of the article).— *Ed.*

traverse—the Neisse, the Katzbach, the Deichsel, and the Bober—
to rapid torrents, and making the roads almost impracticable.
Thus it occurred, that with the aid of the country militia in the
mountains on the left flank of the Silesian army, the battle on the
Katzbach, insignificant in itself, resulted in the capture of 18,000
to 20,000 prisoners, above 200 pieces of artillery, and more than
300 ammunition, hospital, and baggage wagons, with baggage, &c.

After the battle Blücher did every thing to instigate his forces to
exert their utmost strength in the pursuit of the enemy, justly
representing to them that "with some bodily exertion they might
spare a new battle."[a] Sept. 3, he crossed the Neisse, with his army,
and on the 4th proceeded by Bischofswerda to concentrate at
Bautzen. By this move he saved the grand army, which, routed at
Dresden, Aug. 27, and forced to retreat behind the Erzgebirge,
was now disengaged,[228] Napoleon being compelled to advance with
reenforcements toward Bautzen, there to take up the army
defeated on the Katzbach, and to offer battle to the Silesian army.
During his stay in the S. E. corner of Saxony, on the right bank
of the Elbe, Blücher, by a series of retreats and advances, always
shunned battle when offered by Napoleon, but always engaged
when encountering single detachments of the French army. Sept.
22, 23, and 24, he executed a flank march on the right of the
enemy, advancing by forced marches to the lower Elbe, in the
vicinity of the army of the north. Oct. 2, he bridged the Elbe at
Elster with pontoons, and on the morning of the 3d his army
defiled. This movement, not only bold, but even hazardous,
inasmuch as he completely abandoned his lines of communication,
was necessitated by supreme political reasons, and led finally to
the battle of Leipsic,[229] which, but for Blücher, the slow and
overcautious grand army would never have risked.

The army of the north, of which Bernadotte was the commander-in-chief, was about 90,000 strong, and it was, consequently, of
the utmost importance that it should advance on Saxony. By
means of the close connection which he maintained with Bülow
and Wintzingerode, the commanders of the Prussian and Russian
corps forming part of the army of the north, Blücher obtained the
most convincing proofs of Bernadotte's coquetry with the French,
and of the impossibility of inciting him to any activity, so long as
he remained alone on a separate theatre of war. Bülow and
Wintzingerode declared themselves ready to act in spite of
Bernadotte, but to do so they wanted the support of 100,000 men.

----

[a] op. cit., p. 327.—Ed.

Hence Blücher's resolution to venture upon his flank march, in which he persisted despite the orders he had received from the sovereigns to draw near to them on the left, toward Bohemia. He was not to be diverted from his purpose through the obstacles which Bernadotte systematically threw in his way, even after the crossing of the Elbe by the Silesian army. Before leaving Bautzen, he had despatched a confidential officer to Bernadotte, to inform him that, since the army of the north was too weak to operate alone on the left bank of the Elbe, he would come with the Silesian army, and cross at Elster on Oct. 3; he therefore invited him to cross the Elbe at the same time, and to advance with him toward Leipsic. Bernadotte not heeding this message, and the enemy occupying Wartenburg opposite Elster, Blücher first dislodged the latter, and then, to protect himself in case Napoleon should fall upon him with his whole strength, began establishing an intrenched encampment from Wartenburg to Bleddin. Thence he pushed forward toward the Mulde.

Oct. 7, in an interview with Bernadotte, it was arranged that both armies should march upon Leipsic. On the 9th, while the Silesian army was preparing for this march, Bernadotte, on the news of Napoleon's advance on the road from Meissen, insisted upon retreating behind the Elbe, and only consented to remain on its left bank on condition that Blücher would resolve to cross the Saale in concert with him, in order to take up a position behind that river. Although by this movement the Silesian army lost anew its line of communication, Blücher consented, since otherwise the army of the north would have been effectually lost for the allies. Oct. 10, the whole Silesian army stood united with the army of the north on the left bank of the Mulde, the bridges over which were destroyed. Bernadotte now declared a retreat upon Bernburg to have become necessary, and Blücher, with the single view of preventing him from crossing [to] the right bank of the Elbe, yielded again on the condition that Bernadotte should cross the Saale at Wettin and take up a position there. Oct. 11, when his columns were just crossing the high road from Magdeburg to Halle, Blücher being informed that, in spite of his positive promise, Bernadotte had constructed no bridge at Wettin, resolved upon following that high road in forced marches.

Napoleon, seeing that the northern and Silesian armies avoided accepting battle, which he had offered them by concentrating at Duben, and knowing that they could not avoid it without retreating across the Elbe; being at the same time aware that he had but 4 days left before he must meet the grand army, and thus be placed between two fires, undertook a march on the right bank of the Elbe toward Wittenberg, in order by this simulated movement to draw the northern and Silesian armies across the Elbe, and then strike a rapid blow on the grand army. Bernadotte, indeed, anxious for his lines of communication with Sweden, gave his army orders to cross without delay to the right bank of the Elbe, by a bridge constructed at Aken, while, on the same day, Oct. 13, he informed Blücher that the emperor Alexander had, for certain important reasons, put him (Blücher) under his orders. He consequently requested him to follow his movements on the right bank of the Elbe with the Silesian army, with the least possible delay. Had Blücher shown less resolution on this occasion and followed the army of the north, the campaign would have been lost, since the Silesian and northern armies, amounting together to about 200,000 men, would not have been present at the battle of Leipsic. He wrote in reply to Bernadotte, that, according to all his information, Napoleon had no intention whatever of removing the theatre of war to the right bank of the Elbe, but only intended to lead them astray. At the same time he conjured Bernadotte to give up his intended movement across the Elbe. Having, meanwhile, again and again solicited the grand army to push forward upon Leipsic, and offered to meet them there, he received at last, Oct. 15, the long-expected invitation. He immediately advanced toward Leipsic, while Bernadotte retreated toward Petersberg. On his march from Halle to Leipsic on Oct. 16, he routed at Möckern the 6th corps of the French army under Marmont, in a hotly contested battle, in which he captured 54 pieces of artillery. Without delay he sent accounts of the issue of this battle to Bernadotte, who was not present on the 1st day of the battle of Leipsic. On its 2d day, Oct. 17, Blücher dislodged the enemy from the right bank of the Parthe, with the exception of some houses and intrenchments near the Halle gate. On the 18th, at daybreak, he had a conference at Breitenfeld with Bernadotte, who declared he could not attack on the left bank of the Parthe unless Blücher gave him for that day 30,000 men of the Silesian army. Keeping the interest of the whole exclusively in view, Blücher consented without hesitation, but on the condition of remaining himself with these 30,000 men, and thus securing their vigorous cooperation in the attack.

After the final victory of Oct. 19, and during the whole of Napoleon's retreat from Leipsic to the Rhine, Blücher alone gave him an earnest pursuit. While, on Oct. 19, the generals in command met the sovereigns in the market-place of Leipsic, and precious time was spent in mutual compliments, his Silesian army was already marching in pursuit of the enemy to Lützen. On his march from Lützen to Weissenfels, Prince William of Prussia overtook him, to deliver to him the commission of a Prussian field-marshal. The allied sovereigns had allowed Napoleon to gain a start which could never be recovered, but from Eisenach onward, Blücher found himself every afternoon in the room which Napoleon had left in the morning. When about to march upon Cologne, there to cross the Rhine, he was recalled and ordered to blockade Mentz on its left bank; his rapid pursuit as far as the Rhine having broken up the confederation of the Rhine,[230] and disengaged its troops from the French divisions in which they were still enrolled. While the head-quarters of the Silesian army was established at Höchst, the grand army marched up the upper Rhine. Thus ended the campaign of 1813, whose success was entirely due to Blücher's bold enterprise and iron energy.

The allies were divided as to the plan of operations now to be followed; the one party proposing to stay on the Rhine, and there to take up a defensive position; the other to cross the Rhine and march upon Paris. After much wavering on the part of the sovereigns, Blücher and his friends prevailed, and the resolution was adopted to advance upon Paris in a concentric movement, the grand army being to start from Switzerland, Bülow from Holland, and Blücher, with the Silesian army, from the middle Rhine. For the new campaign, 3 additional corps were made over to Blücher, viz., Kleist's, the elector of Hesse's, and the duke of Saxe-Coburg's. Leaving part of Langeron's corps to invest Mentz, and the new reenforcements to follow as a second division, Blücher crossed the Rhine Jan. 1, 1814, on 3 points, at Mannheim, Caub and Coblentz, drove Marmont beyond the Vosges and the Saar, in the valley of the Moselle, posted York's corps between the fortresses of the Moselle, and with a force of 28,000 men, consisting of Sacken's corps and a division of Langeron's corps, proceeded by Vaucouleurs and Joinville to Brienne, in order to effect his junction with the grand army by his left. At Brienne, Jan. 29, he was attacked by Napoleon, whose forces mustered about 40,000, while York's corps was still detached from the Silesian army, and the grand army, 110,000 strong, had only reached Chaumont. Blücher had consequently to face the greatly superior forces of Napoleon, but the latter neither attacked him with his usual vigor, nor hindered his retreat to Trannes, save by some cavalry skirmishes. Having taken possession of Brienne, placed part of his troops in its vicinity, and occupied Dienville, La Rothière, and Chammenil, with 3 different corps, Napoleon would, on Jan. 30, have been able to fall upon Blücher with superior numbers, as the latter was still awaiting his reenforcements. Napoleon, however, kept up a passive attitude, while the grand army was concentrating by Bar-sur-Aube, and detachments of it were strengthening Blücher's left flank. The emperor's inactivity is explained by the hopes from the negotiations of the peace congress of Châtillon, which he had contrived to start, and through the means of which he expected to gain time.[231] In fact, after the junction of the Silesian army with the grand army had been effected, the diplomatic party insisted that during the deliberations of the peace congress the war should be carried on as a feint only. Prince Schwarzenberg sent an officer to Blücher to procure his acquiescence, but Blücher dismissed him with this answer:

"We must go to Paris. Napoleon has paid his visits to all the capitals of Europe; should we be less polite? In short, he must descend from the throne [...] and [...] until he is hurled from it we shall have no rest."[a]

He urged the great advantages of the allies attacking Napoleon near Brienne, before he could bring up the remainder of his troops, and offered himself to make the attack, if he were only strengthened in York's absence. The consideration that the army could not subsist in the barren valley of the Aube, and must retreat if it did not attack, caused his advice to prevail. The battle was decided upon, but Prince Schwarzenberg, instead of bearing upon the enemy with the united force at hand, only lent Blücher the corps of the crown prince of Württemberg (40,000 men), that of Gyulay (12,000), and that of Wrede (12,000). Napoleon, on his part, neither knew nor suspected any thing of the arrival of the grand army. When about 1 o'clock, Feb. 1, it was announced to him that Blücher was advancing, he would not believe it. Having made sure of the fact, he mounted his horse with the idea of avoiding the battle, and gave Berthier orders to this effect. When, however, between old Brienne and Rothière, he reached the young guard,[232] who had got under arms on hearing the approaching cannonade, he was received with such enthusiasm that he thought fit to improve the opportunity, and exclaimed, "L'artillerie en avant!"[b] Thus, about 4 o'clock, the affair of La Rothière commenced in earnest. At the first reverse, however, Napoleon no longer took any personal part in the battle. His

---

[a] Müffling, op. cit., p. 419.— Ed.
[b] op. cit., p. 423.— Ed.

infantry having thrown itself into the village of La Rothière, the combat was long and obstinate, and Blücher was even obliged to bring up his reserve. The French were not dislodged from the village till 11 o'clock at night, when Napoleon ordered the retreat of his army, which had lost 4,000 or 5,000 men in killed and wounded, 2,500 prisoners, and 53 cannon. If the allies, who were then only 6 days' march from Paris, had vigorously pushed on, Napoleon must have succumbed before their immensely superior numbers; but the sovereigns, still apprehensive of cutting Napoleon off from making his peace at the congress of Châtillon, allowed Prince Schwarzenberg, the commander-in-chief of the grand army, to seize upon every pretext for shunning a decisive action.

While Napoleon ordered Marmont to return on the right bank of the Aube toward Ramerupt, and himself retired by a flank march upon Troyes, the allied army split into 2 armies, the grand army advancing slowly upon Troyes, and the Silesian army marching to the Marne, where Blücher knew he would find York, beside part of Langeron's and Kleist's corps, so that his aggregate forces would be swelled to about 50,000 men. The plan was for him to pursue Marshal Macdonald, who had meanwhile appeared on the lower Marne, to Paris, while Schwarzenberg was to keep in check the French main army on the Seine. Napoleon, however, seeing that the allies did not know how to use their victory, and sure of returning to the Seine before the grand army could have advanced far in the direction of Paris, resolved to fall upon the weaker Silesian army. Consequently, he left 20,000 men under Victor and Oudinot in face of the 100,000 men of the grand army, advanced with 40,000 men, the corps of Mortier and Ney, in the direction of the Marne, took up Marmont's corps at Nogent, and on Feb. 9 arrived with these united forces at Sézanne. Meanwhile Blücher had proceeded by St. Ouen and Sommepuis on the little road leading to Paris, and established, Feb. 9, his head-quarters at the little town of Vertus. The disposition of his forces was this: about 10,000 men at his head-quarters; 18,000, under York, posted between Dormans and Château Thierry, in pursuit of Macdonald, who was already on the great post road leading to Paris from Epernay; 30,000 under Sacken, between Montmirail and La Ferté-Sous-Jouarre, destined to prevent the intended junction of Sébastiani's cavalry with Macdonald, and to cut off the passage of the latter at La Ferté-Sous-Jouarre; the Russian general, Olsuvieff, cantoned with 5,000 men at Champaubert. This faulty distribution, by which the Silesian army was drawn up in a very extended position, *en échélon*, resulted from the contradictory motives which actuated Blücher. On the one hand, he desired to cut off Macdonald, and prevent his junction with Sébastiani's cavalry; on the other hand, to take up the corps of Kleist and Kapzewitch, who were advancing from Châlons, and expected to unite with him on the 9th and 10th. The one motive kept him back, the other pushed him on.

Feb. 9, Napoleon fell upon Olsuvieff, at Champaubert, and routed him. Blücher, with Kleist and Kapzewitch, who had meanwhile arrived, but without the greater part of their cavalry, advanced against Marmont, despatched by Napoleon, and followed him in his retreat upon La Fère Champenoise, but on the news of Olsuvieff's discomfiture, returned in the same night, with his 2 corps, to Bergères, there to cover the road to Châlons. After a successful combat on the 10th, Sacken had driven Macdonald across the Marne at Trilport, but hearing on the night of the same day of Napoleon's march to Champaubert, hastened back on the 11th toward Montmirail. Before reaching it he was, at Vieux Maisons, obliged to form against the emperor, coming from Montmirail to meet him. Beaten with great loss before York could unite with him, the two generals effected their junction at Viffort, and retreated, Feb. 12, to Château Thierry, where York had to stand a very damaging rear-guard engagement, and withdrew thence to Oulchy-la-Ville. Having ordered Mortier to pursue York and Sacken on the road of Fismes, Napoleon remained on the 13th at Château Thierry. Uncertain as to the whereabout of York and Sacken and the success of their engagements, Blücher had, from Bergères, during the 11th and 12th, quietly watched Marmont posted opposite him at Etoges. When informed, on the 13th, of the defeat of his generals, and supposing Napoleon to have moved off in search of the grand army, he gave way to the temptation of striking a parting blow upon Marmont, whom he considered Napoleon's rear-guard. Advancing on Champaubert, he pushed Marmont to Montmirail, where the latter was joined on the 14th by Napoleon, who now turned against Blücher, met him at noon at Veauchamps, 20,000 strong, but almost without cavalry, attacked him, turned his columns with cavalry, and threw him back with great loss on Champaubert. During its retreat from the latter place, the Silesian army might have reached Etoges before it grew dark, without any considerable loss, if Blücher had not taken pleasure in the deliberate slowness of the retrograde movement. Thus he was attacked during the whole of his march, and one detachment of his forces, the division of Prince Augustus of

Preussen, was again beset from the side streets of Etoges, on its passage through that town. About midnight Blücher reached his camp at Bergères, broke up, after some hours' rest, for Châlons, arrived there about noon, Feb. 15, and was joined by York's and Sacken's forces on the 16th and 17th. The different affairs at Champaubert, Montmirail, Château Thierry, Veauchamps, and Etoges, had cost him 15,000 men and 27 guns; Gneisenau and Müffling being alone responsible for the strategetical faults which led to these disasters.

Leaving Marmont and Mortier to front Blücher, Napoleon, with Ney, returned in forced marches to the Seine, where Schwarzenberg had driven back Victor and Oudinot, who had retreated across the Yères, and there taken up 12,000 men under Macdonald, and some reenforcements from Spain. On the 16th they were surprised by the sudden arrival of Napoleon, followed on the 17th by his troops. After his junction with the marshals he hastened against Schwarzenberg, whom he found posted in an extended triangle, having for its summits Nogent, Montereau, and Sens. The generals under his command, Wittgenstein, Wrede, and the crown prince of Württemberg, being successively attacked and routed by Napoleon, Prince Schwarzenberg took to his heels, retreated toward Troyes, and sent word to Blücher to join him, so that they might in concert give battle on the Seine. Blücher, meanwhile, strengthened by new reenforcements, immediately followed this call, and entered Méry Feb. 21, and waited there the whole of the 22d for the dispositions of the promised battle. He learned in the evening that an application for a truce had been made to Napoleon, through Prince Liechtenstein, who had met with a flat refusal. Instantly despatching a confidential officer to Troyes, he conjured Prince Schwarzenberg to give battle, and even offered to give it alone, if the grand army would only form a reserve; but Schwarzenberg, still more frightened by the news that Augereau had driven Gen. Bubna back into Switzerland, had already ordered the retreat upon Langres. Blücher understood at once that a retreat upon Langres would lead to a retreat beyond the Rhine; and, in order to draw Napoleon off from the pursuit of the dispirited grand army, resolved upon again marching straight in the direction of Paris, toward the Marne, where he could now expect to assemble an army of 100,000 men, Wintzingerode having arrived with about 25,000 men in the vicinity of Rheims, Bülow at Laon with 16,000 men, the remainder of Kleist's corps being expected from Erfurt, and the rest of Langeron's corps, under St. Priest, from Mentz.

It was this second separation on the part of Blücher from the grand army, that turned the scale against Napoleon. If the latter had followed the retreating grand army instead of the advancing Silesian one, the campaign would have been lost for the allies. The passage of the Aube before Napoleon had followed him, the only difficult point in Blücher's advance, he effected by constructing a pontoon bridge at Anglure on Feb. 24. Napoleon, commanding Oudinot and Macdonald, with about 25,000 men, to follow the grand army, left Herbisse on the 26th, together with Ney and Victor, in pursuit of the Silesian army. On the advice sent by Blücher, that the grand army had now but the 2 marshals before it, Schwarzenberg stopped his retreat, took heart, turned round upon Oudinot and Macdonald, and beat them on the 27th and 28th. It was Blücher's intention to concentrate his army at some point as near as possible to Paris. Marmont, with his troops, was still posted at Sézanne, while Mortier was at Château Thierry. On Blücher's advance, Marmont retreated, united on the 26th with Mortier at La Ferté-Sous-Jouarre, thence to retire with the latter upon Meaux. Blücher's attempt, during 2 days, to cross the Ourcq, and, with a strongly advanced front, to force the 2 marshals to battle, having failed, he was now obliged to march on the right bank of the Ourcq. He reached Oulchy-le-Château March 2, learned in the morning of the 3d [about] the capitulation of Soissons, which had been effected by Bülow and Wintzingerode, and, in the course of the same day, crossed the Aisne, and concentrated his whole army at Soissons. Napoleon, who had crossed the Marne at La Ferté-Sous-Jouarre, 2 forced marches behind Blücher, advanced in the direction of Château Thierry and Fismes, and, having passed the Vesle, crossed the Aisne at Berry-au-Bac, March 6, after the recapture of Rheims by a detachment of his army. Blücher originally intended to offer battle behind the Aisne, on Napoleon's passage of that river, and had drawn up his troops for that purpose. When he became aware that Napoleon took the direction of Fismes and Berry-au-Bac, in order to pass the Silesian army by the left, he decided upon attacking him from Craonne on the flank, in an oblique position, immediately after his debouching from Berry-au-Bac, so that Napoleon would have been forced to give battle with a defile in his rear. Having already posted his forces, with the right wing on the Aisne, with the left on the Lette, half way from Soissons to Craonne, he resigned this excellent plan on making sure that Napoleon had, on the 6th, been allowed by Wintzingerode to pass Berry-au-Bac unmolested, and had even pushed a detachment on the road to Laon. He now thought it necessary to accept no decisive battle except at Laon.

To delay Napoleon, who, by Corbeny, on the causeway from Rheims, could reach Laon as soon as the Silesian army from Craonne, Blücher posted the corps of Woronzoff between the Aisne and the Lette, on the strong plateau of Craonne, while he despatched 10,000 horse under Wintzingerode, to push on by Fetieux toward Corbeny, with the order to fall upon the right flank and rear of Napoleon, as soon as the latter should be engaged in attacking Woronzoff. Wintzingerode failing to execute the manoeuvre intrusted to him, Napoleon drove Woronzoff from the plateau on the 7th, but himself lost 8,000 men, while Woronzoff escaped with the loss of 4,700, and proved able to effect his retreat in good order. On the 8th, Blücher had concentrated his troops at Laon, where the battle must decide the fate of both armies. Apart from his numerical superiority, the vast plain before Laon was peculiarly adapted for deploying the 20,000 horse of the Silesian army, while Laon itself, situated on the plateau of a detached hill, which has on every side a fall of 12, 16, 20 to 30 degrees, and at the foot of which lie 4 villages, offered great advantages for the defence as well as the attack. On that day, the left French wing, led by Napoleon himself, was repulsed, while the right wing, under Marmont, surprised in its bivouacs at nightfall, was so completely worsted, that the marshal could not bring his troops to a halt before reaching Fismes. Napoleon, completely isolated with his wing, numbering 35,000 men only, and cooped up in a bad position, must have yielded before far superior numbers flushed with victory. Yet on the following morning, a fever attack and an inflammation of the eyes disabled Blücher, while Napoleon yet remained in a provocatory attitude, in the same position, which so far intimidated the men who now directed the operations, that they not only stopped the advance of their own troops which had already begun, but allowed Napoleon to quietly retire at nightfall to Soissons.

Still the battle of Laon had broken his forces, physically and morally. He tried in vain by the sudden capture, on March 13, of Rheims, which had fallen into the hands of St. Priest, to restore himself. So fully was his situation now understood, that when he advanced, on the 17th and 18th, on Arcis-sur-Aube, against the grand army, Schwarzenberg himself, although but 80,000 strong against the 25,000 under Napoleon, dared to stand and accept a battle, which lasted through the 20th and 21st. When Napoleon broke it off, the grand army followed him up to Vitry, and united in his rear with the Silesian army. In his despair, Napoleon took a last refuge in a retreat upon St. Dizier, pretending thus to endanger, with his handful of men, the enormous army of the allies, by cutting off its main line of communication and retreat between Langres and Chaumont; a movement replied to on the part of the allies by their onward march to Paris. On March 30 took place the battle before Paris, in which the Silesian army stormed Montmartre. Though Blücher had not recovered since the battle of Laon, he still appeared at the battle for a short time, on horseback, with a shade over his eyes, but, after the capitulation of Paris, laid down his command, the pretext being his sickness, and the real cause the clashing of his open-mouthed hatred against the French with the diplomatic attitude which the allied sovereigns thought fit to exhibit. Thus he entered Paris, March 31, in the capacity of a private individual. During the whole campaign of 1814, he alone among the allied army represented the principle of the offensive. By the battle of La Rothière he baffled the Châtillon pacificators; by his resolution at Méry he saved the allies from a ruinous retreat; and by the battle of Laon he decided the first capitulation of Paris.

After the first peace of Paris[233] he accompanied the emperor Alexander and King Frederic William of Prussia on their visit to England, where he was fêted as the hero of the day. All the military orders of Europe were showered upon him: the king of Prussia created for him the order of the iron cross; the prince regent of England[a] gave him his portrait, and the university of Oxford the academical degree of LL. D.[b]

In 1815 he again decided the final campaign against Napoleon. After the disastrous battle of Ligny, June 16, though now 73 years of age, he prevailed upon his routed army to form anew and march on the heels of their victor, so as to be able to appear in the evening of June 18 on the battle field of Waterloo,[234] an exploit unprecedented in the history of war. His pursuit, after the battle of Waterloo, of the French fugitives, from Waterloo to Paris, possesses one parallel only, in Napoleon's equally remarkable pursuit of the Prussians from Jena to Stettin. He now entered Paris at the head of his army, and even had Müffling, his quartermaster-general, installed as the military governor-general of Paris. He insisted upon Napoleon's being shot, the bridge of Jena blown up, and the restitution to their original owners of the treasures plundered by the French in the different capitals of

---

[a] George.— *Ed.*
[b] Legum Doctor (Doctor of Laws).— *Ed.*

Europe. His first wish was baffled by Wellington, and the second by the allied sovereigns, while the last was realized. He remained at Paris 3 months, very frequently attending the gambling tables for *rouge-et-noir*.[a] On the anniversary of the battle on the Katzbach, he paid a visit to Rostock, his native place, where the inhabitants united to raise a public monument in his honor. On the occurrence of his death the whole Prussian army went into mourning for 8 days.

Le vieux diable,[b] as he was nicknamed by Napoleon, "Marshal Forwards," as he was styled by the Russians of the Silesian army, was essentially a general of cavalry. In this speciality he excelled, because it required tactical acquirements only, but no strategetical knowledge. Participating to the highest degree in the popular hatred against Napoleon and the French, he was popular with the multitude for his plebeian passions, his gross common sense, the vulgarity of his manners, and the coarseness of his speech, to which, however, he knew, on fit occasions, how to impart a touch of fiery eloquence. He was the model of a soldier. Setting an example as the bravest in battle and the most indefatigable in exertion; exercising a fascinating influence on the common soldier; joining to his rash bravery a sagacious appreciation of the ground, a quick resolution in difficult situations, stubbornness in defence equal to his energy in the attack, with sufficient intelligence to find for himself the right course in simpler combinations, and to rely upon Gneisenau in those which were more intricate, he was the true general for the military operations of 1813-'15, which bore the character half of regular and half of insurrectionary warfare.

Written between September 17 and October 30, 1857

First published in *The New American Cyclopaedia*, Vol. III, 1858

Reproduced from *The New American Cyclopaedia*

---

[a] Red and black.— *Ed.*
[b] The old devil.— *Ed.*

Frederick Engels

ARTILLERY[235]

The invention of gunpowder, and its application to throwing heavy bodies in a given direction, are now pretty generally conceded to have been of eastern origin. In China and India, saltpetre is the spontaneous excrescence of the soil, and, very naturally, the natives soon became acquainted with its properties. Fireworks made of mixtures of this salt with other combustible bodies were manufactured at a very early period in China, and used for purposes of war as well as for public festivities. We have no information at what time the peculiar composition of saltpetre, sulphur, and charcoal became known, the explosive quality of which has given it such an immense importance. According to some Chinese chronicles, mentioned by M. Paravey in a report made to the French academy in 1850,[a] guns were known as early as 618 B.C.; in other ancient Chinese writings, fire-balls projected from bamboo tubes, and a sort of exploding shell, are described. At all events, the use of gunpowder and cannon for warlike purposes does not appear to have been properly developed in the earlier periods of Chinese history, as the first authenticated instance of their extensive application is of a date as late as 1232 of our era, when the Chinese, besieged by the Mongols in Kaï-fong-fu, defended themselves with cannon throwing stone balls, and used explosive shells, petards, and other fireworks based upon gunpowder.

The Hindoos appear to have had some sort of warlike fireworks as early as the time of Alexander the Great, according to the

---

[a] This presumably refers to Ch. H. de Paravey's book *Mémoire sur la découverte très-ancienne en Asie et dans l'Indo-Perse de la poudre à canon et des armes à feu.—Ed.*

evidence of the Greek writers Aelian, Ctesias, Philostratus, and Themistius. This, however, certainly was not gunpowder, though saltpetre may have largely entered into its composition. In the Hindoo laws some sort of fire-arms appears to be alluded to; gunpowder is certainly mentioned in them, and, according to Prof. H. H. Wilson, its composition is described in old Hindoo medical works. The first mention of cannon, however, coincides pretty nearly with the oldest ascertained positive date of its occurrence in China. Chased's poems, about 1200, speak of fire-engines throwing balls, the whistling of which was heard at the distance of 10 coss (1,500 yards). About 1258 we read of fireworks on carriages belonging to the king of Delhi. A hundred years later the use of artillery was general in India; and when the Portuguese arrived there, in 1498, they found the Indians as far advanced in the use of fire-arms as they themselves were.

From the Chinese and Hindoos the Arabs received saltpetre and fireworks. Two of the Arabic names for saltpetre signify *China salt,* and *China snow.* Chinese red and white fire is mentioned by their ancient authors. Incendiary fireworks are also of a date almost contemporaneous with the great Arabic invasion of Asia and Africa.[236] Not to mention the *maujanitz,* a somewhat mythical fire-arm said to have been known and used by Mohammed, it is certain that the Byzantine Greeks received the first knowledge of fireworks (afterward developed in the Greek fire) from their Arab enemies. A writer of the 9th century, Marcus Gracchus, gives a composition of 6 parts of saltpetre, 2 of sulphur, 1 of coal, which comes very near to the correct composition of gunpowder.[a] The latter is stated with sufficient exactness, and first of all European writers, by Roger Bacon, about 1216, in his *Liber de Nullitate Magiae,*[237] but yet for fully a hundred years the western nations remained ignorant of its use. The Arabs, however, appear to have soon improved upon the knowledge they received from the Chinese. According to Conde's history of the Moors in Spain,[b] guns were used, 1118, in the siege of Saragossa, and a culverin of 4 lb. calibre, among other guns, was cast in Spain in 1132.[238] Abd-el-Mumen is reported to have taken Mohadia, near Bona, in Algeria, with fire-arms, in 1156, and the following year Niebla, in Spain, was defended against the Castilians with fire-machines throwing bolts and stones. If the nature of the engines used by the Arabs in the 12th century remains still to be investigated, it is

---

[a] Marcus Graecus, *Liber ignium ad comburendos hostes.*—*Ed.*
[b] J. A. Conde, *Historia de la dominacion de los Arabes en España,* t. I-III.—*Ed.*

quite certain that in 1280 artillery was used against Cordova, and
that by the beginning of the 14th century its knowledge had
passed from the Arabs to the Spaniards. Ferdinand IV took
Gibraltar by cannon in 1308. Baza in 1312 and 1323, Martos in
1326, Alicante in 1331, were attacked with artillery, and carcasses
were thrown by guns in some of these sieges. From the Spaniards
the use of artillery passed to the remaining European nations. The
French, in the siege of Puy Guillaume in 1338, had guns, and in
the same year the German knights in Prussia used them.[239] By
1350, fire-arms were common in all countries of western,
southern, and central Europe. That artillery is of eastern origin, is
also proved by the manufacture of the oldest European ordnance.
The gun was made of bars of wrought iron welded longitudinally
together, and strengthened by heavy iron rings forced over them.
It was composed of several pieces, the movable breech being fixed
to the flight after loading. The oldest Chinese and Indian guns
are made exactly in the same way, and they are as old, or older,
than the oldest European guns. Both European and Asiatic
cannon, about the 14th century, were of very inferior construction, showing artillery to have still been in its infancy. Thus, if it
remains uncertain when the composition of gunpowder and its
application to fire-arms were invented, we can at least fix the
period when it first became an important engine in warfare; the
very clumsiness of the guns of the 14th century, wherever they
occur, proves their novelty as regular war-machines. The European guns of the 14th century were very unwieldy affairs. The
large-calibred ones could only be moved by being taken to pieces,
each piece forming a wagon-load. Even the small-calibred guns
were exceedingly heavy, there being then no proper proportion
established between the weight of the gun and that of the shot,
nor between the shot and the charge. When they were brought
into position, a sort of timber framework or scaffolding was
erected for each gun to be fired from. The town of Ghent had a
gun which, with the framework, measured 50 feet in length.
Gun-carriages were still unknown. The cannons were mostly fired
at very high elevations, like our mortars, and consequently had
very little effect until shells were introduced. The projectiles were
generally round shot of stone, for small calibres sometimes iron
bolts. Yet, with all these drawbacks, cannon was not only used in
sieges and the defence of towns, but in the field also, and on
board ships of war. As early as 1386 the English took 2 French
vessels armed with cannon. If the guns recovered from the *Mary
Rose* (sunk 1545) may serve as a clue, those first ship guns were

simply let into and secured in a log of wood hollowed out for the purpose, so as to be incapable of elevation.

In the course of the 15th century, considerable improvements were made, both in the construction and application of artillery. Cannon began to be cast of iron, copper, or brass. The movable breech was falling into disuse, the whole gun being cast of a piece. The best founderies were in France and Germany. In France, too, the first attempts were made to bring up and place guns under cover during a siege. About 1450 a sort of trench was introduced, and shortly after the first breaching batteries were constructed by the brothers Bureau, with the aid of which the king of France, Charles VII, retook in one year all the places the English had taken from him. The greatest improvements were, however, made by Charles VIII of France. He finally did away with the movable breech, cast his guns of brass and in one piece, introduced trunnions, and gun-carriages on wheels, and had none but iron shot. He also simplified the calibres, and took the lighter regularly into the field. Of these, the double cannon was placed on a 4-wheeled carriage drawn by 35 horses; the remainder had 2-wheeled carriages, the trails dragging on the ground, and were drawn by from 24 down to 2 horses. A body of gunners was attached to each, and the service so organized as to constitute the first distinct corps of field artillery; the lighter calibres were movable enough to shift about with the other troops during action, and even to keep up with the cavalry. It was this new arm which procured to Charles VIII his surprising successes in Italy. The Italian ordnance was still moved by bullocks; the guns were still composed of several pieces, and had to be placed on their frames when the position was reached; they fired stone shot, and were altogether so clumsy that the French fired a gun oftener in an hour than the Italians could do in a day. The battle of Fornovo (1495), gained by the French field artillery,[240] spread terror over Italy, and the new arm was considered irresistible. Machiavelli's *Arte della Guerra* was written expressly, in order to indicate means to counteract its effect by the skilful disposition of the infantry and cavalry. The successors of Charles VIII, Louis XII and Francis I, continued to improve and lighten their field artillery. Francis organized the ordnance as a distinct department, under a grand-master of the ordnance. His field-guns broke the hitherto invincible masses of the Swiss pikemen at Marignano, 1515,[241] by rapidly moving from one flanking position to another, and thus they decided the battle. The Chinese and Arabs knew the use and manufacture of shells, and it is probable that from the latter this knowledge passed to the European nations. Still, the adoption of this projectile, and of the mortar from which it is now fired, did not take place in Europe before the second half of the 15th century, and is commonly ascribed to Pandolfo Malatesta, prince of Rimia. The first shells consisted of 2 hollow metal hemispheres screwed together, the art of casting them hollow was of later invention.

The emperor Charles V was not behind his French rivals in the improvement of field-guns. He introduced limbers, thus turning the two-wheeled gun, when it had to be moved, into a 4-wheeled vehicle capable of going at a faster pace and of surmounting obstacles of ground. Thus his light guns, at the battle of Renty in 1554,[242] could advance at a gallop.

The first theoretical researches, respecting gunnery and the flight of projectiles, also fall in this period. Tartaglia, an Italian, is said to be the discoverer of the fact that the angle of elevation of 45° gives, *in vacuo,* the greatest range. The Spaniards Collado and Ufano also occupied themselves with similar inquiries. Thus the theoretical foundations for scientific gunnery were laid. About the same time Vannocci Biringoccio's inquiries into the art of casting (1540)[a] produced considerable progress in the manufacture of cannon, while the invention of the calibre scale by Hartmann, by which every part of a gun was measured by its proportion to the diameter of bore, gave a certain standard for the construction of ordnance, and paved the way for the introduction of fixed theoretical principles, and of general experimental rules.

One of the first effects of the improved artillery was a total change in the art of fortification. Since the time of the Assyrian and Babylonian monarchies, that art had made but little progress. But now the new fire-arm everywhere made a breach on the masonry walls of the old system, and a new plan had to be invented. The defences had to be constructed so as to expose as little masonry as possible to the direct fire of the besieger, and to admit of a strong artillery being placed on the ramparts. The old masonry wall was replaced by an earthwork rampart, only faced with masonry, and the small flanking town was turned into a large pentagonal bastion. Gradually the whole of the masonry used in fortification was covered against direct fire by outlying earthworks, and by the middle of the 17th century the defence of a fortified place became once more relatively stronger than the attack, until Vauban again gave the ascendant to the latter.

---

[a] V. Biringoccio, *Pirotechnia.—Ed.*

Hitherto the operation of loading had been carried on with loose powder shovelled into the gun. About 1600 the introduction of cartridges, cloth bags containing the prescribed quantity of powder, much abridged the time necessary for loading, and insured greater precision of fire by greater equality of charge. Another important invention was made about the same time, that of grape-shot and case-shot. The construction of field-guns, adapted for throwing hollow shot, also belongs to this period. The numerous sieges occurring during the war of Spain against the Netherlands [243] contributed very much to the improvement of the artillery used in the defence and attack of places, especially as regards the use of mortars and howitzers, of shells, carcasses, and red-hot shot, and the composition of fuzes and other military fireworks. The calibres in use in the beginning of the 17th century were still of all sizes, from the 48-pounder to the smallest falconets bored for balls of $1/2$ lb. weight. In spite of all improvements, field artillery was still so imperfect that all this variety of calibre was required to obtain something like the effect we now realize with a few middle-sized guns between the 6-pounder and the 12-pounder. The light calibres, at that time, had mobility, but no effect; the large calibres had effect, but no mobility; the intermediate ones had neither the one nor the other in a degree sufficient for all purposes. Consequently, all calibres were maintained, and jumbled together in one mass, each battery consisting generally of a regular assortment of cannon. The elevation was given to the piece by a quoin. The carriages were still clumsy, and a separate model was of course required for each calibre, so that it was next to impossible to take spare wheels and carriages into the field. The axletrees were of wood, and of a different size for each calibre. In addition to this, the dimensions of the cannon and carriages were not even the same for one single calibre, there being everywhere a great many pieces of old construction, and many differences of construction, in the several workshops of a country. Cartridges were still confined to guns in fortresses; in the field the cannon was loaded with loose powder, introduced on a shovel, upon which a wad and the shot were rammed down. Loose powder was equally worked down the touchhole, and the whole process was extremely slow. The gunners were not considered regular soldiers, but formed a guild of their own, recruiting themselves by apprentices, and sworn not to divulge the secrets and mysteries of their handicraft. When a war broke out, the belligerents took as many of them into their service as they could get, over and above their peace establishment. Each of these

gunners or bombardiers received the command of a gun, had a
saddle-horse, and apprentice, and as many professional assistants
as he required, beside the requisite number of men for shifting
heavy pieces. Their pay was fourfold that of a soldier. The horses
of the artillery were contracted for when a war broke out; the
contractor also found harness and drivers. In battle the guns were
placed in a row in front of the line, and unlimbered; the horses
were taken out of the shafts. When an advance was ordered, the
limbers were horsed, and the guns limbered up; sometimes the
lighter calibres were moved, for short distances, by men. The
powder and shot were carried in separate carts; the limbers had
not yet any boxes for ammunition. Manoeuvring, loading,
priming, pointing, and firing, were all operations of great
slowness, according to our present notions, and the number of
hits, with such imperfect machinery, and the almost total want of
science in gunnery, must have been small indeed.

The appearance of Gustavus Adolphus in Germany, during the
30 years' war,[244] marks an immense progress in artillery. This
great warrior did away with the extremely small calibres, which he
replaced, first, by his so-called leather guns, light wrought-iron
tubes covered with ropes and leather. These were intended to fire
grape-shot only, which thus was first introduced into field warfare.
Hitherto its use had been confined to the defence of the ditch in
fortresses. Along with grape and case shot, he also introduced
cartridges in his field artillery. The leather guns not proving very
durable, were replaced by light cast-iron 4-pounders, 16 calibres
long, weighing 6 cwt. with the carriage, and drawn by two horses.
Two of these pieces were attached to each regiment of infantry.
Thus the regimental artillery which was preserved in many armies
up to the beginning of this century, arose by superseding the old
small calibred, but comparatively clumsy guns, and was originally
intended for case shot only, though very soon it was also made to
fire round shot. The heavy guns were kept distinct, and formed
into powerful batteries occupying favorable positions on the wings
or in front of the centre of the army. Thus by the separation of
the light from the heavy artillery, and by the formation of
batteries, the tactics of field artillery were founded. It was General
Torstensson, the inspector-general of the Swedish artillery, who
mainly contributed to these results by which field artillery now
first became an independent arm, subject to distinct rules of its
own for its use in battle. Two further important inventions were
made about this time: about 1650, that of the horizontal elevating
screw, as it was used until Gribeauval's times, and about 1697, that

of tubes filled with powder for priming, instead of working powder into the touchhole. Both pointing and loading became much facilitated thereby. Another great improvement was the invention of the prolonge, for manoeuvring at short distances. The number of guns carried into the field during the 17th century, was very large. At Greifenhagen, Gustavus Adolphus had 80 pieces with 20,000 men, and at Frankfort-on-the-Oder, 200 pieces with 18,000 men.[245] Artillery trains of 100 to 200 guns were of very common occurrence during the wars of Louis XIV. At Malplaquet,[246] nearly 300 pieces of cannon were employed on both sides; this was the largest mass of artillery hitherto brought together on a single field of battle. Mortars were very generally taken into the field about this time. The French still maintained their superiority in artillery. They were the first to do away with the old guild system and enrol the gunners as regular soldiers, forming, in 1671, a regiment of artillery, and regulating the various duties and ranks of the officers. Thus this branch of service was recognized as an independent arm, and the education of the officers and men was taken in hand by the state. An artillery school, for at least 50 years the only one in existence, was founded in France in 1690. A hand-book of artilleristic science, very good for the time, was published in 1697 by Saint-Remy.[a] Still the secrecy surrounding the "mystery" of gunnery was so great that many improvements adopted in other countries were as yet unknown in France, and the construction and composition of every European artillery differed widely from any other. Thus the French had not yet adopted the howitzer, which had been invented in Holland and adopted in most armies before 1700. Limber boxes for ammunition, first introduced by Maurice of Nassau, were unknown in France, and indeed but little adopted. The gun, carriage, and limber were too heavy to admit of their being encumbered with the extra weight of ammunition. The very small calibres, up to 3 lbs. inclusive, had indeed been done away with, but the light regimental artillery was unknown in France. The charges used in the artillery of the times hitherto considered were, for guns, generally very heavy; originally equal in weight to the ball. Although the powder was of inferior quality, these charges were still far stronger in effect than those now in use, thus they were one of the chief causes of the tremendous weight of the cannon. To resist such charges the weight of a brass cannon was

---

[a] A reference to *Mémoires d'artillerie,* a collection of works by artillery officers compiled and edited by Saint-Remy.— *Ed.*

often from 250 to 400 times the weight of the shot. Gradually,
however, the necessity of lightening the guns compelled a
reduction of the charge, and about the beginning of the 18th
century, the charge was generally only one-half the weight of the
shot. For mortars and howitzers the charge was regulated by the
distance, and generally very small.

The end of the 17th and beginning of the 18th century was the
period in which the artillery was in most countries finally
incorporated in the army, deprived of its mediaeval character of a
guild, recognized as an arm, and thus enabled to take a more
regular and rapid development. The consequence was an almost
immediate and very marked progress. The irregularity and variety
of calibres and models, the uncertainty of all existing empirical
rules, the total want of well-established principle, now became
evident and unbearable. Accordingly, experiments were
everywhere made on a large scale to ascertain the effects of
calibres, the relations of the calibre to the charge and to the
weight and length of the gun, the distribution of metal in the
cannon, the ranges, the effects of recoil on the carriages, &c.
Between 1730 and 1740, Bélidor directed such experiments at La
Fère in France, Robins in England, and Papacino d'Antoni at
Turin. The result was a great simplification of the calibres, a
better distribution of the metal of the gun, and a very general
reduction of the charges, which were now between $1/3$ and $1/2$ the
weight of the shot. The progress of scientific gunnery went side by
side with these improvements. Galileo had originated the parabolic
theory, Torricelli his pupil, Anderson, Newton, Blondel, Ber-
noulli, Wolff, and Euler, occupied themselves with further
determining the flight of projectiles, the resistance of the air, and
the causes of their deviations. The above-named experimental
artillerists also contributed materially to the advancement of the
mathematical portion of gunnery.

Under Frederick the Great the Prussian field artillery was again
considerably lightened. The short, light, regimental guns, not
more than 14, 16, or 18 calibres long, and weighing from 80 to
150 times the weight of the shot, were found to have a sufficient
range for the battles of those days, decided principally by infantry
fire. Accordingly, the king had all his 12-pounders cast the same
proportional length and weight. The Austrians, in 1753, followed
this example, as well as most other states; but Frederick himself, in
the latter part of his reign, again provided his reserve artillery
with long powerful guns, his experience at Leuthen [247] having
convinced him of their superior effects. Frederick the Great

introduced a new arm by mounting the gunners of some of his batteries, and thus creating horse artillery, destined to give the same support to cavalry as foot-artillery did to infantry. The new arm proved extremely effective, and was very soon adopted by most armies; some, as the Austrians, mounting the gunners in separate wagons as a substitute. The proportion of guns with the armies of the 18th century was still very large. Frederick the Great had, in 1756, with 70,000 men 206 guns, 1762 with 67,000 men 275 guns, 1778 with 180,000 men 811 guns. These guns, with the exception of the regimental ones which followed their battalions, were organized in batteries of various sizes from 6 to 20 guns each. The regimental guns advanced with the infantry, while the batteries were firing from chosen positions, and sometimes advanced to a second position, but here they generally awaited the issue of the battle; they left, as regards mobility, still very much to be desired, and at Kunersdorf,[248] the loss of the battle was due to the impossibility of bringing up the artillery in the decisive moment. The Prussian general, Tempelhof, also introduced field-mortar batteries, the light mortars being carried on the backs of mules; but they were soon again abolished after their uselessness had been proved in the war of 1792 and '93. The scientific branch of artillery was, during this period, cultivated especially in Germany. Struensee and Tempelhof wrote useful works on the subject,[a] but Scharnhorst was the leading artillery-man of his day. His hand-book of artillery is the first comprehensive really scientific treatise on the subject, while his hand-book for officers, published as early as 1787, contains the first scientific development of the tactics of field artillery.[b] His works, though antiquated in many respects, are still classical. In the Austrian service, Gen. Vega, in the Spanish, Gen. Morla, in the Prussian, Hoyer and Rouvroy, made valuable contributions to artilleristic literature.[c] The French had reorganized their artillery according to the system of Vallière in 1732; they retained 24, 16, 12, 8, and 4-pounders, and adopted the 8-inch howitzer. Still there was a great variety of models of construction; the guns were from 22 to 26 calibres long, and weighed about 250 times as much as the

---

[a] K. A. Struensee, *Anfangsgründe der Artillerie*, G. F. Tempelhof, *Le bombardier prussien*.— *Ed.*

[b] G. Scharnhorst, *Handbuch der Artillerie*, Bd. 1-3 and *Handbuch für Officiere. Erster Theil von der Artillerie*.— *Ed.*

[c] G. Vega, *Praktische Anweisung zum Bombenwerfen;* T. Morla, *Tratado de artilleria;* J. G. Hoyer, *Allgemeines Wörterbuch der Artillerie*, Th. 1-2; F. G. Rouvroy, *Vorlesungen über die Artillerie*, Th. 1-3.— *Ed.*

corresponding shot. At length, in 1774, General Gribeauval, who
had served with the Austrians in the 7 years' war, and who knew
the superiority of the new Prussian and Austrian artilleries,
carried the introduction of his new system. The siege artillery was
definitively separated from the field artillery. It was formed of all
guns heavier than 12-pounders, and of all the old heavy
12-pounder guns. The field artillery was composed of 12-pounder,
8-pounder, and 4-pounder guns, all 18 calibres long, weighing 150
times the weight of the shot, and of a 6-inch howitzer. The charge
for the guns was definitely fixed at one-third the weight of the
shot, the perpendicular elevating screw was introduced, and every
part of a gun or carriage was made according to a fixed model, so
as to be easily replaced from the stores. Seven models of wheels,
and 3 models of axletrees, were sufficient for all the various
vehicles used in the French artillery. Although the use of
limber-boxes to carry a supply of ammunition was known to most
artillerists, Gribeauval did not introduce them in France. The
4-pounders were distributed with the infantry, every battalion
receiving 2 of them; the 8 and 12-pounders were distributed in
separate batteries as reserve artillery, with a field-forge to every
battery. Train and artisan companies were organized, and
altogether this artillery of Gribeauval was the first corps of its kind
established on a modern footing. It has proved superior to any of
its day, in the proportions by which its constructions were
regulated, in its material, and in its organization, and for many
years it has served as a model.

Thanks to Gribeauval's improvements, the French artillery,
during the wars of the revolution, was superior to any other, and
soon became, in the hands of Napoleon, an arm of hitherto
unknown power. There was no alteration made, except that the
system of regimental guns was definitively done away with in
1799, and that with the immense number of 6-pounder and
3-pounder guns conquered in all parts of Europe, these calibres
were also introduced in the service. The whole of the field artillery
was organized into batteries of 6 pieces, among which one was
generally a howitzer, and the remainder guns. But if there was
little or no change in the material, there was an immense one in
the tactics of artillery. Although the number of guns was
somewhat diminished in consequence of the abolition of regimental pieces, the effect of artillery in a battle was heightened by its
skilful use. Napoleon used a number of light guns, attached to the
divisions of infantry, to engage battle, to make the enemy show his
strength, &c., while the mass of the artillery was held in reserve,

until the decisive point of attack was determined on; then enormous batteries were suddenly formed, all acting upon that point, and thus preparing by a tremendous cannonade the final attack of the infantry reserves. At Friedland 70 guns, at Wagram 100 guns, were thus formed in line[249]; at Borodino,[a] a battery of 80 guns prepared Ney's attack on Semenovka. On the other hand, the large masses of reserve cavalry formed by Napoleon, required for their support a corresponding force of horse artillery, which arm again received the fullest attention, and was very numerously represented in the French armies, where its proper tactical use was first practically established. Without Gribeauval's improvements, this new use of artillery would have been impossible, and with the necessity for the altered tactics, these improvements gradually, and with slight alterations, found their way into all continental armies.

The British artillery, about the beginning of the French revolutionary war, was exceedingly neglected, and much behind that of other nations. They had two regimental guns to each battalion, but no reserve artillery. The guns were horsed in single team, the drivers walking alongside with long whips. Horses and drivers were hired. The *materiel* was of very old-fashioned construction, and except for very short distances, the pieces could move at a walk only. Horse artillery was unknown. After 1800, however, when experience had shown the inadequacy of this system, the artillery was thoroughly reorganized by Major Spearman. The limbers were adapted for double team, the guns brigaded in batteries of 6 pieces, and in general those improvements were introduced which had been in use for some time already on the continent. No expense being spared, the British artillery soon was the neatest, most solidly, and most luxuriously equipped of its kind; great attention was paid to the newly erected corps of horse artillery, which soon distinguished itself by the boldness, rapidity, and precision of its manoeuvres. As to fresh improvements in the *materiel,* they were confined to the construction of the vehicles; the block-trail gun-carriage, and the ammunition wagon with a limber to it have since been adopted in most countries of the continent.

The proportion of artillery to the other components of an army became a little more fixed during this period. The strongest proportion of artillery now present with an army was that of the Prussians at Pirmasens[250]—7 guns for every 1,000 men. Napoleon considered 3 guns per 1,000 men quite sufficient, and this

---

[a] See this volume, pp. 251-55.— *Ed.*

proportion has become a general rule. The number of rounds to accompany a gun was also fixed; at least 200 rounds per gun, of which $^1/_4$ or $^1/_5$ were case shot. During the peace following the downfall of Napoleon, the artilleries of all European powers underwent gradual improvements. The light calibres of 3 and 4 lbs. were everywhere abolished, the improved carriages and wagons of the English artillery were adopted in most countries. The charge was fixed almost everywhere at $^1/_3$, the metal of the gun at, or near, 150 times the weight of the shot, and the length of the piece at from 16 to 18 calibres. The French reorganized their artillery in 1827. The field-guns were fixed at 8 and 12 lb. calibre, 18 calibres long, charge $^1/_3$, weight of metal in gun 150 times that of the shot. The English carriages and wagons were adopted, and limber-boxes for the first time introduced into the French service. Two kinds of howitzers, of 15 and 16 centimetres of bore, were attached to the 8 and 12-pounder batteries, respectively. A great simplicity distinguishes this new system of field artillery. There are but 2 sizes of gun-carriages, 1 size of limber, 1 size of wheel, and 2 sizes of axletrees to all the vehicles used in the French field batteries. Beside this, a separate mountain artillery was introduced, carrying howitzers of 12 centimetres bore.

The English field artillery now has for its almost exclusive calibre the 9-pounders of 17 calibres long, weight $1^1/_2$ cwt. to 1 pound weight of shot, charge $^1/_3$ the weight of shot. In every battery there are 2 24-pounder $5^1/_2$-inch howitzers. Six-pounder and 12-pounder guns were not sent out at all in the late Russian war.[a] There are 2 sizes of wheels in use. In both the English and French foot artillery the gunners are mounted during manoeuvres on the limber and ammunition wagons.

The Prussian army carries 6 and 12-pounder guns, 18 calibres long, weighing 145 times, and charged with $^1/_3$ the weight of the shot. The howitzers are $5^1/_2$ and $6^1/_2$-inch bore. There are 6 guns and 2 howitzers to a battery. There are 2 wheels and 2 axletrees, and 1 limber. The gun-carriages are of Gribeauval construction. In the foot artillery, for quick manoeuvres, 5 gunners, sufficient to serve the gun, mount the limber-box and the off-horses; the remaining 3 follow as best they can. The ammunition wagons are not, therefore, attached to the guns, as in the French and British service, but form a column apart, and are kept out of range during action. The improved English ammunition wagon was adopted in 1842.

---

[a] The Crimean war of 1853-56.—*Ed.*

The Austrian artillery has 6 and 12-pounder guns, 16 calibres long, weighing 135 times, charged with $^1/_4$ the weight of the shot. The howitzers are similar to those of the Prussian service. Six guns and 2 howitzers compose a battery.

The Russian artillery has 6 and 12-pounder guns, 18 calibres long, 150 times the weight of the shot, with a charge of $^1/_3$ its weight. The howitzers are 5 and 6-inch bore. According to the calibre and destination, either 8 or 12 pieces form a battery, one-half of which are guns, and the other half howitzers.

The Sardinian army has 8-pounder and 16-pounder guns, with a corresponding size of howitzer. The smaller German armies all have 6 and 12-pounders, the Spaniards 8 and 12-pounders, the Portuguese, Swedes, Danes, Belgians, Dutch, and Neapolitans 6 and 12-pounders.

The start given to the British artillery by Major Spearman's reorganization, along with the interest for further improvement thereby awakened in that service, and the wide range offered to artilleristic progress by the immense naval artillery of Great Britain, have contributed to many important inventions. The British compositions for fireworks, as well as their gunpowder, are superior to any other, and the precision of their time fuzes is unequalled. The principal invention latterly made in the British artillery are the shrapnel shells (hollow shot, filled with musket balls, and exploding during the flight), by which the effective range of grape has been rendered equal to that of round shot. The French, skilful as they are as constructors and organizers, are nearly the only army which has not yet adopted this new and terrible projectile; they have not been able to make out the fuze composition, upon which every thing depends.

A new system of field artillery has been proposed by Louis Napoleon, and appears to be in course of adoption in France. The whole of the 4 calibres of guns and howitzers now in use, to be superseded by a light 12-pounder gun, $15^1/_2$ calibres long, weighing 110 times, and charged with $^1/_4$ the weight of the solid shot. A shell of 12 centim. (the same now used in the mountain artillery), to be fired out of the same gun with a reduced charge, thus superseding howitzers for the special use of hollow shot. The experiments made in 4 artillery schools of France have been very successful, and it is said that these guns showed a marked superiority, in the Crimea, over the Russian guns, mostly 6-pounders. The English, however, maintain that their long 9-pounder is superior in range and precision to this new gun, and it is to be observed that they were the first to introduce, but very soon again to abandon, a light 12-pounder for a charge of $^1/_4$ the shot's weight, and which has evidently served Louis Napoleon as a model. The firing of shells from common guns is taken from the Prussian service, where, in sieges, the 24-pounders are made to fire shells for certain purposes. Nevertheless, the capabilities of Louis Napoleon's gun have still to be determined by experience, and as nothing special has been published on its effects in the late war, we cannot here be expected finally to judge on its merits.

The laws and experimental maxims for propelling solid, hollow, or other projectiles, from cannon, the ascertained proportions of range, elevation, charge, the effects of windage and other causes of deviation, the probabilities of hitting the mark, and the various circumstances that may occur in warfare, constitute the science of gunnery. Though the fact, that a heavy body projected *in vacuo,* in a direction different from the vertical, will describe a parabola in its flight, forms the fundamental principle of this science, yet the resistance of the air, increasing as it does with the velocity of the moving body, alters very materially the application of the parabolic theory in gunnery practice. Thus for guns propelling their shot at an initial velocity of 1,400 to 1,700 feet in a second, the line of flight varies considerably from the theoretic parabola, so much so that with them, the greatest range is obtained at an elevation of only about 20 degrees, while according to the parabolic theory it should be at 45 degrees. Practical experiments have determined, with some degree of precision, these deviations, and thus fixed the proper elevations for each class of guns, for a given charge and range. But there are other circumstances affecting the flight of the shot. There is, first of all, the windage, or the difference by which the diameter of the shot must be less than that of the bore, to facilitate loading. It causes first an escape of the expanding gas during the explosion of the charge, in other words, a reduction of the force, and secondly an irregularity in the direction of the shot, causing deflections in a vertical, or horizontal sense. Then there is the unavoidable inequality in the weight of the charge, or in its condition at the moment it is used, the eccentricity of the shot, the centre of gravity not coinciding with the centre of the sphere, which causes deflections varying according to the relative position of the centres at the moment of firing, and many other causes producing irregularity of results under seemingly the same conditions of flight. For field-guns, we have seen that the charge of $^1/_3$ of the shot's weight, and a length of 16-18 calibres are almost universally adopted. With such charges, the point-blank range (the gun being laid horizontal), the shot will touch the ground at about 300 yards distance, and by elevating the gun, this range may be increased up to 3,000 or 4,000 yards. Such a range, however, leaves all probability of hitting the mark out of the question, and for actual and effective practice, the range of field-guns does not exceed 1,400 or 1,500 yards, at which distance scarcely 1 shot out of 6 or 8 might be expected to hit the mark. The decisive ranges, in which alone cannon can contribute to the issue of a battle, are, for round shot and shell, between 600 and 1,100 yards, and at these ranges the probability of striking the object is indeed far greater. Thus it is reckoned that at 700 yards about 50 per cent., at 900 yards about 35 per cent., at 1,100 yards 25 per cent., out of the shots fired from a 6-pounder, will hit a target representing the front of a battalion in column of attack (34 yards long by 2 yards high). The 9 and 12-pounder will give somewhat better results. In some experiments made in France in 1850, the 8-pounders and 12-pounders then in use gave the following results, against a target 30 metres by 3 metres (representing a troop of cavalry) at:—

	500 met.	600 met.	700 met.	800 met.	900 met.
12-p'ders, hits	64 p. ct.	54 p. ct.	43 p. ct.	37 p. ct.	32 p. ct.
8-p'ders, "	67 "	44 "	40 "	28 "	28 "

Though the target was higher by one-half, the practice here remained below the average stated above. With field-howitzers the charge is considerably less in proportion to the weight of the projectile than with guns. The short length of the piece (7 to 10 calibres) and the necessity of firing it at great elevations, are the causes of this. The recoil from a howitzer fired under high elevation, acting downward as well as backward, would, if a heavy charge was used, strain the carriage so as to disable it after a few rounds. This is the reason why in most continental artilleries several charges are in use in the same field-howitzer, thus making the gunner to produce a given range by different combination of charge and elevation. Where this is not the case, as in the British artillery, the elevation taken is necessarily very low, and scarcely exceeding that of guns; the range-tables for the British 24-pounder howitzer, $2\frac{1}{2}$-pound charge, do not extend beyond 1,050 yards, with 4° elevation; the same elevation, for the 9-pounder gun, giving a range of 1,400 yards. There is a peculiar short kind of howitzer in use in most German armies, which is capable of an elevation of from 16 to 20 degrees, thus acting somewhat like a mortar; its charge is, necessarily, but small; it has this advantage over the common, long howitzer, that its shells can be made to drop into covered positions, behind undulations of ground, &c. This advantage is, however, of a doubtful nature against movable objects like troops, though of great importance where the object covered from direct fire is immovable; and as to direct fire, these howitzers, from their shortness (6 to 7 calibres) and small charge, are all but useless. The charge, to obtain various ranges at an elevation fixed by the purpose intended (direct firing or shelling), necessarily varies very much; in the Prussian field artillery, where these howitzers are still used, not less than twelve different charges occur. Withal, the howitzer is but a very imperfect piece of cannon, and the sooner it is superseded by an effective field shell-gun, the better.

The heavy cannon used in fortresses, sieges, and naval armaments, are of various description. Up to the late Russian war, it was not customary to use in siege-warfare heavier guns than 24-pounders, or, at the very outside, a few 32-pounders. Since the siege of Sebastopol, however, siege-guns and ship-guns are the same, or, rather, the effect of the heavy ship-guns in trenches and land-defences has proved so unexpectedly superior to that of the customary light siege-guns, that the war of sieges will henceforth have to be decided, in a great measure, by such heavy naval cannon. In both siege and naval artillery, there are generally found various models of guns for the same calibre. There are light and short guns, and there are long and heavy ones. Mobility being a minor consideration, guns for particular purposes are often made 22 to 25 calibres long, and some of these are, in consequence of this greater length, as precise as rifles in their practice. One of the best of this class of guns is the Prussian brass 24-pounder of 10 feet 4 inches, or 22 calibres long, weighing 60 cwt.; for dismounting practice in a siege, there is no gun like it. For most purposes, however, a length of 16 to 20 calibres is found quite sufficient, and as, upon an average, size of calibre will be preferable to extreme precision, a mass of 60 cwt. of iron or gun-metal will be more usefully employed, as a rule, in a heavy 32-pounder of 16-17 calibres long. The new long iron 32-pounder, one of the finest guns in the British navy, 9 feet long, 50 cwt., measures but $16^{1}/_{2}$ calibres. The long 68-pounder, 112 cwt., pivot-gun of all the large screw 131 gun-ships, measures 10 feet 10 inches, or a trifle more than 16 calibres; another kind of pivot-gun, the long 56-pounder of 98 cwt., measures 11 feet, or $17^{1}/_{2}$ calibres. Still a great number of less effective guns enter into naval armaments even now, bored-up guns of merely 11 or 12 calibres, and carronades of 7-8 calibres long. There is, however, another kind of naval gun that was introduced about 35 years ago by General Paixhans, and has since received an immense importance, the shell-gun. This kind of ordnance has undergone considerable improvement, and the French shell-gun still comes nearest to that constructed by the inventor; it has retained the cylindrical chamber for the charge. In the English service the chamber is either a short frustum of a cone, reducing only very slightly the diameter of the bore, or there is no chamber at all; it measures in length from 10 to 13 calibres, and is intended for hollow shot exclusively; but the long 68-pdrs. and 56-pdrs. mentioned above throw solid shot and shell indiscriminately. In the U.S. navy Capt. Dahlgren has proposed a new system of shell-guns, consisting of short guns of very large calibre (11 and 9 inches bore), which has been partly adopted in the armament of several new frigates. The value of this system has still to be fixed by actual experience, which must determine whether the tremendous effect of such enormous shells can be obtained without the sacrifice of precision, which cannot but suffer from the great elevation required at long ranges. In sieges and naval gunnery, the charges are as variable as the constructions of the guns themselves, and the ends to be attained. In laying a breach in masonry, the heaviest charges are used, and these amount, with some very heavy and solid guns, to one-half the weight of the shot. On the whole, however, one-fourth may be considered a full average charge for siege purposes, increased sometimes to one-third, diminished at others to one-sixth. On board ship, there are generally 3 classes of charges to each gun; the high charge, for distant practice, chasing, &c., the medium charge, for the average effective distances of naval engagements; the reduced, for close quarters and double shotting. For the long 32-pdrs. they are equal to $^{5}/_{16}$, $^{1}/_{4}$, and $^{3}/_{16}$ of the shot's weight. For short light guns and shell-guns, these proportions are of course still more reduced; but with the latter, too, the hollow shot does not reach the weight of the solid one. Beside guns and shell-guns, heavy howitzers and mortars enter into the composition of siege and naval artillery. Howitzers are short pieces intended to throw shell at an elevation up to 12 or 30 degrees, and to be fixed on carriages; mortars are still shorter pieces, fixed to blocks, intended to throw shell at an elevation generally exceeding 20 degrees, and increasing even to 60 degrees. Both are chambered ordnance; i. e. the chamber or part of the bore intended to receive the charge, is less in diameter than the flight or general bore. Howitzers are seldom of a calibre exceeding 8 inches, but mortars are bored up to 13, 15, and more inches. The flight of a shell from a mortar, from the smallness of the charge (1-20th to 1-40th of the weight of the shell), and from its considerable elevation, is less interfered with by the resistance of the air, and here the parabolic theory may be used in gunnery calculations without material deviation from practical results. Shells from mortars are intended to act either by bursting, and, as carcasses, setting fire to combustible objects by the jet of flame from the fuzes, or by their weight as well, in breaking through vaulted and otherwise secured roofs; in the latter case the higher elevation is preferred, giving the highest flight and greatest momentum of fall. Shells from howitzers are intended to act, first by impact, and afterward by bursting. From their great elevation, and the small initial velocity imparted to the shell, and consequent little resistance offered to it by the air, a mortar throws its projectile further than any other kind of ordnance, the object fired at being generally a whole town, there is little precision required; and thus it happens that the effective range of heavy mortars extends to 4,000 yards and upward, from which distance Sveaborg was bombarded by the Anglo-French mortar-boats.[251]

The application of these different kinds of cannon, projectiles, and charges, during a siege, will be treated of under that head[a]; the use of naval artillery constitutes nearly the whole fighting part of naval elementary tactics, and does therefore not belong to this subject; it thus only remains for us to make a few observations on the use and tactics of field artillery.

Artillery has no arms for hand-to-hand fight; all its forces are concentrated in the distant effect of its fire. It is, moreover, in fighting condition as long only as it is in position; as soon as it limbers up, or attaches the prolonge for a movement, it is temporarily disabled. From both causes, it is the most defensive of all the 3 arms; its powers of attack are very limited indeed, for attack is onward movement, and its culminating point is the clash of steel against steel. The critical moment for artillery is therefore the advance, taking position, and getting ready for action under the enemy's fire. Its deployments into line, its preliminary movements, will have to be masked either by obstacles of ground or by lines of troops. It will thus gain a position parallel to the line it has to occupy, and then advance into position straight against the enemy, so as not to expose itself to a flanking fire. The choice of a position is a thing of the highest importance, both as regards

---

[a] See this volume, pp. 336-38.— *Ed.*

the effect of the fire of a battery, and that of the enemy's fire upon it. To place his guns so that their effect on the enemy is as telling as possible, is the first important point; security from the enemy's fire the second. A good position must afford firm and level standing ground for the wheels and trails of the guns; if the wheels do not stand level, no good practice is possible; and if the trail digs into the ground, the carriage will soon be broken by the power of recoil. It must, beside, afford a free view of the ground held by the enemy, and admit of as much liberty of movement as possible. Finally, the ground in front, between the battery and the enemy, must be favorable to the effect of our arms, and unfavorable, if possible, to that of theirs. The most favorable ground is a firm and level one, affording the advantage of ricochet practice, and making the shot that go short strike the enemy after the first graze. It is wonderful what difference the nature of the ground will make in artillery practice. On soft ground the shot, on grazing, will deflect or make irregular rebounds, if they do not stick fast in it at once. The way the furrows run in ploughed land, makes a great difference, especially with canister and shrapnel firing; if they run crossways, most of the shot will bury themselves in them. If the ground be soft, undulating, or broken immediately in front of us, but level and hard further on toward the enemy, it will favor our practice, and protect us from his. Firing down or up inclinations of more than 5 degrees, or firing from the top of one hill to that of another, is very unfavorable. As to our safety from the enemy's fire, very small objects will increase that. A thin fence, scarcely hiding our position, a group of shrubs, or high corn, will prevent his taking correct aim. A small abrupt bank on which our guns are placed will catch the most dangerous of his projectiles. A dyke makes a capital parapet, but the best protection is the crest of a slight undulation of ground, behind which we draw our guns so far back that the enemy sees nothing but the muzzles; in this position every shot striking the ground in front, will bound high over our heads. Still better is it, if we can cut out a stand for our guns into the crest, about 2 feet deep, flattening out to the rear with the slope, so as to command the whole of the external slope of the hill. The French under Napoleon were extremely skilful in placing their guns, and from them all other nations have learnt this art. Regarding the enemy, the position should be chosen so as to be free from flank or enfilading fire; regarding our own troops, it should not hamper their movements. The usual distance from gun to gun in line is 20 yards, but there is no necessity to adhere strictly to any of these rules of the parade-ground. Once in position, the limbers remain close behind their guns, while the wagons, in some services, remain under cover. Where the wagons are used for mounting the men, they too must run the chance of going into effective range. The battery directs its fire upon that portion of the enemy's forces which at the time most menaces our position; if our infantry is to attack, it fires upon either the opposing artillery, if that is yet to be silenced, or upon the masses of infantry if they expose themselves; but if a portion of the enemy advance to actual attack, that is the point to aim at, not minding the hostile artillery which fires on us. Our fire against artillery will be most effective when that artillery cannot reply, *i. e.* when it is limbering up, moving, or unlimbering. A few good shots cause great confusion in such moments. The old rule that artillery, excepting in pressing moments of importance, should not approach infantry to within 300 yards, or the range of small arms, will now soon be antiquated. With the increasing range of modern muskets, field artillery, to be effective, cannot any longer keep out of musket range; and a gun with its limber, horses, and gunners, forms a group quite large enough for skirmishers to fire at, at 600 yards with the Minié or Enfield rifle. The long-established idea, that who wishes to live long must enlist in the artillery, appears to be no longer true, for it is evident that skirmishing from a distance will in future be the most effective way of combating artillery; and where is the battle-field in which there could not be found capital cover for skirmishers within 600 yards from any possible artillery emplacement?

Against advancing lines or columns of infantry, artillery has thus far always had the advantage; a few effective rounds of grape, or a couple of solid shot ploughing through a deep column, have a terribly cooling effect. The nearer the attack comes, the more effective becomes our practice; and even at the last moment we can easily withdraw our guns from an opponent of such slowness, though whether a line of *chasseurs de Vincennes,* advancing at the *pas gymnastique,* would not be down upon us before we had limbered up, must still remain doubtful.

Against cavalry, coolness gives the advantage to artillery. If the latter reserve their grape to within 100 yards, and then give a well-aimed volley, the cavalry will be found pretty far off by the time the smoke has cleared away. At all events, to limber up and try to escape, would be the worst plan; for cavalry would be sure to overtake the guns.

Artillery against artillery, the ground, the calibres, the relative number of guns, and the use made thereof by the parties, will decide. It is, however, to be noticed, that though the large calibre has an undoubted advantage at long ranges, the smaller calibre approaches in its effects those of the large one as the ranges decrease, and at short distances almost equals them. At Borodino, Napoleon's artillery consisted principally of 3 and 4-pounders, while the Russians exulted in their numerous 12-pounders; yet the French small pop-guns had decidedly the best of it.

In supporting either infantry or cavalry, the artillery will have always to gain a position on its flank. If the infantry advances, it advances by half-batteries or sections on a line with the skir-mishers, or rather in advance of it; as soon as the infantry masses prepare to attack with the bayonet, it trots up to 400 yards from the enemy, and prepares the charge by a rapid fire of case shot. If the attack is repelled, the artillery will re-open its fire on the pursuing enemy until compelled to withdraw; but if the attack succeeds, its fire contributes a great deal to the completion of the success, one-half of the guns firing while the other advances. Horse artillery, as a supporting arm to cavalry, imparting to it some of that defensive element which it naturally lacks altogether, is now one of the most favorite branches of all services, and brought to high perfection in all European armies. Though intended to act on cavalry ground, and in company with cavalry, there is no horse artillery in the world which would not be prepared to gallop across a country where its own cavalry would not follow without sacrificing its order and cohesion. The horse artillery of every country forms the boldest and skilfullest riders of its army, and they will take a particular pride, on any grand field-day, in dashing across obstacles, guns and all, before which the cavalry will stop. The tactics of horse artillery consist in boldness and coolness. Rapidity, suddenness of appearance, quickness of fire, readiness to move off at a moment's notice, and to take that road which is too difficult for the cavalry, these are the chief qualities of a good horse artillery. Choice of position there is but little in this constant change of places; every position is good so as it is close to the enemy and out of the way of the cavalry; and it is during the ebbing and flowing of cavalry engagements, that the artillery, skirting the advancing and receding waves, has to show every moment its superior horseman-ship and presence of mind in getting clear of this surging sea across all sorts of ground where not every cavalry dares, or likes to follow.

In the attack and defence of posts, the tactics of artillery are similar. The principal thing is always to fire upon that point from which, in defence, threatens the nearest and most direct danger, or in attack, from which our advance can be most effectually checked. The destruction of material obstacles also forms part of its duties, and here the various calibres and kinds of ordnance are applied according to their nature and effect; howitzers for setting fire to houses, heavy guns to batter down gates, walls, and barricades.

All these remarks apply to the artillery which in every army is attached to the divisions. But the grandest results are obtained by the reserve artillery in great and decisive battles. Held back out of sight and out of range during the greater part of the day, it is brought forward in a mass upon the decisive point as soon as the time for the final effort has come. Formed in a crescent a mile or more in extent, it concentrates its destructive fire upon a comparatively small point. Unless an equivalent force of guns is there to meet it, half an hour's rapid firing settles the matter. The enemy begins to wither under the hailstorm of howling shot; the intact reserves of infantry advance—a last, sharp, short struggle, and the victory is won. Thus did Napoleon prepare Macdonald's advance at Wagram, and resistance was broken before the 3 divisions advancing in a column had fired a shot or crossed a bayonet. And since those great days only can the tactics of field artillery be said to exist.

Written between October 19 and November 27, 1857

First published in *The New American Cyclopaedia*, Vol. II, 1858

Reproduced from *The New American Cyclopaedia*

Karl Marx

BUGEAUD[252]

Bugeaud de la Piconnerie, Thomas Robert, duc d'Isly, marshal of France, born at Limoges, in Oct. 1784, died in Paris, June 10, 1849. He entered the French army as a private soldier in 1804, became a corporal during the campaign of 1805, served as sub-lieutenant in the campaign of Prussia and Poland (1806-'7), was present in 1811, as major, at the sieges of Lerida, Tortosa, and Tarragona, and was promoted to the rank of lieutenant-colonel after the battle of Ordal, in Catalonia.[253] After the first return of the Bourbons Col. Bugeaud celebrated the white lily[a] in some doggerel rhymes; but these poetical effusions being passed by rather contemptuously, he again embraced, during the Hundred Days,[254] the party of Napoleon, who sent him to the army of the Alps, at the head of the 14th regiment of the line. On the 2d return of the Bourbons he retired to Excideuil, to the estate of his father. At the time of the invasion of Spain by the duke of Angoulême[255] he offered his sword to the Bourbons, but the offer being declined, he turned liberal, and joined the movement which finally led to the revolution of 1830.

He was chosen as a member of the chamber of deputies in 1831, and made a major-general by Louis Philippe. Appointed governor of the citadel of Blaye in 1833, he had the duchess of Berry under his charge, but earned no honor from the manner in which he discharged his mission, and became afterward known by the name of the "ex-gaoler of Blaye." During the debates of the chamber of deputies on Jan. 25,[b] 1834, M. Larabit complaining of Soult's

---

[a] Heraldic emblem of the Bourbon dynasty.— *Ed.*
[b] *The New American Cyclopaedia* has "Jan. 16".— *Ed.*

military dictatorship, and Bugeaud interrupting him with the words, "Obedience is the soldier's first duty," another deputy, M. Dulong, pungently asked, "What, if ordered to become a gaoler?" This incident led to a duel between Bugeaud and Dulong, in which the latter was shot.[256] The consequent exasperation of the Parisians was still heightened by his co-operation in suppressing the Paris insurrection of April 13 and 14, 1834.[257] The forces destined to suppress that insurrection were divided into 3 brigades, one of which Bugeaud commanded. In the *rue Transnonain* a handful of enthusiasts who still held a barricade on the morning of the 14th, when the serious part of the affair was over, were cruelly slaughtered by an overwhelming force. Although this spot lay without the circumscription made over to Bugeaud's brigade, and he, therefore, had not participated in the massacre, the hatred of the people nailed his name to the deed, and despite all declarations to the contrary, persisted in stigmatizing him as the "man of the *rue Transnonain.*"

Sent, June 6, 1836, to Algeria, Gen. Bugeaud became invested with a commanding position in the province of Oran, almost independent of the governor-general. Ordered to fight Abd-el-Kader, and to subdue him by the display of an imposing army, he concluded the treaty of the Tafna,[258] allowing the opportunity for military operations to slip away, and placing his army in a critical state before it had begun to act. Bugeaud fought several battles previous to this treaty. A secret article, not reduced to writing, stipulated that 30,000 boojoos (about $12,000) should be paid to Gen. Bugeaud. Called back to France, he was promoted to the rank of lieutenant-general and appointed grand officer of the legion of honor. When the secret clause of the treaty of the Tafna oozed out, Louis Philippe authorized Bugeaud to expend the money on certain public roads, thus to increase his popularity among his electors and secure his seat in the chamber of deputies.

At the commencement of 1841 he was named governor-general of Algeria, and with his administration the policy of France in Algeria underwent a complete change. He was the first governor-general who had an army adequate to its task placed under his command, who exerted an absolute authority over the generals second in command, and who kept his post long enough to act up to a plan needing years for its execution. The battle of Isly (Aug. 14, 1844), in which he vanquished the army of the emperor of Morocco[a] with vastly inferior forces, owed its success

---

[a] Abd-ur-Rahman II.— *Ed.*

to his taking the Mussulmans by surprise, without any previous declaration of war, and when negotiations were on the eve of being concluded.[259] Already raised to the dignity of a marshal of France, July 17, 1843, Bugeaud was now created duke of Isly. Abd-el-Kader having, after his return to France, again collected an army, he was sent back to Algeria, where he promptly crushed the Arabian revolt. In consequence of differences between him and Guizot, occasioned by his expedition into Kabylia, which he had undertaken against ministerial orders, he was replaced by the duke of Aumale, and, according to Guizot's expression, "enabled to come and enjoy his glory in France."[a][260]

During the night of Feb. 23-24, 1848, he was, on the secret advice of Guizot, ordered into the presence of Louis Philippe, who conferred upon him the supreme command of the whole armed force—the line as well as the national guard. At noon of the 24th, followed by Gens. Rulhière, Bedeau, Lamoricière, De Salles, St. Arnaud, and others, he proceeded to the general staff at the Tuileries, there to be solemnly invested with the supreme command by the duke of Nemours. He reminded the officers present that he who was about to lead them against the Paris revolutionists "had never been beaten, neither on the battle-field nor in insurrections," and for this time again promised to make short work of the "rebel rabble." Meantime, the news of his nomination contributed much to give matters a decisive turn. The national guard, still more incensed by his appointment as supreme commander, broke out in the cry of "Down with Bugeaud!" "Down with the man of the *rue Transnonain!*" and positively declared that they would not obey his orders. Frightened by this demonstration, Louis Philippe withdrew his orders, and spent the 24th in vain negotiations. On Feb. 24, alone of Louis Philippe's council, Bugeaud still urged war to the knife; but the king already considered the sacrifice of the marshal as a means to make his own peace with the national guard. The command was consequently placed in other hands, and Bugeaud dismissed. Two days later he placed, but in vain, his sword at the command of the provisional government.[261]

When Louis Napoleon became president he conferred the command-in-chief of the army of the Alps upon Bugeaud, who was also elected by the department of Charente-Inférieure as representative in the national assembly. He published several

---

[a] Quoted from D. Stern's *Histoire de la révolution de 1848* (p. 55). The quotations in the next paragraph are also from this book (pp. 147, 150).— *Ed.*

literary productions, which treat chiefly of Algeria.[a] In Aug. 1852, a monument was erected to him in Algiers, and also one in his native town.

Written in November (not later than the 27th), 1857

First published in *The New American Cyclopaedia*, Vol. IV, 1859

Reproduced from *The New American Cyclopaedia*

---

[a] Th. R. Bugeaud, *L'Algérie. Des moyens de conserver et d'utiliser cette conquête; De la colonisation de l'Algérie,* and others.— Ed.

Karl Marx

BRUNE[262]

Brune, Guillaume Marie Anne, a marshal of the French empire, born at Brives-la-Gaillarde, March 13, 1763, died, in Avignon, Aug. 2, 1815. His father sent him to Paris to study the law, but on leaving the university, financial difficulties caused him to become a printer. In the beginning of the revolution, together with Gauthier and Jourgniac de St. Méard, he published the *Journal général de la Cour et de la Ville*. He soon embraced the party of the revolution, enlisted in the national guard, and became an ardent member of the club of the *cordeliers*.[263] His grand figure, martial air, and boisterous patriotism, rendered him one of the military leaders of the people in the demonstration of 1791 in the Champ de Mars, which was crushed by La Fayette's national guards.[264] Thrown into prison, and the rumor spreading that the partisans of the court had attempted to get rid of him by odious means, Danton was instrumental in procuring his release. To the protection of the latter, among whose partisans he became prominent, he owed a military appointment during the famous days of Sept. 1792,[265] and his sudden promotion, in Oct. 12, 1792, to the rank of colonel and adjutant-major. He served under Dumouriez in Belgium; was sent against the federalists of Calvados, advancing under Gen. Puisaye upon Paris, whom he easily defeated. He was next made a general of brigade, and participated in the battle of Hondschoote.[266] The committee of public safety intrusted him with the mission of putting down the insurrectionary movements in the Gironde, which he did with the utmost rigor.[267]

After Danton's imprisonment, he was expected to rush to the rescue of his friend and protector, but keeping prudently aloof during the first moments of danger, he contrived to shift through the reign of terror. After the 9th Thermidor he again joined the now victorious Dantonists,[268] and followed Fréron to Marseilles and Avignon. On the 13th Vendémiaire (Oct. 5, 1795) he acted as one of Bonaparte's under-generals against the revolted sections of Paris.[269] After having assisted the directory in putting down the conspiracy of the camp at Grenelle (Sept. 9, 1796),[270] he entered the Italian army in the division of Masséna, and distinguished himself during the whole campaign by great intrepidity. Wishing to propitiate the chiefs of the *cordeliers,* Bonaparte attributed part of his success at Rivoli [271] to the exertions of Brune, appointed him general of division on the battle-field, and induced the directory to instal him as commander of the second division of the Italian army, made vacant by Augereau's departure for Paris.

After the peace of Campo Formio[272] he was employed by the directory on the mission of first lulling the Swiss into security, then dividing their councils, and finally, when an army had been concentrated for that purpose, falling upon the canton of Bern, and seizing its public treasury; on which occasion Brune forgot to draw up an inventory of the plunder. Again, by dint of manoeuvres, bearing a diplomatic rather than a military character, he forced Charles Emmanuel, the king of Sardinia, and the apparent ally of France, to deliver into his hands the citadel of Turin (July 3, 1798). The Batavian campaign,[273] which lasted about 2 months, forms the great event of Brune's military life. In this campaign he defeated the combined English and Russian forces, under the command of the duke of York, who capitulated to him, promising to restore all the French prisoners taken by the English from the commencement of the anti-Jacobinic war. After the *coup d'état* of the 18th Brumaire,[274] Bonaparte appointed Brune a member of the newly created council of state, and then despatched him against the royalists of Brittany.

Sent in 1800 to the army of Italy, Brune occupied 3 hostile camps, intrenched on the Volta, drove the enemy beyond this river, and took measures for crossing it instantly. According to his orders, the army was to effect its passage at 2 points, the right wing under Gen. Dupont between a mill situated on the Volta and the village of Pozzolo, the left wing under Brune himself at Monbazon. The second part of the operations meeting with difficulties, Brune gave orders to delay its execution for 24 hours, although the right wing, which had commenced crossing on the other point, was already engaged with far superior Austrian forces. It was only due to Gen. Dupont's exertions that the right wing was not destroyed or captured, and thus the success of the whole campaign imperilled. This blunder led to his recall to Paris.

From 1802 to 1804 he cut a sorry figure as ambassador at Constantinople, where his diplomatic talents were not, as in Switzerland and Piedmont, backed by bayonets. On his return to Paris, in Dec. 1804, Napoleon created him marshal in preference to generals like Lecourbe. Having for a while commanded the camp at Boulogne,[275] he was, in 1807, sent to Hamburg as governor of the Hanseatic towns, and as commander of the reserve of the grand army.[276] In this quality he vigorously seconded Bourrienne in his peculations. In order to settle some contested points of a truce concluded with Sweden at Schlatkow, he had a long personal interview with King Gustavus, who, in fact, proposed to him to betray his master. The manner in which he declined this offer raised the suspicions of Napoleon, who became highly incensed when Brune, drawing up a convention relating to the surrender of the island of Rügen to the French, mentioned simply the French and the Swedish armies as parties to the agreement, without any allusion to his "imperial and royal majesty."[a] Brune was instantly recalled by a letter of Berthier, in which the latter, on the express order of Napoleon, stated

"that such a scandal had never occurred since the days of Pharamond."[b]

On his return to France, he retired into private life. In 1814 he gave his adhesion to the acts of the senate,[277] and received the cross of St. Louis from Louis XVIII. During the Hundred Days[278] he became again a Bonapartist, and received the command of a corps of observation on the Var, where he displayed against the royalists the brutal vigor of his Jacobin epoch. After the battle of Waterloo[279] he proclaimed the king.[c] Starting from Toulon for Paris, he arrived at Avignon, on Aug. 2, at a moment when that town had for 15 days been doomed to carnage and incendiary fires by the royalist mob. Being recognized by them, he was shot, the mob seizing his corpse, dragging it through the streets, and throwing it into the Rhône.

"Brune, Masséna, Augereau, and many others," said Napoleon at St. Helena, "were intrepid depredators."[d]

---

a "Capitulation de l'isle de Rugen, en date du 7 Sept. 1807" (G. F. Martens, *Recueil des principaux Traités*, I, t. VIII, pp. 695-96).— *Ed.*

b Quoted from the article "Brune" published in *Biographie universelle (Michaud) ancienne et moderne*, t. 6, p. 19.— *Ed.*

c Louis XVIII.— *Ed.*

d Las Cases, *Mémorial de Sainte-Hélène*. Probably quoted from the article "Brune" published in *Biographie des célébrités militaires*, t. 1, p. 243.— *Ed.*

In regard to his military talents he remarks:

"Brune was not without a certain merit, but, on the whole, he was a *général de tribune* rather than a terrible warrior."[a]

A monument was erected to him in his native town in 1841.

Written probably between November 27, 1857 and January 8, 1858

First published in *The New American Cyclopaedia,* Vol. IV, 1859

Reproduced from *The New American Cyclopaedia*

---

[a] A. H. Jomini, *Vie politique et militaire de Napoléon,* t. 2, ch. VII, p. 64.— *Ed.*

Karl Marx

BOLIVAR Y PONTE [280]

Bolivar y Ponte, Simon, the "liberator" of Colombia, born at Caracas, July 24, 1783, died at San Pedro, near Santa Martha, Dec. 17, 1830. He was the son of one of the *familias Mantuanas,* which, at the time of the Spanish supremacy, constituted the creole nobility in Venezuela. In compliance with the custom of wealthy Americans of those times, at the early age of 14 he was sent to Europe. From Spain he passed to France, and resided for some years in Paris. In 1802 he married in Madrid, and returned to Venezuela, where his wife died suddenly of yellow fever. After this he visited Europe a second time, and was present at Napoleon's coronation as emperor, in 1804, and at his assumption of the iron crown of Lombardy, in 1805. [281] In 1809 he returned home, and despite the importunities of Joseph Felix Ribas, his cousin, he declined to join in the revolution which broke out at Caracas, April 19, 1810 [282]; but, after the event, he accepted a mission to London to purchase arms and solicit the protection of the British government. Apparently well received by the marquis of Wellesley, then secretary for foreign affairs, he obtained nothing beyond the liberty to export arms for ready cash with the payment of heavy duties upon them. On his return from London, he again withdrew to private life, until, Sept. 1811, he was prevailed upon by Gen. Miranda, then commander-in-chief of the insurgent land and sea forces, to accept the rank of lieutenant-colonel in the staff, and the command of Puerto Cabello, the strongest fortress of Venezuela.

The Spanish prisoners of war, whom Miranda used regularly to send to Puerto Cabello, to be confined in the citadel, having succeeded in overcoming their guards by surprise, and in seizing the citadel, Bolivar, although they were unarmed, while he had a numerous garrison and large magazines, embarked precipitately in the night, with 8 of his officers, without giving notice to his own troops, arrived at daybreak at La Guayra, and retired to his estate at San Mateo. On becoming aware of their commander's flight, the garrison retired in good order from the place, which was immediately occupied by the Spaniards under Monteverde. This event turned the scale in favor of Spain, and obliged Miranda, on the authority of the congress, to sign the treaty of Vittoria, July 26, 1812, which restored Venezuela to the Spanish rule. On July 30 Miranda arrived at La Guayra, where he intended to embark on board an English vessel. On his visit to the commander of the place, Col. Manuel Maria Casas, he met with a numerous company, among whom were Don Miguel Peña and Simon Bolivar, who persuaded him to stay, for one night at least, in Casas's house. At 2 o'clock in the morning, when Miranda was soundly sleeping, Casas, Peña, and Bolivar entered his room, with 4 armed soldiers, cautiously seized his sword and pistol, then awakened him, abruptly told him to rise and dress himself, put him into irons, and had him finally surrendered to Monteverde, who dispatched him to Cadiz, where, after some years' captivity, he died in irons. This act, committed on the pretext that Miranda had betrayed his country by the capitulation of Vittoria, procured for Bolivar Monteverde's peculiar favor, so that when he demanded his passport, Monteverde declared,

"Col. Bolivar's request should be complied with, as a reward for his having served the king of Spain by delivering up Miranda."[a]

He was thus allowed to sail for Curaçoa, where he spent 6 weeks, and proceeded, in company with his cousin Ribas, to the little republic of Carthagena. Previous to their arrival, a great number of soldiers, who had served under Gen. Miranda, had fled to Carthagena. Ribas proposed to them to undertake an expedition against the Spaniards in Venezuela, and to accept Bolivar as their commander-in-chief. The former proposition they embraced eagerly; to the latter they demurred, but at last yielded, on the condition of Ribas being the second in command. Manuel Rodriguez Torrices, the president of the republic of Carthagena, added to the 800 soldiers thus enlisted under Bolivar, 500 men under the command of his cousin, Manuel Castillo. The expedition started in the beginning of Jan. 1813. Dissensions as to the

---

[a] Quoted from *Memoirs of General Miller*, Vol. 2, pp. 277-78.— *Ed.*

supreme command breaking out between Bolivar and Castillo, the latter suddenly decamped with his grenadians. Bolivar, on his part, proposed to follow Castillo's example, and return to Carthagena, but Ribas persuaded him at length to pursue his course at least as far as Bogota, at that time the seat of the congress of New Granada. They were well received, supported in every way, and were both made generals by the congress, and, after having divided their little army into 2 columns, they marched by different routes upon Caracas. The further they advanced, the stronger grew their resources; the cruel excesses of the Spaniards acting everywhere as the recruiting sergeants for the army of the independents. The power of resistance on the part of the Spaniards was broken, partly by the circumstance of $^3/_4$ of their army being composed of natives, who bolted on every encounter to the opposite ranks, partly by the cowardice of such generals as Tiscar, Cajigal, and Fierro, who, on every occasion, deserted their own troops. Thus it happened that San Iago Mariño, an ignorant youth, had contrived to dislodge the Spaniards from the provinces of Cumana and Barcelona, at the very time that Bolivar was advancing through the western provinces. The only serious resistance, on the part of the Spaniards, was directed against the column of Ribas, who, however, routed Gen. Monteverde at Lostaguanes, and forced him to shut himself up in Puerto Cabello with the remainder of his troops.

On hearing of Bolivar's approach, Gen. Fierro, the governor of Caracas, sent deputies to propose a capitulation, which was concluded at Vittoria; but Fierro, struck by a sudden panic, and not expecting the return of his own emissaries, secretly decamped in the night, leaving more than 1,500 Spaniards at the discretion of the enemy. Bolivar was now honored with a public triumph. Standing in a triumphal car, drawn by 12 young ladies, dressed in white, adorned with the national colors, and all selected from the first families of Caracas, Bolivar, bareheaded, in full uniform, and wielding a small baton in his hand, was, in about half an hour, dragged from the entrance of the city to his residence. Having proclaimed himself "dictator and liberator of the western provinces of Venezuela"—Mariño had assumed the title of "dictator of the eastern provinces"—he created "the order of the liberator," established a choice corps of troops under the name of his body-guard, and surrounded himself with the show of a court. But, like most of his countrymen, he was averse to any prolonged exertion, and his dictatorship soon proved a military anarchy, leaving the most important affairs in the hands of favorites, who squandered the finances of the country, and then resorted to odious means in order to restore them. The new enthusiasm of the people was thus turned to dissatisfaction, and the scattered forces of the enemy were allowed to recover. While, in the beginning of Aug. 1813, Monteverde was shut up in the fortress of Puerto Cabello, and the Spanish army reduced to the possession of a small strip of land in the north-western part of Venezuela, 4 months later, in December, the liberator's prestige was gone, and Caracas itself threatened, by the sudden appearance in its neighborhood of the victorious Spaniards under Boves. To strengthen his tottering power, Bolivar assembled, Jan. 1, 1814, a junta of the most influential inhabitants of Caracas, declaring himself to be unwilling any longer to bear the burden of dictatorship. Hurtado Mendoza, on the other hand, argued, in a long oration,

"the necessity of leaving the supreme power in the hands of Gen. Bolivar, until the congress of New Granada could meet, and Venezuela be united under one government."[a]

This proposal was accepted, and the dictatorship was thus invested with some sort of legal sanction.

The war with the Spaniards was, for some time, carried on in a series of small actions, with no decisive advantage to either of the contending parties. In June, 1814, Boves marched with his united forces from Calabozo on La Puerta, where the two dictators, Bolivar and Mariño, had formed a junction, met them, and ordered an immediate attack. After some resistance, Bolivar fled toward Caracas, while Mariño disappeared in the direction of Cumana. Puerto Cabello and Valencia fell into the hands of Boves, who then detached 2 columns (1 of them under the command of Col. Gonzales), by different roads, upon Caracas. Ribas tried in vain to oppose the advance of Gonzales. On the surrender of Caracas to Gonzales, July 17, 1814, Bolivar evacuated La Guayra, ordered the vessels lying in the harbor of that town to sail for Cumana, and retreated with the remainder of his troops upon Barcelona. After a defeat inflicted on the insurgents by Boves, Aug. 8, 1814, at Arguita, Bolivar left his troops the same night secretly to hasten, through by-roads, to Cumana, where, despite the angry protests of Ribas, he at once embarked on board the *Bianchi*, together with Mariño and some other officers. If Ribas, Paez, and other generals had followed the dictators in their flight,

---

[a] Quoted from Ducoudray Holstein, *Memoirs of Simon Bolivar,* Vol. I, pp. 170-71.— *Ed.*

every thing would have been lost. Treated by Gen. Arismendi, on their arrival at Juan Griego, in the island of Margarita, as deserters, and ordered to depart, they sailed for Carupano, whence, meeting with a similar reception on the part of Col. Bermúdez, they steered toward Carthagena. There, to palliate their flight, they published a justificatory memoir,[a] in high-sounding phraseology.

Having joined a plot for the overthrow of the government of Carthagena, Bolivar had to leave that little republic, and proceeded to Tunja, where the congress of the federalist republic of New Granada was sitting.[283] At that time the province of Cundinamarca stood at the head of the independent provinces which refused to adopt the Granadian federal compact, while Quito, Pasto, Santa Martha, and other provinces, still remained in the power of the Spaniards. Bolivar, who arrived at Tunja Nov. 22, 1814, was created by the congress commander-in-chief of the federalist forces, and received the double mission of forcing the president of the province of Cundinamarca to acknowledge the authority of the congress, and of then marching against Santa Martha, the only fortified seaport the Spaniards still retained in New Granada. The first point was easily carried, Bogota, the capital of the disaffected province, being a defenceless town. In spite of its capitulation, Bolivar allowed it to be sacked during 48 hours by his troops. At Santa Martha, the Spanish general Montalvo, having a feeble garrison of less than 200 men, and a fortress in a miserable state of defence, had already bespoken a French vessel, in order to secure his own flight, while the inhabitants of the town sent word to Bolivar that on his appearance they would open the gates and drive out the garrison. But instead of marching, as he was ordered by the congress, against the Spaniards at Santa Martha, he indulged his rancor against Castillo, the commander of Carthagena, took upon himself to lead his troops against the latter town, which constituted an integral part of the federal republic. Beaten back, he encamped upon La Papa, a large hill, about gun-shot distance from Carthagena, and established a single small cannon as a battery against a place provided with about 80 guns. He afterward converted the siege into a blockade, which lasted till the beginning of May without any other result than that of reducing his army, by desertion and malady, from 2,400 men to about 700. Meanwhile a great Spanish expedition from Cadiz had arrived, March 25, 1815,

---

[a] On September 30, 1814.— *Ed.*

under Gen. Morillo, at the island of Margarita, and had been able
to throw powerful reenforcements into Santa Martha, and soon
after to take Carthagena itself. Previously, however, Bolivar had
embarked for Jamaica, May 10, 1815, with about a dozen of his
officers, on an armed English brig. Having arrived at the place of
refuge, he again published a proclamation,[a] representing himself
as the victim of some secret enemy or faction, and defending his
flight before the approaching Spaniards as a resignation of
command out of deference for the public peace.

During his 8 months' stay at Kingston, the generals he had left
in Venezuela, and Gen. Arismendi in the island of Margarita,
stanchly held their ground against the Spanish arms. But Ribas,
from whom Bolivar had derived his reputation, having been shot
by the Spaniards after the capture of Maturin, there appeared in
his stead another man on the stage, of still greater abilities, who,
being as a foreigner unable to play an independent part in the
South American revolution, finally resolved to act under Bolivar.
This was Louis Brion. To bring aid to the revolutionists, he had
sailed from London for Carthagena with a corvette of 24 guns,
equipped in great part at his own expense, with 14,000 stand of
arms and a great quantity of military stores. Arriving too late to be
useful in that quarter, he reembarked for Cayes, in Hayti,[284]
whither many emigrant patriots had repaired after the surrender
of Carthagena. Bolivar, meanwhile, had also departed from
Kingston to Porte au Prince, where, on his promise of emancipat-
ing the slaves, Pétion, the president of Hayti, offered him large
supplies for a new expedition against the Spaniards in Venezuela.
At Cayes he met Brion and the other emigrants, and in a general
meeting proposed himself as the chief of the new expedition, on
the condition of uniting the civil and military power in his person
until the assembling of a general congress. The majority accepting
his terms, the expedition sailed April 16, 1816, with him as its
commander and Brion as its admiral. At Margarita the former
succeeded in winning over Arismendi, the commander of the
island, in which he had reduced the Spaniards to the single spot of
Pampatar. On Bolivar's formal promise to convoke a national
congress at Venezuela, as soon as he should be master of the
country, Arismendi summoned a junta in the cathedral of La Villa
del Norte, and publicly proclaimed him the commander-in-chief of
the republics of Venezuela and New Granada. On May 31, 1816,
Bolivar landed at Carupano, but did not dare prevent Mariño and

---

[a] On May 9, 1815.— Ed.

Piar from separating from him, and carrying on a war against
Cumana under their own auspices. Weakened by this separation,
he set sail, on Brion's advice, for Ocumare, where he arrived July
3, 1816, with 13 vessels, of which 7 only were armed. His army
mustered but 650 men, swelled, by the enrolment of negroes
whose emancipation he had proclaimed, to about 800. At
Ocumare he again issued a proclamation, promising

> "to exterminate the tyrants" and to "convoke the people to name their deputies
> to congress." [a]

On his advance in the direction of Valencia he met, not far
from Ocumare, the Spanish general Morales at the head of about
200 soldiers and 100 militia men. The skirmishers of Morales
having dispersed his advanced guard, he lost, as an eye-witness
records,

> "all presence of mind, spoke not a word, turned his horse quickly round, and
> fled in full speed toward Ocumare, passed the village at full gallop, arrived at the
> neighboring bay, jumped from his horse, got into a boat, and embarked on the
> *Diana*, ordering the whole squadron to follow him to the little island of Buen Ayre,
> and leaving all his companions without any means of assistance." [b]

On Brion's rebukes and admonitions, he again joined the other
commanders on the coast of Cumana, but being harshly received,
and threatened by Piar with trial before a court-martial as a
deserter and a coward, he quickly retraced his steps to Cayes.
After months of exertion, Brion at length succeeded in persuading
a majority of the Venezuelan military chiefs, who felt the want of
at least a nominal centre, to recall Bolivar as their general-in-chief,
upon the express condition that he should assemble a congress,
and not meddle with the civil administration. Dec. 31, 1816, he
arrived at Barcelona with the arms, munitions of war, and
provisions supplied by Pétion. Joined, Jan. 2, 1817, by Arismendi,
he proclaimed on the 4th martial law and the union of all powers
in his single person; but 5 days later, when Arismendi had fallen
into an ambush laid by the Spaniards, the dictator fled to
Barcelona. The troops rallied at the latter place, whither Brion
sent him also guns and reenforcements, so that he soon mustered
a new corps of 1,100 men. April 5, the Spaniards took possession
of the town of Barcelona, and the patriot troops retreated toward
the charity-house, a building isolated from Barcelona, and

---

[a] This quotation from Bolivar's proclamation of July 6, 1816, "To the
Inhabitants of Venezuela", is given according to Ducoudray Holstein's book, op.
cit., Vol. II, p. 6.— *Ed.*

[b] Ducoudray Holstein, op. cit., Vol. II, pp. 10-11.— *Ed.*

intrenched on Bolivar's order, but unfit to shelter a garrison of 1,000 men from a serious attack. He left the post in the night of April 5, informing Col. Freites, to whom he transferred his command, that he was going in search of more troops, and would soon return. Trusting this promise, Freites declined the offer of a capitulation, and, after the assault, was slaughtered with the whole garrison by the Spaniards.

Piar, a man of color and native of Curaçao, conceived and executed the conquest of the provinces of Guiana; Admiral Brion supporting that enterprise with his gun-boats. July 20, the whole of the provinces being evacuated by the Spaniards, Piar, Brion, Zea, Mariño, Arismendi, and others, assembled a provincial congress at Angostura, and put at the head of the executive a triumvirate, of which Brion, hating Piar and deeply interested in Bolivar, in whose success he had embarked his large private fortune, contrived that the latter should be appointed a member, notwithstanding his absence. On these tidings Bolivar left his retreat for Angostura, where, emboldened by Brion, he dissolved the congress and the triumvirate, to replace them by a "supreme council of the nation," with himself as the chief, Brion and Antonio Francisco Zea as the directors, the former of the military, the latter of the political section. However, Piar, the conqueror of Guiana, who once before had threatened to try him before a court-martial as a deserter, was not sparing of his sarcasms against the "Napoleon of the retreat," and Bolivar consequently accepted a plan for getting rid of him. On the false accusation of having conspired against the whites, plotted against Bolivar's life, and aspired to the supreme power, Piar was arraigned before a war council under the presidency of Brion, convicted, condemned to death, and shot, Oct. 16, 1817. His death struck Mariño with terror. Fully aware of his own nothingness when deprived of Piar, he, in a most abject letter, publicly calumniated his murdered friend, deprecated his own attempts at rivalry with the liberator, and threw himself upon Bolivar's inexhaustible fund of magnanimity.

The conquest by Piar of Guiana had completely changed the situation in favor of the patriots; that single province affording them more resources than all the other 7 provinces of Venezuela together. A new campaign, announced by Bolivar through a new proclamation,[a] was, therefore, generally expected to result in the

---

[a] The proclamation of February 7, 1818 entitled "To the Inhabitants of the Plains". The proclamation and a passage from it that follows below are quoted from Ducoudray Holstein's book, op. cit., Vol. II, pp. 74-75.— Ed.

final expulsion of the Spaniards. This first bulletin, which described some small Spanish foraging parties withdrawing from Calabozo as "armies flying before our victorious troops," was not calculated to damp these hopes. Against about 4,000 Spaniards, whose junction had not yet been effected by Morillo, he mustered more than 9,000 men, well armed, equipped, and amply furnished with all the necessaries of war. Nevertheless, toward the end of May, 1818, he had lost about a dozen battles and all the provinces lying on the northern side of the Orinoco. Scattering as he did his superior forces, they were always beaten in detail. Leaving the conduct of the war to Paez and his other subordinates, he retired to Angostura. Defection followed upon defection, and every thing seemed to be drifting to utter ruin. At this most critical moment, a new combination of fortunate accidents again changed the face of affairs. At Angostura he met with Santander, a native of New Granada, who begged for the means of invading that territory, where the population were prepared for a general rise against the Spaniards. This request, to some extent, he complied with, while powerful succors in men, vessels, and munitions of war, poured in from England, and English, French, German, and Polish officers, flocked to Angostura. Lastly, Dr. German Roscio, dismayed at the declining fortune of the South American revolution, stepped forward, laid hold of Bolivar's mind, and induced him to convene, Feb. 15, 1819, a national congress, the mere name of which proved powerful enough to create a new army of about 14,000 men, so that Bolivar found himself enabled to resume the offensive.

The foreign officers suggested to him the plan of making a display of an intention to attack Caracas, and free Venezuela from the Spanish yoke, and thus inducing Morillo to weaken New Granada and concentrate his forces upon Venezuela, while he (Bolivar) should suddenly turn to the west, unite with Santander's guerillas, and march upon Bogota. To execute this plan, he left Angostura Feb. 24, 1819, after having nominated Zea president of the congress and vice-president of the republic during his absence. By the manoeuvres of Paez, Morillo and La Torre were routed at Achaguas, and would have been destroyed if Bolivar had effected a junction between his own troops and those of Paez and Mariño. At all events, the victories of Paez led to the occupation of the province of Barima, which opened to Bolivar the way into New Granada. Every thing being here prepared by Santander, the foreign troops, consisting mainly of Englishmen, decided the fate of New Granada by the successive victories won July 1 and 23, and

Aug. 7, in the province of Tunja.[285] Aug. 12, Bolivar made a triumphal entry into Bogota, while the Spaniards, all the Granadian provinces having risen against them, shut themselves up in the fortified town of Mompox.

Having regulated the Granadian congress at Bogota, and installed Gen. Santander as commander-in-chief, Bolivar marched toward Pamplona, where he spent about 2 months in festivals and balls. Nov. 3, he arrived at Montecal, in Venezuela, whither he had directed the patriotic chieftains of that territory to assemble with their troops. With a treasury of about $2,000,000, raised from the inhabitants of New Granada by forced contributions, and with a disposable force of about 9,000 men, the 3d part of whom consisted of well disciplined English, Irish, Hanoverians, and other foreigners, he had now to encounter an enemy stripped of all resources and reduced to a nominal force of about 4,500 men, $2/3$ of whom were natives, and, therefore, not to be relied upon by the Spaniards. Morillo withdrawing from San Fernando de Apure to San Carlos, Bolivar followed him up to Calabozo, so that the hostile head-quarters were only 2 days' march from each other. If Bolivar had boldly advanced, the Spaniards would have been crushed by his European troops alone, but he preferred protracting the war for 5 years longer.

In October, 1819, the congress of Angostura had forced Zea, his nominee, to resign his office, and chosen Arismendi in his place. On receiving this news, Bolivar suddenly marched his foreign legion toward Angostura, surprised Arismendi, who had 600 natives only, exiled him to the island of Margarita, and restored Zea to his dignities. Dr. Roscio, fascinating him with the prospects of centralized power, led him to proclaim the "republic of Colombia," comprising New Granada and Venezuela, to publish a fundamental law for the new state, drawn up by Roscio, and to consent to the establishment of a common congress for both provinces. On Jan. 20, 1820, he had again returned to San Fernando de Apure. His sudden withdrawal of the foreign legion, which was more dreaded by the Spaniards than 10 times the number of Colombians, had given Morillo a new opportunity to collect reenforcements, while the tidings of a formidable expedition to start from Spain under O'Donnell raised the sinking spirits of the Spanish party. Notwithstanding his vastly superior forces, Bolivar contrived to accomplish nothing during the campaign of 1820. Meanwhile the news arrived from Europe that the revolution in the Isla de Leon[286] had put a forcible end to O'Donnell's intended expedition. In New Granada 15 provinces out of 22 had joined the government of Colombia, and the Spaniards now held there only the fortresses of Carthagena and the isthmus of Panama. In Venezuela 6 provinces out of 8 obeyed the laws of Colombia. Such was the state of things when Bolivar allowed himself to be inveigled by Morillo into negotiations resulting, Nov. 25, 1820, in the conclusion at Truxillo of a truce for 6 months. In the truce no mention was made of the republic of Colombia, although the congress had expressly forbidden any treaty to be concluded with the Spanish commander before the acknowledgment on his part of the independence of the republic.

Dec. 17, Morillo, anxious to play his part in Spain, embarked at Puerto Cabello, leaving the command-in-chief to Miguel de la Torre, and on March 10, 1821, Bolivar notified La Torre, by letter, that hostilities should recommence at the expiration of 30 days. The Spaniards had taken a strong position at Carabobo, a village situated about half-way betwen San Carlos and Valencia; but La Torre, instead of uniting there all his forces, had concentrated only his 1st division, 2,500 infantry and about 1,500 cavalry, while Bolivar had about 6,000 infantry, among them the British legion, mustering 1,100 men, and 3,000 llaneros[287] on horseback, under Paez. The enemy's position seemed so formidable to Bolivar, that he proposed to his council of war to make a new armistice, which, however, was rejected by his subalterns. At the head of a column mainly consisting of the British legion, Paez turned through a footpath the right wing of the enemy, after the successful execution of which manoeuvre, La Torre was the first of the Spaniards to run away, taking no rest till he reached Puerto Cabello, where he shut himself up with the remainder of his troops. Puerto Cabello itself must have surrendered on a quick advance of the victorious army, but Bolivar lost his time in exhibiting himself at Valencia and Caracas. Sept. 21, 1821, the strong fortress of Carthagena capitulated to Santander. The last feats of arms in Venezuela, the naval action at Maracaibo, in Aug. 1823, and the forced surrender of Puerto Cabello, July, 1824, were both the work of Padilla. The revolution of the Isla de Leon, which prevented O'Donnell's expedition from starting, and the assistance of the British legion, had evidently turned the scale in favor of the Colombians.

The Colombian congress opened its sittings in Jan. 1821, at Cucuta, published, Aug. 30, a new constitution, and after Bolivar had again pretended to resign, renewed his powers. Having signed the new constitution, he obtained leave to undertake the campaign of Quito (1822), to which province the Spaniards had retired after their ejection by a general rising of the people from the isthmus of Panama.[288] This campaign, ending in the incorporation of Quito, Pasto, and Guayaquil into Colombia, was nominally led by Bolivar and Gen. Sucre, but the few successes of the corps were entirely owed to British officers, such as Col. Sands. During the campaigns of 1823-'24, against the Spaniards in upper and lower Peru,[a] he no longer thought it necessary to keep up the appearance of generalship, but leaving the whole military task to Gen. Sucre, limited himself to triumphal entries, manifestos, and the proclamation of constitutions. Through his Colombian body-guard, he swayed the votes of the congress of Lima, which, Feb. 10, 1823, transferred to him the dictatorship, while he secured his reelection as president of Colombia by a new tender of resignation. His position had meanwhile become strengthened, what with the formal recognition of the new state on the part of England, what with Sucre's conquest of the provinces of upper Peru, which the latter united into an independent republic, under the name of Bolivia. Here, where Sucre's bayonets were supreme, Bolivar gave full scope to his propensities for arbitrary power, by introducing the "Bolivian Code," an imitation of the *Code Napoléon*.[289] It was his plan to transplant that code from Bolivia to Peru, and from Peru to Colombia—to keep the former states in check by Colombian troops, and the latter by the foreign legion and Peruvian soldiers. By force, mingled with intrigue, he succeeded indeed, for some weeks at least, in fastening his code upon Peru. The president and liberator of Colombia, the protector and dictator of Peru, and the godfather of Bolivia, he had now reached the climax of his renown. But a serious antagonism had broken out in Colombia, between the centralists or Bolivarists and the federalists, under which latter name the enemies of military anarchy had coalesced with his military rivals. The Colombian congress having, at his instigation, proposed an act of accusation against Paez, the vice-president of Venezuela, the latter broke out into open revolt, secretly sustained and pushed on by Bolivar himself, who wanted insurrections, to furnish him a pretext for overthrowing the constitution and reassuming the dictatorship. Beside his body-guard, he led, on his return from Peru, 1,800 Peruvians, ostensibly against the federalist rebels. At Puerto Cabello, however, where he met Paez, he not only confirmed him in his command of Venezuela, and issued a proclamation of amnesty to all the rebels, but openly took their part and rebuked

---

[a] See this volume, pp. 170-71.— *Ed.*

the friends of the constitution; and by decree at Bogota, Nov. 23, 1826, he assumed dictatorial powers.

In the year 1826, from which the decline of his power dates, he contrived to assemble a congress at Panama, with the ostensible object of establishing a new democratic international code.[290] Plenipotentiaries came from Colombia, Brazil, La Plata, Bolivia, Mexico, Guatemala, &c. What he really aimed at was the erection of the whole of South America into one federative republic, with himself as its dictator. While thus giving full scope to his dreams of attaching half a world to his name, his real power was rapidly slipping from his grasp. The Colombian troops in Peru, informed of his making arrangements for the introduction of the Bolivian code, promoted a violent insurrection. The Peruvians elected Gen. Lamar as the president of their republic, assisted the Bolivians in driving out the Colombian troops, and even waged a victorious war against Colombia, which ended in a treaty reducing the latter to its primitive limits, stipulating the equality of the 2 countries, and separating their debts.[291] The congress of Ocaña, convoked by Bolivar, with a view to modify the constitution in favor of his arbitrary power, was opened March 2, 1828, by an elaborate address, insisting on the necessity of new privileges for the executive. When, however, it became evident that the amended project of the constitution would come out of the convention quite different from its original form, his friends vacated their seats, by which proceeding the body was left without a quorum, and thus became extinct. From a country-seat, some miles distant from Ocaña, to which he had retreated, he published another manifesto,[a] pretending to be incensed at the step taken by his own friends, but at the same time attacking the convention, calling on the provinces to recur to extraordinary measures, and declaring that he was ready to submit to any load of power which might be heaped upon him. Under the pressure of his bayonets, popular assemblies at Caracas, Carthagena, and Bogota, to which latter place he had repaired, anew invested him with dictatorial power. An attempt to assassinate him in his sleeping room at Bogota, which he escaped only by leaping in the dark from the balcony of the window, and lying concealed under a bridge, allowed him for some time to introduce a sort of military terrorism. He did not, however, lay hands on Santander, although he had participated in the conspiracy, while he put to death Gen. Padilla, whose guilt was not proved at all, but who, as a man of color, was not able to resist.

---

[a] On June 12, 1828.—*Ed.*

Violent factions disturbing the republic in 1829, in a new appeal to the citizens,[a] Bolivar invited them to frankly express their wishes as to the modifications to be introduced into the constitution. An assembly of notables at Caracas answered by denouncing his ambition, laying bare the weakness of his administration, declaring the separation of Venezuela from Colombia, and placing Paez at the head of that republic. The senate of Colombia stood by Bolivar, but other insurrections broke out at different points. Having resigned for the 5th time, in Jan. 1830, he again accepted the presidency, and left Bogota to wage war on Paez in the name of the Colombian congress. Toward the end of March, 1830, he advanced at the head of 8,000 men, took Caracuta, which had revolted, and then turned upon the province of Maracaibo, where Paez awaited him with 12,000 men, in a strong position. As soon as he became aware that Paez meant serious fighting, his courage collapsed. For a moment he even thought to subject himself to Paez, and declare against the congress; but the influence of his partisans at the congress vanished, and he was forced to tender his resignation, notice being given to him that he must now stand by it, and that an annual pension would be granted to him on the condition of his departure for foreign countries. He accordingly sent his resignation to the congress, April 27, 1830. But hoping to regain power by the influence of his partisans, and a reaction setting in against Joachim Mosquera, the new president of Colombia, he effected his retreat from Bogota in a very slow manner, and contrived, under a variety of pretexts, to prolong his sojourn at San Pedro, until the end of 1830, when he suddenly died.

The following is the portrait given of him by Ducoudray Holstein:

"Simon Bolivar is 5 feet 4 inches in height, his visage is long, his cheeks hollow, his complexion livid brown; his eyes are of a middle size, and sunk deep in his head, which is covered thinly with hair. His mustaches give him a dark and wild aspect, particularly when he is in a passion. His whole body is thin and meagre. He has the appearance of a man 65 years old. In walking, his arms are in continual motion. He cannot walk long, but becomes soon fatigued. He likes his hammock, where he sits or lolls. He gives way to sudden gusts of resentment, and becomes in a moment a madman, throws himself into his hammock, and utters curses and imprecations upon all around him. He likes to indulge in sarcasms upon absent persons, reads only light French literature, is a bold rider, and passionately fond of waltzing. He is fond of hearing himself talk and giving toasts. In adversity, and destitute of aid from without, he is perfectly free from passion and violence of temper. He then becomes mild, patient, docile, and even submissive. In a great

---

[a] Of January 20, 1830.— Ed.

measure he conceals his faults under the politeness of a man educated in the so-called *beau monde,* possesses an almost Asiatic talent for dissimulation, and understands mankind better than the mass of his countrymen."[a]

By decree of the congress of New Granada, his remains were removed in 1842 to Caracas, and a monument erected there in his honor.

See *Histoire de Bolivar, par le Gén. Ducoudray Holstein; continuée jusqu'a sa mort par Alphonse Viollet* (Paris, 1831), *Memoirs of Gen. John Miller (in the service of the Republic of Peru)*[292]; Col. Hippisley's "Account of his Journey to the Orinoco" (Lond. 1819).

Written between December 1857 and January 8, 1858

First published in *The New American Cyclopaedia,* Vol. III, 1858

Reproduced from *The New American Cyclopaedia*

---

[a] op. cit., Vol. I, pp. 232-36.— *Ed.*

Frederick Engels

CAMPAIGN[293]

This term is very often used to denote the military operations which are carried on during a war within a single year; but if these operations take place on 2 or more independent seats of war, it would be scarcely logical to comprise the whole of them under the head of one campaign. Thus what may be loosely called the campaign of 1800 comprises 2 distinct campaigns, conducted each quite independently of the other: the campaign of Italy (Marengo), and the campaign of Germany (Hohenlinden).[294] On the other hand, since the almost total disuse of winter quarters, the end of the year does not always mark the boundary between the close of one distinct series of warlike operations and the commencement of another. There are nowadays many other military and political considerations far more important in war than the change of the seasons. Thus each of the campaigns of 1800 consists of 2 distinct portions: a general armistice extending over the time from July to September divides them, and although the campaign of Germany is brought to a close in Dec. 1800, yet that of Italy continues during the first half of Jan. 1801. Clausewitz justly observes that the campaign of 1812 does evidently not end with Dec. 31 of that year, when the French were still on the Niemen, and in full retreat, but with their arrival behind the Elbe in Feb. 1813, where they again collected their forces, the impetus which drove them homeward having ceased.[a] Still, winter remaining always a season during which fatigue and exposure will, in our latitudes, reduce active armies at an excessive rate, a mutual suspension of operations and recruiting of strength

---

[a] C. Clausewitz, *Vom Kriege* (*Hinterlassene Werke*, Bd. 2, 1833, S. 6).—*Ed.*

very often coincide with that time of the year; and although a campaign, in the strict sense of the word, means a series of warlike operations closely connected together by one strategical plan and directed toward one strategetical object, campaigns may still in most cases very conveniently be named by the year in which their decisive actions are fought.

Written between January 1 and 8, 1858

First published in *The New American Cyclopaedia*, Vol. IV, 1859

Reproduced from *The New American Cyclopaedia*

Frederick Engels

CANNONADE

Cannonade, in a general sense, the act of firing artillery during a battle or a siege. As a technical expression in tactics, a cannonade means an engagement between 2 armies in which the artillery alone is active, and the other arms are either passive or do not, at least, overstep the bounds of mere demonstration. The most celebrated instance of this kind is the cannonade of Valmy, in 1792.[295] Kellermann awaited the attack of the Prussian army on a range of heights, his artillery placed in front of his troops. The Prussians drew up on the opposite range of the hills, brought forward their artillery, and the cannonade began. Several times the Prussian infantry formed for the attack and advanced a little; but, the French remaining firm, the Prussians withdrew again before coming within musket range. Thus the day passed, and the next day the Prussian army began their general retreat. In most general engagements such cannonades occur. They often form the 1st act of the performance; they serve to fill up the intervals between a repulsed attack and another attempt to dislodge the enemy; and they form the *finale* of most drawn battles. In most cases they serve more for purposes of demonstration than for any thing else, causing by a great waste of ammunition at long ranges that almost incredibly small proportion of hits to misses which characterizes the artillery practice of modern battles.

Written before January 8, 1858

First published in *The New American Cyclopaedia,* Vol. IV, 1859

Reproduced from *The New American Cyclopaedia*

Frederick Engels

CAPTAIN

Captain, the rank designating a commander of a company in infantry, or of a squadron or troop in cavalry, or the chief officer of a ship of war. In most continental armies in Europe captains are considered subalterns; in the British army they form an intermediate rank between the field officer and the subaltern, the latter term comprising those commissioned officers only whose rank does not imply a direct and constant command. In the U.S. army the captain is responsible for the arms, ammunition, clothing, &c., of the company under his command. The duties of a captain in the navy are very comprehensive, and his post is one of great responsibility. In the British service he ranks with a lieut.-colonel in the army, until the expiration of 3 years from the date of his commission, when he takes rank with a full colonel. In the old French service he was forbidden to leave his ship under pain of death, and was to blow it up rather than let it fall into the hands of an enemy. The title of captain is also applied to masters of merchant or passenger vessels, and to various petty officers on ships of the line, as captain of the forecastle, of the hold, of the main and fore tops, &c. The word is of Italian origin, meaning a man who is at the head of something, and in this sense it is often used as synonymous with a general-in-chief, especially as regards his qualities for command.

Written before January 8, 1858

First published in *The New American Cyclopaedia,* Vol. IV, 1859

Reproduced from *The New American Cyclopaedia*

Frederick Engels

CARABINE [296]

$Carabine$, or $carbine$, a short barrelled musket adapted to the use of cavalry. In order to admit of its being easily loaded on horseback, the barrel ought not to be more than 2 feet 6 inches long, unless it be breech-loading; and to be easily managed with one hand only, its weight must be less than that of an infantry musket. The bore, too, is in most services rather less than that of the infantry fire-arm. The carabine may have either a smooth or a rifled bore; in the first case, its effect will be considerably inferior to that of the common musket; in the second, it will exceed it in precision for moderate distances. In the British service, the cavalry carry smooth-bored carabines; in the Russian cavalry, the light horse all have rifled carabines, while of the cuirassiers $^1/_4$ have rifled, and the remaining $^3/_4$ smooth barrels to their carabines. The artillery, too, in some services (French and British especially), carry carabines; those of the British are on the principle of the new Enfield rifle.[a] Carabine-firing was at one time the principal mode of cavalry fighting, but now it is principally used on outpost duty, and with cavalry skirmishing. In French military works, the expression $carabine$ always means an infantry rifle, while for a cavalry carabine the word $mousqueton$ is adopted.

Written between January 8 and 22, 1858

First published in The New American Cyclopaedia, Vol. IV, 1859

Reproduced from The New American Cyclopaedia

---

[a] On the Enfield rifle see Engels' work The History of the Rifle in this volume. — Ed.

Frederick Engels

CARCASS

Carcass, a shell filled with inflammable composition, the flame of which issues through 3 or 4 holes, and is so violent that it can scarcely be extinguished. They are thrown from mortars, howitzers, and guns, in the same way as common shells, and burn from 8 to 10 minutes. The composition is either melted over a fire, and poured hot into the shell, or it is worked into a compact mass by the aid of liquid grease, and then crammed into the shell. The fuse holes are stopped with corks or wooden stoppers, through which a tube, filled with fuse-composition, passes into the shell. Formerly these carcasses were cast with a partition or diaphragm, like the present shrapnell shells, the bottom part being destined to receive a bursting charge of gunpowder; but this complication is now done away with. Another kind of carcasses was formerly in use, constructed like a light ball, on two circular iron hoops, crossing each other at right angles, over which canvas was spread, thus forming an imperfectly spheroidal body, which was filled with a similar composition, containing mostly gunpowder and pitch. These carcasses, however, have been abandoned, because their great lightness made it almost impossible to throw them to any distance, or with any precision. The compositions for filling our modern carcasses vary considerably, but they each and all consist chiefly of saltpetre and sulphur, mixed with a resinous or fatty substance. Thus the Prussian service uses 75 parts saltpetre, 25 parts sulphur, 7 parts mealed powder, and 33 parts colophony. The British use saltpetre 100 parts, sulphur 40 parts, rosin 30 parts, antimony 10 parts, tallow 10 parts, turpentine 10 parts. Carcasses are chiefly used in bombardments, and sometimes against shipping, though in this latter use they have been almost entirely superseded by red-hot shot, which is easier prepared, of greater precision and of far more incendiary effect.

Written between January 8 and 22, 1858

First published in *The New American Cyclopaedia*, Vol. IV, 1859

Reproduced from *The New American Cyclopaedia*

Frederick Engels
CARRONADE

Carronade, a short piece of iron ordnance, first constructed at the Carron foundery, Scotland, in 1779, for the use of the British navy, and first employed against the United States.[297] The carronades have no trunnions, but a loop under the middle of the piece, by which they are fastened to the carriage. The bore has a chamber, and the muzzle is scooped out like a cup. They are very short and light, there being about 60 or 70 lbs. of the gun to 1 lb. of the weight of the solid shot, the length varying from 7 to 8 calibres. The charge, consequently, cannot but be weak, and ranges from $^1/_{16}$ to $^1/_8$ the weight of the shot.

Carronades, on their first introduction, found great favor with naval men. Their lightness and insignificant recoil allowed great numbers of them to be placed on board the small men-of-war of those times. Their ranges appeared proportionably great, which was caused: 1, by a reduced windage, and, 2, by their great angle of dispart, arising from the thickness of metal around the breech, and the shortness of the gun; and the great weight of metal projected by them rendered them at close quarters very formidable. They were adopted in the U.S. service about 1800. It was, however, soon discovered that this kind of cannon could not compete with longer and heavier guns, throwing their projectiles with full charge and at low elevations. Thus, it has been ascertained that the common long guns of the British service have at 2° elevation, and the shell guns at 3°, the same range as the carronades of corresponding calibre at 5° (viz., about 1,200 yards). And, as the chance of hitting decreases as the elevation increases, the use of carronades beyond 1,200 yards and an elevation of 5° is completely out of the question; whereas, long guns may with considerable effect be used at ranges up to a mile, and even 2,000 yards. This was strikingly exemplified by the 2 contending squadrons on Lakes Erie and Ontario, during the Anglo-American war of 1812-'14.[298] The American vessels had long guns, while the British were mainly armed with carronades. The Americans manoeuvred so as to keep just out of range of the British carronades, while their own long guns told heavily on the hulls and rigging of their opponents. In consequence of these defects, carronades have now become almost obsolete. On shore they are used by the British, now and then, on the flanks of bastions and in casemates, where but a short extent of ditch is to be flanked by grape principally. The French navy possesses a carronade with trunnions (*carronade à tourillons*); but this is in reality a powerful gun.

Written between January 8 and 22, 1858

First published in *The New American Cyclopaedia*, Vol. IV, 1859

Reproduced from *The New American Cyclopaedia*

Frederick Engels

CARTOUCH

Cartouch (Fr. *cartouche*), in old military works, used sometimes as synonymous with case or grape shot. It is also now and then used to designate the cartridge-box of the infantry soldier.—In architecture and sculpture, a block or modillion in a cornice, and generally an ornament on which there is some device or inscription.

Written between January 8 and 22, 1858

First published in *The New American Cyclopaedia*, Vol. IV, 1859

Reproduced from *The New American Cyclopaedia*

Frederick Engels

CARTRIDGE

Cartridge, a paper, parchment, or flannel case or bag containing the exact quantity of gunpowder used for the charge of a fire-arm, and to which, in some instances, the projectile is attached. Blank cartridge, for small arms, does not contain a bullet; ball cartridge does. In all small-arm cartridge the paper is used as a wad, and rammed down. The cartridge for the French Minié and British Enfield rifle is steeped in grease at one end, so as to facilitate ramming down. That of the Prussian needle gun contains also the fulminating composition exploded by the action of the needle.[a] Cartridges for cannon are generally made of flannel or other light woollen cloth. In some services, those for field service at least have the projectile attached to the cartridge by means of a wooden bottom whenever practicable; and the French have partially introduced this system even into their naval service. The British still have cartridge and shot separated, in field as well as in naval and siege artillery.

An ingenious method of making paper cartridges without seams has been lately introduced into the royal arsenal, Woolwich, England. Metallic cylindrical hollow moulds, just large enough for a cartridge to slip over, are perforated with a multitude of small holes, and being introduced into the soft pulp of which cartridge paper is made, and then connected with an exhausted receiver of an air-pump, are immediately covered with a thin layer of the pulp. This, on being dried, is a complete paper tube. The moulds are arranged many together; and each one is provided with a

---

[a] On the Minié and Enfield rifles and the needle gun see Engels' work *The History of the Rifle* in this volume.— *Ed.*

worsted cover, like the finger of a glove, upon which the pulp collects, and this being taken off with it serves as the lining with which the best cartridges are provided.

A kind of cartridge is in use for sporting pieces, made of a network of wire containing the shot only. It is included in an outer case of paper. The charge of shot is mixed with bone dust to give compactness. When the piece is fired, the shot are carried along to a much greater distance without scattering than if charged in any other way.

Written between January 8 and 22, 1858

First published in *The New American Cyclopaedia*, Vol. IV, 1859

Reproduced from *The New American Cyclopaedia*

Frederick Engels

CASE SHOT

Case shot, or *canister shot*, consists of a number of wrought-iron balls, packed in a tin canister of a cylindrical shape. The balls for field service are regularly deposited in layers, but for most kinds of siege and naval ordnance they are merely thrown into the case until it is filled, when the lid is soldered on. Between the bottom of the canister and the charge a wooden bottom is inserted. The weights of the balls vary with the different kinds of ordnance, and the regulations of each service. The English have, for their heavy naval guns, balls from 8 oz. to 3 lbs.; for their 9-pound field-gun, $1\,^1/_2$ oz. and 5 oz. balls, of which respectively 126 and 41 make up a canister for one discharge. The Prussians use 41 balls, each weighing $^1/_{32}$ of the weight of the corresponding round shot. The French had up to 1854 nearly the same system; how they may have altered it since the introduction of the new howitzer gun, we are unable to tell. For siege and garrison artillery, the balls are sometimes arranged round a spindle projecting from the wooden bottom, either in a bag in the shape of a grape (whence the name grape shot), or in regular layers with round wooden or iron plates between each layer, the whole covered over with a canvas bag.

The most recently introduced kind is the spherical case shot, commonly called from their inventor, the British general Shrapnel, shrapnel shells. They consist of a thin cast-iron shell (from $^1/_3$ to $^3/_4$ inch thickness of iron), with a diaphragm or partition in the middle. The lower compartment is destined to receive a bursting charge, the upper one contains leaden musket balls. A fuse is inserted containing a carefully prepared composition, the accuracy of whose burning off can be depended upon. A composition is run between the balls, so as to prevent them from shaking. When used in the field, the fuse is cut off to the length required for the distance of the enemy, and inserted into the shell. At from 50 to 70 yards from the enemy the fuse is burnt to the bottom, and explodes the shell, scattering the bullets toward the enemy precisely as if common case shot had been fired on the spot where the shell exploded. The precision of the fuses at present attained in several services is very great, and thus this new projectile enables the gunner to obtain the exact effect of grape at ranges where formerly round shot only could be used. The common case is most destructive up to 200 yards, but may be used up to 500 yards; its effect against advancing lines of infantry or cavalry at close quarters is terrible; against skirmishers it is of little use; against columns round shot is oftener applicable. The spherical case, on the other hand, is most effective at from 600 to 1,400 yards, and with a proper elevation and a long fuse, may be launched at still greater ranges with probability of effect. From its explosion near the enemy, by which the hailstorm of bullets is kept close together, it may successfully be used against troops in almost any but the skirmishing formation. After the introduction of the spherical case shot, it was adopted in almost all European services as soon as a proper fuse composition was invented by each, this forming the only difficulty; and of the great European powers, France is the only one which has not yet succeeded in this particular. Further experiments, accidents, or bribes will, however, no doubt soon place this power in possession of the secret.

Written between January 8 and 22, 1858

First published in *The New American Cyclopaedia*, Vol. IV, 1859

Reproduced from *The New American Cyclopaedia*

Frederick Engels

BERME[299]

Berme, in fortification, a horizontal bank of ground left standing between the upper interior edge of the ditch and the exterior slope of the parapet of a work. It is generally made about 3 feet wide. Its principal object is to strengthen the parapet, and to prevent the earth of which it is composed from rolling down into the ditch, after heavy rain, thaw, &c. It may also serve sometimes as an exterior communication round the works. It is, however, not to be overlooked that the berme serves as a very convenient resting and collecting place for storming and scaling parties, in consequence of which it is entirely done away with in many systems of permanent fortification, and in others protected by a crenellated wall, so as to form a covered line of fire for infantry. In field fortification, or the construction of siege-batteries, with a ditch in front, a berme is generally unavoidable, as the scarp of the ditch is scarcely ever revetted, and without such an intermediate space, both scarp and parapet would soon crumble under the changes of the weather.

Written between January 23 and 29, 1858

First published in *The New American Cyclopaedia*, Vol. III, 1858

Reproduced from *The New American Cyclopaedia*

Frederick Engels

BLENHEIM [300]

Blenheim, or *Blindheim,* a village about 23 miles from Augsburg, in Bavaria, the theatre of a great battle, fought Aug. 13, 1704, between the English and Austrians, under Marlborough and Prince Eugene, and the French and Bavarians, under Marshal Tallard, Marsin, and the elector of Bavaria.[a] The Austrian states being menaced by a direct invasion on the side of Germany, Marlborough marched from Flanders to their assistance. The allies agreed to act on the defensive in Italy, the Netherlands, and the lower Rhine, and to concentrate all their available forces on the Danube. Marlborough, after storming the Bavarian intrenchments on the Schellenberg, passed the Danube, and effected his junction with Eugene, after which both at once marched to attack the enemy. They found him behind the Nebel brook, with the villages of Blenheim and Kitzingen strongly occupied in front of either flank. The French had the right wing, the Bavarians held the left. Their line was nearly 5 miles in extent, each army having its cavalry on its wings, so that a portion of the centre was held by both French and Bavarian cavalry. The position had not yet been properly occupied according to the then prevailing rules of tactics. The mass of the French infantry, 27 battalions, was crammed together in Blenheim, consequently in a position completely helpless for troops organized as they were then, and adapted for line fighting in an open country only. The attack of the Anglo-Austrians, however, surprised them in this dangerous condition, and Marlborough very soon drew all the advantages from it which the occasion offered. Having in vain attacked

---

[a] Maximilian II Maria Emanuel.— *Ed.*

Blenheim, he suddenly drew his main strength toward his centre, and with it broke through the centre of his opponents. Eugene made light work of the thus isolated Bavarians, and undertook the general pursuit, while Marlborough, having completely cut off the retreat of the 18,000 Frenchmen blocked up in Blenheim, compelled them to lay down their arms. Among them was Marshal Tallard. The total loss of the Franco-Bavarians was 30,000 killed, wounded, and prisoners; that of the victors, about 11,000 men. The battle decided the campaign, Bavaria fell into the hands of the Austrians, and the prestige of Louis XIV was gone.

This battle is one of the highest tactical interest, showing very conspicuously the immense difference between the tactics of that time and those of our day. The very circumstance which would now be considered one of the greatest advantages of a defensive position, viz., the having [of] 2 villages in front of the flanks, was with troops of the 18th century the cause of defeat. At that time, infantry was totally unfit for that skirmishing and apparently irregular fighting which now makes a village of masonry houses, occupied by good troops, almost impregnable. This battle is called in France, and on the continent generally, the battle of Höchstädt, from a little town of this name in the vicinity, which was already known to fame by a battle fought there on Sept. 20 of the preceding year.[301]

Written between January 23 and 29, 1858

First published in *The New American Cyclopaedia,* Vol. III, 1858

Reproduced from *The New American Cyclopaedia*

Frederick Engels

BORODINO[302]

Borodino, a village on the left bank of the river Kolotcha, in Russia, about 2 miles above its junction with the Moskva. From this village the Russians name the great battle, in 1812, which decided the possession of Moscow; the French call it the battle of the Moskva, or of Mozhaisk. The battle-field is on the right bank of the Kolotcha. The Russian right wing was covered by that river from its junction with the Moskva to Borodino; the left wing was drawn back, *en potence,* behind a brook and ravine descending from the extreme left, at Utitsa, toward Borodino. Behind this ravine, 2 hills were crowned with incomplete redoubts, or lunettes, that nearest the centre called the Rayevski redoubt, those on the hill toward the left, 3 in number, called the Bagration lunettes. Between these 2 hills, another ravine, called from a village behind it that of Semionovskoye, ran down from the Russian left toward the former ravine, joining it about 1,000 yards before it reached the Kolotcha. The main road to Moscow runs by Borodino; the old road, by Utitsa, to Mozhaisk, in rear of the Russian position. This line, about 9,000 yards in extent, was held by about 130,000 Russians, Borodino being occupied in front of the centre. Gen. Kutusoff was the Russian commander-in-chief; his troops were divided into 2 armies, the larger, under Barclay de Tolly, holding the right and centre, the smaller, under Bagration, occupying the left. The position was very badly chosen; an attack on the left, if successful, turned the right and centre completely; and if Mozhaisk had been reached by the French before the Russian right had retreated, which was possible enough, they would have been hopelessly lost. But Kutusoff, having once rejected the capital position of Tsarevoye Zaimishtche, selected by Barclay, had no other choice.[303]

The French, led by Napoleon in person, were about 125,000 strong: after driving the Russians, Sept. 5, 1812, N. S. (Aug. 24,

O. S.), from some slight intrenchments on their left, they were arranged for battle on the 7th. Napoleon's plan was based upon the errors of Kutusoff; merely observing the Russian centre, he concentrated his forces against their left, which he intended to force, and then cut his way through toward Mozhaisk. Prince Eugène was accordingly ordered to make a false attack upon Borodino, after which Ney and Davout were to assail Bagration and the lunettes named from him, while Poniatowski was to turn the extreme left of the Russians by Utitsa; the battle once well engaged, Prince Eugène was to pass the Kolotcha, and attack the Rayevski lunette. Thus the whole front actually attacked did not exceed in length 5,000 yards, which allowed 26 men to each yard of front, an unprecedented depth of order of battle, which accounts for the terrible losses of the Russians by artillery fire. About day-break Poniatowski advanced against Utitsa, and took it, but his opponent, Tutchkoff, again expelled him; subsequently, Tutchkoff having had to send a division to the support of Bagration, the Poles retook the village. At 6 o'clock Davout attacked the proper left of the Bagration intrenchments. Under a heavy fire from 12-pounders, to which he could oppose only 3 and 4-pounders, he advanced. Half an hour later, Ney attacked the proper right of these lunettes. They were taken and retaken, and a hot and undecided fight followed.

Bagration, however, well observed the great force brought against him, with their powerful reserves, and the French guard in the background. There could be no mistake about the real point of attack. He accordingly called together what troops he could, sending for a division of Rayevski's corps, for another of Tutchkoff's corps, for guards and grenadiers from the army reserve, and requesting Barclay to despatch the whole corps of Baggehufvud. These reenforcements, amounting to more than 30,000 men, were sent at once; from the army reserve alone, he received 17 battalions of guards and grenadiers, and 2 12-pound batteries. They could not, however, be made available on the spot before 10 o'clock, and before this hour Davout and Ney made their second attack against the intrenchments, and took them, driving the Russians over the Semionovskoye ravine. Bagration sent his cuirassiers forward; an irregular struggle of great violence followed, the Russians regaining ground as their reenforcements arrived, but again driven beyond the ravine as soon as Davout engaged his reserve division. The losses on both sides were immense; almost all the general officers were killed or wounded, and Bagration himself was mortally hit. Kutusoff now at last took some part in the battle, sending Dokhturoff to take the command of the left, and his own chief of the staff, Toll, to superintend the arrangements for defence on the spot. A little after 10 the 17 battalions of guards and grenadiers, and the division of Va-siltchikoff, arrived at Semionovskoye; the corps of Baggehufvud was divided, one division being sent to Rayevski, another to Tutchkoff, and the cavalry to the right. The French, in the mean time, continued their attacks; the Westphalian division advanced in the wood toward the head of the ravine, while Gen. Friant passed this ravine, without, however, being able to establish himself there. The Russians now were reenforced ($^{1}/_{2}$ past 10) by the cuirassiers of Borosdin from the army reserve, and a portion of Korff's cavalry; but they were too much shattered to proceed to an attack, and about the same time the French were preparing a vast cavalry charge. On the Russian centre Eugène Beauharnais had taken Borodino at 6 in the morning, and passed over the Kolotcha, driving back the enemy; but he soon returned, and again crossed the river higher up in order to proceed, with the Italian guards, the division of Broussier (Italians), Gérard, Morand, and Grouchy's cavalry, to the attack on Rayevski, and the redoubt bearing his name. Borodino remained occupied. The passage of Beauharnais's troops caused delay; his attack could not begin much before 10 o'clock. The Rayevski redoubt was occupied by the division Paskiewitch, supported on its left by Vasiltchikoff, and having Dokhturoff's corps for a reserve. By 11 o'clock, the redoubt was taken by the French, and the Paskiewitch division completely scattered, and driven from the field of battle. But Vasiltchikoff and Dokhturoff retook the redoubt; the division of Prince Eugene of Württemberg arrived in time, and now Barclay ordered the corps of Ostermann to take position to the rear as a fresh reserve. With this corps the last intact body of Russian infantry was brought within range; there remained now, as a reserve, only 6 battalions of the guard. Eugène Beauharnais, about 12 o'clock, was just going to attack the Rayevski redoubt a second time, when Russian cavalry appeared on the left bank of the Kolotcha.[304] The attack was suspended, and troops were sent to meet them. But the Russians could neither take Borodino, nor pass the marshy bottom of the Voina ravine, and had to retreat by Zodock,[a] without any other result than having to some extent crossed Napoleon's intentions.

---

[a] Engels treats Zodock as a geographical name. Actually it is a distorted form of the Russian word *zadok*, which means *rear, back*, and should here be interpreted as "the back fields" (or "pasture").— *Ed.*

In the mean time, Ney and Davout, posted on the Bagration hill, had maintained a hot fire across the Semionovskoye ravine on the Russian masses. All at once the French cavalry began to move. To the right of Semionovskoye, Nansouty charged the Russian infantry with complete success, until Sievers's cavalry took him in flank and drove him back. To the left, Latour-Maubourg's 3,000 horse advanced in 2 columns; the first, headed by 2 regiments of Saxon cuirassiers, rode twice over 3 Russian grenadier battalions just forming square, but they were also taken in flank by Russian cavalry; a Polish cuirassier regiment completed the destruction of the Russian grenadiers, but they too were driven back to the ravine, where the second column, 2 regiments of Westphalian cuirassiers, and 1 of Polish lancers, repelled the Russians. The ground thus being secured, the infantry of Ney and Davout passed the ravine. Friant occupied Semionovskoye, and the remainder of the Russians who had fought here, grenadiers, guards, and line, were finally driven back and their defeat completed by the French cavalry. They fled in small disorderly bands toward Mozhaisk, and could only be collected late at night; the 3 regiments of guards alone preserved a little order. Thus the French right, after defeating the Russian left, occupied a position directly in rear of the Russian centre as early as 12 o'clock, and then it was that Davout and Ney implored Napoleon to act up to his own system of tactics, and complete the victory, by launching the guards by Semionovskoye on the Russian rear. Napoleon, however, refused, and Ney and Davout, themselves dreadfully shattered, did not venture to advance without reenforcements.

On the Russian side, after Eugène Beauharnais had desisted from the attack on the Rayevski redoubt, Eugene of Württemberg was sent to Semionovskoye, and Ostermann, too, had to change front in that direction so as to cover the rear of the Rayevski hill toward Semionovskoye. When Sorbier, the French chief of artillery, saw these fresh troops, he sent for 36 12-pounders from the artillery of the guard, and formed a battery of 85 guns in front of Semionovskoye. While these guns battered the Russian masses, Murat drew forward the hitherto intact cavalry of Montbrun and the Polish lancers. They surprised Ostermann's troops in the act of deploying, and brought them into great danger, until the cavalry of Kreutz repelled the French horse. The Russian infantry continued to suffer from the artillery fire; but neither party ventured to advance. It was now about 2 o'clock, and Eugène Beauharnais, reassured as to the hostile cavalry on his left, again attacked the Rayevski redoubt. While the infantry attacked it in front, cavalry was sent from Semionovskoye to its rear. After a hard struggle, it remained in the hands of the French; and a little before 3 o'clock the Russians retreated. A general cannonade from both sides followed, but the active fighting was over. Napoleon still refused to launch his guard, and the Russians were allowed to retreat as they liked. The Russians had all their troops engaged, excepting the 2 first regiments of the guards, and even these lost by artillery fire 17 officers and 600 men. Their total loss was 52,000 men, beside slightly wounded and scattered men who soon found their way back; but on the day after the battle their army counted only 52,000 men. The French had all their troops engaged, with the exception of the guards (14,000 infantry, 5,000 cavalry and artillery); they thus beat a decidedly superior number. They were, beside, inferior in artillery, having mostly 3 and 4-pounders, while $^1/_4$ of the Russian guns were 12-pounders, and the rest 6-pounders. The French loss was 30,000 men; they took 40 guns, and only about 1,000 prisoners. If Napoleon had launched his guard, the destruction of the Russian army, according to Gen. Toll, would have been certain.[a] He did not, however, risk this last reserve, the nucleus and mainstay of his army, and thus, perhaps, missed the chance of having peace concluded in Moscow.

The above account, in such of its details as are at variance with those commonly received, is mainly based upon the "Memoirs of Gen. Toll," whom we have mentioned as Kutusoff's chief of the staff. This book contains the best Russian account of the battle, and is indispensable for its correct appreciation.

Written between January 23 and 29, 1858

First published in *The New American Cyclopaedia*, Vol. III, 1858

Reproduced from *The New American Cyclopaedia*

---

[a] See Th. Bernhardi, *Denkwürdigkeiten aus dem Leben des kaiserl. russ. Generals von der Infanterie Carl Friedrich Grafen von Toll*, Bd. 2, S. 117-18. The account of the battle mentioned below is on pp. 58-119 of this book.— *Ed.*

Frederick Engels

BRIDGE-HEAD[305]

Bridge-Head, or *tête-de-pont,* in fortification, a permanent or field work, thrown up at the further end of a bridge in order to protect the bridge, and to enable the party holding it to manoeuvre on both banks of the river. The existence of bridge-heads is indispensable to those extensive modern fortresses situated on large rivers or at the junction of 2 rivers. In such a case the bridge-head is generally formed by a suburb on the opposite side and regularly fortified; thus, Castel is the bridge-head of Mentz, Ehrenbreitstein that of Coblentz, and Deutz that of Cologne. No sooner had the French got possession, during the revolutionary war, of Kehl, than they turned it into a bridge-head for Strasbourg. In England, Gosport may be considered the bridge-head of Portsmouth, although there is no bridge, and though it has other and very important functions to fulfil. As in this latter case, a fortification on the further side of a river or arm of the sea is often called a bridge-head, though there be no bridge; since the fortification, imparting the power of landing troops under its protection and preparing for offensive operations, fulfils the same functions, and comes, strategetically speaking, under the same denomination. In speaking of the position of an army behind a large river, all the posts it holds on its opposite bank are called its bridge-heads, whether they be fortresses, intrenched villages, or regular field works, inasmuch as every one of them admits of the army debouching in safety on the other side. Thus, when Napoleon's retreat from Russia, in 1813, ceased behind the Elbe, Hamburg, Magdeburg, Wittenberg, and Torgau were his bridge-heads on the right bank of that river. In field fortification, bridge-heads are mostly very simple works, consisting of a *bonnet à prêtre*,[a] or sometimes a horn-work or crown-work, open toward the river, and with a redoubt close in front of the bridge. Sometimes a hamlet, a group of farm-houses, or other buildings close to a bridge, may be formed into a sufficient bridge-head by being properly adapted for defence; for, with the present light-infantry tactics, such objects, when at all capable of defence, may be made to offer a resistance as great, or greater, than any field works thrown up according to the rules of the art.

Written in the first half of February 1858

First published in *The New American Cyclopaedia*, Vol. III, 1858

Reproduced from *The New American Cyclopaedia*

---

[a] See this volume, p. 138.— *Ed.*

Frederick Engels

BUDA [306]

Buda, or *Ofen*, a city on the west bank of the Danube, formerly the capital of Hungary, and now that of the circle of Pesth; pop. of the town and its 7 suburbs, including that of Alt Ofen, which was annexed in 1850, 45,653, exclusive of the garrison and the students. It is distant from Vienna, in a straight line, 135 miles S. E., and from Belgrade 200 miles N. W. It was formerly connected with the city of Pesth, which lies on the opposite side of the river, by a bridge of boats, and since 1849 by a suspension bridge 1,250 feet long; a tunnel to connect the bridge with the fortress has been in course of construction since 1852. Buda is about 9 miles in circuit, and built around the Schlossberg, an isolated and shelving rock. Its central and highest part, called the fortress, is the most regular portion of the town, and contains many fine buildings and squares. This fortress is surrounded by walls, from which the several suburbs extend toward the river. The principal edifices of the city are the royal palace, a quadrangular structure 564 feet in length, and containing 203 apartments; the church of the ascension of the virgin, and the garrison church, both Gothic structures; the arsenal, the state palace, and the town hall. Buda contains 12 Roman Catholic churches, a Greek church, and a synagogue, several monasteries and convents, a theatre, and many important military, educational, and benevolent institutions. There are several publishing houses and 3 journals established here. The observatory, with the printing establishment of the university of Pesth,[307] is built upon an eminence to the south of the town, 516 feet above the level of the Mediterranean, and no expense has been spared to furnish it with the best instruments. There are in various parts of the suburbs sulphurous hot springs, and relics remain of baths constructed here by the Romans and Turks, the former tenants of the place. The principal trade of the town is in the wines (chiefly red wines, resembling those of Burgundy) which are produced from the vineyards upon the neighboring heights, to the amount, it is computed, of 4,500,000 gallons annually. There are also cannon founderies, and a few manufactures of silk, velvet, cottons, woollens, and leather. The boats of the Danube steamboat navigation company are built here, giving employment to about 600 persons. Buda is the usual residence of the governor of Hungary, and of the public authorities.

It has been thought that this city occupies the site of the old Aquincum mentioned in the "Itinerary" of Antoninus.[308] During the Hungarian monarchy, Buda was the residence of its kings, by whom it was enlarged and adorned, especially by Matthias the Great. It was taken by the Turks under Solyman the Magnificent in 1526, but was recovered the next year. It fell again into the hands of the Turks in 1529, and remained in their possession till 1686, when it was finally recovered by Charles of Lorraine, and in 1784 was again made the seat of government.

Buda has been beleaguered not less than 20 times in the course of her history. The last siege took place in May, 1849, when the Hungarian army under Görgey had driven back the Austrian troops to the western frontier of the kingdom. Two plans were discussed as to further operations: first, to follow up the advantages gained, by a vigorous pursuit of the enemy on his own ground, to disperse his forces before the Russians, then marching on Hungary, could arrive, and to attempt to revolutionize Vienna; or, to remain on the defensive in front of Comorn, and to detach a strong corps for the siege of Buda, where the Austrians on their retreat had left a garrison. Görgey maintains that this latter plan was insisted on by Kossuth and Klapka[a]; but Klapka professes to know nothing of Kossuth having sent such an order, and denies that he himself ever advised this step.[b] From a comparison of Görgey's and Klapka's writings we must, however, confess that there still remains considerable doubt as to who is to be blamed for the march on Buda, and that the evidence adduced by Klapka is by no means conclusive. Görgey also says that his resolution was further determined by the total want of field-gun ammunition and

---

[a] A. Görgei, *Mein Leben und Wirken in Ungarn in den Jahren 1848 und 1849,* S. 56-59.— *Ed.*

[b] G. Klapka, *Memoiren,* S. 14, 10-11.— *Ed.*

other stores, and by his own conviction that the army would refuse to pass the frontier. At all events, all offensive movements were arrested, and Görgey marched with 30,000 men to Buda. By this move the last chance of saving Hungary was thrown away. The Austrians were allowed to recover from their defeats, to reorganize their forces, and 6 weeks afterward, when the Russians appeared on the borders of Hungary, they again advanced, 127,000 strong, while 2 reserve corps were still forming. Thus, the siege of Buda forms the turning point of the Hungarian war of 1848-'49, and if there ever really were treasonable relations between Görgey and the Austrians, they must have taken place about this time.

The fortress of Buda was but a faint remnant of that ancient stronghold of the Turks, in which they so often had repulsed all attacks of the Hungarian and imperial armies. The ditches and glacis were levelled; there remained but the main ramparts, a work of considerable height, faced with masonry. It formed in its general outline an oblong square, the sides of which were more or less irregularly broken so as to admit of a pretty efficient flanking fire. An intrenchment of recent construction led down from the eastern front to the Danube, and protected the waterworks supplying the fortress with water. The garrison consisted of 4 battalions, about a company of sappers, and the necessary allotment of gunners, under Major-Gen. Hentzi, a brave and resolute officer. Seventy-five guns were mounted on the ramparts. On May 4, after having effected the investment of the place, and after a short cannonade from heavy field-guns, Görgey summoned the garrison to surrender. This being refused, he ordered Kmety to assail the water-works; under the protection of the fire of all disposable guns, his column advanced, but the artillery of the intrenchment, enfilading its line of march, soon drove it back. It was thus proved that an attack by main force would never carry the place, and that an artillery attack was indispensable in order first to form a practicable breach. But there were no guns at hand heavier than 12-pounders, and even for these the ammunition was deficient. After some time, however, 4 24-pounders and 1 18-pounder, and subsequently 6 mortars, arrived from Comorn. A breaching battery was constructed on a height 500 yards from the N. W. angle of the rampart, and began its fire, May 15. Previous to that day, Hentzi had bombarded the town of Pesth[a] without any provocation, or without the chance of deriving any advantage

---

[a] Pesth was bombarded on May 13, 1849.— Ed.

from this proceeding. On the 16th the breach was opened, though scarcely practicable; however, Görgey ordered the assault for the following night, one column to assault the breach, 2 others to escalade the walls, and a 4th, under Kmety, to take the waterworks. The assault was everywhere unsuccessful. The artillery attack was resumed. While the breaching battery completed its work, the palisadings around the waterworks were shattered by 12-pounders, and the interior of the place was bombarded. False attacks were made every night to alarm the garrison. Late on the evening of the 20th another assault was prepared. The 4 columns and their objects of attack remained the same, and before daybreak on the 21st they advanced on the fortress. After a desperate struggle, during which Hentzi himself led the defence of the breach and fell mortally wounded, the breach was carried by the 47th Honved[309] battalion, followed by the 34th, while Kmety stormed the waterworks, and the troops of the 3d army corps under Knezich escaladed the walls near the Vienna gate. A severe fight in the interior of the fortress ensued, but soon the garrison surrendered. Of 3,500 men, about 1,000 were killed, the rest were made prisoners. The Hungarians lost 600 men during the siege.

Written in the first half of February 1858

First published in *The New American Cyclopaedia*, Vol. IV, 1859

Reproduced from *The New American Cyclopaedia*

Frederick Engels

CAMP[310]

Camp, a place of repose for troops, whether for one night or a longer time, and whether in tents, in bivouac, or with any such shelter as may be hastily constructed. Troops are cantoned when distributed among villages, or when placed in huts at the end of a campaign. Barracks are permanent military quarters. Tents were deemed unwholesome by Napoleon, who preferred that the soldier should bivouac, sleeping with his feet toward the fire, and protected from the wind by slight sheds and bowers. Major Sibley, of the American army, has invented a tent which will accommodate 20 cavalry soldiers, with their accoutrements, all sleeping with their feet toward a fire in its centre. Bivouac tents have been introduced into the French service since 1837. They consist of a tissue of cotton cloth impregnated with caoutchouc, and thus made water-proof. Every man carries a portion of this cloth, and the different pieces are rapidly attached together by means of clasps. In the selection of a camp, good water within a convenient distance is essential, as is the proximity of woods for firewood and means of shelter. Good roads, canals, or navigable streams are important to furnish the troops with the necessaries of life, if they are encamped for a long period. The vicinity of swamps or stagnant water is to be avoided. The ground to be suitable for defence must admit of manoeuvres of troops. As far as possible the cavalry and infantry should be established on a single line, the former upon the wings, the latter in the centre. The shelters or huts are arranged, as nearly as the nature of the ground admits, in streets perpendicular to the front, and extending from one end of the camp to the other. In arranging a camp, however, no universal rule can be laid down, but the commander must decide according to circumstances whether to form his army in 1 or 2 lines, and upon the relative positions of infantry, cavalry, and artillery. The guards of camps are: 1, the camp-guard, which serves to keep good order and discipline, prevent desertions, and give the alarm; 2, detachments of infantry and cavalry, denominated pickets, stationed in front and on the flanks, which intercept reconnoitring parties of the enemy, and give timely notice of a hostile approach; and 3, grand guards, or outposts, which are large detachments posted in surrounding villages, farm-houses, or small field works, from which they can watch the movements of the enemy. They should not be so far from the camp as to be beyond succor in case of attack. Immediately after arriving on the ground, the number of men to be furnished for guards and pickets are detailed; the posts to be occupied by them are designated; the places for distribution of provisions mentioned; and, in general, all arrangements made concerning the interior and exterior police and service of the camp.

One of the most ancient camps mentioned in history is that of the Israelites at their exodus from Egypt. It formed a large square, divided for the different tribes, had in the middle the camp of the Levites with the tabernacle,[311] and a principal gate or entrance, which, with an adjacent open space, was at the same time a forum and market-place.[a] But the form, the dimensions, and the intrenchments of the regular military camps of the Hebrews, or their enemies, can scarcely be traced.

The camp of the Greeks before Troy was close upon the sea-shore, to shelter their ships drawn upon the land, divided into separate quarters for the different tribes, and fortified with ramparts fronting the city and the sea, and externally with a high mount of earth, strengthened with wooden towers against the sallies of the besieged. The bravest of their chiefs, as Achilles and Ajax, were posted at the extremities.[b] The camp of the Lacedæmonians was circular, and not without the regular precautions of sentries and videttes.

The Roman camp varied according to the season of the year, the length of time it was to be occupied, the number of legions, as well as the nature of the ground, and other circumstances. A historian of the time of the empire mentions camps of every shape, circular, oblong, &c.[c]; but the regular form of the Roman

---

[a] Numbers, 1:2.— *Ed.*

[b] Homer, *The Iliad.—Ed.*

[c] Flavius Josephus, *The Jewish War*, Book III, Ch. 5. Engels used the German edition, *Des Flavius Josephus Geschichte des jüdischen Krieges,* Stuttgart, 1856, in which the relevant passage occurs on p. 365.— *Ed.*

camp was quadrangular. Its place was determined by augurs and according to the 4 quarters, with the front to the rising sun; it was measured with a gnomon[312]; a square of 700 feet was regarded as sufficient for 20,000 men. It was divided into an upper and lower part, separated by a large open space, and by 2 chief lines (*decumana* and *cardo*), running from E. to W., and from N. to S., and by several streets. It had 4 gates, the principal of which were the decuman and the prætorian, which no soldier could pass without leave, under pain of death, and was surrounded with a rampart, separated by a space of 200 feet from the inner camp, a ditch, and a mound of earth. All these intrenchments were made by the soldiers themselves, who handled the pickaxe and the spade as dexterously as the sword or the lance; they levelled the ground, and fixed the palisades, which they carried along, around the intrenchments into a kind of hedge of irregular points. In the middle of the upper division was the pavilion of the general (*praetorium*), forming a square of 200 feet; around it the *auguraculum*, the *quaestorium*, or quarters of the treasurers of the army, the *forum*, serving as a market and meeting place, and the tents of the *legati*, those of the tribunes opposite their respective legions, and of the commanders of foreign auxiliary troops. In the lower division were the tents of the inferior officers and the legions, the Roman horse, the *triarii*, the *principes*, the *hastati*,[a] &c.; and on the flanks the companies of foreign horse and foot, carefully kept apart. The tents were covered with skins, each containing 10 soldiers, and their *decanus;* the centurions and standard-bearers at the head of their companies. In the space between the 2 divisions, which was called *principia*, were the platform of the general, for the exercise of justice as well as for harangues, the altar, the sacred images, and the not less sacred military ensigns. In exceptional cases the camp was surrounded with a wall of stones, and sometimes even the quarters of the soldiers were of the same material. The whole camp offered the aspect of a city; it was the only fortress the Romans constructed. Among the most permanent memorials of the Roman occupation of Britain is the retention of the Latin *castra* (camp), as, in whole or part, the name of a great number of places first occupied by them as military posts, as Doncaster, Leicester, Worcester, Chester, Winchester, &c.

The camps of the barbarous nations of antiquity were often surrounded with a fortification of wagons and carts, as for

---

[a] See this volume, pp. 97-98.— *Ed.*

instance, that of the Cimbri, in their last battle against the Romans (101 B. C.), which camp was so fiercely defended, after their defeat, by their wives.[313]

An *Intrenched Camp* is a camp surrounded by defensive works, which serves also as a fortification, and is intended accordingly for prolonged use.

Written probably before February 18,1858

First published in *The New American Cyclopaedia*, Vol. IV, 1859

Reproduced from *The New American Cyclopaedia*

Frederick Engels

CATAPULT

Catapult (Gr. κατά, against, and πάλλω, to hurl), an ancient military engine for throwing stones, darts, and other missiles, invented in Syracuse, in the reign of Dionysius the elder. It acted upon the principle of the bow, and consisted of wood frame-work, a part of which was elastic, and furnished with tense cords of hair or muscle. Catapults were of various sizes, being designed either for field-service or bombardments. The largest of them projected beams 6 feet long and weighing 60 lbs. to the distance of 400 paces, and Josephus gives instances of their throwing great stones to the distance of $^1/_4$ of a mile.[a] The Romans employed 300 of them at the siege of Jerusalem.[314] From the time of Julius Caesar it is not distinguished by Latin authors from the *ballista*, which was originally used only for throwing masses of stone.

Written probably before February 18, 1858

First published in *The New American Cyclopaedia*, Vol. IV, 1859

Reproduced from *The New American Cyclopaedia*

---

[a] Flavius Josephus, *The Jewish War*, Book V, Ch. 6. Engels used the German edition, *Des Flavius Josephus Geschichte des jüdischen Krieges*, Stuttgart, 1856, in which the relevant passage occurs on p. 558.— *Ed.*

Frederick Engels

COEHORN[315]

Coehorn, or *Cohorn*, *Menno van*, baron, a Dutch general and engineer, born in Friesland in 1641, died at the Hague, May 17, 1704. At the age of 16 he received a captain's commission, distinguished himself at the siege of Maestricht, and afterward at the battles of Senef, Cassel, St. Denis, and Fleurus.[316] During the intervals of active duty he devoted much attention to the subject of fortification, with the view of equalizing the chances between besiegers and besieged, the new system of his contemporary Vauban having given great advantages to the latter. While comparatively a young man he gained a name as an engineer, and by the time he had reached middle life was recognized as the best officer of that arm in the Dutch service. The prince of Orange promised him a colonelcy, but being rather remiss in fulfilling the pledge, he retired in disgust with the intention of offering his services to the French. His wife and 8 children, however, were arrested by the order of the prince as hostages for his return, which quickly brought him back, whereon he received the promised rank, and was afterward appointed, successively, as general of artillery, director-general of fortifications, and governor of Flanders.

His whole life was spent in connection with the defences of the Low Countries. At the siege of Grave, in 1674, he invented and for the first time made use of the small mortars, called cohorns, for throwing grenades, and in the succeeding year elicited the applause of Vauban by successfully crossing the Meuse, and carrying a bastion which was considered as protected by the river. After the peace of Nimeguen (1678),[317] he was employed in strengthening various already strong places; Nimeguen, Breda, Mannheim, since dismantled, and Bergen-op-Zoom attest the value of his system. The last-named place he considered his masterpiece, although it was taken after a long siege in 1747, by Marshal de Lowendal. During the campaigns from 1688 to 1691,[318] he was in active service. The siege of Namur, in 1692, gave him an opportunity to test his system against that of Vauban, for these two great engineers were there opposed to each other, Coehorn in defending a work which he had constructed to protect the citadel, and Vauban in attempting to reduce it. Coehorn made an obstinate defence, but being dangerously wounded, was compelled to surrender to his rival, who handsomely acknowledged his bravery and skill. He was afterward engaged at the attack on Trarbach, Limburg, and Liège, and in 1695 aided in retaking Namur. In the war of the Spanish succession[319] he besieged successively Venloo, Stephensworth, Ruremonde, Liège, and in 1703 took Bonn, on the Rhine, after 3 days' cannonade of heavy artillery aided by a fire of grenades from 500 cohorns. Next he passed into Dutch Flanders, where he gained several successes over the French, and directed the siege of Huy. This was his last service, for he died soon afterward of apoplexy, while waiting a conference with the duke of Marlborough on the plan of a new campaign.

Coehorn's greatest work, *Nieuwe Vestingbouw*, was published at Leeuwarden, in folio, 1685, and translated into several foreign languages. His plans are mostly adapted to the Dutch fortresses, or to those which are similarly situated on ground but a few feet above water level. Wherever it was practicable, he encircled his works with two ditches, the outermost full of water; the inner dry, and usually of the width of about 125 feet, serving as a *place d'armes* for the besieged, and in some cases for detachments of cavalry. The theory of his system, both of attack and defence, was the superiority of a combined mass over isolated fire. Professionally, Coehorn was accused of wasteful expenditure of life, in which respect he contrasted unfavorably with Vauban, who was sparing of men. Personally, he was blunt, honest, brave, and a hater of adulation. He refused inducements offered by several foreign governments. Charles II of England knighted him. He was buried at Wijkel, near Sneek, in Friesland, and a monument was dedicated there to his memory.

Written probably before February 18, 1858

First published in *The New American Cyclopaedia*, Vol. V, 1859

Reproduced from *The New American Cyclopaedia*

Frederick Engels

BIDASSOA [320]

Bidassoa, a small river of the Basque provinces of Spain, noted for the battles fought upon its banks, between the French under Soult and the English, Spaniards, and Portuguese, under Wellington. After the defeat of Vittoria in 1813,[321] Soult collected his troops in a position, the right of which rested on the sea opposite Fuenterrabia, having the Bidassoa in front, while the centre and left extended across several ridges of hills toward St. Jean de Luz. From this position he once attempted to relieve the blockaded garrison of Pampeluna, but was repulsed. San Sebastian, besieged by Wellington, was now hard pressed, and Soult resolved to raise the siege. From his position of the lower Bidassoa it was but 9 miles to Oyarzun, a village on the road to San Sebastian; and if he could reach that village the siege must be raised. Accordingly, toward the end of Aug. 1813, he concentrated 2 columns on the Bidassoa. The one on the left, under Gen. Clausel, consisting of 20,000 men and 29 guns, took a position on a ridge of hills opposite Vera (a place beyond which the upper course of the river was in the hands of the allies), while Gen. Reille with 18,000 men, and a reserve of 7,000 under Foy, took his station lower down, near the road from Bayonne to Irun. The French intrenched camp to the rear was held by d'Erlon with 2 divisions, to ward off any turning movement of the allied right.

Wellington had been informed of Soult's plan, and had taken every precaution. The extreme left of his position, sheltered in front by the tidal estuary of the Bidassoa, was well intrenched, though but slightly occupied; the centre, formed by the extremely strong and rugged ridges of San Marcial, was strengthened with field-works, and held by Freire's Spaniards, the lst British division standing as a reserve on their left rear near the Irun road. The right wing, on the rocky descents of the Peña de Haya mountain, was held by Longa's Spaniards and the 4th Anglo-Portuguese division; Inglis's brigade of the 7th division connecting it with the light division at Vera, and with the troops detached still further to the right among the hills. Soult's plan was, that Reille should take San Marcial (which he intended forming into a bridge-head for ulterior operations), and drive the allies toward their right, into the ravines of Peña de Haya, thus clearing the high road for Foy, who was to advance along it straight on Oyarzun, while Clausel, after leaving a division to observe Vera, should pass the Bidassoa a little below that place, and drive whatever troops opposed him up the Peña de Haya, thus seconding and flanking Reille's attack.

On the morning of Aug. 31, Reille's troops forded the river in several columns, carried the first ridge of San Marcial with a rush, and advanced toward the higher and commanding ridges of that group of hills. But in this difficult ground his troops, imperfectly managed, got into disorder; skirmishers and supports became mingled, and in some places crowded together in disordered groups, when the Spanish columns rushed down the hill and drove them back to the river. A second attack was at first more successful, and brought the French up to the Spanish position; but then its force was spent, and another advance of the Spaniards drove them back into the Bidassoa in great disorder. Soult having learned in the mean time that Clausel had made good his attack, slowly conquering ground on Peña de Haya, and driving Portuguese, Spaniards, and British before him, was just forming columns out of Reille's reserves and Foy's troops for a third and final attack, when news came that d'Erlon had been attacked in his camp by strong forces. Wellington, as soon as the concentration of the French on the lower Bidassoa left no longer any doubt of the real point of attack, had ordered all troops in the hills on his extreme right to attack whatever was before them. This attack, though repulsed, was very serious, and might possibly be renewed. At the same time, a portion of the British light division was drawn up on the left bank of the Bidassoa so as to flank Clausel's advance. Soult now gave up the intended attack, and drew Reille's troops back across the Bidassoa. Those of Clausel were not extricated till late in the night, and after a severe struggle to force the bridge at Vera, the fords having become impassable by a heavy fall of rain on the same day, the allies took San Sebastian, except the citadel, by storm, and this latter post surrendered on Sept. 9.

The second battle of the Bidassoa took place Oct. 7, when

BATTLES OF THE BIDASSOA, AUGUST 31 AND OCTOBER 7, 1813

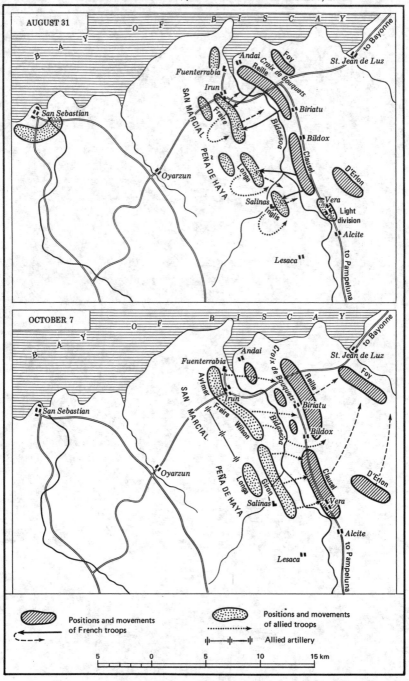

AUGUST 31

to Bayonne
B · A · Y · O · F · B · I · S · C · A · Y
St. Jean de Luz
Andai
Foy
Croix de Bouquets
Reille
Fuenterrabia
Irun
SAN MARCIAL
Freire
Biriatu
Bidassoa
Bildox
San Sebastian
Clausel
D'Erlon
PEÑA DE HAYA
Longa
Oyarzun
Salinas
Vera
Inglis
Light division
Alcite
Lesaca
to Pampeluna

OCTOBER 7

to Bayonne
B · A · Y · O · F · B · I · S · C · A · Y
St. Jean de Luz
Andai
Fuenterrabia
Croix de Bouquets
Foy
SAN
Aylmer
Reille
Irun
Freire
Biriatu
MARCIAL
Wilson
Bidassoa
Bildox
San Sebastian
Clausel
D'Erlon
PEÑA DE HAYA
Oyarzun
Longa
Girón
Salinas
Vera
Alcite
Lesaca
to Pampeluna

Positions and movements
of French troops

Positions and movements
of allied troops

Allied artillery

5   0   5   10   15 km

Wellington forced the passage of that river. Soult's position was about the same as before; Foy held the intrenched camp of St. Jean de Luz, d'Erlon held Urdax and the camp of Ainhoa, Clausel was posted on a ridge connecting Urdax with the lower Bidassoa, and Reille stood along that river from Clausel's right down to the sea. The whole front was intrenched, and the French were still employed in strengthening their works. The British right stood opposed to Foy and d'Erlon; the centre, composed of Girón's Spaniards and the light division, with Longa's Spaniards and the 4th division in reserve, in all 20,000 men, faced Clausel; while on the lower Bidassoa Freire's Spaniards, the 1st and 5th Anglo-Portuguese divisions, and the unattached brigade of Aylmer and Wilson, in all 24,000 men, were ready to attack Reille. Wellington prepared every thing for a surprise. His troops were drawn up well sheltered from the view of the enemy during the night before Oct. 7, and the tents of his camp were not struck. Beside, he had been informed by smugglers of the locality of 3 fords in the tidal estuary of the Bidassoa, all passable at low water, and unknown to the French, who considered themselves perfectly safe on that side.

On the morning of the 7th, while the French reserves were encamped far to the rear, and of the one division placed in 1st line many men were told off to work at the redoubts, the 5th British division and Aylmer's brigade forded the tidal estuary, and marched toward the intrenched camp called the Sansculottes. As soon as they had passed to the other side, the guns from San Marcial opened, and 5 more columns advanced to ford the river. They had formed on the right bank before the French could offer any resistance; in fact, the surprise completely succeeded; the French battalions, as they arrived singly and irregularly, were defeated, and the whole line, including the key of the position, the hill of Croix de Bouquets, was taken before any reserves could arrive. The camp of Biriatu and Bildox, connecting Reille with Clausel, was turned by Freire's taking the Mandale hill, and abandoned. Reille's troops retreated in disorder until they were stopped at Urogne by Soult, who arrived in haste with the reserves from Espelette. While still there, he was informed of an attack on Urdax; but he was not a moment in doubt about the real point of attack, and marched on the lower Bidassoa, where he arrived too late to restore the battle. The British centre, in the mean time, had attacked Clausel, and gradually forced his positions by both front and flank attacks. Toward evening he was confined to the highest point of the ridge, the Grande Rhune, and that hill he abandoned next day. The loss of the French was about 1,400, that of the allies about 1,600 killed and wounded. The surprise was so well managed that the real defence of the French positions had to be made by 10,000 men only, who, on being vigorously attacked by 33,000 allies, were driven from them before any reserves could come to their support.

Written in February (not later than the 23rd), 1858

First published in *The New American Cyclopaedia*, Vol. III, 1858

Reproduced from *The New American Cyclopaedia*

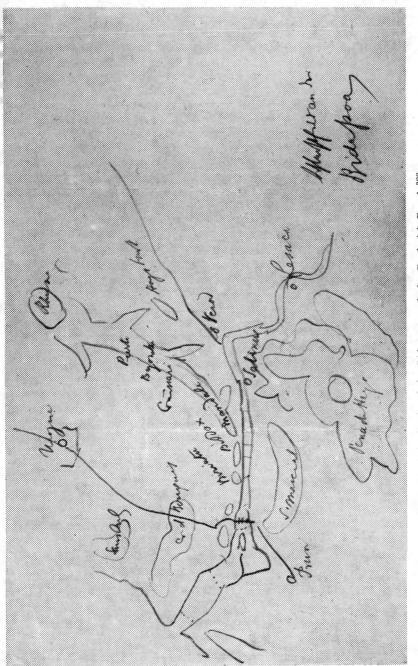

Chart of the battle of the Bidassoa made by Frederick Engels [322]

Frederick Engels

BRESCIA [323]

Brescia, a province of Lombardy, bounded N. by Bergamo and Tyrol, W. by Verona and Mantua, S. by Cremona, E. by Lodi and Bergamo. Area, 1,300 sq. m.; pop. 350,000. The fertility of the soil is favorable to the choicest productions, and one of the most important branches of industry is the trade in silk, of which 1,000,000 pounds are annually produced; the number of silk manufactories is 27, and of silk weaving establishments 1,046. About 70,000 lbs. of very superior wool are raised annually, and there are not less than 45 woollen manufactories, 40 manufactories of woollen and cotton goods, 13 of cloth, 27 of gold, silver, and bronze, 12 of hardware and porcelain, 7 printing establishments, 137 manufactories of iron and other metals (Brescia steel enjoying a world-wide reputation), and 77 of fire-arms and weapons, the excellency of which gave to Brescia, in former times, the name of *l'Armata*.[a] Butter, cheese, wheat, maize, hay, flax, chestnuts, oil, and wine, afford additional elements of prosperity. The trade of the province is principally carried on in the capital of the same name.

The town (anc. *Brixia*) has a population of 40,000, and is situated on the rivers Mella and Garza, at the foot of a hill. The strong castle on the top of the hill was in former times called the falcon of Lombardy. It is a well-built, pleasant, and animated town, noted for its abundant supply of fountains, of which there are not less than 72 in the streets and squares, beside some 100 in private houses. The ancient cathedral, and the other churches, contain many paintings of the great Italian masters. The new

---

[a] Armoury, arsenal.— *Ed.*

cathedral, or *Duomo Nuovo*, was begun in 1604, but the vaulting of the cupola was only completed in 1825. The chief ornament of the church of Santa Afra is "The Woman Taken in Adultery," by Titian. There are, on the whole, over 20 churches, all noted for their treasures of art. Among the remarkable public buildings, is the *Palazzo della Loggia* in the *Piazza Vecchia*, intended for the town hall, the beautiful façade of which suffered much from the bombardment in April, 1849. The Palazzo Tosi was presented to the town by Count Tosi, and contains, among many famous pictures, the celebrated "Saviour," by Raphael. The picture galleries in the Palazzo Averoldi, Fenaroli, Lecchi, Martinengo, and in other palaces, are equally noted for their artistic attractions. A whole street, *Il Corso del Teatro*, has the fronts of the 2d stories decorated with scriptural, mythological, and historical paintings. The *Biblioteca Quirinina*, founded in the middle of the 18th century by Cardinal Quirini, contains upward of 80,000 volumes, beside a vast collection of curious manuscripts and objects of antiquity. The most unique monument of Brescia is the cemetery (*Campo Santo*), the finest in Italy, built in 1810, consisting of a semi-circular area in front, surrounded by tombs, and a row of cypresses. Brescia is the seat of the provincial government, of a bishopric, of a tribunal of commerce, and of other courts of law. There are various charitable institutions, a theological seminary, 2 gymnasiums, a lyceum, a botanical garden, a cabinet of antiquities and one of natural history, an agricultural society, several academies, the philharmonic being one of the oldest in Italy, a casino, a fine theatre, and a large booth outside of the town for the annual fair—a period of great activity and rejoicing. The weekly journal of Brescia is called *Giornale della provincia Bresciana*. A Roman temple of marble was excavated in the vicinity in 1822. Brescia is connected by railway with Verona, and other Italian cities.

The town is supposed to have been founded by the Etruscans. After the fall of the Roman empire it was pillaged by the Goths, and eventually passed into the hands of the Franks. Otho the Great raised it to the rank of a free imperial city, but the contests between the Guelphs and the Ghibellines[324] became a source of trouble to the town. Having been for some time under the sway of the lords of Verona, it fell in 1339 into the power of the Milanese. In 1426 it was taken by Carmagnola; in 1438 besieged by Piccinino; in 1509 it surrendered to the French; in 1512 it was captured by the Venetian general Gritti, but eventually liberated by Gaston de Foix. Subjected to 3 more sieges during the 16th century, it remained in the possession of Venice until the fall of that republic.[325] During the Napoleonic era it was the capital of the department of Mella. In the revolution of 1849, the Brescians rose in arms against the power of Austria, to which they had been subjected since 1814. The town was bombarded, March 30, by General Haynau, and held out until the noon of April 2, when it was compelled to surrender, and to pay a ransom of $1,200,000, in order to avert utter destruction.

Written in February (not later than the 24th), 1858

First published in *The New American Cyclopaedia*, Vol. III, 1858

Reproduced from *The New American Cyclopaedia*

Frederick Engels

BURMAH[326]

Burmah, or the Kingdom of Ava, an extensive state in the S. E. of Asia, beyond the Ganges, formerly much larger than at present. Its former limits were between lat. 9° and 27° N., ranging upward of 1,000 miles in length, and over 600 in breadth. At present the Burmese territory reaches from lat. 19° 25' to 28° 15' N., and from long. 93° 2' to 100° 40' E.; comprising a space measuring 540 miles in length from N. to S., and 420 miles in breadth, and having an area of about 200,000 sq. m. It is bounded on the W. by the province of Aracan, surrendered to the British by the Burmese treaty of 1826, and by the petty states of Tiperah, Munnipoor, and Assam, from which countries it is separated by high mountain ridges; on the S. lies the newly acquired British province of Pegu,[327] on the N. upper Assam and Thibet, and on the E. China. The population, according to Capt. Henry Yule, does not exceed 3,000,000.[a]

Since the cession of Pegu to the British, Burmah has neither alluvial plains nor a seaboard, its southern frontier being at least 200 miles from the mouths of the Irrawaddy, and the country rising gradually from this frontier to the north. For about 300 miles it is elevated, and beyond that it is rugged and mountainous. This territory is watered by three great streams, the Irrawaddy, its tributary the Khyen-dwem, and the Salwin. These rivers have their sources in the northern chain of mountains, and run in a southerly course to the Indian ocean.

Though Burmah has been robbed of its most fertile territory,

---

[a] H. Yule, A Narrative of the Mission Sent by the Governor-General of India to the Court of Ava in 1855, p. 290.— Ed.

that which remains is far from unproductive. The forests abound in valuable timber, among which teak, used for ship building, holds a prominent place. Almost every description of timber known in India is found also in Burmah. Stick lac of excellent quality, and varnish used in the manufacture of lacquered ware, are produced. Ava, the capital, is supplied with superior teak from a forest at 15 days' distance. Agriculture and horticulture are everywhere in a remarkably backward state; and were it not for the wealth of the soil and the congeniality of the climate, the state would be very poor. Fruits are not cultivated at all, and the crops are managed with little skill. Of garden vegetables, the onion and the capsicum are the most generally cultivated. Yams and sweet potatoes are also found, together with inconsiderable quantities of melons, cucumbers, and egg-plants. The young shoots of bamboo, wild asparagus, and the succulent roots of various aquatic plants, supply to the inhabitants the place of cultivated garden fruits. Mangoes, pineapples, oranges, custard-apples, the jack (a species of breadfruit), the papaw, fig, and the plantain (that greatest enemy of civilization), are the chief fruits, and all these grow with little or no care. The chief crops are rice (which is in some parts used as a circulating medium), maize, millet, wheat, various pulses, palms, sugar-cane, tobacco, cotton of short staple, and indigo. Sugar-cane is not generally cultivated, and the art of making sugar is scarcely known, although the plant has been long known to the people. A cheap, coarse sugar is obtained from the juice of the Palmyra palm, of which numerous groves are found, especially south of the capital. Indigo is so badly managed as to be entirely unfit for exportation. Rice in the south, and maize and millet in the north, are the standard crops. Sesamum is universally raised for cattle. On the northern hills the genuine tea-plant of China is cultivated to considerable extent; but, singularly, the natives, instead of steeping it, as they do the Chinese tea, eat the leaf prepared with oil and garlic. Cotton is raised chiefly in the dry lands of the upper provinces.

The dense forests of Burmah abound in wild animals, among which the chief are the elephant, the one-horned rhinoceros, the tiger and leopard, the wild hog, and several species of deer. Of birds, the wild cock is common; and there are also varieties of pheasants, partridges, and quails. The domestic animals are the ox, the horse, and the buffalo. The elephant also is used as a draught animal. The camel is not known. A few goats and sheep are found, but the breed is little cared for. Asses are also little used. Dogs are neglected in the Burmese economy, but cats are numerous. Horses are used exclusively for riding, and are rarely more than thirteen hands high. The ox is the beast of draught and burden in the north; the buffalo in the south.

Of minerals, gold, carried down in the sands of the mountains, is found in the beds of the various streams. Silver mines are wrought at Bor-twang, on the Chinese frontier. The amount of gold and silver obtained annually has been estimated to approach $1,000,000. Iron is abundant in the eastern portion of Laos, but is so rudely wrought that from 30 to 40 per cent. of the metal is lost in the process of forging. The petroleum pits on the banks of the Irrawaddy produce 8,000,000 pounds per annum. Copper, tin, lead, and antimony are known to exist in the Laos country, but it is doubtful if any of these metals are obtained in considerable quantities, owing to the ignorance of the people of the methods of working ores. The mountains near the city of Ava furnish a superior quality of limestone; fine statuary marble is found 40 miles from the capital, on the banks of the Irrawaddy; amber exists so plentifully that it sells in Ava at the low price of $1 per pound; and nitre, natron, salt, and coal are extensively diffused over the entire country, though the latter is little used. The petroleum, which is produced in such abundance, is used by all classes in Burmah for burning in lamps, and as a protection against insects. It is dipped up in buckets from narrow wells sunk to a depth of from 210 to 300 feet; it bubbles up at the bottom like a living spring of water. Turpentine is found in various portions of the country, and is extensively exported to China. The oriental sapphire, ruby, topaz, and amethyst, beside varieties of the chrysoberyl and spinelle, are found in 2 districts in the beds of rivulets. All, over $50 in value, are claimed by the crown, and sent to the treasury; and no strangers are allowed to search for the stones.

From what has been said, it is evident that the Burmese have made but little advance in the practice of the useful arts. Women carry on the whole process of the cotton manufacture, using a rude loom, and displaying comparatively little ingenuity or skill. Porcelain is imported from China; British cottons are imported, and even in the interior undersell the native products; though the Burmese melt iron, steel is brought from Bengal; silks are manufactured at several places, but from raw Chinese silk; and while a very great variety of goods is imported, the exports are comparatively insignificant, those to China, with which the Burmese carry on their most extensive commerce, consisting of raw cotton, ornamental feathers, chiefly of the blue jay, edible swallows' nests, ivory, rhinoceros and deer's horns, and some minor species of precious stones. In return for this, the Burmese import wrought copper, orpiment, quicksilver, vermilion, iron pans, brass wire, tin, lead, alum, silver, gold and gold leaf, earthenware, paints, carpets, rhubarb, tea, honey, raw silk, velvets, Chinese spirits, musk, verdigris, dried fruits, paper, fans, umbrellas, shoes, and wearing apparel. Gold and silver ornaments of a very rude description are made in various parts of the country; weapons, scissors, and carpenters' tools are manufactured at Ava; idols are sculptured in considerable quantities about 40 miles from Ava, where is found a hill of pure white marble. The currency is in a wretched condition. Lead, silver, and gold, all uncoined, form the circulating medium. A large portion of the commerce is carried on by way of barter, in consequence of the difficulties attending the making of small payments. The precious metals must be weighed and assayed at every change of hands, for which bankers charge about $3\frac{1}{2}$ per cent. Interest ranges from 25 to 60 per cent. per annum. Petroleum is the most universal article of consumption. For it are exchanged saltpetre, lime, paper, lacquer ware, cotton and silk fabrics, iron and brass ware, sugar, tamarinds, &c. The yonnet-ni (the standard silver of the country) has generally an alloy of copper of 10 or 15 per cent. Below $^{85}/_{100}$ the mixture does not pass current, that degree of fineness being required in the money paid for taxes.

The revenues of the empire proceed from a house tax, which is levied on the village, the village authorities afterward assessing householders according to their respective ability to pay. This tax varies greatly, as from 6 tikals per householder in Prome to 27 tikals in Tongho. Those subject to military duty, the farmers of the royal domain, and artificers employed on the public works, are exempt. The soil is taxed according to crops. The tobacco tax is paid in money; other crops pay 5 per cent. in kind. The farmers of the royal lands pay over one-half their crops. Fishing ports on lake and river are let either for a stated term or for a proportion of dried fish from the catch. These various revenues are collected by and for the use of the officers of the crown, each of whom receives, according to his importance, a district greater or less, from the proceeds of which he lives. The royal revenue is raised from the sale of monopolies of the crown, among which cotton is the chief. In the management of this monopoly, the inhabitants are forced to deliver certain articles at certain low prices to the crown officers, who sell them at an enormous advance. Thus, lead is delivered by the producers at the rate of 5 tikals per bis, or 3.6

lbs., and his majesty sells it at the rate of 20 tikals. The royal revenues amount, so it is stated, to about 1,820,000 tikals, or £227,500 per annum, to which must be added a further sum of £44,250, the produce of certain tolls levied in particular districts. These moneys keep the royal household. This system of taxation, though despotic, is singularly simple in its details; and a further exemplification of simplicity in government, is the manner in which the army is made to maintain itself, or, at least, to be supported by the people. The modes of enlistment are various; in some districts the volunteer system being adhered to, while in others, every 16 families are forced to furnish 2 men armed and equipped. They are further obliged to furnish to these recruits, monthly, 56 lbs. of rice and 5 rupees. In the province of Padoung every soldier is quartered upon 2 families, who receive 5 acres of tax-free land, and have to furnish the man of war with half the crops, and 25 rupees per annum, beside wood and other minor necessities. The captain of 50 men receives 10 tikals (the tikal is worth $1 $1/_4$, or $2 $1/_2$ rupees) each from 6 families, and half the crop of a 7th. The bo, or centurion, is maintained by the labor of 52 families, and the bo-gyi, or colonel, raises his salary from his own officers and men. The Burman soldier fights well under favoring circumstances, but the chief excellence of a Burman army corps lies in the absence of the *impedimenta;* the soldier carries his bed (a hammock) at one end of his musket, his kettle at the other, and his provisions (rice) in a cloth about his waist.

In physical conformation, the Burmese appear to be of the same race which inhabits the countries between Hindostan and China, having more of the Mongolian than of the Hindoo type. They are short, stout, well proportioned, fleshy, but active; with large cheek-bones, eyes obliquely placed, brown but never very dark complexion, coarse, lank, black hair, abundant, and more beard than their neighbors, the Siamese. Major Allen, in a memoir to the East India government,[a] gives them credit for frankness, a strong sense of the ridiculous, considerable readiness of resource, little patriotism, but much love of home and family; comparatively little prejudice against strangers, and a readiness to acquire the knowledge of new arts, if not attended with too much mental exertion. They are sharp traders, and have a good deal of a certain kind of enterprise; are temperate, but have small powers of endurance; have more cunning than courage; though not

---

[a] Major Allen, *Report on the Northern Frontier of Pegu, dated 18th July, 1854* (H. Yule, op. cit., pp. 250-51).— *Ed.*

blood-thirsty by nature, have borne phlegmatically the cruelties of their various kings; and without being naturally liars and cheats, are yet great braggarts and treacherous.

The Burmese are Buddhists by faith, and have kept the ceremonies of their religion freer from intermixture with other religions than elsewhere in India and China. The Burmese Buddhists avoid, to some extent, the picture worship practised in China, and their monks are more than usually faithful to their vows of poverty and celibacy. Toward the close of the last century, the Burman state religion was divided by 2 sects, or offshoots from the ancient faith. The first of these entertained a belief similar in some respects to pantheism, believing that the godhead is diffused over and through all the world and its creatures, but that it appears in its highest stages of development in the Buddhists themselves. The other rejects entirely the doctrine of the metempsychosis, and the picture worship and cloister system of the Buddhists; considers death as the portal to an everlasting happiness or misery, according to the conduct of the deceased, and worships one supreme and all-creating spirit (*Nat*). The present king,[a] who is a zealous devotee to his faith, has already publicly burned 14 of these heretics, both parties of whom are alike outlawed. They are, nevertheless, according to Capt. Yule, very numerous, but worship in secret.

The early history of Burmah is but little known. The empire attained its acme of power in the 11th century, when the capital was in Pegu. About the beginning of the 16th century the state was split into several minor and independent governments, which made war upon each other; and in 1554, when the king Tshen-byoo Myayen took Ava, he had subdued to himself all the valley of the Irrawaddy, and had even subjected Siam. After various changes, Alompra, the founder of the present dynasty (who died in 1760), once more raised the empire to something like its former extent and power. Since then the British have taken from it its most fertile and valuable provinces.

The government of Burmah is a pure despotism, the king, one of whose titles is lord of life and death, dispensing imprisonment, fines, torture, or death, at his supreme will. The details of the government are carried out by the hlwot-dau, or council of state, whose presiding officer is the pre-nominated heir-apparent to the throne, or if there is no heir named, then a prince of the blood

---

[a] Mindon.— *Ed.*

royal. In ordinary times the council is composed of 4 ministers, who have, however, no distinct departments, but act wherever chance directs. They form also a high court of appeal, before whom suits are brought for final adjudication; and in their individual capacity, they have power to give judgment on cases which are not brought up to the collective council. As they retain 10 per cent. of the property in suit for the costs of the judgment, they derive very handsome incomes from this source. From this and other peculiarities of the Burmese government, it is easily seen that justice is rarely dealt out to the people. Every office-holder is at the same time a plunderer; the judges are venal, the police powerless, robbers and thieves abound, life and property are insecure, and every inducement to progress is wanting. Near the capital the power of the king is fearful and oppressive. It decreases with distance, so that in the more distant provinces the people pay but little heed to the behests of the lord of the white elephant, elect their own governors, who are ratified by the king, and pay but slight tribute to the government. Indeed, the provinces bordering on China display the curious spectacle of a people living contentedly under two governments, the Chinese and Burmese taking a like part in the ratification of the rulers of these localities, but, wisely, generally settling on the same men. Notwithstanding various British embassies have visited Burmah, and although missionary operations have been carried on there more successfully than elsewhere in Asia, the interior of Burmah is yet a complete *terra incognita*, on which modern geographers and map-makers have ventured some wild guesses, but concerning which they know very little in detail.

(See "Narrative of the Mission sent by the Governor-General of India, to the Court of Ava, 1855," by Capt. Henry Yule. London, 1858.)

Written between February and March 9, 1858

First published in *The New American Cyclopaedia*, Vol. IV, 1859

Reproduced from *The New American Cyclopaedia*

Frederick Engels

BOMARSUND [328]

Bomarsund, a narrow channel between the island of Ålands[a] and Vardo, at the entrance of the gulf of Bothnia. The Russian fortifications to the harbor of Bomarsund were destroyed by the British and French fleets during the war of 1854.[b] The channels leading up to Bomarsund were blockaded at the end of July by 4 British ships and a few small steamers. Shortly afterward strong detachments of the allied fleets arrived, with the admirals Napier and Parseval-Deschênes, followed, Aug. 7, by the line-of-battle ships with Gen. Baraguay d'Hilliers and 12,000 troops, mostly French. The Russian commander, Gen. Bodisco, was compelled to surrender on Aug. 16, the allies continuing to occupy the island until the end of the month, when the whole of the fortification was blown up. The trophies of the victors were 112 mounted guns, 79 not mounted, 3 mortars, 7 field guns, and 2,235 prisoners. The principal military interest offered by this siege is its setting completely at rest the question as to the employment of uncovered masonry in fortifications with land-fronts.

Written between February 24 and March 19, 1858

First published in *The New American Cyclopaedia,* Vol. III, 1858

Reproduced from *The New American Cyclopaedia*

---

[a] See this volume, p. 9.—*Ed.*
[b] During the Crimean war of 1853-56.—*Ed.*

Karl Marx

BÜLOW [329]

Bülow, Friedrich Wilhelm, Count von Dennewitz, a Prussian general, born Feb. 16, 1755, died Feb. 25, 1816. At the earliest period of Napoleon's European wars, he was engaged against him. In 1808 he was made a general of brigade. In 1813 he was ennobled for his victories at Möckern,[a] Luckau, Gros-Beeren, and Dennewitz.[b] He subsequently distinguished himself in Westphalia, Holland, and Belgium, and contributed essentially (as Wellington warmly acknowledged[c]) to the victorious close of the battle of Waterloo,[330] in which he commanded the 4th division of the allied army.

Written at the end of March 1858

First published in *The New American Cyclopaedia,* Vol. IV, 1859

Reproduced from *The New American Cyclopaedia*

---

a Known also as the battle of Dannigkow.— *Ed.*
b For details on this battle see this volume, pp. 156, 402 and 403.— *Ed.*
c A. Wellington, "To Earl Bathurst, Waterloo, June 19th, 1815" (*Selections from the Dispatches and General Orders of Field Marshal the Duke of Wellington,* p. 860).— *Ed.*

Karl Marx and Frederick Engels

BERESFORD[331]

Beresford, William Carr, viscount, British general, born in Ireland, Oct. 2, 1768, died in Kent, Jan. 8, 1854. The illegitimate son of George, 1st marquis of Waterford, he entered the army at the age of 16, and served in Nova Scotia until 1790. During this period, he lost one of his eyes from an accidental shot by a brother officer. He served at Toulon, Corsica, the West Indies (under Abercromby), the East Indies, and Egypt, under Baird. On his return, in 1800, he was made colonel by brevet. He subsequently was employed in Ireland, at the conquest of the Cape of Good Hope, and (as brigadier-general) against Buenos Ayres, in 1806, where he was compelled to surrender, but finally escaped. In 1807 he commanded the forces which captured Madeira, and was made governor of that island.[332] In 1808 he became major-general, and, having arrived in Portugal with the English forces, was intrusted with the whole organization of the Por-tuguese army, including the militia. He was one of the commis-sioners for adjusting the terms of the celebrated convention of Cintra; was present during the retreat on, and battle of, Coruña, where he covered the embarkation of Sir John Moore's troops[333]; and, in March, 1809, was appointed marshal and generalissimo of the Portuguese army, soon raised by him into an excellent force, whether of attack or defence. He fought all through the Peninsular war, until its close in 1814, vigorously supporting Wellington. On the only considerable occasion, however, when he held the chief command, at the battle of Albuera, in 1811, he displayed very poor generalship, and the day would have been lost but for the act of a subaltern[a] in disobedience of his orders.[b] He took part in the victories of Salamanca, Vittoria, Bayonne, Orthes, and Toulouse.[334] For these services he was created a field-marshal of Portugal, duke of Elvas, and marquis of Santo Campo. In 1810 he was chosen member of parliament for the county of Waterford (he never took his seat), and, in 1814, was created Baron Beresford of Albuera and Dungannon; in 1823 he was advanced to the dignity of viscount.

In 1814 he went on a diplomatic mission to Brazil, where, in 1817, he repressed a conspiracy.[335] On his return, he successively became lieutenant-general of the ordnance, general of the army, and (from 1828 to 1830) master-general of the ordnance. Having assisted Don Miguel, in 1823[336], he was deprived of his baton as field-marshal of Portugal. In politics, he was actively, though silently, a decided tory. His military efficiency chiefly consisted in his successful reorganization of the Portuguese troops, whom, by great skill and unwearied exertions, he finally rendered sufficiently firm and well disciplined to cope even with the French. In 1832 he married his cousin, Louisa, daughter of the archbishop of Tuam, and widow of Thomas Hope, the millionaire banker, and author of "Anastasius." He left no children, and the title became extinct at his death.

Written between March 11 and April 9, 1858

First published in *The New American Cyclopaedia*, Vol. III, 1858

Reproduced from *The New American Cyclopaedia*

---

[a] Henry Hardinge.— *Ed.*
[b] See this volume, pp. 10-11.— *Ed.*

Frederick Engels

CAVALRY [337]

Cavalry (Fr. *cavalerie,* from *cavalier,* a horseman, from *cheval,* a horse), a body of soldiers on horseback. The use of the horse for riding, and the introduction of bodies of mounted men into armies, naturally originated in those countries to which the horse is indigenous, and where the climate and gramineous productions of the soil favored the development of all its physical capabilities. While the horse in Europe and tropical Asia soon degenerated into a clumsy animal or an undersized pony, the breed of Arabia, Persia, Asia Minor, Egypt, and the north coast of Africa attained great beauty, speed, docility, and endurance. But it appears that at first it was used in harness only; at least in military history the war chariot long precedes the armed horseman. The Egyptian monuments show plenty of war chariots, but with a single exception no horsemen; and that exception appears to belong to the Roman period. Still it is certain that at least a couple of centuries before the country was conquered by the Persians,[a] the Egyptians had a numerous cavalry, and the commander of this arm is more than once named among the most important officials of the court. It is very likely that the Egyptians became acquainted with cavalry during their war with the Assyrians; for on the Assyrian monuments horsemen are often delineated, and their use in war with Assyrian armies at a very early period is established beyond a doubt. With them, also, the saddle appears to have originated. In the older sculptures the soldier rides the bare back of the animal; at a later epoch we find a kind of pad or cushion introduced, and finally a high saddle similar to that now used all

---

[a] In 525 B.C.—*Ed.*

over the East. The Persians and Medians, at the time they appear in history, were a nation of horsemen. Though they retained the war chariot, and even left to it its ancient precedence over the younger arm of cavalry, yet the great numerical strength of the mounted men gave the latter an importance it had never possessed in any former service. The cavalry of the Assyrians, Egyptians, and Persians consisted of that kind which still prevails in the East, and which, up to very recent times, was alone employed in northern Africa, Asia, and eastern Europe, irregular cavalry. But no sooner had the Greeks so far improved their breed of horses by crosses with the eastern horse, as to fit them for cavalry purposes, than they began to organize the arm upon a new principle. They are the creators of both regular infantry and regular cavalry. They formed the masses of fighting men into distinct bodies, armed and equipped them according to the purpose they were intended for, and taught them to act in concert, to move in ranks and files, to keep together in a definite tactical formation, and thus to throw the weight of their concentrated and advancing mass upon a given point of the enemy's front. Thus organized, they proved everywhere superior to the undrilled, unwieldy, and uncontrolled mobs brought against them by the Asiatics. We have no instance of a combat of Grecian cavalry against Persian horsemen before the time the Persians themselves had formed bodies of a more regular kind of cavalry; but there can be no doubt that the result would have been the same as when the infantry of both nations met in battle. Cavalry, at first, was organized by the horse-breeding countries of Greece only, such as Thessalia and Boeotia; but, very soon after, the Athenians formed a body of heavy cavalry, beside mounted archers for outpost and skirmishing duty. The Spartans, too, had the *élite* of their youth formed into a body of horse-guards; but they had no faith in cavalry, and made them dismount in battle, and fight as infantry. From the Greeks of Asia Minor, as well as from the Greek mercenaries serving in their army, the Persians learned the formation of regular cavalry, and there is no doubt that a considerable portion of the Persian horse that fought against Alexander the Great were more or less trained to act in compact bodies in a regular manner. The Macedonians, however, were more than a match for them. With that people horsemanship was an accomplishment indispensable to the young nobility, and cavalry held a high rank in their army. The cavalry of Philip and Alexander consisted of the Macedonian and Thessalian nobility, with a few squadrons recruited in Greece proper. It was composed of heavy horsemen—*cataphractae*—armed with helmet and breast-plate, cuisses, and a long spear. It usually charged in a compact body, in an oblong or wedge-shaped column, sometimes also in line. The light cavalry, composed of auxiliary troops, was of a more or less irregular kind, and served like the Cossacks now-a-days for outpost duty and skirmishing.

The battle of the Granicus (334 B.C.) offers the first instance of an engagement in which cavalry played a decisive part. The Persian cavalry was placed at charging distance from the fords of the river. As soon as the heads of columns of the Macedonian infantry had passed the river, and before they could deploy, the Persian horse broke in upon them and drove them headlong down again into the river. This manoeuvre, repeated several times over with perfect success, shows at once that the Persians had regular cavalry to oppose to the Macedonians. To surprise infantry in the very moment of its greatest weakness, viz., when passing from one tactical formation into another, requires the cavalry to be well in hand, and perfectly under the control of its commanders. Irregular levies are incapable of it. Ptolemy, who commanded the advanced guard of Alexander's army, could make no headway until the Macedonian cuirassiers passed the river, and charged the Persians in flank. A long combat ensued, but the Persian horsemen being disposed in one line without reserves, and being at last abandoned by the Asiatic Greeks in their army, were ultimately routed. The battle of Arbela (331 B.C.)[a] was the most glorious for the Macedonian cavalry. Alexander in person led the Macedonian horse, which formed the extreme right of his order of battle, while the Thessalian horse formed the left. The Persians tried to outflank him, but in the decisive moment Alexander brought fresh men from the rear so as to overlap them in their turn; they at the same time left a gap between their left and centre. Into this gap Alexander at once dashed, separating their left from the remainder of the army, rolling it up completely, and pursuing it for a considerable distance. Then, on being called upon to send assistance to his own menaced left, he rallied his horse in a very short time, and passing behind the enemy's centre fell upon the rear of his right. The battle was thus gained, and Alexander from that day ranks among the first of the cavalry generals of all times. And to crown the work, his cavalry pursued the fugitive enemy with such ardor that its advanced guard stood the next day 75 miles in advance of the battle-field. It is very

---

[a] See this volume, p. 23.— *Ed.*

curious to observe that the general principles of cavalry tactics were as well understood at that time as they are now. To attack infantry in the formation of the march, or during a change of formation; to attack cavalry principally on its flank; to profit by any opening in the enemy's line by dashing in and wheeling to the right and left, so as to take in flank and rear the troops placed next to such a gap; to follow up a victory by a rapid and inexorable pursuit of the broken enemy—these are among the first and most important rules that every modern cavalry officer has to learn. After Alexander's death we hear no more of that splendid cavalry of Greece and Macedon. In Greece infantry again prevailed, and in Asia and Egypt the mounted service soon degenerated.

The Romans never were horsemen. What little cavalry they had with the legions was glad to fight on foot. Their horses were of an inferior breed, and the men could not ride. But on the southern side of the Mediterranean a cavalry was formed, which not only rivalled, but even outshone that of Alexander. The Carthaginian generals, Hamilcar and Hannibal, had succeeded in forming, beside their Numidian irregular horsemen, a body of first-rate regular cavalry, and thus created an arm which almost everywhere insured them a victory. The Berbers of north Africa are, up to the present day, a nation of horsemen, at least in the plains, and the splendid Barb horse which carried Hannibal's swordsmen into the deep masses of the Roman infantry, with a rapidity and vehemence unknown before, still mounts the finest regiments of the whole French cavalry, the *chasseurs d'Afrique,* and is by them acknowledged to be the best war-horse in existence. The Carthaginian infantry was far inferior to that of the Romans, even after it had been long trained by its two great chiefs; it would not have had the slightest chance against the Roman legions, had it not been for the assistance of that cavalry which alone made it possible for Hannibal to hold out 16 years in Italy[338]; and when this cavalry had been worn out by the wear and tear of so many campaigns, not by the sword of the enemy, there was no longer a place in Italy for him. Hannibal's battles have that in common with those of Frederick the Great, that most of them were won by cavalry over first-rate infantry; and, indeed, at no other time has cavalry performed such glorious deeds as under those two great commanders. From what nation, and upon what tactical principles, Hamilcar and Hannibal formed their regular cavalry, we are not precisely informed. But as their Numidian light horse are always clearly distinguished from the heavy or regular cavalry, we may conclude that the latter was not composed of Berber tribes. There were very likely many foreign mercenaries and some Carthaginians; the great mass, however, most probably consisted of Spaniards, as it was formed in their country, and as even in Caesar's time Spanish horsemen were attached to most Roman armies. Hannibal being well acquainted with Greek civilization, and Greek mercenaries and soldiers of fortune having before his time served under the Carthaginian standards, there can scarcely be a doubt that the organization of the Grecian and Macedonian heavy cavalry served as the basis for that of the Carthaginian. The very first encounter in Italy settled the question of the superiority of the Carthaginian horse. At the Ticinus (218 B.C.), the Roman consul Publius Scipio, while reconnoitring with his cavalry and light infantry, met with the Carthaginian cavalry led by Hannibal on a similar errand. Hannibal at once attacked. The Roman light infantry stood in first line, the cavalry formed the second. The Carthaginian heavy horse charged the infantry, dispersed it, and then fell at once on the Roman cavalry in front, while the Numidian irregulars charged their flank and rear. The battle was short. The Romans fought bravely, but they had no chance whatever. They could not ride; their own horses vanquished them; frightened by the flight of the Roman skirmishers, who were driven in upon them and sought shelter between them, they threw off many of their riders and broke up the formation. Other troopers, not trusting to their horsemanship, wisely dismounted and attempted to fight as infantry. But already the Carthaginian cuirassiers were in the midst of them, while the inevitable Numidians galloped round the confused mass, cutting down every fugitive who detached himself from it. The loss of the Romans was considerable, and Publius Scipio himself was wounded. At the Trebia, Hannibal succeeded in enticing the Romans to cross that river, so as to fight with this barrier in their rear. No sooner was this accomplished than he advanced with all his troops against them and forced them to battle. The Romans, like the Carthaginians, had their infantry in the centre; but opposite to the 2 Roman wings formed by cavalry, Hannibal placed his elephants, making use of his cavalry to outflank and overlap both wings of his opponents. At the very outset of the battle, the Roman cavalry, thus turned and outnumbered, was completely defeated; but the Roman infantry drove back the Carthaginian centre and gained ground. The victorious Carthaginian horse now attacked them in front and flank; they compelled them to desist from advancing, but could not break them. Hannibal, however, knowing the solidity of the Roman legion, had sent 1,000 horsemen and 1,000 picked foot soldiers under his brother Mago by a roundabout way to their rear. These fresh troops now fell upon them and succeeded in breaking the second line; but the first line, 10,000 men, closed up, and in a compact body forced their way through the enemy, and marched down the river toward Placentia, where they crossed it unmolested. In the battle of Cannae (216 B.C.), the Romans had 80,000 infantry and 6,000 cavalry; the Carthaginians, 40,000 infantry and 10,000 cavalry. The cavalry of Latium formed the Roman right wing, leaning on the river Aufidus; that of the allied Italians stood on the left, while the infantry formed the centre. Hannibal, too, placed his infantry in the centre, the Celtic and Spanish levies again forming the wings, while between them, a little further back, stood his African infantry, now equipped and organized on the Roman system. Of his cavalry, he placed the Numidians on the right wing, where the open plain permitted them, by their superior mobility and rapidity, to evade the charges of the Italian heavy horse opposed to them; while the whole of the heavy cavalry, under Hasdrubal, was stationed on the left, close to the river. On the Roman left, the Numidians gave the Italian cavalry plenty to do, but from their very nature as irregular horse could not break up their close array by regular charges. In the centre, the Roman infantry soon drove back the Celts and Spaniards, and then formed into a wedge-shaped column in order to attack the African infantry. These, however, wheeled inward, and charging the unwieldy mass in line, broke its impetus; and there the battle, now, became a standing fight. But Hasdrubal's heavy horse had, in the mean time, prepared the defeat of the Romans. Having furiously charged the Roman cavalry of the right wing, they dispersed them after a stout resistance, passed, like Alexander at Arbela, behind the Roman centre, fell upon the rear of the Italian cavalry, broke it completely, and, leaving it an easy prey to the Numidians, formed for a grand charge on the flanks and rear of the Roman infantry. This was decisive. The unwieldy mass, attacked on all sides, gave way, opened out, was broken, and succumbed. Never was there such complete destruction of an army. The Romans lost 70,000 men; of their cavalry, only 70 men escaped. The Carthaginians lost not quite 6,000, $^2/_3$ of whom belonged to the Celtic contingents, which had had to bear the brunt of the first attack of the legions. Of Hasdrubal's 6,000 regular horse, which had won the whole of the battle, not more than 200 men were killed and wounded.

The Roman cavalry of later times was not much better than that of the Punic wars.[339] It was attached to the legions in small bodies, never forming an independent arm. Beside this legionary cavalry, there were in Caesar's time Spanish, Celtic, and German mercenary horsemen, all of them more or less irregular. No cavalry serving with the Romans ever performed things worthy of mention; and so neglected and ineffective was this arm, that the Parthian irregulars of Khorassan remained extremely formidable to Roman armies. In the eastern half of the empire, however, the ancient passion for horses and horsemanship retained its sway; and Byzantium remained, up to its conquest by the Turks,[a] the great horse mart and riding academy of Europe. Accordingly, we find that during the momentary revival of the Byzantine empire, under Justinian, its cavalry was on a comparatively respectable footing; and in the battle of Capua, in A.D. 554, the eunuch Narses is reported to have defeated the Teutonic invaders of Italy principally by means of this arm.[340]

The establishment, in all countries of western Europe, of a conquering aristocracy of Teutonic origin, led to a new era in the history of cavalry. The nobility took everywhere to the mounted service, under the designation of men-at-arms (*gens d'armes*), forming a body of horse of the heaviest description, in which not only the riders but also the horses were covered with defensive armor of metal. The first battle at which such cavalry appeared was that at Poitiers, where Charles Martel, in 732, beat back the torrent of Arab invasion. The Frankish knighthood, under Eudes, duke of Aquitania, broke through the Moorish ranks and took their camp. But such a body was not fit for pursuit; and the Arabs, accordingly, under shelter of their indefatigable irregular horse, retired unmolested into Spain. From this battle dates a series of wars in which the massive but unwieldy regular cavalry of the West fought the agile irregulars of the East with varied success. The German knighthood measured swords, during nearly the whole of the 10th century, with the wild Hungarian horsemen, and totally defeated them by their close array at Merseburg in 933, and at the Lech in 955.[341] The Spanish chivalry, for several centuries, fought the Moorish invaders of their country, and ultimately conquered them. But when the occidental "heavies" transferred the seat of war, during the crusades,[342] to the eastern homes of their enemies, they were in their turn defeated, and in most cases completely destroyed; neither they nor their horses could stand the climate, the immensely long marches, and the

---

[a] Byzantium was finally conquered by the Turks in 1453.— *Ed.*

want of proper food and forage. These crusades were followed by a fresh irruption of eastern horsemen into Europe, that of the Mongols. Having overrun Russia, and the provinces of Poland, they were met at Wahlstatt in Silesia, in 1241, by a combined Polish and German army.[343] After a long struggle, the Asiatics defeated the worn-out steel-clad knights, but the victory was so dearly bought that it broke the power of the invaders. The Mongols advanced no further, and soon, by divisions among themselves, ceased to be dangerous, and were driven back. During the whole of the middle ages, cavalry remained the chief arm of all armies: with the eastern nations the light irregular horse had always held that rank; with those of western Europe, the heavy regular cavalry formed by the knighthood was in this period the arm which decided every battle. This preeminence of the mounted arm was not so much caused by its own excellence, for the irregulars of the East were incapable of orderly fight, and the regulars of the West were clumsy beyond belief in their movements; it was principally caused by the bad quality of the infantry. Asiatics as well as Europeans held that arm in contempt; it was composed of those who could not afford to appear mounted, principally of slaves or serfs. There was no proper organization for it; without defensive armor, with a pike and sword for its sole weapons, it might now and then by its deep formation withstand the furious but disorderly charges of eastern horsemen; but it was resistlessly ridden over by the invulnerable men-at-arms of the West. The only exception was formed by the English infantry, which derived its strength from its formidable weapon, the long-bow. The numerical proportion of the European cavalry of these times to the remainder of the army was certainly not as strong as it was a few centuries later, nor even as it is now. Knights were not so exceedingly numerous, and in many large battles we find that not more than 800 or 1,000 of them were present. But they were generally sufficient to dispose of any number of foot soldiers, as soon as they had succeeded in driving from the field the enemy's men-at-arms. The general mode of fighting of these men-at-arms was in line, in single rank, the rear rank being formed by the esquires, who wore, generally speaking, a less complete and heavy suit of armor. These lines, once in the midst of the enemy, soon dissolved themselves into single combatants, and finished the battle by sheer hand-to-hand fighting. Subsequently, when firearms began to come into use, deep masses were formed, generally squares; but then the days of chivalry were numbered.

During the 15th century, not only was artillery introduced into the field of battle, while part of the infantry, the skirmishers of those times, were armed with muskets, but a general change took place in the character of infantry. This arm began to be formed by the enlistment of mercenaries who made a profession of military service. The German *Landsknechte* and the Swiss were such professional soldiers, and they very soon introduced more regular formations and tactical movements. The ancient Doric and Macedonian phalanx was, in a manner, revived; a helmet and a breastplate somewhat protected the men against the lance and sword of the cavalry; and when, at Novara (1513),[344] the Swiss infantry drove the French knighthood actually from the field, there was no further use for such valiant but unwieldy horsemen. Accordingly, after the insurrection of the Netherlands against Spain,[345] we find a new class of cavalry, the German *Reiters* (*reitres* of the French), raised by voluntary enlistment, like the infantry, and armed with helmet and breastplate, sword and pistols. They were fully as heavy as the modern cuirassiers, yet far lighter than the knights. They soon proved their superiority over the heavy men-at-arms. These now disappear, and with them the lance; the sword and short firearms now form the general armature for cavalry. About the same time (end of the 16th century) the hybrid arm of dragoons was introduced, first in France, then in the other countries of Europe. Armed with muskets, they were intended to fight, according to circumstances, either as infantry or as cavalry. A similar corps had been formed by Alexander the Great under the name of the *dimachae,* but it had not yet been imitated. The dragoons of the 16th century had a longer existence, but toward the middle of the 18th century they had everywhere lost their hybrid character, except in name, and were generally used as cavalry. The most important feature in their formation was that they were the first body of regular cavalry which was completely deprived of defensive armor. The creation of real hybrid dragoons was again attempted, on a large scale, by the emperor Nicholas of Russia; but it was soon proved that, before the enemy, they must always be used as cavalry, and consequently Alexander II very soon reduced them to simple cavalry, with no more pretensions to dismounted service than hussars or cuirassiers. Maurice of Orange, the great Dutch commander, formed his *Reiters* for the first time in something like our modern tactical organization. He taught them to execute charges and evolutions in separate bodies, and in more than one line; to wheel, break off, form column and line, and change front, without disorder, and in separate squadrons and troops. Thus a cavalry fight was no longer decided by one charge of the whole mass, but by the successive charges of separate squadrons and lines supporting each other. His cavalry was formed generally 5 deep. In other armies it fought in deep bodies, and where a line formation was adopted it was still from 5 to 8 deep.

The 17th century, having completely done away with the costly men-at-arms, increased the numerical strength of cavalry to an enormous extent. At no other period was there so large a proportion of that arm in every army. In the 30 years' war[346] from $^2/_5$ to nearly $^1/_2$ of each army was generally composed of cavalry; in single instances there were 2 horsemen to 1 foot soldier. Gustavus Adolphus stands at the head of cavalry commanders of this period. His mounted troops consisted of cuirassiers and dragoons, the latter fighting almost always as cavalry. His cuirassiers, too, were much lighter than those of the emperor, and soon proved their incontestable superiority. The Swedish cavalry were formed 3 deep; their orders were, contrary to the usage of the cuirassiers of most armies, whose chief arm was the pistol, not to lose time in firing, but to charge the enemy sword in hand. At this period the cavalry, which during the middle ages had generally been placed in the centre, was again placed, as in antiquity, on the wings of the army, where it was formed in 2 lines. In England, the civil war[347] gave rise to 2 distinguished cavalry leaders. Prince Rupert, on the royalist side, had as much "dash" in him as any cavalry general, but he was almost always carried too far, lost his cavalry out of hand, and was himself so taken up with what was immediately before him, that the general always disappeared in the "bold dragoon." Cromwell, on the other hand, with quite as much dash where it was required, was a far better general; he kept his men well in hand, always held back a reserve for unforeseen events and decisive movements, knew how to manoeuvre, and thus proved generally victorious over his inconsiderate opponent. He won the battles of Marston Moor and Naseby by his cavalry alone.

With most armies the use of the firearm still remained the chief employment of cavalry in battle, the Swedes and English alone excepted. In France, Prussia, and Austria, cavalry was drilled to use the carabine exactly as infantry used the musket. They fired on horseback, the line standing still all the while, by files, platoons, ranks, &c.; and when a movement for a charge was made, the line advanced at a trot, pulled up at a short distance from the enemy, gave a volley, drew swords, and then charged. The effective fire of the long lines of infantry had shaken all confidence in the charge of a cavalry which was no longer protected by armor; consequently, riding was neglected, no movements could be executed at a quick pace, and even at a slow pace accidents happened by the score to both men and horses. The drill was mostly dismounted work, and their officers had no idea whatever of the way of handling cavalry in battle. The French, it is true, sometimes charged sword in hand, and Charles XII of Sweden, true to his national tradition, always charged full speed without firing, dispersing cavalry and infantry, and sometimes even taking field works of a weak profile. But it was reserved for Frederick the Great and his great cavalry commander, Seydlitz, to revolutionize the mounted service, and to raise it to the culminating point of glory. The Prussian cavalry, heavy men on clumsy horses, drilled for firing only, such as Frederick's father[a] had left them to his son, were beaten in an instant at Mollwitz (1741). But no sooner was the first Silesian war[348] brought to a close than Frederick entirely reorganized his cavalry. Firing and dismounted drill were thrown into the background, and riding was attended to.

"All evolutions are to be made with the greatest speed, all wheels to be done at a canter. Cavalry officers must above all things form the men into perfect riders; the cuirassiers to be as handy and expert on horseback as a hussar, and well exercised in the use of the sword."[b]

The men were to ride every day. Riding in difficult ground, across obstacles, and fencing on horseback, were the principal drills. In a charge, no firing at all was allowed until the 1st and 2d lines of the enemy were completely broken.

"Every squadron, as it advances to the charge, is to attack the enemy sword in hand, and no commander shall be allowed to let his troops fire under penalty of infamous cashiering; the generals of brigades to be answerable for this. As they advance, they first fall into a quick trot, and finally into a full gallop, but well closed; and if they attack in this way, his majesty is certain that the enemy will always be broken." "Every officer of cavalry will have always present to his mind that there are but 2 things required to beat the enemy: 1, to charge him with the greatest possible speed and force, and 2, to outflank him."

These passages from Frederick's instructions sufficiently show the total revolution he carried out in cavalry tactics. He was

---

[a] Frederick William I.— Ed.

[b] Here and below Engels is freely quoting from Frederick II's instructions, in particular from "Instruction für die Cavallerie im Falle eines Gefechts" of March 17, 1742, "Instruction für die Obersten und sämmtliche Officiere von Regimentern der Husaren" of March 21, 1742, "Disposition, wie sich die Officiere von der Cavallerie in einem Treffen gegen den Feind zu verhalten haben" of July 25, 1744, and others.— Ed.

seconded admirably by Seydlitz, who always commanded his cuirassiers and dragoons, and made such troops of them that, for vehemence and order of charge, quickness of evolutions, readiness for flank attacks, and rapidity in rallying and reforming after a charge, no cavalry has ever equalled the Prussian cavalry of the 7 years' war.[349] The fruits were soon visible. At Hohenfriedberg the Baireuth regiment of dragoons, 10 squadrons, rode down the whole left wing of the Austrian infantry, broke 21 battalions, took 66 stand of colors, 5 guns, and 4,000 prisoners. At Zorndorf, when the Prussian infantry had been forced to retreat, Seydlitz, with 36 squadrons, drove the victorious Russian cavalry from the field, and then fell upon the Russian infantry, completely defeating it with great slaughter. At Rossbach, Striegau, Kesselsdorf, Leuthen, and in 10 other battles, Frederick owed the victory to his splendid cavalry.[350]

When the French revolutionary war broke out, the Austrians had adopted the Prussian system, but not so the French. The cavalry of the latter nation had, indeed, been much disorganized by the revolution, and in the beginning of the war the new formations proved almost useless. When their new infantry levies were met by the good cavalry of the English, Prussians, and Austrians, they were, during 1792 and '93, almost uniformly beaten. The cavalry, quite unable to cope with such opponents, was always kept in reserve until a few years' campaigning had improved them. Since 1796 and afterward every division of infantry had cavalry as a support; still, at Würzburg, the whole of the French cavalry was defeated by 59 Austrian squadrons (1796).[351] When Napoleon took the direction of affairs in France, he did his best to improve the French cavalry. He found about the worst material that could be met with. As a nation, the French are decidedly the worst horsemen of Europe, and their horses, good for draught, are not well adapted for the saddle. Napoleon himself was but an indifferent rider, and neglected riding in others. Still he made great improvements, and after the camp of Boulogne,[352] his cavalry in great part, mounted on German and Italian horses, was no despicable adversary. The campaigns of 1805 and 1806-'7 allowed his cavalry to absorb almost all the horses of the Austrian and Prussian armies, and beside, reenforced Napoleon's army by the excellent cavalry of the confederation of the Rhine and the grand duchy of Warsaw.[353] Thus were formed those enormous masses of horsemen with which Napoleon acted in 1809, 1812, and the latter part of 1813, which, though generally designated as French, were in great part composed of

Germans and Poles. The cuirass, which had been entirely done away with in the French army shortly before the revolution, was restored to a portion of the heavy cavalry by Napoleon. In other respects the organization and equipment remained nearly the same, except that with his Polish auxiliaries he received some regiments of light horse, armed with the lance, the costume and equipment of which were soon imitated in other armies. But in the tactical use of cavalry he introduced a complete change. According to the system of composing divisions and army corps of all 3 arms, a portion of the light cavalry was attached to each division or corps; but the mass of the arm, and especially all the heavy horse, were held together in reserve for the purpose of striking at a favorable moment a great decisive blow, or, in case of need, of covering the retreat of the army. These masses of cavalry, suddenly appearing on a given point of the battle-field, have often acted decisively; still, they never gained such brilliant successes as the horsemen of Frederick the Great. The cause of this is to be looked for partly in the changed tactics of infantry, which, by selecting chiefly broken ground for its operations, and always receiving cavalry in a square, made it more difficult for the latter arm to achieve such great victories as the Prussian horsemen had obtained over the long, thin infantry lines of their opponents. But it is also certain that Napoleon's cavalry was not equal to that of Frederick the Great, and that Napoleon's cavalry tactics were not in every instance an improvement upon those of Frederick. The indifferent riding of the French compelled them to charge at a comparatively slow pace, at a trot or a collected canter; there are but few instances where they charged at a gallop. Their great bravery and close ranks made up often enough for the curtailed impetus, but still their charge was not what would now be considered good. The old system of receiving hostile cavalry standing, carabine in hand, was in very many cases retained by the French cavalry, and in every such instance were they defeated. The last example of this happened at Dannigkow (April 5, 1813),[354] where about 1,200 French cavalry thus awaited a charge of 400 Prussians, and were completely beaten in spite of their numbers. As to Napoleon's tactics, the use of great masses of cavalry with him became such a fixed rule, that not only was the divisional cavalry weakened so as to be completely useless, but also in the employment of these masses he often neglected that successive engagement of his forces which is one of the principal points in modern tactics, and which is even more applicable to cavalry than to infantry. He introduced the cavalry charge in

column, and even formed whole cavalry corps into one monster
column, in such formations that the extrication of a single
squadron or regiment became an utter impossibility, and that any
attempt at deploying was entirely out of the question. His cavalry
generals, too, were not up to the mark, and even the most brilliant
of them, Murat, would have cut but a sorry figure if opposed to a
Seydlitz. During the wars of 1813, '14, and '15, cavalry tactics had
decidedly improved on the part of Napoleon's opponents. Though
to a great extent following Napoleon's system of holding cavalry in
reserve in large masses, and therefore very often keeping the
greater portion of the cavalry entirely out of an action, still in
many instances a return to the tactics of Frederick was attempted.
In the Prussian army the old spirit was revived. Blücher was the
first to use his cavalry more boldly, and generally with success.
The ambuscade of Haynau (1813),[a] where 20 Prussian squadrons
rode down 8 French battalions and took 18 guns, marks a turning
point in the modern history of cavalry, and forms a favorable
contrast to the tactics of Lützen,[355] where the allies held 18,000
horse entirely in reserve until the battle was lost, although a more
favorable cavalry ground could not be found.

The English had never adopted the system of forming large
masses of cavalry, and had therefore many successes, although
Napier himself admits that their cavalry was not so good at that
time as that of the French.[b] At Waterloo[356] (where, by the way, the
French cuirassiers for once charged at full speed), the English
cavalry was admirably handled and generally successful, except
where it followed its national weakness of getting out of hand.
Since the peace of 1815, Napoleon's tactics, though still preserved
in the regulations of most armies, have again made room for those
of Frederick. Riding is better attended to, though still not at all to
the extent it should be. The idea of receiving the enemy carabine
in hand is scouted; Frederick's rule is everywhere revived, that
every cavalry commander who allows the enemy to charge him,
instead of charging himself, deserves to be cashiered. The gallop is
again the pace of the charge; and the column attack has made way
for charges in successive lines, with dispositions for flank attack,
and with a possibility of manoeuvring with single detachments
during the charge. Still much remains to be done. A greater
attention to riding, especially across country, a nearer approach in

---

[a] See this volume, p. 174.— Ed.

[b] W. F. P. Napier, *History of the War in the Peninsula and in the South of France, from the Year 1807 to the Year 1814*, Vol. III, p. 272.— Ed.

the saddle and the seat to those of the hunting-field, and above all, a reduction of the weight carried by the horse, are improvements called for in every service without exception.

From the history of cavalry let us now turn to its present organization and tactics. The recruiting of cavalry, as far as the men are concerned, is not different upon the whole from the way the other arms recruit themselves in each country. In some states, however, the natives of particular districts are destined to this service: thus in Russia, the Malorussians (natives of Little Russia)[a]; in Prussia, the Poles. In Austria, the heavy cavalry is recruited in Germany and Bohemia, the hussars exclusively in Hungary, the lancers mostly in the Polish provinces. The recruiting of the horses, however, deserves especial notice. In England, where the whole cavalry does not require in time of war above 10,000 horses, the government finds no difficulty in buying them; but in order to insure to the service the benefit of horses not worked till nearly 5 years old, 3-year-old colts, mostly Yorkshire bred, are bought and kept at government expense in depots till they are fit to be used. The price paid for the colts (£20 to £25), and the abundance of good horses in the country, make the British cavalry certainly the best mounted in the world. In Russia a similar abundance of horses exists, though the breed is inferior to the English. The remount officers buy the horses by wholesale in the southern and western provinces of the empire, mostly from Jewish dealers; they re-sell those that are unfit, and hand over to the various regiments such as are of its color (all horses being of the same color in a Russian regiment). The colonel is considered as it were proprietor of the horses; for a round sum paid to him he has to keep the regiment well mounted. The horses are expected to last 8 years. Formerly they were taken from the large breeding establishments of Volhynia and the Ukraine, where they are quite wild; but the breaking them for cavalry purposes was so difficult that it had to be given up. In Austria the horses are partly bought, but the greater portion have of late been furnished by the government breeding establishments, which can part every year with above 5,000 5-year-old cavalry horses. For a case of extraordinary effort, a country so rich in horses as Austria can rely upon the markets of the interior. Prussia, 60 years ago, had to buy almost all her horses abroad, but now can mount the whole of her cavalry, line and Landwehr,[357] in the interior. For the line, the horses are bought at 3 years old, by remount commissaries, and sent into depots until

---

[a] The Ukrainians.— *Ed.*

old enough for service; 3,500 are required every year. In case of mobilization of the Landwehr cavalry, all horses in the country, like the men, are liable to be taken for service; a compensation of from $40 to $70 is however paid for them. There are 3 times more serviceable horses in the country than can be required. France, of all European countries, is the worst off for horses. The breed, though often good and even excellent for draught, is generally unfit for the saddle. Government breeding studs (*haras*) have been long established, but not with the success they have had elsewhere; in 1838 these studs, and the remounting depots connected with them, could not furnish 1,000 horses to the service, bought or government bred. Gen. La Roche-Aymon considered that there were not altogether 20,000 horses in France between 4 and 7 years old, fit for cavalry service.[a] Though the depots and studs have of late been much improved, they are still insufficient to fully supply the army. Algeria furnishes a splendid breed of cavalry horses, and the best regiments of the service, the *chasseurs d'Afrique,* are exclusively mounted with them, but the other regiments scarcely get any. Thus in case of a mobilization, the French are compelled to buy abroad, sometimes in England, but mostly in northern Germany, where they do not get the best class of horses, though each horse costs them nearly $100. Many condemned horses from German cavalry regiments find their way into the ranks of the French, and altogether the French cavalry, the *chasseurs d'Afrique* excepted, is the worst mounted in Europe.

Cavalry is essentially of 2 kinds: heavy and light. The real distinctive character of the 2 is in the horses. Large and powerful horses cannot well work together with small, active, and quick ones. The former in a charge act less rapidly, but with greater weight; the latter act more by the speed and impetuosity of the attack, and are moreover far more fit for single combat and skirmishing, for which heavy or large horses are neither handy nor intelligent enough. Thus far the distinction is necessary; but fashion, fancy, and the imitation of certain national costumes, have created numerous subdivisions and varieties, to notice which in detail would be of no interest. The heavy cavalry, at least in part, is in most countries furnished with a cuirass, which, however, is far from being shot proof; in Sardinia, its first rank carries a lance. Light cavalry is partly armed with the sword and carabine,

_____
   [a] La Roche-Aymon, *De la cavalerie, ou des changements nécessaires dans la composition, l'organisation et l'instruction des troupes à cheval,* première partie, p. 140.— *Ed.*

partly with the lance. The carabine is either smooth-bored or rifled. Pistols are added in most cases to the armature of the rider; the United States cavalry alone carries the revolver. The sword is either straight, or curved to a greater or less degree; the first preferable for thrusts, the second for cuts. The question as to the advantages of the lance over the sword is still under discussion. For close encounter the sword is undoubtedly preferable; and in a charge the lance, unless too long and heavy to be wielded, can scarcely act at all, but in the pursuit of broken cavalry it is found most effective. Of nations of horsemen, almost all trust to the sword; even the Cossack abandons his lance when he has to fight against the expert swordsmen of Circassia. The pistol is useless except for a signal shot; the carabine is not very effective, even if rifled, and never will be of much real use until a breech-loading one is adopted; the revolver in skilful hands is a formidable weapon for close encounter; still the queen of weapons for cavalry is a good, sharp, handy sword.

Beside the saddle, bridle, and armed rider, the cavalry horse has to carry a valise with reserve clothing, camp utensils, grooming tackle, and in a campaign also food for the rider and forage for itself. The sum total of this burden varies in different services and classes of cavalry, between 250 and 300 lbs. for the heavy marching order, a weight which will appear enormous when compared with what private saddle horses have to carry. This overweighting the horses is the weakest point of all cavalry. Great reforms are everywhere required in this respect. The weight of the men and accoutrements can and must be reduced, but as long as the present system lasts, this drag upon the horses is always to be taken into account whenever we judge of the capabilities of exertion and endurance of cavalry. Heavy cavalry, composed of strong but, if possible, comparatively light men, on strong horses, must act principally by the force of a well-closed, solid charge. This requires power, endurance, and a certain physical weight, though not as much as would render it unwieldy. There must be speed in its movements, but no more than is compatible with the highest degree of order. Once formed for the attack, it must chiefly ride straight forward; but whatever comes in its path must be swept away by its charge. The riders need not be, individually, as good horsemen as those of light cavalry; but they must have full command over their horses, and be accustomed to ride straight forward and in a well-closed mass. Their horses, in consequence, must be less sensible to the leg, nor should they have their haunches too much under them; they should step out well in their trot, and be accustomed to keep well together in a good, long hand gallop. Light cavalry, on the contrary, with nimbler men and quicker horses, has to act by its rapidity and ubiquity. What it lacks in weight must be made up by speed and activity. It will charge with the greatest vehemence; but when preferable, it will seemingly fly in order to fall upon the enemy's flank by a sudden change of front. Its superior speed and fitness for single combat render it peculiarly fit for pursuit. Its chiefs require a quicker eye and a greater presence of mind than those of heavy horse. The men must be, individually, better horsemen; they must have their horses perfectly under control, start from a stand into a full gallop, and again stop in an instant; turn quick, and leap well; the horses should be hardy and quick, light in the mouth, and obedient to the leg, handy at turning, and especially broken in for working at a canter, having their haunches well under them. Beside rapid flank and rear attacks, ambuscades, and pursuit, the light cavalry has to do the greater part of the outpost and patrolling duty for the whole army; aptness for single combat, the foundation of which is good horsemanship, is therefore one of its principal requirements. In line, the men ride less close together, so as to be always prepared for changes of front and other evolutions.

The English have nominally 13 light and 13 heavy regiments (dragoons, hussars, lancers; the 2 regiments of life-guards alone are cuirassiers); but in reality all their cavalry, by composition and training, are heavy cavalry, and little different in the size of men and horses. For real light cavalry service they have always used foreign troops—Germans in Europe, native irregulars in India. The French have 3 kinds: light cavalry, hussars and chasseurs, 174 squadrons; line cavalry, lancers and dragoons, 120 squadrons; reserve cavalry, 78 squadrons, cuirassiers and carabineers. Austria has 96 squadrons of heavy cavalry, dragoons and cuirassiers; and 192 squadrons of light, hussars and lancers. Prussia has, of the line, 80 squadrons of heavy horse, cuirassiers and lancers; and 72 squadrons of light horse, dragoons and hussars; to which may be added, in case of war, 136 squadrons of lancers of the first levy of the Landwehr. The second levy of the Landwehr cavalry will scarcely ever be formed separately. The Russian cavalry consists of 160 heavy squadrons, cuirassiers and dragoons; and 304 light squadrons, hussars and lancers. The formation of the dragoon corps for alternate mounted and infantry duty has been abandoned, and the dragoons incorporated with the heavy cavalry. The real light cavalry of the Russians, however, are the Cossacks, of whom they always have more than enough for all the outpost, reconnoitring, and irregular duties of their armies. In the U.S. army there are 2 regiments of dragoons, 1 of mounted riflemen, and 2 styled cavalry; all of which regiments, it has been recommended, should be called regiments of cavalry. The U.S. cavalry is really a mounted infantry.

The tactical unity in cavalry is the squadron, comprising as many men as the voice and immediate authority of one commander can control during evolutions. The strength of a squadron varies from 100 men (in England) to 200 men (in France); those of the other armies also being within these limits. Four, 6, 8, or 10 squadrons form a regiment. The weakest regiments are the English (400 to 480 men); the strongest the Austrian light horse (1,600 men). Strong regiments are apt to be unwieldy; too weak ones are very soon reduced by a campaign. Thus the British light brigade at Balaklava,[358] not 2 months after the opening of the campaign, numbered in 5 regiments of 2 squadrons each scarcely 700 men, or just half as many as one Russian hussar regiment on the war footing. Peculiar formations are: with the British the troop or half squadron, and with the Austrians the division or double squadron, an intermediate link which alone renders it possible for one commander to control their strong regiments of horse.

Until Frederick the Great, all cavalry was formed at least 3 deep. He first formed his hussars, in 1743, 2 deep, and at the battle of Rossbach had his heavy horse formed the same way. After the 7 years' war this formation was adopted by all other armies, and is the only one now in use. For purposes of evolution the squadron is divided into 4 divisions; wheeling from line into open column of divisions, and back into line from column, form the chief and fundamental evolution of all cavalry manoeuvres. Most other evolutions are only adapted either for the march (the flank march by threes, &c.), or for extraordinary cases (the close column by divisions or squadrons). The action of cavalry in battle is eminently a hand-to-hand encounter; its fire is of subordinate importance; steel—either sword or lance—is its chief weapon; and all cavalry action is concentrated in the charge. Thus the charge is the criterion for all movements, evolutions, and positions of cavalry. Whatever obstructs the facility of charging is faulty. The impetus of the charge is produced by concentrating the highest effort both of man and horse into its crowning moment, the moment of actual contact with the enemy. In order to effect this, it is necessary to approach the enemy with a gradually increasing velocity, so that

the horses are put to their full speed at a short distance from the
enemy only. Now the execution of such a charge is about the most
difficult matter that can be asked from cavalry. It is extremely
difficult to preserve perfect order and solidity in an advance at
increasing pace, especially if there is much not quite level ground
to go over. The difficulty and importance of riding straight
forward is here shown; for unless every rider rides straight to his
point, there arises a pressure in the ranks, which is soon rolled
back from the centre to the flanks, and from the flanks to the
centre; the horses get excited and uneasy, their unequal speed and
temper comes into play, and soon the whole line is straggling
along in any thing but a straight alignment, and with any thing
but that closed solidity which alone can insure success. Then, on
arriving in front of the enemy, it is evident that the horses will
attempt to refuse running into the standing or moving mass
opposite, and that the riders must prevent their doing so;
otherwise the charge is sure to fail. The rider, therefore, must not
only have the firm resolution to break into the enemy's line, but
he must also be perfectly master of his horse. The regulations of
different armies give various rules for the mode of advance of the
charging cavalry, but they all agree in this point, that the line, if
possible, begins to move at a walk, then trot, at from 300 to 150
yards from the enemy canter, gradually increasing to a gallop, and
at from 20 to 30 yards from the enemy full speed. All such
regulations, however, are subject to many exceptions; the state of
the ground, the weather, the condition of the horses, &c., must be
taken into consideration in every practical case. If in a charge of
cavalry against cavalry both parties actually meet, which is by far
the most uncommon case in cavalry engagements, the swords are
of little avail during the actual shock. It is the momentum of one
mass which breaks and scatters the other. The moral element,
bravery, is here at once transformed into material force; the
bravest squadron will ride on with the greatest self-confidence,
resolution, rapidity, *ensemble,* and solidity. Thus it is that no
cavalry can do great things unless it has plenty of "dash" about it.
But as soon as the ranks of one party are broken, the swords, and
with them individual horsemanship, come into play. A portion at
least of the victorious troop has also to give up its tactical
formation, in order to mow with the sword the harvest of victory.
Thus the successful charge at once decides the contest; but unless
followed up by pursuit and single combat, the victory would be
comparatively fruitless. It is this immense preponderance of the
party which has preserved its tactical compactness and formation,

over the one which has lost it, which explains the impossibility for irregular cavalry, be it ever so good and so numerous, to defeat regular cavalry. There is no doubt that so far as individual horsemanship and swordsmanship is concerned, no regular cavalry ever approached the irregulars of the nations of horse-warriors of the East; and yet the very worst of European regular cavalries has always defeated them in the field. From the defeat of the Huns at Châlons (451) to the sepoy mutiny of 1857,[359] there is not a single instance where the splendid but irregular horsemen of the East have broken a single regiment of regular cavalry in an actual charge. Their irregular swarms, charging without concert or compactness, cannot make any impression upon the solid, rapidly moving mass. Their superiority can only appear when the tactical formation of the regulars is broken, and the combat of man to man has its turn; but the wild racing of the irregulars toward their opponents can have no such result. It has only been when regular cavalry, in pursuit, have abandoned their line formation and engaged in single combat, that irregulars, suddenly turning round and seizing the favorable moment, have defeated them; indeed, this stratagem has made up almost the whole of the tactics of irregulars against regulars, ever since the wars of the Parthians and the Romans. Of this there is no better example than that of Napoleon's dragoons in Egypt, undoubtedly the worst regular cavalry then existing, which defeated in every instance the most splendid of irregular horsemen, the Mamelukes.[360] Napoleon said of them, 2 Mamelukes were decidedly superior to 3 Frenchmen; 100 Frenchmen were a match for 100 Mamelukes; 300 Frenchmen generally beat 300 Mamelukes; 1,000 Frenchmen in every instance defeated 1,500 Mamelukes.[a]

However great may be the superiority in a charge of that body of cavalry which best preserves its tactical formation, it is evident that even this body must, after the successful charge, be comparatively disordered. The success of the charge is not equally decisive on every point; many men are irretrievably engaged in single combat or pursuit; and it is comparatively but a small portion, mostly belonging to the second rank, which remains in some kind of line. This is the most dangerous moment for cavalry; a very small body of fresh troops, thrown upon it, would snatch the victory from its hands. To rally quickly after a charge is therefore the criterion of a really good cavalry, and it is in this

---

[a] *Mémoires pour servir à l'histoire de France, sous Napoléon, écrits à Sainte-Hélène*, Tome premier, p. 262.—*Ed.*

point that not only young but also otherwise experienced and brave troops are deficient. The British cavalry, riding the most spirited horses, are especially apt to get out of hand, and have almost everywhere suffered severely for it (*e.g.,* at Waterloo and Balaklava). The pursuit, on the rally being sounded, is generally left to some divisions or squadrons, specially or by general regulations designated for this service; while the mass of the troops re-form to be ready for all emergencies. For the disorganized state, even of the victors, after a charge, is inducement enough to always keep a reserve in hand which may be launched in case of failure in the first instance; and thus it is that the first rule in cavalry tactics has always been, never to engage more than a portion of the disposable forces at a time. This general application of reserves will explain the variable nature of large cavalry combats, where the tide of victory ebbs and flows to and fro, either party being beaten in his turn until the last disposable reserves bring the power of their unbroken order to bear upon the disordered, surging mass, and decide the action. Another very important circumstance is the ground. No arm is so much controlled by the ground as cavalry. Heavy, deep soil will break the gallop into a slow canter; an obstacle which a single horseman would clear without looking at it, may break the order and solidity of the line; and an obstacle easy to clear for fresh horses will bring down animals that have been trotted and galloped about without food from early morning. Again, an unforeseen obstacle, by stopping the advance and entailing a change of front and formation, may bring the whole line within reach of the enemy's flank attacks. An example of how cavalry attacks should not be made, was Murat's great charge at the battle of Leipsic.[361] He formed 14,000 horsemen into one deep mass, and advanced on the Russian infantry which had just been repulsed in an attack on the village of Wachau. The French horse approached at a trot; about 600 or 800 yards from the allied infantry they broke into a canter; in the deep ground the horses soon got fatigued, and the impulse of the charge was spent by the time they reached the squares. Only a few battalions which had suffered severely were ridden over. Passing round the other squares, the mass galloped on through the second line of infantry, without doing any harm, and finally arrived at a line of ponds and morasses which put a stop to their progress. The horses were completely blown, the men in disorder, the regiments mixed and uncontrollable; in this state two Prussian regiments and the Cossacks of the guard, in all less than 2,000 men, surprised their flanks and drove them all pell mell back again. In this instance there was neither a reserve for unforeseen emergencies, nor any proper regard for pace and distance; the result was defeat.

The charge may be made in various formations. Tacticians distinguish the charge *en muraille,* when the squadrons of the charging line have none or but very small intervals between each other; the charge with intervals, where there are from 10 to 20 yards from squadron to squadron; the charge *en échelon,* where the successive squadrons break off one after the other from one wing, and thus reach the enemy not simultaneously but in succession, which form may be much strengthened by a squadron in open column on the outward rear of the squadron forming the first *échelon;* finally, the charge in column. This last is essentially opposed to the whole of the former modes of charging, which are all of them but modifications of the line attack. The line was the general and fundamental form of all cavalry charges up to Napoleon. In the whole of the 18th century, we find cavalry charging in column in one case only, *i.e.* when it had to break through a surrounding enemy. But Napoleon, whose cavalry was composed of brave men but bad riders, had to make up for the tactical imperfections of his mounted troops by some new contrivance. He began to send his cavalry to the charge in deep columns, thus forcing the front ranks to ride forward, and throwing at once a far greater number of horsemen upon the selected point of attack than could have been done by a line attack. The desire of acting with masses, during the campaigns succeeding that of 1807, became with Napoleon a sort of monomania. He invented formations of columns which were perfectly monstrous, and which, happening to be successful in 1809, were adhered to in the later campaigns, and helped to lose him many a battle. He formed columns of whole divisions either of infantry or of cavalry, by ranging deployed battalions and regiments one behind the other. This was first tried with cavalry at Eckmühl,[362] in 1809, where 10 regiments of cuirassiers charged in column, 2 regiments deployed in front, 4 similar lines following at distances of about 60 yards. With infantry, columns of whole divisions, one battalion deployed behind the other, were formed at Wagram.[363] Such manoeuvres might not be dangerous against the slow and methodical Austrians of the time, but in every later campaign, and with more active enemies, they ended in defeat. We have seen what a pitiable end the great charge of Murat at Wachau, in the same formation, came to. The disastrous issue of d'Erlon's great infantry attack at Waterloo was caused by its being made with this formation.[364] With cavalry the monster column appears especially faulty, as it absorbs the most valuable resources into one unwieldy mass, which, once launched, is irretrievably out of hand, and, whatever success it may have in front, is always at the mercy of smaller bodies well in hand that are thrown on its flanks. With the materials for one such column, a second line and one or two reserves might be prepared, the charges of which might not have such an effect at first, but would certainly by their repetition ultimately obtain greater results with smaller losses. In most services, indeed, this charge in column has either been abandoned, or it has been retained as a mere theoretical curiosity, while for all practical purposes the formation of large bodies of cavalry is made in several lines at charging intervals, supporting and relieving each other during a prolonged engagement. Napoleon, too, was the first to form his cavalry into masses of several divisions, called corps of cavalry. As a means of simplifying the transmission of commands in a large army, such an organization of the reserve cavalry is eminently necessary; but when maintained on the field of battle, when these corps had to act in a body, it has never produced any adequate results. In fact, it was one of the main causes of that faulty formation of monster columns which we have already mentioned. In the present European armies, the cavalry corps is generally retained, and in the Prussian, Russian, and Austrian services, there are even established normal formations and general rules for the action of such a corps on the field of battle, all of which are based on the formation of a first and second line and a reserve, together with indications for the placing of the horse artillery attached to such a body.

We have hitherto spoken of the action of cavalry so far only as it is directed against cavalry. But one of the principal purposes for which this arm is used in battle, in fact its principal use now-a-days, is its action against infantry. We have seen that in the 18th century infantry, in battle, scarcely ever formed square against cavalry. It received the charge in line, and if the attack was directed against a flank, a few companies wheeled back, en potence, to meet it. Frederick the Great instructed his infantry never to form square except when an isolated battalion was surprised by cavalry; and if in such a case it had formed square,

"it may march straight against the enemy's horse, drive them away, and, never heeding their attacks, proceed to its destination."

The thin lines of infantry in those days met the cavalry charge with full confidence in the effect of their fire, and indeed repelled it often enough; but where they once got broken, the disaster was irreparable, as at Hohenfriedberg and Zorndorf. At present, when the column has replaced the line in so many cases, the rule is that infantry always, where it is practicable, form square to receive cavalry. There are indeed plenty of instances in modern wars where good cavalry has surprised infantry in line and has to fly from its fire; but they form the exception. The question now is, whether cavalry has a fair chance of breaking squares of infantry. Opinions are divided; but it appears to be generally admitted that, under ordinary circumstances, a good, intact infantry, not shattered by artillery fire, stands a very great chance against cavalry, while with young foot soldiers, who have lost the edge of their energy and steadiness by a hard day's fighting, by heavy losses and long exposure to fire, a resolute cavalry has the best of it. There are exceptions, such as the charge of the German dragoons at Garcia Hernandez (in 1812),[365] where each of 3 squadrons broke an intact French square; but as a rule, a cavalry commander will not find it advisable to launch his men on such infantry. At Waterloo, Ney's grand charges with the mass of the French reserve cavalry on Wellington's centre, could not break the English and German squares, because these troops, sheltered a good deal behind the crest of the ridge, had suffered very little from the preceding cannonade, and were almost all as good as intact. Such charges, therefore, are adapted for the last stage of a battle only, when the infantry has been a good deal shattered and exhausted both by actual engagement and by passivity under a concentrated artillery fire. And in such cases they act decisively, as at Borodino[a] and Ligny,[366] especially when supported, as in both these cases, by infantry reserves.

We cannot enter here into the various duties which cavalry may be called upon to perform on outpost, patrolling, and escorting service, &c. A few words on the general tactics of cavalry, however, may find a place. Infantry having more and more become the main stay of battles, the manoeuvres of the mounted arm are necessarily more or less subordinate to those of the former. And as modern tactics are founded upon the admixture and mutual support of the 3 arms, it follows that for at least a portion of the cavalry, all independent action is entirely out of the question. Thus the cavalry of an army is always divided into 2 distinct bodies: divisional cavalry and reserve cavalry. The first consists of horsemen attached to the various divisions and corps of

---

infantry, and under the same commander with them. In battle, its office is to seize any favorable moments which may offer themselves to gain an advantage, or to disengage its own infantry when attacked by superior forces. Its action is naturally limited, and its strength is not sufficient to act any way independently. The cavalry of reserve, the mass of the cavalry with the army, acts in the same subordinate position toward the whole infantry of the army as the divisional cavalry does toward the infantry division to which it belongs. Accordingly, the reserve cavalry will be held in hand till a favorable moment for a great blow offers itself, either to repel a grand infantry or cavalry attack of the enemy, or to execute a charge of its own of a decisive nature. From what has been stated above, it will be evident that the proper use of the cavalry of reserve is generally during the latter stages of a great battle; but then it may be and often has been decisive. Such immense successes as Seydlitz obtained with his horse are completely out of the question now; but still, most great battles of modern times have been very materially influenced by the part cavalry has played in them. But the great importance of cavalry lies in pursuit. Infantry supported by artillery need not despair against cavalry so long as it preserves its order and steadiness; but once broken, no matter by what cause, it is a prey to the mounted men that are launched against it. There is no running away from the horses; even on difficult ground, good horsemen can make their way; and an energetic pursuit of a beaten army by cavalry is always the best and the only way to secure the full fruits of the victory. Thus, whatever supremacy in battles may have been gained by infantry, cavalry still remains an indispensable arm, and will always remain so; and now, as heretofore, no army can enter the lists with a fair chance of success unless it has a cavalry that can both ride and fight.

Written between January 14 and June 22, 1858

First published in *The New American Cyclopaedia*, Vol. IV, 1859

Reproduced from *The New American Cyclopaedia*

Frederick Engels

FORTIFICATION [367]

This subject is sometimes divided into defensive fortification, which provides the means of rendering a given locality, permanently or for a short time only, capable of defence; and offensive fortification, which contains the rules for conducting a siege. We shall, however, treat of it here under the three heads of *permanent fortification*, or the mode of putting a locality, in time of peace, in such a state of defence as to compel the enemy to attack it by a regular siege; the art of *sieges*; and *field fortification*, or the construction of temporary works to strengthen a given point in consequence of the momentary importance which it may acquire under the peculiar circumstances of a campaign.

I. PERMANENT FORTIFICATION

The oldest form of fortification appears to be the stockade, which up to the end of the 18th century was still the national system with the Turks (*palanka*), and is even now in full use in the Indo-Chinese peninsula among the Burmese. It consists of a double or triple row of stout trees, planted upright and near each other in the ground, forming a wall all around the town or camp to be defended. Darius in his expedition among the Scythians, Cortes at Tabasco in Mexico, and Capt. Cook in New Zealand, all came in contact with such stockades. Sometimes the space between the rows of trees was filled up with earth; in other instances the trees were connected and held together by wicker work. The next step was the erection of masonry walls instead of stockades. This plan secured greater durability, at the same time that it rendered the assault far more difficult; and from the days of Nineveh and

Babylon down to the close of the middle ages, masonry walls formed the exclusive means of fortification among all the more civilized nations. The walls were made so high that escalade was rendered difficult; they were made thick enough to offer a lengthened resistance to the battering ram, and to allow the defenders to move about freely on the top, sheltered by a thinner masonry parapet with battlements, through the embrasures of which arrows and other missiles might be shot or thrown against the assailants. To increase the defence, the parapet was soon built overhanging, with holes between the projecting stones on which it rested, so as to allow the besieged to see the foot of the wall and reach an enemy who might have got so far by direct missiles from above. The ditch, no doubt, was also introduced at an early period, surrounding the whole wall, and serving as the chief obstacle against access to it. Finally, the defensive capabilities of masonry walls were developed to the highest point by adding at intervals towers which projected from the wall, thus giving it a flanking defence by missiles thrown from them at such troops as assailed the space between two towers. Being in most cases higher than the wall, and separated from its top by cross parapets, they commanded it and formed each a small fortress, which had to be taken singly after the defenders had been driven from the main wall itself. If we add to this, that in some cities, especially in Greece, there was a kind of citadel, on some commanding height inside the walls (acropolis), forming a reduit and second line of defence, we shall have indicated the most essential points of the fortification of the masonry epoch.

But from the 14th to the end of the 16th century the introduction of artillery fundamentally changed the modes of attacking fortified places. From this period dates that immense literature on fortification which has produced systems and methods innumerable, part of which have found a more or less extensive practical application, while others, and not always the least ingenious, have been passed over as merely theoretical curiosities, until at later periods the fruitful ideas contained in them have been again drawn into daylight by more fortunate successors. This has been the fate, as we shall see, of the very author who forms, if we may say so, the bridge between the old masonry system and the new system of earthworks merely revetted with masonry in those places which the enemy cannot see from a distance.[a] The first effect of the introduction of artillery was an

---

[a] This refers to the German engineer Daniel Speckle and his book *Architectura von Vestungen.— Ed.*

increase in the thickness of the walls and in the diameter of the towers at the expense of their height. These towers were now called roundels (*rondelli*), and were made large enough to hold several pieces of cannon. To enable the besieged to work cannon on the wall too, a rampart of earth was thrown up behind it so as to give it the necessary width. We shall soon see how this earthwork gradually encroached on the wall, so as in some cases to supersede it altogether. Albert Dürer, the celebrated German painter, developed this system of roundels to its highest perfection. He made them perfectly independent forts, intersecting the continuity of the wall at certain intervals, and with casemated batteries enfilading the ditch; of his masonry parapets, not more than 3 feet high is uncovered (visible to the besieger and subject to his direct fire); and in order to complete the defence of the ditch, he proposed *caponnières*, casemated works on the sole of the ditch, hidden from the eyes of the besiegers, with embrasures on either side so as to enfilade the ditch as far as the next angle of the polygon. Almost all these proposals were new inventions; and if none except the casemates found favor with his age, we shall see that in the latest and most important systems of fortification they have all been adopted and developed according to the altered circumstances of modern times.

About the same time, a change was adopted in the shape of the enlarged towers from which modern systems of fortification may be considered to date. The round shape had the disadvantage that neither the curtain (the piece of wall between two towers) nor the next adjoining towers could reach with their fire every point in front of an intermediate tower; there were small angles close to the wall, where the enemy, if he once reached them, could not be touched by the fire of the fortress. To avoid this, the tower was changed into an irregular pentagon, with one side turned toward the interior of the fortress, and 4 toward the open country. This pentagon was called a bastion. To prevent repetitions and obscurity, we shall now at once proceed to give the description and nomenclature of bastionary defence, based on one of those systems which show all its essential particulars.

Fig. 1 (see next page) represents 3 fronts of a hexagon fortified according to Vauban's first system. The left side represents the mere outline as used in the geometrical delineation of the work; the right gives the ramparts, glacis, &c., in detail. The entire side of the polygon $f'f''$ is not formed by a continuous rampart; at each end, the portions d' f' and e'' f'' are left open and the space thus arising is closed by the projecting pentagonal bastion

d' b' a' c' e'. The lines a' b' and a' c' form the faces, the
lines b' d' and c' e' the flanks of the bastion. The points
where faces and flanks meet are called the shoulder points. The
line a' f', which goes from the centre of the circle to the point
of the bastion, is called the capital. The line e'' d', forming part
of the original circumference of the hexagon, is the curtain. Thus
every polygon will have as many bastions as sides. The bastion may
be either full, if the whole pentagon is filled up with earth as high
as the *terreplein* of the rampart (the place where the guns stand),
or hollow (empty) if the rampart slopes down, immediately behind
the guns, into the interior. In fig. 1, d b a c e is a full bastion; the

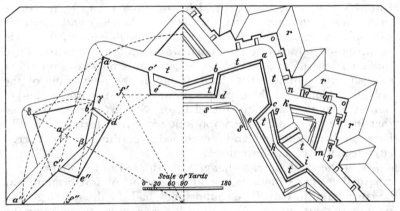

FIG. 1

next one to the right, of which one half only is seen, is a hollow
one. Bastions and curtains together constitute the enceinte, or
body of the place. In them we notice, on the terreplein, first the
parapet, constructed in front so as to shelter the defenders, and
then the ramps, on the interior slope (s s), by which the
communications with the interior are kept up. The rampart is
high enough to cover the houses of the town from direct fire, and
the parapet thick enough to offer lengthened resistance to heavy
artillery. All round the rampart is the ditch t t t t, and in it are
several classes of outworks. First, the ravelin or demilune k l m, in
front of the curtain, a triangular work with two faces, k l and l m,
each with a rampart and parapet to receive artillery. The open
rear of any work is called the gorge; thus in the ravelin, k m, in
the bastion d e, is the gorge. The parapet of the ravelin is about 3
or 4 feet lower than the parapet of the body of the place, so that it
is commanded by it, and the guns of the latter may in case of need

fire away over it. Between the curtain and ravelin there is a long and narrow detached work in the ditch, the *tenaille, g h i,* destined principally to cover the curtains from breaching fire; it is low and too narrow for artillery, and its parapet merely serves for infantry to flank the ditch fire into the lunette in case of a successful assault. Beyond the ditch is the covered way, *n o p,* bounded on the inner side by the ditch and on the outer side by the interior slope of the glacis, *r r r,* which from its highest inner boundary line or crest (*crête*) slopes very gradually down into the field. The crest of the glacis is again 3 feet or more lower than the ravelin, so as to allow all the guns of the fortress to fire over it. Of the slopes in these earthworks the exterior one of the body of the place and of the outworks in the ditch (scarp), and the exterior one of the ditch (from the covered way downward) or counterscarp, are generally revetted with masonry. The salient and reentering angles of the covered way form large, roomy, sheltered spots, called places of arms; they are called either salient (*o*) or reentering (*n p*), according to the angles at which they are situated. To prevent the covered way from being enfiladed, traverses or cross parapets are constructed across it at intervals, leaving only small passages at the end nearest the glacis. Sometimes there is a small work constructed to cover the communication across the ditch from the tenaille to the ravelin; it is called a *caponnière,* and consists of a narrow pathway covered on either side by a parapet, the exterior surfaces of which slope down gradually like a glacis. There is such a caponnière between the tenaille *g h i* and the ravelin *k l m,* fig. 1.

The section given in fig. 2 will assist in rendering this description clearer. A is the terreplein of the body of the place, B is the parapet, C the masonry revetment of the scarp, D the ditch, E the *cunette,*[a] a smaller and deeper ditch drawn across the middle of the larger one, F the masonry revetment of the counterscarp, G the covered way, H the glacis. The steps shown behind the parapet and glacis are called banquettes, and serve as stands for infantry to step on and fire over the protecting parapet. It will be readily observed from the diagram that the guns placed on the flanks of the bastions sweep the whole ditch in front of the adjoining bastions. Thus the face a' b' is covered by the fire of the flank c'' e'', and the face a' c' by the flank b d. On the other hand, the inner faces of two adjoining bastions cover the faces of the ravelin between them, by keeping the ditch in front of

---

[a] Or cuvette.— *Ed.*

the ravelin under their fire. Thus there is no portion of the ditch unprotected by a flanking fire; in this consists the original and great step in advance by which the bastionary system inaugurates a new epoch in the history of fortification.

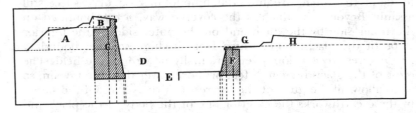

FIG. 2

The inventor of bastions is not known, nor is the precise date at which they were introduced; the only thing certain is that they were invented in Italy, and that San Michele in 1527 constructed two bastions in the rampart of Verona. All statements respecting earlier bastions are doubtful. The systems of bastionary fortification are classed under several national schools; the first to be mentioned is of course that which invented bastions, the Italian. The first Italian bastions bore the stamp of their origin; they were nothing but polygonal towers or roundels; they scarcely altered the former character of the fortification, except as regarded the flanking fire. The enceinte remained a masonry wall, exposed to the direct fire of the enemy; the rampart of earth thrown up behind served chiefly to give room to place and handle artillery, and its inner slope was also revetted with masonry, as in the old town walls. It was not till a later day that the parapet was constructed of earthworks, but even then the whole of its outer slope up to the top was revetted with masonry exposed to the direct fire of the enemy. The curtains were very long, from 300 to 550 yards. The bastions were very small, the size of large roundels, the flanks always perpendicular to the curtains. Now as it is a rule in fortification that the best flanking fire always comes from a line perpendicular to the line to be flanked, it is evident that the chief object of the old Italian flank was to cover, not the short and distant face of the adjoining bastion, but the long straight line of the curtain. Where the curtain became too long, a flat, obtuse-angled bastion was constructed on the middle of it, and called a platform (*piatta forma*). The flanks were not constructed on the shoulder point, but a little retired behind the rampart of the faces, so that the shoulder points projected and were supposed to shelter them; and each flank had two batteries, a lower one, and a higher one a little to the rear; sometimes even a casemate in the scarp wall of the flank on the bottom of the ditch. Add to this a ditch, and you have the whole of the original Italian system; there were no ravelins, no tenailles, no covered way, no glacis. But this system was soon improved. The curtains were shortened, the bastions were enlarged. The length of the inner side of the polygon (f' f', fig. 1) was fixed at from 250 to 300 yards. The flanks were made longer, $^1/_6$ of the side of the polygon, $^1/_4$ of the length of the curtain. Thus, though they remained perpendicular to the curtain and had other defects, as we shall see, they now began to give more protection to the face of the next bastion. The bastions were made full, and in their centre a cavalier was often erected, that is, a work with faces and flanks parallel to those of the bastion, but with a rampart and parapet so much higher as to admit of its firing over the parapet of the bastion. The ditch was very wide and deep, the counterscarp running generally parallel to the face of the bastion; but as this direction of the counterscarp prevented the part of the flank nearest the shoulder from seeing and flanking the whole of the ditch, it was subsequently done away with, and the counterscarp was traced so that its prolongation passed through the shoulder point of the next bastion. The covered way was then introduced (first in the citadel of Milan, in the 2d quarter of the 16th century, first described by Tartaglia in 1554[a]). It served as a place of concentration as well as of retreat for sallying parties, and from its introduction the scientific and energetic use of offensive movements in the defence of fortresses may be said to date; to increase its utility the places of arms were introduced, which give more room, and of which the reentering angles also give a capital flanking fire to the covered way. To render the access to the covered way still more difficult, rows of palisades were erected on the glacis, one or two yards from its crest, but in this position they were soon destroyed by the enemy's fire; after the middle of the 17th century, therefore, they were placed, at the suggestion of the Frenchman Maudin, on the covered way, covered by the glacis. The gates were in the middle of the curtain; to cover them, a crescent-shaped work was placed in the middle of the ditch in front of them; but for the same reason that the towers were transformed into bastions, the half-moon (*demi-lune*) was soon

---

[a] A reference to Book 6 of Nicolò Tartaglia's *Quesiti, et inventioni di verse.*— *Ed.*

changed into a triangular work—the present ravelin. This was still very small, but became larger when it was found that not only did it serve as a bridge-head across the ditch, but also covered flanks and curtains against the enemy's fire, gave a cross fire in front of the capitals of the bastions, and effectually flanked the covered way. Still they were made very small, so that the prolongation of their faces reached the body of the place in the curtain point (the extremity of the curtain). The principal faults of the Italian mode of fortification were the following: 1. The bad direction of the flank. After the introduction of ravelins and covered ways, the curtain became less and less the point of attack; the faces of the bastions now were chiefly assailed. To cover these well, the prolongation of the faces should have met the curtain at the very point where the flank of the next bastion was erected, and this flank should have been perpendicular or nearly so to this prolonged line (called the line of defence). In that case there would have been an effective flanking fire all along the ditch and front of the bastion. As it was, the line of defence was neither perpendicular to the flanks nor did it join the curtain at the curtain point; it intersected the curtain at $1/4$, $1/3$, or $1/2$ of its length. Thus, the direct fire of the flank was more likely to injure the garrison of the opposite flank than the assailants of the next bastion. 2. There was an evident want of provision for a prolonged defence after the enceinte had been breached and successfully assaulted at one single point. 3. The small ravelins but imperfectly covered the curtains and flanks, and received but a poor flanking fire from them. 4. The great elevation of the rampart, which was all faced or revetted with masonry, exposed, in most cases, a height of 15 to 20 feet of masonry to the direct fire of the enemy, and of course this masonry was soon destroyed. We shall find that it took almost two centuries to eradicate this prejudice in favor of uncovered masonry, even after the Netherlands had proved its uselessness. The best engineers and authors belonging to the Italian school were: San Michele (died 1559), fortified Napoli di Romania in Greece, and Candia, and built Fort Lido near Venice; Tartaglia (about 1550); Alghisi da Carpi, Girolamo Maggi, and Giacomo Castriotto, who about the end of the 16th century all wrote on fortification.[a] Paciotto of Urbino built the citadels of Turin and Antwerp (1560-'70). The later Italian authors on fortification, Marchi, Busca, Floriani, Rossetti,

---

[a] G. Alghisi, *Delle fortificationi*; G. Maggi and G. Castriotto, *Della fortificatione delle citta.*—Ed.

introduced many improvements, but none of these were original. They were mere plagiarists of more or less skill; they copied most of their devices from the German Daniel Speckle, and the remainder from the Netherlanders. They all belong to the 17th century, and were completely eclipsed by the rapid development of fortificatory science which at that time took place in Germany, the Netherlands, and France.

The defects of the Italian system of fortification were soon discovered in Germany. The first man to point out the chief defect of the elder Italian school, the small bastions and long curtains, was a German engineer, Franz, who fortified for Charles V the town of Antwerp. In the council held to try the plan, he insisted upon larger bastions and shorter curtains, but was outvoted by the duke of Alva and the other Spanish generals, who believed in nothing but the routine of the old Italian system. Other German fortresses were distinguished by the adoption of casemated galleries upon the principle of Dürer, as Küstrin, fortified in 1537-'58, and Jülich, fortified a few years later by an engineer known under the name of Master John (*Meister Johann*). But the man who first broke completely through the fetters of the Italian school and laid down the principles on which the whole of the subsequent systems of bastionary fortification are founded, was Daniel Speckle, engineer to the town of Strasbourg (died 1589). His chief principles were: 1. That a fortress becomes stronger the more sides there are to the polygon which forms the enceinte, the different fronts being thereby enabled to give a better support to each other; consequently, the nearer the outline to be defended comes to a straight line, the better. This principle, demonstrated as an original discovery with a great show of mathematical learning by Cormontaigne, was thus very well known to Speckle 150 years earlier. 2. Acute-angled bastions are bad; so are obtuse-angled; the salient angle should be a right one. Though correct in his opposition to acute salients (the smallest admissible salient angle is now generally fixed at 60°), the partiality of his time for right-angled salients made him hostile to the obtuse salient, which is indeed very advantageous and unavoidable in polygons with many sides. In fact, this appears to have been merely a concession to the prejudices of his time, for the diagrams of what he considers his strongest method of fortification all have obtuse-angled bastions. 3. The Italian bastions are far too small; a bastion must be large. Consequently, Speckle's bastions are larger than those of Cormontaigne. 4. Cavaliers are necessary in every bastion and on every curtain. This was a consequence of the system of siege of his time, in which high cavaliers in the trenches played a great part. But in Speckle's intention, the cavaliers were to do more than resist these; they are real *coupures* provided beforehand in the bastion, forming a second line of defence after the enceinte has been breached and stormed. The whole of the credit generally given to Vauban and Cormontaigne for cavaliers forming permanent coupures, is therefore in reality due to Speckle. 5. A portion, at least, of the flank, and better still the whole of the flank of a bastion, must be perpendicular to the line of defence, and the flank be erected in the point where the line of defence crosses the curtain. This important principle, the alleged discovery of which forms the greater part of the glory of the French engineer Pagan, was thus publicly proclaimed 70 years before Pagan. 6. Casemated galleries are necessary for the defence of the ditch; consequently Speckle has them both on the faces and flanks of the bastion, but only for infantry; if he had made them large enough for artillery, he would in this respect have been fully up to the latest improvements. 7. To be useful, the ravelin must be as large as possible; accordingly, Speckle's ravelin is the largest ever proposed. Now, Vauban's improvements upon Pagan consist partly, and Cormontaigne's improvements upon Vauban consist almost entirely, in the successive enlargement of the ravelin; but Speckle's ravelin is a good deal larger than even Cormontaigne's. 8. The covered way is to be strengthened as much as possible. Speckle was the first to see the immense importance of the covered way, and he strengthened it accordingly. The crests of the glacis and of the counterscarp were formed *en crémaillère* (like the edge of a saw), so as to render enfilading fire ineffective. Cormontaigne, again, took up this idea of Speckle's; but he retained the traverses (short ramparts across the covered way against enfilading fire), which Speckle rejected. Modern engineers have generally come to the conclusion that Speckle's plan is better than Cormontaigne's. Speckle, beside, was the first to place artillery on the places of arms of the covered way. 9. No piece of masonry is to be exposed to the eye and direct fire of the enemy, so that his breaching batteries cannot be established before he has arrived on the crest of the glacis. This most important principle, though established by Speckle in the 16th century, was not generally adopted until Cormontaigne; even Vauban exposes a good deal of his masonry. (See C, fig. 2.) In this short abstract of Speckle's ideas the fundamental principles of all modern bastionary fortification are not only contained but plainly stated, and his system, which even now would afford very good defensive works, is truly wonderful considering the time in which he lived. There is not a celebrated engineer in the whole history of modern fortification who cannot be proved to have copied some of his best ideas from this great original source of bastionary defence. Speckle's practical engineering skill was shown in the construction of the fortresses of Ingolstadt, Schlettstadt, Hagenau, Ulm, Colmar, Basel, and Strasbourg, all of which were fortified under his direction.

About the same epoch, the struggle for the independence of the Netherlands[368] gave rise to another school of fortification. The Dutch towns, whose old masonry walls could not be expected to resist a regular attack, had to be fortified against the Spaniards; there was, however, neither time nor money for the erection of the high masonry bastions and cavaliers of the Italian system. But the nature of the ground offered other resources in its low elevation above the water horizon, and consequently the Dutch, expert in canal and dike building, trusted to the water for their defence. Their system was the exact counterpart of the Italian: wide and shallow wet ditches, from 14 to 40 yards across; low ramparts without any masonry revetment, but covered by a still lower advanced rampart (*fausse-braie*) for the stronger defence of the ditch; numerous outworks in the ditch, such as ravelins, half moons (ravelins in front of the salient of the bastion), horn and crown works*; and finally, a better use of the accidents of the ground than with the Italians. The first town fortified entirely by earthworks and wet ditches was Breda (1533). Subsequently the Dutch method received several improvements: a narrow zone of the scarp was revetted with masonry, as the wet ditches, when frozen over in winter, were easily passed by the enemy; locks and sluices were constructed in the ditch, so as to let the water in at the moment when the enemy had begun to sap the hitherto dry bottom; and finally, sluices and dikes were constructed for a systematic inundation of the country around the foot of the glacis. The writers on this elder Dutch method of fortification are

---

* A horn work is a bastionary front, two half bastions, a curtain, and a ravelin advanced in front of the main ditch and closed on each side by a straight line of rampart and ditch, which is aligned upon the faces of the bastions of the enceinte so as to be completely flanked by their fire. A crown work consists of two such advanced fronts (one bastion flanked by two half bastions); a double crown work has three fronts. In all these works it is necessary that their rampart should be at least as much lower than that of the enceinte as the rampart of the ravelin to maintain the command of the enceinte over them. The adoption of such outworks, which of course were exceptions, was regulated by the nature of the ground.

Marolois (1627), Freitag (1630), Völker (1666), Melder (1670). An
application of Speckle's maxims to the Dutch method was
attempted by Scheither, Neubauer, Heidemann, and Heer (all
from 1670 to 1690, and all of them Germans).

Of all the different schools of fortification, the French has
enjoyed the greatest popularity; its maxims have found practical
application in a greater number of still existing fortresses than
those of all the other schools put together. Still, there is no school
so poor in original ideas. There is neither a new work nor a new
principle in the whole of the French school which is not borrowed
from the Italians, the Dutch, or the Germans. But the great merit
of the French is the reduction of the art to precise mathematical
rules, the symmetrical arrangement of the proportions of the
different lines, and the adaptation of the scientific theory to the
varied conditions given by the locality to be fortified. Errard of
Bar-le-Duc (1594), commonly called the father of French fortification, has no claim to the appellation; his flanks form an acute
angle with the curtain, so as to be still more ineffective than those
of the Italians. A more important name is Pagan (1645). He was
the first to introduce in France, and to popularize, Speckle's
principle that the flanks should be perpendicular to the lines of
defence. His bastions are roomy; the proportions between the
lengths of faces, flanks, and curtains are very good; the lines of
defence are never longer than 240 yards, so that the whole of the
ditch, but not the covered way, is within musket range from the
flanks. His ravelin is larger than that of the Italians, and has a
reduit or keep in its gorge, so as to admit of resistance when its
rampart has already been taken. He covers the faces of the
bastions with a narrow detached work in the ditch, called a
counter-guard, a work which had already been used by the Dutch
(the German Dilich appears to have first introduced it). His
bastions have a double rampart on the faces, the second to serve
as a coupure; but the ditch between the two ramparts is entirely
without flanking fire. The man who made the French school the
first in Europe was Vauban (1633-1707), marshal of France.
Although his real military glory rests upon his two great
inventions in the attack of fortresses (ricochet fire and parallels),
still he is popularly better known as a constructor of them. What
we have said of the French school is true of Vauban's method in
the highest degree. We see in his constructions as great a variety
of forms as is compatible with the bastionary system; but there is
nothing original among them, much less any attempt to adopt
other forms than the bastionary. But the arrangement of the

details, the proportions of the lines, the profiles, and the adaptation of the theory to the ever-varying requirements of the locality, are so ingenious, that they appear perfection in comparison to the works of his predecessors, so that scientific and systematic fortification may be said to date from him. Vauban, however, did not write a line on his method of fortification, but from the great number of fortresses constructed by him the French engineers have tried to deduce the theoretical rules he followed, and thus have been established 3 methods, called Vauban's first, second, and third system.

Fig. 1 gives the first system in its greatest simplicity. The chief dimensions were: the outer side of the polygon, from the point of one bastion to that of the next, 300 yards (on an average); on the middle of this line, a perpendicular α β, $1/6$ of the first; through β, the lines of defence from a'' and a', a'' d' and a' e''. From the points a'' and a', $2/7$ of a'' a' measured on the lines of defence gives the faces a'' c'' and a' b'. From the shoulder points c'' and b' arcs with the radius c'' d' or b' e'' were drawn between the lines of defence, giving the flanks b' d' and c'' e''. Draw e'' d', the curtain. The ditch: with radius 30 yards, an arc in front of the point of the bastion, prolonged by tangents drawn to this arc from the shoulder points of the adjoining bastions, gives the counterscarp. The ravelin: from the curtain point e'', with radius e'' γ (γ, a point on the opposite face 11 yards beyond the shoulder-point), draw the arc γ δ, until it crosses the prolongation of the perpendicular α β; this gives the point of the ravelin; the chord to the arc just described gives the face, which is continued from the point until it reaches the prolongation of the tangent forming the counterscarp of the main ditch; the gorge of the ravelin is fixed by this line equally, so that the whole of the ditch remains free for the fire of the flanks. In front of the curtain, and there alone, Vauban retained the Dutch *fausse-braie*; this had already been done by the Italian Floriani before him, and the new work had been called *tenaille (tenaglia)*. Its faces were in the direction of the lines of defence. The ditch in front of the ravelin was 24 yards wide, the counterscarp parallel to the faces of the ravelin, and the point rounded off. In this manner Vauban obtained roomy bastions, and kept his flanked salient angles well within musket range; but the simplicity of these bastions renders the defence of the place impossible as soon as the face of one bastion is breached. His flanks are not so good as Speckle's or Pagan's, forming an acute angle with the lines of defence; but he does away with the 2 and 3 tiers of uncovered guns which figure in most of the Italian and early French flanks, and which were never very useful. The tenaille is intended to strengthen the defence of the ditch by infantry fire, and to cover the curtain from direct breaching fire from the crest of the glacis; but this is very imperfectly done, as the breaching batteries in the reentering place of arms (*n*, fig. 1) have a full view of the piece of the curtain next to the flank at *e*. This is a great weakness, as a breach there would turn all the coupures prepared in the bastion as a second line of defence. It arises from the ravelin being still too small. The covered way, constructed without *crémaillères*, but with traverses, is much inferior to Speckle's; the traverses prevent not only the enemy, but also the defence, from enfilading the covered way. The communications between the different works are on the whole good, but still not sufficient for energetic sallies. The profiles are of a degree of strength which is still generally adopted. But Vauban still clung to the system of revetting the whole of the outside of the rampart with masonry, so that at least 15 feet high of masonry was uncovered. This mistake is made in many of Vauban's fortresses, and once made can only be remedied at an enormous expense by widening the ditch in front of the faces of the bastions, and constructing earthwork counterguards to cover the masonry. During the greater part of his life Vauban followed his first method; but after 1680 he introduced two other methods, having for their object to admit of a prolonged defence after the bastion was breached. For this purpose he took up an idea of Castriotto's, who had proposed to modernize the old tower and wall fortification by placing detached bastions, isolated, in the ditch, in front of the towers. Both Vauban's second and third methods agree in this. The ravelin is also made larger, the masonry is a little better covered; the towers are casemated, but badly; the fault that the curtain may be breached between bastion and tenaille is maintained, and renders the detached bastion partly illusory. Still, Vauban considered his second and third methods as very strong. When he handed over to Louis XIV the plan for the fortification of Landau (second system), he said:

"Sire, here is a place that all my art would not suffice to take."[a]

This did not prevent Landau from being taken 3 times during Vauban's life (1702, 1703, 1704), and again shortly after his death (1713).[369]

The errors of Vauban were rectified by Cormontaigne, whose

---

[a] A. Zastrow, *Geschichte der beständigen Befestigung*, S. 168.— *Ed.*

method may be considered as the perfection of the bastionary system. Cormontaigne (1696-1752) was a general of engineers. His larger bastions permit the construction of permanent coupures and second lines of defence; his ravelins were nearly as large as those of Speckle, and fully covered that portion of the curtain which Vauban had left exposed. In polygons of 8 and more sides his ravelins were so far advanced that their fire took in the rear the besiegers' works against the next bastion as soon as he reached the crest of the glacis. In order to avoid this, two ravelins have to be conquered before one bastion can be breached. This mutual support of the large ravelins becomes more and more effective the more the line to be defended approaches a straight one. The reentering place of arms was strengthened by a reduit. The crest of the glacis is drawn *en crémaillère*, as with Speckle, but traverses are maintained. The profiles are very good, and the masonry is always covered by the earthworks in front. With Cormontaigne the French school closes, as far as the construction of bastionary defences, with outworks within the ditch, is concerned. A comparison of the gradual development of bastionary fortification from 1600 to 1750, and of its final results as laid down by Cormontaigne, with the principles of Speckle, as stated above, will tend to elucidate the wonderful genius of the German engineer; for although outworks in the ditch have been multiplied to an enormous degree, yet not a single important principle has been discovered during all these 150 years which had not been already clearly and distinctly enunciated by Speckle.

After Cormontaigne, the school of engineers of Mézières (about 1760) made some slight alterations in his system, the principal of which is the return to Speckle's old rule that the flanks must be perpendicular to the lines of defence. But the principal point for which the school of Mézières is remarkable is that they for the first time construct outworks beyond the covered way. On fronts particularly open to attack they place at the foot of the glacis, on the capital of the bastion, a detached ravelin called a lunette, and thereby approach for the first time to the modern system of permanent intrenched camps. In the beginning of the 19th century Bousmard, a French emigrant who served in Prussia and was killed at Dantzic in 1807,[370] tried still to improve upon Cormontaigne; his ideas are rather complicated, and the most remarkable is that his ravelin, which is very large, is advanced to the foot of the glacis almost so as to take the place and functions, to a certain degree, of the lunette just described.

A Dutch engineer of Vauban's time, who more than once

opposed him in siege warfare with equal honor, Baron Coehorn,[a] gave a further development to the old Dutch method of fortification. His system gives a stronger defence even than Cormontaigne's, by the clever combination of wet and dry ditches, the great facilities offered to sorties, the excellent communications between the works, and the ingenious reduits and coupures in his ravelins and bastions. Coehorn, a great admirer of Speckle, is the only engineer of note who was honest enough to acknowledge how much he owed to him.

We have seen that even before the introduction of bastions, Albert Dürer used caponnières to afford a stronger flanking fire. In his fortified square he even entirely trusts to these caponnières for the defence of the ditch; there are no towers on the corner of the fort; it is a plain square with none but salient angles. To make the enceinte of a polygon entirely coincident with its outline, so as to have all salient and no reentering angles, and to flank the ditch by caponnières, constitutes what is called polygonal fortification, and Dürer must be considered as its father. On the other hand, a star-shaped enceinte, in which salient and reentering angles follow upon each other regularly, and in which each line is both flank and face at once, flanking the ditch of the next line with the portion next to the reentering angle, and commanding the field with the portion next the salient—such an outline constitutes tenaille fortification. The older Italians and several of the older Germans had proposed this form, but it was not developed till afterward. The system of George Rimpler (engineer to the emperor of Germany,[b] killed in defending Vienna against the Turks in 1683 [371]) forms a kind of intermediate stage between the bastionary and tenaille system. What he calls intermediate bastions constitute in reality a perfect line of tenailles. He declared himself energetically against open batteries with a mere earth parapet in front, and insisted on casemated batteries wherever they could be erected; especially on the flanks, where 2 or 3 tiers of well covered guns would thus have a far greater effect than the 2 or 3 tiers of guns in open flank batteries, which could never act together. He also insisted on batteries, that is, *reduits*, in the places of arms of the covered way, which Coehorn and Cormontaigne adopted, and especially a double and triple line of defence behind the salient angles of the enceinte. In this manner his system is remarkably in advance of his time; the whole of his enceinte consists of

---

[a] See this volume, pp. 267-68.— *Ed.*
[a] Leopold I.— *Ed.*

independent forts, each of which has to be taken separately, and large defensive casemates are used in a manner which reminds us, almost in the details even of their application, of the more recent constructions in Germany. There is no doubt that Montalembert owed as much to Rimpler as the bastionary system of the 17th and 18th century to Speckle. The author who first fully developed the advantages of the tenaille over the bastionary system was Landsberg (1712); but it would lead us too far if we were to enter into his arguments or describe his fortificatory outline. Of the long series of skilful German engineers who followed Rimpler and Landsberg, we may name the Mecklenburg colonel Buggenhagen (1720), the inventor of blockhouse traverses, or traverses hollowed out and adapted for casemated musketry fire; and the Württemberg major Herbort (1734), inventor of defensive barracks, large barracks in the gorge of salient works, proof against vertical fire, with embrasured casemates on the side facing the enceinte, and barracks and store rooms on the side facing the town. Both these constructions are now very largely used.

Thus we see that the German school, with almost the only exception of Speckle, was from its origin adverse to bastions, which it sought to replace chiefly by tenailles, and that it attempted at the same time to introduce a better system of inner defence, chiefly by the use of casemated galleries, which again were considered as the height of absurdity by French engineering authorities. One of the greatest engineers, however, that France ever produced, the marquis de Montalembert (1713-'99), major-general of cavalry, passed over with drums beating and colors flying into the camp of the German school, to the great horror of the whole French engineering corps, who, up to the present date, decry every word he has written. Montalembert severely criticized the defects of the bastionary system[a]; the ineffectuality of its flanking fire; the almost certainty it offered to the enemy that his shots if they missed one line must do harm in another; the want of protection against vertical fire; the perfect uselessness of the curtain as to fire; the impossibility of having good and large coupures in the gorges of the bastions, proved by the fact that no fortress of his time had any of the multifarious permanent coupures proposed by the theorists of the school; and the weakness, bad connection, and want of mutual support of the

---

[a] M. R. Montalembert, *La fortification perpendiculaire, ou essai Sur plusieurs manieres de fortifier la ligne droite, le triangle, le quarré, & tous les polygônes*, t. 1, pp. 73-88.— *Ed.*

outworks. Montalembert therefore preferred either the tenaille or the polygonal system. In either case the body of the place consisted of a row of casemates, with one or two tiers of guns, the masonry of which was covered from direct fire by a counterguard of *couvre-face* of earthwork extending all around and having a second ditch in its front; this ditch was flanked by casemates in the reentering angles of the couvre-face covered by the parapet of the reduit or lunette in the reentering place of arms. The whole system was based upon the principle of opposing, by means of casemated guns, such an overwhelming fire to the enemy the moment he reached the crest of the glacis, or of the couvre-face, that he could not possibly succeed in erecting his breaching batteries. That casemates could do this he maintained against the unanimous condemnation of French engineers, and he afterward even compiled systems of circular and tenaille fortifications in which all earthworks were rejected and the whole defence intrusted to high casemated batteries with from 4 to 5 tiers of guns, the masonry of which was to be protected by the fire of its batteries only. Thus, in his circular system, he contrives to concentrate 348 guns on any point 500 yards from the fortress, and expects that such an immense superiority of fire would put the possibility of erecting siege batteries entirely out of the question. In this, however, he has found no adherents, except in the construction of the sea fronts of coast forts; here the impossibility of breaching strong casemated walls by the guns of ships was pretty well demonstrated by the bombardment of Sebastopol.[372] The splendid forts of Sebastopol, Cronstadt, Cherbourg, and the new batteries on the entrance of Portsmouth harbor (England), and almost all modern forts for harbor defence against fleets, are constructed according to Montalembert's principle. The partly uncovered masonry of the Maximilian towers at Lintz (Austria)[373] and of the reduits of the detached forts of Cologne are imitated from Montalembert's less happy projects. In the fortification of steep heights (Ehrenbreitstein in Prussia, for instance) the uncovered masonry forts have also been sometimes adopted, but what resistance they will be able to make must be decided by actual experience.

The tenaille system has never, to our knowledge at least, found practical application, but the polygonal system is in great favor in Germany, and has been applied to most modern constructions there; while the French tenaciously cling to Cormontaigne's bastions. The enceinte, in the polygonal system, is generally a plain earthwork rampart with revetted scarp and counterscarp, with large caponnières in the middle of the fonts, and with large defensive barracks behind the rampart and covered by it to serve as coupures. Similar defensive barracks have also been erected as coupures in many bastionary works, to close the gorges of the bastions; the rampart serving as a counterguard to protect the masonry from distant fire.

Of all Montalembert's proposals, however, that of detached forts has had the greatest success, and initiated a new era, not only in fortification, but in the attack and defence of fortresses, and even in general strategy. Montalembert proposed to surround large fortresses in important situations by a single or double chain of small forts, on commanding elevations, which, though isolated in appearance, would still support each other by their fire, and, by the facility they gave for large sorties, would render a bombardment of the place impossible, and when required form an intrenched camp for an army. Vauban had already introduced permanent intrenched camps under the guns of fortresses, but their intrenchments consisted of long continuous lines, which, if broken through at one point only, were completely at the mercy of the enemy. But these intrenched camps of Montalembert's were capable of a far greater resistance, for each fort had to be taken singly, and before 3 or 4 at least were conquered, no enemy could open his trenches against the place. Moreover, the siege of each of the forts could be interrupted at every moment by the garrison, or rather the army encamping behind the forts, and thus a combination of active campaigning and regular fortress warfare was secured, which must greatly strengthen the defence. When Napoleon led his armies hundreds of miles through the enemy's country, never heeding the fortresses which had all been constructed according to the old system, and when in return the allies (1814 and 1815) marched straight on toward Paris, leaving almost unnoticed in their rear the triple belt of fortresses with which Vauban had endowed France, it became evident that a system of fortification was antiquated which confined its outworks to the main ditch or at the outside to the foot of the glacis. Such fortresses had lost their power of attraction over the large armies of modern times. Their means of doing harm did not extend beyond the range of their cannon. It thus became necessary to find some new means to break the impetuous movement of modern invading armies, and Montalembert's detached forts were applied on a large scale. Cologne, Coblentz, Mentz, Rastadt, Ulm, Königsberg, Posen, Lintz, Peschiera, and Verona were severally transformed into large intrenched camps, capable of holding from

60,000 to 100,000 men, but defensible, in case of need, by far smaller garrisons. At the same time, the tactical advantages of the locality to be fortified were placed in the background by the strategetical considerations which now decided the situation of fortresses. Such places only were fortified as might directly or indirectly stop the progress of a victorious army, and which, being large towns in themselves, offered great advantages to an army by being the centre of the resources of whole provinces. Situations on large rivers, especially at the points of junction of two considerable rivers, were chosen in preference, as they compelled the attacking army to divide its forces. The enceinte was simplified as much as possible, and outworks in the ditch were almost entirely done away with; it was sufficient to have the enceinte safe against an irregular attack. The principal battle-field lay around the detached forts, and they were to be defended not so much by the fire from their ramparts, as by the sallies of the garrison of the fortress itself. The largest fortress constructed upon this plan is Paris; it has a simple bastioned enceinte with bastioned forts, almost all squares; there is no outwork, not even a ravelin, in the whole fortification. No doubt, the defensive strength of France has gained 30 per cent. by this new and immense intrenched camp, large enough to afford a refuge for three beaten armies. The intrinsic value of the different methods of fortification has lost a great deal of its importance by this improvement; the cheapest will now be the best; for the defence is now based, not upon the passive system of awaiting the enemy behind the walls until he opens his trenches, and then cannonading them, but upon the active one of taking the offensive with the concentrated strength of the garrison against the necessarily divided forces of the besieger.

II. SIEGES

The art of sieges had been brought to a certain perfection by the Greeks and Romans. They tried to breach the walls of fortresses by the battering ram, and approached them under cover of strongly roofed galleries, or in case of need by a lofty construction which was to command walls and towers by its greater height, and offer a safe approach to the storming columns. The introduction of gunpowder did away with these contrivances; the fortresses having now ramparts of less elevation, but a fire effective at long distances, the approaches were made by trenches, leading in zigzags or curved lines toward the glacis; batteries being erected at various spots so as to silence if possible the fire of the besieged and to batter down his masonry. Once arrived on the crest of the glacis, a high trench cavalier was erected, with the intention of commanding the bastions and their cavaliers, and then by a crushing fire to complete the breach and prepare for the assault. The curtain was the point generally attacked. There was, however, no system in this mode of attack until Vauban introduced parallels of ricochet firing, and regulated the process of sieges in the manner which is in use even now, and still denominated Vauban's attack. The besieger, after investing the place with a sufficient force on all sides, and choosing the fronts to be attacked, opens the first parallel during the night (all siege works are chiefly carried on at night) at about 600 yards from the fortress. A trench parallel to the sides of the besieged polygon is drawn around at least 3 of these sides and fronts; the earth, being thrown up on the side toward the enemy and propped upon the sides of the ditch with gabions (willow-work baskets filled with earth), forms a kind of parapet against the fire of the fortress. In this first parallel the ricochet batteries for enfilading the long lines of the attacked fronts are constructed. Taking for the object of the siege a bastioned hexagon, there should be ricochet batteries to enfilade the faces of 2 bastions and 3 ravelins, in all the batteries, one for each face. These batteries throw their shot so as to pass just over the parapet of the works and along the faces in their whole length, taking them in flank and endangering guns and men. Similar batteries are constructed to enfilade the branches of the covered way, and mortars and howitzers are placed in\ battery to throw shells into the interior of the bastions and ravelins. All these batteries are covered by earthwork parapets. At the same time, at two or more places, zigzag trenches are pushed forward toward the place, taking care to avoid all enfilading fire from the town; and so soon as the fire of the place shows signs of slacking, the second parallel, about 350 yards from the works, is opened. In this parallel the dismounting batteries are constructed. They serve to completely destroy the artillery and embrasures on the faces of the fortress; there will be 8 faces to attack (2 bastions and their ravelins, and the inner faces of the adjoining ravelins), for each of which there is a battery, constructed parallel to the attacked faces, and each embrasure exactly opposite to an embrasure of the fortress. From the second parallel fresh zigzags are pushed toward the town; at 200 yards the half parallel is constructed, forming new enlargements of the zigzags armed with mortar batteries; and at last, at the foot of the glacis, the third parallel. This is armed with heavy mortar batteries. By this time the fire of the place will have been nearly silenced, and the approaches, in varied forms of curved or angular lines, to avoid ricochet fire, are carried up to the crest of the glacis, which it reaches opposite the points of the two bastions and of the ravelin. A lodgment or trench and parapet is then formed in the salient place of arms to enfilade the ditch by infantry fire. If the enemy is active and daring in his sorties, a 4th parallel connecting the salient places of arms across the glacis becomes necessary. Otherwise a sap is pushed from the 3d parallel to the reentering places of arms, and the crowning of the glacis, or the construction of a trench all along the covered way on the crest of the glacis, is completed. Then the counter batteries are constructed in this *couronnement* in order to silence the fire of the flank, which enfilades the ditch, and after them the breaching batteries against the point and faces of the bastions and ravelin. Opposite the points to be breached, a mining gallery is constructed leading down from the trenches through the glacis and counterscarp into the ditch; the counterscarp is blown in, and a fresh trench constructed across the ditch to the foot of the breach, covered on the side whence the enfilading fire of the flank comes by a parapet. As soon as both breach and passage of the ditch are complete, the assault takes place. This is in the case of a dry ditch; across a wet ditch, a dike has to be constructed with fascines, covered equally by a parapet on the side of the flank of the adjoining bastion. If on taking the bastion it is found that there is a further intrenchment or coupure in the rear, a lodgment has to be effected, fresh batteries to be constructed on the breach, and a fresh breach, descent, and passage of the ditch and assault to be made. The average resistance of a bastioned hexagon of Vauban's first method against such a siege is calculated to be from 19 to 22 days if there are no coupures, and 27 or 28 days if it is provided with coupures. Cormontaigne's method is expected to hold out 25 or respectively 35 to 37 days.

III. FIELD FORTIFICATION

The construction of field works is as old as the existence of armies. The ancients were even far more expert in this art than our modern armies; the Roman legions, before an enemy, intrenched their camp every night. During the 17th and 18th centuries we see also a very great use of field works, and in the wars of Frederick the Great pickets on outpost duty generally threw up slightly profiled redans. Yet even then, and it is still more the case now, the construction of field works was confined to the strengthening of a few positions selected beforehand with a view to certain eventualities during a campaign. Thus Frederick the Great's camp at Bunzelwitz, Wellington's lines at Torres Vedras, the French lines of Weissenburg, and the Austrian intrenchments in front of Verona in 1848.[374] Under such circumstances, field works may exercise an important influence upon the issue of a campaign by enabling an inferior army successfully to resist a superior one. Formerly the intrenched lines, as in Vauban's permanently intrenched camps, were continuous; but from the defect that if pierced and taken at one point the whole line was useless, they are now universally composed of one or more lines of detached redoubts, flanking each other by their fire, and allowing the army to fall upon the enemy through the intervals as soon as the fire of the redoubts has broken the energy of his assault. This is the principal use of field works; but they are also employed singly, as bridge-heads to defend the access to a bridge, or to close an important pass to small parties of the enemy. Omitting all the more fanciful shapes of works which are now out of date, such fortifications should consist of works either open or closed at the gorge. The former will either be redans (two parapets with a ditch in front forming an angle facing the enemy) or lunettes (redans with short flanks). The latter may be closed at the gorge by palisadings. The principal closed field work now in use is the square redoubt, either as a regular or an irregular quadrangle, closed by a ditch and parapet all round. The parapet is made as high as in permanent fortification (7 to 8 feet), but not so thick, having to resist field artillery only. As none of these works has a flanking fire in itself, they have to be disposed so that they flank each other within musket range. To do this effectually, and strengthen the whole line, the plan now most generally adopted is to form an intrenched camp by a line of square redoubts flanking each other, and also a line of simple redans, situated in front of the intervals of the redoubts. Such a camp was formed in front of Comorn, south of the Danube, in 1849, and was defended by the Hungarians for 2 days against a far superior army.[375]

Written between April and June 10, 1859   Reproduced from *The New American Cyclopaedia*

First published in *The New American Cyclopaedia*, Vol. VII, 1859

Frederick Engels

INFANTRY [376]

Infantry, the foot soldiers of an army. Except among nomadic tribes, the great mass, if not the entire strength of all armies, has always consisted of foot soldiers. Thus even with the first Asiatic armies, with the Assyrians, Babylonians, and Persians, infantry made up, numerically at least, the main body. With the Greeks at first the whole army was composed of infantry. What little we know of the composition, organization, and tactics of ancient Asiatic infantry, has already been stated in the article *Army*,[a] to which we refer for many details which it would be useless to repeat here. In this article, we shall restrict ourselves to the most important tactical features only in the history of the arm; we therefore at once begin with the Greeks.

I. GRECIAN INFANTRY

The creators of Grecian tactics were the Dorians [377]; among them, the Spartans brought to perfection the ancient Doric order of battle. Originally, the whole of the classes which composed a Dorian community were subjected to military service; not only the full citizens who formed the aristocracy, but also the subject *periaeci*,[378] and even the slaves. They were all formed into the same phalanx, but each in a different position. The full citizens had to appear heavily armed, with defensive armor, with helmet, cuirass, and cuissarts of brass, with a large wooden shield covered with leather, high enough to protect the whole person, and with a lance and sword. They formed, according to their numbers, the first or

---

[a] See this volume, pp. 85-89.— *Ed.*

first and second ranks of the phalanx. Behind them stood the
subjects and slaves, so that every Spartan squire had his retainers
in his rear; these were without the costly defensive armor, relying
on the protection afforded to them by the front ranks and their
shields; their offensive weapons were slings, javelins, knives,
daggers, and clubs. Thus the Doric phalanx formed a deep line,
the hoplites or heavy infantry in front, the *gymnetae* or light
infantry in the rear ranks. The hoplites had to bear down the
enemy by the charge of their spears; once in the midst of the
hostile body, they drew their short swords, and worked their way
forward at close quarters, while the gymnetae, who first prepared
the charge by throwing stones and javelins over the heads of the
front ranks, now assisted the onward pressure of the hoplites by
disposing of the wounded and straggling enemies. The tactics of
such a body were thus very simple; tactical manoeuvring there was
scarcely any; the courage, tenacity, bodily strength, and individual
agility and skill of the men, especially the hoplites, decided every
thing.

This patriarchal union of all classes of the nation in the same
phalanx disappeared soon after the Persian wars,[379] principally
from political causes; the consequence was that the phalanx was
now formed exclusively of hoplites, and that the light infantry,
where it continued to exist, or where a new light infantry was
formed, fought separately as skirmishers. In Sparta, the Spartan
citizens along with the *periaeci* formed the heavy armed phalanx;
the helots[380] now followed with the baggage, or as shield-bearers
(*hypaspistae*). For a while this phalanx was made to suffice for all
the exigencies of battle; but soon the skirmishers of the Athenians,
in the Peloponnesian war,[381] compelled the Spartans to provide
themselves with troops of a similar kind. They did not, however,
form gymnetae of their own, but sent out the younger portion of
their men on skirmishing duty. When, toward the end of that war,
the number of citizens and even of periaeci had become greatly
reduced, they were compelled to form phalanxes of heavily armed
slaves, commanded by citizens. The Athenians, after banishing
from the phalanx the gymnetae, formed of the poorer citizens, of
retainers and slaves, created special corps of light infantry,
consisting of gymnetae or *psiles*, destined for skirmishing, and
armed exclusively for distant fighting, slingers (*sphendonetae*),
archers (*toxotae*), and javelin-throwers (*akontistae*), the latter also
called *peltastae* from the small shield (*pelta*) which they alone
carried. This new class of light infantry, originally recruited from
the poorer citizens of Athens, very soon came to be formed almost

exclusively of mercenaries and the contingents of the allies of Athens.[382] From the moment these skirmishers were introduced, the clumsy Doric phalanx was no longer fit to act alone in battle. Its materials, too, had been constantly deteriorating; in Sparta, by the gradual extinction of the warlike aristocracy; in the other towns, by the influence of commerce and wealth, which gradually undermined the ancient contempt of death. Thus, the phalanx, formed of a not very heroic militia, lost most of its old importance. It formed the background, the reserve of the line of battle, in front of which the skirmishers fought, or behind which they retired when pressed, but which scarcely ever was expected to come itself to close quarters with the enemy. Where the phalanx was formed of mercenaries, its character was not much better. Its clumsiness made it unfit for manoeuvring, especially in ground but lightly broken, and its whole use was passive resistance. This led to two attempts at reform made by Iphicrates, a general of mercenaries. This Grecian *condottiere*[383] exchanged the old, short spears of the hoplites (from 8 to 10 feet long) for considerably longer ones, so that, with closed ranks, the lances of 3 or 4 ranks projected in front and could act against the enemy; thus, the defensive element of the phalanx was considerably strengthened. On the other hand, to create a force fit for deciding battles by close yet rapid attack, he armed his peltastae with light defensive armor and a good sword, and drilled them in the evolutions of the phalanx. When ordered to charge, they advanced at a pace unattainable by the phalanx of hoplites, gave a volley of javelins at 10 or 20 yards, and broke into the enemy with the sword. The simplicity of the ancient Doric phalanx had thus made way for a far more complicated order of battle; the action of the general had become an important element of victory; tactical manoeuvres had become possible. Epaminondas was the first to discover the great tactical principle which up to the present day decides almost all pitched battles: the unequal distribution of the troops on the line of front, in order to concentrate the main attack on one decisive point. Hitherto the battles of the Greeks had been delivered in parallel order; the strength of the front line was the same on all points; if one army was superior in numbers to the one opposed to it, either it formed a deeper order of battle, or it overlapped the other army on both wings. Epaminondas, on the contrary, destined one of his wings for attack and the other for defence; the attacking wing was composed of his best troops, and of the mass of his hoplites, formed in a deep column and followed by light infantry and by the cavalry. The other wing was of course considerably weaker, and was kept back, while the attacking one broke through the enemy, and the column, either deploying or wheeling into line, rolled them up with the assistance of the light troops and horsemen.

The progress established by Iphicrates and Epaminondas was still further developed when Macedonia had taken the lead of the Hellenic race and led them against Persia. The long lances of the hoplites appear still further lengthened in the Macedonian *sarissa*. The *peltastae* of Iphicrates appear again in an improved form in Alexander's *hypaspistae*. Finally, the economy of forces, as applied to the order of battle by Epaminondas, was extended by Alexander to a combination of the various arms such as Greece with her insignificant cavalry could never have produced. Alexander's infantry was composed of the phalanx of hoplites, which formed the defensive strength of the order of battle; of the light skirmishing infantry, which engaged the enemy all along the front, and also contributed to the following up of the victory; and of the hypaspistae, to which belonged his own body guard, which, though lightly equipped, were still capable of regular phalangitic manoeuvring, and formed that kind of average infantry which is more or less adapted to both close and extended order. Still, neither Greece nor Macedonia had produced a movable infantry which could be relied upon when opposed to a solid phalanx. Here, Alexander brought in his cavalry. The attacking wing was formed by the mass of his heavy cavalry, chosen from the Macedonian nobility, and with them acted the hypaspistae; they followed the charge of the horsemen, and rushed into the gap they had made, securing the success obtained by them, and establishing themselves in the midst of the enemy's position. After the conquest of the centre of the Persian empire, Alexander used his hoplites chiefly for garrisoning the conquered towns. They soon disappeared from the army which subdued by its bold and rapid marches the tribes of Asia to the Indus and Jaxartes. That army was formed chiefly of cavalry, hypaspistae, and light infantry; the phalanx, which could not have followed on such marches, became at the same time superfluous from the nature of the enemy to be conquered. Under the successors of Alexander, his infantry, as well as his cavalry and tactics, were completely and rapidly deteriorated. The two wings of the order of battle were formed exclusively of cavalry, and the centre of infantry; but the latter was so little relied on, that it was covered by elephants. In Asia, the prevailing Asiatic element soon got the upper hand, and rendered the armies of the Seleucidae all but worthless; in

Europe, the Macedonian and Greek infantry regained some solidity, but with it came a return to the former exclusive phalangitic tactics. Light troops and cavalry never recovered, while much trouble and ingenuity were wasted in vain attempts to give to the phalanx that mobility which from its very nature it could never attain; until finally the Roman legion put an end to the whole system.

The tactical organization and manoeuvres of the phalanx were simple enough. Being generally 16 deep (under Alexander), a line of 16 files formed a complete square, and this, the *syntagma*, formed the unit of evolutions; 16 syntagmas, or 256 files, formed a phalangarchy of 4,096 men, 4 of which again were to form the complete phalanx. The phalangarchy, in order of battle, formed in line 16 deep; it passed into the order of march by facing right or left, or by wheeling into syntagmas, in each case forming a close column 16 in front. When in line, the depth could be increased and front decreased by double files, the even files placing themselves behind the odd ones; and the opposite movement was performed by double ranks, reducing the depth from 16 to 8 men per file. Countermarching by files was employed when the enemy suddenly appeared in the rear of the phalanx; the inversion caused by this (every file being in a wrong place in its own section or syntagma) was sometimes set right by a countermarch by ranks in each section. Add to this the handling of the lance, and we have enumerated the various items of the drill of the ancient hoplites. It is a matter of course that the lighter troops, though not exactly destined to fight in close order, still were exercised in the phalangitic movements.

II. ROMAN INFANTRY

The Latin word *legio* was originally used to express the totality of the men selected for field service, and thus was synonymous with army. Subsequently, when the extent of the Roman territory and the power of the enemies of the republic required larger armies, they were divided into several legions, each of which had a strength similar to that of the original Roman army. Up to the time of Marius, every legion was composed of both infantry and cavalry, the latter about $1/10$ of the former in strength. Originally the infantry of the Roman legion appears to have been organized similarly to the ancient Doric phalanx, fighting in a deep line, the patricians and richer citizens in heavy armor forming the front ranks, the poorer and lighter armed plebeians behind them. But about the time of the Samnite wars the legion began to undergo a change of organization, which soon placed it in perfect contrast to the Grecian phalanx, and of which, after it had attained its full development in the Punic wars,[384] Polybius gives us a full account.[a] The legion, of which 4 were generally levied for each campaign, was now composed of 4 classes of infantry, *velites, hastati, principes*, and *triarii;* the first, formed from recruits, were light infantry; the triarii, from veterans, were the reserve of the army; the other two classes, forming the main fighting body or infantry of the line, composed the remainder of the army, and differed in this, that the principes were selected from those men who, after the triarii, had seen most service. The velites wore leather caps, light round shields for defensive armor, and carried swords and a number of light javelins; the remaining 3 classes had brass helmets, leather body armor covered with brass plates, and brass cuissarts. The hastati and principes, beside a short sword, carried two *pila* or javelins, a light one and a very heavy one; this latter formed the specific arm of attack of the Roman infantry. It was of thick, heavy wood, with a long iron point, weighing in all at least 10 pounds, and with the point nearly 7 feet long. It could be thrown at very short distances only, say 8 or 12 yards, but from its weight its effect was formidable to the light defensive armor of those times. The triarii, beside the sword, carried lances instead of pila. Every legion contained 1,200 hastati, divided into 10 *manipuli* or companies of 120 men each; the same number of principes, similarly divided; 600 triarii, in 10 manipuli of 60 each; and 1,200 velites, 40 of whom were attached to each of the 30 manipuli, and formed the rear ranks unless otherwise employed. The hastati formed the first line, each manipulus being deployed in line, probably 6 deep, with an interval from the next manipulus equal to its front, which, as the room allotted for every man in a rank was 6 feet, extended about 120 feet, the whole line extending 2,400 feet. Behind them, in second line, were placed the 10 manipuli of the principes, covering the intervals of the manipuli of the first line, and behind the principes the triarii, each line at an appropriate distance from the one in front of it. The velites skirmished before the front and flanks. By doubling files, the order of battle could be reduced to one half its original extent of front, or 1,200 feet. The whole of this order of battle was calculated for attack.

Capable, by the smallness of the tactical units and by the great

---

[a] Polybius, *Histories,* Book 6.— *Ed.*

liberty thereby secured to all its movements, of fighting in almost any kind of ground, it was immensely superior to the Grecian phalanx, which required a level plain, and had been very soon reduced by its own clumsiness to a mere formation for defense. The legion advanced; at 8 or 12 yards the hastati, probably doubling their ranks for the occasion, threw their heavy pila into the phalanx, whose lances could not yet reach the Romans, and, having thereby broken the closed order of the phalangites, rushed upon them sword in hand. If a single manipulus got into disorder, the effect was not transmitted to the neighboring companies; if the combat continued without immediate decision, the principes marched up into the intervals, threw their pila, and broke in upon the enemy with the sword, thus giving the hastati an opportunity of disentangling themselves and reforming behind the triarii. In an extreme case, these latter advanced, either to finally decide the victory or to secure an orderly retreat. The velites, in company with the cavalry, did outpost duty, engaged the enemy in the beginning of the battle by skirmishing, and followed up the pursuit. The light pilum of the hastati and principes appears to have been principally used in defensive positions, to create disorder in the ranks of an advancing enemy before he was close enough for the heavy pilum. Marches to the front were begun from either wing, the first manipulus of hastati in front, followed by the first respectively of principes and triarii, then the 3 second manipuli in the same order, and so forth; marches to a flank were made in 3 columns, each of the 3 classes of infantry forming a column; the baggage was on the side furthest from the enemy. If the latter appeared from the side where the triarii marched, the army halted, and faced toward the enemy, the principes and hastati passing through the intervals of the manipuli of the triarii and taking up their proper positions.

When, after the second Punic war, the continued wars and extended conquests of the Romans, combined with important social changes in Rome and Italy generally, rendered the universal liability to military service almost impracticable, the Roman armies began gradually to be composed of voluntary recruits from the poorer classes, thus forming soldiers by profession instead of the old militia in which all the citizens were included. The army hereby entirely changed its character; and, the elements from which it was composed becoming deteriorated, a new organization became more and more a necessity. Marius carried out this new organization. The Roman horse ceased to exist. What little cavalry remained was composed of barbarian mercenaries or allied contingents.[385] The distinction of the 4 classes of infantry was done away with. The velites were replaced by allied contingents or barbarians, and the remainder of the legion formed of one and the same class of infantry of the line, armed like the hastati or principes, but without the light pilum. The manipulus was replaced, as a tactical unit, by the cohort, a body averaging 360 men, and formed originally by the fusion of 3 manipuli into one; so that the legion was now divided into 10 cohorts, which were generally disposed in 3 lines (4, 3, and 3 cohorts respectively). The cohort was formed 10 deep, with 3 to 4 feet front for each file, so that the total extent of front of the legion was very much reduced (about 1,000 feet). Thus, not only were the tactical movements much simplified, but the influence of the commander of the legion was made much more immediate and powerful. The armament and equipment of every soldier was lightened, but on the other hand he was made to carry the greater part of his baggage on wooden forks invented for the purpose by Marius (*muli Mariani*); the *impedimenta* of the army were thus considerably reduced. On the other hand, the concentration of 3 manipuli into one cohort could not but reduce the facility of manoeuvring in broken ground; the absence of the light pilum reduced the capability for defence; and the abolition of the velites, not always fully replaced by foreign auxiliaries or mercenaries, or by the *antesignani* (men selected from the legion for light infantry service by Caesar, but left without arms for distant fighting), diminished the chances of maintaining an engagement and still evading a decision. Rapid, resolute attack became the only form of combat fitted for these legions. Still the Roman infantry continued to consist of Romans, or at least Italians; and in spite of the decline of the empire under the Caesars, it maintained its ancient renown so long as the national character was left intact. But when Roman citizenship was no longer a necessary condition for admission into a legion, the army soon lost its standing. As early as the times of Trajan, barbarians, partly from the Roman provinces, partly from unconquered countries, formed the main force of the legions, and from that moment the character of the Roman infantry was lost. The heavy armor was thrown away; the pilum was replaced by the lance; the legion, organized into cohorts, was again fused into an unwieldy phalanx; and as a general unwillingness to come to close quarters was a characteristic of the infantry of this period, the bow and javelin were now used, not for skirmishing only, but also for the closed order of infantry of the line.

III. THE INFANTRY OF THE MIDDLE AGES

The decline of the Roman infantry found a continuation in that of the Byzantine foot soldiers. A kind of forced levy was still maintained, but with no other result than to form the very dregs of the army. Barbarian auxiliaries and mercenaries composed its better portions, but even these were of no great value. The hierarchic and administrative organization of the troops was perfected to an almost ideal state of bureaucracy, but with the same result that we now see in Russia: a perfect organization of embezzlement and fraud at the expense of the state, with armies costing enormous sums and existing in part only on paper. The contact with the irregular horse of the East reduced both the importance and quality of the infantry more and more. Mounted archers became the favorite arm; the greater part if not all of the infantry were also equipped with the bow beside the lance and sword. Thus, fighting at a distance became the fashion, hand-to-hand encounters being regarded as out of date. The infantry was considered such rubbish that it was intentionally kept away from the field of battle, and used for garrison duty principally; most of the battles of Belisarius were fought by the cavalry exclusively, and when the infantry partook in them, it was sure to run away. His tactics were entirely based upon the principle of avoiding a combat at close quarters, and of tiring out the enemy. If he succeeded in this against the Goths, who had no distance arms at all, by choosing broken ground in which their phalanx could not act, he was beaten by the Franks, whose infantry had something of the old Roman mode of fighting about them, and by the Persians, whose cavalry was certainly superior to his.

The German invaders of the Roman empire originally consisted for the greater part of infantry, and fought in a kind of Doric phalanx, the chiefs and wealthier men in the front ranks, the others behind them. Their arms were the sword and lance. The Franks, however, carried short, double-edged battle axes, which they threw, like the Roman pilum, into the hostile mass the moment before they charged sword in hand. They and the Saxons retained for some time a good and respected infantry; but gradually the Teutonic conquerors everywhere took to cavalry service, and left the duty of the foot soldiers to the conquered Roman provincials; thus the infantry service became despised as an attribute of slaves and serfs, and the character of the foot soldier necessarily sunk in proportion. By the end of the 10th century cavalry was the only arm which really decided battles all over Europe; infantry, though far more numerous in every army than cavalry, was nothing better than an ill-armed rabble with hardly any attempt at organization. A foot soldier was not even considered a soldier; the word *miles* became synonymous with horseman. The only chance for maintaining a respectable infantry lay with the towns, especially in Italy and Flanders. They had a militia of their own which was necessarily formed of infantry; and as its service for the protection of the towns, in the midst of the never-ending feuds among the surrounding nobles, was a permanent one, it was soon found convenient to have a force of paid mercenaries instead of a militia composed of the citizens, this latter force being reserved for extraordinary occasions. Still, we do not find that the contingents of the towns showed any marked superiority over the rabble of footmen collected by the nobles, and in battle always left to protect the baggage. This holds good, at least, for the classic period of chivalry. In the cavalry of these times, every knight appeared armed cap-à-pied,[a] covered all over with armor, and mounting a similarly armed horse. He was accompanied by an esquire rather more lightly armed, and by sundry other mounted men without any armor and armed with bows. In order of battle, these forces were ranged upon a principle similar to that of the ancient Doric phalanx—the heavily armed knights in the first, the esquires in the second rank, the mounted archers behind them. These last, from the nature of their arm, were soon employed in dismounted fighting, which became more and more the rule with them, so that their horses were mainly used for locomotion, not for a charge. The English archers, armed with the long-bow, while those of southern Europe carried the cross-bow, especially excelled in this mode of fighting on foot, and it was very likely this circumstance which soon led to an extension, in this service, of dismounted fighting. No doubt, in their long campaigns in France, the horses of the heavily armed knights got soon knocked up and unfit to serve for more than means of transport. In this plight it was natural that the worst mounted *gendarmes* should dismount and form a phalanx of lances, to be filled up by the better portion of the footmen (especially the Welsh); while those whose horses were still fit for a charge, now formed the actual fighting cavalry. Such an arrangement appeared very well adapted for defensive battles, and upon it were based all the battles of the Black Prince,[b] and, as is well

---

[a] From head to foot.— *Ed.*
[b] Edward, Prince of Wales.— *Ed.*

known, with perfect success. The new mode of fighting was soon adopted by the French and other nations, and may be considered as almost the normal system of the 14th and 15th centuries. Thus, after 1,700 years, we are brought back almost to the tactics of Alexander; with this difference only, that with Alexander cavalry was a newly introduced arm which had to strengthen the declining capabilities of the heavy infantry, while here the heavy infantry, formed by dismounted horsemen, was a living proof that cavalry was on the decline, and that a new day had dawned for infantry.

IV. THE REVIVAL OF INFANTRY

From the Flemish towns, then, the first manufacturing district of the world, and from the Swiss mountains, arose the first troops which, after centuries of decline, again deserved the name of infantry. The French chivalry succumbed as much to the weavers and fullers, the goldsmiths and tanners of the Belgian cities, as the Burgundian and Austrian nobility to the peasants and cowherds of Switzerland. Good defensive positions and a light armament did the most, supported as they were in the case of the Flemish by numerous fire-arms, and in that of the Swiss by a country almost impracticable to the heavily armed knights of the time. The Swiss carried principally short halberts, which might be used as well for thrusting as for striking, and were not too long for hand-to-hand fight; subsequently they also had pikes, and cross-bows and fire-arms; but in one of their most celebrated battles, at Laupen (1339),[386] they had no arms for distant fighting but stones. From defensive encounters in their inaccessible mountains, they soon came to offensive battles in the plain, and with these to more regular tactics. They fought in a deep phalanx; defensive armor was light, and in general confined to the front ranks and the flank files, the centre being filled up by men without armor; the Swiss phalanx, however, was always formed in 3 distinct bodies, an advanced guard, a main body, and a rear guard, so that greater mobility and the chance of varied tactical arrangements were secured. They soon became expert in taking advantage of the accidents of ground, which, coupled with the improvement in fire-arms, protected them against the onslaught of cavalry, while against infantry armed with long lances they devised various means to work an entrance somewhere through the forest of lances, after which their short heavy halberts gave them an immense advantage, even against men cased in armor. They very soon learned, especially when assisted by artillery and small fire-arms, to hold out in squares or cross-shaped bodies against the charges of cavalry; and as soon as an infantry was again capable of doing that, the days of chivalry were numbered.

About the middle of the 15th century the struggle of the cities against the feudal nobility had been everywhere taken up by the princes of the larger monarchies now consolidating, and consequently the latter had begun to form armies of mercenaries both for putting down the nobles and for carrying out independent objects of foreign policy. Beside the Swiss, the Germans, and soon after them most other European nations, began to furnish large contingents of mercenaries, raised by voluntary enlistment, and selling their services to the highest bidder without any regard to nationality. These bands formed themselves tactically upon the same principle as the Swiss; they were armed chiefly with pikes, and fought in large square battalions, as many men deep as there were in the front rank. They had to fight, however, under different circumstances from the Swiss who defended their mountains; they had to attack as well as to hold out in defensive positions; they had to encounter the enemy in the plains of Italy and France as well as in the hills; and they very soon found themselves face to face with the now rapidly improving small-arms. These circumstances caused some deviations from the old Swiss tactics, which were different according to the different nationalities; but the chief characteristics, the formation in 3 deep columns, figuring in name, if not always in reality, as advanced guard, main body, and rear guard or reserve, remained common to all. The Swiss retained their superiority until the battle of Pavia,[387] after which the German *Landsknechte,* who had already for some time been nearly if not fully equal to them, were considered the first infantry of Europe. The French, whose infantry had as yet never been good for any thing, tried very hard during this period to form a serviceable national body of foot soldiers; but they succeeded with the natives of two provinces only, the Picards and the Gascons. The Italian infantry of this period never counted for any thing. The Spaniards, however, among whom Gonsalvo de Córdova during the wars with the Moors of Granada[388] first introduced the Swiss tactics and armament, very soon rose to considerable reputation, and after the middle of the 16th century began to pass for the best infantry of Europe. While the Italians, and after them the French and Germans, extended the length of the pike from 10 to 18 feet, they retained shorter and more handy lances, and their agility made them very formidable with sword and dagger in close encounter. This reputation they upheld in western Europe—France, Italy, and the Netherlands at least—to the close of the 17th century.

The contempt of the Swiss for defensive armor, based upon traditions of a different time, was not shared by the pikemen of the 16th century. As soon as a European infantry was formed in which the different armies were becoming more and more equal to each other in military qualities, the system of lining the phalanx with a few men covered with breastplates and helmets proved to be insufficient. If the Swiss had found such a phalanx impenetrable, this was no longer the case when it was met by another phalanx quite its equal. Here a certain amount of defensive armor became of some importance; so long as it did not too much impede the mobility of the troops, it was a decided advantage. The Spaniards, moreover, had never participated in this contempt for breastplates, and they began to be respected. Accordingly, breastplates, helmets, cuissarts, brassarts, and gauntlets began again to form a part of the regular equipment of every pikeman. To it was added a sword, shorter with the Germans, longer with the Swiss, and now and then a dagger.

V. THE INFANTRY OF THE 16TH AND 17TH CENTURIES

The long-bow had for some time disappeared from the continent of Europe, excepting Turkey; the cross-bow made its last appearance among the French Gascons in the first quarter of the 16th century. It was everywhere replaced by the matchlock musket, which, in different degrees of perfection, or rather imperfection, now became the second arm of the infantry. The matchlocks of the 17th century, unwieldy and defectively constructed machines, were of very heavy caliber, to secure, beside range, at least some precision, and the force to penetrate the breastplate of a pikeman. The form generally adopted about 1530 was the heavy musket fired off from a fork, as a man could not have taken aim without such a support. The musketeers carried a sword, but no defensive armor, and were used either for skirmishing or in a kind of open order, to hold defensive positions or to prepare the charge of the pikemen for the attack of such positions. They soon became very numerous in proportion to the pikemen; in the battles of Francis I in Italy they were far inferior to the pikemen in numbers, but were at least in equal numbers with them 30 years later. This increase in the number of musketeers compelled the invention of some tactical method of regularly encasing them in the order of battle. This was done in the system of tactics called the Hungarian ordinance, invented by the imperial troops in their wars with the Turks in Hungary. The musketeers, being unable to defend themselves at close quarters, were always placed so as to be able to retire behind the pikemen. Thus they were sometimes placed on either wing, sometimes on the 4 corners of the wings; very often the whole square or column of pikemen was surrounded by a rank of musketeers, who found protection under the pikes of their rear men. Finally, the plan of having the musketeers on the flanks of the pikemen got the upper hand in the new tactical system introduced by the Dutch in their war of independence.[389] This system is distinguished especially by the subdivision of the 3 great phalanges in which every army was formed according to both the Swiss and Hungarian tactics. Each of them was formed upon 3 lines, the middle one of which was again subdivided into a right and a left wing, separated from each other by a distance equal at least to the extent of front of the first line. The whole army being organized in half regiments, which we will call battalions, each battalion had its pikemen in the centre and its musketeers on the flanks. The advanced guard of an army, consisting of 3 regiments, would thus be formed as follows: two half regiments in contiguous line in the first line; behind each of their wings another half regiment; further to the rear, and covering the first line, the remaining two half regiments also in contiguous line. The main body and rear guard might be placed either on the flank or behind the advanced guard, but would be formed on the same plan. Here we have a return in a certain degree to the old Roman formation in 3 lines and distinct small bodies.

The imperialists, and with them the Spaniards, had found the necessity of dividing their large armies into more than the 3 masses already mentioned; but their battalions or tactical units were much larger than the Dutch, fought in column or square instead of in line, and had not had a regular formation for order of battle until during the Dutch war of independence the Spaniards began to form them in what is known as a Spanish brigade. Four of these large battalions, each consisting often of several regiments, formed in square, surrounded with a rank or two of musketeers, and having wings of musketeers at the corners, were disposed at proper intervals on the 4 corners of a square, one corner being turned toward the enemy. If the army was too large to be comprised in one brigade, two could be formed; and thus arose 3 lines, having 2 battalions in the first, 4 (sometimes only 3) in the second, and 2 in the third. As in the Dutch system, we find here the attempt to return to the old Roman system of 3 lines.

Another great change took place during the 16th century; the heavy cavalry of the knights was broken up and replaced by a mercenary cavalry, armed similarly to our modern cuirassiers, with cuirass, helmet, sword, and pistols. This cavalry, greatly superior in mobility to their predecessors, became thereby more formidable to infantry also; still the pikemen of the time were never afraid of it. By this change cavalry became a uniform arm, and entered in a far larger proportion into the composition of armies, especially during the period we now have to consider, viz., the 30 years' war.[390] At this time the system of mercenary service was universal in Europe; a class of men had been formed who lived upon war and by war; and though tactics might have gained thereby, the character of the men, the material composing armies as well as their *morale*, had certainly suffered. Central Europe was overrun by *condottieri* of all kinds, who took religious and political quarrels for their pretext to plunder and devastate the whole country. The character of the individual soldier had entered upon that degradation which went on increasing until the French revolution finally swept away this system of mercenary service. The imperialists formed their battles upon the Spanish brigade system, having 4 or more brigades in line, thus forming 3 lines. The Swedes under Gustavus Adolphus formed in Swedish brigades, each consisting of 3 battalions, one in front and two a little to the rear, each deployed in line, and having the pikes in the centre and the musketeers on the wings. They were so disposed (both arms being represented in equal numbers) that by forming a contiguous line either could cover the other. Supposing the order given to form a contiguous line of musketeers, the two wings of that arm of the centre or front battalion would cover their own pikes by stepping before them, while those of the two other battalions would, each on its flank, advance into alignment with the first. If an attack of cavalry was apprehended, all the musketeers retired behind the pikemen, while the two wings of these latter advanced into alignment with the centre, and thus formed a contiguous line of pikes. The order of battle was formed of two lines of such brigades, composing the centre of the army, while the numerous cavalry was stationed on the two wings, and intermixed with small bodies of musketeers. The characteristic of this Swedish system is that the pikemen, who in the 16th century had been the great offensive arm, had now lost all capacity of attack. They had become a mere means of defence, and their office was to screen

the musketeers from a charge of cavalry; it was this latter arm
again which had to do all the attacking work. Thus, infantry had
lost, cavalry had regained ground. But then Gustavus Adolphus
put an end to the firing which had become a favorite mode of
fighting for cavalry, and ordered his horse always to charge at full
speed and sword in hand; and from that time to the resumption
of fighting in broken ground every cavalry which adhered to these
tactics was able to boast of great successes over infantry. There can
be no greater condemnation of the mercenary infantry of the 17th
and 18th centuries than that; and yet it was, for all purposes of
battle, the most disciplined infantry of all times.

The general result of the 30 years' war upon European tactics
was that both the Swedish and the Spanish brigades disappeared,
and armies were now disposed in two lines, the cavalry forming
the wings and the infantry the centre. The artillery was placed
before the front or in the intervals of the other arms. Sometimes a
reserve of cavalry, or of cavalry and infantry, was retained. The
infantry was deployed in line, 6 deep; the muskets were so much
lightened that the fork could be dispensed with, and cartridges
and cartridge boxes had been everywhere adopted. The mixing up
of musketeers and pikemen in the same infantry battalions now
gave rise to the most complicated tactical movements, all founded
upon the necessity of forming what was called defensive battalions,
or what we should call squares against cavalry. Even in a simple
square, it was no trifle to get the 6 ranks of pikemen from the
centre so drawn asunder that they completely surrounded on all
sides the musketeers, who, of course, were defenceless against
cavalry; but what must it have been to form in a similar way the
battalion into a cross, an octagon, or other fanciful shapes! Thus it
happened that the drilling system of this period was the most
complicated ever seen, and nobody but a soldier for life ever had
any chance of attaining even the commonest proficiency in it. At
the same time, it is obvious that, before the enemy, all these
attempts at forming a body capable of resisting cavalry were
perfectly useless; any decent cavalry would have been in the midst
of such a battalion before one fourth of the movements could
have been gone through.

During the latter half of the 17th century, the number of
pikemen was very much reduced in proportion to that of
musketeers; for from the moment that they had lost all power of
attack, the musketeers were the really active part of the infantry.
Moreover, it was found that the Turkish cavalry, the most
formidable of the time, very often broke into the squares of

pikemen, while they were quite as often repulsed by the well aimed fire of a line of musketeers. In consequence, the imperialists did away with all pikes in their Hungarian army, and replaced them sometimes by *chevaux de frise*, which were put together on the field, the musketeers carrying the blades as part of their regular equipment. In other countries, too, cases occurred of armies being sent into the field without a single pikeman, the musketeers trusting to their fire and the assistance of their own cavalry when threatened with a charge of horse. Still, two inventions were required to do away entirely with the pike: the bayonet, invented in France about 1640, and improved in 1699 so far as to be the handy weapon now in use; and the flint lock, invented about 1650.[a] The former, though certainly an imperfect substitute for the pike, enabled the musketeer to give himself, to a certain degree, that protection which he had hitherto been supposed to find in the pikemen; the second, by simplifying the process of loading, enabled him to do much more than make up by rapid firing for the imperfections of the bayonet.

VI. THE INFANTRY OF THE 18TH CENTURY

With the superseding of the pike, all defensive armor disappeared from infantry equipment, and this arm was now composed of one class of soldiers only, armed with the flint-lock musket and bayonet. This change was accomplished in the first years of the Spanish war of succession,[391] coinciding with the first years of the 18th century. At the same time, we now find everywhere standing armies of considerable magnitude, recruited as much as possible by voluntary enlistment coupled with kidnapping, but in case of need also by forced conscription. These armies were now regularly organized in battalions of from 500 to 700 men, as tactical units, subdivided for special purposes into companies; several battalions forming a regiment. Thus the organization of infantry now began to take a more stable and settled form. The handling of the flint lock requiring far less space than that of the old matchlock, the old open order was done away with, and the files were closed well up to each other, in order to have as many firing men as possible in the same space. For the same reason, the intervals between the various battalions in line of battle were reduced to a minimum, so that the whole front formed one stiff and uninterrupted line, the infantry, in two lines, in the centre, the cavalry on the wings.

---

[a] *The New American Cyclopaedia* has 1670 here.— *Ed.*

Firing, formerly done by ranks, every rank after having fired retiring to the rear to reload, was now done by platoons or companies, the 3 front ranks of each platoon firing simultaneously as the word of command was given. Thus an uninterrupted fire could be maintained by every battalion against the enemy in front of it. Every battalion had its distinct place in this long line, and the order giving to each its place was called the order of battle. The great difficulty now was to organize the marching order of the army so that it could always with facility pass from the marching to the fighting order, every portion of the line getting at once and quickly into its proper place. Encampments within reach of the enemy were arranged with a view to the same object. Thus the art of marching and encamping armies made great progress during this epoch; still the stiffness and unwieldiness of the order of battle formed a heavy clog upon all the movements of an army. At the same time, its formality, and the impossibility of handling such a line in any but the most level plains, still more restricted the choice of ground for battle fields; but as long as both parties were bound by the same fetters, this was no disadvantage for either. From Malplaquet[392] to the outbreak of the French revolution, a road, a village, or a farm yard was tabooed to infantry; even a ditch or a hedge was considered almost a drawback by those who had to defend them.

The Prussian infantry is the classic infantry of the 18th century. It was principally formed by Prince Leopold of Dessau. During the war of the Spanish succession, the line of infantry had been reduced from 6 deep to 4 deep. Leopold did away with the 4th rank, and formed the Prussians 3 deep. He also introduced the iron ramrod, which enabled his troops to load and fire 5 times in a minute, while other troops scarcely fired 3 times. At the same time they were drilled to fire while advancing, but as they had to stop for firing, and as the alignment of the whole long line had to be maintained, the step was but slow—what is called the goose step. Firing began at 200 yards from the enemy; the line advanced at the goose step, stepping shorter and redoubling fire the nearer it got to the enemy, until the latter either gave way, or was so far shaken that a cavalry charge from the wings, and an advance with the bayonet of the infantry, drove him from his position. The army was always ranged on two lines, but, there being scarcely any intervals in the first line, it became very difficult for the second to come to the aid of the first when wanted. Such was the army and such were the tactics which Frederick II of Prussia found at his disposal on his accession. There appeared to be very little chance for a man of genius to improve upon this system, unless he broke through it, and that Frederick, in his position and with the material he had for soldiers, could not do. Still he contrived to organize his mode of attack and his army so that he could, with the resources of a kingdom less than Sardinia now is, and with scanty pecuniary support from England, carry on a war against almost all Europe. The mystery may be easily explained. Hitherto the battles of the 18th century had been parallel battles, both armies being deployed on lines parallel to each other, struggling in a plain, fair, stand-up fight, without any stratagems or devices of art; the only advantage accruing to the stronger party being that his wings overlapped those of his opponent. Frederick applied to the line order of battle the system of oblique attack invented by Epaminondas. He chose one wing of the enemy for the first attack, and brought against this one of his wings, overlapping that of the enemy, and part of his centre, at the same time keeping back the rest of his army. Thus not only had he the advantage of outflanking the enemy, but also of crushing by superior forces the troops exposed to his attack. The other troops of the enemy could not come to the assistance of those attacked; for not only were they tied to their places in the line, but as the attack on the one wing proved successful, the remainder of the army entered into line and engaged the hostile centre in front, while the original attacking wing fell upon its flank after disposing of the wing. This was indeed the only imaginable method by which it was possible, while maintaining the system of lines, to bring a superior force upon any one part of the enemy's line of battle. Every thing, then, depended upon the formation of the attacking wing; and as far as the rigidity of the order of battle admitted of it, Frederick always strengthened it. He very often placed in front of the first line of infantry of the attacking wing an advanced line formed of his grenadiers or élite troops, so as to insure success as much as possible at the first onset.

The second means which Frederick took to improve his army was the reorganization of his cavalry. The teachings of Gustavus Adolphus had been forgotten; cavalry, instead of relying on the sword and the impetuosity of the charge, with rare exceptions had returned to fighting with the pistol and the carbine. The wars in the beginning of the 18th century had thus not been rich in successful charges of horsemen; the Prussian cavalry was especially neglected. But Frederick returned to the old plan of charging sword in hand and at full gallop, and formed a cavalry unequalled in history; and to this cavalry he owed a very great part of his successes. When his army became the model of Europe, Frederick, in order to blind the military men of other nations, began to complicate to an astonishing degree the system of tactical evolutions, all of them unfit for actual war, and intended only to hide the simplicity of the means which had procured him victory. He succeeded so well in this that nobody was more blinded than his own subordinates, who actually believed that these complex methods of forming line were the real essence of his tactics; and thus Frederick, beside laying the foundation for that pedantry and martinetism which have since distinguished the Prussians, actually prepared them for the unparalleled disgrace of Jena and Auerstädt.[393]

Beside the infantry of the line, which we have so far described, and which always fought in closed ranks, there was a certain class of light infantry, but this did not appear in great battles. Its task was the war of partisans; for this the Austrian Croats were admirably adapted, while for every other purpose they were useless. Upon the model of these half savages from the military frontier against Turkey,[394] the other European states formed their light infantry. But skirmishing in great battles, such as was practised by the light infantry of antiquity and of the middle ages, even up to the 17th century, had completely disappeared. The Prussians alone, and after them the Austrians, formed a battalion or two of riflemen, composed of gamekeepers and forest guards, all dead shots, who in battle were distributed over the whole front and fired at officers; but they were so few that they scarcely counted. The resuscitation of skirmishing is the product of the American war of independence.[395] While the soldiers of European armies, held together by compulsion and severe treatment, could not be trusted to fight in extended order, in America they had to contend with a population which, untrained to the regular drill of line soldiers, were good shots and well acquainted with the rifle. The nature of the ground favored them; instead of attempting manoeuvres of which at first they were incapable, they unconsciously fell into skirmishing. Thus, the engagement of Lexington and Concord[396] marks an epoch in the history of infantry.

VII. THE INFANTRY OF THE FRENCH REVOLUTION AND OF THE 19TH CENTURY

When the European coalition invaded revolutionary France, the French were in a similar position to that of the Americans a short time before, except that they had not the same advantages of ground. In order to fight the numerous armies, invading or threatening to invade the country, upon the old line principle, they would have required well drilled men, and these were scarce, while undrilled volunteers were plentiful. As far as time allowed, they were exercised in the elementary evolutions of linear tactics; but as soon as they got under fire, the battalions deployed in line dissolved themselves, unconsciously, into thick swarms of skirmishers, seeking protection against fire from all accidents of ground, while the second line formed a kind of reserve which often enough was involved in the fight from the very beginning of the engagement. The French armies, moreover, were very differently organized from those opposed to them. They were formed, not into an unbending monotonous line of battalions, but into army divisions, each of which was composed of artillery, cavalry, and infantry. The great fact was all at once rediscovered that it matters not whether a battalion fights in its "correct" place in the order of battle, so that it advances into line when ordered, and fights well. The French government being poor, tents and the immense baggage of the 18th century were done away with; bivouacking was invented, and the comforts of the officers, which in other armies formed a large portion of the impediments, were reduced to what they could carry on their backs. The army, instead of being fed from magazines, had to depend upon requisitions on the country passed through. Thus the French attained a mobility and a facility of forming order of battle quite unknown to their enemies. If beaten, they were out of the reach of pursuit in a few hours; if advancing, they could appear on unexpected points, on the flanks of the enemy, before he got notice. This mobility, and the jealousy among themselves of the chiefs of the coalition, gave them breathing time to drill their volunteers, and to elaborate the new tactical system which was rising among them.

From the year 1795 we find this new system taking the definite form of a combination of skirmishers and close columns. The formation in line was subsequently added, though not for a whole army as hitherto, but for single battalions only, which deployed in line whenever an opportunity appeared to require it. It is evident that this latter manoeuvre, requiring more steadiness of drill, was the last to be resumed by the irregular bands of the French revolution. Three battalions formed a demi-brigade, 6 a brigade; 2 or 3 brigades of infantry a division, to which were added 2 batteries of artillery and some cavalry; several such divisions formed an army. Whenever a division met the enemy, the skirmishers of its advanced guard established themselves in a defensive position, the advanced guard forming their reserve until the division came up. The brigades then formed upon two lines and a reserve, but every battalion in column, and with no stated intervals; for the protection of rents in the order of battle there was the cavalry and the reserve. The line of battle was no longer necessarily a straight and uninterrupted one; it might be bent in all directions, as the ground required, for now there was no longer a selection of naked level plains for battle fields; on the contrary, the French preferred broken ground, and their skirmishers, forming a chain in front of the whole line of battle, threw themselves into every village, farm yard, or copse that they could get hold of. If the battalions of the first line deployed, they generally all turned now soon skirmishers; those of the second line always remained in column, and generally charged in this formation against the thin lines of the enemy with great success. Thus, the tactical formation of a French army for battle gradually came to consist of two lines, each formed of battalions in close column, placed en échiquier,[a] with skirmishers before the front, and a compact reserve in the rear.

It was at this stage of development that Napoleon found the tactics of the French revolution. As soon as his accession to political power allowed him to do so, he began to develop the system still further. He concentrated his army in the camp of Boulogne,[397] and there gave them a regular course of drill. He especially practised them in the formation of compact reserve masses on a small space of ground, and in the quick deployment of these masses for entering into line. He formed 2 or 3 divisions into one army corps so as to simplify the command. He invented and brought to its highest perfection the new marching order, which consists in spreading the troops over so great an extent of ground that they can subsist on the stores it contains, still keeping so well together that they can be united on any given point before the part which is attacked can be crushed by the enemy. From the campaign of 1809, Napoleon began to invent new tactical formations, such as deep columns of entire brigades and divisions, which however signally failed and were never again revived. After 1813 this new French system became the common property of all nations on the continent of Europe. The old line system, and the system of recruiting mercenaries, had both been abandoned. Everywhere the liability of every citizen to military service was acknowledged, and everywhere the new tactics were introduced.

---

[a] Chequer-wise.— Ed.

In Prussia and Switzerland every one had actually to serve; in the other states a conscription was introduced, the young men drawing lots to determine who should serve; everywhere reserve systems were introduced, by dismissing a portion of the men, when drilled, to their homes, so as to have a large number of drilled men at disposal in case of war, with little expense in peace.

Since that time several changes have occurred in the armament and organization of infantry, produced partly by the progress of the manufacture of small arms, partly by the collision of French infantry with the Arabs of Algeria. The Germans, always fond of the rifle, had increased their battalions of light riflemen; the French, driven by the necessity of having in Algeria an arm of greater range, at last in 1840 formed a battalion of riflemen armed with an improved rifle of great precision and range. These men, drilled to perform all their evolutions and even long marches in a kind of trot (*pas gymnastique*), soon proved themselves of such efficiency that new battalions were formed. In this manner a new light infantry was created, not from sporting shots and game-keepers, but from the strongest and most agile men; precision of fire and long range were combined with agility and endurance, and a force was formed which, as far as it went, was certainly superior to any other infantry in existence. At the same time, the *pas gymnastique* was introduced into the infantry of the line, and what even Napoleon would have considered the height of folly, running, is now practised in every army as an essential part of infantry drill.

The success of the new rifle of the French riflemen (Delvigne-Poncharra) soon produced new improvements.[a] The conical bullet was introduced for rifled arms. New means were invented by Minié, Lorenz, and Wilkinson, to make the bullet glide down easily into the bore, and still to expand it, when once down, so as to fill up the grooves with its lead, and thus to give it the lateral rotation and force on which the effect of the rifle depends; on the other hand, Dreyse invented the needle gun, to be loaded at the breech, and not requiring a separate priming. All these rifles were capable of hitting at 1,000 yards, and quite as easily loaded as a common smooth-bore musket. Then the idea arose of arming the whole of the infantry with such rifles. England was the first to carry out this idea; Prussia, which had prepared for this step long before, followed; then Austria and the smaller German states; at last

---

[a] For details on the rifles mentioned here and below see Engels' *The History of the Rifle*, this volume, pp. 436-39.— *Ed.*

France. Russia, and the Italian and Scandinavian states, are still behind. This new armament has completely changed the aspect of warfare, but not in the way expected by tactical theorists, and for a very simple mathematical reason. It can be easily proved, by constructing the flight of these bullets, that an error of 20 or 30 yards in the estimation of the distance of the object will destroy all chance of hitting beyond 300 or 350 yards. Now, while on the practice ground the distances are known, on the battle field they are not, and they change every moment. Infantry posted in a defensive position, and having had time to pace off the distances of the most conspicuous objects before the front, will thus have an immense advantage, at from 1,000 to 300 yards, over an attacking force. This can only be obviated by advancing rapidly and without firing, at full trot, to some 300 yards, when the fire of the two parties will be equally effective. At this distance firing will become so murderous between two well posted lines of skirmishers, and so many bullets will hit the pickets and reserves, that a plucky infantry can do no better than seize the first opportunity to make a rush at the enemy, giving a volley at 40 or 50 yards. These rules, first proved theoretically by the Prussian Major Trotha,[a] have been practically tried by the French in their late war against the Austrians,[398] and with success. They will, therefore, form part and parcel of modern infantry tactics, especially if they prove to be of equally good effect when tried against such a rapidly loading arm as the Prussian needle gun. The arming of all infantry with one and the same rifle gun will tend to do away with the distinctions, still existing, of light and line infantry, by forming an infantry capable of any service. In this will evidently consist the next improvement of this arm.

Written between the end of August and October 10, 1859

First published in The New American Cyclopaedia, Vol. IX, 1860

Reproduced from The New American Cyclopaedia

---

[a] Trotha, Beitrag zur Erörterung der Frage: Welchen nothwendigen Einfluss haben die jetzt gebräuchlichen weittragenden Handfeuerwaffen auf das Gefecht der Infanterie?—Ed.

Frederick Engels

NAVY [399]

Navy, a collective term for the vessels of war belonging to a sovereign or nation. The war fleets of the ancients, though often numerous, were insignificant when compared with those of the present day, in regard to the size of the ships, their powers of locomotion, and their aptitude for offence. The sea-going vessels of Phoenicia and Carthage, of Greece and Rome, were flat-bottomed barges, unable to live in a gale of wind; sea room, in a squall, was destruction to them; they crept along the coasts, casting anchor at night in some cove or creek. To cross over from Greece to Italy, or from Africa to Sicily, was a dangerous operation. The ships, unfit to carry the press of sail to which our modern men-of-war are accustomed, were provided with but little canvas; the oars were relied upon to propel them sluggishly through the waves. The compass had not yet been discovered; latitudes and longitudes were unknown; and landmarks and the pole star were the only guides in navigation. The implements for offensive warfare were equally inefficient. Bows and arrows, javelins, clumsy ballistas and catapults, were the only arms that could be used at a distance. No serious harm could be done to an enemy at sea until the two fighting ships came into actual contact. Thus, there were but two modes of naval fighting possible: to manoeuvre so that the sharp, strong, iron-pointed prow of your own ship should be driven with full force against the enemy's broadside in order to run him down; or else to run on broadside to broadside, fasten the two ships together, and board the enemy at once. After the first Punic war, which destroyed the naval superiority of the Carthaginians, [400] there is not a single naval engagement in ancient history offering the slightest professional interest, and Roman dominion soon put an end to the possibility of further naval contests in the Mediterranean.

The real birthplace of our modern navies is the German ocean.[a] About the time when the great mass of the Teutonic tribes of central Europe rose to trample down the decaying Roman empire and to regenerate western Europe, their brethren on the northern shores, the Frisians, Saxons, Angles, Danes, and Northmen, began to take to the sea. Their vessels were firm, stout sea boats, with a prominent keel and sharp lines, relying mostly on sails alone, and not afraid to face a gale in the middle of that rough northern sea. It was with this class of vessels that the Anglo-Saxons passed from the mouths of the Elbe and Eider to the shores of Britain, and that the Northmen undertook their roving expeditions, extending to Constantinople on the one side and America on the other. With the construction of ships that dared cross the Atlantic, navigation underwent a complete revolution; and before the middle ages had passed away, the new sharp-bottomed sea boats had been adopted on all the coasts of Europe. The vessels in which the Northmen made their excursions were probably of no very large size, perhaps not exceeding 100 tons burden in any case, and carrying one or at the outside two masts, fore-and-aft rigged.

For a long time both ship building and navigation appear to have remained stationary; during the whole of the middle ages vessels were small; and the bold spirit of the Northmen and the Frisians had passed away; whatever improvements were made were owing to Italians and Portuguese, who now became the boldest sailors. The Portuguese discovered the route by sea to India; two Italians in foreign service, Columbus and Cabot, were the first since the times of Leif the Northman to cross the Atlantic. Long sea voyages now became a necessity, and they required large ships; at the same time the necessity of arming vessels of war and even merchantmen with heavy artillery, equally tended to increase size and tonnage. The same causes which had produced standing armies on land, now produced standing navies afloat; and it is from this time only that we can properly speak of navies. The era of colonial enterprise which now opened for all seafaring nations, also witnessed the formation of large fleets of war to protect the newly formed colonies and their trade; and a period followed richer in naval struggles and more fruitful to the development of naval armaments than any that preceded it.

---

[a] North Sea.— *Ed.*

The foundation of the British navy was laid by Henry VII, who built the first ship called *The Great Harry*. His successor[a] formed a regular standing fleet, the property of the state, the largest ship of which was called the *Henry Grace de Dieu*. This vessel, the largest ever built up to that time, carried 80 guns, partly on two regular flush gun decks, partly on additional platforms both forward and astern. She was provided with 4 masts; her tonnage is variously stated at from 1,000 to 1,500. The whole of the British fleet, at the death of Henry VIII, consisted of about 50 sail, with an aggregate tonnage of 12,000, and manned by 8,000 sailors and marines. The large ships of the period were clumsy contrivances, deep-waisted, that is to say, provided with towering forecastles and poops, which rendered them exceedingly top-heavy. The next large ship we hear of is the *Sovereign of the Seas*, afterward called the *Royal Sovereign*, built in 1637. She is the first vessel of whose armament we get something like an accurate account. She had 3 flush decks, a forecastle, a half deck, a quarter deck, and a round house; on her lower deck she carried 30 guns, 42 and 32-pounders; 30 on her middle deck, 18 and 9-pounders; on her upper deck 26 lighter guns, probably 6 and 3-pounders. Beside these, she carried 20 chase guns and 26 guns on her forecastle and half deck. But on her regular home establishment this armament was reduced to 100 guns, the full complement being evidently too much for her. As to the smaller vessels, our information is very scanty.

In 1651 the navy was classed in 6 rates; but beside them there continued to exist numerous classes of unrated ships, such as shallops, hulks, and later bombs, sloops, fire ships, and yachts. In 1677 we find a list of the whole English navy; according to which, the largest first rate three-decker carried 26 42-pdrs., 28 24-pdrs., 28 9-pdrs., 14 6-pdrs., and 4 3-pdrs.; and the smallest two-decker (fifth rate) carried 18 18-pdrs., 8 6-pdrs., and 4 4-pdrs., or 30 guns in all. The whole fleet consisted of 129 vessels. In 1714, we find 198 vessels; in 1727, 178; and in 1744, 128. Afterward, as the number of vessels increases, their size also gets larger, and the heaviness of the armament is augmented with the tonnage.

The first English ship answering to our modern frigate was built by Sir Robert Dudley, as early as the end of the 16th century; but it was not till fully 80 years later that this class of ships, first used by the southern European nations, was generally adopted in the

---

[a] Henry VIII.— *Ed.*

British navy. The particular fast-sailing qualities of frigates were little understood, for some time, in England. British ships were generally overgunned, so that their lower ports were but 3 feet from the water's edge, and could not be opened in a rough sea, and the sailing capacities of the vessels were also greatly impaired. Both the Spaniards and the French allowed more tonnage in proportion to the number of guns; the consequence was that their ships could carry heavier caliber and more stores, had more buoyancy, and were better sailers. The English frigates of the first half of the 18th century carried as many as 44 guns, of 9, 12, and a few of 18 lbs. caliber, with a tonnage of about 710. By 1780 frigates of 38 guns (mostly 18-pdrs.) and of 946 tons were built; the improvement here is obvious. The French frigates of the same epoch, with a similar armament, averaged 100 tons more. About the same time (the middle of the 18th century) the smaller men-of-war were more accurately classed in the modern way as corvettes, brigs, brigantines, and schooners.

In 1779 a piece of ordnance was invented (probably by the British Gen. Melville) which changed to a great extent the armaments of most navies. It was a very short gun, with a large caliber, approaching in its shape a howitzer, but intended to throw solid shot, with small charges, at short ranges. From these guns being first manufactured by the Carron iron company, in Scotland, they were called carronades. The shot from this gun, useless at long ranges, had fearful effects upon timber at close quarters; from its reduced velocity (by the reduced charge), it made a larger hole, shattered the timber far more, and made numerous and more dangerous splinters. The comparative lightness of the guns, too, made it easy to find room for a few of them on the quarter deck and forecastle of vessels; and as early as 1781 there were 429 ships in the British navy provided with from 6 to 10 carronades over and above their regular complement of guns. In reading the accounts of naval engagements during the French and American wars, it should be borne in mind that the British never include the carronades in the number of guns given as a ship's complement: so that, for instance, a British frigate, stated to be a 36-gun frigate, may in reality have carried 42 or more guns, including the carronades. The superior weight of metal which the carronades gave to the British broadsides, helped to decide many an action fought at close quarters during the war of the French revolution. But after all, carronades were merely a makeshift to increase the strength of the comparatively small-sized men-of-war of 80 years ago. As soon as the size of the ships was increased for each rating, they were again cast aside, and are now comparatively superseded.

In this particular, the construction of men-of-war, the French and Spaniards were decidedly ahead of the English. Their ships were larger and designed with far better lines than the British; their frigates especially were superior both in size and sailing qualities; and for many years the English frigates were copied from the French frigate *Hebe*, captured in 1782. In the same proportion as the vessels were lengthened, the high towering erections at the bow and stern, the forecastles, quarter decks, and poops, were reduced in height, the sailing qualities of the ships being increased thereby; so that gradually the comparatively elegant and swift-sailing lines of the present men-of-war came to be adopted. Instead of increasing the number of guns to these larger ships, the caliber was increased, and so were the weight and length of each gun, in order to admit of the use of full charges, and to receive the greatest point-blank range, so as to allow of the fire being opened at long distances. The small calibers below 24 lbs. disappeared from the larger vessels, and the remaining calibers were simplified, so as to have no more than two calibers, or at the outside three, on board of any one vessel. In ships of the line, the lower deck, being the strongest, was armed with guns of the same caliber as the upper decks, but of greater length and weight, in order to have at least one tier of guns available for the greatest possible range.

About 1820 the French Gen. Paixhans made an invention which has been of great importance in naval armaments. He constructed a gun of large caliber provided with a narrow chamber at the breech for the insertion of the powder, and began to fire hollow shot, at low elevations, from these "shell guns" (*canons obusiers*). Hitherto hollow shot had been fired against ships from howitzers in shore batteries only; though in Germany the practice of firing shell horizontally from short 24-lb. and even 12-lb. guns had been long in use against fortifications. The destructive effects of shells against the wooden sides of vessels were well known to Napoleon, who at Boulogne[401] armed most of his gun boats for the expedition to England with howitzers, and laid it down as a rule that ships must be attacked with projectiles which will burst after hitting. Now, Paixhans' shell guns gave the means of arming ships with cannon which, by throwing their shells as nearly as possible horizontally, could be used at sea, ship against ship, with nearly the same probability of hitting as the old round-shot guns. The new gun was soon introduced into all navies, and, after undergoing various improvements, now constitutes an essential portion of the armament of all large men-of-war.

Shortly afterward the first attempts were made to apply steam to the propulsion of ships of war, as it had already been applied by Fulton to that of commercial vessels. The progress from the river steamer to the coasting steamer, and gradually to the ocean steamer, was slow; in the same ratio was the progress of war steamers retarded. As long as paddle boats were the only steamers in existence, this was justifiable. The paddles and part of the engine were exposed to the enemy's shot, and could be disabled by a single lucky hit; they took up the best portion of the broadside room of the vessel; and the weight of engine, paddles, and coal so much reduced the capacity of the ship, that a heavy armament of numerous long guns was entirely out of the question. A paddle steamer, therefore, could never be a ship of the line; but its superior speed might permit it to compete with frigates, which are expected to hover on the flanks of an enemy, to collect the fruits of a victory, or to cover a retreat. Now a frigate has just the size and armament which enable it to go fearlessly on any independent roving errand, while its superior sailing qualities enable it to withdraw in time from an unequal contest. The sailing qualities of any frigate were far outstripped by the steamer; but without a good armament the steamer could not fulfil its mission. Regular broadside fighting was out of the question; the number of guns must, for want of space, be always inferior to that of a sailing frigate. Here, if anywhere, the shell gun was in its place. The diminished number of guns on board a steam frigate was counterbalanced by their weight of metal and caliber. Originally these guns were intended to throw shells only, but recently they have been made so heavy, especially the chase guns (at the bow and stern of the vessel), that they can, with full charges, throw solid shot also to considerable distances. Moreover, the reduced number of guns admits of traversing platforms and railways being laid down on the deck, by means of which all or most of the guns can be brought to bear in almost any direction; a provision by which the strength of a steam frigate for an attack is nearly doubled, and a 20-gun steam frigate can bring at least as many guns into action as a 40-gun sailing frigate with but 18 working guns for each single broadside. Thus the large modern paddle-steamer frigate is a most formidable ship; the superior caliber and range of her guns, added to her velocity, enable her to cripple an opponent at a distance where scarcely any effective return of fire is possible to the sailing vessel; while the weight of her metal comes in with crushing power when it is to her advantage finally to force the fighting. Still the disadvantage remains that her whole motive force is exposed to direct fire, and offers a large object to aim at.

For smaller vessels, corvettes, advice boats and other light craft, not counting in a naval battle, but very useful throughout a campaign, steam was at once found of great advantage, and there were many such paddle boats constructed in most navies. It was the same with transport ships. Where landings were intended, steamers not only reduced the length of passage to a minimum, but permitted one to calculate to a moral certainty the time of arrival at any given place. The transport of bodies of troops was now made a matter of great simplicity, especially as every naval country had a large fleet of commercial steamers to fall back upon for transport vessels in case of necessity. It was on these considerations that Prince de Joinville, in his well known pamphlet, ventured to maintain that steam had altered the condition of naval warfare to such an extent as to render an invasion of England by France no longer an impossibility.[402] Still, so long as the ships used for decisive action, the ships of the line, remained exclusively sailing vessels, the introduction of steam could work but little change in the conditions under which great naval battles were fought.

The invention of the screw propeller was destined to supply the means of revolutionizing naval warfare entirely, and to transform all war fleets into steam fleets. It was fully 13 years after the invention of the screw before the first step in this direction was made. The French, always superior to the English in naval design and construction, were the first to do it. Finally in 1849 the French engineer Dupuy-Delôme constructed the first screw line-of-battle ship, the *Napoléon,* of 100 guns and 600 horse power. This ship was not intended to depend upon steam only; unlike the paddles, the screw allowed a ship to retain all the lines and rigging of a sailing vessel, and to be moved, at will, by steam alone, by sails alone, or by both combined. She could, therefore, always save her coal for emergencies by having recourse to her sails, and was thus far less dependent upon the proximity of coaling stations than the old paddle-wheel steamer. On this account, and because her steam power was too weak to give her the full speed of a paddle steamer, the *Napoléon* and other vessels of this class were called auxiliary steam vessels; since then, however, ships of the line have been constructed which have steam power enough to give them all the speed of which the screw propeller is capable. The success of the

Napoléon soon caused screw ships of the line to be built both in France and England. The Russian war[a] gave a new impulse to this radical change in naval construction; and when it was found that most strong-built ships of the line could, without too much difficulty, be fitted with a screw and engines, the transformation of all navies into steam fleets became only a matter of time. No large naval power now thinks of constructing any more large sailing vessels; almost all ships newly laid down are screw steamers, excepting the few paddle steamers which for certain purposes are still required; and before 1870 sailing ships of war will be almost as completely antiquated as the spinning wheel and the smooth-bore musket are now.

The Crimean war called into existence two new naval constructions. The first of these is the steam gun boat or mortar boat, originally constructed by the English for the contemplated attack on Cronstadt; it is a small vessel drawing from 4 to 7 feet of water, and armed with one or two heavy long-range guns or a heavy mortar; the former to be used in shallow and intricate waters generally, the latter in the bombardment, from a long distance, of fortified naval arsenals. They answered exceedingly well, and will no doubt play an important part in future naval campaigns. The mortar boat, as proved at Sveaborg,[403] totally alters the relations of attack and defence between fortresses and ships, by giving the ships that power of bombarding the former with impunity which they never before possessed; at 3,000 yards, from which the shells of the mortar boats can hit an object as large as a town, they are themselves quite secure from their smallness of surface. The gun boats, on the contrary, when acting in concert with coast batteries, will strengthen the defence, and will also provide naval warfare with those light skirmishers which were hitherto wanting to it.

The second innovation is the iron-sided, shot-proof floating batteries, first constructed by the French, for the attack of coast defences. They were tried at Kinburn only, and their success, even against the rickety parapets and rusty cannon of that little place, was not so very signal.[404] Still, the French appeared to be so well satisfied with them, that they have gone on ever since experimenting upon steel-plated vessels. They have constructed gun boats with a kind of shot-proof steel parapet on the forecastle, which shelters the gun and its crew; but if the floating batteries were unwieldy and had to be towed, these gun boats always had their

---

[a] The Crimean war of 1853-56.— *Ed.*

heads in the water and were not at all seaworthy. They have however produced a steel-plated steam frigate called *La Gloire,* which is said to be shot-proof, of very good speed, and quite capable of living in a gale. The most exaggerated statements are made with regard to the probable revolution these shot-proof frigates will create in naval warfare. We are told that ships of the line are antiquated, and that the power to decide great naval actions has passed over to these frigates with a single battery of guns, covered in shot-proof on all sides, against which no wooden three-decker can stand. This is not the place to argue these questions; but we may observe that it is far easier to invent and put on board ship rifled artillery heavy enough to smash iron or steel plates, than it is to construct vessels cased with metal thick enough to withstand the shot or shell from these guns. As to the *Gloire,* it is not certain after all that she is fit to live in a gale, and from her incapacity for holding coal it is said that she cannot keep the sea under steam for more than 3 days. What her British competitor, the *Warrior,* will do, remains to be seen. No doubt, by reducing the armament and coal, and by altering the mode of construction, it may be possible to render a ship entirely shot-proof at long and medium ranges, and a fair steamer; but in an age when the science of artillery makes such rapid strides, it is very doubtful whether such ships will be worth constructing in the long run.[405]

The revolution in artillery which the rifled gun is now effecting appears to be a far more important matter for naval warfare than any thing that can be effected by steel-plated ships. Every rifled gun that deserves the name gives such a precision at long ranges that the ancient inefficiency of naval firing at such ranges appears to be fast becoming a matter of the past. Moreover, the rifled cannon, by admitting elongated shot and reduced charges, allows a considerable reduction in the bore and weight of broadside guns; or otherwise, the bore remaining the same, gives results far greater. The elongated shot from a 56 cwt. rifled 32-pounder will surpass the round shot from a 113 cwt. smooth-bore 10-inch gun, not only in weight, but also in penetration, range, and precision. The power of attack of every vessel is at least tripled if it be armed with rifled ordnance. Moreover, the great desideratum has always been to invent a useful percussion shell which should explode the very moment it penetrates a ship's side. The rotation of round shot has rendered this impracticable; the percussion fuze was not always in the proper position when the shell struck, and then it did not go off. But an elongated shot from a rifled cannon, rotating round its longitudinal axis, must always strike head foremost; and a simple percussion cap on the fuze head bursts the shell the moment it enters the ship's side. It is not probable that any steel-clad ship yet invented can brave two such broadsides from a two-decker with impunity; not to speak of the shells which enter the ports and must explode between decks. Rifled ordnance must to a great degree put a stop to such close-fought actions as were those in which carronades could be useful; manoeuvring will once more regain the ascendant; and as steam now makes the contending vessels independent of wind and tide, naval warfare will in future much more approach the method and be subject to the tactics of land battles.

The vessels of war of which modern navies are composed are classed in various ratings, from first to sixth rates; but as these ratings are both variable and arbitrary, it will be better to class them in the common way as ships of the line, frigates, sloops, brigs, schooners, &c. Ships of the line are the largest men-of-war afloat, destined to form the line of battle in a general action, and to decide the struggle by the weight of metal thrown into the enemy's ships. They are either 3-deckers or 2-deckers; that is to say, they have either 3 or 2 covered decks armed with guns. These decks are called the lower, middle, and main or upper deck. The upper deck, which was formerly covered in at the quarter deck and forecastle only, is now covered in by a continuous open deck from stem to stern. This open deck, which is still called the quarter deck and forecastle (the position amidships being called the gangway), also carries artillery, mostly carronades; so that in reality a 2-decker carries 3, and a 3-decker 4 tiers of guns. The heaviest guns are, of course, placed on the lower deck; and the guns become lighter in proportion as the batteries are more elevated above the water. The caliber being mostly the same, this is obtained by reducing the weight of the guns themselves, in consequence of which those on the upper decks can only stand reduced charges, which implies that they can be used only at shorter ranges. The only exception to this rule is in the case of chase guns, which are placed at the bow and stern of a ship, and which, even if placed on the forecastle or quarter deck, are still as long and heavy as possible, as they are required to act at the longest ranges practicable. Thus, the bow and stern guns of English ships of the line are composed either of 8 or 10-inch shell guns, or of 56-pdr. (bore 7.7 inches) or 68-pdr. (bore 8.13 inches) solid shot guns, one of which is placed on the forecastle on a traversing platform. There are in the English navy generally 6

stern and 5 bow guns to a first rate; the remaining armament of
such a ship is as follows:

Position.	Description.	W'ght.	Length.	No.
Lower deck	8-inch shell guns.	65 cwt.	9 ft. 0 in.	4
" "	32-pounder guns.	56 "	9 6	28
Middle deck..............	8-inch shell guns.	65 "	9 0	2
" "	32-pounder guns.	50 "	9 0	32
Upper deck.............	" "	42 "	8 ·0	34
Forecastle and ⎫	" "	45 "	8 6	6
quarter deck.⎭	" carronades	17 "	4 0	14
Total....................	.....	.....	.....	120

The armament of the smaller ratings of vessels of the line is
arranged upon the same principle. For the sake of comparison, we
also give that of a French first rate, viz.: lower deck, 32 long 30-lb.
guns; middle deck, 4 80-lb. shell guns, and 30 short 30-lb. guns;
upper deck, 34 30-lb. shell guns; forecastle and quarter deck, 4
30-lb. shell guns, and 16 30-lb. carronades; in all, 120 guns. The
French 80-lb. shell gun has a larger bore than the 8-inch English
gun by 0.8 inch; the 30-lb. shell gun and the 30-lb. gun have a
slightly larger bore than the English 32-pdr., so that the advantage
of weight of metal would lie with the French. The smallest ship of
the line now carries 72 guns; the largest frigate carries 61.

A frigate is a ship with only one covered deck carrying guns,
and another open deck above it (forecastle and quarter deck)
which is equally provided with guns. The armament, in the
English service, is generally of 30 guns (either all shell guns or
part shell guns and part long 32-pdrs.) on the gun deck, and 30
short 32-pdrs. on the forecastle and quarter deck, with a heavy
pivot gun on a traversing platform at the bow. Frigates being
mostly sent on detached service, where they are always likely to
become engaged single-handed against hostile frigates sent on the
same errand, it has been a great point with most naval nations to
make them as large and powerful as possible. In no class of vessels
is the increase in size so remarkable as in this. The United States,
requiring a cheap navy strong enough to enforce respect, were the
first to see the great advantage to be drawn from a fleet of large
frigates, each of them superior to any frigate which other nations
could bring against it. The superiority of the American ship
builders in producing swift vessels was also taken advantage of,
and the last war against England (1812-'14)[406] showed in many

well contested engagements what formidable antagonists these American frigates were. Up to the present day the U.S. frigates are considered models of this class of vessels, although the difference in size when compared with other navies is not by far so marked as it was 30 or 40 years ago.

The next class of men-of-war are called corvettes. They have but one tier of guns, placed on an open deck; but the larger class are provided with a forecastle and quarter deck (not connected, however, by a continuous deck amidships), where they carry a few guns more. Such corvettes, therefore, almost correspond to what a frigate was 80 years ago, before the two elevated extremities of the vessel were connected by a flush deck. These corvettes are still strong enough to carry the same caliber of guns as the larger vessels. They also carry 3 masts, all square-rigged. Of smaller vessels, brigs and schooners carry from 20 guns to 6. They have but two masts, square-rigged in brigs, fore-and-aft rigged in schooners. The caliber of their guns is necessarily smaller than that of the larger ships, and does not generally exceed 18 or 24-pdrs. going down as low as 12 and 9-pdrs. Vessels of this small power of offence cannot be sent where serious resistance is anticipated. In European waters they are becoming generally superseded by small steamers, and they can be of actual service only on such coasts as those of South America, China, &c.,where they have to meet powerless antagonists, and where they merely serve to represent the flag of a powerful naval nation.

The armaments given above are merely those adopted at present, but they will undoubtedly be changed in every respect during the next 10 years by the general adoption of rifled ship guns.[407]

Written in October and November, before November 23, 1860

First published in *The New American Cyclopaedia,* Vol. XII, 1861

Reproduced from *The New American Cyclopaedia*

FROM THE PREPARATORY MATERIALS
FOR THE ARTICLES
IN *THE NEW AMERICAN CYCLOPAEDIA*[408]

Frederick Engels

SUMMARY OF JOHN W. KAYE'S
HISTORY OF THE WAR IN AFGHANISTAN[409]

AFGHANISTAN WAR. J. W. KAYE, *HISTORY OF THE WAR
IN AFGHANISTAN*, 1851, 2 Vols.

From 1818 Dost Mohammed Khan of the Barukzye tribe
(Douranee tribe, as also the Populzyes, then the dynasty of the
Suddozyes, but ousted by Dost Mohammed) ruled in Kabul after
many civil wars. In Peshawar and Kandahar brothers of Dost
Mohammed also ruled. The one in Peshawar, Azim Khan,
attacked the Sikhs but Runjeet Singh defeated him and seized
Peshawar from him so that it further became a tributary of the
Sikhs.

Herat alone remained under an ancient Suddozye dynasty. This
was attacked by Mohamed Shah of Persia with Russian advice and
aid. Agitation among the English. Fear of a Russian invasion of
India, for Persia had been completely played into the hands of the
Russians by English policy.

Even earlier, in 1835, Lord Auckland, Governor-General [of
India], sent Alexander Burnes to Kabul as ambassador, under the
pretext of a trade mission. The Persians wanted to have Dost
Mohammed also on their side, but Dost was for the English
alliance. But when it came to particulars the English demanded
everything and would promise nothing in return. The Pole
Vitkievicz intervened, promised everything and demanded little,
and Burnes finally had to leave, whereupon Vitkievicz and the
Persians momentarily gained the upper hand (garbled "blue
books"[410]).

The Indian Governor, in Simla at the time, under the influence
not of the Indian Council, but of W. H. Macnaghten, secretary to

the Government, Henry Torrens and J. Colvin, his private
secretaries. Macnaghten and Colvin very ambitious, particularly
the former. In its Russophobia this conclave decided to restore
Shah Soojah, who had been ousted back in 1809 and was living on
pension in Loodhianah, to the throne of Afghanistan and to
conclude an alliance with the Sikhs to this end. This was done.
The army gathered. Runjeet Singh was ready. Shah Soojah began
to organise a recruited army under English officers.

Meanwhile small expedition to Karrak (near Bushire) in the
Persian Gulf was enough at the very last moment, September 4-9,
1838, when Herat had almost fallen, to push the Persians back.
They retired, and now *au fond* no more fear of Russian power in
Afghanistan. But the English had advanced too far, and so the
expedition was undertaken, although only with a few troops.

October 1, 1838 proclamation containing the Governor-
General's declaration of war—scarcely public, when the news of
the relief of Herat arrived.

The army which actually marched: 2 brigades Bengal army,
13th Queen's Infantry Regiment, 16th, 31st, 35th, 37th, 42nd,
48th native infantry under Sir W. Cotton, 16th Lancers and
Indian irregular cavalry, 9,500 men in all.

One brigade Bombay army, 4th Dragoons, 2nd and 17th
Queen's regiments, a native infantry regiment and some artillery
via the Indus.

Shah Soojah's army: 2 cavalry, 4 infantry regiments, 1 mounted
battery—6,000 men under Major-General Simpson (Crimea?[a]).

The Bengal troops and Shah Soojah's troops marched through
Sindh, on which a levy was imposed for the benefit of Runjeet
Singh and Shah Soojah, to Shikarpur, where they were to meet
the Bombay troops. Sir J. Keane commander-in-chief.[b]—The
Sikhs, with Shah Soojah's son Timur Khan, through the Khyber
Pass towards Kabul. Having marched off from Lahore in
mid-December, by February 20 Cotton in Shikarpur, where the
Shah's army was already. The English Bengal army 9,500 men,
3,800 camp-followers,[b] 30,000 pack-camels.

Macnaghten's political agents and emissaries with Shah Soojah.[c]
Burnes among them.

Many camels already lost in Shikarpur.

---

[a] This remark refers to Simpson's participation in the Crimean war of
1853-56.— *Ed.*

[b] Engels uses the English word.— *Ed.*

[c] Macnaghten himself joined the army as British envoy at the Shah's
Court.— *Ed.*

Beginning of March through the *Bolan* Pass. To Dadur 146 miles, 16 marches. The camels were dropping for want of forage. Food supplies ditto. The Baluchistan robbers on flank and at rear. Particularly from Dadur to Quetta, 60 miles through the pass. In Quetta on March 26. Here the cavalry was due to stop, but nothing to eat. Burnes set out to Mehrab Khan of Khelat, who promised everything, but said that the land was poor.

On March 7 the Shah's troops marched from Shikarpur. The Bombay brigade also followed, and Sir J. Keane, who arrived with it in Quetta on April 6. Nothing for it but forthwith to Kandahar. Left on April 7, over the Kodjuk Pass. Kohun-dil-Khan and his brothers fled, and the army entered Kandahar on April 25.

The army paid for everything and nationalised very liberally. In the process Macnaghten squandered a lot of money on bribery[a] but to no avail. No enthusiasm for Shah Soojah.[b]

June 27 from Kandahar for Kabul via Ghuznee, which was the impregnable fortress of Afghanistan, and was reached on July 21. Through treachery it came to Keane's knowledge that one gate, the Kabul, was not walled up on the inside. He had left his siege guns in Kandahar, and had only light field guns. This news alone made capture possible. While mock assaults on the impregnable façade and a bombardment deceived the garrison, the gate was blown up with sacks of gunpowder and stormed by the 13th Regiment (under Dennie and Sale). After fierce resistance the fortress fell.

Dost Mohammed moved to Maidan, a very strong position, and then even closer to the English. But his army broke up, and Dost Mohammed fled to Bokhara, where the Khan had him seized.

The Sikhs did nothing, but as Dost Mohammed did not support the Afridis, they allowed Timur Khan through with a very few motley[a] troops (under Capt. Wade). Arrived in Kabul on September 3.

On August 6 Shah Soojah and the English had entered Kabul. On September 18 the Bombay brigade marched back. On October 3 three companies of infantry, the 16th Lancers, 3rd Bengal Cavalry, 4th Local Horse[c] and one battery of artillery of the Bengal division were also repulsed. Distribution of the rest: Kabul: 13th Queen's Infantry, 35th Native Infantry, 3 cannon light foot.

---

[a] Engels uses the English word.— *Ed.*

[b] This sentence is in English in the manuscript.— *Ed.*

[c] Engels uses the English words "Local Horse".— *Ed.*

Jellalabad: 48th Native Infantry, some cavalrymen and sappers.

Ghuznee: 16th Native Infantry, 1 squadron irregular cavalry and what was available of Shah Soojah's troops.

Kandahar: 42nd and 43rd Native Infantry, 1 squadron irregular cavalry, 1 battery and some of Shah Soojah's troops available (Nott in command).

What had become of the 31st and 37th Native Infantry *non liquet*.[a] Bameean particularly through the Shah's good Gurkha Regiment [411] and one battery mounted artillery (!! taken in hand!).

The Afghans furious at the invasion by the Kafirs, Shah Soojah hated or indifferent. English intervention in government and administration makes things even worse. The Douranees around Kandahar had reckoned on Shah Soojah giving them back their former preponderance and rights of plunder suppressed by Dost Mohammed. This was not permitted by the English. The Douranees furious about this. The Afridis in the Khyber Pass irritated instead of being paid. In Khelat, Mehrab Khan was attacked at Macnaghten's instigation for being a traitor (!), and Khelat stormed by Willshire, who seemed to have remained in the area with the 2nd and 17th Queen's and 31st Native Infantry together with cavalry and artillery. Mehrab Khan fell and part of the country annexed by Shah Soojah.

Rewards now showered from England.

In winter Macnaghten checked the revenue.[b] Very bad. Almost everything had to be met by English subsidies. The Russian expedition to Khiva now known, and its strength greatly exaggerated because of the success in Afghanistan.[412] Runjeet Singh died in Punjab, having already been fatally ill when the [English] expedition set out, and his sons and grandsons intrigued against each other and against the English. In Herat, Yar Mohamed, Shah Kamran's vizier, let the English pay him, and intrigued against them in Afghanistan. In Afghanistan itself the Douranees not pacified, and Khelat in open rebellion. In Bokhara, Stoddart, English envoy, arrested, maltreated and forced to embrace Islam. In the northern mountains on the other side of the Hindu Kush near Khulum the supporters of Dost Mohammed among the Uzbek tribes in unrest (hitherto they had been dubious vassals of Afghanistan).

Admittedly, the Russian expedition was a failure, as Macnaghten ascertained in *July*, but it was now also established that Nao Nehal

---

a Not clear (Engels' remark).— *Ed.*

b Here, in the left margin, Engels made the following note: "Book IV. 1840 Jan."— *Ed.*

Singh, heir apparent and actual ruler of the Sikhs, was in direct correspondence and intrigues with the enemies of Shah [Soojah], that he had given asylum to Ghilzye refugees, etc., and was at the same time preparing the betrayal by Yar Shah, who was on intimate terms with the Persians and made himself out to be the most obedient servant of the Shah in Shah.[a]

Auckland had returned to Calcutta, where Sir Jasper Nicolls was commander-in-chief[b] and at the same time a member of the Council. The latter proved that the armed forces in India were already extremely weak. Macnaghten continued to demand that Herat should be conquered and Peshawar taken from the Sikhs, but now of course in vain. He wanted to macadamise the Punjab to enable troops to march through and to create a direct link with India, and continued to demand money and reinforcements, the latter, however, always being denied him. Macnaghten blamed all bad luck on Herat and the Sikhs; in Afghanistan, he claimed, all was in vain since Shah Soojah was very popular!

Meanwhile, in Afghanistan constant insurrections. The Ghilzyes rose again in spring 1840. Captain Anderson, Bengal artillery, defeated them May 16 on the Turnuk river, and Macnaghten promised them a subsidy of £3,000 p.a., yet still they persisted in unrest.

In Khelat the Baluchis rose and recaptured Khelat.

By now all the Englishmen in Afghanistan convinced of the untenability of the position, only Macnaghten obstinately maintained all was well.

In August Conolly sent to Khokand and Khiva.

In the Hindu Kush Azim Khan, Dost Mohammed's son, and shortly afterwards Jubbar Khan, Dost Mohammed's brother, came with Dost Mohammed's family, respectively surrendering and submitting to the English in Bameean. At the same time various engagements with the Uzbeks in the mountains between Bameean and Kamurd, with varying success. Finally Dost Mohammed escaped from Bokhara and went to Khulum, where he gathered an army. Bajgah, a weak outpost in the mountains beyond Kamurd, had to be evacuated August 30 by the Gurkha Regiment of Shah Soojah. A newly formed Afghan regiment went over to Dost Mohammed 2-3 days later. Kabul was ready to break away, the Sikhs were intriguing these directly against the English and giving financial support to Dost Mohammed.

---

[a] Mohamed Shah of Persia.— *Ed.*

[b] Engels uses the English word.— *Ed.*

On September 14 Brig. Dennie arrived in Bameean with the
35th Native Infantry. On the 18th he attacked Dost Mohammed's
Uzbeks, etc., who were debouching from the mountains on
Bameean, and utterly routed them. The wullee (chief) of Khulum
pledged not to give Dost Mohammed asylum and concluded
peace.

But Dost Mohammed reappeared in Kohistan (in the eastern
Hindu Kush). At the end of September Sale marched towards the
Ghorebund Pass against him. On September 29 a number of
fortifications in the pass captured (near Tootundurrah), on
October 3 Joolgah (a fortified village) stormed but repulsed. Dost
Mohammed was everywhere and nowhere, it was often said 40-50
miles from Kabul, where the Balahissar were being armed. At
length Dost Mohammed turned up with a fair-sized army in
Nijrow (where?). Sale marched against him, encountered him at
Purwandurrah and pursued him with his cavalry (Natives[a]) as he
retreated. The latter, attacked by Dost Mohammed's horsemen,
fled immediately (November 2) and were pursued as far as
Kamurd. Thereupon Sale broke off the engagement.

After this victory, however, Dost Mohammed rode to Kabul and
surrendered to Macnaghten.

In October-November unrest in Zemindawer (north-west[a] of
Kandahar) among the Parsewan inhabitants because of the
collection of taxes due from the time of Dost Mohammed, and the
cavalry escort of Shah Soojah's army defeated by these inhabitants.

End of December 1840 Nott sent troops from Kandahar against
them, and on January 3, 1841 the Zemindawer Douranees beaten.
(This insurrection directly instigated by Yar Mohamed in Herat,[b]
who promised to come.) Todd (envoy in Herat) now left his post,
as nothing more could be done with Yar Mohamed, who was
openly admitting his treachery and just demanding more money—
but Auckland disavowed Todd and dismissed him!

The Douranees continued in unrest, and the Ghilzyes also rose
again. The English decided to fortify Khelat in Ghilzye once
again; the Ghilzyes refused to suffer this and banded together.
Nott sent 400 men of the 38th Native Infantry. On May 19 the
Ghilzyes were defeated at Assiai-Ilmee but this failed to bring
calm.

Aktur Khan of Zemindawer with 3,000 men defeated outside
Ghiresk by Woodburn with chiefly Afghan troops (5th Afghan

---

[a] Engels uses the English word.— Ed.
[b] Here, in the left margin, Engels has "1841".— Ed.

Infantry, 2 guns, and a few Afghan cavalrymen, who absconded) (in July).

Aktur Khan and another Douranee chief, Akrum Khan, back into the field. Defeated on August 17. This pacified the Douranees for some time.

On August 5 Chambers also defeated the Ghilzyes with Indian cavalry, and Macnaghten was triumphant.

"All quiet from Dan to Beersheba."[a]

The English in Kabul encamped outside the town, the camp miserably fortified, untenable, dominated everywhere. Elphinstone, an old, sick general, had been in command since early 1841, when Cotton resigned. The ramparts could be surmounted on horseback! All around: gardens, houses and defile paths. The stores were kept separately in a fort, and between it and the camp lay an empty fort with a walled garden, which seemed to be made for a hostile party[b] to cut off the communications. All this through the fault of the politicals[c] who would not permit the occupation of the Bala Hissar.[d]

The English officers and soldiers had intrigued a good deal with the women of Kabul, and the men of Kabul could get no redress.[e] Widespread fury of the Mohammedans, who finally decided to seek revenge. This at the heart of the fury against the invaders.[c]

Macnaghten saw everything, as he wrote September 20, 1841, in "*couleur de rose*".[f] Meanwhile in September another minor insurrection suppressed in Kohistan.

The Indian finances ruined by the Afghan war. Every year £1¼ million went to Afghanistan, and Nicolls maintained that either the Punjab had to be conquered or the force in Afghanistan to be brought up to 25,000. A new Indian loan issued. 9,000 Indian troops encamped between Karachi and Quetta, 16,000 infantry and Shah troops in Afghanistan itself. Now a ministerial crisis in England, prospects of a Tory administration opposed to all trans-Indus expeditions. (Macnaghten so blind that when the loan was issued he asked if it was intended for the Chinese

---

[a] From Macnaghten's letter to Robertson, August 20, 1841 (J. W. Kaye, *History of the War in Afghanistan*, Vol. I, p. 602).— *Ed.*

[b] Engels uses the English words "hostile party".— *Ed.*

[c] Engels uses the English word.— *Ed.*

[d] Kabul's citadel which became Shah Soojah's residence.— *Ed.*

[e] Engels uses the English words "could get no redress" (paraphrase of Kaye's words).— *Ed.*

[f] J. W. Kaye, op. cit., Vol. I, pp. 616-17.— *Ed.*

war![a])—The 44th Queen's Regiment under Shelton sent to Kabul in the spring.

Macnaghten appointed Governor of Bombay. Before departing he saw the necessity of restricting expenditure. Firstly by curtailing the subsidies to the chieftains of the Ghilzyes, Kohistanees, Momunds, Kaubulees, Kuzzilbashes. *This* decided it. The summoning of the chieftains to Kabul resulted immediately in a conspiracy, and they decided that the Ghilzyes in the mountains to the south of Jellalabad should rise first. This they did.

Macnaghten, however, decided, *as all was quiet,* to send some of the troops to India. One regiment in Kabul and one in Kandahar were sufficient succour[b] [to Shah Soojah's troops]. So he set out, on his return joining up with troops who were to take punitive measures on the way.

On October 9 the 35th Regiment Native Infantry, a cavalry squadron and two guns set out.... At Bootkhak the camp attacked. On the 10th Sale followed [Monteith] with the 13th Infantry Regiment and on October 13 arrived at the pass of Khurd-Kabul. Heavy fighting, but the English pushed through and Sale returned to Bootkhak. Monteith with the 35th Native Infantry was attacked every night in the mountains and robbed of all his camels. Admittedly peace concluded with the chieftains and promised to continue paying the old subsidies, but no go.[c] The tribes went on fighting and the chieftains laughed up their sleeves. From Tezeen to Gundamuck continual fighting, and it flared up again on the other side of the Jugdulluck. There the outlet from the defile was captured.

Sale was in Gundamuck. *Macnaghten* still considered it unimportant.

Kaye, *War in Afghanistan,* Vol. II.

The conspiracy of the chieftains in Kabul was known to Burnes and Macnaghten (the latter had not yet left) but nothing was done. On the evening of November 1 a meeting of the conspirators, decision to start an insurrection in the town in the morning, beginning with an attack on the residence of Burnes, who lived in the town.

November 2 Burnes' house destroyed and he and his guards

---

[a] Cf. Macnaghten's letter to Major Rawlinson of April 20, 1841 (J. W. Kaye, op. cit., Vol. I, pp. 620-21). The Chinese war—the war waged by England against China from 1840 to 1842 (so-called First Opium War).— *Ed.*

[b] Engels uses the English word.— *Ed.*

[c] Engels uses the English expression.— *Ed.*

murdered. The English did nothing. *Ordre, contre-ordre, désordre.*[a] Elphinstone weak. Shah Soojah wanted no troops in the Bala Hissar! and they gave in to him!

November 3. Not until 3 p.m. **three** companies and **2** guns sent against the town! Repulsed, of course.[b]

The fortified camp of the English (bastioned stockade continued[c]!) much too big for the few troops there, moreover dominated. Food supplies in a fort 400 yards removed from the S.W. corner of the camp!! Between the two lay an old earth fort with walled gardens, which was not occupied, and Macnaghten forbade its occupation!! This place (Mohamed Sheriff's Fort) immediately occupied by the Afghans, the camp fired upon and the commissariat fort attacked (only 80 men inside!).

November 4 three **rei**[d] companies sent to the commissariat fort forced to turn back. Likewise a cavalry expedition sent to *fetch* (!) the garrison out of the commissariat fort. In the night the garrison evacuated the commissariat fort, which was immediately plundered. All the medical stores, beer, wine, etc., were lost together with the food supplies. A more distant fort where corn had been stored had already been evacuated the night of the 3rd on account of the weakness of the garrison and water shortage.

The Kohistan Regiment of Shah Soojah in Kardurrah rebelled and killed their officers.

November 5 Elphinstone already talking of *bribing* the enemy and of negotiations!

November 6 Mohamed Sheriff's Fort finally captured and destroyed. Otherwise nothing happened. Some corn purchased in the surrounding villages. Elphinstone writes to Macnaghten:

"Our case is not yet desperate [...] but it goes very fast."[e]

Mohun Lal, Burnes' moonshee, sent as negotiator to the mountain tribes, in order to *bribe* the chieftains. But also secretly to pay rewards *for the heads of the most furious* (10,000 rupees a piece[f]).

---

[a] Napoleon's words.— *Ed.*
[b] Engels uses the English expression "of course".— *Ed.*
[c] Engels uses the English word.— *Ed.*
[d] The abbreviation "rei" used by Engels may stand for the English "reinforced".— *Ed.*
[e] From Elphinstone's letter to Macnaghten of November 6, 1841 (J. W. Kaye, op. cit., Vol. II, p. 39). The quotation is in English in the manuscript.— *Ed.*
[f] Engels uses the English words "rupees a piece".— *Ed.*

Elphinstone quite ill, at a loss, undecided, depending on whoever spoke last, *ordre, contre-ordre, désordre.*

November 9 Brig. Shelton, who was in the Bala Hissar with the Shah's troops, called to the camp as second in command [a] and as *ad latus* [b] of Elphinstone, but the two constantly at loggerheads. Sale's brigade was now to return from Gundamuck, to relieve them.

November 10 the Afghans *en masse* on the dominating foothills, fired into the camp. At Macnaghten's insistence, 1,000 men were to attack. No sooner were they assembled than counter-order from Elphinstone. Eventually sent however. A small fort captured, but the troops in the open field fled from the Afghan horsemen (Europeans! and natives [c]). However, the enemy finally repulsed.

November 13 the Afghans again on the mountain, bombarding the camp from the heights of Beh-meru with 2 guns. Macnaghten wanted to attack, Shelton did not, overruled, [c] and 16 companies, $2^1/_2$ squadrons, 2 guns sent out, among them Shelton himself. The Afghan horsemen charged again and again through the English infantry, repulsing them and being repulsed themselves by the cavalry. The infantry then followed and took the heights and the 2 guns. *Last success of the English.*

November 15 Pottinger arrived from Kohistan wounded: the Shah's Gurkha Regiment *annihilated* by the mountain tribes.

November 17 news that Sale was marching towards Jellalabad. Last hope gone west. Now only a choice between occupation of the Bala Hissar, retreat or capitulation. Shelton succeeded in asserting his view that the Bala Hissar should *not* be occupied (his reasons childish), which alone would have made wintering possible.

November 23 second engagement at Beh-meru. The English marched out, totally defeated, lost 2 guns. The artillery alone fought well, the infantry, Europeans and Sepoys, **cowardly.** Chased back in disorder over the plain into the camp by the Afghans.

Now they could no longer (in Elphinstone's opinion) enter the Bala Hissar without sacrificing some of the 700 wounded and sick and almost all the stores, [c] ammunition and food. On half rations for the past few days! Therefore negotiations. The Afghan chieftains demand (November 24) unconditional surrender. Rejected.

---

[a] Engels uses the English phrase.— *Ed.*
[b] Assistant.— *Ed.*
[c] Engels uses the English word.— *Ed.*

Mahomed Akbar Khan, Dost Mohammed's son, arrived in Kabul and became chief of the Afghans. He immediately took steps to cut off all the supplies[a] of the English, and succeeded. Abdullah Khan and Meer Musjedee, the two chieftains on whose heads the English had placed a reward, eliminated before the end of November. The first was wounded at Beh-meru by a dubious shot (second engagement) and was then allegedly given poison; the second probably poisoned or suffocated. The rewards claimed, but the English refused payment.

December 1-8 shortages in camp. Horses dying. March on Jellalabad declared impossible. Likewise a capitulation, which, it was said, could provide no protection against the tribes in the mountains. Macnaghten now wants [to move to] the Bala Hissar. December 5 the Afghans burnt the English bridge over the Kabul, $1/4$ mile from the camp, without the English attempting to prevent them. December 6 Mohamed Sheriff's Fort evacuated. (5,000 men still fit for duty.[b]) [The garrison of the fort consisting] of 100 men [were put to flight by] 20 Afghans who had climbed up the walls of the fort!!

The generals pressed for capitulation or retreat, which was admittedly almost impossible. Macnaghten hesitated. On the 10th news that the relief force from Kandahar, for which they had been hoping, could not get through. On the 11th everything eaten up down to the last scrap. The soldiers had become so cowardly that they were no longer fit for fighting.

December 11 capitulation. *The whole of Afghanistan to be evacuated.* The British troops in Kabul to go to Peshawar. Shah Soojah to accompany them or remain, as he chooses. Dost Mohammed returns. 4 British officers as hostages. Nevertheless, peace and friendship between Afghanistan and England (even a clause inserted stating that the Afghans were not to enter into any alliance without the consent of the English). The treaty accepted in the main by word of mouth.

During the entire period of the English defensive and sluggish offensive the Afghans distinguished by their use of long-range long flintlocks (jezails). They were always out of range of the poor smoothbore muskets of the English.

December 13 the Bala Hissar evacuated by the English.

December 16 the forts round the camp (small Afghan fortifications) evacuated in return for deliveries of supplies, which proved

---

[a] Engels uses the English word.— *Ed.*

[b] Engels uses the English expression "fit for duty".— *Ed.*

to be very scanty.[a] The Afghans suspicious, sent nothing and scoffed at the treaty.

December 18 *snow.* December 19 dispatch of Macnaghten's order that Ghuznee, Kandahar, Jellalabad should be evacuated. The chieftains disunited and suspicious. On December 22 Mahomed Akbar Khan had the proposal put to them that they should associate with the English, leave Shah Soojah on the throne, make him, Mahomed Akbar Khan, vizier and immediately defeat the other Afghan tribes, and let the English remain until the spring, when they should retire peacefully. Macnaghten walked into the trap, arrived on the 23rd to conclude the matter—and was *murdered.* The generals sat back and let this happen!

January 1 [1842] the treaty at last. The English to march, as soon as they have cattle, accompanied by Afghan chieftains. The troops in Jellalabad to march even earlier. Those in Ghuznee via Kabul, those in Kandahar direct [to India]. 6 British officers as hostages. The Afghans to conclude no alliance without the consent of the English, but may, in return, claim English help too (if this not ratified, the Afghans to do as they like). All guns except 6 horse-drawn and three small mule-drawn (mountain) guns to remain, likewise all remaining similar weapons, ammunition and stores.[a]

In addition all the cash[a] (19 lakhs) remains, and bills of exchange for 14 lakhs signed for individual chieftains, to whom Macnaghten was alleged to have promised this.

Immediate warning from all parties that they would be attacked during the march. But *que faire?*[b] At first Pottinger refused to conclude this treaty, since reinforcements were on the way from India and there was great dissension among the chieftains, nor did the treaty offer any guarantee of a safe withdrawal. But a council of war (December 25) ordered it.

Written in July 1857

Published for the first time

Printed according to the manuscript

Translated from the German

---

a Engels uses the English word.—*Ed.*
b What was to be done?—*Ed.*

Karl Marx

EXCERPTS FROM THE ARTICLE "BLUM" PUBLISHED
IN *MEYER'S CONVERSATIONS-LEXICON*[413]

Mr. (Meyer)—Popular (i.e. pulpit) *eloquence. Steger.*

Blum (Robert) born in Cologne, November 10, 1807. His father (unsuccessful budding theologian) [became a] journeyman[a] cooper. "Mother, a servant from the country, earned additional income by sewing." Father † 1815: "entire responsibility for supporting the 3 children fell to the mother". In 1816 she married an absolutely brutal bargee[b] (first smuggler, later a soldier in the service of Spain and Portugal). Unhappy marriage. Appalling peak of distress in the famine year of 1816-17. 1817 [Robert Blum] sent to elementary school. 1819 communion; then employed as acolyte, "which entailed free tuition in the church school" as well as bringing in money. Clash with the priests because of embezzlement and over transubstantiation. Breach of the sacred seal of confession. End of his religious activity. Artisan first as goldsmith, then girdler; journeyman's travels; "finally had to return to Cologne. There found work in a lantern factory". "The boss, F. W. Schmitz, [...] transferred him to the office", took him on trips to London, Württemberg, Bavaria; lived for six months in Munich. Then to Berlin; studied there diligently (1829-30). *Self-taught.*[c] Military service in the meantime. "In April 1830 Blum had to join the fusilier battalion of the 24th Infantry Regiment in Prenzlau, [...] only for 6 weeks, [...] was placed on the reserve." Meanwhile Schmitz to Belgium and France. Blum had to return to Cologne, where his father ill and unable to earn. Becomes a theatre employee (to help the family[a]) under director Ringelhardt. "As such he had to handle all the dealings between director and actors, [...] to deliver parts and money, to announce performances and rehearsals." "In addition" Blum "was a poet, and was in touch with several respected editorial boards.[...] The then precarious times allowed him to be less sensitive at times to this [in]congruity, earned him a standing in the social life of Cologne far exceeding his material circumstances at the time". Blum one of those who set the tone for the politicising circles of Cologne. Writes for freedom "in the face of the 'tremendous'[d] obstacles raised by censorship".... "His own studies at this time

---

[a] Marx uses the English word.— *Ed.*
[b] Kaspar Gd. Schilder.— *Ed.*
[c] In the manuscript this word is written above the line.— *Ed.*
[d] This word is given in quotes by Marx.— *Ed.*

included nothing less than the entire dramatic literature insofar as it was available at the Cologne Theatre Library." In 1831 Ringelhardt left Cologne. Blum a bailiff's clerk. In the winter again a theatre employee. Became theatre secretary and assistant cashier for Ringelhardt in Leipzig; after a few years head cashier. Writes contributions to *Komet, Abend-Zeitung* and *Elegante Zeitung*.[a] The *Theaterlexikon* with Herlossohn and Marggraff, *Verfassungsfreund* with Steger (3rd issue confiscated, and that was the end of that), the pocket book *Vorwärts.*

Blum's political activity began in 1837, when, as spokesman of the deputation at the Leipzig citizens' celebration for deputies Todt and Dieskau, he presented them with cups of honour. In 1840 among the first founders of the Schiller Association, from 1841 its president, promoter of this "fine annual celebration". "In 1840 takes part in the initial preparations for the Writers' Association, its co-president from 1841." *Sächsische Vaterlands-Blätter.* "Buys himself a property which, according to the stipulations of the Constitution, makes him eligible to the town council and the Provincial Diet." *Ronge's letter calling for a reform* of the Catholic Church[b]; Blum supported it in the *Vaterlands-Blätter;* from 1845 heads a community of the German-Catholic Society.

(Up to here *Blum's* own biography both in *Meyer* and *Steger.*)

On August 12, 1845 a detachment of riflemen (Leipzig) fired on a crowd in the midst of which excesses against a prince of the royal house[c] had earlier been committed, 7 people killed, not one of them a rioter; the civil guard partly not summoned, partly held aside on the square itself. Terrible unrest in the morning meetings of citizens and students to storm the riflemen's barracks.

"Blum [...] spoke in favour of observing the legal procedures. Everyone followed him to the riflemen's house, where for several days orderly discussions took place on how to exact atonement for the blood that had been shed." Blum taken to court for various speeches. The *Sächsische Vaterlands-Blätter* suppressed. In 1847 Blum also prosecuted for a protest of the Leipzig citizens against the extraordinary assembly of the estates of 1847 as being unconstitutional. Blum gives up his job as theatre cashier and founds a bookseller's. Writes *Weihnachtsbaum* (biographies of free-thinking Germans) and a *Staatslexikon für das deutsche Volk.* "In autumn 1847 elected an unpaid member of the municipal council by the Leipzig city councilmen. The district board withheld its confirmation"; written appeal by Blum. "His political activity in Leipzig now devoted to the *'Oratory Society',* which he founded with men of like mind." *February 1848* worked ["to overthrow the government"]. "Central figure of his party for all Saxony." Founds the *Fatherland Association,* soon more than 40,000 members; resumes publication of the *Vaterlands-Blätter.* Blum vice-president in the Preliminary Parliament, averts the threatening breach between north and south. "Opposed to the mass withdrawal of the Left." Member of the Committee of Fifty. Elected to the Frankfurt Parliament. Blum's "coquetry in all directions" and vacillation. In his report on his activity in parliament [he wrote]: "We want, then, the *republic* at the head of the whole state. But while we want this, we decidedly reject the idea of ever laying a hand on the transformation of conditions in

---

[a] *Zeitung für die elegante Welt.—Ed.*

[b] A reference to the open letter of Johannes Ronge, founder of the "German Catholics" movement, to Bishop Arnoldi of Trier, dated October 16, 1844.— *Ed.*

[c] Johann of Saxony.— *Ed.*

the individual states—we would consider that a misfortune and a piece of folly. Our fatherland is constructed in such a way that its tribes must remain independent; on this rests its most beautiful life. And there is not a man in Germany who would commit the folly, if he could, of intervening in the conditions of the individual states in favour of republican forms.... No, my fellow citizens! It is a lie that has made us think of the creation of individual republics; we would be the first to oppose efforts of an entirely republican National Assembly to intervene in the individual states."

"When the news of the Vienna rising reached Frankfurt, Blum was the first to propose issuing an address. [...] Extreme Left and Left came together. [...] Blum, Fröbel, Dr. Trampusch and Moritz Hartmann were chosen to deliver the address. On *October 13* they left Frankfurt, [...] 17th October in Vienna. The City Council received them at a plenary meeting. Blum acts as spokesman. [...] From his reports in the *Reichstagszeitung* one sees that the movement completely captivated him." Glowing admiration for the Viennese; enters the hall armed. "Commands a barricade in the days of the fighting. [...] After the storming of Vienna Blum stays calmly in his hotel when it is surrounded by soldiers", he is taken prisoner. "Blum denied not a single speech or action" in front of his judges. On November 8 death by the rope, the bullet substituted out of mercy. Early on November 9 shot in the Brigittenau. Leaves a widow[a] and 4 children. Solemn memorial ceremony. Collection of 40,000 talers for them. *"Stormy meeting of the National Assembly on November 14"; von Schmerling:* "Those who venture into peril perish in it."[b] "Stern features."[c]

Excerpts made in late
August and September 1857

Published for the first time

Printed according to the manuscript

Translated from the German

---

[a] Eugenie Blum.—*Ed.*

[b] Schmerling quoted this dictum of Jesus Sirach (3:27) in his speech in the National Assembly (November 17, 1848) on the occasion of Robert Blum's shooting.—*Ed.*

[c] This concerns an extant portrait of Blum.—*Ed.*

Karl Marx

EXCERPTS MADE FOR THE ARTICLE "BOURRIENNE"[414]

(*BIOGRAPHIE UNIVERSELLE. SCHLOSSER.*)
(*ENGLISH CYCLOPAEDIA 1856*)

Bourrienne (Louis Antoine Fauvelet de), biographer of Napoleon Bonaparte,[a] "born in Sens, July 9, 1769, the same year as Napoleon, also entered the same year, 1778, the military school in Brienne". Approximately 6 years together in this house. "Of the 2, Bourrienne, [...] the more promising scholar: [...] in 1783, when Bonaparte, then about to leave the school, took a prize for mathematics, Bourrienne gained 7 premiums for languages and other accomplishments."[b]

We find the signs of Bonaparte's future greatness most clearly disclosed in Bourrienne in the very passages where the latter thrusts himself forward and leads us to believe that luck favoured Bonaparte when it really ought to have favoured the author of the memoirs. Bourrienne brings the greatness of his hero into full relief by constantly thrusting himself alongside him or in front of him.

"Adopting diplomacy, 1789, to Vienna as clerk or attaché to the embassy of the Marquis de Noailles, ambassador of Louis XVI, at the court of the Austrian Emperor Joseph; after a few months to Leipzig, to study international law and the English and German languages"; then to Warsaw, well received (1791) at the court of King Poniatowski; translates there, in literary fit, Kotzebue's *L'Inconnu;* 1792 return to Paris[c]; again he meets up with Bonaparte; both of them fare poorly; talks pitifully of Napoleon's financial difficulties. Bourrienne obtains post as *secrétaire d'ambassade à* Stuttgart, but scarcely arrived there, "when the overthrow of Louis XVI's throne caused him to lose this post".

---

[a] The words "biographer of Napoleon Bonaparte" are in English in the manuscript.—*Ed.*
[b] Marx quotes in English from *The English Cyclopaedia.—Ed.*
[c] Here Marx paraphrases, partly in English and partly in German, a passage from *The English Cyclopaedia.—Ed.*

Bourrienne evaded the dangers of the terror by a prolonged stay abroad.

Placed on the list of émigrés. 1794 marries in Leipzig. 1795 returns to Paris with his wife, Bonaparte then out of employment[a] as *général de brigade à l'armée d'Italie.*

With his customary pettiness Bourrienne again misrepresents his meeting with Bonaparte in Paris.

October 5, 1795 (13th Vendémiaire[415]) gives power[b] to Bonaparte, "placed at the head of the army of the interior" (i.e. of Paris); Bourrienne reproaches Bonaparte saying that he "had become colder towards his friends".[c]

On Bourrienne's own admission this applies only to people like him, who boasted about their acquaintanceship with Bonaparte or desired to obtain through it in an underhand way offices and posts which they did not deserve.

Bourrienne arrested (February 1796) as an "émigré, his name not having been crossed off the fatal list". His wife turns to Bonaparte; the latter very cold. "The pity of a justice of the peace saved Bourrienne." Bonaparte (1796) commander-in-chief of the army in Italy; Bourrienne writes to him; Bonaparte invites him[d]; "it was at the end of the campaign of 1797, at the moment when the preliminaries of Léoben were being signed,[416] that Bourrienne arrived at the headquarters at Gratz". From the first day writes[b] at the dictation of Napoleon, follows him after the Peace of Campo Formio to Rastatt, Paris, Egypt, "returns with him", with him during the Marengo campaign,[417] "received the title of Councillor of State. Lodged at the Tuileries in the same apartment and almost the same room as the first consul, at all hours of the day and night he had to answer his call and the orders of the most active man", etc. No money "was enough for the insatiable Bourrienne; he abused [...] his credit in order to obtain unlawful gains". Bonaparte "reproaches him severely". "Bankruptcy of the firm of Coulon, [...] who thanks to him had been charged with supplying all the equipment of the cavalry." Bankruptcy to the tune of 3 million. The head of the firm disappeared. "Bourrienne accused of causing his flight, and even his death, either in order to share the deficit with him or to appropriate it all for himself. A criminal action was about to be brought against him by the creditors when he was saved by the pretended disgrace with which Bonaparte punished him, and by an honourable exile to Hamburg"—1802, with the "title of French chargé d'affaires in the district of Lower Saxony. His mission in this post, according to the instructions of the Minister of Police, was above all to observe the actions and the secret relations of the royalist agents in the different cabinets of the Continent with England" (army contractors[e] of Coulon). Later Bourrienne in Hamburg, his mission being to

---

[a] Marx uses the English words "out of employment".— *Ed.*
[b] Marx uses the English word.— *Ed.*
[c] Marx quotes in English from *The English Cyclopaedia.*— *Ed.*
[d] Marx uses the English words "Bonaparte invites him".— *Ed.*
[e] Marx uses the English words.— *Ed.*

implement the continental system,ᵃ i.e. "to stop and seize all merchandise and capital suspected of coming from England". "Complaints against Bourrienne for extortion and embezzlement" (among the claimants Emperor Alexander himself on behalf of the Duke of Mecklenburg). Bonaparte sends M. Augier de la Sauzaye as "commissary to inquire and report".ᵇ His report "that one could safely make the chargé d'affaires return 2 millions; he [...] had apparently laid the Duke of Mecklenburg under contribution [...] for 40,000 friedrichsdors and 2 bonds for a similar amount; [...] Hamburg senate 750,000 marks banco (about 2 millionsᶜ)— Napoleon reduced it [...] to 1 million". "Bourrienne [...] had to refund to the Imperial Treasury"ᵇ "but he did not have much of it left; a taste for excessive expenditure, [...] imprudent speculations in commerce and on the Stock Exchange"; utterly disgraced and ruined.ᵈ

Showed great joy at the fall of Napoleon.

"Was one of the first to hasten over to Talleyrand, who made him postmaster-generalᵉ on April 1. [...] The Provisional Government⁴¹⁸ also refunds him the million." "Louis XVIII dismisses him from that post."ᵇ But March 1815, at the rumour of Napoleon's return from Elba, Louis XVIII's prefect of police; "after a week has to flee"; by decree of Lyons March 13 Napoleon includes him among the members of the Provisional Government not affected by the amnesty. Follows Louis XVIII to Belgium, "appointed his minister in Hamburg, probably again with an observation mission". "On his return to Paris appointed"ᵇ councillor; then minister of state; elected member of the *Chambre introuvable*⁴¹⁹ by the department of Yonne; likewise 1821 to the Chamber, member and spokesman of the budget commission, seeming very strange that "a man known for his corruption and extravagance is charged with examining the finances of the state. [...] His affairs so bad that obliged to flee to avoid the legal proceedings of his creditors" (1828). At the home of the Duchess de Brancas, at Fontaine-l'Evêque, near Charleroi, here "writes his memoirs, put in order and edited by Max de Villemarest, Paris 1829, 10 vols. in 8*vo*". Went mad after the July revolution. † February 7 in a lunatic asylum (hospital for the insane)ᶠ in Normandy, near Caen. "He could never write the word 'Millions' without a kind of nervous agitation, and fidgeting in his chair."ᵇ

(*Biographie universelle. English Cyclopaedia No. 5—entirely copied from this.*)

Written in September 1857

Published for the first time

Printed according to the manuscript

Translated from the French and German

ᵃ Marx uses the English words "continental system".—*Ed.*
ᵇ Marx quotes in English from *The English Cyclopaedia.*—*Ed.*
ᶜ Marx uses the English words.—*Ed.*
ᵈ Marx uses the English words "disgraced" and "ruined".—*Ed.*
ᵉ Marx uses the English term.—*Ed.*
ᶠ Marx uses the English words "in a lunatic asylum (hospital for the insane)".—*Ed.*

Karl Marx

ROUGH DRAFT OF THE ARTICLE "BRUNE" [420]

Brune (Guillaume-Marie-Anne), Marshal, was born at Brives-la-Gaillarde, in the department of Corrèze, in 1763. His father, an advocate, sent him to Paris, there to study the law. On leaving the university, financial difficulties induced him to become an apprentice-compositor, and in such quality, in 1788, he printed a literary essay of his own entitled: "Voyage pittoresque et sentimental dans plusieurs provinces occidentales de la France". Having acquired a small press of his own (*Setzerei*[a]), he published, in the first time of the Revolution, together with Jourgniac de St.-Méard and Gauthier, the *Journal général de la Cour et de la Ville*, one of the aristocratic papers which disappeared after the 10th of August.[421] Brune, however, soon turned his back to this aristocratic print, enlisted in the guard-national, there drew attention upon himself by his martial figure and the ardour of his patriotism, became an adept of the club of the Jacobins, and decided partizan of Danton. To the protection of the latter he owed, during the famous days of September 1792, his appointment as adjunct to the *adjutants généraux* of the Interior, and his sudden promotion (on October 12, 1792) to the rank of colonel-adjutant-general. In this quality he first served under Dumouriez in Belgium. Sent afterwards against the federalists of Calvados, advancing under General Puisaye, he carried an easy victory since the federalist army, from different causes, melted down to a handful of men. In reward for his exploit, he wanted now to be created minister-of-war, but was put off with the advancement to the rank of general of brigade, in which quality he assisted at the battle of Hondschoote. The Committee of the Public Weal called him back,

---

[a] Composing-room.— *Ed.*

and intrusted him with the mission of putting down the symptoms of insurrection manifesting themselves in the Gironde, a task he vigorously executed.

After Danton's imprisonment, Brune was expected to put himself at the head of a mob in order to deliver his friend, but he stood prudently aloof. The storm having passed away, he insinuated himself with the family Duplays, with whom Robespierre lived, and thus contrived to be not molested during the reign of terror. After the 9th Thermidor, he again appeared on the public stage in company of Robespierre's deadliest enemy, Fréron, whom he followed as "pacificator" to Marseilles and Avignon. On the 13th Vendémiaire he was employed by Barras as one of the under-generals (*mitraillade*[a]), commanding the royalist sections of Paris under the command-in-chief of Bonaparte. After the affair of September 9, 1796, in which he had displayed all his energy against the Babouvists, he joined Bonaparte in Italy, and commanded a brigade of division under Masséna. He distinguished himself by his intrepidity during the whole of this campaign. (Sieh[b] Schlosser.[422]) Brune's old connexion with the Dantonists, whose ranks were composed of bold adventurers, made it desirable to Bonaparte to secure him as one of his tools. Hence he made him general-of-division on the battle-field of Rivoli, mentioned him honourably in the bulletins, and induced the Directory to confide him the second division of the Italian army, become vacant by the depart of Augereau.

After the peace of Campo Formio he was sent by the Directory to lull the Swiss into security, to divide their councils, to fall at the proper moment upon the canton of Berne with an army concentrated for this purpose, and there to plunder the treasury of Berne, which latter delicate mission peculiarly answered Brune's rapacious instincts. In plundering the treasury of Berne, Brune took care to forget drawing up an inventory of it. It was again by manoeuvres of a diplomatic rather than a military character that, as commander of the army in Italy, he persuaded Charles Emmanuel, the king of Sardinia, then the apparent ally of France, to deliver into his hands the citadel of Turin (3 July 1798).

The Batavian campaign against the Anglo-Russians who had invaded Holland,—a campaign lasting 2 months, opened on 22 Août[c] 1799, the capitulation of the Duke of York, signed on the

---

[a] Grape-shot fire.— *Ed.*
[b] See.— *Ed.*
[c] August.— *Ed.*

18th October of the same year—forms the great event in Brune's military life. An English squadron debarked on the coasts of Holland with 45,000 men under the Duke of York; Brune's army 25,000 men only; Brune charged the generals Daendels and Dumonceau, the one of the defence of the province of Holland, the other of the Eastern provinces, reserving for himself a reserve with which he would be able to turn on any points menaced. The Anglo-Russians having disembarked their *matériel* after a lively combat with Daendels, entered the Texel, occupied the Helder and seized upon the Dutch fleet, Brune concentrated his forces before Alkmaar and attacked the allied on the 9th September, but without success. On the 18th, the Anglo-Russians, in their turn, attempted dislodging him, but a Russian column being cut off and forced to capitulate, the Duke of York retreated, and both armies re-occupied their prior positions. (This battle at Bergen.) Both armies did nothing from the battle of Bergen to the 2nd of October. This inactivity a great fault on the part of the army which was more numerous and which received its provisions by the sea only. Brune profited by it for strengthening his position and swelling his army. The vigorous attack made by the enemy under Abercromby, on the 2nd of October, in which Brune was near being cut off his retreat, he lost 4,000 men, and was obliged to transfer his headquarters to Beverwikcop-Zee and Kiommen-Dig, where Brune occupied an excellent position. It was only on the 6th that the Gallo-Batavian lines were again attacked. York took Limmen and Askerloot, while the Russians rendered themselves masters of Bakkum; but when they had arrived before Castricum, Brune routed them completely. A cavalry charge completed their defeat, and threw them back into their positions. (This: battle of Beverwyk.) York retired to his encampment behind the Zyp. Having destroyed the maritime establishments, cut upon the *digues*,[a] laid fire to the buildings of the East India Company,[423] he embarked himself for England; and in order to see this operation not troubled, he negotiated a capitulation, ignominious for the English, which stipulated, among other things, the free and unconditional *renvoi*[b] of 8,000 French made prisoners before this campaign.

In 1800 he was sent to the army of Italy *en remplacement de Masséna*.[c] After the battle of Marengo an armistice had been

---

a Dams.— *Ed.*
b Return, delivery.— *Ed.*
c In the place of Masséna.— *Ed.*

concluded with the Austrians. The hostilities recommenced on 24 November. Brune seized upon 3 entrenched (*retranchés*) camps at the Volta, threw the enemy beyond this river, and prepared instantly to traverse it. According to his orders, his army ought to pass at two points, one between the *moulin*[a] of the Volta and the village of Pozzolo, the other at Monbazon. This second part of the operation having encountered difficulties, Brune gave order to delay it for 24 hours, although the right wing, which had commenced to pass at the other point, had already engaged with the Austrians. It was but due to the exertions of General Dupont that the whole right wing was not captured or destroyed, and Brune forced to retreat without ever crossing the Mincio. Napoleon says that from this moment it had become evident that Brune was not made for the command-in-chief of armies.

Returned to the state-council, a member of which he had been since its creation, he was nominated president of the section of war. From 1802 to 1804, as French ambassador at Constantinople, he cut a sad figure. Recalled in December 1804, he was, on his return to Paris, appointed marshal of the Empire. He commanded for a while the camp at Boulogne. Being sent to Hamburg in 1807 as governor of the Hanseatic towns and commander of the reserve of the grand army, he vigorously seconded Bourrienne in his extortions and "concussions". A truce having been concluded at Schlatkow now between the French and the King of Sweden, he had, with regard to some contested points, a long interview with Gustavus, King of Sweden, near Anklam, in Pomerania, which seems to have given rise to suspicions on the part of Napoleon. When, afterwards, in the surrender of the island of Rügen by the Swedish general Toll, agreeably to a convention with Brune, the latter omitted in the text of the convention the titles of the Emperor Napoleon, and mentioned simply the French army and the Swedish army as parties to the agreement, Napoleon highly incensed. Berthier, by express order, had to write him that "no such scandal had ever been since the time of Pharamond".[b] (He made mention of the "French army" instead of "the army of his Imperial and Royal Majesty".[c]) He lost his commandment, and retired to the department of Escaut to preside over an electoral college. One moment his indiscreet complaints of the imperial

---

[a] Mill.— *Ed.*

[b] Marx quotes from the article "Brune" published in *Biographie universelle (Michaud) ancienne et moderne*, t. 6, p. 19.— *Ed.*

[c] "Capitulation de l'isle de Rugen, en date du 7 Sept. 1807" (G. F. Martens, *Recueil des principaux Traités*, I, t. VIII, pp. 695-96).— *Ed.*

injustice threatened him with being ordered to restitute part of his *plunder.* Now cajoled Berthier, *courtisait*[a] the emperor.

In 1814 he sent his adhesion to the acts of the senate against Napoleon and act of adhesion to Louis XVIII,[b] who gave him the cross of St. Louis; but as the royal favours went not farther, Brune became again Bonapartist. During the "Hundred Days", he commanded under Napoleon a corps of observation on the Var, in which quality he developed all his brutal vigour against the Royalists. After the battle of Waterloo he proclaimed the king, and leaving his corps, was travelling from Toulon to Avignon on the way to Paris, when a furious mob forced its way into the inn at Avignon, where Brune was, insulted him as one of the Septembriseurs of 1792, blocked him up, removed the obstacles which he had thrown up, penetrated to his room, and shot him. The mob seized up his cadaver, dragged it through the streets, and threw it into the Rhône.

Nothing more notorious than his cupidity and greed.[c]

"For more than a fortnight Avignon was consigned to turmoil, carnage and fire when, on August 2, 1815, Brune arrived there with two aides-de-camp and stopped for breakfast at the Hotel Palais-Royal where the horse relay station was. Recognised by an army veteran who had pointed him out to the curious, he regained his carriage about an hour later. A hundred steps from the town gates, where his passport was checked, the populace set upon him, throwing stones at his carriage and forcing him to return to the hotel he had just left. The crowd in the square kept swelling, and clamoured for the head of the man who had been pointed out to it as the assassin of the Princesse de Lamballe.'[d]

Napoleon said at Saint Helena:

"Brune, Masséna, Augereau, and many others were intrepid depredators."[e]

Written in December 1857

Published for the first time

Reproduced from the manuscript

---

[a] Flattered.— *Ed.*

[b] *Le Moniteur universel,* Nos. 94 and 98, April 4 and 8, 1814.— *Ed.*

[c] The beginning of this sentence is in German, the end is in French; the remaining part of the manuscript is also in French.— *Ed.*

[d] *Les Événements d'Avignon,* Paris, 1818. Quoted from *Biographie universelle (Michaud) ancienne et moderne,* t. 6, p. 19.— *Ed.*

[e] Las Cases, *Mémorial de Sainte-Hélène.* Probably quoted from the article "Brune" published in *Biographie des célébrités militaires,* t. 1, p. 243.— *Ed.*

Karl Marx

EXCERPTS FROM THE ARTICLE "BÜLOW" PUBLISHED IN *MEYER'S CONVERSATIONS-LEXICON*[424]

Bülow (Friedrich Wilhelm, Baron von, from 1814 Count of Dennewitz, Royal Prussian general of infantry, etc.) born February 16, 1755 at the Bülow family estate of Falkenberg in the Altmark. In his 14th year he entered the regiment of Count Lottum in Berlin as a Junker. 1772 ensign, 1777 second, 1786 first lieutenant. 1793 staff captain and tutor of Prince Ludwig Ferdinand of Prussia,

in which capacity he took part in the 1793 campaign, soon promoted to major. During the siege and capture of Mainz (1793) he provided brilliant proof of his courage.

In 1806, as lieutenant-colonel, to which rank he was promoted in 1805, he took part in the defence of Thorn under General L'Estocq and at the battle of Waltersdorf found the opportunity to bring himself and his battalion to the fore. In 1808 he became major-general

and commander of a Pomeranian brigade which he had been given temporarily at the beginning of the year as colonel. 1811 he was posted to the West Prussian brigade at Marienwerder and at the outbreak of the Franco-Russian war[a] he was made interim Governor-General of East and West Prussia.

At the beginning of the 1813 campaign lieutenant-general, entrusted with the siege of Stettin. Relieved by General Tauenzien, he then allied himself with generals York and Wittgenstein, marching to confront the French army detachment that had moved to the right bank of the Elbe under the viceroy of Italy.[b] He fought the first successful battle at Möckern[c] on April 5, shortly afterwards capturing Halle,

which, however, he was soon forced to evacuate again owing to the retreat of the allied army.

[a] Of 1812.— *Ed.*
[b] Eugène Beauharnais.— *Ed.*
[c] Known also as the battle of Dannigkow.— *Ed.*

Withdrew across the Elbe in order to take over the defence of Berlin, which Oudinot was threatening.

Victory at Luckau on June 4 crowned the enterprise.

"After the ceasefire commanded the 3rd Prussian Army Corps under the supreme command of the Crown Prince of Sweden."[a] At the head of the 3rd Prussian Army Corps "saved Berlin a second time by the battle of Grossbeeren on August 23"; shielded Berlin for the third time by the battle of Dennewitz, September 6,

in which he forced Marshal Ney to retreat to Wittenberg.

"After laying siege to Wittenberg he fought with the northern army in the battle of Leipzig. [...] While the allied armies advanced over the Rhine he broke into Holland, took Doesburg, Jütphen, Arnheim by storm, setting up his headquarters in Utrecht on December 2, and invested Gorkum and Herzogenbusch. In 1814 he marched from Breda, was victorious at Hogstraten on January 11, bombarded Antwerp, entered Brussels, captured la Fère and Soissons, joined up with the Silesian army, commanded the centre at the battle of Laon, March 9 and 10." Knight of the Order of the Black Eagle, appointed general of infantry. "After the peace he was made Governor-General of West and East Prussia and on the renewed outbreak of war in 1815 was given the 4th Prussian Army Corps. Owing to a delayed order not present at the battle of Ligny (June 15),[b] but after his union with Blücher, achieved by a forced march, he helped to decide the outcome of the battle of Belle Alliance.[425] For this the Boor[c] appointed him Honorary Colonel of the 15th Regiment of the Line, which he had led so bravely and which was to bear his name. January 11, 1816 Bülow returned to his governorship, † February 25 of inflammation of the liver at Königsberg."

King made him a Grand Knight of the Iron Cross, elevating him and his descendants to the rank of counts in Paris in 1814. Took part in the Battle of the Nations.[426] Then departed for Holland, from which country he expelled the French.

Written between March 1 and 18, 1858

First published in: Marx and Engels, *Works,* Second Russian Edition, Vol. 44, Moscow, 1977

Printed according to the manuscript

Translated from the German

Published in English for the first time

FREDERICK ENGELS

ARTICLES
FOR THE *ALLGEMEINE MILITÄR-ZEITUNG* AND
THE VOLUNTEER JOURNAL,
FOR LANCASHIRE AND CHESHIRE

Allgemeine Militär-Zeitung.

Herausgegeben von einer Gesellschaft deutscher Offiziere und Militärbeamten.

TO THE EDITOR
OF THE *ALLGEMEINE MILITÄR-ZEITUNG*[427]

6, Thorncliffe Grove, Oxford Road,
Manchester, August 24, 1860

TO THE EDITOR OF THE *ALLGEMEINE MILITÄR-ZEITUNG*
IN DARMSTADT

As a subscriber to your esteemed journal and encouraged by the appreciative review of my pamphlet *Po and Rhine* (Duncker, Berlin)[a] published therein last year,[428] I take the liberty of sending you herewith an article that may be of interest to your readers.[b] If I could help you in any way with news items, occasional articles and so forth, I should be glad to do so; I might soon be in a position to supply you with interesting information on the Whitworth gun, etc.[429] That England's rapid military progress is also of significance to Germany is something of which you will in any case be aware: save for Russia, England is, in the final count, our only natural and necessary ally against Bonapartism.

If you ask a service-record of your contributors, then I am truly in poor case. As a one-year volunteer in the Artillery Brigade of the Prussian Guard I did not rise above the rank of bombardier. Later, in Baden, I took part in the campaign of 1849 on the side of the insurgents.[430] Since my period of service, however, I have constantly busied myself with military matters.

Should you find my paper worthy of acceptance, I should be much obliged if you would at once mail me a proof copy in a

---

[a] "*Po und Rhein*. Berlin, 1859. Verlag von Franz Duncker", *Allgemeine Militär-Zeitung*, Nos. 95-96, November 26, 1859.— *Ed.*

[b] See this volume, pp. 409-16.— *Ed.*

wrapper, and I shall immediately publish it in translation in English newspapers as an excerpt from the *Allgemeine M.-Z.*, which could not but be of benefit to your journal; otherwise I would beg you to return the manuscript to me. Since my copy of the *A. M.-Z.* comes to me through a bookseller and never arrives till a month after publication, any other course would mean undue delay and the article would lose all interest here.

Might I recommend that my most recent pamphlet, *Savoy, Nice and the Rhine,*[a] published in April, should be accorded an early if impartial review in your paper?

I remain, Sir,

Your most obedient servant

Frederick Engels

First published in: Marx and Engels, *Works,* First Russian Edition, Vol. XXV, Moscow, 1934

Printed according to the original

Translated from the German

Published in English for the first time

---

[a] See present edition, Vol. 16.— *Ed.*

THE VOLUNTEER JOURNAL,
for Lancashire and Cheshire.

No. 2. | MANCHESTER, FRIDAY, SEPTEMBER 14, 1860. | PRICE THREEPENCE.

A REVIEW OF ENGLISH VOLUNTEER RIFLEMEN [a] [431]

England, as well as Germany, is arming to repel the attack with which Bonapartism threatens her; the British volunteer riflemen arose from the same cause which made Prussia double the number of her battalions of the line. It will, therefore, be of interest to the German military public, to receive some detailed information on the present state and the fitness for actual service of the British volunteer army; for this army, from its very origin, and in virtue of its fundamental idea, is an enemy of Bonapartism, an ally of Germany.

A very few battalions excepted, this army of volunteers dates from the latter half of last year (1859); the great body has not been put in uniform and drilled more than a twelvemonth. At present its strength, on paper, is 120,000 men; but if we may draw conclusions from what is the fact in some districts, there will not be more than 80,000 men really effective and drilled; the

---

[a] In *The Volunteer Journal* this article has the following introductory note,[432] written by the author himself: "The *Allgemeine Militär-Zeitung,* published at Darmstadt, and considered the first military paper in Germany, in its number of the 8th September, gives an account, by a correspondent, of the Newton Review, and of the rifle movement in general. The following is a translation of this article (prepared specially for the *Volunteer Journal*), which no doubt will prove interesting to the volunteers of Lancashire and Cheshire, and especially to those who were present at the review. As may be expected, this account is not made up of that unqualified praise which the British press generally gives as its contribution to the movement; still the character of the contemporary in question ought to be a sufficient guarantee that it is not written by an incompetent hand, and the sympathetic tone of the whole article proves that the writer had no inclination for wanton fault-finding. As to the suggestions contained in the article, we shall leave our readers to form their own opinion upon them." — *Ed.*

remainder take no interest in the matter, and had better be erased from the lists.

The organisation is very simple. Wherever 60 to 100 volunteers (in the artillery 50 to 80) are brought together, in any locality, they form themselves into a company, subject to the consent of the Lord-Lieutenant of the county. They elect candidates for officers (a captain, a lieutenant, and an ensign), on whom the Lord-Lieutenant, in most cases, confers their respective commissions; but there have also been instances of rejection. Several companies may form themselves into a battalion, in which case the Lord-Lieutenant appoints the major and lieutenant-colonel, mostly according to the wishes of the officers, or according to seniority among the captains. Thus there are corps varying from one to eight companies and more, numbered in the order of their formation in their respective counties; but only full battalions of eight companies receive a lieutenant-colonel. The officers may, all of them, be appointed from among the volunteers, and they are not subjected to any examination. The adjutant,[433] however, must be an officer from the line or militia, and he alone receives regular pay.* The volunteers find their own clothing, &c., but if desired, the Government furnishes them with rifle and bayonet by way of loan. The colour and cut of the uniform is fixed by the various corps themselves, subject to the approval of the Lord-Lieutenant. The corps have also, upon the whole, to find their own drill and practice grounds, ammunition, instructors, and music.

The uniforms of the various infantry or rifle corps are mostly dark green, dark or light grey, or brown drab. The shape is something intermediate between the French and English pattern; for a head-dress they mostly wear the French *kepi,* or the French or English officer's cap. The artillery is dressed in dark blue, and has adopted, for appearance's sake, the rather unserviceable and lumbering fur-cap or busby of the horse artillery. There are also a few mounted rifles whose uniform imitates that of the English cavalry, but they are a mere article of luxury.

At the time when the formation of these rifle corps was first agitated, the whole matter savoured very strongly of our own national and civic guards[434]; there was a great deal of playing at

---

* To the allowance of £180 granted by the Government, most of the battalions add considerable sums; I know adjutants, lieutenants of the line, who receive £300 or 2,000 talers and even more. [Engels' note in the *Allgemeine Militär-Zeitung*.]

soldiers; the way in which officers were manufactured,[a] and the appearance and helplessness of some of these[b] officers, when on duty, were rather amusing. It may well be imagined, the men did not always elect the most capable, or even those who had the movement most at heart. During the first six months, almost all battalions and companies made the same effect upon the beholder as our own defunct civic guard of 1848.

This, then, was the material handed over to the drill-sergeants, in order to shape it into a body of serviceable field troops. The manual and platoon was gone through mostly[c] at nights, between seven and nine o'clock, in covered rooms and by gas-light, twice or three times a week. On Saturday afternoons, if possible, the whole body made a short march, and went through company movements. To drill on Sunday was forbidden both by law and custom. The instructors were sergeants and corporals of the line, the militia, or pensioners; and they, too, had to form the officers into shape. But the English non-commissioned officer is an excellent man in his way. There is, on duty, less swearing and coarse language in the English army than in any other; on the other hand, punishment is so much the more certain to be applied. The non-commissioned imitates the commissioned officer, and thus adopts manners far superior to those of our German sergeants. Then he does not serve because of the prospect of some pettifogging office in the civil service being held out to him, as is the case with us; he has engaged himself voluntarily for twelve years, and promotion, up to the rank of sergeant-major even, offers him considerable fresh advantages at every step; in every battalion one or two commissions (adjutant and paymaster) are mostly reserved to old non-commissioned officers; and, on active service, every sergeant may attach the golden star to his collar by distinguishing himself before the enemy. The drill-sergeants belonging to this class of men have, indeed, upon the whole, made the volunteers what it was possible to make them in so short a time; they have not only made them steady in company movements, but also licked the officers into shape.

---

[a] Instead of the words "the way in which officers were manufactured" the *Allgemeine Militär-Zeitung* has "favouritism [*Klüngel*] in the election of officers", with an editorial footnote explaining the word *Klüngel:* "An expression which is not quite clear to many of our readers, although our correspondent in Manchester has not forgotten it. It is of old-Cologne origin and means the connection of the most notable families with the city regiment."— *Ed.*

[b] The *Allgemeine Militär-Zeitung* has "new" instead of "some of these".— *Ed.*

[c] The *Allgemeine Militär-Zeitung* has here: "Drilling was exercised usually".— *Ed.*

In the meantime, the single companies, at least in the large
towns, formed themselves into battalions, and received adjutants
from the regular troops. Similar to the Austrian, the English
subaltern is far less theoretically educated than the North German;
but, same as the Austrian, if he likes his profession, he knows his
duty exceedingly well. Among the adjutants who have passed over
from the line to the volunteers, there are men who, as instructors,
could not be better; and the results which they obtained in a very
short time in their battalions are surprising indeed. Up to the
present time, however, only a minority of the volunteers have
been formed into permanent battalions, and, as a matter of
course, these are considerably superior to the mass of companies
not so formed.

The volunteers of Lancashire and Cheshire had organised a
review at Newton, half way between Manchester and Liverpool,
for the 11th of August, the commanding general of the district,
Sir George Wetherall, taking the command. The volunteers who
met here were the contingents of the manufacturing districts
around Manchester; there were not very many present either from
Liverpool or from the neighbouring agricultural districts of
Cheshire. To judge from our own German recruiting experience,
these corps must have been physically below the average; but it is
not to be forgotten that by far the minority of the volunteers
belong to the working classes.

The soil of Newton race-course, of itself spongy enough, had
been considerably softened by the continuous rains; it was very
uneven and very sticky. On one side of it there is a small brook,
with here and there some thick gorse on its banks. The ground
was just right for a parade of young volunteers; they most of them
stood ankle deep in water and mud, and the officers' horses often
sank into the clay until above the fetlock-joint.

The 57 corps which had sent in their adhesion were divided into
four brigades; the first of four, the remainder of three battalions
each; every battalion of eight companies. Lieutenant-colonels of
the line commanded the brigades; officers of volunteers were
appointed to the battalions. The first brigade had three battalions
deployed, the fourth in column behind the centre. The three
remaining brigades stood in second line, nine battalions in
contiguous columns of companies at quarter distance, right in
front.

After saluting the general, a change of front to the left was to
be effected, under shelter of the battalion which stood in column
behind the first line. To effect this, the two centre companies of

the battalion deployed in front of it, wheeled outwards, upon which the column passed through the opening thus formed, and then extended along the watercourse,—four companies skirmishing, and four forming the supports. The ground and the gorse were both so wet that the men could not be expected to take a correct advantage of the ground; besides, most battalions of volunteers are still occupied with the ABC only of skirmishing and outpost duty, so that it would not be fair to measure them by too high a standard in this respect. In the meantime, the deployed line effected its change of front around its own centre as a pivot; the two centre companies of the middle battalions wheeled a quarter of a circle,—the one forwards, the other backwards,—after which the remaining companies took up the new alignment. The two battalions on the wings of the first line formed columns at quarter distance,[a] marched into the alignment, and deployed again. It may be imagined what a time was occupied by this complicated and rather clumsy manoeuvre. At the same time, the right battalion of the line of columns advanced straight on until halted behind the new right wing of the first line; the remaining battalions faced to the right and followed in double files (fours right), each battalion turning to the front, and following the right battalion as soon as arrived on the spot originally occupied by this right battalion. When the last column has thus arrived upon the new alignment, each column independently wheeled to the left, and thus restored the front of the line of columns.

The third brigade now advanced from the centre of this line of columns; arrived about two hundred paces behind the first or deployed line, the three battalions opened out to deploying distance and deployed in their turn. The chain of skirmishers, in the meantime, having gained considerable ground, both deployed lines advanced a couple of hundred paces, upon which the first line was relieved by the second. This is effected by the first line forming fours right, and the head of each company disengaging and wheeling to the right; files in the second line give way, thus affording room for the first line to pass through[b]; after which, companies form front and wheel into line. This is one of those

---

[a] The *Allgemeine Militär-Zeitung* has here the following text in brackets: "the closest column known to the English".— *Ed.*

[b] In the *Allgemeine Militär-Zeitung* after the words "This is effected by" the following text is given: "the two lines facing to the right and forming double files, fours right, in the first line the head of each company wheeling right and in the second the head of each company wheeling left, and so the two lines passing through each other".— *Ed.*

drill-ground movements which are superfluous wherever they are practicable, and which are not practicable where they would be necessary. After this, the four brigades were drawn together again[a] into a mass of columns, and the troops marched past the general in open column of companies (25 to 35 files front). We shall not attempt to criticise this system of evolutions[b] which, no doubt, will appear rather old-fashioned to our readers. It is evident that, whatever may be its value in an army of the line, with twelve years' service, it is certainly less adapted than any other for volunteers who can afford a few spare hours per week only for their drill. What interests us most on this occasion, is the manner in which these movements were performed by the volunteers; and here we must say that, although there was a slight hitch here and there, upon the whole, these evolutions were gone through steadily and without confusion. The most defective parts were, the wheeling in column and the deployments, which latter were done very slowly; in both evolutions, it was visible that the officers were not sufficiently formed and not yet at home in their duty. But, on the other hand, the advance in line, this chief and cardinal movement of British tactics, was good beyond all expectation; the English appear, indeed, to have quite an exceptional talent for this movement, and to learn it uncommonly quick. The marching-past also came off, upon the whole, very well,—and what was most amusing, it came off under a drenching shower of rain. There were a few mistakes against British military etiquette,[c] and besides, by the fault of the officers, distances were very badly kept.

Excepted a sham-fight[d] organised in London, by some over-sanguine commanders of volunteers, and gone through rather wildly, this was the first time that a larger body of volunteers performed evolutions which had something more in view than eventual marching-past. If we consider that the great mass of the troops present at Newton consisted of corps which, counting one, two, or at the outside three companies, are not formed into permanent battalions, have no officers from the regulars, have been drilled by drill-sergeants alone, and have only now and then been brigaded together in a battalion, we shall have to allow that

---

[a] The *Allgemeine Militär-Zeitung* has here: "in a similar way corresponding to the line tactics".— *Ed.*

[b] The *Allgemeine Militär-Zeitung* has "this kind of elementary tactics" instead of "this system of evolutions".— *Ed.*

[c] The *Allgemeine Militär-Zeitung* has here: "the rather complex English military etiquette".— *Ed.*

[d] Instead of "a sham-fight" the *Allgemeine Militär-Zeitung* has "a series of manoeuvres with an enemy".— *Ed.*

the volunteers have done everything that was possible, and that they are no longer on the same level with our civic guards. As a matter of course, the corps which form permanent battalions, and are directed by adjutants from the line (for the adjutants, so far, are the virtual commanders of battalions), were also those which went most steadily through their evolutions at the review.

The men upon the whole looked well. There were, indeed, some companies as puny as Frenchmen, but others surpassed in stature the average of the present British line. Mostly, however, they were very unequal in size and breadth of chest. The pallor peculiar to the inhabitants of towns gave to most of them a rather unpleasantly unwarlike look, but eight days' encampment would soon get the better of that. The uniforms, some of them a little over-ornamental, made a very good effect in the mass.

The first year's drill has taught the volunteers so much of the elementary movements, that they may now enter upon skirmishing and rifle practice. They will be far more handy at both these kinds of work than the English line, so that by summer, 1861, they would form a very useful army, if only their officers knew more about their business.

This is the weak point of the whole formation. Officers cannot be manufactured in the same time and with the same means as privates. Up to now it has been proved that the willingness and the zeal of the mass may be relied upon, as far as is required for making every man a soldier as far as necessary. But this is not sufficient for the officers. As we have seen, even for simple battalion movements, wheeling in column, deployments, keeping distance (so important in the English system of evolutions, where open columns are very often employed[a]), the officers are not by far sufficiently formed. What is to become of them on outpost and skirmishing duty, where judgment of ground is everything, and where so many other difficult matters are to be taken into consideration? How can such men be entrusted with the duty of taking care of the safety of an army on the march? Government has made it binding upon every officer of volunteers to go to Hythe for three weeks, at least. So far, so good; but that will neither teach him to conduct a patrol, nor to command a picket. And yet the volunteers are chiefly to be used for light infantry service—for that very kind of duty which requires the cleverest and most reliable of officers.

---

[a] The *Allgemeine Militär-Zeitung* has here: "(so important in the English line tactics)".— *Ed.*

If the whole movement is to lead to something, this is the point where Government will have to step in. All companies which are still existing,—singly, or by twos and threes,—ought to be compelled to combine together in permanent battalions, to engage adjutants from the regulars. These adjutants should be bound to give to all the officers of their respective battalions a regular course of instruction in elementary tactics, light infantry service in all its branches, and the regulations affecting the internal routine of service in a battalion. The officers should be bound, besides attending Hythe,[a] to do duty, for at least three weeks, with a regiment of the line or militia[b] in some encampment; and, finally, they should, after a certain time, be all made to pass an examination, proving that they have learnt at least the most indispensable part of their business. Such a course of instruction and examination of the officers; further, a medical examination of the men, in order to weed out those who are physically unfit for field-service (and there is not a few); and an annual revision of the company-lists, for the removal of those men who do not attend drill, who only play at soldiers and will not learn their duty;—if this was done, the 120,000 men now existing on paper would be considerably reduced, but you would have an army worth three times the one which now counts 120,000 men on paper.

Instead of that, it is reported that the military authorities[c] are busy discussing the important question, whether it would not be desirable to clothe, at the first opportunity, all rifle volunteers in the so very desirable brick colour of the line.

Written between August 11 and 24, 1860

First published in the *Allgemeine Militär-Zeitung*, No. 36, September 8, 1860; published in Engels' translation in *The Volunteer Journal, for Lancashire and Cheshire*, No. 2, September 14, 1860 and in the collection *Essays Addressed to Volunteers*, London-Manchester, 1861

Reproduced from the collection, checked with the text in the *Allgemeine Militär-Zeitung* and *The Volunteer Journal*

---

[a] The *Allgemeine Militär-Zeitung* has "the shooting school" instead of "Hythe".— *Ed.*

[b] The words "or militia" do not occur in the *Allgemeine Militär-Zeitung*.— *Ed.*

[c] The *Allgemeine Militär-Zeitung* has "the War Ministry" instead of "the military authorities".— *Ed.*

THE FRENCH LIGHT INFANTRY [435]

If ever our volunteers should have to exchange bullets with an enemy, that enemy will be,—everybody knows it,—French infantry; and the finest type, the *beau idéal* of a French foot-soldier, is the light infantry soldier, especially the *chasseur*.

The French chasseur is not only the model for his own army; the French give the law, to a certain degree, to all European armies in matters regarding light infantry service; thus the chasseur becomes, in a certain sense, a model for all European light infantry.

In both these qualities, as a possible opponent, and as, hitherto, the most perfect specimen of a light infantry soldier, the French chasseur is a subject of high interest to the British volunteer. The sooner our volunteer gets acquainted with him the better.

CHAPTER I

Up to 1838 there was not a rifle in use in the French army. The old rifle, with its close-fitting bullet, which had to be hammered down, and made loading a difficult and slow operation, was no weapon for the French. When Napoleon once examined the firelocks of a German battalion of rifles, he exclaimed:—"Surely this is the most unfortunate arm to give into the hands of a soldier." The old rifle was, certainly, unfit for the great mass of the infantry. In Germany and Switzerland, a few chosen battalions were always armed with it, but they were exclusively used as sharpshooters, to pick off officers, to fire on sappers constructing a bridge, &c.; and great care was taken to form these corps from the sons of gamekeepers, or other young men who had been trained to the use of the rifle long before they entered the army. The chamois-hunters of the Alps, the keepers of the great deer forests of Northern Germany, formed excellent material for these battalions, and they, too, were the model for the rifles of the English line.

What the French formerly used to call light infantry, were men equipped and drilled exactly the same as the regiments of the line; consequently, in 1854, a decree of Louis Napoleon deprived these 25 regiments of the name of light infantry, and embodied them in the line, where they now number from the 76th to the 100th regiment.

There was, indeed, in every battalion of infantry a company of *voltigeurs*, formed of the best and most intelligent soldiers of small stature; the *élite* of the taller men being formed into the company of grenadiers. They are the first to extend when skirmishers are required, but in every other respect they are armed and drilled like the remainder of the battalion.

After the conquest of Algiers, in 1830,[a] the French found themselves face to face with an enemy armed with the long musket, common to most Eastern nations. The smooth-bore muskets of the French were inferior to them in range. The French columns, on the march, were surrounded on every side by mounted Bedouins in the plains, by Kabyle skirmishers in the mountains; the bullets of these enemies told on the columns, while they themselves were out of effective range of the French fire. Skirmishers, in the plains, could not move far from their columns, for fear of being surprised and cut up by the rapid Arab horsemen.

When the English army got into Afghanistan,[b] it made acquaintance with these same long muskets. The Afghan shots, though from matchlocks only, did fearful execution in the English ranks, both in the camp at Kabul and during the retreat through the hills, at distances utterly unattainable to poor old Brown Bess.[436] The lesson was a severe one[c]; protracted conflicts with the tribes on the north-western frontier of British India might be expected; yet nothing was done to arm the English soldiers sent to that frontier with a weapon able to cope at long range with the Eastern matchlock.

---

[a] See this volume, pp. 64-67.— *Ed.*

[b] On the Anglo-Afghan war of 1838-42 see this volume, pp. 44-48.— *Ed.*

[c] *The Volunteer Journal* has here one more sentence: "the war was to be renewed", probably inserted by the editors. Engels deleted it when printing the article in the *Essays Addressed to Volunteers.—Ed.*

Not so the French. No sooner was the defect found out than steps were taken to remedy it. The Duke of Orleans, the son of Louis Philippe, on his matrimonial tour through Germany in 1836, took occasion to study the organisation of the two battalions of rifles of the Prussian guard. He saw at once that here was a starting point, issuing from which he might succeed in forming the very class of troops required for Algeria. He occupied himself at once with the subject. The old French prejudice against the rifle placed many obstacles in his way. Fortunately, the inventions of Delvigne and Poncharra, in his own country, came to his help; they had produced a rifle which could be loaded almost as quickly and easily as the smooth-bore musket, while it exceeded the latter by far, both in range and precision. In 1838, the Duke obtained permission to form a company according to his own ideas; in the same year this company was increased to a full battalion; in 1840 it was sent to Algeria to prove what it could do in actual war; and it stood the test so well, that in the same year nine more battalions of chasseurs were formed. Finally, in 1853, ten other battalions were organised, so that the whole chasseur force of the French army now consists of twenty battalions.

The peculiar military qualities of the Bedouins and Kabyles, who undoubtedly were models of light horsemen and of infantry skirmishers, very soon induced the French to try the enlistment of natives, and to conquer Algeria by setting Arab to fight Arab. This idea gave origin, among others, to the corps of the Zouaves. They were formed principally of natives, as early as 1830, and remained a chiefly Arab corps up to 1839, when they deserted in masses into the camp of Abd-el-Kader, who had just raised the standard of holy war.[437] There remained, then, merely the cadres and the twelve French soldiers of each company, besides the two exclusively French companies attached to each battalion. The vacancies had to be filled up by Frenchmen, and since that date the Zouaves have remained an exclusively French corps, destined to take permanent garrison in Africa. But the original stock of old French Zouaves had adopted so much of the native character that the whole corps has ever since remained, in its entire spirit and habits, a specially Algerian corps, endowed with a nationality of its own, and quite distinct from the remainder of the French army. They are recruited mostly from substitutes,[438] and thus they are most of them professional soldiers for life. They, too, essentially belong to the light infantry of the army, and have, therefore, been long since provided with rifles. There are now three regiments or nine battalions of them in Africa, and one regiment (two battalions) of

Zouaves of the Guard.

Since 1841, new attempts were made to enlist native Algerians for the local army. Three battalions were formed, but they remained weak and incomplete till 1852, when more encouragement was given to native enlistment; and this succeeded so far that, in 1855, three regiments, or nine battalions, could be formed. These are the *Turcos* or *Tirailleurs indigènes*, of whom we have heard so much during the Crimean and Italian wars.[439]

Thus, not counting the foreign legion (now disbanded, but to all appearances re-forming) and the three penal battalions, the French army contains 38 battalions, especially formed and trained for light service. Of these, the chasseurs, the Zouaves, and the Turcos, each have their distinguishing characteristics. Troops like the last two classes have too strongly marked a local character ever to exercise a great influence upon the mass of the French army; still, their furious onslaught—during which they still, as has been proved in Italy, remain perfectly in hand, and even anticipate by their own military tact the orders of their chief—will always remain a brilliant example to the remainder of the troops. It is also a fact that the French, in their practice of the detail of skirmishing, and their mode of taking advantage of ground, have adopted a great deal from the Arabs. But that class of light infantry which has remained essentially French, and has thereby become, as we said before, a model to the army, are the chasseurs.[a]

CHAPTER II[b]

The very first page of the French Drill Regulations of 1831, proves what little men the French army is composed of.

> Slow time, each step 65 centimètres (25 inches), and 76 paces in a minute.
> Quick time, same length of step, and 100 paces in a minute.
> Charging time (*pas de charge*), same length of step, and 130 paces in a minute.

The step of 25 inches is undoubtedly the shortest, and the celerity of 100 paces in a minute the most sluggish adopted in any army for field-movements. While the French battalion moves over 208 feet of ground in a minute, an English, Prussian, or Austrian battalion would move over 270 feet, or thirty per cent. more. Our long step of 30 inches would be too much for the short legs of Frenchmen. The same at a charge: the French advance, in a

---

[a] *The Volunteer Journal* further has: "of whom more in our next number".—*Ed.*
[b] *The Volunteer Journal* has the sub-heading "The Chasseurs".—*Ed.*

minute, 271 feet, or as much as the English at simple quick time, while the English, at their double of 36 inches, and 150 per minute, would get over 450 feet, or sixty per cent. more. This fact alone shows that the standard size of the men cannot be reduced beyond a certain limit without affecting the efficiency and mobility of an army.

With such short legs, short steps, and slow marching time, no light infantry could be formed. When the chasseurs were first organised, care was taken from the very beginning to select the best infantry material in the country; they were all well-built, broad-shouldered, active men, from 5ft. 4in. to 5ft. 8in. in height, and mostly chosen from the mountainous parts of the country. By the regulations for chasseur drill and evolutions (published in 1845), the length of the step for the quick march was retained, but the time increased to 110 in a minute; the double (*pas gymnastique*) was regulated at 33 inches (83 centimètres) each step, and 165 in a minute; but for deployments, formation of square, or other urgent occasions, its time is to be increased to 180 in a minute. Even at this latter pace, the chasseur would cover but 45 feet more ground in a minute than the English soldier at his double. But it is less by extraordinary rapidity of motion that extraordinary results are attained, than by the length of time for which the chasseurs can continue this accelerated motion; besides, in cases of great urgency, rallying, &c., they are ordered to run as fast as they can.

The double is the principal thing practised in the chasseur battalions. The men are first taught to mark the time at 165 and 180 per minute, during which they shout One! Two! or Right! Left! which is supposed to regulate the action of the lungs, and to prevent inflammations. They are then made to march forward at the same rate, and the distance is gradually increased until they can go over a French league of 4,000 metres (two miles and a half) in twenty-seven minutes. If some of the recruits are found too weak in wind and limb for such exercise, they are sent back to the infantry of the line. The next step is the practice of leaping and running, in which latter pace the greatest possible rapidity has to be obtained for short distances; both the *pas gymnastique* and the running being practised first on the level drill-ground, or on the road, and afterwards across country, with jumping over rails and ditches. After such preparation only are the men entrusted with their arms, and now the whole course of double, running, and leaping is again gone through with rifle in hand, and in heavy marching order, the knapsack and pouch weighted to the same extent as in the field; and thus they are made to continue for a full hour at the *pas gymnastique,* during which time they have to cover at least five miles of ground. A foreign officer in plain clothes once attempted to keep pace with such a battalion of chasseurs in heavy marching order; but, untrained as he was, he could scarcely keep up for one hour; the chasseurs marched on, alternately at quick time and at the *pas gymnastique,* and went that day over twenty-two miles of country.

The whole of the field movements and evolutions have to be gone through at the double; advance in line, forming column and square, wheeling, deployments, and everything, so that the men keep in their places as steadily at this pace as at the ordinary quick time. The time for all evolutions is 165 in a minute, only in deployments and wheelings it is accelerated to 180.

The following is the opinion of a Prussian field officer of the chasseurs:—

"On the Champ-de-Mars, I saw a few companies of chasseurs manoeuvring at the side of a regiment of the line. What a contrast, from their mobility, from the whole style of their movements, to that regiment! At the first glance you see that they are a picked body, chosen from the best men of the wood and mountain districts; they are all well-knit, compact, strong, and yet so wonderfully nimble. As they flit about with astonishing rapidity, you recognise their enterprising spirit, their daring pluck, their quick intellect, their indefatigable endurance, though, certainly, you also recognise their immense conceit and French vanity. And wherever you see them, in Strasbourg, in Paris, or in any other garrison, they always make the same impression, they look as if cast in the same mould. At their head I saw none but young officers; a few only of the captains appeared thirty-five; most of them less, and even the field-officers not older. Their rapid mobility shows neither constraint nor effort; constant exercise appears to have made it their second nature, with such ease and freedom do these battalions go through their movements. Their blood has a more tranquil flow, their breath is less disturbed than with others. Single orderlies in a street would pass, in a short time, all persons walking before them; and at the same quick pace, whole battalions, at the merry sound of the bugle, defile through the streets. Whenever you see them, on the drill-ground, on the march out or home, never did they appear tired to me. Ambition, in this matter, may go hand in hand with habit.

"If quickness of motion and steadiness of aim appear to be irreconcilable, the chasseurs seem to have overcome this apparent incompatibility. I have not myself seen them practising at the target; but, according to the judgment of experienced officers, their performances in this line are not to be thought little of. If their steadiness of aim is at all disturbed, it certainly must be so in a degree very little affecting their efficiency on the field of battle. In Africa, where many an engagement was preceded by similar marches at the double, they have always known how to hit their opponents; and this proves that the special system of training to which they are subjected, tends to properly develop the powers of the body, and does not destroy steadiness of aim. With troops not so trained, this would, of course, be very different.

"The great advantages of this system of training are evident. Many are the cases in war in which it may be of decisive importance that your infantry should be capable of quicker locomotion than it is at present; for instance, in preceding the enemy in the occupation of an important position; in rapidly attaining a commanding point; in supporting a body attended by superior forces; or in surprising the enemy by making a detachment suddenly appear in a direction quite unexpected by him."

The Algerian war had made evident to the French military authorities the immense superiority of an infantry trained in this long-continued running. Since 1853, the question was debated whether this system should not be applied to the whole army. General de Lourmel (killed before Sebastopol,[440] 5th November, 1854) had specially drawn the attention of Louis Napoleon to it. Soon after the Crimean war, the *pas gymnastique* was introduced in all French infantry regiments. The time, indeed, is slower, and probably the step, too, shorter, than with the chasseurs; besides, the long-continued runs of the chasseurs are much reduced in the line. This was a necessity; the unequal bodily strength and size of the line made the capabilities of the weaker and smaller men the standard of the performance of the whole. But, still, the old sluggish rate of marching can now be overcome at an emergency; a mile or so may now and then be trotted, and, especially, the aptitude of the men to go through their evolutions at the double, admits of that charge, at a run, for some six or eight hundred yards, which carried the French, last year, in a few instants, over those very distances at which the excellent Austrian rifles were most dangerous. The *pas gymnastique* has done a great deal towards the winning of Palestro, Magenta, and Solferino.[441] The run itself gives a vigorous moral impulse to the men; a battalion charging might hesitate when marching at quick time, but the same battalion, trained so as not to arrive out of breath, will, in most cases, go on fearlessly, will arrive comparatively unscathed, and will certainly make a far greater moral impression on a standing enemy, if it charges at a run.

The extreme perfection of the chasseurs in running may pass for a special arm like theirs, but it would be both impracticable and useless to the mass of the infantry of the line. Nevertheless, the English line, with its better material of men, might easily be made to far surpass the French line in this respect; and, like every healthy exercise, this would have a capital effect on the men, bodily and morally. An infantry which cannot alternately run a mile and walk a mile for a couple of hours, will soon be considered slow. As to the volunteers, the great difference of age and bodily strength existing in their ranks, would make it difficult to obtain even this result, but there can be no doubt that gradual training for the double, at distances from half a mile to a mile, would hurt nobody's health, and improve wonderfully their efficiency for the field.

CHAPTER III

Nothing is neglected in France to develop the physical, mental, and moral powers of every individual recruit, and especially of every chasseur, in such a manner as to form him into as perfect a soldier as possible. Everything is attended to that can make him strong, active, and nimble, that can give him a rapid glance for advantages of ground, or quickness of decision in difficult situations; everything that will heighten his confidence in himself, his comrades, his arms. Drill, therefore, is but a small portion of a soldier's duties in France; and to our notions, a French battalion on the drill-ground marches, wheels, and does the manual in a shockingly loose manner. But this appears to be a consequence of the national character, and has not, so far, been attended with any bad results. English or German troops seem, themselves, to prefer a stricter system of drill; they obey the command more instantaneously, and, after a certain amount of drilling, will always exhibit more precision in all their movements than the French will ever attain. For the remainder, the system of tactical movements for the drill-ground is nearly the same in France as in England, though it is vastly different on a field of battle.

One of the chief occupations of the French soldier is gymnastic exercise. There is a central military gymnasium in Paris, which forms the teachers for the whole army. There are fifteen to twenty officers from different regiments, and besides, one sergeant from every regiment of the line or battalion of chasseurs, who remain for six months, and are then relieved by others. The course of exercises gone through is not very different from what is practised in other countries; there appears to be only one original exercise, the escalading of walls, either by putting hands and feet in holes produced by cannon-balls, or by a pole leaned against the wall, or else by means of a rope with a hook thrown over it. This kind of exercise is undoubtedly of practical value, and will contribute a great deal to make the men rely on the use of their hands and feet. The bayonet exercise is also taught in this school; but it is confined to the practising of the various points and guards; the men are never made to actually defend themselves one against the other or against cavalry.

Every garrison, in France, has the necessary conveniences for gymnastic exercise. There is, first of all, a piece of ground set apart for the more common gymnastics, with all the necessary appliances; to this the whole of the soldiers are marched in turns, and have to go through a regular course of instruction as part of their duty. The introduction of this kind of exercise is not yet very old, and is entirely imitated from the chasseurs, who were the first to be put to gymnastics; after the system had answered so well with them, it was extended to the whole army.

There is, besides, in every barracks a fencing-room and a dancing-room. In the first, fencing with the small-sword and broad-sword is taught; in the other, dancing and wrestling which the French call "la boxe." Every soldier may choose which of these exercises he will be taught, but one of them he must learn. Dancing and the small-sword are generally preferred. Single-stick is also taught now and then.

All these exercises, as well as gymnastics, properly so called, are not taught because they are considered necessary in themselves; they are practised because they develop the bodily strength and agility of the soldier generally, and give him greater self-confidence. The fencing and dancing-rooms, so far from being the scenes where tedious duty is performed, are, on the contrary, an attraction, tending to keep the soldier in the barracks even in his leisure hours; he will go there for amusement; if, in the ranks, he was but a machine, here, sword in hand, he is an independent man, trying his individual skill against his comrades; and whatever confidence in his own quickness and agility he gains here, it is so much gain for outpost and skirmishing duty, where he is, also, more or less reduced to his own resources.

The new system of skirmishing adopted by the chasseurs has not only been adopted in the whole French army since, but it has also served as a model for many European armies, among others, for the improved practice adopted in the British army during and after the Crimean war. We shall, therefore, notice but a few of the principal traits, especially as in an engagement the French very often act quite differently, partly in accordance with general orders (as in 1859, in Italy), partly because every latitude is left to officers to act entirely according to circumstances, and partly because all drill regulations must undergo considerable alterations in battle. The skirmishers act in groups of four, each group deploying into one single line, with five paces interval from man to man. The interval between the groups is at least five paces (forming a continuous line, with one man at every five paces), and at most forty paces from group to group. The non-commissioned officers take up a position ten paces behind their sections; the officers, each attended by a guard of four men and a bugler, twenty or thirty paces to the rear. If only part of a company is extended, the captain takes his station half-way between the skirmishers and the support. Taking advantage of cover is the principal thing to be attended to; the dressing of the line as well as the exactness of the intervals are sacrificed to it. The whole line of skirmishers is directed by the bugle alone, the signals numbering twenty-two; besides which, each chasseur battalion, and every company in it, has a distinctive signal of its own, which is made to precede the signal of command. The officers carry a whistle, which they are, however, to use in extreme cases only; it gives five signals—Caution! Advance! Halt! Retire! Rally!—and is the original of the whistle which some volunteers have adopted as part and parcel of every man's accoutrements, thus depriving their officers of the use of the whistle when it might be necessary. The skirmishers rally by groups of four, if attacked by skirmishing cavalry; by sections and sub-divisions, in irregular compact masses; on the support, where they form a kind of company square; or on the battalion, in case the latter is to act in line or to form square. These various forms of rallying are practised very much, and the French excel in them; and their variety does not create any confusion, as the men are instructed to get rallied any way they can in case of imminent danger, and then to profit of favourable movements to join the larger body to which the signal had called them. The squares are sometimes two, sometimes four deep.

Compared to the old-fashioned system, as adopted in almost all armies before the chasseurs were organised, this new method had an immense superiority. But it is not to be forgotten that it is, after all, nothing but a set of drill-ground regulations. There is no room in it, as far as it goes, for the intelligence of the individual soldier; and if it was practised on a level plain, it would be compatible with as great pedantry as might satisfy the stiffest martinet. The lines are formed with regular intervals,—they advance, retire, change front and direction same as any battalion in line, and the men are moved by the bugle as so many puppets by a wire. The real practice ground for skirmishers is before the enemy, and here the French had a splendid school for their light infantry in the fearfully broken ground of Algeria, defended by the Kabyles, the bravest, most tenacious, and most wary skirmishers the world ever saw. Here it was that the French developed to the highest degree that instinct for extended fighting and taking advantage of cover which they have shown in every war since 1792; and here the Zouaves especially turned to the best account the lessons given to them by the natives, and served as models to the whole army. Generally a chain of skirmishers is supposed to advance in something like a deployed line, crowding together, perhaps, on points offering good cover, and thinning where they have to pass open ground; occupying the enemy's skirmishers in front, only now and then taking advantage of a hedge or so to put in a little flank fire, and, withal, not expected nor even attempting to do much besides occupying their opponents. Not so the Zouaves. With them, extended order means the independent action, subordinate to a common object, of small groups; the attempt at seizing advantages as soon as they offer; the chance of getting near the enemy's masses, and disturbing them by a well-sustained fire; and, in small engagements, the possibility of deciding them without calling in the masses at all. With them, surprise and ambush are the very essence of skirmishing. They do not use cover merely to open fire from a comparatively sheltered position; they principally use it to creep, unseen, close up to the enemy's skirmishers, jump up suddenly, and drive them away in disorder; they use it to get on the flanks of their opponents, and there to appear unexpectedly in a thick swarm, cutting off part of their line, or to form an ambush, into which they entice the hostile skirmishers, if following too quick upon their simulated retreat. In decisive actions, such artifices will be applicable in the many pauses occurring between the great efforts to bring on decision; but in petty warfare, in the war of detachments and outposts, in collecting information respecting the enemy, or securing the rest of their own army, such qualities are of the highest importance. What the Zouaves are one example will show. In outpost duty, in all armies, the rule is that, especially during the night, the sentries must not sit, nor much less lay down, and are to fire as soon as the enemy approaches, in order to alarm the pickets. Now read the Duke of Aumale's description of a camp of Zouaves*:—

"At night, even the solitary Zouave placed on the brow of yonder hill, and overlooking the plain beyond, has been drawn in. You see no videttes; but wait till the officer goes his rounds, and you will find him speak to a Zouave who is lying flat on the ground, just behind the brow, and watchful of everything. You see yonder group of bushes; I should not be at all surprised if on examination you were to find there ensconced a few couples of Zouaves; in case a Bedouin should creep up into these bushes in order to espy what is going on in the camp, they will not fire, but despatch him quietly with the bayonet, in order not to shut the trap."

* *Revue des deux Mondes,* 15th March, 1855.

What are soldiers who have learnt their outpost duty in peace garrisons only, and who cannot be trusted to keep awake except standing or walking, to men trained in a war of ruse and stratagem, against Bedouins and Kabyles? And with all these deviations from the prescribed system, the Zouaves have been surprised only once by their wary enemies.

England has, in the north-west frontier of India, a district very similar, in its military features, to Algeria. The climate is nearly the same, so is the nature of the ground, and so is the border population. Frequent forays and hostile encounters do occur there; and that district has formed some of the best men in the British service. But that these long and highly instructive encounters should not have had any lasting influence upon the mode in which all kinds of light service are carried on in the British army; that after twenty and more years of fighting with Afghans and Beloochees, that part of the service should have been found so defective that French examples had to be hurriedly imitated in order to bring the infantry, in this respect, into a state of efficiency; this is, certainly, strange.

The French chasseurs have introduced into the French army:— 1. The new system of dress and accoutrements; the tunic, the light shako, the waist belts, instead of the cross belts. 2. The rifle, and the science of its use; the modern school of musketry. 3. The prolonged application of the double, and its use in evolutions. 4. The bayonet exercise. 5. Gymnastics; and, 6. Together with the Zouaves, the modern system of skirmishing. And if we will be sincere, for how much of all this, so far as it exists in the British army, are we not indebted to the French?

There is still plenty of room for improvements. Why should not the British army come in for its share? Why should not the north-western frontier of India, even now, form the troops employed there into a corps capable of doing that for the English army which the chasseurs and Zouaves have done for the French?

Written between mid-September and mid-October 1860

First published in *The Volunteer Journal, for Lancashire and Cheshire*, Nos. 3, 5, 7, September 21, October 5 and 20, 1860; reprinted in the collection *Essays Addressed to Volunteers*, London-Manchester, 1861

Reproduced from the collection, checked with the text in *The Volunteer Journal*

VOLUNTEER ARTILLERY [442]

The subject of volunteer artillery is one of great importance, and ought to be widely discussed; the more so, as the part which the volunteer artillery is to take in the defence of the country does not appear to have been, as yet, very clearly defined.[a]

Now, it is evident that the first question to be settled is the proper sphere of action of the volunteer artillery. Unless this be done, there will never be any uniform system of training in the different corps; and as the science of artillery comprises the most multifarious subjects, the whole of which it would be difficult indeed, theoretically and practically, to teach to all the volunteer officers and privates, the different corps, when wanted for action, would arrive with very different qualifications for the duties to be performed by them; and many a company, on being put to a particular task, would be found to be very little qualified to carry it out.

In the following observations we do not by any means profess to say what volunteer artillery ought, or ought not to be; we merely wish to point out some of the conditions under which volunteer, as

---

[a] In *The Volunteer Journal* the first paragraph reads as follows (its text is, probably, partially or wholly written by the editors): "We give, in another column of this week's journal, some remarks from the London correspondent of the *Manchester Weekly Express,* on volunteer artillery. The subject is one of great importance, and ought to be widely discussed; the more so, as the part which the volunteer artillery is to take in the defence of the country, does not appear to have been, as yet, very clearly defined. The very article to which we refer, while it wishes to see the formation of artillery corps confined to the sea-board, still expects volunteer gunners to act as a kind of field artillery, not confining themselves to the attendance upon heavy guns in fortified places, but also galloping about with 'light six-pounders or Whitworth's twelves'." — *Ed.*

well as any other artillery, has to be formed, to open the field for that discussion which we invite, and from which, ultimately, an understanding must arise, as to the proper sphere of action of volunteer artillery corps.

All artillery is divided into field artillery which has to operate with the infantry and cavalry in the field, and is provided with horsed guns; and into siege or fortress artillery which works heavy guns in stationary and protected batteries, for the attack or defence of fortified places. If in a regular army, the length of service of the men, and the special scientific education of the officers, renders it possible to train the whole body to both branches of the service, so far, at least, that on an emergency every company can be put to any duty; this is not the case with volunteers, who, officers as well as men, can devote but a portion of their time to their military duties. In France, in Austria, in Prussia, field artillery is kept quite distinct from garrison or siege artillery. If this is the case in regular standing armies, surely there must be some reason for it which will operate far stronger in an army of volunteers.

The fact is this: the mere handling of a field gun is not so different from that of a heavy gun in battery that the privates of a volunteer company could not easily learn both. But the nature of the duties of the officers in either case is so very different, that nothing less than a professional education and long practice could qualify a man to do both equally well. In an officer of field artillery, a rapid military glance, a thorough judgment of ground and of distances, a perfect knowledge of the effect of his guns, enabling him to hold out against an attack to the last moment without losing any guns, a long experience of what horses can do, and of the way to treat them in a campaign; and, finally, a good deal of dash combined with prudence, are the chief qualities. In an officer of garrison or siege artillery, scientific acquirements, theoretical knowledge of artillery in all its branches, of fortification, mathematics, and mechanics, an ability of turning everything into use, a patient and strict attention to the erection and repair of earthworks, and to the effects of a concentrated fire, and a courage more tenacious than dashing will be required. Give the command of a bastion to a captain of a 9-pounder battery, and it will take the best man a deal of training before he is up to the work; put an officer who has attended for a couple of years to nothing but siege guns, at the head of a battery of horse artillery, and it will take a long while before he has worn off his methodical slowness and recovered the dash required for his new arm. With non-commissioned officers lacking the scientific education of their superiors, the difficulty will be still greater.

Of the two, the garrison artillerist seems to be the easiest formed. Civil engineers possess all the preliminary scientific knowledge required for the business, and will very soon learn the application to artillery of the scientific principles with which they are conversant. They will easily learn the handling of the different machines used in moving heavy ordnance, the construction of batteries, and the rules of fortification. They will, therefore, form the class from which volunteer artillery officers should be chiefly selected, and will be especially adapted for garrison artillery. It will be the same with the non-commissioned officers and gunners. All men who have had much to do with machinery, such as engineers, mechanics, blacksmiths, will form the best material, and on this ground the great manufacturing centres ought to form the best corps. Practice with heavy guns may be an impossibility in the interior of the country, but the sea is not so very far from our Lancashire and Yorkshire inland towns that occasional trips to the sea-side might not be organised for the purpose; besides, with heavy guns in battery, where the first graze of every shot can be seen, and the men can correct themselves, actual target practice is not of such paramount importance.

There is another thing against the attempt at getting up volunteer field artillery—the expense of the guns and the horsing of them. A few companies combining amongst themselves may, indeed, be able to raise the expense of horsing a couple of guns for the summer months, and drill with them in turns, but neither men nor officers will thereby be formed into efficient field artillerists. The expense of equipping a field-battery of six guns is generally reckoned about equal to that of getting up a whole battalion of infantry; no company of volunteer artillery could afford such an outlay; and considering the disgrace attached to the loss of a gun on the battle-field, it may well be doubted whether any government would ever be inclined, in case of invasion, to entrust volunteer artillery with field guns, horses and drivers, on the terms on which rifle volunteers are supplied with small arms.

On these and other grounds, we cannot but come to the conclusion that the proper sphere for the volunteer artillery is the manning of heavy guns in stationary batteries on the coast. An attempt at field artillery may be inevitable in inland towns, to keep up the interest in the movement, and it will certainly do no harm to either officers or men to be made acquainted, as far as possible, with the handling of horsed light guns; but we confess we have, from our own personal experience in the arm, our great doubts as to their eventual proficiency in field service. Still, they will have learned a great many things which will be quite as useful to them in the use of heavy guns, and they will soon be up to the mark when placed in charge of them.

There is another point we wish to allude to. Artillery, far more than infantry and cavalry, is an essentially scientific arm, and as such its efficiency will chiefly depend upon the theoretical and practical knowledge of the officers. We have no doubt that by this time Major Griffiths' *Artillerist's Manual* will be in the hands of every officer of volunteer artillery. The contents of that book show with what a variety of subjects an artillery officer, and even a non-commissioned officer, has to make himself familiar before he can lay claim to any proficiency in his arm; yet that book is merely a short abstract of what an efficient artillerist ought to know. Besides the regular company and battalion drill, common to infantry and artillery, there is the knowledge of the many different calibres of ordnance, their carriages and platforms, charges, ranges, and various projectiles; there is the construction of batteries, and the science of sieges; permanent and field fortification; the manufacture of ammunition and fireworks; and, finally, that science of gunnery which, at the present moment, is receiving such wonderful and new additions by the introduction of rifled guns. All these things have to be learnt both theoretically and practically, and they are all of equal importance; for whenever the volunteer artillery are embodied for active service, they will come to a dead lock unless all these branches have been attended to. Of all volunteer corps, therefore, the artillery is the one in which the efficiency of the officers is of the greatest importance; and we do hope and trust that they will exert themselves to the utmost to attain that practical experience and theoretical knowledge without which they must be found wanting on the day of trial.

Written in the first half of October 1860

First published in *The Volunteer Journal, for Lancashire and Cheshire*, No. 6, October 13, 1860; reprinted in the collection *Essays Addressed to Volunteers*, London-Manchester, 1861

Reproduced from the collection, checked with the text in *The Volunteer Journal*

THE HISTORY OF THE RIFLE[443]

I

The rifle is a German invention, dating as far back as the close of the fifteenth century. The first rifles were made with apparently no other object than to facilitate the loading of the arm with an almost tight-fitting bullet. To this end, the grooves were made straight, without any spiral turning, and merely served to diminish the friction of the bullet in the bore. The bullet itself was surrounded by a piece of greased woollen or linen cloth (the plaster), and was thus hammered down without too much difficulty. These rifles, primitive as they were, must have given far better results than the smooth-bore small arms of the period, with their bullets of considerably smaller diameter than the bore.

Later on, the character of the arm was totally altered by the spiral turn given to the grooves, which transformed the bore of the barrel into a sort of female screw; the bullet, by the tight-fitting plaster, being made to follow the grooves, took the spiral turn as well, and thus retained a spiral rotation round its line of flight. It was soon found that this mode of fixing the rotation of the bullet vastly increased both the range and accuracy of the arm, and thus the spiral grooves very soon superseded the straight ones.

This, then, was the kind of rifle which remained in general use for more than two hundred years. If we except hair-triggers and more carefully worked sights, it scarcely underwent any improvement up to 1828. It was greatly superior to the smooth-bore musket in accuracy, but not so very much in range; beyond 400 or 500 yards, it could not be relied upon. At the same time, it was comparatively difficult to load; the hammering down of the bullet was a very tedious operation; the powder and plastered bullet had each to be put separately into the barrel, and not more than one round per minute could be fired. These drawbacks made it unfit for the generality of an army, especially at a time like the eighteenth century, when all battles were decided by the rapid firing of deployed lines. With such tactics, the old smooth-bore musket, with all its glaring imperfections, was still a far preferable arm. Thus we find that the rifle remained the favourite implement of the deer-stalker and chamois-hunter, and that it was used as an exceptional arm of war, for a few battalions of sharpshooters, in such armies only as could recruit these battalions from a sufficient number of trained sportsmen among the population.

The wars of the American and French Revolutions[444] created a great change in tactics. Henceforth extended order was introduced in every engagement; the combination of skirmishers with lines or columns became the essential characteristic of modern fighting. The masses, during the greater part of the day, are kept back; they are held in reserve or employed in manoeuvring so as to concentrate on the weak point of the enemy; they are only launched in decisive moments; but, in the meantime, skirmishers and their immediate supports are constantly engaged. The mass of the ammunition is spent by them, and the objects they fire at are seldom larger than the front of a company; in most cases, they have to fire at single men well hidden by covering objects. And yet, the effect of their fire is most important; for every attack is both prepared, and, in the first instance, met by it; they are expected to weaken the resistance of detachments occupying farm houses or villages, as well as to take the edge off the attack of a charging line. Now, with old "Brown Bess,"[445] none of these things could be done effectively. Nobody can ever have been under the fire of skirmishers, armed with smooth-bore muskets, without taking home an utter contempt for its efficiency at medium ranges. Still, the rifle in its old shape was not fitted for the mass of skirmishers. The old rifle, in order to facilitate the forcing down of the bullet, must be short, so short that it was but a poor handle to a bayonet; consequently, riflemen were used in such positions only when they were safe against an attack with the bayonet, or by cavalry.

Under these circumstances, the problem at once presented itself: to invent a gun which should combine the range and accuracy of the rifle, with the rapidity and ease of loading, and with the length of barrel of the smooth-bore musket; an arm, which is at the same time a rifle and a handy arm of war, fit to be placed into the hands of every infantry soldier.

Thus we see that with the very introduction of skirmishing into modern tactics, arose the demand for such an improved arm of war. In the nineteenth century, whenever a demand for a thing arises, and that demand be justified by the circumstances of the case, it is sure to be supplied. It was supplied in this case. Almost all improvements in small arms made since 1828 tended to supply it.

Before, however, we attempt to give an account of those improvements which have created such great and numerous changes in rifled fire-arms, by dropping the old system of forcing the bullet home, we may be allowed to cast a glance at the attempts made to improve the rifle while maintaining the old method of loading.

The rifle with oval bore which is known in England as the Lancaster rifle, has been in use on the Continent for more than forty years. We find it mentioned in a German military book printed in 1818. In Brunswick, Colonel Berner improved it and had the whole infantry of that duchy armed with it in 1832. The ovality was but slight, and the oval bullet was forced home in the old fashion. This oval bullet, however, was to be used in skirmishing only. For volley firing, the men were provided with spherical bullets of smaller calibre, which rolled down the barrel quite as easy as any musket ball. Still, the inconveniences of this system are obvious. It is merely remarkable as the first instance of giving rifled muskets to the whole of the infantry in any one army.

In Switzerland, a civil engineer and officer of rifles, M. Wild, improved the rifle considerably. His bullet was smaller in proportion to the bore than usual, and was made to take the rifling by means of the plaster only; a disk on the ramrod prevented it from entering the bore too deep, and thus driving the bullet so close on the charge that the powder got crushed; the spirality of the grooves was reduced and the charge increased. Wild's rifle gave very good results up to above 500 yards, with a very flat trajectory; besides, it allowed of more than 100 shots being fired without fouling. It was adopted in Switzerland, Württemberg, and Baden, but is now, of course, antiquated and relinquished.[a]

The most modern and the best rifle constructed upon the forcing principle is the new Swiss sharpshooters' regulation rifle. This arm has adopted the American principle of a very small

---

[a] In *The Volunteer Journal* the word "superseded" is used here.— *Ed.*

calibre; its bore is not more than 10.50 millimètres, or 0.42 of an inch. The barrel is but 28 inches long, and has eight flat grooves (one turn in 34 inches). The ramrod is provided with the disk as introduced by Wild. The bullet is cylindro-ogival, and very long; it is forced home by means of a greased plaster. The charge is comparatively strong, and of a very coarse-grained powder. This arm has shown the most astonishing effects; and in the trial of various rifles recently made by the Dutch Government, its range, accuracy, and lowness of trajectory, were found to be unequalled. In fact, at a range of 600 yards, the highest point of its trajectory is only 8 feet 6 inches, so that the whole of the flight, at that range, is dangerous space for cavalry, and that even for infantry the last 100 yards of the trajectory are dangerous space; in other words, an error in judging distance of 100 yards, at 600 yards range, would not prevent the bullet from hitting an object six feet high. This is a result far surpassing that of any other rifled musket; the very best of them require an elevation, which raises the highest points of the trajectory, for 600 yards, to 13 to 20 feet, and reduces the dangerous space to from 60 to 25 yards. This extraordinary flatness of trajectory is produced by the small calibre of the arm, which admits of a very elongated bolt-shaped shot, and of a comparatively powerful charge; with a small bore, the rifle may be made very strong, without being clumsy, the shot may be long, without being heavy, and the charge may be powerful, relatively, without producing too severe a recoil. It is certain that the forced loading has nothing to do with the admirable shooting of the arm; indeed, it forms its only drawback, and prevents it from being used as the general arm of infantry. The Swiss have, therefore, restrained it to their companies of sharpshooters, in whose hands, no doubt, it will answer uncommonly well.

We shall next show how the rifle came to be made into a weapon fit to be placed into the hands of every infantry soldier.

II

Delvigne, a French officer, was the originator of the first attempt to make the rifle a weapon fit for general infantry use. He saw clearly that to do this, the bullet must slip down the barrel as easy, or nearly so, as the bullet of a smooth-bore musket, and be made, afterwards, to change its shape so as to enter into the grooves.

To obtain this end, he constructed, as early as 1828, a rifle with a chamber at the breech; that is to say, the extreme end of the bore at the breech, where the powder lies, was made of considerably smaller diameter than the remaining part of the barrel. This chamber was adopted from howitzers and mortars which had always been so constructed; but while, in ordnance, it merely served to keep well together the small charges used for mortars and howitzers, it answered quite a different purpose in Delvigne's rifle. The powder having been dropped down into the chamber, the bullet, smaller than the bore, was made to roll down after it; but, arrived on the edge of the chamber, it could not pass any further, and remained supported on it; and a few smart blows with the ramrod were sufficient to force the soft lead of the bullet sideways into the grooves, and to enlarge its diameter so much that it fitted tight in the barrel.

The greatest inconvenience in this system was, that the bullet lost its spherical shape, and became somewhat flattened, in consequence of which it was apt to lose the lateral rotation impressed upon it by the grooves, which impaired its precision considerably. To remedy this, Delvigne invented elongated shot (cylindro-conical), and although the experiments with this kind of shot were not, at first, very successful in France, it answered very well in Belgium, Austria, and Sardinia, in which countries Delvigne's rifle, with various improvements, was given to the Chasseur battalions instead of the old rifle. Although his rifle is at present almost everywhere superseded, Delvigne's improvements embrace the two great principles on which all succeeding inventors have been obliged to rely. Firstly, that in muzzle-loading rifles, the shot must go down with a certain windage, so as to admit of easy loading, and must change its shape, so as to enter the grooves, only after it has been rammed home; and secondly, that elongated shot are the only projectiles adapted for modern rifles. Delvigne thus at once put the question on its proper footing, and fully deserves the name of the father of the modern rifle.

The advantages of elongated shot over spherical bullets are numerous, so long as their lateral rotation (around its longitudinal axis) can be secured to the former, which is accomplished in a satisfactory manner by almost every modern rifle. The elongated shot offers a far smaller section, in proportion to its weight, to the resistance of the atmosphere than the spherical bullet. Its point can be so shaped as to reduce that resistance to a minimum. Like a bolt or an arrow, it is to a certain degree supported by the air below it. The consequence is, that it loses far less of its initial

velocity by the resistance of the air, and that, consequently, it will
reach a given distance with a far lower trajectory (that is to say,
with a line of flight far more dangerous to the enemy) than any
round shot of the same diameter.

Another advantage is, that the elongated shot offers a far
greater surface of contact to the sides of the barrel than the round
shot. This makes the former take the rifling far better, and
therefore admits of a reduced pitch of the rifling as well as of a
reduced depth of groove. Both these circumstances facilitate the
cleaning of the arm, and at the same time permit the use of full
charges without increasing the recoil of the gun.

And finally, as the weight of the elongated shot is so much
greater than that of the round bullet, it follows that the calibre, or
diameter of bore, of the gun can be considerably reduced, while it
still remains capable of firing a projectile equal in weight to the
old round bullet. Now, if the weight of the old smooth-bore
musket and that of its bullet be considered as the standard
weights, a rifle for elongated shot of this weight can be made
stronger than the old musket in the same proportion as the bore
has been reduced, and it will still not exceed the weight of the old
musket. The gun being stronger, it will stand the charge so much
the better; it will have less recoil, and, consequently, the reduced
bore will admit of relatively stronger charges, whereby a greater
initial velocity, and, consequently, a lower line of flight will be
secured.

The next improvement was made by another French officer,
Colonel Thouvenin. He clearly perceived the inconvenience of
leaving the shot, while being rammed into the grooves, supported
on a circular projection touching its edges. He therefore did away
with the edges of the chamber, boring out the whole of the bore
to one uniform diameter as heretofore. In the middle of the screw
closing the bore, he fixed a short strong steel pin, or peg, which
projected into the bore, and around which the powder was to fall;
on the blunt top of this peg the shot was to be supported while the
ramrod hammered it into the grooves. The advantages of this
system were considerable. The expansion of the shot, by the blows
of the ramrod, was far more regular than in Delvigne's rifles. The
arm could afford a greater windage, which facilitated loading. The
results obtained with it were so satisfactory that, as early as 1846,
the French *Chasseurs à pied* were armed with Thouvenin's rifles;
the Zouaves and other light African infantry followed; and as it
was found that the old smooth-bore muskets could, with little
expense, be transformed into Thouvenin's rifles, the carbines of

the French foot-artillery were all altered accordingly. The Prussian rifles were armed with Thouvenin's rifle in 1847; those of Bavaria in 1848; and most of the smaller States of Northern Germany followed the example, in some cases arming even portions of the line with this excellent weapon. In all these rifles there is visible a certain approach to unity of system, in spite of all their variations as to calibre, &c.; the number of grooves is reduced (mostly to 4), and the pitch generally is from three-quarters of a turn to one turn in the whole length of the barrel.

Still, Thouvenin's rifle had its drawbacks. The force required to drive, by repeated blows, the lead of the shot, laterally, into the grooves was incompatible with that length of barrel which the common musket of infantry of the line must always have as an effective handle to a bayonet. It was, besides, very difficult for skirmishers, crawling or kneeling, to apply that force. The resistance offered to the explosive force by the shot, jammed as it is in the grooves just in front of the powder, increases the recoil, and thereby restricts the gun to a comparatively small charge. Finally, the peg always remains an undesirable complication of the arm; it renders the cleaning of the space around it very difficult, and is liable to get out of order.

Thus the principle of compressing the shot by blows from the ramrod gave very satisfactory results, for the time being, in the system of Delvigne, and better results, again, in that of Thouvenin. Still it could not assert its superiority, for an arm for general infantry use, over the old smooth-bore gun. Other principles had to be resorted to before a rifle fit for every soldier's hands could be produced.

III

Delvigne, whose rifle we described in the preceding article, found it advisable to hollow out his elongated bullets from the base, in order to reduce their weight to something like that of the old spherical bullet. Though he very soon found that this hollow projectile was incompatible with the system of expanding the shot by mechanical blows, his experiments sufficed to prove to him that the gas developed by the explosion, on entering the cavity formed in the bullet, had a tendency to expand the walls of this hollow portion so as to make the bullet fit the barrel exactly and take the rifling.

It was this discovery which was taken up in 1849 by the then Captain Minié. He did entirely away with the peg or pillar at the bottom of the bore, and restored to the rifle the simplicity which it had possessed before Delvigne and Thouvenin; relying entirely upon the expansive action of the explosion upon the hollow portion of his bullet. This bullet was cylindro-ogival, with two ring-shaped indentations round the cylindrical portion,* and hollowed out conically from the base; a cup-shaped hollow iron plug (*culot*) closed the hollow portion, and was driven into it by the force of the explosion, thereby effectively expanding the lead. The bullet had sufficient windage to go easily down, even when surrounded by the greased paper cartridge.

Here, then, we have at last a rifle and a bullet constructed upon principles which render it possible to give this arm to every foot soldier. The new arm loads as easily as the smooth-bore musket, and has an effect far superior to that of the old rifle, which it equals in precision, but far exceeds in range. The rifle with expansion bullet is undoubtedly—of all muzzle-loaders—the best arm for general use as well as for sharpshooters, and it is owing to this circumstance that it owes its very great success, its adoption in so many services, and the many attempts that have been made to improve the shape of the shot or the grooving of the rifle. The Minié bullet, in consequence of its being hollowed out, can be made but little heavier than the old round bullet of the same calibre; the bullet lying loose on the powder, and being only gradually expanded as it passes through the barrel, the recoil is far less than with either the old or the Delvigne and Thouvenin rifles, in every one of which the shot is jammed fast in the barrel, and has to be dislodged by the full force of the explosion; consequently the Minié rifle can apply a relatively stronger charge. The grooves have to be made very shallow, which facilitates the cleaning of the barrel; the length of axis in which one full turn of the grooves is made has to be pretty great, in consequence of which the number of rotations, and also the friction with the air (which takes place at every rotation), is diminished, whereby the initial velocity is better preserved. The hollow base-end of the shot also brings its centre of gravity more forward; and all these circumstances combine to produce a comparatively low trajectory.

The general adoption of the Minié rifle was, in fact, owing to another circumstance: That, by a very simple process, all old smooth-bore muskets could be transformed into rifles fit for Minié

---

* These indentations (*cannelures*) had been invented by Tamisier, another French officer. Besides reducing the weight of the bullet and the friction in the barrel, they were found to balance the shot in the air, similar to the wings of an arrow, and thus to lower the trajectory.

bullets. When the Crimean war [446] made it desirable, in Prussia, that the whole infantry should at once be armed with rifled muskets, and the requisite number of needle-guns had not yet been manufactured, 300,000 old muskets were rifled and rendered fit for Minié ammunition in less than a year.

The French Government were the first to arm a few battalions with the Minié rifle; but the grooves were progressive, that is to say, they were deeper at the breech than at the muzzle, so that whatever lead had entered the grooves at the breech, was again compressed by the shallowing grooves during its progress through the barrel, while at the same time from within the expanding force of the powder continued to act. Thus such an amount of friction was created that very often the solid point of the shot was torn off and sent out of the barrel while the hollow base-end remained fast in the grooves. This, and other defects, induced the Government to renounce any further attempt to introduce the Minié rifle.

In England, as early as 1851, 28,000 of these rifles were constructed, similar to those tried in France; the bullets were slightly conical, with ogival point, with a round hollow plug, and without indentations, as it was intended to *press* them. The results were very unsatisfactory, chiefly in consequence of the shape of the bullet; until, in 1852, new experiments were made, from which, finally, the Enfield rifle and bullets proceeded, which will be again alluded to hereafter. The Enfield rifle is but one of the modifications of the Minié. It has, since 1854, definitively superseded all smooth-bore muskets in the British army.

In Belgium, the Minié rifle, with slight alterations, has been adopted since 1854 for riflemen, and latterly for the line also.

In Spain, in 1853, the rifles received the Minié, which has since also been given to the line.

In Prussia, in 1855-56, the Minié rifle was provisionally given to the line, as already stated. It has since been completely superseded by the needle-gun.

In the smaller German States, the Minié rifle was also adopted, with very few exceptions.

In Switzerland, the Prélat rifle, destined to arm the whole of the infantry with the exception of the sharpshooters, is but a modification of the Minié.

And in Russia, finally, the Government is just now occupied in replacing the old smooth-bore muskets by Minié rifles of a very good model.

In almost every one of these countries has the number, depth, and pitch of the grooves, and the shape of the bullet, undergone various modifications of detail, to describe the most important of which will be the purport of our next chapter.

IV

We again recapitulate the principle of Minié's system: A rifled musket, with shallow grooves, is loaded with an elongated bullet, which is so much smaller in diameter than the bore, that it glides down easily. This bullet is hollowed out from its base, that is to say, from the end resting on the powder. On firing, the gas suddenly developed by the explosion enters into this hollow part, and by its pressure against its comparatively thin sides, *expands* the lead so as to make it fit the bore and enter into the grooves; the bullet, therefore, must follow the turn of these grooves, and retain the lateral rotation characteristic of all rifle bullets. This is the principle, the essential part in all the different rifles firing expansion bullets; and it is common to them all. But in matters of detail, a great many modifications have been made by various inventors.

Minié himself adopted the plug. This plug was a little, round, cup-shaped piece of sheet-iron, driven into the mouth of the hollow part of the bullet. It was intended to be driven deeper into the hollow by the explosion, and thus to assist and render more certain the expansion of the shot. It was, however, soon found that this cup-shaped plug had great inconveniences. It separated very often from the bullet on leaving the muzzle, and in its irregular line of flight it slightly wounded sometimes troops belonging to the firing party and placed a little in advance laterally. It also sometimes turned over while being driven into the lead, and thus caused an irregular expansion, and thereby a deviation of the shot from the line of aim. As it had been proved that the expansion of the shot might be obtained without any plugs at all, experiments were made to fix the best shape of an expansion bullet without plug. The Prussian Captain Neindorff appears to have been the first to propose such a bullet (in 1852). The hollow of this projectile is cylindrical, but widened out towards the base, in the shape of a tun-dish. This shot gave very good results as to range and precision, but it was soon found that the plug served another purpose besides expansion—it preserved the thin sides of the hollow shot from getting crushed during transport and rough handling; while Neindorff's bullets became deformed during transport, and then gave very bad results. In most German services, therefore, the hollow iron plug was maintained, but it was made of a long, pointed, sugar-loaf shape, and then answered very well, never turned over, and scarcely ever got separated from the leaden shot. The Enfield bullet, as is well known, has a solid wooden plug. In some States, however, the experiments with bullets without plugs were continued, and such bullets adopted for the service. This was the case in Belgium, France, Switzerland, and Bavaria. The chief object in all these experiments was to fix a shape for the hollow part of the bullet which would prevent crushing while it allowed expansion. Thus the hollow was formed in the shape of a bell (Timmerhans, in Belgium), of a three-sided prism (Nessler, in France), with a cross-shaped section (Plönnies, in Darmstadt), &c. But it appears almost impossible to unite the two elements, solidity and expansibility, in any modification of an expansion shot without a plug, unless the calibre be considerably reduced.[a] The new Bavarian projectile (Major Podewils'), which has a plain cylindrical hollow, and very strong sides to it, appears, so far, to answer best, but the Bavarian rifle also has a small bore.[b]

In countries where old smooth-bore muskets were rifled for Minié bullets, the large calibre of the old musket became, of course, compulsory. But where entirely new rifles were provided for the army, the calibre was considerably reduced, from considerations to which we have alluded in a former article. The English Enfield rifle has a calibre of 14.68 millimètres, the South-German rifle (adopted in Württemberg, Bavaria, Baden, and Hesse-Darmstadt) of 13.9 mm. The French alone, in their rifles for the guard, retained the calibre of their smooth-bore muskets (17.80 mm.).

The Enfield rifle is a very fair specimen of the expansion system. Its calibre is small enough to admit of a shot twice the length of its diameter, and still not much heavier than the old round musket bullet. Its workmanship is very good, and superior to that of almost all rifles served out to Continental troops. The bullet has very good proportions; against the wooden plug it is objected that it may either swell, and thereby increase the diameter of the shot, or shrink, and then fall out; but we think these objections futile. If the swelling of the plug presented any inconvenience, it would have been found out long since; and in case of its shrinking, the make of the cartridge prevents its falling

---

[a] The words "unless the calibre be considerably reduced" do not occur in *The Volunteer Journal.—Ed.*

[b] The words "but the Bavarian rifle also has a small bore" do not occur in *The Volunteer Journal.—Ed.*

out. The results obtained with the Enfield rifle are about on a par
with those of the best Continental expansion rifles.

The objections to the Enfield, as a rifle with expansion bullets,
are these: That the calibre might still be smaller, giving a longer
bullet for the same weight and a stronger barrel with the same
weight; that five grooves are proved to be better than three; that
the barrel of the long Enfield, at least, is too delicate, towards the
muzzle, to be used as a handle for a bayonet; that the bullet, from
having no ring-shaped indentations, must suffer an enormous
amount of friction in the barrel, and thereby runs the risk of
having the solid point torn off, while the ring-shaped hollow part
sticks fast to the grooves.

To change the calibre is a very serious matter; and without that
it will be very difficult to give the muzzle end of the barrel more
solidity. This appears to us the most serious objection. All other
objections appear unimportant; the number of grooves, and the
shape of the bullet may be altered any time without inconvenience; and even as it is, the Enfield has proved itself a very useful
arm of war.

We have, so far, compared the Enfield with such rifles only
which use expansion bullets; the comparison with rifles based
upon different principles we must reserve for a future occasion,
when we shall have examined the various other constructions now
in use.

V

In 1852, an English gun-maker, Mr. Wilkinson, and an Austrian
officer of artillery, Capt. Lorenz, simultaneously, but each
independently of the other, invented another method of making a
loose-fitting elongated bullet increase its diameter by the force of
the explosion, so as to make it fit the bore closely, and follow the
turn of the grooves. This method consisted in making the
explosion *compress* the bullet lengthways instead of expanding it.

Take a soft or elastic ball, place it on a table, and make it fly off
with a smart blow of the hand. The first effect of the blow, even
before it starts the ball, will be a change in its shape. Light as it is,
the weight of the ball offers resistance enough to become flattened
on the side where it receives the blow; it is compressed in one
direction, and, consequently, its size must increase in another
direction, similar to what it does when you completely flatten it. As
the blow acts upon the elastic ball, so is the explosion of the
powder expected to act upon the *compression bullet* of Lorenz and
Wilkinson. The weight, the *vis inertiae* of the bullet is made the

means, which, by its resistance to the force of the explosion, compresses the bullet lengthways, and thereby makes it larger sideways; when the shot comes out, it is shorter and thicker than when it was put in.

An elongated bullet of solid lead, in order to offer sufficient resistance, and thus to be sufficiently compressed to take the grooves, would have to be very heavy—in other words, very long in proportion to its thickness. Even with a small calibre such a bullet would be too heavy for war, as the men would be overweighted with ammunition if they carried the usual number of rounds. To remedy this, two very deep ring-shaped indentations are cut into the cylindrical part of the bullet. Take an Enfield bullet, remove the plug, fill the cavity with molten lead, and when cold, cut these two indentations, close to each other and close to the flat end, into the cylindrical part of the projectile, leaving the three remaining portions of the bullet strung, as it were, upon a common axis of solid lead. The bullet will then consist of two very flat truncated cones, pointing forward, and of the heavy solid point, all of which are solidly connected with each other. This bullet will answer as a compression bullet. The resistance against the explosion will be offered by the heavy fore part or point of the bullet; the head of the rear cone will be driven, by the force of the powder, into the base of the cone in front of it, whose head, again, will be driven into the rear end of the point; and thus the shot, being shortened and compressed in the direction of its length, will be made so much thicker that it closes on all sides to the bore and takes the rifling.

From this it is evident that the solid point is the principal portion of the compression bullet. The longer and heavier it is, the more resistance will it offer, and, consequently, the more certain will be the compressive effect of the explosion. So long as the calibre of the rifle is small, say rather less than the Enfield, it will be possible to make compression bullets not heavier in metal than expansion bullets; but with the calibre grows the surface of the base of the bullet, or in other words the surface exposed to the immediate action of the powder; and this is the cause why, with large calibres, compression bullets will always have to be too heavy to be of any use; otherwise the force of the explosion, by overcoming the resistance of the bullet, would throw it out of the barrel before it had time to become properly compressed. Large calibred, smooth-bore muskets may, therefore, be altered into rifles for expansion shot, but they will never do for compression bullets.

With small calibres and flat grooves, the compression system gives excellent results. The forward position of the centre of gravity is very favourable to a low trajectory. The compression bullet has all the advantages of the expansion system, as far as regards ease and rapidity of loading, and smallness of recoil. The bullet is solid, and can stand transport and rough usage well enough; its shape allows of its being pressed, instead of cast. The only drawback is that it requires a very small windage, of not more than about 0·01 of an inch, and a great regularity both in the size of the bores and that of the bullets, as evidently the compressive effect does not increase the circumference of the shot by near as much as the expansive effect; and thus, with a greater windage, or old barrels, it would be doubtful whether the bullet becomes compressed enough to take the rifling. But this small windage is no great objection, as many rifles with expansion shot have no greater windage (the Enfield, too, for instance, has only 0·01 of an inch), and there is now no difficulty in constructing both barrels and bullets of very exact and regular dimensions.

The Austrian army has adopted the compression bullet for the whole of the infantry. The calibre is small, 13·9 millimètres, or 0·546 of an inch (0·031 less than the Enfield); the barrel has four very flat grooves (an even number of grooves, though decidedly objectionable in expansion rifles, is found to answer better in compression rifles than an odd number), with one turn in about six feet six inches (almost the same as the Enfield). The bullet weighs about 480 grains (50 grains less than the Enfield), and the charge is 1-6th of its weight (with the Enfield, about 1-8th of the weight of the bullet). This arm stood its trial in the Italian campaign of 1859,[447] and the great number of French soldiers, and especially officers, who succumbed to it, testify to its excellence. It has a considerably lower trajectory than the Enfield, which is owing to the proportionally stronger charge, to the smaller calibre producing a more elongated shot, and, may be, to the action of the two ring-shaped indentations.

Saxony, Hanover, and one or two small German States have also adopted, for their light infantry, rifles from which compression bullets constructed on Lorenz's principle are fired.

In Switzerland, besides the sharpshooters' rifle mentioned before, there has been adopted a rifle of the same calibre (10·51 millimètres or 0·413 of an inch, 0·164 smaller than the Enfield) for compression shot. This rifle is used by the light companies of the infantry battalions. The bullet is on Lorenz's model, and the results given by this rifle, in lowness of trajectory, range and precision, class it second only to the Swiss sharpshooters' rifle above alluded to, whose bullet, forced home in the old fashion, has the flattest trajectory of any known rifle. At 500 yards, the Swiss compression bullet fired from this rifle gives a dangerous space of 130 yards! *

So far, there can be no doubt that the compression-system has given better results than the expansion system, as it has hitherto certainly produced the lower trajectory. It is, however, equally doubtless that this is not owing to the system in itself, but to other causes, among which the smallness of the calibre is the principal one. With an equally small calibre, the expansion bullet must produce as low a line of flight as its hitherto more successful competitor. This will soon be made evident. The rifles of the four States of South-Western Germany (Bavaria, &c.) have the same calibre as those of Austria, so that they may in case of need use Austrian ammunition, and *vice versa*. But, in adopting the same diameter of bore, they have all of them adopted expansion bullets; and the practice tables of both classes of shot will thus afford a fair test of the merits of either. If, as we expect, the expansion bullet will then give as good results as its competitor, it will deserve the preference; for—1st, it is more certain of taking the rifling, under any circumstances; 2nd, it may be made lighter, with the same bore, than compression shot; and, 3rd, it is less affected by the enlargement of the bore, which takes place in all gun-barrels after having been in use for a certain time.

VI

All the rifles which we have hitherto described, were muzzle-loaders. There have been, however, in former times, a great many kinds of fire-arms which were loaded at the breech. Breech-loading in cannon preceded muzzle-loading; and most old armouries will contain rifles and pistols two or three hundred years old, with a moveable breech, into which the charge could be introduced without being passed through the barrel by a ramrod. The great difficulty always was to join the moveable breech in

* By dangerous space is understood that portion of the flight of a bullet in which it is never higher than the height of a man, say six feet. Thus, in this instance, a shot aimed at the bottom of a target six feet high and 500 yards distant, would hit any object, six feet high, standing in the line of aim anywhere between 370 and 500 yards from the man firing. In other words, with the 500 yards sight, an error of 130 yards in judging the distance of the object may be made, and still the object will be hit if the line of aim was taken correctly.

such a way to the barrel that it could be easily separated and put on again, and that the mode of fixing it was solid enough to stand the explosion. With the deficient mechanical contrivances of those times, it was no wonder that these two requisites could not be combined. Either the parts fixing the breech on to the barrel were deficient in solidity and durability, or the process of unfixing and re-fixing it was fearfully slow. No wonder, then, that these arms were thrown aside, that muzzle-loading did its work quicker, and that the ramrod ruled supreme.

When, in modern times, military men and gun-makers were bent upon the construction of a fire-arm which should combine the quick and easy loading of the old musket with the range and precision of the rifle, it was natural that breech-loading should again receive attention. With a proper system of fixing the breech, all difficulties were overcome. The shot, a little larger in diameter than the bore, could then be placed, together with the charge, in the breech, and on being pushed forward by the explosion, would press itself through the bore, fill the grooves with its excess of lead, take the rifling, and exclude all possibility of windage. The only difficulty was the mode of fixing the breech. But what was impossible in the 16th and 17th centuries need not be despaired of now.

The great advantages of a breech-loader, supposing that difficulty overcome, are obvious. The time required for loading is considerably reduced. No drawing, turning round, and returning ramrod. One motion opens the breech, another brings the cartridge into its place, a third closes the breech again. A rapid fire of skirmishers, or a quick succession of volleys, so important in many decisive circumstances, are thus secured in a degree which no muzzle-loader can ever equal.

With all muzzle-loaders the art of loading is rendered difficult as soon as the soldier, in skirmishing, is kneeling or laid down behind some covering object. If he keeps behind his shelter he cannot hold his gun in a vertical position, and a great part of his charge will stick on to the sides of the bore while running down; if he holds his gun straight up he has to expose himself. With a breech-loader he can load in any position, even without turning his eye from the enemy, as he can load without looking at his gun. In line, he can load while advancing; pour in volley after volley during the advance, and still arrive upon the enemy with a gun always loaded. The bullet can be of the simplest construction, perfectly solid, and will never run any of the chances by which both compression and expansion shots miss taking the grooves, or experience other unpleasant accidents. The cleaning of the gun is uncommonly facilitated. The chamber, or place where the powder and bullet lie, which is the part always most exposed to fouling, is here laid completely open, and the barrel or tube, open at both ends, can be easily inspected and cleaned to perfection. The parts about the breech being necessarily very heavy, as otherwise they could not withstand the explosion, bring the centre of gravity of the rifle nearer the shoulder, and thereby facilitate a steady aim.

We have seen that the only difficulty consisted in the proper closing of the breech. There can be no doubt that this difficulty has now been fully overcome. The number of breech-loaders brought out during the last twenty years is wonderful, and some of them, at least, fulfil all reasonable expectations, both as to the efficiency and solidity of the breech-loading apparatus, and as to the ease and rapidity with which the breech can be fixed and unfixed. As arms of war, however, there are at present only three different systems in use.

The first is the gun now used by the infantry in Sweden and Norway. The breech-loading apparatus appears to be sufficiently handy and solid. The charge is fired by a percussion cap, both cock and piston being at the *under* side of the chamber piece. Of the practice made by this gun we have not been able to obtain any particulars.

The second is the revolver. The revolver, same as the rifle, is a very old German invention. Centuries ago, pistols with several barrels were made, provided with a revolving apparatus, which, after every shot, made a fresh barrel turn into the position required for the action of the lock upon it. Colonel Colt, in America, again took up the idea. He separated the chambers from the barrels, so that one barrel did for all the revolving chambers, thus making the arm breech-loading. As most of our readers will have handled one of these Colt's pistols, it will be unnecessary to describe them; besides, the complicated nature of the mechanism would render any detailed account impossible without diagrams. This arm is fired by percussion caps; and the round bullet, rather larger than the bore of the barrel, takes the grooves while being pressed through it. Colt's invention having become popular, a great number of revolving small-arms have been invented, but only Deane and Adams have really simplified and improved it as an arm of war. Still, the whole thing is extremely complicated, and applicable, for war purposes, to pistols only. But, with a few improvements, this revolver will become a necessity for all cavalry, and for sailors when boarding, while for artillery it will be far more useful than any carbine. As it is, its effects at close quarters are terrible; and not only have the American cavalry been provided with them, but they have also been introduced into the British, American, French, Russian, and other navies.

The Swedish gun, as well as the revolver, is fired from without by common percussion caps. The third class of breech-loaders, the much talked-of Prussian needle-gun, does entirely away with these too; the charge is fired from within.

The needle-gun was invented by a civilian, Mr. Dreyse, of Sömmerda, in Prussia. After having first invented the method of firing a gun by means of a needle suddenly penetrating an explosive substance fixed in the cartridge, he completed his invention, as early as 1835, by constructing a breech-loader, supplied with this needle-firing apparatus. The Prussian Government at once bought up the secret, and succeeded in keeping it to themselves up to 1848, when it became public; in the meantime they resolved upon giving this arm, in case of war, to all their infantry, and commenced manufacturing needle-guns. At present, the whole infantry of the line, and the greater portion of the Landwehr [448] are armed with it, while all the light cavalry are at this moment receiving breech-loading needle-carbines.

Of the breech-loading mechanism we will only say that it seems to be the simplest, handiest, and most durable of all those that have, so far, been proposed. It has now been tried for years, and the only fault that can be found with it is this, that it does not last quite so long, and will not bear quite so many rounds as the fixed breech of a muzzle-loader. But this is a fault which appears unavoidable in all breech-loaders, and the necessity of renewing, a little sooner than with the old arms, a few pieces of the breech, cannot in any way detract from the great merits of the arm.

The cartridge contains bullet, powder, and the explosive composition, and is placed, *unopened*, into the chamber, which is slightly wider than the rifled barrel. A simple motion of the hand closes the breech, and at the same time cocks the gun. There is, however, no cock outside. Behind the charge, in a hollow iron cylinder, lies a strong, pointed steel needle, acted upon by a spiral spring. The cocking of the gun consists in merely drawing back, compressing, and holding fast this spring; when the trigger is drawn, it sets the spring loose, which at once sends the needle quickly forward into the cartridge, which it pierces, instantaneously explodes the explosive composition, and thus fires the charge. Thus, loading and firing with this gun consists of five motions only: opening the breech, placing the cartridge in it, closing the breech, presenting, and firing. No wonder that, with such a gun, five well-aimed rounds can be fired in a minute.

The projectiles first used for the needle-gun had a very unfavourable shape, and, consequently, gave a very high trajectory. This defect has been very successfully remedied a short time ago. The shot is now much longer, and has the shape of an acorn taken from its cup. It is of considerably smaller diameter than that of the bore; its rear-end is embedded in a kind of cup, or bottom, of a soft material, so as to give it the requisite thickness. This cup sticks on to the bullet while in the barrel, takes the rifling, and thus gives the shot the lateral rotation, while at the same time it considerably diminishes friction in the barrel, and yet does away with all windage. The practice of the gun has been so much improved thereby, that the same sight, which formerly served for 600 paces (500 yards), now serves for 900 (750 yards); certainly an immense lowering of the trajectory.

Nothing is further from the truth than that the needle-gun is of a very complicated construction. The pieces composing the breech-loading apparatus and the needle-lock are not only far less numerous, but also far stronger than those composing a common percussion-lock, which yet nobody thinks too intricate for war and rough usage. Moreover, while the taking to pieces of a common percussion-lock is an affair requiring considerable time and sundry instruments, a needle-lock can be taken to pieces and refitted in an incredibly short time, and with no other instruments than the soldier's ten fingers. The only piece liable to break is the needle itself. But every soldier carries a reserve-needle, which he can fit to the lock at once, without having to take it to pieces, and even during an action. We are also informed that Mr. Dreyse has rendered the breaking of the needle a very unlikely thing, by an improvement in the lock, which makes the needle go back to its sheltered position as soon as it has done its work of exploding the charge.

The trajectory of the present Prussian needle-gun will be about the same as that of the Enfield rifle; its calibre is a little larger than that of the Enfield. With a reduction of calibre to that of the Austrian, or better still, the Swiss sharpshooters' rifle, there is no doubt that it would equal any of these arms in range, precision, and flatness of trajectory, while its other enormous advantages would remain to it. The breech-loading apparatus could even be made much stronger than at present, and the centre of gravity of the gun would be brought still nearer to the shoulder of the aiming soldier.

The introduction into an army of an arm capable of such rapid firing will necessarily produce many speculations as to what changes this will produce in tactics; especially among people so fond of speculating as the North Germans. There has been no end of controversies on the pretended revolution in tactics which the needle-gun was to produce. The majority of the military public, in Prussia, at last came to the result that no charge could be made against a battalion firing needle-gun volleys in rapid succession, and that consequently it was all up with the bayonet. If this foolish notion had prevailed, the needle-gun would have brought upon the Prussians many a severe defeat. Fortunately, the Italian war proved to all who could see, that the fire from modern rifles is not necessarily so very dangerous to a battalion charging with spirit, and Prince Frederick Charles of Prussia has taken occasion therefrom to remind his comrades that passive defence, if ever so well armed, is always sure of defeat. The tide of military opinion has turned. People again begin to see that men, and not muskets, must win battles; and if any real change in tactics will be made by the new gun, it will be a return to a greater use of deployed lines (where the ground admits of it), and even to that charge in line which, after having won most of the battles of Frederick the Great, had become almost unknown to the Prussian infantry.

VII

Having now passed in review the different systems upon which the various rifles, now in use in European armies, are constructed, we cannot take leave of our subject without saying a few words with respect to a rifle which, although not introduced into any service, enjoys a well-deserved popularity for its astonishing precision at long ranges. We mean, of course, the Whitworth rifle.

Mr. Whitworth, if we are not mistaken, claims as original two principles in the construction of his fire-arms—the hexagonal bore and the mechanical fit of the projectile in the bore. The bore, instead of having a circular, has a hexagonal section throughout, and a very strong pitch or turn, as is shown on the surface of one of the hexagonal bullets. The bullet itself is of a hard metal, fits the bore as nice as possible, and is not expected to alter its shape in consequence of the explosion, as its six corners make it follow the twist of the grooves with unerring certainty. To prevent windage, and to lubricate the bore, a cake or bottom of greasy matter is inserted between the powder and the charge; this grease melts from the heat of the explosion, while travelling, behind the bullet, towards the muzzle.

Now, in spite of the undeniably excellent results which Mr. Whitworth has obtained with his rifle, we believe that this principle is inferior to either that of expansion, or of compression, or of breech-loading with a bullet larger in diameter than the bore. That is to say, we believe that either a rifle for expansion-shot, or one for compression-shot, or one constructed on the system of the Prussian needle-gun, would beat a Whitworth rifle if the workmanship was equally good, the calibre equally small, and all other circumstances alike. Mr. Whitworth's mechanical fit may be ever so nice, he cannot make it as close as the change in the shape of the bullet during and after the explosion makes it. There is in his rifles with hard bullets always that which a rifle is meant radically to avoid, namely, windage and consequent escape of gas; even the melting grease cannot entirely do away with that, especially in a rifle which, from long use, has become a trifle larger in the bore. There is a very distinct limit to all mechanical fit in such a case, and that is, the fit must be loose enough to let the bullet go down easily and quickly, even after a couple of dozen rounds. The consequence is that these hexagonal bullets do fit but loosely, and although we do not know exactly what the amount of windage is, still the fact that they will go down quite easily without any grease and with a piece of paper wrapped round them, makes it probable that it is not much less (if less at all) than that of the Enfield bullet, which is the one-hundredth part of an inch. Mr. Whitworth, in contriving this rifle, seems to have had chiefly two leading ideas: firstly, to do away with all possibility of getting the grooves loaded; and, secondly, to do away with all the accidents which may prevent a cylindrical bullet from taking the rifling— because they prevent either expansion or compression taking place—by adapting the shape of the bore and that of the shot to each other beforehand. The obstruction of the grooves by particles of lead torn off from the bullet may occur in *all* rifles with soft leaden bullets; the accidents preventing a bullet from taking the grooves in the correct way may occur in either compression or expansion rifles, but not in breech-loaders on the Prussian principle. But neither of these inconveniences is so great that they cannot be overcome, and that, in order to avoid them, the first principle in rifle making should be sacrificed, viz., that the bullet takes the rifling without leaving any windage.

In saying so, we are backed by an excellent authority, namely by Mr. Whitworth himself. We are informed that Mr. Whitworth has dropped his principle of mechanical fit as far as his rifle is concerned, and certain it is that at present most people fire from his rifle not a hard, solid, hexagonal bullet, but a soft, leaden, cylindrical bullet. This bullet is hollowed out at its base similar to the Enfield bullet, but it has no plug; it is very long (the one 480 grains, three times as long as its diameter, the other, 530 grains, three and a half times its diameter), and *takes the rifling by the effect of the explosion.* Here, then, we have Mr. Whitworth's principle of *mechanical fit* entirely abandoned for that of *expansion,* and the Whitworth rifle turned into a subordinate species of the genus Minié quite as much as the Enfield ever was. Remains the hexagonal bore; and how will that answer for an expansion rifle?

The hexagonal bore has, of course, six grooves, and we have seen that an even number of grooves has been found to answer, for expansion bullets, not so well as an uneven one, as it is not desirable that two grooves should be diametrically opposite to each other. Then the grooves in most expansion-rifles are very shallow—in the Enfield, for instance, scarcely visible. In the hexagon the difference between the diameter of the inner circle (representing the bore at large) and that of the outer circle (drawn through the six corners) is about 2-13ths, or rather less than one-sixth part of the former; or, in other words, the lead has to expand nearly one-sixth of its diameter before it can properly close to the corners of the hexagonal bore. From this it would appear that the hexagonal bore, although exceedingly ingenious for the system of mechanical fit, is about the most unlikely to answer for the system of expansion.

Still it answers, as the results of almost every rifle contest prove. How is this possible, if Mr. Whitworth has abandoned the essential point of his principle, and now applies a principle for which his rifle is not adapted?

First of all, there is the excellence of the workmanship. It is well known that for accuracy in the most minute and even micrometrical details, Mr. Whitworth stands unrivalled. As his engineering tools, so are his rifles; perfect models in the construction of their detail. Look at the sight on the muzzle of his rifles, and at that of any other class! There is no comparison: and in rifles firing at 1,000 yards range, this is an immense advantage.

Secondly, and chiefly: the calibre of the Whitworth rifle is 0.451 of an inch minimum bore (what we have called the inner circle). The Enfield is 0.577; the Swiss sharpshooters' rifle, which we have more than once mentioned as giving the lowest trajectory known, is 0.413. Now, look at the difference in the shape of the bullet.

The Whitworth expansion bullet of 530 grains is about three-eighths of an inch longer than the Enfield bullet of the same weight; while the former is about three and a half times its own diameter in length, the latter is scarcely twice its own diameter. It is evident that a bullet of the same weight and with the same charge will cut better through the air, that is, give a lower trajectory if it is thin and long, than if it is short and thick. Then, the charge of the Enfield is 68 grains of powder; for the Whitworth, charges of 60, 70, and 80 grains are used, but we have been told by good shots who are in the habit of using this rifle that 80 grains are required to make the bullet expand well and give good results at long ranges. Thus we have a charge for the Whitworth fully one-sixth stronger than for the Enfield, and that charge would act better (even with equal weight), as it explodes in a more confined space and acts upon a far smaller surface of the bullet.

Here, then, we have another specimen of the immense advantage of a small bore, which gives a long, thin, bolt-shaped shot. Whoever of my readers has attentively followed our inquiries into the advantages of the various rifles, will have long since come to the conclusion that the shape of the bullet is of far more importance than the system on which either shot or rifle is designed; and that in order to have a portable soldier's bullet of the best shape, we must have a *small bore*. This is the lesson the Whitworth rifle again teaches us.

We may also learn from it that, with a small bore, the long, heavy point of the bullet offers resistance enough to allow the hollow tail end to expand with certainty, and without the assistance of a plug. The Whitworth bullet has but a small cavity at its base, and no plug; it has to expand at least three times as much as any other expansion bullet; and still, with 80 grains of powder (which the rifle stands without too much kicking), it does take the rifling quite sufficiently.

That Mr. Whitworth's rifle will ever become a weapon of war, we very much doubt; indeed, we think the hexagonal bore will soon go out altogether. If volunteers who had become practically convinced of the superior shooting of the Whitworth rifle as compared with the present Enfield, have proposed that they should be armed with the former, they have certainly far overshot the mark. We think it utterly unfair to compare the two species of arms. The Whitworth is an arm of luxury, which costs at least twice as much as the Enfield to produce. In its present state it is too delicate a weapon to be placed into every soldier's hands; but take, for instance, the delicate sight from the muzzle, replacing it by one fit for rough usage, and its accuracy at long ranges will be considerably diminished. To arm both army and volunteers with the Whitworth, one of two things must be done; either the calibre of the regulation small-arms must remain the same as now, and then a Whitworth, with the bore of the present Enfield, would give far worse results than the present Whitworth, or the bore must be reduced, say to that of the present Whitworth, and then it is probable that an Enfield with that reduced bore, on the making of which as much had been spent as on a Whitworth, would give as good or better results.

VIII

We conclude with a short recapitulation of the different systems of rifles now in use, and of the principles which we may consider as established with regard to this arm.

The different systems of rifles are as follows: —

1. The system of forcible loading, the tight fitting bullet and plaster being hammered down by strong blows of the ramrod. This is the oldest plan of making a bullet take the rifling. It has now been almost universally abandoned for arms of war; the principal and very remarkable exception being the new Swiss sharpshooters' rifle, which has a very small calibre and a long, bolt-shaped shot, and which gives, of all rifles now in use, the lowest trajectory. It is not intended for an arm for the mass of the infantry, but for select bodies only, and requires careful loading in order to give the highly favourable results which distinguish it above all other rifles now known.

2. The system of flattening the loose fitting bullet against some obstacle at the bottom of the breech (either the rim of a narrowing chamber—Delvigne—or a peg placed in the middle of the chamber—Thouvenin) and thus driving it into the grooves. This plan, for a time very generally favoured, is now becoming more or less superseded by the following systems. Let us observe, at the same time, that it requires a rather large calibre, as otherwise the chamber becomes too narrow.

3. The system of expansion, the loose fitting, elongated shot being hollowed out from the base, and the gas created by the explosion entering into the cavity and blowing it up, so to say, to a sufficient degree to make the bullet fit the bore and take the rifling. This system now is in general favour, and is still capable of great improvement, as has latterly been shown by the excellent

result which Mr. Whitworth obtained with his rifle since he adopted the principle of expansion.

4. The system of compression, in which the same result is obtained by providing the bullets with deep, circular indentations, which allow the explosive force, while opposed by the weight of the heavy fore part of the projectile, to compress it lengthways, and thereby give it the required increase of diameter. This plan, although evidently less safe than the expansion principle, has given excellent results with small calibres, as has been proved in Austria and Switzerland. Still, the compression-bullet, fired from the Swiss sharpshooters' rifle above alluded to, does not give quite as good results as the tight-fitting plaster bullet from the same arm.

5. The breech-loading system, which has advantages of its own over all other systems of rifles in the mode of loading and firing, offers, at the same time, the greatest certainty of the bullet taking the rifling, as the chamber and bullet may be made slightly larger than the rest of the bore, and thus the bullet cannot get to the muzzle without being pressed into the grooves. This system, indeed, appears to be destined gradually to supersede all other systems.

We do not count Mr. Whitworth's system of mechanical fit, as it has been abandoned as far, at least, as small arms are concerned; and with these alone we have now to do. If the various systems are classed according to their intrinsic merits, we should say that the breech-loading needle-gun stands highest; next, the expansion system; then the compression system. The two first systems may be considered to be superseded; for even if forcible loading, in Switzerland, so far gives better results, with the same calibre, than compression, we should not at all be inclined to give *to the system* the credit of these results without a very searching examination; and, besides, the Swiss sharpshooters' plaster bullet is acknowledged to be unfit for the mass of the infantry.

At the same time, we have seen that since the introduction of elongated bullets, the system on which either rifle or shot is constructed is of but secondary importance in obtaining great range, low trajectory, and accuracy of flight. As long as bullets were round, the system of rifling was of greater importance, for then all bullets were met by the resistance of the air under nearly equal circumstances, and the influences of a stronger pitch of rifling, of deeper or more numerous grooves, &c., were comparatively far more important than now. But with elongated shot, a new element appears on the ground. The bullet may be made longer or shorter, within pretty wide limits, and now the question is which shape of bullet is most advantageous? On theoretical grounds it is clear that the same mass of lead, started with the same initial velocity, will better retain that velocity if its shape is long and thin, than if it is short and thick; supposing always that the lateral rotation which a rifle would give it, is there to prevent its going head over heels. The resistance of the air is the retarding force; it gradually diminishes the original velocity imparted to the bullet by the powder, and thus gives the ever-increasing force of gravity, so to speak, a greater hold upon the projectile. The initial velocity depends upon the charge, and in some degree upon the construction of the arm; this we may, therefore, consider to be fixed; the force of gravity is also fixed, and a given quantity; remains, as variable, the shape of the bullet to enable it to dart through the air with the least amount of resistance; and to evade atmospheric resistance, as we have said, a long and thin shot is far better fitted than a short and thick one of the same weight.

Now, the maximum weight of the bullet for military purposes is also a given quantity. A man must be able to carry, at least, sixty rounds over and above his arms and accoutrements. To produce the best-shaped bullet, therefore, out of this given weight of lead (say 530 grains), the length must be increased and the thickness diminished;—in other words, the bore of the rifle must be made less. Up to a certain point this will hold good without exception. Look at the 530 grains in the Enfield and at the same weight in the Whitworth bullet; a single glance explains why the latter has a so much lower trajectory (that is, retains its initial velocity so much better), and will, therefore, hit a target at a 1,000 yards with ease, while the Enfield cannot be trusted at that distance. And yet, the two are both expansion bullets, and the general construction of the Whitworth is certainly not the best adapted for expansion. Or look at the Swiss sharpshooters' rifle, with a bore still smaller than the Whitworth, and giving still better results and a still lower trajectory, be its bullet rammed home with a plaster, or let down loosely and compressed by the explosion. Or take the Prussian needle-gun; by reducing the diameter and increasing the length of the bullet, and guiding it in the wide bore by a bottom or wad, the same sight which formerly marked the 600 yards' range, now carries the bullet to 900 yards. We shall, therefore, be pretty safe in considering it as an established fact that, in a general way, the efficiency of rifles, no matter on what system they are constructed, will be in the inverse ratio of the diameters of their bores. The smaller the bore, the better the rifle, and *vice versa*.

With these observations we take leave of a subject which may have appeared rather dry to many of our readers. Still its importance is very great. No intelligent soldier ought to be ignorant of the principles on which his arms are constructed, and are expected to act. What we have attempted to expose here, the non-commissioned officers of most continental armies are expected to know; and surely, the majority of the volunteers, "the intelligence of the country," ought to be as well up in the knowledge of their fire-arms as they!

Written between the end of October 1860 and the first half of January 1861

First published in *The Volunteer Journal, for Lancashire and Cheshire*, Nos. 9, 11, 14, 15, 17, 18, 19, 20, November 3 and 17, December 8, 15 and 29, 1860, January 5, 12 and 19, 1861; reprinted in the collection *Essays Addressed to Volunteers*, London-Manchester, 1861

Reproduced from the collection, checked with the text in *The Volunteer Journal*

VOLUNTEER ENGINEERS:
THEIR VALUE AND SPHERE OF ACTION [449]

The volunteer army has had, for some time, its infantry and artillery in considerable numbers; it has had its small complement of cavalry too; and now, the last branch of military service, the engineering branch, is gradually being taken up. The subject of volunteer engineers is at present very widely discussed, and it deserves the attention it enjoys. The corps of Royal Engineers is too weak already for the numerous duties it has to perform at home and in the colonies. What will it be in case of a war, and anticipated invasion? Then the numerous fortifications which now are in course of erection, and by means of which the dockyards are being surrounded by vast entrenched camps, will require a considerable number of engineer officers and men for their garrison; and the army in the field, swelled to twice or three times its present number by the addition of the volunteers, will also be in want of a certain complement of engineers, to give it its full liberty of action before the enemy. Unless the corps of Royal Engineers is considerably increased, the duties of this branch of the service must either be imperfectly performed, or they must be performed by volunteers trained for them beforehand.

The number of engineers to be attached to an army in the field is, after all, not very numerous; three or four companies to an army corps of two divisions (16 to 24 battalions of infantry, with a due proportion of cavalry and artillery) would be quite sufficient. Supposing a field-army of 40,000 of the line, 20,000 militia, and

100,000 volunteers, in all 160,000, or 200 battalions, this would give from eight to ten corps, and require about thirty companies of engineers. We will suppose ten companies to be furnished by the Royal Engineers; this would leave twenty companies to be supplied by the volunteer movement. About the same number more volunteer engineers would be sufficient to assist the royals in the defence of the fortified dockyards; so that something like forty companies of volunteer engineers would appear an ample complement for the present strength of the volunteer infantry and artillery. If the number of volunteers should so far increase as to enable them to appear in the field, after deducting garrisons, with more than 100,000 men, one additional engineer for every hundred additional riflemen would be enough; giving 200 engineers (or three companies) for every army corps of 20,000 men.

For the present, then, forty companies, or about 3,000 effectives, would be the maximum engineer force which it might be advisable to create. And it will require a great deal of energy to make them engineers not only in name, but also in reality. We find already now that among artillery volunteers a great deal of time is devoted to company and battalion drill, carbine in hand, although all this work serves for parade purposes only, and will never avail them one jot on active service, be it with field-guns, or be it in fortifications. And we are afraid it will be the same with the engineers. They should, above all things, bear in mind that every hour spent on company drill, beyond what is required to give them a military bearing, a ready and instantaneous obedience to orders, and the capability of moving in good order on a march, is an hour lost to them; that they have quite different things to learn, and that on these, and not on steady marching past, depends their efficiency. They will have to acquaint themselves— men as well as officers—with the elements of field and permanent fortification; they will have to practise the construction of trenches and batteries, and the making and repairing of roads. If means can be found, they will have to construct military bridges, and even to dig mines. Some of these branches, it is to be feared, can only be taught theoretically, as fortresses in England are scarce, and pontoons also; and not every volunteer can be expected to go to Portsmouth or Chatham to study fortification or assist at the laying down of a pontoon bridge. But there are others which it is in the power of every company to practise. If there was a company of engineers formed here in Manchester, we could show them plenty of lanes in as bad a state as any to be passed by a column in war, and where those whom it concerns would very likely be only too glad to allow them to practise road-making to their heart's content. It would not be very difficult for them to find a plot of land on which they could construct a few field-works, dig trenches, and erect batteries; especially as such a plot of land would offer both the artillery and rifle volunteers an opportunity of practising such parts of their service as they could otherwise not be made to go through. They might even find spots where they would be allowed occasionally to throw a small bridge of *chevalets*[a] over one of those high-banked rivers of our neighbourhood, which offer such capital facilities for this kind of bridges wherever their bottom is firm. Such things, and many others of the same kind, should constitute their chief practice; company drill should be gone through rapidly at first, and only taken up again when the corps have got on fairly with their real engineering business; then, in the second winter, the nights may be used for drill with advantage. But if the engineers make it a point, from the beginning, to compete with the rifles in the style of marching past, and in battalion evolutions, to the detriment of their specific education; if the attention of the officers is directed more towards the duties of an infantry officer than to professional education— then the volunteer engineers may depend upon it that in a campaign they will far oftener be used as infantry than as engineers.

There will be little difficulty in finding very efficient officers, if they are selected from the only class fit for the post—the civil engineers. A few months' theoretical study, and an occasional journey to Chatham, Portsmouth, or Aldershot, will soon make them conversant with most branches of military engineering, and the military education of their companies will help them on. They will learn by teaching. Their own profession compels them to know all the principles of military engineering, and as they *must* be very intelligent and well-informed men, the application of these principles to military subjects will give them but little difficulty.

We have read a statement in the *Army and Navy Gazette*[b] respecting some immense military engineering organisation, which is to comprise all the lines of railway in the country, and to

---

a Piers.— *Ed.*

b "The Transport Service", *The Army and Navy Gazette,* November 10, 1860.— *Ed.*

promise vast results in case of an invasion.[a] The shape in which this plan is presented before the public is excessively vague; so far we do not see the immense advantages that are ascribed to it, and rather think that two different things have been mixed up together. No doubt it is of the highest importance to study the strategical bearings of every single line of railway in the kingdom, as well as of the whole network of railways combined. This is so important that we should consider it a grave delinquency if it had not been done long ago, and if there were not now lying in the archives of the Horse Guards,[450] as well as of the various district commanders, very extensive papers embodying the results of these studies. But this is the duty of the staff, and not of the engineers. As to forming the engineers, firemen, platelayers, and navvies of every railway line into a corps of military engineers, we do not see the great advantage of this. These men have already, so to say, a military organisation, and are under stricter discipline than any volunteer corps in the country. What they are expected to do in their quality as volunteer engineers, they are quite as capable of doing in their present capacity. And as in time of war their presence at their present posts would be far more indispensable than now, there can be no earthly use in training them to special branches of military engineering.

These remarks apply to the plan only as far as it has been made public; if it should turn out, hereafter, that it contains other features, we must, of course, reserve our opinion. We may be permitted, however, to point out another advantage to which the vast amount of engineering intelligence in this country may be turned. Most armies have, besides the officers connected with the Sappers and Miners, a number of engineer officers unattached to any companies, and doing special duties. Why not give the civil engineers of England a chance of preparing themselves for this service? The College of Civil Engineers might be made the means to effect this purpose. A few courses of lectures on military engineering, and a short practical course with a company of engineers would do all that is required; an examination, strictly confined to military subjects, and which in this case would be absolutely necessary, might be made the principal test of admission to the Corps of Unattached Volunteer Engineer Officers; the Government to have, of course, the power to reject candidates

---

[a] *The Volunteer Journal* has here: "The principal features of the plan are reproduced in last week's *Volunteer Journal*." The reference is to the article "A Volunteer Engineer Corps" in issue No. 11 for November 17, 1860.— *Ed.*

considered ineligible. Such officers would be of great service, for it is upon the intelligence of the officers that in this case everything depends; and on an emergency they would better get on with a few volunteer riflemen or artillerymen, placed under their command for the execution of some engineering work, than regular engineer officers with a section or two of infantry of the line told off to them for the same kind of duty.

Written between November 19 and December 1, 1860

First published in *The Volunteer Journal, for Lancashire and Cheshire*, Nos. 12 and 13, November 24 and December 1, 1860; reprinted in the collection *Essays Addressed to Volunteers*, London-Manchester, 1861

Reproduced from the collection, checked with the text in *The Volunteer Journal*

FRENCH ARMAMENTS[451]

According to the *Almanach de Gotha*,[a] which is as good an authority on the subject as can be found anywhere, the war footing of the French army for 1860-61 has been fixed as follows:—

1. *Infantry: Guards*—12 battalions of Grenadiers, 16 ditto of Voltigeurs, 2 of Zouaves, 1 of Chasseurs; in all 31 battalions. *Line*—103 regiments of 4 battalions, in all 412 battalions; 3 regiments of *Zouaves*, 2 of the *Foreign Legion*, 3 of *Turcos* (or native Algerian rifles), at 3 battalions each, 24 battalions; *Chasseurs*, 20 battalions; *Zephyrs*, or light African (disciplinary) battalions, 3; *Pompiers* (firemen) of Paris, 1 battalion. In all 491 battalions; or in time of war ....

<table>
<tr><td></td><td>Men.</td></tr>
<tr><td>time of war</td><td>515,037</td></tr>
<tr><td>2. Cavalry: 6 regiments, or 37 squadrons, of the Guard; 58 regiments, or 358 squadrons, of the Line; in all 395 squadrons</td><td>100,221</td></tr>
<tr><td>3. Artillery: 22 regiments—227 batteries (of which 146 are batteries of 6 guns—876 guns are field artillery)</td><td>66,007</td></tr>
<tr><td>4. Engineers</td><td>15,443</td></tr>
<tr><td>5. Train: Sanitary troops, commissariat</td><td>24,561</td></tr>
<tr><td>6. Gendarmes</td><td>24,172</td></tr>
<tr><td>7. Staffs, invalids, military schools, &c.</td><td>17,324</td></tr>
<tr><td>Total</td><td>762,765</td></tr>
</table>

---

[a] "Armée française en 1860-1861", *Almanach de Gotha. Annuaire diplomatique et statistique pour l'année 1861*, pp. 507-10.— *Ed.*

This is the war footing. The peace establishment is as follows:—

Infantry	255,248
Cavalry	61,023
Artillery	39,023
Engineers	7,467
Train, &c.	11,489
Gendarmes, invalids, &c.	41,496
	415,746 men.

In January, 1859, a short time before the Italian war [152] broke out, the *Constitutionnel* published an official *status* of the French army, showing a war establishment of 568,000 men, with a peace establishment of 433,000.[a] How, then, has it been possible within two years to augment the war footing by 200,000 men, while the peace footing has been actually reduced?

Again, the annual contingent of able-bodied young men disposable for the army is about 160,000. Of these, under Louis Philippe, between 40,000 and 60,000 were actually enrolled, and found sufficient to keep the army up, in spite of the losses in Algeria. Later on, 80,000, and even 100,000 and more, have been enrolled; the Empire which is peace [b] consumed twice the amount of food for powder than the constitutional monarchy or the republic had required. The time of service is seven years; but, even supposing that of late 100,000 men had been enrolled annually (which is above the average), this would, for seven years, give 700,000 men only; and deducting from these the losses during campaigns and from other causes, there would be scarcely as many as 600,000 men. How, then, are the remaining 163,000 found?

The answer to these two questions is comprised in the late acts of the French Emperor. Before the Italian war, the regiments, hitherto formed in three battalions of eight companies each, are formed in four battalions of six companies each; thus, by merely changing the distribution of the 24 companies of a regiment, four battalions are got instead of three. The size of a battalion has a maximum; above 1,000 men it becomes too strong for one man to command it with his voice, and too unwieldy for quick manoeuvr-

---

[a] See L. Boniface, "Paris, 29 janvier", *Le Constitutionnel*, No. 30, January 30, 1859.— *Ed.*

[b] A reference to Louis Bonaparte's words "L'Empire c'est la paix" ("The Empire is peace") from his speech made at Bordeaux on October 9, 1852.— *Ed.*

ing. But the size of a company is far more variable; whether 100 or 250 men, is a matter of choice, not of necessity. By forming the fourth battalions in the way indicated, with the same number of officers and sergeants, the regiment was enabled to muster 4,000 instead of 3,000 strong, as soon as the men were found. During the war, the regiments went out in the strength of three fighting battalions, the fourth forming the depôt. Thus, in the fourth battalions of the 100 regiments of the line, the means were found to place 100,000 men more than the old *cadres* could employ. After the war, the fourth battalions were dissolved, but they have been reinstated again a short time ago. Three more infantry regiments (101st, 102nd, 103rd) have been formed, offering room for 17,000 men more. These new formations account for 112,000 men; and the 51,000 men which remain to be accounted for may constitute the figure to which the army in January, 1859, in consequence of previous losses, was short of its full war complement. This would show that there are *cadres* now, in the French infantry alone, sufficient to organise the enormous number of men stated above, without any recourse to new formations. But where are the men to be found who are to fill up these *cadres*?

The regular enrolments of the last seven years will have left on the rolls from 550,000 to 600,000 men. The annual contingent available is about 160,000 men. One year's levy would leave but 50,000 men short, in the worst case; and in case of need, there are the young men who, during the last six years, have been entirely liberated from service by drawing favourable lots at the conscription.[453] These might be made available to the tune of some 300,000 at least, but as long habit has made such men consider themselves freed for ever from the obligation to serve, as they are partly married, partly scattered all over the country and hard to find, such a measure would be both unpopular and difficult to carry out.

How, then, does Louis Napoleon make up for the deficiency? By introducing a modification of the Prussian reserve system. Of the 160,000 men available every year, a portion, say one-half, is taken to fill up the vacancies of the standing army. The remainder is enrolled on the reserve list; they are embodied and drilled, the first year two months, the second and third years one month each; they remain liable to be called out for seven years in all, same as the line. Now, we have some reason to believe that if the military surgeons are not over strict in passing the men, and in time of war they get often exceedingly lenient, the annual contingent of

160,000 able-bodied men might, by a stretch, be raised to 200,000; but that we will for the present leave out of the question. In seven years, 160,000 men annually would give an army of 1,112,000 men, and deducting a good round number for losses, there would be fully *one million of soldiers.* Thus we see that by the new reserve system lately introduced, Louis Napoleon's troops will in a couple of years outgrow the organised bodies ready to receive them. That eventuality, however, is also provided for. In future the four battalions of a regiment are *all* to be fighting battalions; a fifth battalion is now forming under the name of battalion of instruction, and under the pretext of drilling the men put on the reserve list. This new organisation finds room for 103,000 men more, raising the number of men which can be usefully employed by existing corps or cadres to 863,000 men.

Not satisfied with this, the French Government propose to form one more regiment of guards and 17 of infantry of the line; these 18 regiments represent 90 more battalions, or 90,000 men.

Thus, before this year is out, we are sure, from what is known even now, that the French army will be so organised as to be able to stow away comfortably in its battalions, squadrons, and batteries, not less than 953,000 men. And as to finding the men to fill up these organisations, we have seen that up to 700,000 men can be found even this year, without falling back upon men liberated in former years; but, if the universal liability to service, either in the line or reserve, be once acknowledged, it will be easy enough to apply the same principle to the men liberated in the last six years (Napoleon has done the same over and over again in his time); and then there can be no doubt that the full 953,000 men will be soon together.

Here, then, we have the man who unintentionally caused the volunteer movement, responding to it by quietly and noiselessly organising an army of a million of men, and at the same time laying down twenty iron-cased frigates on the stocks, maybe to escort a fraction of that army across the Channel.

Written at the end of January 1861   Reproduced from the journal

First published in *The Volunteer Journal,*
for Lancashire and Cheshire, No. 22, February 2, 1861

ON THE MORAL ELEMENT IN FIGHTING.
BY MARSHAL BUGEAUD [454]

[*The Volunteer Journal, for Lancashire and Cheshire*, No. 23, February 9, 1861]

The following lines are translated from the instructions which the then Colonel Bugeaud,[a] of the 56th French regiment, wrote down for his officers. It is, without any exception, the best thing the Marshal has ever written. It lays down, with a masculine energy unsurpassed in the military literature of any country, and with a clearness such as only long experience in war can give, those principles of infantry-fighting which even now are invariably acted upon by the French; and which, so far, have given them the victory over armies which, from long habits of peace, appear to have trusted more to scientific tactics than to arousing all the moral energies of the soldiers. These principles are not new, nor are they in any way exclusively French; but they are here grouped well together, and expressed in fine manly language. They do not in any way supersede the science of tactics, but they form a very necessary complement to it; and they are, besides, most of them so self-evident, and require so little military science to be understood, that they will be perfectly intelligible to the majority of the volunteers.

Gentlemen,—The art of engaging a body of troops has a powerful influence on the issue of a combat; by it, good dispositions are crowned with success, and defective ones deprived of their worst consequences. There is between troops of highly developed moral faculties, energetically conducted, penetrated with the real principles of fighting, and troops constituted and instructed as most European troops are, the same difference which exists between adults and children. That is a

---

[a] A reference to the section "Principes phisiques et moraux du combat de l'infanterie" of the book *Aperçus sur quelques détails de la guerre.—Ed.*

truth of which I have been convinced by twenty engagements. You will recognise it like myself, I hope, and you will assist me, with all the means in your power, to raise the 56th to that high elevation of both soul and instruction that no imperial or royal guards in the world could resist us for five minutes on ground equally fair to both parties.

Most of you, gentlemen, have seen engagements of infantry which amounted merely to a timid exchange of fire, at very long range, by troops placed parallel to each other.

Either party appeared to expect victory from chance, or from the fright which its bullets might cause to their opponents. Millions of cartridges were fired away without any other results but killed and wounded on either side, until some circumstance or other, mostly independent of the troops engaged, determined the retreat of one of the two lines. Men who have thus exhausted their fire and seen their ranks decimated, are but little disposed to new efforts, and easily put to flight by fresh troops, acting upon better principles.

That is not the way of fighting of solidly instructed infantry. We shall now try to establish those principles which must give us an immense superiority over all infantries of Europe.

These principles, gentlemen, are not mere bookworm speculations; experience has made me adopt them ever since the commencement of the Peninsular war, in 1808, and they have always ensured success to me, against the Spaniards, the English,* and the Austrians. I hope you will adopt them, because they are in harmony with what you must have yourselves observed in the engagements where you were present; you will do your best to penetrate your subordinates with them; and when these principles are in the very soul of the whole regiment, from the drummers to the colonel, the 56th may consider itself invincible; it may be defeated by the re-union of several arms acting at once against it, but never by infantry alone, though that infantry should far outnumber its strength.

Fighting has its moral and its physical part. The first appears to me the most essential; but let us begin by treating of the second.

To fire at long range is the type of bad infantry; good infantry saves its fire. It is because this fire constitutes its greatest strength that an infantry should not throw it away, and should be taught to aim with the greatest accuracy. If the moment for firing has not arrived, keep yourself out of range, or hide your troops. When that moment arrives, march on to meet your enemy with an energy and coolness that permit you to execute anything. If your opponent, against all probability, should stand firm and allow you to come very near him without firing himself, then you give the first volley, and take good care that your men always load two bullets to a round. I have owed, more than once, success to the use of the two bullets. In the heat of action I might forget to order it, but you will think of it; I attach great importance to this. With that cool determination, and with this fire of two bullets to the round, you will seldom have to fire a second volley, whether in attacking a position or in repelling a body of troops charging you.

Whoever knows a little about war, will know that it cannot be otherwise. If you arrive close upon your enemy with loaded arms, when they have exhausted their fire, how could they resist? Their moral courage is terror-struck by the fear of a volley at close quarters, which cannot but be terrible, and they will give way. Then

---

* Marshal Bugeaud commanded, as major or lieutenant-colonel, a battalion in the army of Marshal Suchet, in Catalonia. It is well known that this portion of the French force in Spain was the most successful, and maintained its position longer than any other.

give your volley, enter into their ranks, and *make prisoners,* which is better than killing; *while you kill one man with the bayonet, you might have taken six prisoners.* These struggles cost the conqueror but little; you lose a few men in advancing, but as soon as you have closed upon and upset your enemy, you don't lose a man. This system of tactics, gentlemen, will guarantee to you the victory, and if the whole army were penetrated with them, it would conquer, no matter how bad the general dispositions might be. These dispositions are not within our province; but when we are told the point where we are to strike, we must strike so as to crush everything before us. That was the tactics of Duguay-Trouin, and this mode of fighting contributed more than all his other talents towards forcing his brilliant reputation. He arrived close upon the enemy's vessel with all his guns loaded, and his men laid down on deck; as soon as he touched his opponent, his men sprang up, and swept the hostile decks by a superior fire, which made boarding an easy matter.

[*The Volunteer Journal, for Lancashire and Cheshire,* No. 24, February 16, 1861]

Besides the above-mentioned, we must employ still other means, for we ought to have as many odds as possible in our favour. A good use of skirmishers will be a powerful auxiliary; their actions must always precede that of the masses, be it for attack or for defence. When you attack, they will find out such accidents of ground as the eye could not reconnoitre from a distance; they will throw upon the enemy's ranks a shower of bullets which will disturb them, and prevent them from aiming with precision upon the line which advances without firing. They will have to be directed as much as possible towards those points where the decisive combat will *not* take place. If, however, they should be required to act in front of the attacking line, they will finally withdraw towards its flanks, in order not to impede its action, and then attempt to gain the flanks of the enemy, in order to demoralise him and to make prisoners, or else they will retire by the intervals of the battalions, or lay down flat on the ground, in order to let the line pass over them.

The fire of skirmishers should no more be thrown away than that of lines. It is not a question of merely exchanging bullets: these bullets should contribute towards success. To this effect, a moment before the attack of the line, the skirmishers will be shown the positions they will have to occupy, before they commence firing; and as soon as they have commenced firing, the line will advance to the attack. You will feel that if the skirmishers were left to themselves for any length of time very near the enemy's forces, they would be driven back, and the end in view would not be attained; you would have to reinforce them in order to repel the enemy's skirmishers, who had driven them in, and that would be a serious inconvenience. It is, then, of the highest importance never to engage skirmishers but *apropos;* and the proper moment will almost invariably be that of the attack. In case the enemy incommodes us before that moment by his skirmishers, we shall drive them in by sudden and short, but rough, attacks. You will be sure of making them give way if, instead of opposing to them a parallel line of skirmishers, as is generally done, you out-flank and turn them; or if you pierce their line by a company running at them in a cluster. This is the consequence of a moral effect, which I try to explain to myself in this way: —

Skirmishers cannot have that moral force, that sense of cohesion, which results from the contact of elbow to elbow, and from the unity of command. Every skirmisher, to a certain degree, commands himself, and consults his own forces only. He sees a numerous cluster of men running at him; he is too weak to resist; he gives way. His neighbours, right and left, do the same; and are followed again by their neighbours, who run from unconscious imitation, or because they fear to be cut off; they rally farther to the rear, in order to recommence firing.

Our charging company will not return this fire; it will either retire again, or take shelter behind some accident of ground. *Nothing is so stupid, so damaging, as these everlasting engagements of skirmishers, which lead to nothing at all; you use up your men and your ammunition, without advancing matters, and often, at the decisive moment, you lack the means which you have thus squandered.* I insist upon this because waste of ammunition is the greatest fault of our infantry, as well as of all others. Many times, after half-an-hour's firing, and before anything is decided, you have everywhere the cry that cartridges are running short; men leave the ranks to get some, and that often is the cause of defeat. Sixty rounds per man should suffice for the greatest battle. In 1815, the 14th of the line, then commanded by Colonel Bugeaud, was under fire in the Alps for eight hours, and kept one-third of its cartridges. The enemy fired all the eight hours long, but the 14th never replied but by single volleys, and that only when the Austrians, who attacked us, were close to its position. *The volley was invariably, and at once, followed by a charge with the bayonet,* which settled that attack, without further skirmishing and stray firing. Both parties returned to their previous positions, which were very near each other; the Austrians continued to fire, but the 14th abstained until again attacked.

This example has also for its object to make you appreciate the true principles of fighting when defending a position, viz., always to attack, yourself, at the last decisive moment; but here, as much as when you are attacking, there is another extremely effective means to determine the victory, and that is, to avoid, as much as ever possible, parallel fighting, which equalises advantages in a certain manner, and cannot be decided in our favour except by moral superiority, and our better-fed fire of two bullets to each round. We shall, therefore, at the decisive moment, try to envelop the flanks of the enemy. When on the defensive, in broken ground, this is easy enough. As soon as the enemy's attack is well developed, we send a portion of our reserves, in column, towards the flanks of the position, and at the decisive moment these troops show themselves, advance, and deploy, so as to take the enemy in flank; we detach skirmishers towards his rear, and as soon as each battalion or wing has deployed, it charges at once, so as not to give the enemy the time to ward off the attack. Charged at the same time both in front and flank, he ought to be quickly defeated.

The same means may be employed when we are attacking. Two small columns would march behind the two flanks of the deployed line, and, when arrived near enough to the enemy, would form in line, too, so as to prolong it and form a sort of crescent, overlapping and embracing his line; or, if you have not troops enough for that purpose, the flank battalions of the advancing line might wheel into open column while on the march, gain the flanks of the enemy, re-form in line, and charge, the intervals left by them being filled up by skirmishers. This movement appears to me very well adapted for the purpose, and very practicable, if the commander of the battalion knows well how to judge his distance, so as to commence it neither too soon nor too late. Of course, if darkness or broken ground permit you to gain, unseen, the flanks of your enemy, that is to be taken advantage of in preference.

When retreating, be particularly sparing of your ammunition. While you defend yourself by firing, you lose ground—you do not get any nearer to your destination. There are even occasions *when you will have to run* in order to get out of your opponent's reach. This is often the only means of escaping destruction. How many bodies of troops have been annihilated for having made a slow and measured retreat, which was falsely called methodical? The only sensible method is to do everything to attain your end: on a retreat, this end is to get quickly out of reach of your opponent, because circumstances do not any longer permit you to fight; but your end can never be to involve yourselves, through a misunderstood feeling of honour, into a struggle which cannot but be disastrous, and from which you often will find it impossible again to disentangle yourselves. In this case, flight is the only methodical course of proceeding. There is an example of it from the history of one of our greatest modern captains.

During Marshal Masséna's retreat from Portugal, Marshal Ney was ordered to keep back the English with the rear-guard, in order to give the baggage-train time to pass a *défilé*. He performed this task with his usual energy; but the English army receiving reinforcement after reinforcement, the position was no longer tenable. On leaving it he would have to descend into a narrow valley, and to re-ascend another hill-side beyond it; during this time his troops would have remained under the fire of the enemy, who, of course, would at once have occupied the abandoned position. The marshal thought that a slow retreat would subject him to great losses; he therefore ordered the colours of the battalions, the orderlies of the staff, &c., to mark out on the hill to the rear a new line to be traced by officers of the staff. No sooner was this done than he sent his battalions, at a run, across the valley to fill up this line, which was thus re-formed as if by enchantment. Without this admirable precaution we should have lost many men, and probably the affair would have ended in our being routed. At the same time, it is evident that this manoeuvre is inapplicable wherever you have to fear any cavalry; in such a case, you will have to get on as quick as you can, all the while maintaining a respectable order in your ranks.

I have often heard it said by pretended tacticians that a retreat ought to be made at slow time; this principle has always appeared to me false. No doubt there are occasions when a portion of the army will have to stop the enemy, in order to give the remainder time to get out of the way; but, then, you will not have to march at slow time, you will have to fight, and very often to advance and charge, in order to restore the moral courage of your men, and to diminish that of the enemy. But when that portion of the army has performed its part, when the end is gained, when the growing accumulation of the enemy's forces render it impossible to that portion to fight on, then it will soon have to retire as quick as circumstances will permit.

We shall, therefore, learn to run away methodically, though in disorder, and to reform our ranks promptly; to form in line at the double, on one of the flanks of the enemy, in inverted or correct order; and always to aim with the utmost precision.

[The Volunteer Journal, for Lancashire
and Cheshire, No. 26, March 2, 1861]

Moral force has always appeared to me to be superior to physical force. You prepare this moral force by elevating the soul of the soldier, by imparting to him a love of glory, a feeling for the honour of his regiment, and especially in developing that patriotism, the germ of which lies in every man's breast. With men thus trained, you can with ease perform great things, if you have known how to gain their confidence. To obtain that, you will have to fulfil towards them all your duties, to make them your friends, to talk often with them on war and warfare, and to prove to them that you are capable of leading them well. Under fire, you will have to give to them a brilliant example of courage and coolness.

You should pay every attention to whatever circumstance may tend to raise the moral courage of your own men and to weaken that of your opponents. It is for this purpose that *the 56th will never permit itself to be attacked; it will always, at the decisive moment, take the initiative of the fight, and charge.* For the defensive, it will place itself in rear of the line on which it intends the struggle to take place, in order to advance to it at the decisive moment. In such a case you see the power of moral influences; every physical advantage is in favour of a troop posted in a locality strong both by nature and art; and yet, this posted troop will almost invariably be dislodged if it confines itself to a stand-still fight. Morally as well as physically, it may be said that *a good defensive must always be carried on offensively.* Offensive movements on the flanks and rear of your opponent, tell almost invariably; even if executed by a mere handful of men, they singularly affect the *morale* of the enemy. For these movements there can be no better manoeuvre than the formation of close columns in rear of the flanks of the charging line, which columns deploy and envelop the enemy as soon as you come to close quarters. And because these manoeuvres are so very telling, you will have to put your own men on their guard against them, by pointing out to them that they themselves may be attacked in this manner, and by showing to them how this will be guarded against. You will also have to tell them that cries of alarm may be raised in the rear, such as—"We are surrounded," "We are cut off," &c.; you will inform them that the supernumeraries, and besides them, sections of picked men to the rear, have strict orders to bayonet or shoot down any emissaries of the enemy or any bad soldier of our own who should raise such cries; that such hostile detachments as might venture to threaten our flanks and rear, will soon be disposed of by our reserves, and that your own men, for the moment, have nothing to think of but how to conquer that enemy who is straight before them.

By raising the *morale* of your men, you will further make sure that your ranks will not be thinned by men pretending to look after the wounded. When the fight is over, if we are at hand, we shall take every care of them; but our first task and our first duty is to conquer. The wounded of a victorious army are never abandoned; those of a beaten army are made to undergo a thousand evils. To occupy ourselves with the wounded during battle is therefore false mercy, and generally a mere cloak for cowardice. The officers here again will have to give the example of devotion in repelling, if wounded, any attentions offered to them by soldiers who ought to fight.

At the battle of Austerlitz,[455] a great number of our wounded privates were seen sending back to their battalions their comrades who offered to take them to the dressing places.

One of the best means of maintaining the moral courage of the soldier is the brilliant conduct of the officers, in every phase of an engagement. Is the regiment halted under the fire of artillery? they should walk up and down proudly in front of their men, and keep their spirits up by merry talk or by words of energy. Is it time to rush upon the enemy? they should prepare them for it, repeat to them the principles laid down above on the use of their fire, and recommend them to keep together as much as possible in hand to hand fighting, and to rally promptly at the first signal.

There is one good means to prevent your men from beginning to fire too soon; it is simply this, that the mounted officers march in front of the line. "Soldiers," the colonel might say, "you will not fire on your officers! I shall not pass to your rear until it will be time to commence firing." Troops thus led will always be brave, and will rarely be vanquished, because they will rarely find an enemy having their moral firmness and their principles of fighting.

If cavalry presents itself, the soldiers should be reminded of the strength of our square, which renders them invulnerable. As far as I am concerned, I declare to you I heartily wish that at the first engagement at which we may assist, we may be charged by cavalry, so sure am I that this would be an opportunity of glory for the 56th.

The moral courage of soldiers is never more severely tried than on a retreat. It has often been said that the French are little fitted for this kind of fighting, which would be tantamount to saying that the French are bad soldiers. This is absurd. Numberless facts have proved, during the last forty years, that the French, when well commanded, can make brilliant retreats. The national character has often been accused when the fault ought to have been laid at the door of the generals who make bad dispositions, or were unfit to call forth the moral energy of the troops.

An old proverb says: "Make a sheep of yourself, and you will be shorn." You must make lions of yourselves on a retreat; and when you will have given three or four hard knocks to an enemy who pursues you too hard, you will be respected. With a little experience of warfare it is easy to have some of those rear-guard successes which tend so much to revive the moral courage of a retreating army, and to make the pursuers excessively timid. On a retreat, you have always the choice of the ground on which to fight; there you mass and group your forces, so as easily to envelop the head of the enemy's column, which will have become very long during the pursuit. The part to be performed by every one must be well traced beforehand, and the fighting must be quick and dashing. No indecision or hesitation must be shown; the head of the enemy's column must be crushed, and then you retire quickly, in order not to become engaged with the reinforcements which will be continually arriving.

Gentlemen, I have said enough to make you appreciate the power of moral force. This moral force arises from the confidence an officer knows how to inspire to his subordinates; it is made to grow by acts of tact, of intelligence, and of courage. You will take care to give to your soldiers, in time of peace, a good opinion of what you will be capable of in time of war. You will attain this if you do not confine yourselves to inspections and reviews, or to a mere dreary drill—all matters, no doubt, very useful, but without any influence upon the *morale* of the soldier. You will reason with your men on our past wars, recount to them the distinguished actions of our brave army, excite in them the wish to emulate them, and, in one word, do everything in order to inspire them with the love of glory.

Written in February 1861   Reproduced from the journal

First published in *The Volunteer Journal,
for Lancashire and Cheshire,* Nos. 23, 24
and 26, February 9 and 16, March 2, 1861

PREFACE TO THE COLLECTION
ESSAYS ADDRESSED TO VOLUNTEERS[456]

The following articles were originally written for *The Volunteer Journal for Lancashire and Cheshire,* and are now republished, in their present shape, at the desire of the Proprietors of that paper, who seem to consider them worthy of a larger circulation among the Volunteers, than could be given to them in a periodical of a more or less local character. Whether this opinion be correct, remains for the public to decide.

It will hardly be necessary to premise that the facts contained in articles such as those on the Rifle, on French Light Infantry, &c., are neither new nor original; on the contrary, such articles are necessarily, to a great extent, compilations from other sources, which it will, however, not be necessary to enumerate; the only portion of these papers which may be considered original, are the conclusions at which the author arrives and the opinions he expresses.

F. E.

Manchester, March 9th, 1861

First published in the collection *Essays Addressed to Volunteers,* London-Manchester, 1861

Reproduced from the collection

ESSAYS

ADDRESSED TO VOLUNTEERS.

[Reprinted from the "Volunteer Journal for Lancashire and Cheshire."]

LONDON:

W. H. SMITH AND SON, 186, STRAND.

MANCHESTER: W. H SMITH AND SON, 12, BROWN STREET.

1861.

Title page of the collection *Essays Addressed to Volunteers*

NEW SERIES.
Published every Saturday Morning, price One Penny.

THE VOLUNTEER JOURNAL
FOR LANCASHIRE AND CHESHIRE.

THE GENERAL CONTENTS COMPRISE:—

A Chronicle of the Week, recording the most important proceedings of the several corps of the two counties, reported by special correspondents, and embracing information upon rifle ranges, administrative organisation, official inspections, rifle contests, musketry and gunnery practice, formation of new corps, appointments and promotions, &c.

Descriptive articles on the more important general events, reviews, rifle meetings, &c.

Original contributions upon various topics of permanent interest and value to the volunteer service.

Notices of improvements and new inventions in guns and gunnery.

Editorial Comments; Government Notices; Official Papers; Correspondence; and information on all national events connected with the development of the volunteer force.

The following are among the Contents of the first volume of the *Journal*, viz.:—from September, 1860, to February, 1861.

DESCRIPTIVE PAPERS AND REPORTS.

ESSAYS AND EDITORIAL ARTICLES.

First page of an advertisement giving the contents of the first volume of *The Volunteer Journal*

VOLUNTEER GENERALS [457]

There has been one thing wanting to the volunteer movement, and that is a fair and intelligent, but plain and outspoken criticism by competent outsiders. The volunteers have been to such a degree the pets of the public and the press, that such a criticism became an absolute impossibility. Nobody would have listened to it; everybody would have declared it unfair, ungenerous, untimely. The shortcomings of volunteer performances were almost invariably passed over in silence, while every corps was extolled to the skies for whatever it did go through tolerably well. The politeness of people, with any regard for impartiality, was most fearfully taxed; everywhere they had to give their opinion upon some volunteer affair or other, and unless they were prepared to utter the most fulsome and unqualified praise, they were lucky if they escaped being thought conceited snobs. How often have the volunteers been insulted by the stupid piece of flattery that they were fit to fight any troops in the world? How often have they been told that no division of the line could have done better what they did at Hyde Park, Edinburgh, Newton, or Knowsley?

Now, setting aside such absurd flattery, which at all times would have been ridiculous, we are quite prepared to admit that a fair trial had to be given to the volunteers before a fair opinion could be passed on their proficiency. But that time has passed long ago. If the volunteer movement, after nearly two years' existence, cannot yet bear criticism, it will never be able to bear it. The great reviews of last summer, in our opinion, mark the period at which the movement passed from infancy into adolescence; by these reviews the volunteers themselves actually provoked criticism; and yet that criticism, with one or two exceptions, was not publicly exercised by those who ought to have done so.

The effects, as well of this absence of plain and outspoken criticism as of this unmitigated adulation, are now visible enough. There will be scarcely a single volunteer corps of eighteen months' standing which does not consider itself, in the silence of its own conviction, quite as good as it has any business to be. The men, after having gone through the simplest battalion movements, through the routine work of skirmishing on a level piece of ground, and through a little rifle shooting, will be but too apt to say that they can do all these things as well as the line; and what the officers think of themselves has been shown by the race for promotion to captaincies, majorities, and lieutenant-colonelcies, which has been going on in almost every corps. Everybody considered himself perfectly fit for any commission he might be able to procure; and, as in the majority of cases, it was certainly not merit which made the man, we need not wonder that, in a good many instances, we have anything but the right man in the right place. Officers and men so firmly believed in what a benevolent press and public chose to call the perfection of their performances, that they began to think soldiering an uncommonly easy thing; and it is a wonder their own mushroom-perfection did not make them consider a standing army, composed of long-trained officers and soldiers, quite unnecessary in a country where perfect soldiers could be manufactured far easier on the volunteer plan.

The first distinct proof of the damage done to the movement by its friends in the press, was the sham fight last summer in London. Some enterprising colonels of volunteers thought the time had come to give their men a foretaste of what fighting looked like. Of course, the wiseacres among the regulars shook their heads, but that did not signify. These regulars bore an ill-will to the volunteer movement; they were envious of them; the success of the Hyde Park review almost made them go mad; they feared the sham fight would come off better than anything the line had ever done in that branch, &c. Had not the men gone through the manual and platoon, battalion drill, and skirmishing? And the officers, though mere civilians a short time ago, were they not now efficient captains, majors, and colonels? Why should they not lead a brigade or a division, as well as a battalion? Why should they not play a little at generals, having so well succeeded in the lower grades?

Thus did the sham fight come off, and a regular sham it was, according to all accounts. The thing was gone through with a supreme contempt for all accidents of ground, with a splendid disregard for the effects of fire, and with a perfectly ludicrous exaggeration of all the impossibilities which are inherent in every sham fight. The men learned nothing by it; they took home with them an idea of fighting totally the reverse of reality, an empty stomach, and tired legs: the latter two, perhaps, the only things which might be considered in any way useful to incipient warriors.

Such childishness was pardonable in the boyhood of the movement. But what shall we say to the return of similar attempts at this present time? Our indefatigable London self-made volunteer generals are at work again. Their own laurels of last summer do not let them rest. A mere sham fight on an ordinary scale no longer satisfies their ambition. This time a great decisive action is to be fought. An army of 20,000 volunteers will be thrown from London upon the south coast, will repel an invasion, and return to London the same evening, so as to be able to attend to business next morning. All this, as the *Times*[a] very properly observes, without any organisation, without staff, commissariat, land transport, regimental train—nay, without knapsacks, and without all those necessaries for campaigning which a line soldier carries in that receptacle! However, this is but one side of the question; it shows only one striking feature of the incredible self-confidence which our volunteer generals have the satisfaction of possessing. How the mere tactical knowledge, the art of handling the troops, is to be procured, the *Times* does not inquire. Yet this is quite as important a point. The drill of volunteers, so far, has been gone through on level ground only; but battle-fields generally are anything but level and unbroken, and it is just the taking advantage of this broken and undulating ground which forms the basis of all practical tactics, of the whole art of disposing troops in action. Now, this art, which has to be learned theoretically and practically, how are the volunteer generals, colonels, and captains to know it? Where have they been taught it? So little has this groundwork of practical tactics been attended to, that we do not know of a single corps which has been instructed, practically, in skirmishing in broken ground. What, then, can become of all such attempts at sham fights but a performance, which, satisfactory, perhaps, to ignorant spectators, will be most certainly useless to the men made to go through it, and which cannot but tend to make the volunteer movement look ridiculous in the eyes of military men assisting at such a spectacle.

---

[a] A reference to the article on the volunteer movement beginning with the words "It would be nothing less than a misfortune" and published in *The Times*, No. 23879, March 13, 1861.— *Ed.*

To our astonishment, we find that even in practical Manchester an attempt is made to manufacture volunteer generals. No doubt we are not quite so advanced as our friends the Cockneys; we are not to have a sham fight, but a mere field-day of all the Manchester volunteers—something, it appears, in the style of the Newton review; and the affair is to come off on some comparatively level piece of ground. Now we wish it to be understood that, so far from disapproving this, we think, on the contrary, that half-a-dozen such field-days every year would do the Manchester volunteers a deal of good. We would add, that we should even consider it desirable that these field-days should come off in ground a little more broken, so as to allow the manoeuvres (against a supposed enemy) to come off with more variation, and to gradually give officers and men the habit of manoeuvring in broken ground. Such manoeuvres would give the adjutants excellent opportunities for afterwards connecting with them, at officers' drill, a few practical lectures on the mode of taking advantage of ground in fighting. So far, then, we not only approve of the plan, but should even wish to see it extended and regularised. But, then, we are informed by a paragraph, which appeared last Saturday[a] in a local paper, that on this occasion the volunteers will do everything for themselves. That is to say, they are going to have a volunteer commander-in-chief, volunteer generals of brigade, and a volunteer staff. Here, then, we have the attempt to import into Manchester the London system of manufacturing volunteer generals, and to that we decidedly object. With all due respect to the commanding officers of regiments in Manchester, we say they have yet a great deal to learn before they become—and we make here no exception—fully efficient commanders of battalions; and if, before they have made themselves fully equal to the responsibility already undertaken by them, they aspire to act for a day in higher commands, we say that they do that which would be the greatest curse to the volunteer movement, namely, playing at soldiers, and that they degrade the movement. At the head of their battalions they would be in their places, they would be able to look after their men, and they would learn something themselves. As Brummagem generals, they would be of no real use, neither to their men nor to themselves. All honour to the adjutants[458] of our Manchester regiments, who deserve the greater part of the credit of having made their regiments what they are; but their place is with their respective regiments, where,

---

[a] March 9, 1861.— *Ed.*

as yet, they cannot be spared, while they would be of no real use to those regiments if they played, for a day, at adjutant, general, and brigade-major—a thing which surely would not give them, personally, any particular satisfaction.

When we have in Manchester the head-quarters of the northern division of the army, with a numerous and efficient staff—when we have an infantry and a cavalry regiment garrisoned here— surely there is no necessity of recurring to such extraordinary pranks. We think it would be both more conformable to military subordination, and also more in the interest of the volunteers themselves, not to collect in such numbers, under arms, without offering the command to the general of the district, and leaving to him the choice of appointing staff and line officers to the division and brigades. No doubt the volunteers would be met in the same friendly spirit as they have been on former occasions. They would then have men at the head of the division and brigades who understand their business, and can point out mistakes when they occur; and they would also preserve their own organisation unbroken. No doubt this would preclude colonels from acting as generals, majors as colonels, and captains as majors; but it would have the great advantage of keeping out of Manchester that manufacture of Brummagem generals for which London is now getting an unenviable notoriety.

Written between March 13 and 16, 1861   Reproduced from the journal

First published in *The Volunteer Journal,
for Lancashire and Cheshire*, No. 28, March
16, 1861

BRIGHTON AND WIMBLEDON [459]

The performances of the volunteer forces of London and neighbourhood on Easter Monday[a] appear to have fully borne out our anticipations expressed in the article on "Volunteer Generals."[b] The attempt of Lord Ranelagh to gather for a day, under his own command, all the volunteers of his district at once created a split among the different corps. An opposition candidate for the commandership-in-chief started up in the person of Lord Bury; to the sham fight at Brighton he opposed a field day at Wimbledon. Great was the division among the various corps; and the consequence was, that some went to Brighton under Lord Ranelagh, some to Wimbledon under Lord Bury, some to the same place, but independently, some to Richmond, and some to Wanstead. There would be no harm in this dispersion alone. Every corps is quite independent of the other, and has a right to enjoy its holiday after its own fashion. But there must arise, and has arisen, a great deal of harm from the acrimonious debates, the personal bickerings, and animosities which have preceded this split, and which are sure to continue for some time. Commanding officers have taken their post for one side or the other; their men have equally taken part, and not always with their commanders; so that the majority of the London volunteers are broken up into two great parties—the Ranelagh and the Bury faction. At Brighton, a great many men of the corps which had been ordered to Wimbledon appeared without arms, but in uniform, to protest against the decision and order of their own immediate superiors;

---

[a] April 1, 1861.— *Ed.*
[b] See this volume, pp. 479-83.— *Ed.*

and Lord Ranelagh, enjoying this mark of sympathy amazingly, had them even formed into a provisional battalion, and, with an exquisite military taste not hitherto met with in any army, allowed them to march past with his own men. So, at least, reports the *Daily Telegraph.*[a]

Now, we ask, what right have either Lord Ranelagh or Lord Bury to put themselves forward as candidates for volunteer generals, and thereby to cause dissensions among bodies hitherto acting harmoniously together? Both these officers have served in the regulars; if they had the ambition to become generals, there was for them, as for others, the usual way of aspiring to that position; and, from their social position, they stood a chance ten times better than the great bulk of their other comrades. They knew very well, when entering the volunteers, that the highest active rank compatible with that service is that of lieutenant-colonel; that in case the volunteers were ever called out to act, they would be brigaded together with the line and militia, and placed under the command of brigadiers from the line; that the very nature of the British military organisation renders it impossible to appoint general officers from any other branch of the forces than the line. In aspiring to the position of temporary volunteer generals, they aspire to places which neither they nor any other volunteer officer will ever be called on to fill, and which they, from want of experience in the handling of masses of troops, must be incapable of filling. But if, in order to play the general for a day, they disturb the harmony between the various corps of their district, and risk to do the movement serious harm, they deserve even stronger and more unequivocal condemnation.

In all large gatherings of volunteers, hitherto, it has been the usage of offering the command in chief and the appointment of brigadiers and divisionary generals, to the military commander of the district. We have said in our previous article that we fully approve of this proceeding, because it is in accordance with military etiquette and subordination, and because it ensures efficient commanders. Now we see that it does more. Had the command of the Easter performance been entrusted to the proper authorities, there would have been no split, and all this bickering would have been saved. But the London commanders appear to have imbued their men with a highly ludicrous fear of the Horse Guards.[460] "For God's sake, keep the Horse Guards out!" is their cry. We in the north have not been so particular. We have always

_____

[a] "The Sham Fight at Brighton", *The Daily Telegraph,* April 2, 1861.— *Ed*

been on capital terms with our natural military superiors, and have found the benefit of it; we hope, too, that the old system may be continued, and save us from those ridiculous quarrels now dividing the London force.

How jealous the Londoners were of the Horse Guards is shown by the uproar created by the presence at Brighton of General Scarlett, who was deputed by the Horse Guards to report upon the proceedings. The wise men of the different corps shook their heads in the most serious manner. To send that general here was an attempt on the part of the Horse Guards to put in the thin end of the wedge. The most fearful consequences were predicted if this were allowed to pass as a matter of course. The volunteers ought to protest; and, indeed, it was proposed that General Scarlett was not entitled to the salute which was due to the lord-lieutenant of the county only. The matter was finally settled by both coming up and receiving the salute in common. But that such questions could be discussed, shows how much some volunteers do mistake their position.

Thus we see, that neither as regards discipline within the corps, nor subordination or even deference to superior officers, has this Easter affair been of any benefit to the London volunteers.

In turning to the various field days, we must premise that we can only go by the reports of the London press, which are exceedingly incomplete and obscure as to military features; and if we should make mistakes in facts, it cannot, therefore, be laid to our charge.

Lord Ranelagh's five brigades took up a position east of Brighton, facing the town, after having marched past. They were very small, each numbering three battalions of 400 men on an average. With this force a ridge of hills was to be occupied, which was far too extensive for such a small number. Now, in this case, if 7,000 men accept a combat, the supposition is, that the enemy is not of a very great superiority in numbers, as otherwise they would retire on their reserves. Consequently, the commander would form his troops in a first and second line, and a reserve, as usual; supporting his flank as best he could, and trusting to his reserves and to the main body (supposed to be in his rear) for the repulse of any outflanking movements on the part of the enemy. But as it would appear by almost all reports, Lord Ranelagh extended the whole of his 7,000 men in one single line! He had a programme made out for three times that number, and as only 7,000 had come instead of 20,000, he made the small number occupy the whole extent of ground marked out for the expected larger number. If this has been actually done, it would settle at once and for ever Lord Ranelagh's claims to generalship, volunteer or other. We are most unwilling to believe that he should have committed such an absurdity, but we have never seen the almost unanimous statement of the press contradicted, and, therefore, must believe it to be the case. We are even told that there *was* a small reserve of a few companies, but that two-thirds of it were at once called into the first line, so that scarcely the ghost of a second line, or reserve, was on the field.

This first line, with its *supposed* second line and *supposed* reserve, was attacked by a supposed enemy who was received by skirmishers, and after these had been thrown back, by file-firing from the right of companies. Why the volunteers are taught file-firing in sham-fights is more than we can tell. We believe that all soldiers who have seen service will agree with us that file-firing, of some use at the time when the lines advanced at the goose-step, is now completely antiquated, that it never can be of any good in front of the enemy, and that there is no useful intermediate link between the fire of skirmishers and the volley.

The imaginary enemy repulsed the defensive line. How the action of the second line and reserves (which must, after all, have been *supposed* to support the first line) was represented, we are at a loss to understand. The battalions had to suppose, not only that they were repulsed, but also that they were relieved. A second line of hills to the rear was then occupied and lost, but at a third accident of ground matters took a turn, and imaginary reinforcements coming up, the enemy was beaten back but not seriously pursued.

We are told by the *Times* that the movements gone through were of the simplest nature.[a] The following is a summary which the correspondent of the *Telegraph* got from an officer, as a report of the movements of his battalion:—

"Having arrived in fours, the ranks formed quarter-distance column in front of No. 1; column wheeled to the left and deployed again on No. 1, advanced in line, covered by No. 1, halted, the assembly was sounded and the skirmishers came in; firing from the right of companies; line retired, and from the proper right of companies passed by fours to the rear; front turn into column; formed quarter-distance column in rear of No. 1; marched by sub-divisions round the centre; opened out to wheeling distance from the rear; left wheeled into line and fired a volley; moved in column of companies from the right along the rear; lined to the front on No. 1; formed quarter-distance column in front of No. 1; deployed on No. 2; then No. 1 advanced to the front, and the remainder right wheeled; formed quarter-distance column in rear of No. 1; fours left, and so left the hill."

---

[a] A reference to the article "The Review at Brighton", *The Times*, No. 23896, April 2, 1861.— *Ed.*

Of the way in which these movements were carried out, we only know that, as usual with volunteers, distances very often were lost, and companies got asunder when forming line.

At Wimbledon, Lord Grosvenor manoeuvred his battalion early in the morning, and marched off when Lord Bury's two brigades (under 4,000) arrived. These went through a very simple performance, but very well adapted to give the men an idea of events and evolutions such as will occur in actual war. The whole is so well described in Colonel M'Murdo's address[a] that we have merely to add that here, too, we find file-firing used to fill up the interval between the retreat of the skirmishers and the opening of volley firing—a thing we most decidedly consider faulty in every respect. The Duke of Wellington rather let his men lie flat down in such moments than stand up to be shot at by artillery and return a weak, ineffectual, and, to themselves, demoralising file-fire.

For the remainder, we concur entirely with Colonel M'Murdo's admirable address, with which we conclude these remarks. We hope all volunteers will note and bear in mind what he says on company drill. The elementary instruction of volunteers must necessarily be less perfect than that of the regular soldier, but it is nevertheless of the highest importance in giving solidity to battalions. The greatest attention to company drill alone can make up in some degree for this unavoidable defect.

Colonel M'Murdo says:—

Volunteers, to men of understanding it is not necessary that the movements which you have gone through to-day should be fully explained, but I think it necessary to call your attention to the nature of the two positions which you have taken up in the course of the field movements through which you have gone. The first position which you took up was naturally one of very great strength—so great that two-thirds of the enemy would have been non-effective. His cavalry could not have acted with effect, nor could his artillery have injured you except by a vertical fire. It was supposed that the enemy, finding that too strong a position, endeavoured to reach the plateau on which we now stand by turning our flank up one of those long valleys in the direction of Wimbledon. It was necessary, therefore, that you should quit the strong position which you formerly held by changing your front to the left. The enemy had a double object in view. He desired to come upon plain level ground, by which means he could bring both his artillery and his cavalry to bear in the action, as well as his infantry; he also desired, by turning your left flank, to reach the Wimbledon Road, by which he could march through you on London. It is my desire to point out to you the difference in the two positions which you held. It was a very different thing when

_____

[a] This refers to McMurdo's speech at Wimbledon on April 1, 1861, which was quoted in the article "Field Day at Wimbledon" (*The Times,* No. 23896, April 2, 1861). Below Engels freely quotes from this speech.—*Ed.*

you were along that rugged crest of a hill, where neither cavalry nor artillery could reach you. You checked the enemy there, and any number of bold men could have checked an enemy there; but here you are brought, as it were, on a sort of billiard table, where you might be exposed to the operations of, perhaps, the best troops in Europe. I observed, in forming the line here, that some battalions were a little unsteady. I do not blame them for it, because they have as yet had very little practice. Still they were unsteady; and if they were unsteady in coming into line to-day, what would be the case if this plain were swept by the artillery of an enemy, if you were choking with thirst, many of your comrades falling around you, and suddenly, through the dust and smoke, you felt the very ground shake under you by a heavy charge of the enemy's cavalry. Consider how liable young troops would be to be unsteady under such circumstances. What is it that overcomes all this? It is discipline, and discipline alone. By the term discipline I do not mean the correction of bad conduct—I mean that habitual union, that combination of mind and body brought to bear upon a certain object; that combination of mind and body that sets the whole in action, and makes a company, a battalion, or a brigade, act like a machine. Now this can only be acquired by company drill; it can only be acquired by paying great attention to individual drill, because I consider a company to be the unit of an army, and when individuals are well drilled and steady the company is steady, and the whole army will be steady. All that you have learned in the way of shooting, all your zeal, all your patriotism, will be of no avail in the day of battle without a thorough knowledge of your company drill. Company drill and nothing but company drill will do, and therefore I beg you to consider that excellence in shooting is not everything, because nothing will do unless you have perfect steadiness of formation under fire. Gentlemen, you have had a hard day's work on the wet ground, and therefore I will no longer detain you, but leave you to return to those homes which you are so well able to protect.

Written between April 2 and 6, 1861   Reproduced from the journal

First published in *The Volunteer Journal,*
for Lancashire and Cheshire, No. 31, April
6, 1861

Signed: *F. E.*

COMPANY DRILL

In our last number but one we called the especial attention of volunteers to the remarks of Colonel M'Murdo on company drill.[a] We now recur to the subject as we think it is high time that its importance should be fully appreciated by every rifleman in the country.

The other day we took occasion to witness the battalion drill of a volunteer corps, which, on the whole, stands decidedly above the average of the force of this district in proportionate number of effectives, good attendance at drill, attention to duty on the part of officers, and, consequently, in general efficiency. To our great surprise, we found that there was very little progress beyond what we had seen this same corps perform some six months ago. The battalion movements came off slightly better than at the close of last season, but the manual and platoon were gone through in a rather slovenly manner. Even in shouldering arms, every man looked as if acting without any consciousness that he was to act in concert with some 400 men right, left, and in rear of him. In making ready and presenting, every rifle seemed to take a pride in coming to the proper position independently of its neighbours; and, altogether, a quiet disregard of the one—two, or one—two—three, by which the execution of each word of command is to be characterised, appeared the general order of the day.

In one corner of the barrack-yard in which this took place, we happened to see a squad of a line regiment fall in for drill under a sergeant. They were, we suppose, the awkward squad of the battalion, ordered for extra drill. What a difference! The men

---

[a] See this volume, pp. 488-89.— *Ed.*

stood like statues; not a limb moved till the word was given, and then those limbs only moved which had to execute the command—the remainder of the body remained perfectly still. When the command struck their ears, every arm moved simultaneously, every motion into which the execution of the command was divided was perfectly distinct, and was gone through at the same moment by every man. The whole squad, in fact, moved like one man. Those gentlemen who are so fond of boasting that the volunteers can do all their work quite as well as the line, would do well to go and study the line a little; they would then soon find out that between the best volunteers and the worst drilled line regiment there is still an enormous difference.

But what, it will be said, is the use of such perfection of drill to the volunteers? They are not intended to have it, they cannot be expected to have it, and they will not require it. No doubt this is quite correct. The very attempt to make volunteers emulate the line in perfection of drill would be the ruin of the movement. But drilled the volunteers must be, and so far drilled that common simultaneous action shall become quite mechanical, quite a matter of course with them; so far, that all their movements and motions can be gone through steadily, simultaneously, by all, and with a certain degree of military bearing. In all these points the line will remain the model which they will have to look up to, and company drill will have to be the means by which the required efficiency can alone be obtained.

Take the manual and platoon. That on any given word of command, the whole of the rifles in the battalion should be moved simultaneously, and in the manner prescribed, is not a mere matter of appearance. We must suppose that all volunteer corps are now so far advanced that the men can go through this exercise without positively hurting each other, or knocking their rifles together. But even beyond this, a mere slovenly way of going through the different motions has, undoubtedly, a great moral effect upon the battalion under drill. Why should any one man be particularly attentive to the command, if he has blunders committed right and left, and rifles coming up or down in a straggling way long after he has performed the command? What confidence, before the enemy, can a man on the left wing have in his comrades on the right wing, unless he knows they will load, make ready, and present together with him on the command being given, and will be ready again, as soon as he himself shall be, either to fire again or to charge? Moreover, every experienced soldier will tell you that the habit of such simultaneous action—

the certainty of the officer's command being responded to by those two or three round distinct sounds, denoting that every man acts at the same time as his comrades—has a very great moral influence on the battalion. It brings home to the senses of the men the fact that they really are like one body; that they are perfectly in the hand of the commander, and that he can employ their strength at the shortest notice and with the greatest effect.

Again, take the movements of large or small bodies of troops. Unless every man is so far confirmed in his drill that every movement he may be required to go through is done almost mechanically on the word being given, a battalion will never move steadily. A soldier who has still to ransack his memory or his intellect to make out what kind of thing the command given asks him to do, will do more harm than good in a battalion. So will a man who, either from habit or some other cause, is apt to think that certain movements will necessarily be followed by others; he will often receive a command quite different to what he expected, and then he will very probably blunder. Now, these defects can only be overcome by constant company drill. There the officer in command can put the small body under his orders, in a quarter of an hour's time, through so many different movements and formations, and can vary the order of passing from one to the other to such an extent, that the men, never knowing what is to come, will soon learn to be attentive and to respond quite mechanically to the word of command. In a battalion, all movements are necessarily much slower, and therefore on the whole less instructive to the men, though more so to the officers; but it is an acknowledged fact that men, perfect in their company drill, will, under good officers, learn their battalion movements perfectly in a very short time. The more the men are tossed about in company movements by a competent quick-eyed instructor, the steadier will they afterwards be in the battalion. And it requires no pointing out how important perfect steadiness in a battalion is: a volley may be given rather irregularly, and still take effect; but a battalion thrown into disorder in forming square, deploying, wheeling in column, &c., may at any time be hopelessly lost if in front of an active and intelligent enemy.

Then there is the important point of distances. It is an indispensable fact that no volunteer officer or soldier has an eye for distances. In marching in open or quarter distance column, in deploying, every battalion drill shows how difficult to the officers it is to keep the correct distance. In re-forming column from square, the men of the centre sections almost always lose their distance; they step back too far or too little, and the wheel backwards is consequently done in a very irregular way. The officers can learn to keep distance in the battalion only, though company movements in sub-divisions and sections will tend to improve them; but the men, to learn how to re-form column from square (a movement of the greatest importance before the enemy), will have to practise it in their companies.

There is another point to be considered, and that is the military bearing of the men. We do not only mean the erect, proud, and yet easy position of each individual man under arms, but also that quick simultaneous action in company and battalion movements which is as necessary to a body on the move as to a battalion handling its rifles at a stand-still. Volunteers appear quite satisfied if they manage, somehow or other, to get into their proper places in something like the prescribed time, including, generally, a few seconds of respite. No doubt this is the principal point, and in the first year of the existence of a volunteer corps anybody would be perfectly satisfied with it. But there is for every move a certain fixed mode of doing it, prescribed by the regulations, and this is supposed to be that mode by which the object in view can be attained in the shortest possible time, with the greatest convenience to all concerned, and, consequently, with the highest degree of order. The consequence is, that every deviation from the prescribed mode is necessarily connected by a slight degree of disorder and want of regularity, which not only makes an impression of slovenliness upon the beholder, but also implies a certain loss of time, and makes the men think that the detail of the regulations is mere humbug. Let any man see a body of volunteers advance by double files from the centre and front, form company, or go through any other change of formation, and he will at once see what kind of negligent habits we are attaining. But such faults, which may be suffered in an old line regiment, which has a good sub-stratum of solid drill, and will be made to go through the same drill again and shake off its easy ways, are far more dangerous in a body of volunteers, where that solid foundation of detail-drill is unavoidably wanting. Their slovenly habits, which have to be tolerated in the beginning, as the men *must* be hurried through all elementary work, will increase and multiply unless regularly and assiduously checked by strict company drill. It will be impossible to drive such habits out entirely, but at all events they may be, and ought to be, so far checked as not to gain ground. As to the individual bearing of the men, that we suppose will gradually improve, though we very much doubt whether that

494 Frederick Engels

peculiar waving of a line, marking time, seen in all volunteer drills, will ever disappear. We allude to a certain habit of moving the upper part of the body in marking time, which appears common to all volunteers we have yet seen. No sooner goes up the right foot, than up goes the right shoulder and down goes the left; with the left foot, the left shoulder moves upwards, and thus the whole line waves to and fro like a ripe corn-field under a mild zephyr, but not very much like a body of sturdy soldiers prepared to meet the enemy.

We believe we have said enough to call attention to the subject. Every volunteer who has the movement at heart, will agree with us as to the necessity of regular and diligent company drill; for, let us repeat it, the volunteer force has been unavoidably neglected in its elementary education, and it requires great attention and a deal of work to make up in some manner for this defect.

Written in mid-April 1861

First published in *The Volunteer Journal, for Lancashire and Cheshire*, No. 33, April 20, 1861

Signed: *F. E.*

Reproduced from the journal

RIFLES AND RIFLE-SHOOTING

THE LANCASTER AND ENFIELD RIFLES

The recent contest between Lieut. Wallinger and the sergeants of the Royal Engineers, reported in our numbers for April 6th and 13th,[a] has recalled public attention to the merits of the Lancaster rifle, especially as a service weapon. In the match at Chatham the sergeants fired with the ordinary military 577 oval-bore Lancaster carbine of the Royal Engineers, the cost of which is about £4. To match such a weapon with the highly-finished Whitworth, costing about £25, is evidently unfair. A more equal comparison might be instituted between the Lancaster and the ordinary Enfield, because the difference in the cost of these two weapons is not very material, and the price of the Lancaster would probably be reduced to an equality with the Enfield if it were manufactured in as great numbers at the Government factories. The question then remains, is it a better rifle? A writer in the *London Review*, reasoning from general principles, and judging also from actual experience, answers in the affirmative; and we invite attention to the following passages from his article on the subject:—

The law which governs accurate rifle-shooting or practice is very simple. It is only necessary to establish an equation between the length and diameter of the ball, and to give to that ball an adequate rotatory motion around its polar axis, when unfailing accuracy must be the result, irrespective of the precise method by which

---

[a] A reference to the articles "Lancaster v. Whitworth Rifles" and "Lancaster or Whitworth", published in *The Volunteer Journal, for Lancashire and Cheshire*, Nos. 31 and 32, April 6 and 13, 1861. This reference is probably made by the *Volunteer Journal* editors.— *Ed.*

the rotatory or rifle motion is given. That is to say, the interior of the rifle barrel may be cut into any number or any shape of grooves, or no grooves at all, so long as the equation is preserved, and the bullet acquires a proper rotatory motion, and then the accuracy in every case will be equal. The consideration, however, that must determine the proper arm for a soldier involves as first conditions that the weapon should not exceed a certain weight and dimension, and that it should be easily loaded and easily cleaned. It therefore follows, that to be easily loaded, the bearing surface, in the act of loading, should be as small as possible; and that, in the shape given to the rifling, as far as practicable, all angles should be avoided. We know no other form that so perfectly carries out this proposition as the spiral oval, inasmuch as the bearing surfaces in the act of loading are but two, and no form offers so great facilities for cleaning with the unavoidably scanty means at the disposition of the soldier during active service. This opinion seems to be borne out by the results of the Indian campaign,[461] and by the trials at Malta, Gibraltar, and other foreign stations. In India the Enfield rifle is said to have completely "shut up" at many critical periods of the campaign. The papers and private letters and official reports teemed with complaints; yet with the same ammunition, under the same circumstances, the oval-bore rifles with which the Royal Engineers were armed never failed to perform their duty to the satisfaction of both officers and men.

When the Enfield rifle is made with a diminished bore and an elongated bullet is used, comparably with the Whitworth the effect is just as good; yet the Enfield service-rifle, as it now exists, must be regarded as an attempt to satisfy impossible conditions. The officers charged with the construction of this arm were not permitted to reduce the calibre of the weapon below a given limit. Hence the adoption of the standard bore of ·577. As a consequence of this too great diameter of bore, an inherent difficulty presented itself, namely, that of securing a perfectly and unfailingly hermetical fit between the interior of the bore and the ball when driven from the barrel by the explosion of the powder. Let us examine the actual result of the imperfect conditions exhibited in the Enfield rifle. The weight of the ball is fixed at 530 grains, the charge of powder at 70 grains, the calibre, as before stated, at ·577. Now, the effect of 70 grains of powder acting on the large cross-section of the ball, will not and does not give pressure sufficient to produce in every case sufficient expansion of the ball into the grooves. Careful experiment shows that not 10 per cent. of the bullets are equally and fully expanded on every side. Sometimes one groove is distinctly marked, sometimes two, and in only one-tenth of the total rounds are they fully expanded, hence the inaccuracy of the shooting of the ·577 bore service-rifle.

Now, the perfect conditions of accurate practice from rifles grooved in *any form* may be described as follows:—That the bore should be ·5 inch, the length of ball 1·12 inches, rotation or twist 1 in 18 inches, charge of powder 90 to 100 grains (No. 6), weight of ball identical, namely 530 grains. The force exerted under this condition upon the cross-section of the ball may be considered as plus, therefore there is an unfailing and unerring fit between the ball and the bore, and it arises in this way: the diminished diameter of the bore gives increased length of ball, and no wooden plug is necessary as in the service bullets to drive out the metal. The bullet is therefore an homogeneous solid of about three diameters long. In the explosion the expansive force of the powder is first exerted on the rear or posterior section of the ball (*a*), and the transmission of the motive force, although almost instantaneous, is nevertheless met by the *vis inertiae* of the mass of metal constituting the ball, exerted in the whole length (from *a* to *b*), and backed by the counter resistance of the air in the barrel.

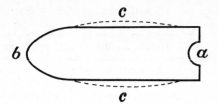

Bullet for small-bore rifle

It is at a glance evident that this resistance must be evinced in the middle portion of the bullet or part of greatest resistance (*c*), and consequently, by a perfectly natural expansion there, the bullet would be slightly shortened, say about one-tenth of an inch, while the central portion would be increased in diameter sufficiently to fit hermetically the form of the interior of the barrel, whatever its shape might be.

When these more perfect conditions are fulfilled, not once in 500 times is there any defective expansion, the ball invariably taking the form of the rifle, and thus there results the most excellent rifle practice.

These remarks apply to all rifles of every description.

What is it these favourable conditions do for a rifle, and why do they give more accurate shooting? Having shown how the interior of the bore is perfectly fitted by the bullet, we will endeavour to trace its results. One of the main achievements in the construction of a rifle is to get a "low trajectory," that is, that the curve the bullet describes in its flight should be as near an approach to a straight line as possible, and, as a necessary sequence, a high velocity is absolutely necessary, so that gravitation may have the minimum of effect in depressing the ball in its passage. Now, the effect of diminution of the calibre achieves the first result, and by the employment of a larger charge of powder on the small cross-section of the ball, the highest velocity and the most accurate results are obtained.

With respect to the methods of rifling, it will be inferred from what we have already said that so long as the ball gets a proper "spin" on leaving the barrel, it matters not in itself how that rotation is given, whether by an hexagonal bore, as in the Whitworth, an oval, as in the Lancaster, or by three grooves, as in the Enfield. Neither is a number of grooves necessary, for if *one* has a sufficient grip on the bullet to turn it, the requisite condition is fulfilled. Still, there are inherent defects in the manners of grooving which may easily be shown. If the rifling be angular, there is a loss of power in effecting the expansion necessary to fill up the angles, besides the probable escape there of the propelling gas. Moreover each angle is a line of weakness to the barrel; so with any number of grooves, and proportionally to their depths are the same defects manifested. The spiral oval, therefore, of the Lancaster gun is theoretically the best, as presenting the form to which the bullet will most readily adapt itself with the slightest expansion.

That the Lancaster rifle must have great merits appears from the fact, that, before the adoption of the Enfield pattern, the Lancaster rifle, then in competition with it, was recommended in preference by four separate and distinct committees. It was submitted for approval to the Commander-in-Chief, and by him sent for final decision to Hythe. The first report from the officers of the School of Musketry there was most favourable; the second report decided in favour of the Enfield. The reason then assigned for this decision was that the balls "stripped." Subsequently, however, the following facts are said to have transpired. The first 10,000 rounds of Pritchett ammunition, with which the first trials there were conducted, were of the proper standard diameter. With these cartridges admirable shooting resulted. In the second experiment the same ammunition was not employed, the former having been made in 1853, the latter in 1854; the experimenting officers at Hythe being entirely unconscious of any difference in the ammunition, not having been informed that in the bullets made in the latter year there was a difference of ·007 less in the diameter, as compared with the bullet of 1853.

This fact was not detected until a year and a-half after the final decision in favour of the Enfield, when Colonel (then Captain) Fitzroy Somerset tested the pattern of the Royal Engineer oval-bore carbine. It is easy to see that the diameter of the diminished Pritchett bullet being less than the proper standard, it would, in many instances, especially when there was any excess of hardness in the lead, pass out of the barrel without acquiring a rotatory motion, that is, it would not sufficiently expand to fill the interior of the barrel, whether of a Lancaster or any other rifle.

That the Whitworth is too expensive for army use, and requires more delicate treatment than it is likely to get in actual service, we think few will question, and the tests should therefore be applied to the Lancaster and Enfield or other patterns respectively, which are fitted for the rough usage of warfare. The way of doing this, however, will not be by rifle-matches, but by firing from a fixed rest, with equal quantities of powder, and with bullets of the same weight and cast, thus making all such conditions equal, and leaving the test open only to the respective merits of the weapons themselves.

The preceding remarks refer to two different questions: 1. Which is the best proportion between the diameter and the length of an elongated rifle-shot to be fired from *any* rifle? And, 2. What are the merits of the Lancaster or oval-bore rifle?

As to question No. 1, we are far from agreeing with the author, that the proportions of his best bullet are preferable to all others. The rifles which, so far, have given the best results—the Swiss and the Whitworth—have both a smaller calibre than 0·5, and a greater proportional length of shot. We cannot, however, here enter into a discussion on a point of such a general nature.

As to question No. 2, we cannot see what positive evidence the author gives of *any* superiority of the Lancaster rifle over the Enfield. That the carbines of the Engineers "shut up" less often than the Enfield rifles of the infantry, is easily explained by the fact that the infantry are a hundred times more numerous, in any army, than the Engineers; and that the latter do not use their carbines once when the line use their rifles a hundred times; because Engineers are there for other purposes altogether than to act as infantry.

That a long and heavy expansion-shot, hollowed out sufficiently at the rear end, with a full charge, can be made to take almost any shape of rifling, is proved in the instance of the Whitworth; here the amount of expansion required is extremely great, and still the bullet takes the hexagonal shape at its rear end. No doubt, therefore, such a bullet can be made to expand sufficiently to fill up an oval bore, if the difference of the two diameters be not too great. But why on that account the Engineer carbine should be better than the Enfield is more than we can perceive. The ideal bullet of our author has nothing whatever to do with this carbine—it would not fit it; and if even with a reduction of calibre, our author considers an increased charge of 90 to 100 grains of powder necessary to make his bullet fully take the oval bore, we think that looks much like a silent admission that the present charge of 70 grains does *not* always ensure a full expansion of the bullet in the oval bore of the Engineers' carbine. Our author does not say what is to become of the increased recoil from the increased charge; still we know that 80 to 90 grains give, in the Whitworth, a not very pleasant amount of recoil, which, in rapid firing, very soon affects the steadiness of aim.

The uncommonly good results given by the Engineers' carbine in the Chatham match, as well as some exceedingly good shooting with Lancaster rifles by private gentlemen, mentioned at times in the press, make it desirable that the capabilities of the oval-bore expansion rifle, and its fitness for a service weapon, should again be tried. We, for our part, believe that it will be found to have its faults too, and that the principle of the rifling is a very secondary matter indeed in military muskets. Instead of quibbling with the Enfield about such minor matters, why not come to the point at once, and say that its greatest and most important defect is its *large calibre*? Change that, and you will find all other improvements but matters of detail.

Written at the end of April 1861

First published in *The Volunteer Journal, for Lancashire and Cheshire*, No. 35, May 4, 1861

Signed: *F. E.*

Reproduced from the journal

ALDERSHOT AND THE VOLUNTEERS

The Duke of Cambridge, in his speech at the London Rifle Brigade dinner,[a] said he should be very glad to see the volunteers at Aldershot.[462] The only difficulty, to him, appeared to be, how to get them there. We propose to venture a few suggestions how to overcome this difficulty.

It is, undoubtedly, quite out of the question to send to Aldershot, or any other camp, whole corps of volunteers. The elements of which they are composed preclude every chance of it. There is no company, much less a battalion, a majority of whose members could spare as much as a fortnight, at one and the same time, for such a purpose.

But if we cannot get the volunteers to Aldershot in bodies, could they not go there singly, and yet learn a great deal? We think they could, if the thing was arranged so as to offer every facility to volunteers to avail themselves of the opportunity.

We believe the great majority of the volunteers to be composed of men who can, now and then, get relieved from their usual avocations for a fortnight in a year. A great many take a regular holiday of that duration, and even longer. Among these there are certainly a considerable number who would not at all object—on the contrary—to spend, for once, their time and their money at Aldershot, if they were received there. Thus, there would be no difficulty whatever, between May and the end of September, to keep at Aldershot a floating population of volunteers amounting, at all times, to the strength of a decent battalion at least. If we can,

---

then, get this floating population to the camp, how can this be utilised?

We propose that a range of huts or tents be set apart for say 600 volunteers, and that a captain, or, better still, a major, from the line be appointed to the command of this volunteer camp, with an adjutant and sergeant-major to assist him. The camp to be opened say in May, as soon as a sufficient number of volunteers have given in their names; if the camp is full, further applicants to be admitted as there may be room for them, the whole of such volunteers to be formed into a battalion; a blouse of a prescribed cut and colour to be worn over the tunics, so as to give the whole a uniform look. As there is sure to be an excess of officers, there will be no other chance but to make officers do duty, for the time being, as sergeants and even privates. Far from considering this a drawback, we should consider it an advantage. No volunteer officer is so well grounded in his personal drill that such a momentary relapse into the ranks would be useless to him; let him recollect that every line officer has to shoulder the rifle for a certain period year after year. The distribution of the temporary officers' posts in the battalion might be easily regulated: the senior captains present might begin, and afterwards others might take their posts by rotation. The major in command could perhaps be intrusted with a deal of discretionary power in nominating to these appointments, in order to ensure a lively emulation among the officers present. These, however, are matters of detail, the arrangement of which would cause but little trouble if the idea was once taken up in good earnest.

Such a battalion, with its floating population, would never attain any very great efficiency, and the major in command, as well as his assistants, would have no easy post of it. But it would ensure one object: that among the volunteer army generally, and among the officers and sergeants specially, a nucleus would be formed of men who have at all events really been soldiers, if only for a fortnight. This may look a contemptibly short period; yet we have no doubt that every man would feel immensely different on leaving, to what he did on reaching Aldershot. There is an immense difference between drilling once or twice a week after the whole day has been spent on business and other matters, and drilling, even for a fortnight only, morning, noon, and night in a camp. During that fortnight, every volunteer present will have no other business to look after but his military education; he will be confirmed in his drill to a degree which no length of the present volunteer drill can raise him up to; and, besides, he will see a great deal more of soldiering than he ever could expect to see in his own corps, unless it encamped on purpose. On leaving Aldershot, every man will think that he has learned during that fortnight at least as much as during the whole of his preceding volunteer service. In due time there will be scarcely a company of volunteers in which one or more members have not been down to Aldershot; and everybody must see to what an extent such an infusion of better educated elements will improve the steadiness and the military manners, too, of the various corps.

We have supposed that the course of instruction for every man is to be a fortnight, merely because almost everybody might find means to spare that short time. But there could be nothing to prevent allowing such volunteers as can afford it, to stop at the camp for a full month.

As a matter of course, the volunteers in camp would have to keep themselves. The Government ought to find tents and camping utensils, and might, perhaps, make arrangements for the delivery of rations, to be paid for by the men. In this way, without costing the country anything to speak of, the affair would be cheap for the volunteers, and everything put upon a regular camp footing.

We have no doubt that, were the experiment once made, the volunteers would at once cordially respond to it; the batallion would be kept up always to its full complement, and, perhaps, the necessity for similar battalions, at other camps, or at Aldershot, would soon arise. If the excess of officers became very considerable, a special "officers' battalion" might be formed at one of the camps, with a somewhat longer period of attendance, and we believe such a battalion would answer well for at least one season.

There is, however, another mode of making the camps, and the line generally, useful for volunteer officers: by attaching, temporarily, such officers to battalions of the regulars. This might be done without taking the officers too far from their homes; during the period of such attachment (say a month) the volunteer officer to do duty as if actually serving in the regiment. No doubt means might be found to allow at least one volunteer officer at a time to be thus attached to a battalion, without in any way infringing upon the habits and position of the line officers, who have always shown the best possible spirit towards the volunteers. If this point was taken up, we should consider it advisable to allow no volunteer officer to be attached to the line who had not shown, in some manner or other, that he was fit to profit by it; for he would go there, not to be taught the rudiments, but to be confirmed and perfected in what he knows already, and to learn matters which he cannot learn in his corps.

Both our suggestions—the formation of floating battalions at the camps, and the permission for duly qualified volunteer officers to be attached to the line for a month—have in view the education of the officers chiefly. We repeat, again and again, that the officers form the weak points of the volunteer army; we add, that it now must be evident to all that the present system of volunteer education *cannot make the officers, as a body, efficient,* and that, therefore, new means of instruction must be found if the force is, not only not to retrograde, but to improve.

We throw out these suggestions for no other purpose but to invite attention to the question. We have no wish to lay before the public a fixed plan, with all details worked out, all eventualities provided for, ready to be put into practice at once. That would be the business of others, if the matter was taken up seriously. But we mean to say, the whole volunteer movement was an experiment, and unless people are prepared to experimentalise a little more in order to find out the proper way to improve the new army which has resulted from that experiment, the movement must ultimately come to a dead lock.

Written at the end of April and the beginning of May 1861

First published in *The Volunteer Journal, for Lancashire and Cheshire*, No. 36, May 11, 1861

Signed: *F. E.*

Reproduced from the journal

THE WAR OFFICE AND THE VOLUNTEERS

We believe that in all Great Britain, nowhere has there been among volunteers a greater readiness and alacrity to conform to all War Office orders and regulations, to take up a proper position with regard to the regular army, to work the movement in harmony with the authorities, than in Lancashire, and among other towns, in Manchester. When armouries were ordered to be provided, the order was carried out, although it unavoidably implied great inconvenience in a large town. Whatever orders were sent down were obeyed at once and without a murmur. When our volunteers met in large masses, they anticipated the Duke of Cambridge's desire, and requested the military authorities of the district to take the command and organise the brigades. The desire for efficiency made our Lancashire volunteers criticise all Government interference with a favourable eye; they knew that uniformity and regularity were above all things requisite, and they looked upon every War Office circular as a step towards ensuring these requisites. The *Volunteer Journal,* from its very first number, has not ceased to recommend a willing and cheerful obedience to War Office orders, and to advocate the great advantages of perfect harmony between the volunteers and the military authorities, both local and central. While in other localities, especially in London, there were mysterious rumours abroad respecting the baneful influence of the Horse Guards,[463] the attempts of the authorities to get in the thin end of the wedge, &c., we have never been swayed by such considerations for a single moment. We have given the Commander-in-Chief, the Secretary for War, and all their subordinates, full credit for sincerity when they asserted their willingness to support the movement in every possible shape and form.

But we cannot close our eyes to the fact, that latterly one or two little matters have occurred which look as if there really had been some change in the view men in authority take of the volunteer movement, especially since Lord de Grey and Ripon gave up the Under-Secretaryship for War. A few weeks ago, we believe it was on Whit-Monday,[a] Lord Ranelagh reviewed in Regent's Park such of the London volunteers as would come on his invitation. Now, we have more than once strongly condemned Lord Ranelagh's attempts at playing general.[b] He might have applied to Colonel M'Murdo, the inspector-general of volunteers, to review his men, or to recommend another qualified officer for the purpose. However, right or wrong as regards propriety, he went with his men to the park; the affair had been publicly announced, and was so well known that a large crowd of spectators assembled. There were among this crowd people who behaved in a most shameful manner; they pressed round the volunteers, broke their ranks, rendered evolutions impossible, threw stones, and some even, it is stated, attempted to wound the officers' horses with pointed instruments. When this commenced, the officers in charge naturally looked out for the police, but out of the 6,000 men constituting the army of Sir Richard Mayne, we are told that *not one man was there*! The consequence was, that Lord Ranelagh's review was a total failure, owing to the interference of the crowd. Now, if the matter had been allowed to take its course, it is quite possible that it would have proved as much a failure on its own merits, as Lord Ranelagh's previous attempts had invariably done. As it was, Lord Ranelagh was made a martyr of, and strongly recommended to the sympathy of all volunteers.

There can be no doubt that the total absence of the police from this publicly-announced review was not quite accidental. It has been stated in the press that they must have had orders to keep away; and we know that in London, among volunteers, it is very generally believed that the Horse Guards had something to do with this affair, and that it is desired at the Horse Guards to undermine the volunteer movement in every possible way. The feeling in London is very strong upon the matter, and we confess the facts of the case—which, as far as we are aware, it has never

---

[a] May 20, 1861.—*Ed.*
[b] See this volume, pp. 479-83 and 484-89.—*Ed.*

been attempted to excuse or explain away—are well adapted to create such a feeling.

This week we have to record another affair which certainly does not look as if the authorities intended to do, as they promised, everything in their power to assist the volunteers. It has been announced, some time ago, that one of our Manchester regiments intended to go into camp for a short period. We believe this announcement was not made before it had been ascertained that it could be carried out. It is commonly reported that verbal application was made to the authorities for tents, &c., and that this application was granted; and that, moreover, the terms had been fixed upon which it had been granted. We believe these arrangements were come to not more than two or three weeks ago. On the strength of this, all other arrangements as to the ground for encampment, canteen, officers' mess, and other matters, were entered into; and when everything is straight, and the formal application for the tents is made, the Government all at once draw back, and declare they cannot furnish any tents at all!

As a matter of course, this upsets the whole plan, and the expense and trouble incurred by the regiments has all been wasted; and we all know that volunteer regiments have every reason to be careful of their small balance, if any, at the banker's. We are told that so many volunteer regiments are said to have applied for tents that the Government cannot possibly find tents for all, and that therefore none can be furnished to any corps. Whether this be correct or not, the Government ought to know that a bargain is a bargain, and that posterior events could not relieve them from engagements already undertaken. But rumour, which is now beginning to do its work in Manchester quite as much as in London, says that this is a mere idle pretext, and that the Government do not want the volunteers to go under canvas at all; that even if the corps in question were to provide tents or huts at their own expense, and from an independent source, the encampment would not be looked on with a favourable eye in high quarters.

Such occurrences are certainly not adapted to promote that cordiality between the authorities and the volunteers which is so essential to the further success of the movement. The movement is too powerful for any Government to put down; but want of confidence in the authorities on the part of the volunteers, and hidden opposition on the part of the authorities, can very soon create considerable confusion, and hamper its progress for a time.

This ought not to be allowed. There are a great many volunteer officers in Parliament. Let them get up in their places and take care that the Government give such explanations as will at once put the matter right, and show the volunteers that they will have to expect cordial support instead of hidden hostility.

Written at the beginning of June 1861

First published in *The Volunteer Journal, for Lancashire and Cheshire*, No. 40, June 8, 1861

Signed: *F. E.*

Reproduced from the journal

WALDERSEE ON THE FRENCH ARMY [464]

[*The Volunteer Journal, for Lancashire and Cheshire*, No. 42, June 22, 1861]

A short time ago there was published, in Berlin, a book on "The French Army on the Drill-ground and in the Field,"[a] which created a great sensation, and rapidly passed through several editions. Although the author merely calls himself "an old officer," it is no mystery that the book is written by General Count Waldersee, late Minister of War in Prussia. He is a man of very high standing in the Prussian army, where he has particularly distinguished himself by revolutionising the old pedantic system of teaching the soldier skirmishing, patrolling, outpost, and light infantry duty generally. His new method, to which we may revert on some other occasion, is now introduced in that army. It is remarkable for doing away with all pedantry of forms, and exclusively appealing to the intellectual resources of the soldier in the performance of a duty which can only be carried out well by the intelligent and harmonious co-operation of a number of men. An officer who lays so much stress on the intellectual training of every individual soldier, very naturally took great interest, at all times, in the French army, as the one which is most famous for the individual military intelligence of its men; and we need not, therefore, be astonished if we find that he has made that army the especial object of his studies, and that he has many friends and acquaintances in its ranks, from whom he can obtain valuable information. After the successes of the French against one of the best and bravest European armies, in the Italian campaign of 1859,[465] it became a question of European interest to what circumstances such extraordinary and unvaried victories were

---

owing; and in the above publication General Waldersee gives what he considers to be an elucidation of the subject.

The following is taken from an account of the general character of the French army:—

It partakes of all the good qualities, but also of all the faults and weaknesses, of the French character. Animated by a genuine warlike spirit, it is full of combativeness, thirst for action and for glory, brave and plucky, as it has shown at all times, and more recently on the battle-fields of Algeria, the Crimea, and Italy. Everywhere there have been occasions on which both officers and soldiers—particularly among the picked troops—have performed wonders of bravery; and the performances of the French soldiers generally, in these campaigns, are worthy of the highest respect.

Of great bodily and mental mobility—which, however, is often enough increased to a continuous restlessness—the French soldier is indefatigable and persevering in battle, as well as in hard work of all kinds.

Self-confident in the highest degree, full of ambition and vanity, every individual soldier has but one desire—to march upon the enemy. He knows no difficulties; he goes by the old French proverb, "If the thing is possible, it is as good as done; if it is impossible, it will be done somehow." Without much reflection—often, indeed, very inconsiderately—he advances, convinced there are no difficulties he cannot overcome. Thus, with the dash and impetuosity inherent to his nation, he always presses for the attack, in which is his chief strength. Besides this, the French soldier is intelligent, handy, particularly adapted for individual fighting, and accustomed to act on his own responsibility. He is inventive and clever in embarrassing situations; he has a peculiar knack of making himself comfortable in a bivouac; of improving bridges, &c., under fire; of putting, at a moment's notice, houses and villages into a defensible state, and of defending them afterwards with the greatest tenacity.

War is the life-element of an army. The French Government very wisely consider war as the normal state of the troops, and, therefore, at all times and under all circumstances treat them with the same strictness and severity as if actually on a campaign. The regiments are concentrated in camp as frequently as possible, and besides are made to change garrisons constantly, so as not to allow any peace habits to grow up among them. In the same spirit, the drill of the men is exclusively adapted for the purposes of war, and nothing whatever is done for purposes of parade. No corps is ever judged from its style of marching past, and it is, therefore, rather surprising to foreign officers to see French battalions march past—even before the Emperor[a]—with a slovenly gait, in undulating front lines, the men stepping with different feet, and marching at ease with sloped arms.

But the picture has its dark as well as its bright side. All these good military qualities which urge on the French soldier to advance impetuously, show their brilliant effects *only so long as you allow him to advance*. The *sentiment individuel,* which is at the root of all his qualifications for attack, has its great disadvantages too. The soldier, being principally busied with himself, goes along with the mass as long as it advances successfully; but if this mass be forcibly, and, perhaps, unexpectedly, made to retire, its cohesion, the connection of every individual with his comrade, is soon severed, and the more so as, in such a case, the careless tactical training of the troops—of which, more hereafter—renders all steadiness impossible, and leads to confusion and utter dissolution.

---

[a] Napoleon III.—*Ed.*

Add to this that the French are naturally given to envy, and, with all their
national levity in critical moments, are apt to be suspicious of others. The French
soldier follows his officers eagerly and willingly into battle, but only so long as these
officers are in front of him, and literally lead him on. This is what the soldiers
expect, and when advancing under fire they express it by shouting, "Epaulettes to
the front!" Thus field officers and generals have generally to march to the charge
in front of their troops—the very place, certainly, for a general—and this explains
the excessive losses the French always have had in officers. But if a retreat becomes
inevitable, confidence in the officers will soon disappear, and, in extreme cases,
make room for open disobedience. From these causes, a retreat, energetically
forced upon a French army, has always been disastrous to it, and will ever be so.

General Waldersee might have added a great deal more on the
facility with which the confidence of the French soldier in his
officers melts away under adverse circumstances. The confidence
of the men in their immediate superiors, even after repeated
unsuccess, is the best standard of discipline. Measured by this, the
French are not much better than totally undisciplined levies. It is a
matter of course for them that they never can be beaten except by
"treachery"; and whenever they lost a battle and had to retreat
more than a few hundred yards—whenever the enemy surprised
them by an unexpected move, they regularly raised the cry, "We
are betrayed!" So much is this part and parcel of the national
character, that Napoleon, in his memoirs (written long after the
fact, at St. Helena),[a] could impute, by insinuation, some kind of
treacherous action to most of his generals; and that French
historians—military and otherwise—could amplify these insinua-
tions into the most wonderful romances. As the nation of the
generals, so does the soldier think of his regimental and company
officers. A few hard knocks, and discipline is completely at an
end; and thus it is that, of all armies, the French have made the
most disastrous retreats.

[*The Volunteer Journal, for Lancashire
and Cheshire*, No. 44, July 6, 1861]

Of the mode of recruiting the soldiers and officers, Waldersee
gives the following account:—

The French soldier is recruited by drawing lots among the young men of the
country; but every man has the right of paying a sum fixed by Government for a
substitute. This sum flows into a fund administered by the Government, from
which the substitute receives a small sum as bounty on enlisting, and the remainder
on the expiration of his term, the interest being paid to him during his time of

---

[a] *Mémoires pour servir à l'histoire de France, sous Napoléon, écrits à Sainte-Hélène*, Paris,
1823.— Ed.

service. The sum owing to him may, however, be partially or totally forfeited by crime or bad conduct. Thus the Government have the selection of substitutes entirely in their own hands, and are in the habit of enlisting, as much as possible, men only who have already served one term of seven years, and who have proved themselves reliable and well conducted. A great many old soldiers are thus secured to the army, and from them most of the non-commissioned officers are selected. The term of service is seven years; of this time, however, the greater portion of the men are but four or five years actually with the colours, spending the remainder on furlough.

The non-commissioned officers are selected with great care and tested with great regard by the officers. They are mostly distinguished, not only by an excellent character and a perfect knowledge of the details of their duty, but also by intelligence, independence, a fine soldier-like bearing, and a certain dignity, especially in their relations with the privates, over whom they know very well how to maintain the great authority which the regulations have given them. As every non-commissioned officer is eligible for a commission, they manage to keep the privates at a respectful distance, while, on the other hand, they use every effort to distinguish themselves and give a good example to their subordinates.

At present the majority of the non-commissioned officers consist of substitutes. A few only are made corporals and sergeants during their first term of service, and among them, particularly those young men who, having had a good education, and finding themselves excluded by the great throng of candidates from the military schools, enlist voluntarily in the army in order to try for a commission. Such young men very soon advance to the position of non-commissioned officers, and on passing the practical military examination prescribed for sergeants before they can be made sub-lieutenants, very often receive a commission after having served from two to four years.

The generality of officers promoted from the ranks receive their commissions after from 9 to 12, and often after from 15 to 20 years only. Of 170 such officers, taken at random, 16 received commissions after from 2 to 4, 62 after 5 to 8, 62 after 9 to 12, and 30 after from 13 to 20 years' service. The first 16 belonged to the class of educated young men; the 62 who received commissions after from 5 to 8 years, were promoted for distinction before the enemy. Thus, in time of peace, promotion from the ranks, even in France, is slow work.

The officers recruit themselves partly from the ranks, as stated above, and partly (in times of peace principally), from the military schools, where the young men have to attend for two years, after which, on passing a severe examination, they at once receive commissions. These two classes of officers keep at a great distance from each other; the pupils of the military colleges and the educated men promoted from the ranks, looking down with disrespect upon the old sub-lieutenants and lieutenants who gained their epaulettes by long service; the officers, even of the same battalion, form anything but that compact body which they do in almost every other army. Yet those men who were raised from the comparatively less educated portion of the ranks (and who now, after the heavy losses in the Crimea and Italy, form the greater portion of the subalterns), are very useful in their way. Though very often positively ignorant, and sometimes rough, and scarcely above the sergeant in character or manners, they are generally clever within their sphere of action, perfectly at home in their duty, conscientious, strict, and punctual; they know exceedingly well how to treat the soldier, how to take care of him, how to stimulate him by their example, both in garrison life and under fire. Besides this, they at present mostly possess a good deal of experience in camp life, marching and fighting.

On the whole, the French officer is intelligent and eager for war; he knows what he is about, and—especially under fire—he knows how to act on his own responsibility, and how to excite the men by the example of his own bravery. Add to this—for the majority of them—a good deal of campaigning and fighting experience, and we must say that they are possessed of qualities which place them very high in their profession.

Promotion is given either by seniority or by selection. In peace, two by seniority to one by selection; in war, the reverse. But selection is generally limited to the educated class of officers, while the mass of those raised from the ranks are promoted by seniority only, and thus attain their captaincy at a rather advanced age. This is about the highest step they ever reach, and they are generally quite satisfied to be able to retire on a captain's pension.

Thus it happens that in the French army you see a good many subalterns of from 30 to 40, and a good many captains approaching 50; while among field-officers and generals there are a great many comparatively young men. This is no doubt a great advantage; and the continued wars in Africa, the Crimea, and Italy, having considerably quickened promotion, have brought still more young men into high commands.

To show the proportion in which promotion to the higher grades is dealt out to the two classes of officers, the following statement of officers killed and wounded, or employed in high commands in Italy, will be read with interest:—From the military schools: 34 generals, 25 colonels commanding regiments, 28 other field-officers, 24 captains, 33 lieutenants and sub-lieutenants. From the ranks: 3 generals, no colonels commanding, 8 field-officers, 66 captains, 95 subalterns.

The generals proceed less from the staff and the scientific or select corps than from the generality of the field-officers. They therefore are mostly wanting in military instruction of a higher order; a few among them only have *les vues larges.*[a] Badly up in strategy, they are rather clumsy in handling large bodies of troops, and therefore much in want of superior orders or scientific assistance; so that very often in the field, as on the drill-ground, they receive a regular programme of the movements to be gone through for engaging in action. On the other hand, they are full of common sense, and ready at inventing expedients; they know the practical part of their duty, are zealous, ambitious, and devoted to the service. Their habit of acting independently gives them the necessary vigour under fire. They know no difficulties; act at once on every emergency, without awaiting or sending for orders; are not afraid of responsibility; and, brave like every Frenchman, they always personally lead on their troops.

Most of them have fought in Algeria, the Crimea, and Italy, and, therefore, are in possession of a valuable store of warlike experience. Of the generals engaged in Italy in 1859 there were twenty-eight old Africans, eighteen of whom had also fought in the Crimea. One general alone (Partouneau) made his first campaign in Italy.

This continued fighting has endowed the French army with a younger body of generals than any other army can boast of. To keep this up in time of peace, lieutenant-generals retire on half-pay at 65, and major-generals at 60 years of age.

In short, the French generals must be regarded as comparatively young and bodily active, intelligent, energetic, experienced in war and well adapted for it, though but a few have, so far, shown themselves unusually clever and well acquainted with the handling of large bodies of troops, and though neither the Crimean nor the Italian war have developed any extraordinary military genius.

---

[a] Broad views.—*Ed.*

[*The Volunteer Journal, for Lancashire and Cheshire,* No. 46, July 20, 1861]

Passing to the drill-practice of the French, our author says:—

The recruit, boorish and clumsy as he is when joining his regiment, nevertheless often enough, before a fortnight is over, and before even he may have received his full equipment, stands sentry with the dignity and authority of an old trooper, and very soon becomes formed by the careful *individual training* which he is made to go through. Though company and battalion drill leave very much to be desired, every individual soldier is carefully trained to gymnastic and bayonet exercise, fencing with the small sword, and long running at double-quick time.... On the drill-ground the infantry is generally without steadiness, loose, and therefore rather slow; but on a march it is exceedingly quick, and broken to long marches, great portions of which are made at the double; which pace is very often used in action, and to no mean advantage. These are the performances by which the excellence of a body of troops is judged in France; it is never judged by its drill, much less by mere marching past. The fact is, the French cannot march past in good order, because they are defective in that drill in detail which, after all, is necessary to every good body of troops.

Talking about drill, our author gives the following anecdote of Napoleon I:—

Napoleon was well aware of the drawbacks inherent to this loose system of drill, and did his best to redress it. Under his iron rod, precision of drill was adhered to as much as it was possible with Frenchmen—though he himself was no very good drill-master. One day, at Schönbrunn, in 1809, he had the idea of drilling himself a battalion of his guards; to make them *faire la théorie,* as the French call it. He drew his sword, and gave the word; but after having ordered a few movements, he got his men into such utter confusion that he called out, putting his sword back into the scabbard, "The devil take your——theory! Set that mess right again." *(Que le diable emporte votre f——théorie! Redressez cette cochonnerie!)*

About the "Turcos," the native Algerian troops, we find the following remarkable statement:—

According to reports received from French officers, the Turcos above all disliked an engagement with the Austrian Rifles. Whenever they met them, they not only refused to advance, but threw themselves down, and, like the camels of the desert, could not be induced either by threats or by blows, to rise to the attack.

On the drill-ground of an infantry regiment—

Recruit-drill is gone through in a very pedantic manner, but still very superficially; little attention is paid to the bearing of the individual men, and thus, the regulations are carried out (in company and battalion-drill) in a positively slovenly manner. Very little care is taken that the men stand properly at attention, that the dressing is good, the line well closed up, or even that the men step out with the same foot. It appears to be sufficient that the men be *there,* and arrive together, somehow or other. An army accustomed to such a loose system of drill will certainly not show to any great extent the disadvantages it entails, so long as it continues to advance. Still, this system must exercise a very bad influence on discipline and order in action; and whenever a retreat under fire becomes inevitable, it may bring on the most serious consequences. This is the reason why the attempt at a retreat in good order has so often proved dangerous to the French, and why a retreat forced upon them by a solid, well-schooled army will always prove disastrous to them.

After disposing of the drill, General Waldersee gives an epitome of Marshal Bugeaud's principles of fighting (the same which we have in great part translated in preceding numbers of the *Volunteer Journal,* under the heading, "On the moral elements in fighting").[a] With these principles he fully coincides, attempting at the same time to prove—and not without success—that most of them are old practical rules, to be found already in the instructions of Frederick the Great. We pass over this, as well as over a lengthy strategical criticism of the campaign in Italy in 1859 (in which not less than eighteen distinct blunders of General Gyulay are shown up), in order to come to the observations on the mode of fighting of the French in that campaign.

The most essential principles of this method are:

1. To act on the offensive whenever this is in any way possible.

2. To treat protracted firing with contempt, and to pass as soon as ever possible to a charge with the bayonet, at the double.

This being once known, it has been very generally concluded that the French always and everywhere, with a complete disregard of all tactical forms, had rushed upon the Austrians, and that they had always instantly, and without further ado, run them down or driven them away.

But the history of the campaign is there to prove that this was far from being the case. On the contrary, it shows:

1. That the French certainly did in most cases, not always, attack their opponents impetuously in double quick time, but that scarcely ever did they conquer them at the first charge. Not only were they generally unsuccessful in this, but in most cases they were defeated with loss in several repeated attacks, so that during action they retreated nearly as often as they advanced.

2. That often enough they charged without firing, but, once repelled, they were obliged to carry on the engagement by firing, which firing lasted for some time, though interrupted by repeated bayonet charges. At Magenta and Solferino[466] such firing engagements lasted several hours.

The author now gives, from reports received both from French and Austrian officers, an account of the tactical formations applied by the French during the Italian campaign, by extracts from which we shall conclude this article.

---

[a] See this volume, pp. 469-75.— *Ed.*

[*The Volunteer Journal, for Lancashire and Cheshire*, No. 62, November 8, 1861]

Our author, after describing the general character and principles of fighting of the French army, proceeds to give an account of the tactical formations employed by them in the Italian campaign of 1859.

A French army division is composed of two brigades, the first of which has a battalion of chasseurs, and two regiments (of three battalions each) of the line, while the second has only two regiments (or six battalions) of the line. Each battalion has six companies.

In the line of battle, the first brigade forms the first line, the battalions being formed in columns at half distance with full deploying intervals between them, and covered by a line of skirmishers. The second brigade stands in second line, 250 yards to the rear, the battalions equally in columns at half distance, but with only half deploying intervals between them; they are generally placed behind one of the *wings* of the first line.

The formation of column generally adopted in the Italian war was what the French call column of divisions—two companies with them being called a division. The six companies are ranged two in front, two at half-distance behind them, and again two companies at half-distance behind the second pair of companies. This column may either be formed on the two centre companies or on the two extreme companies of either wing. With the Guards, who were all picked men, it was always formed on the two centre companies, and thereby (same as in the English double column on the two centre sub-divisions) the time both for forming column and for deployment was abridged by one-half; but with the line it was generally formed on the two right companies. The reason was, that by this method the "grenadier" company (No. 1) was placed in the front of the column, while the light or "voltigeur" company (No. 6) came to the rear. Thus these two companies, consisting of picked men, formed, so to speak, a framework in which the less reliable four "centre companies" were encompassed; and, moreover, in case the two rear companies were ordered to extend as skirmishers, the light company was one of them, while the grenadier company, in the front line, remained together unless the whole battalion had to extend.

For an army fighting chiefly, not in line, but by a combination of skirmishes and columns, this formation offers great advantages. One-third of the men (the two front companies) are always in a position to make use of their fire-arms, while at the same time deployment is simple and can be got through very quickly. The great distance between the component parts of the column (half company distance or about 40 yards) tends very much to reduce the ravages which artillery makes in closer columns; and when it is borne in mind that, as a rule, two companies were extended, so that the whole column consisted of two companies in front, and two at 40 yards behind them, it is seen that this formation approaches the line as much as possible; the two rear companies acting rather as a reserve or second line to the two front ones than as that bodily support which is generally supposed to be given by the rear men to the front line in continental columns of attack. Moreover, although deployments into line did now and then occur in the Italian campaign, the ground in Lombardy is such that fighting in line is positively impossible. In these small fields, intersected by hedges, ditches, and stone walls, and covered, besides the corn, with mulberry trees connected one with another by vine branches; in a country where the lanes, running between high walls, are so narrow that two carts can scarcely pass each other—in such a country all regular formations often cease so soon as troops advance to close with the enemy. The only thing necessary is to have plenty of skirmishers in front, and to dash with the compact masses on to the most important points. Now, for such a purpose, there could be no better formation than that selected by the French. One-third of the battalion skirmishing—no supports, the column at 100 yards to the rear being support enough—the whole advancing rapidly, the skirmishers, when near enough, clearing the front of the battalion and hovering on its wings; the first line giving a volley and charging; the second, 40 yards to the rear, following as a reserve and keeping as much order as the ground will allow. We must admit that this method seems very well adapted for all purposes of attack in such ground, and will keep the men as much as possible together, and under the control of their officers.

Wherever the ground was open enough to admit of regular movements, the attack was carried out in this way—the skirmishers engaged the enemy until the order was given for the column to advance; the supports—if supports there were—forming on the flanks of the line of skirmishers, and extending themselves to the front of either wing, in order to envelop and give cross-fire to an advancing enemy; when the column came up to the line of skirmishers, the latter crowded in the intervals of battalions, advancing in a line with the head of the column; at twenty yards from the enemy the head of the column fired a volley and charged. When the ground was very thickly covered, as many as three or four companies of a battalion were extended, and cases are reported (at Magenta, the Turcos) where whole battalions extended as skirmishers.

Against an Austrian bayonet attack, a method similar to that prescribed by the British regulations for street firing (battalion drill, section 62) was sometimes employed. The leading companies of the column gave a volley, faced outwards, and filed to the rear, where they re-formed; the succeeding companies did the same, until, after the rear companies had fired their volley and cleared the front, the whole battalion charged the enemy.

In decisive moments, the soldiers were ordered to deposit their knapsacks on the ground, but to provide themselves with some bread and all the ammunition they contained, which they stored away about their persons as best they could. This is the origin of the fable, "That the Zouaves carried their cartridges habitually in their breeches' pockets."

At Magenta, the Zouaves and the 1st Grenadier Guards deployed for a time, and fired by files and by ranks; at Solferino, too, the division of Voltigeurs of the Guards (twelve battalions) deployed in a single line before going into action, but when actually engaged, they seem to have been in the usual column. As both these deployments were made under the immediate command and in the presence of Louis Napoleon, there can scarcely be any doubt that he ordered them from some recollection of English line manoeuvres; but in both cases the predilection of the French officers for their own national mode of fighting and the nature of the ground, appear to have prevailed as soon as the real tug of war came on.

In the attack of a village, several columns, preceded by thick swarms of skirmishers, were launched; the weaker column, destined to attack the front of the position, was held back to the last, while stronger columns turned the flanks of the village. The troops who *took* the place at once occupied and fortified it, while *the reserves* pursued the enemy. To defend a village, the French trusted more to the reserves behind it or on its flanks than to a strong garrison in the houses themselves.

With this abstract of the tactical formations of the French army of Italy in 1859, we take leave of Count Waldersee's work.

Although England is far less rough ground for fighting than Lombardy, still her numerous fences, ditches, clusters of trees, and coppices, combined with the undulating nature of the ground, and the deep wooded ravines cut into it, make her a far rougher battle-field than the large uninterrupted plains of Northern France, Belgium, and Germany. If ever a French army should attempt a descent on English soil, there can be little doubt that the formations of its infantry would be very similar to those employed in Italy; and that is the reason why we think these formations not without interest to English volunteers.

Written between the second half of June and the beginning of November 1861

First published in *The Volunteer Journal, for Lancashire and Cheshire,* Nos. 42, 44, 46 and 62, June 22, July 6 and 20, November 8, 1861

Signed: *F. E.*

Reproduced from the journal

A MILITARY CRITICISM OF THE NEWTON REVIEW[467]

Last year's Newton review[a] was a great success, the greater because beset by difficulties of all kinds. It was the first attempt to bring together the volunteers of Lancashire in a body; the railway arrangements were anything but what they should have been; the ground was in an execrable state; the weather was very bad. In spite of all this, the thing went off uncommonly well, and our volunteers went home, wet, hungry, thirsty, but with the proud consciousness that they had surprised everybody by the cool, steady, and soldierlike manner in which they had gone through their work.

Can as much be said of this year's review? We are afraid it cannot. The railway arrangements were excellent; the ground was in capital order; the weather was fine; the volunteers had gone through another year's drill; and yet, we are sure, most of them went home less satisfied with their day's work and their day's success than last year. Whose fault was that?

When the troops arrived on the ground, the flags marking out the positions of the various brigades were in their places, and generally the battalion aids were at once placed. But a good many of the battalions, especially those which arrived first, were moved about, halted, again moved, and again halted for a long time before they were brought to their proper places. The consequence was that corps which were from half an hour to an hour on the ground before the review commenced, could not find time to pile arms and dismiss their men for even a few minutes to get refreshment. This was certainly not the fault of the commanders of battalions.

---

[a] August 11, 1860.— Ed.

After the general salute, the evolutions commenced. But there were scarcely any evolutions. The first brigade deployed, and went through a series of firings one round by companies from centre to flank, one volley by battalions, three rounds file-firing. In the meantime the second brigade deployed, and after the firing was over, relieved the first line. This was done by both lines forming fours deep, and the fours of the second line passing through the spaces of the first. The regulations themselves characterise this movement as one adapted for *parade purposes* only, and never to be applied on service (p. 113). Then the second brigade went through the same course of firing, while the third brigade deployed to form a second line, and the first brigade fell back to the rear in column. We noticed that the first brigade was a very long while over this, and only got out of the way when the firing of the second brigade was nearly over. Then the third, and afterwards the fourth brigade advanced and took their turn of firing, after which the whole body formed in mass of columns and marched past.

Thus, it is evident, instead of evolutions, there were but two points in which the volunteers present could show their proficiency—the firing and the marching past. Now, we protest against blank cartridge firing being made a test by which to judge such a body as the volunteers assembled at Newton. There were regiments which have fired immense numbers of blank cartridges, and which, consequently, long ago obtained considerable success in sharp, round volleys. There were others which are quite as well, perhaps better, up in their company and battalion drill and in target practice, but which scarcely ever fired blank cartridge before. And there were a great number of the small country corps, formed into battalions for the occasion, which never had a chance of firing a battalion volley, for the very simple reason that, so far, they have not been able to go even through battalion drill. Volley-firing, as far as it is to be judged by the sound only, and not by the effect, is of all the duties of a soldier by far the easiest; an otherwise steady battalion will learn it in a very short time, and if the great majority of the battalions present gave very bad volleys, indeed, we must say we are more pleased with it than otherwise, inasmuch as it shows that they have not wasted their time with practising an art which they can learn in a week at any time, and which is very apt to be indulged in as a plaything and an advertisement.

The only good point in the programme was that it gave the whole of the infantry present something to do. Otherwise it was very poor indeed. There was no skirmishing, scarcely any evolutions, and there was a test of efficiency set up which was not only delusive, but positively unfair to the mass of the corps present. As to the gallant cavalry charge which concluded the manoeuvres, we better say nothing of it. The public took it for a capital joke.

In the marching past we noticed again the everlasting weakness of volunteers—the utter disregard to distances. Only one regiment came past with anything like proper distances, and it was *not* the one which had distinguished itself so much by its volleys. Now, we think that proper distance-keeping is both more difficult and more important, in the present style of volunteer drill, than sharp volleys. Upon the whole, the marching past showed less improvement upon last year than one had a right to expect; but we are bound to say that in this respect the smaller corps from the country had made the greatest progress. This deserves so much the more a public acknowledgment as these small corps have to struggle against the greatest difficulties, are mostly deprived of the assistance of adjutants, and have no higher military authority to go by than their drill-sergeant.

We noticed with regret the progress of the scarlet coat, and even the bear-skin cap, among the Lancashire volunteers; it seems to indicate a hankering after show, which cannot do the movement any good. This is a subject, however, which would bear us too far away from Newton, and we shall, therefore, return to it on some other occasion.

Written between August 3 and 10, 1861   Reproduced from the journal

First published in *The Volunteer Journal,
for Lancashire and Cheshire,* No. 49,
August 10, 1861

Signed: *F. E.*

VOLUNTEER OFFICERS

"Lieutenant A. B., dishonourably discharged; Second Lieutenant C. D., struck off the list; Captain E. F., dismissed the United States service,"—such are a few specimens of the latest items of military news we receive by wholesale from America.

The United States have had a very large volunteer army in the field for the last eight months; they have spared neither trouble nor expense to make this army efficient; and, moreover, it has had the advantage of being posted, almost all that time, in sight of the outposts of an enemy who never dared to attack it in a mass or pursue it after a defeat.[468] These favourable circumstances ought to make up, to a very large extent, for the disadvantages under which the United States volunteers were organised; for the poor support they got from a very small army of the line, forming their nucleus; and for the want of experienced adjutants and drill instructors. For we must not forget that in America there were many men both fit and ready to assist in the organisation of the volunteers—partly German officers and soldiers who had undergone regular training and seen service in the campaigns of 1848-49, partly English soldiers emigrated during the last ten years.

Now, if under these circumstances a regular weeding of the officers becomes necessary, there must be some weakness inherent, not to the volunteer system in itself, but to the system of officering volunteers by men chosen indiscriminately by themselves from among themselves. It is only after an eight months' campaign in the face of the enemy that the United States Government ventures to call upon volunteer officers to qualify themselves, in some degree, for the duties they undertook to perform when they accepted their commissions; and see what an amount of voluntary or forced resignations, what a heap of dismissals, more or less dishonourable, is the consequence. No doubt, if the United States army of the Potomac were opposed to a force steadied and kept together by a due proportion of professional soldiers, it would have been dispersed long ago, in spite of its numbers and of the undoubted individual bravery of the men composing it.

These facts may well serve as a lesson to the volunteers of England. Some of our readers may recollect that, from the very starting of the *Volunteer Journal*,[a] we maintained that the officers were the weak point of the volunteer system, and insisted upon an examination, after a certain time, calling upon the officers to prove that they were at least in a fair way of becoming fit for performing the duties they had undertaken. Most of the gentlemen who had taken upon themselves to command and to instruct men in a line of business of which they were as perfectly ignorant at the time as the men themselves—most of these gentlemen scorned the idea. That was the time when all Government assistance and Government interference were equally scorned. But since then the call upon the pockets of these same gentlemen has been heavy enough to make them apply for pecuniary assistance from Government; and, as Governments run, this means, at the same time, a call for Government interference. Moreover, a two years' experience has brought out pretty plainly the defects of the present system of officering volunteer corps; and we are now informed by a metropolitan commanding officer,[b] and apparently upon authority, that before long the volunteer officers will be called upon to prove their fitness for command before a board of examination.

We heartily wish this to be the case. The fact is, the English volunteer officers, too, do require weeding to a certain extent. Look at a line regiment at drill, and compare it to a volunteer battalion. What it takes the volunteers an hour and a half to go through, the line men go through in less than half an hour. We have seen a deal of square-forming by some of the best volunteer regiments in the country, and we cannot help saying they must be wretched cavalry that would not have cut them up each time before they had their flanks ready for firing. That was not the fault of the men. They appeared to know their duty as well as could be expected, and to do it sometimes even as mechanically as

---

[a] See this volume, pp. 415-16.— *Ed.*
[b] Colonel Money.— *Ed.*

you see in a line regiment. But the men had to wait for the company officers, who appeared to hesitate about the word of command to be given, and about the moment when they ought to give it. Thus, hesitation and sometimes confusion was thrown into a formation which, above all others, requires a promptness, both of command and of execution, imparted by long practice only. Now, if this be the case after two years' practice, is this not a proof that there are plenty of volunteer officers holding responsible situations which they are not fit to hold?

Again, the commanders of battalions have lately received some very high praise from the hands of highly competent authority.[a] It was said that they appeared to be up to their work, while the company officers were not always so. We are not at all inclined, as will have been seen above, to dispute the latter statement; but we must say that if the high authority alluded to had seen the lieutenant-colonels and majors, not at a great review, but at plain battalion drill, the opinion given would probably have been slightly different. At a great review, no field officer in command of a battalion, if not perfectly up to his work, would attempt to act on his own responsibility. He has his adjutant—who knows what he is about—for a prompter; and he is prompted by him accordingly, and goes through his work creditably, while the poor captain has to bungle through his performance without any prompter at all. But look at the same field officer at battalion drill. There he has no vigilant general's eye watching him; there he reigns supreme; and there the adjutant, often enough, has to take the post assigned to him by the Queen's[b] regulations, and must keep his advice to himself until asked for it, or until the mess is complete. This is the place where you see the volunteer field officer in his true light. He is there to instruct his men in battalion drill; but not being himself perfect in that science, he profits of their being there to instruct himself in it. As the old saying goes, *docendo discimus.*[c] But if the teacher is not well on his legs in the art he has to teach, blunders and confusion are apt to occur, and, unfortunately, do occur often enough. It will not contribute either to the proficiency in drill of a volunteer battalion, or to its confidence in its commander, if the men find out that battalion drill, for them, means nothing but giving their field officer in command an opportunity of learning his drill himself, while they are tossed

---

[a] The reference is probably to General George Wetherall.— *Ed.*
[b] Victoria.— *Ed.*
[c] We learn by teaching.— *Ed.*

about here and there, without any purpose even, and expected to rectify, by their superior knowledge, the blunders of their superior officer.

We do not mean to say that commanding officers of volunteers have not put themselves to some trouble to learn their duty; but we do mean to say that if company officers cannot be manufactured out of civilians as easily as private soldiers, field officers are far more difficult to manufacture. We must come to the conclusion, on the mere ground of battalion drill experience, that none but professional soldiers are fit to command battalions. And if we consider that drill is but one part of a field officer's duty, that the commander of a battalion, being liable to be detached for independent duty, where he has to act on his own responsibility, requires a knowledge of higher tactics, we must say that we should be very sorry to see the lives of 600 or 1,000 men entrusted to the guidance of such civilians as now form the great majority of commanders of battalions.

Depend upon it, if the English volunteers ever will have to face an enemy, it will not be under the favourable circumstances which now permit the American Government to clear the ranks of their volunteer officers from the most incapable subjects. If the English volunteers are called out, it will be to fight, not a volunteer army like themselves, but the most highly disciplined and most active army in Europe. The very first engagements will be decisive; and, depend upon it, if any hesitation or confusion arises, either by the wrong commands of the colonels, or by the uncertainty of the captains, that will be taken advantage of at once. There will be no time for weeding when once before the enemy, and therefore we hope it will be done while there is time.

Written in mid-November 1861   Reproduced from the journal

First published in *The Volunteer Journal,
for Lancashire and Cheshire*, No. 64,
November 22, 1861

Signed: *F. E.*

LESSONS OF THE AMERICAN WAR

When, a few weeks back, we drew attention to the process of weeding which had become necessary in the American volunteer army,[a] we were far from exhausting the valuable lessons this war[469] is continually giving to the volunteers on this side of the Atlantic. We therefore beg leave again to revert to the subject.

The kind of warfare which is now carried on in America is really without precedent. From the Missouri to Chesapeake Bay, a million of men, nearly equally divided into two hostile camps, have now been facing each other for some six months without coming to a single general action. In Missouri, the two armies advance, retire, give battle, advance, and retire again in turns, without any visible result; even now, after seven months of marching and counter-marching, which must have laid the country waste to a fearful degree, things appear as far from any decision as ever. In Kentucky, after a lengthened period of apparent neutrality,[470] but real preparation, a similar state of things appears to be impending; in Western Virginia, constant minor actions occur without any apparent result; and on the Potomac, where the greatest masses on both sides are concentrated, almost within sight of each other, neither party cares to attack, proving that, as matters stand, even a victory would be of no use at all. And unless circumstances foreign to this state of things cause a great change, this barren system of warfare may be continued for months to come.

How are we to account for this?

The Americans have, on either side, almost nothing but volunteers. The little nucleus of the former United States' regular

---

[a] See this volume, pp. 521-24.—*Ed.*

army has either dissolved, or it is too weak to leaven the enormous mass of raw recruits which have accumulated at the seat of war. To shape all these men into soldiers, there are not even drill-sergeants enough. Teaching, consequently, must go on very slow, and there is really no telling how long it may take until the fine material of men collected on both shores of the Potomac will be fit to be moved about in large masses, and to give or accept battle with its combined forces.

But even if the men could be taught their drill in some reasonable time, there are not officers enough to lead them. Not to speak of the company officers—who necessarily cannot be taken from among civilians—there are not officers enough for commanders of battalions, even if every lieutenant and ensign of the regulars were appointed to such a post. A considerable number of civilian colonels are therefore unavoidable; and nobody who knows our own volunteers will think either M'Clellan or Beauregard over timid if they decline entering upon aggressive action or complicated strategical manoeuvres with civilian colonels of six months' standing to execute their orders.

We will suppose, however, that this difficulty was, upon the whole, overcome; that the civilian colonels, with their uniforms, had also acquired the knowledge, experience, and tact required in the performance of their duties—at least, as far as the infantry is concerned. But how will it be for the cavalry? To train a regiment of cavalry, requires more time, and more experience in the training officers, than to get a regiment of infantry into shape. Suppose the men join their corps, all of them, with a sufficient knowledge of horsemanship—that is to say, they can stick on their horses, have command over them, and know how to groom and feed them—this will scarcely shorten the time required for training. Military riding, that control over your horse by which you make him go through all the movements necessary in cavalry evolutions, is a very different thing from the riding commonly practised by civilians. Napoleon's cavalry, which Sir William Napier ("History of the Peninsular War" [Vol. III, p. 272]) considered almost better than the English cavalry of the time, notoriously consisted of the very worst riders that ever graced a saddle; and many of our best cross-country riders found, on entering mounted volunteer corps, that they had a deal to learn yet. We need not be astonished, then, to find that the Americans are very deficient in cavalry, and that what little they have consists of a kind of Cossacks or Indian irregulars (rangers), unfit for a charge in a body.

For artillery, they must be worse off still; and equally so for engineers. Both these are highly scientific arms, and require a long and careful training in both officers and non-commissioned officers, and certainly more training in the men too, than infantry does. Artillery, moreover, is a more complicated arm than even cavalry; you require guns, horses broken in for this kind of driving, and two classes of trained men—gunners and drivers; you require, besides, numerous ammunition-waggons, and large laboratories for the ammunition, forges, workshops, &c.; the whole provided with complicated machinery. The Federals[471] are stated to have, altogether, 600 guns in the field; but how these may be served, we can easily imagine, knowing that it is utterly impossible to turn out 100 complete, well-appointed, and well-served batteries out of nothing in six months.

But suppose, again, that all these difficulties had been overcome, and that the fighting portion of the two hostile sections of Americans was in fair condition for their work, could they move even then? Certainly not. An army must be fed; and a large army in a comparatively thinly-populated country such as Virginia, Kentucky, and Missouri, must be chiefly fed from magazines. Its supply of ammunition has to be replenished; it must be followed by gunsmiths, saddlers, joiners, and other artisans, to keep its fighting tackle in good order. All these requisites shone by their absence in America; they had to be organised out of almost nothing; and we have no evidence whatever to show that even now the commissariat and transport of either army has emerged from babyhood.

America, both North and South, Federal and Confederate, had no military organisation, so to speak. The army of the line was totally inadequate, by its numbers, for service against any respectable enemy; the militia was almost non-existent. The former wars of the Union never put the military strength of the country on its mettle; England, between 1812 and 1814, had not many men to spare, and Mexico defended herself chiefly by the merest rabble.[472] The fact is, from her geographical position, America had no enemies who could anywhere attack her with more than 30,000 or 40,000 regulars at the very worst; and to such numbers the immense extent of the country would soon prove a more formidable obstacle than any troops America could bring against them; while her army was sufficient to form a nucleus for some 100,000 volunteers, and to train them in reasonable time. But when a civil war called forth more than a million of fighting men, the whole system broke down, and everything had to be begun at the beginning. The results are before us. Two immense, unwieldy bodies of men, each afraid of the other, and almost as afraid of victory as of defeat, are facing each other, trying, at an immense cost, to settle down into something like a regular organisation. The waste of money, frightful as it is, is quite unavoidable, from the total absence of that organised groundwork upon which the structure could have been built. With ignorance and inexperience ruling supreme in every department, how could it be otherwise? On the other hand, the return for the outlay, in efficiency and organisation, is extremely poor; and could that be otherwise?

The British volunteers may thank their stars that they found, on starting, a numerous, well-disciplined, and experienced army to take them under its wings. Allowing for the prejudices inherent to all trades, that army has received and treated them well. It is to be hoped that neither the volunteers nor the public will ever think that the new service can ever supersede, in any degree, the old one. If there are any such, a glance at the state of the two American volunteer armies ought to prove to them their own ignorance and folly. No army newly formed out of civilians can ever subsist in an efficient state unless it is trained and supported by the immense intellectual and material resources which are deposited in the hands of a proportionately strong regular army, and principally by that organisation which forms the chief strength of the regulars. Suppose an invasion to threaten England, and compare what would be then done with what is unavoidably done in America. In England, the War-office, with the assistance of a few more clerks, easily to be found among trained military men, would be up to the transaction of all the additional labour an army of 300,000 volunteers would entail; there are half-pay officers enough to take, say three or four battalions of volunteers each under their special inspection, and, with some effort, every battalion might be provided with a line-officer as adjutant[473] and one as colonel. Cavalry, of course, could not be improvised; but a resolute reorganisation of the artillery volunteers—with officers and drivers from the Royal Artillery—would help to man many a field-battery. The civil engineers in the country only wait for an opportunity to receive that training in the military side of their profession which would at once turn them into first-rate engineer officers. The commissariat and transport services are organised, and may soon be made to supply the wants of 400,000 men quite as easily as those of 100,000. Nothing would be disorganised, nothing upset; everywhere there would be aid and assistance for the volunteers, who would nowhere have to grope in the dark; and—barring some of those blunders which England cannot do without when first she plunges into a war—we can see no reason why in six weeks everything should not work pretty smoothly.

Now, look to America, and then say what a regular army is worth to a rising army of volunteers.

Written at the end of November and the beginning of December 1861

First published in *The Volunteer Journal, for Lancashire and Cheshire,* No. 66, December 6, 1861

Signed: *F. E.*

Reproduced from the journal

THE WAR IN AMERICA[474]

The real opening of the campaign in this war dates from the advance of the Union forces in Kentucky. Not before Missouri and Western Virginia had been finally reconquered did this advance commence. The Secessionist[475] troops held three strong positions—entrenched camps—in the State of Kentucky: Columbus, on the Mississippi, on their left; Bowling Green, in the centre; Mill Springs, on the Cumberland River, on their right. Their line thus extended fully 250 miles as the crow flies. By road, the distance certainly was 300 miles east and west. Such an extended line precluded all possibility of these corps supporting each other, and gave the Federal forces a chance of attacking each of them separately with superior forces. There was no great risk in such a course, as none of the three Secessionist corps were strong enough to advance, even if unopposed, beyond the Ohio River. The great mistake in the Secessionist position was the attempt to occupy everything, and the consequent dissemination of the troops. One strong central entrenched camp, destined to be the prepared battle-field for a decisive action, and held by the main body, would have defended Kentucky far more efficiently; for it must either have attracted the main body of the Federals, or placed them in a disadvantageous position if they attempted to march past it without noticing this strong concentration of troops. As it was, the Federals attempted to attack these three camps one after another, and to manoeuvre their enemy out of them, so as to compel him to fight in the open. This plan was completely in accordance with the rules of military art, and it was executed with a vigour and rapidity which deserves much commendation, as well as the perfect success obtained. Towards the middle of January, a body of 15,000 Federals moved upon Mill Springs, which was held by about 10,000 Confederates. The Federals manoeuvred so as to make their adversaries believe that but a weak force was in the neighbourhood, and the Confederate general, Zollicoffer, at once took the bait thrown out to him. He marched out of his works, attacked the first Federal body he met, but very soon found that he had to do with a force superior to his own in numbers, and at least its equal in spirit and discipline. He fell, and his troops were as completely routed as the Federals had been at Bull Run.[476] But this time the victory was followed up far differently. The beaten army were pursued very closely until they arrived, broken, demoralised, and deprived of their field artillery and baggage, at their camp of Mill Springs. The camp was constructed on the northern shore of the Cumberland River, so that the troops, in case of another defeat, had no retreat but by a few steamers and boats across the river. We shall find that almost all these Secessionist camps were thus placed on the enemy's side of a river. Such an encampment is perfectly correct, and of the greatest utility—when there is a bridge. The camp, in that case, serves as a bridge-head, and gives to its occupants the chance of throwing their forces at will on either bank of the river, by which alone they obtain a perfect command over it. But to do the same thing when there is no bridge, is to place your troops in a position where they have no retreat after an unlucky engagement, and when, therefore, they will either have to surrender or to be massacred and drowned, same as the Federals were whom General Stone's treachery had sent across the Potomac at Balls Bluff.[477]

Accordingly, when the defeated Secessionists reached their camp at Mill Springs, the fact at once became patent to them that unless they could beat off an attack on their entrenchments, they would have to surrender very speedily. After the experience of the morning, they had no longer any confidence in their powers of resistance; and when the Federals, next morning, advanced to attack the entrenched camp, they found that the enemy had taken advantage of the night to cross the river, abandoning camp, baggage, artillery, and stores. Thus the extreme right of the Confederate line was driven back into Tennessee; and Eastern Kentucky, where the population are chiefly Union men, was reconquered for the Union.

About the same time—the second half of January—the preparations for dislodging the Secessionists from Columbus and Bowling Green were commenced. A strong fleet of mortar-boats and iron-clad gunboats had been got ready, and the news was spread everywhere that they were to accompany the march of a strong army down the Mississippi, from Cairo to Memphis and New Orleans. A ridiculously conspicuous reconnaissance was made towards Columbus. The retreat of this strong body of troops, which did not effect anything, even looked like a serious check to the Union troops. But it seems that all these demonstrations on the Mississippi were mere blinds. When everything was ready, the gunboats were quietly removed into the Ohio, and thence into the Tennessee River, which they steamed up to Fort Henry. This place, together with Fort Donelson, on the Cumberland River, formed a second line of defence of the Secessionists in Tennessee. The position was well chosen; for if they had retreated behind the Cumberland River, this would have covered their front, and the Tennessee River their left flank, while the narrow strip of land between the two would have been sufficiently covered by the two camps just named. But the rapid action of the Federals broke through the second line before even the left and centre of the first was attacked.

In the first week of February, the Federal gunboats appeared before Fort Henry, and shelled it with such effect that it at once surrendered. The garrison escaped to Fort Donelson, the land force of the expedition not being strong enough to invest the place. Then the gunboats steamed down the Tennessee again, up the Ohio, and up the Cumberland, towards Fort Donelson; only one gunboat boldly steamed up the Tennessee, right through the heart of the State of Tennessee, skirting the State of Mississippi, and penetrating as far as Florence, in Northern Alabama, where a series of flats and swamps (the so-called mussel shoals) stop further navigation. The single fact of one gunboat performing this long journey (at least 150 miles) and returning without ever being attacked, proves in itself that there must be, along this river at least, a strongly prevailing Union sentiment, which no doubt will tell very powerfully if the Federals should penetrate so far.

The naval expedition up the Cumberland now concerted its movements with those of the land forces under Generals Halleck and Grant. The Secessionists at Bowling Green were deceived as to the Federal movements, and remained quiet and confident in their camp, while a week after the fall of Fort Henry, Fort Donelson was invested on the land side by 40,000 Federals and menaced on the river by a powerful fleet of gunboats. Same as Mill Springs and Fort Henry, the entrenched camp of Fort Donelson was constructed with its rear to the river and no bridge for a retreat. It was the strongest place the Federals had as yet attacked. The works were not only constructed with much greater care, but, besides, it was large enough to shelter the 20,000 men which held it. On the first day of the attack, the gunboats silenced the fire of the batteries facing the river and shelled the interior of the works, while the land forces drove in the enemy's outposts and compelled the main body to take shelter close under the guns of their works. On the second day, the gunboats, having suffered severely the day before, appear to have done little work, but the land forces had to fight a long and sometimes severe battle with the columns of the garrison, which tried to break through their right in order to keep open the line of retreat towards Nashville. But a vigorous attack of the Federal right upon the Secessionist left, and strong reinforcements sent to the Federal left, decided the victory in favour of the assailants. Several outworks had been stormed; the garrison, hemmed in within their inner lines of defence, without any chances of retreat, and evidently not in a condition to resist an assault next morning, surrendered on the third day unconditionally. General Floyd escaped on the evening of the second day, it is said, with 5,000 men. It is not quite clear how that was possible; the number is too large to have been stowed away on steamers during the night; but still they may have successively crossed the river, and escaped along its right bank. The whole of the artillery, baggage, and stores, together with 13,300 prisoners, fell into the hands of the Unionists; 1,000 more prisoners were made next day, and on the appearance of the Federal advanced guard, Clarksville, a town higher up the river, surrendered with great quantities of stores, collected there for the Secessionist troops.

Whether Nashville has also fallen, appears very uncertain, and we can scarcely believe it. As it is, these successes of the Federals, in the short space of three weeks, are quite enough for them to be satisfied with. Columbus, the only place the Secessionists now hold in Kentucky, they can continue to hold at very great risks only. If they lose a decisive battle in Tennessee, the garrison of Columbus cannot escape being compelled to surrender, unless the Federals commit very great blunders. And that the Confederates are now compelled to fight a decisive battle in Tennessee, is one of the great results of the Federal victories. They have concentrated, we are told, 65,000 men at and about Nashville; it may be that they have succeeded in collecting even a larger force. But the combined troops of Halleck, Grant, Buell, and Thomas, together with the reserve now hurrying up from the camps of instruction in Kentucky, Ohio, Indiana, and Illinois, will enable the Federals to outnumber them; and with their *morale* necessarily much raised above that of their adversaries by the late successes, and with a strong Union party among the population to keep them well informed of the movements of the enemy, we do not see that they have any reason to be afraid of the issue.

Written between March 7 and 14, 1862

Reproduced from the journal

First published in *The Volunteer Journal, for Lancashire and Cheshire*, No. 80, March 14, 1862

AN INSPECTION OF ENGLISH VOLUNTEERS[478]

[*Allgemeine Militär-Zeitung,*
No. 44, November 1, 1862]

Two years have passed since you permitted me to report in your journal on the review of volunteers in Newton in August 1860.[a] It may be of interest to your readers to learn something further, after such a lapse of time, on the strength and tactical training of the *English militia.*

On a suitable occasion, perhaps soon, I shall go into the strength and present organisation of the volunteers; I limit myself today to saying that the official effective strength of the volunteer army is 162,800 men, stronger, that is, than ever before, and I proceed at once to describe, by an example, the tactical training of this army.

On August 2 Colonel McMurdo, Inspector General of all volunteers, held a review at Heaton Park, one hour from Manchester, of the contingent raised by that city. The troops consisted of the First, Second and Third Manchester "regiments" (6th, 28th and 40th Lancashire Corps) and the "regiments" raised by the suburbs of Ardwick and Salford (33rd and 56th Lancashire). Only three of these so-called "regiments" (the First and Third Manchester and the Ardwick Corps) were in battalion strength; the other two together made up a battalion; these battalions varied from 18 to 21 squads per company, each battalion was made up of eight companies and was about 400 strong on the average, including officers. Also present were the volunteer cavalry (32 men) and artillery (two amusette one-pounders lent by Mr. Whitworth and about 150 men, constituted as infantry to guard the guns), likewise from Manchester. In most

---

a See this volume, pp. 409-16.— *Ed.*

of the battalions the infantry could have been stronger by 100-150 men, but the commanders seem to have seen to it that the untrained men stayed at home.

The terrain (the southern portion of the park belonging to the Earl of Wilton, where horse races were previously held) is a hilly ridge dropping from west to east; it is bounded by valley bottoms on the right and left which, in front of the eastern foot of the hill, combine to form a flat meadow some 800 paces square. The brook running along the northern foot of the hill, beyond which the land rises again, limited the terrain on that side; in every other direction it was enclosed by the woods up against the park wall. The terrain is quite open in character except for fenced or free-standing shrubbery as well as isolated trees and a swampy place here and there.

Colonel McMurdo's reviews, contrary to most usual reviews of volunteers, are always conducted without a programme prepared in advance and known to the troops; the gentlemen never know in advance what they will be called on to do. Accordingly, the manoeuvres they are ordered to perform are only such as are actually employed in face of the enemy, excluding any kind of tactical sophistication. McMurdo, the son-in-law of Sir Charles Napier, the conqueror of Sind,[479] and his chief of staff in India, is no pedant but a thoroughly practical soldier, and all his actions with the volunteers prove that he is just the man for his present position.

The brigade received the inspector in line, as usual. After the initial formalities, he had quarter-distance columns formed (the usual column in England for manoeuvres of bodies of troops outside the range of enemy fire), then had the ranks closed to centre and the front of the line of the column shifted forward to the right, so that the flat meadow mentioned above and the woods of the eastern wall of the park lay to the front. During these manoeuvres, which were executed rapidly and without disorder, the cavalry deployed in extended formation, went through the woods and opened fire on the supposed enemy, but soon drew back. Now the battalion on the right wing (6th Lancashire) was sent forward, four companies deployed and four in support; the next two battalions (the combined 28th and 56th Lancashire and the 33rd Lancashire) deployed, while the battalion on the left wing (40th Lancashire) remained in column formation and took up a position, along with the cavalry, 200 paces to the rear, as reserve. The two guns were placed on the edge of a hill on the right wing of the line of skirmishers. Until the order to advance was given, the skirmishers, the supporting troops and the deployed line lay flat on the ground. In this posture the brigade made a genuinely military impression such as one is not accustomed to find in usual volunteer manoeuvres; one could see that a real soldier was in command.

The signal to advance and fire sounded for the line of skirmishers. The combat in loose order was not executed particularly well. The men, accustomed to deploying to a pattern on the open plain of their drill-ground, were much too anxiously concerned with their alignment to think of cover. Natural features and thickets were so much Greek to them. Besides, there were the fenced bushes, which were not to be entered and completely confused the men; one company remained halted before one such thicket in the narrow valley and fired into it with the utmost composure, while the rest of the line had long since gone around and was already beyond it. In addition, the line of skirmishers swung gradually all the way over to the left flank, so that the woods into which the cavalry had charged were attacked very little or not at all and the front of the deployed line was more and more exposed. Since the initial disposition and course of the manoeuvre did not seem in any way to call for this movement, I must presume that it was due to a misunderstanding. The artillery advanced, firing, with the right wing of the skirmishers, laid itself for the most part open; and if my field glasses did not deceive me, the wheels of the gun carriages were often tilted on the slope.

The skirmishers were also reinforced for a moment by deployment of the supporting troops and then called back; the deployed line had gone forward in the meantime and opened fire by squads. The fire of the right wing, especially the 28th Lancashire, was very heavy and almost too fast; in the centre, at the right wing of the 33rd Lancashire, it was sluggish and interrupted by long pauses, and rather irregular on the left wing. Here one part of the line stood just behind an undulation of the ground almost twice the height of a man, but that did not stop them from rattling away at it merrily. Meanwhile, the 40th Lancashire had come up from its position in the reserve to 200 paces behind the line, and deployed; to the right of it, the reassembled 6th Lancashire spread out. Both let the left-wing sections of the companies swing back to the rear in order to make room for the passage through of the first line, now breaking off by companies in double files and falling back. I must say that I have never been able to take kindly to this manoeuvre prescribed

in the regulations; on this occasion it made a worse impression
than ever on me. The regulations prescribe that the first line, as it
draws back, wheels about and goes up in line, up to a company in
frontage, to the second line, which is likewise deployed; the first
line then breaks off by companies and passes through the gaps
formed as described above. If the first line is pulling back only
because it is out of ammunition, is little unnerved and need not
fear any immediate attack, such a manoeuvre can be executed at
the double; for an active adversary, however, this would certainly
be the moment to send in his main body. Here, however, the
thing was not even done according to the regulations. The
first line broke off at once in companies and had to retire a
full two hundred paces in this formation, which was rather
untidily executed into the bargain, without being covered by
skirmishers.

The 6th and 40th Lancashire regiments for their part now
opened up fire by squads, which was considerably more uniform
and better sustained than that of the two other battalions. After
perhaps four or five cartridges per man had been shot off—the
artillery had kept up a continuous fire from the right wing of
whatever unit formed the first line at the time—halt was sounded
and this ended the first act of the manoeuvres. So far Colonel
McMurdo had handled his brigade as a detached body engaged in
independent combat with a supposed enemy; the positions and
movements were all related to the opposite terrain held by the
enemy. From this point on he drew up the four battalions in a
single line, operating as the first line of a larger unit. The limited
space no longer made it possible to take the terrain opposite into
account, and in order to keep the men together in mass
movement, there was no further deployment of skirmishers.

[*Allgemeine Militär-Zeitung*, No. 45, November 8, 1862]

At the beginning, the first line changed front forward to the
left, which brought it into the prolongation of the above-
mentioned northern valley. The other battalions deployed to the
left of it and the entire line opened fire by squads. It was then
extended more and more to the left, while from the right wing on
the battalions broke off in companies one after another, marched
behind the front to the left wing, and reformed there. After the
left wing had in this way been shifted almost to the woods of the
western wall of the park, the front was drawn back 90 degrees to

the right, with the left wing as pivot. With the exception of the battalion on the left wing, this manoeuvre was executed, as usual, by assembling the battalions in quarter-distance columns, marching along the line of the new direction and deploying, and was done very quickly and in perfect order, even though on a steep slope. As the battalions deployed again, I went right along the front of the 40th Lancashire Corps and saw each company come up into the line of direction, and I must say that our best-drilled continental troops of the line might have done this more elegantly and "smartly" but certainly not more calmly or quickly. In the course of the manoeuvre Colonel McMurdo expressed his appreciation out loud several times to the battalion. The 6th Lancashire Corps too deployed rapidly and in order; I have seen French troops of the line execute this manoeuvre much more carelessly.

After some squad firing the brigade advanced in echelons from the left flank with 100 paces distance between the battalions, halted and formed a square at the double. This was not executed particularly well since the march through the thickets had separated the men to some extent. The battalions deployed again, advanced into alignment with the battalion on the left wing, each gave a salvo, which by and large was solid enough, and now the entire brigade advanced in a single line. I could wish that some of the officers, so numerous in Germany, who hold that movements in line cannot be executed with young troops, could have seen the frontal march of this line of 640 squads. The terrain was as rugged as one could wish. The front ran across a hilly ridge that fell off rather steeply on three sides, the ground was full of holes and humps, and there were many single trees. None the less the line went forward several hundred paces in perfect order, fairly well aligned, in close order and without deviation, especially the two centre battalions (6th and 40th), and Colonel McMurdo, both on the spot and later to his staff officers, expressed his complete satisfaction with this manoeuvre. Finally he had the attack sounded, and now off they went, as volunteer troops do, running at top speed a hundred paces or so down the slope into the open field, more like a race than an attack. When the halt was sounded, the 40th Lancashire Corps was compact and in order, though poorly aligned, the Sixth not in such good order. On the wings, however, especially the left, things were very disorderly; the men were badly disarrayed, many had fallen, and one man in the front rank was wounded in the calf, since at that point part of the second rank had also fixed bayonets. This ended the manoeuvres; the troops formed up to defile, defiled and went home.

I believe that an example like this will give the readers of the *Allgemeine Militär-Zeitung* a much more vivid picture of the character and the degree of training of these volunteers than any doctrinaire discussions. Although the number of troops concentrated there was small, just for that reason it was possible to execute more practical manoeuvres than would otherwise be possible here with larger masses of volunteers; sufficient space for the latter is never to be found here. In addition, the battalions present constituted a very good average sample of the English volunteer corps: two of them, as will have been seen, were considerably more advanced than the other two and represented the consolidated battalions of the larger cities; the other two, which were more backward in their training if only because of their less homogeneous composition, were more representative of the units formed in the country and smaller towns. On the whole it can be said that the volunteers have adequately learned the principal battalion manoeuvres; they form columns and deploy, and they move in columns and in line with sufficient, and occasionally great assurance. On the other hand, it would be well to spare them the artificial marches and counter-marches still contained in the English regulations, as in so many others. Open-order combat, always the weak side of the English, is known to the volunteers only to the extent that it could be taught them on the drill-ground, but in this respect too there are significant differences among the various battalions. The errors that came to light in this inspection do not differ in any way, as we have seen, from the errors seen daily in the training exercises of our continental peacetime armies, even though those armies have the advantage of being led by officers who have grown grey on the field of manoeuvre. In this connection it should not be overlooked that the officers of the English volunteers are still the weak side of the entire corps, although here too considerable improvement can be seen. One who rejoices in the *march past* will find that the volunteers are further advanced in this art too than he would have expected. Finally, as to their performance on the firing range, they can beyond question bear comparison with any standing army in Europe and certainly have an average of more good shots per battalion than most troops of the line. All in all, the experiment is to be regarded, after three years, as completely successful. Almost without any expense to the Government, England has created an organised army of 163,000 men for the country's defence—an army that has gone so far in its training that, depending on the varying degree of training of the battalions, it needs only three to six weeks of encampment and exercises to become a thoroughly dependable field force. And in the worst of cases any attempt at invasion would be bound to give the English at least that much time!

Written probably between August 2 and 8, 1862

First published in the *Allgemeine Militär-Zeitung*, Nos. 44 and 45, November 1 and 8, 1862

Signed: *F. E.*

Printed according to the newspaper

Translated from the German

Published in English for the first time

NOTES
AND
INDEXES

NOTES

[1] In April 1857 Charles Dana, one of the founders of *The New American Cyclopaedia*, invited Marx to contribute to it. On Engels' advice, Marx agreed to write a number of articles, and Engels promised to help him with those on military and military-historical subjects. Subsequently Engels undertook most of these articles so that Marx could complete his economic research. Marx wrote primarily biographical essays on military figures and on politicians, for which Engels also helped him to elucidate the military aspect. Marx's and Engels' work together for the *Cyclopaedia*, like their joint reporting for the *New-York Daily Tribune*, is an example of the close collaboration between the founders of scientific communism.

The New American Cyclopaedia was "a popular dictionary of general knowledge" prepared by a group of progressive bourgeois journalists and publishers on the *New-York Daily Tribune* editorial board and edited by Charles Dana and George Ripley. It was published in 16 volumes by D. Appleton and Company, New York, in 1858-63 and reprinted in 1868 and 1869. A number of prominent US and European scholars wrote for it. Despite the eclecticism typical of this and other bourgeois encyclopaedias, many articles in *The New American Cyclopaedia* reflected progressive democratic views. Marx and Engels wrote their articles from revolutionary-proletarian, materialist positions notwithstanding the editors' demand not to express their party point of·view. But because of this demand Marx limited the range of his subjects mainly to military problems and to the study of different countries, giving up the idea of writing essays on the history of German philosophy, the Napoleonic Code, Chartism, socialism and communism, which he thought it inadmissible to deal with even in a spirit of apparent neutrality. It may have been for this reason also that Marx did not contribute the article "Aesthetics" as originally planned.

The articles in *The New American Cyclopaedia* were published anonymously, and only volumes II, V and XVI contained lists of the authors of major articles. Marx is also mentioned as the author of the articles "Army", "Artillery", "Bernadotte", "Bolivar", "Cavalry", "Fortification", "Infantry", and "Navy" (actually these articles were written by Engels, except for "Bernadotte" and "Bolivar"). Marx's and Engels' authorship of other articles has been established on the basis of the Marx-Engels correspondence, Charles Dana's letters to Marx, Marx's notebooks, where the dispatch of articles to New York was entered, and other material (conspectuses, extracts for articles, etc.). In all, the authorship of 81 articles has been established. Some of them may have been abridged by the *Cyclopaedia*'s editors, who in some cases interfered with the text.

Marx and Engels contributed to *The New American Cyclopaedia* from July 1857 to November 1860, and their articles (those known to us) were published in volumes I-V, VII, IX and XII. They were also included, unchanged, in the 1868-69 edition of the *Cyclopaedia* but were not reprinted any more during their authors' lifetime. A collection of them was not published until 1933 in the Soviet Union in: Marx and Engels, *Works*, First Russian Edition, Vol. XI, Part II.

The most complete publication of these articles was in volumes 14 (1959) and 44 (1977) of the Second Russian Edition of the *Works* of Marx and Engels. However, this publication left out some articles—"Austerlitz", "Augereau", and "Badajos", of which Engels was erroneously regarded as the author. When preparing the Russian edition, the editors established the true authorship of a number of articles wrongly attributed to Marx and Engels by some bibliographers. Thus the articles "Abd-el-Kader" and "Chartism" were written by William Humphrey, "Austerlitz" by Henry W. Herbert, "Epicurus" by Hermann Raster, "Socialism" by Parke Godwin, and "Hegel" by Henry Smith. The article "Aesthetics" could not have been by Marx either, for it conflicts with the views expressed by Marx on the subject in his works.

In the present English edition, the articles by Marx and Engels from *The New American Cyclopaedia* are published on the basis of research carried out during the preparation of the Second Russian Edition of their *Works*.

p. XXIX

2 "Abensberg" is the first in the provisional list of articles for *The New American Cyclopaedia* written by Engels overleaf his letter to Marx of May 28, 1857, to be agreed on with Dana with respect to his initial request (see present edition, Vol. 40). Besides this theme Engels listed the following: Aboukir, Axle (artillery), Acre (St. Jean d'Acre, its siege), Actium (battle of), Adjutant, Afghanistan (invasion by English), Åland Isles—see Bomarsund, Albuera (battle of), Aldenhoven, Alessandria (fortress and sieges), Algeria (French conquest of and English bombardment of), Almeida (siege of in Peninsular war), Amusette (artillery), Anglesey (Marquis of), Attack (in battle and siege), Antwerp (fortress and sieges), Approaches, Arbela (battle of), Arquebuse, Aspern and Essling (battle of 1809), Augereau (Marshal), Advanced Guard. In his letter to Marx, July 11, 1857, Engels said that he had begun writing articles according to the list (by that time it had probably been slightly changed) and promised to send him by July 14 the articles "Abensberg", "Adjutant", "Alma" and "Ammunition" (the last two were not mentioned in the list), "and more such stuff, thus finishing off the whole of A (except 'Algeria' and 'Afghanistan') up to Ap and Aq". On July 14 Marx thanked Engels for the first, and on July 24 for the second, batch of articles he had received. Judging by an entry in Marx's notebook about the dispatch of the first batch, this material was sent off to New York on July 24. Some articles mentioned in the list ("Axle", "Approaches", "Advanced Guard") were not published in the *Cyclopaedia* and were probably not written by Engels. There is no indication that Engels wrote the articles "Anglesey" and "Augereau".   p. 3

3 The defeat of the Austrian army at Abensberg was an episode in the five-day *battle of Regensburg* (from April 19 to 23) during the Austro-French war of 1809 (a war waged by France against the fifth European coalition: Austria, Britain,

Portugal and Spain). It was followed by the Austrians' defeat at Landshut on April 21 and at Eckmühl on April 22, and their retreat from Regensburg on April 23 under pressure from French troops. Nevertheless, the Austrian army retained its fighting capacity and put up a stubborn resistance to the French advance on Vienna.   p. 3

4 Acre was captured by Richard Coeur de Lion in 1191 during the third crusade (1189-92). The *crusades* were military colonialist expeditions by the big West European feudal lords and Italian trading cities under the religious banner of recovering Jerusalem and other "Holy Lands" from the Mohammedans. Peasants also took part in the crusades, hoping thus to be freed from feudal oppression. History knows eight main crusades (1096-99, 1147-49, 1189-92, 1202-04, 1217-21, 1228-29, 1248-54 and 1270). Not only Mohammedan states in Syria, Palestine, Egypt and Tunisia but also the Christian Byzantine Empire were the objects of the crusaders' aggressive strivings. The crusaders' conquests in the Eastern Mediterranean were not lasting, and were recovered by the Mohammedans.

The *Knights of St. John* (also Hospitallers)—members of a Catholic military order founded by the crusaders in Palestine early in the twelfth century. After the defeat at Acre in 1291 they transferred their seat to Cyprus, then, early in the fourteenth century, to Rhodes and in 1530 to Malta (from that time on it was also called the order of Malta); since the nineteenth century its seat has been in Rome.   p. 4

5 The abortive siege of Acre by the French (from March 21 to May 20, 1799) was an episode in the Egyptian expedition of the French army and navy under General Bonaparte, started in 1798 with a view to conquering Egypt and Syria from Turkey and preparing a base for a blow against the British possessions in India. Napoleon's successes in Egypt were reduced to naught by the destruction of the French fleet by the British squadron under Admiral Nelson at Aboukir on August 1, 1798, the victories of the Russo-Austrian forces under Suvorov over the French in Northern Italy, and the successful actions of the Russian squadron under Admiral Ushakov in the Mediterranean. Napoleon returned to France in the autumn of 1799 and the army left in Egypt was forced to capitulate to the British in 1801.   p. 4

6 A reference to the military clashes between Turkey and the Egyptian ruler Mehemet Ali, who revolted against the Sultan. Syria was seized by Egypt during the Turkish-Egyptian war of 1831-33, but was restored to Turkey with the military support of the European powers during the war of 1839-41.

                                                                                                    p. 4

7 Under the *Brundisium agreement* concluded by Octavian, Mark Antony and Lepidus in 40 B.C. the Roman state was divided among these triumvirs. Antony received the Eastern provinces, Octavian the Western provinces (together with Illyria), and Lepidus became ruler of Africa (in 36 B.C. he was ousted from power by Octavian). The agreement remained in force until the open conflict between Antony and Octavian in 31 B.C.   p. 5

8 Engels informed Marx of his intention to write this article ("Airey") in a letter dated May 28, 1857. The letter contained a list of themes planned for the beginning of their contribution to *The New American Cyclopaedia* (the theme in question was not in the list). In this letter Engels asked Marx for information about Airey's military career prior to the Crimean campaign. Marx's extracts

from several sources have survived, in particular from the *Opening Address of Major-General Sir Richard Airey, K.C.B., Quartermaster-General of the Forces. Before the Board of General Officers Assembled at the Royal Hospital, Chelsea*, London, 1856, which were used in this article.

Marx may have put the finishing touches to the text sent to New York, and the article can be regarded as written jointly by Marx and Engels. But it is also possible that Engels himself used the extracts made for him by Marx.

p. 7

9 Under the *Frederikshamm Peace Treaty* of September 1809, which concluded the Russo-Swedish war of 1808-09, Sweden ceded Finland and the Åland Islands to Russia. p. 9

10 The *battle of Bomarsund* in August 1854, during the Crimean war, is described by Engels in two articles in the *New-York Daily Tribune* (see present edition, Vol. 13, pp. 379-88) and in an item in *The New American Cyclopaedia* (see this volume, p. 287). p. 9

11 A reference to the *battle of Hangut*, a peninsula at the exit of the Gulf of Finland, which took place on July 25-27, 1714, between the Russian and Swedish fleets during the Northern war (1700-21). The battle ended in a victory for the Russians. p. 9

12 During the Peninsular war between Britain and Napoleonic France (1808-14), the fortress of *Badajos* (Southwestern Spain) was three times besieged by the Anglo-Spanish-Portuguese allied army under Wellington. Alongside the regular hostilities, the Spanish and Portuguese peoples waged a national liberation war against the French invaders. Captured by the French in March 1811, Badajos was besieged by the allies on May 4. The siege lasted 10 days and was raised in view of Soult's approaching army. At the end of this article Engels says that the siege of Badajos was raised a few days after the battle of Albuera (May 16, 1811), an inaccuracy which was revealed after publication of the article and which is explained (see Engels' letter to Marx of February 18, 1858) by a mistake in one of the sources used by Engels. On May 25, following the victory at Albuera, the allies resumed the siege but on June 17 they lifted it because of the approaching French reserves. The allies laid siege to Badajos for a third time on March 16, 1812 and took it on April 6 after successfully storming it.

p. 10

13 The *battle of Neerwinden* (Belgium) on March 18, 1793 was fought between the French army and an Austrian force advancing after the victory at Aldenhoven during the war of revolutionary France against the anti-French European coalition (Austria, Prussia, Britain and others). It ended in a victory for the Austrians. p. 12

14 Engels' letter to Marx of May 28, 1857 shows that in this article he also intended to describe the battle of Aldenhoven of October 2, 1794, in which the French defeated the Austrians. Either Engels did not do so or the editors of the *Cyclopaedia* abridged the text. p. 12

15 *The New American Cyclopaedia* has two items under this title. The first item reads as follows: "ALESSANDRIA. I. A division of Piedmont, containing about 550,000 inhabitants, growing maize, wine, silk, madder, and flax."

Item II is by Engels (who in his letter to Marx of May 28, 1857 said that he was going to write about fortresses and sieges) and is the one reproduced in this volume.   p. 13

16 The unsuccessful siege of *Alessandria* by the French in 1657 was an episode in the Franco-Spanish war of 1635-59. Northern Italy, the greater part of which (the Duchy of Milan) had fallen into the hands of the King of Spain by 1635, was one of its theatres.

The seizure of Alessandria by Prince Eugene of Savoy in October 1706 was a military operation by the allied Austrian and Savoy troops against the French in the *War of the Spanish Succession* (1701-14) caused by the struggle for the division of the then decaying feudal Spain's European and colonial possessions, and by the naval and colonial rivalry between Britain and France. France and Spain, whose crown passed to Philip Bourbon, grandson of Louis XIV, after the extinction of the male line of the Spanish Habsburgs, were opposed by a coalition of Britain, the Austrian Habsburgs (to which dynasty the Emperor of Germany also belonged), the Netherlands, the Duchy of Savoy, Portugal, Prussia and other German states. As a result of the war the Spanish possessions in Northern Italy passed to the Austrian Habsburgs while the fortress of Alessandria was ceded to the Duchy of Savoy.   p. 13

17 Annexed to France in September 1802 Piedmont was ruled, together with Genoa annexed in 1805, by a French military governor. In 1814 the independence of Piedmont was restored under the rule of the Savoy dynasty. The territory of the former Genoese Republic was united to it by decision of the Vienna Congress of 1815.   p. 13

18 "Alma" did not figure in the provisional list of articles for *The New American Cyclopaedia* contained in Engels' letter to Marx of May 28, 1857. But on July 11, 1857 Engels wrote to Marx that in a few days he was going to send him an item on this subject, together with other articles under A. Marx apparently sent it to New York with the first batch of articles on July 24, 1857. Charles Dana acknowledged receipt in a letter of September 2, 1857.   p. 14

19 There are three items bearing this title in *The New American Cyclopaedia:* "ALMEIDA. I. A town of Portugal", "II. A seaport town of Brazil" and "ALMEIDA, Francisco de, the first Portuguese viceroy of India". The provisional list of articles in Engels' letter to Marx of May 28, 1857, contains the note: "Almeida (siege of in Peninsular war)", which provides grounds for regarding Engels as the author of the first item. The battle mentioned in it was fought during the Peninsular war of 1808-14 (see Note 12).   p. 19

20 The events mentioned in the text belong to the period of the bourgeois revolution in the Netherlands (1566-1609), in which the struggle of the bourgeoisie and the masses against the feudal system was linked with the war of national liberation against absolutist Spain which had subjugated the Netherlands (now Belgium and Holland) in the sixteenth century. In the course of the war with Spain, the Northern Provinces formed the Dutch Republic (the United Provinces of the Netherlands) and won independence, while the Southern Netherlands remained under the Spaniards. In 1576 Antwerp was burned down by the Spaniards, the following year it was recaptured by the insurgents, and in 1579 it joined the anti-Spanish United Northern Provinces. However, in 1585 it was retaken by the Spaniards.   p. 21

[21] In the autumn of 1832 the Anglo-French fleet blockaded the Dutch ports, and the French army laid siege to the fortress of *Antwerp* to force Holland to fulfil the terms of the London Treaty of 1831. The treaty provided for recognition of the independence of Belgium which had separated from the Kingdom of the Netherlands as a result of the bourgeois revolution of 1830, and for the transfer of Antwerp to the Belgians. The fortress capitulated in late December 1832.   p. 21

[22] Evidence indicates that the articles "Arbela", "Arquebuse", "Aspern" and "Attack" belong to the second batch of articles beginning with A (according to the provisional list in Engels' letter to Marx of May 28, 1857), which he forwarded to Marx immediately after the first batch "up to Ap and Aq" received by Marx on July 14, 1857. On July 24 Marx wrote to Engels that he had received the new material, and judging by an entry in his notebook, he dispatched it, together with the first batch of articles, to New York.

Among the preparatory materials collected by Engels for the article "Army" there is an extract from the article "Arbela", published in the third volume of *The Encyclopaedia Britannica* (Edinburgh, 1853), which he probably used when writing this article.   p. 23

[23] The *battle of Arbela* on October 1, 331 B.C. completed the military rout of the Persia of the Achaemenids and the conquest of its territories by Alexander of Macedon. It was preceded by two big battles between the Macedonian and Persian armies: in May 334 B.C. on the Granicus river (Northwestern Asia Minor) and in November 333 B.C. at Issus (a town in Cilicia on the road from Asia Minor to Syria). These battles were won by the Macedonians.   p. 23

[24] The *battle of Bosworth* (Leicestershire, England) on August 22, 1485 was fought between the soldiers of Henry Tudor, distant relative of the House of Lancaster, and the army of Richard III, of the House of York. Richard III was defeated and killed and Henry Tudor was proclaimed King Henry VII. This battle ended the War of the Roses (1455-85) between the House of York, whose emblem was a white rose, and the Lancastrians with a red rose as their emblem.
                                                                      p. 24

[25] The *battle of Agincourt* (Azincourt) on October 25, 1415 was fought during the Hundred Years' War, a series of wars between England and France lasting from 1337 to 1453, and ended in a victory for the English. The cause of the war was the struggle of the two countries over the possession of the commercial and industrial towns of Flanders, the main consumer of English wool, and the English kings' claims to the French throne. In the first period of the war the English managed to seize a considerable part of Southwestern France, but during the 1360s and 1370s almost the whole of this territory was liberated. In 1415 the English feudal lords resumed hostilities and soon seized all of Northern France, including Paris. However, as a result of a popular war against the foreign invaders, the English were driven out of the whole of France with the exception of Calais.   p. 24

[26] The *battle of Pavia* (Northern Italy) took place on February 24, 1525 between the armies of Francis I of France, then an ally of Henry VIII of England, and of Charles V (Emperor of Germany and King of Spain). The French were defeated and Francis I himself taken prisoner. The battle was one of the major events in the Italian wars waged (with intervals) from 1494 to 1559 between France, on the one hand, and Spain and the German (Holy Roman) Empire, on

the other, over the possession of Italy. As a result of these wars France was forced to give up its claims to Italy, the greater part of which fell into the hands of the Spanish Habsburgs.   p. 24

27 The *English civil wars* during the bourgeois revolution of the mid-seventeenth century were waged between the Royalists, who strove to restore the absolute power of Charles I, and the Parliamentarians. At the beginning of the first civil war (1642-46) the Parliamentary army, whose leaders favoured compromise with the Royalists, suffered defeats. But after the reorganisation of the armed forces by Oliver Cromwell, and thanks to the activity of the masses, there was a turn in the war and the King was defeated. In the spring of 1648 a second civil war broke out following Royalist revolts and the actions in support of Charles I by the Scottish feudal aristocracy. It ended in August 1648 with new victories by the revolutionary army. In 1649 Charles I was beheaded, and a republic was established in England.   p. 25

28 Engels refers here to the campaign against Austria during the war of Napoleonic France against the fifth anti-French coalition (Britain, Austria, Spain and Portugal) in 1809.

   The *grand army* (*grande armée*)—the name given in 1805 to the group of the armed forces of the French Empire operating in the main theatres of the Napoleonic wars. Besides French troops, it included contingents from various countries conquered by Napoleon (Italy, Holland, the German states and Poland).
                                                                                               p. 27

29 On the five-day *battle of Regensburg* (Bavaria), April 19-23, 1809 see Note 3.
                                                                                               p. 27

30 In the *battle at Waterloo* (Belgium) on June 18, 1815 Napoleon's army was routed by the Anglo-Dutch and Prussian armies under Wellington and Blücher, and this decided the final victory of the seventh anti-French coalition (Britain, Russia, Austria, Prussia, Sweden, Spain and other states). Victory was ensured by the endurance of the British infantrymen who rebuffed the numerous attacks of the French, and by Blücher's army which came in time to the aid of the Anglo-Dutch forces.   p. 31

31 A reference to the *battle of Leipzig* on October 16-19, 1813 between the armies of the sixth European coalition (Russia, Austria, Prussia, Britain, Sweden, Spain and other states) and of Napoleonic France. This "battle of the nations" ended in victory for the anti-French coalition and led to Germany's liberation from Napoleon's rule.   p. 33

32 This refers to the continued hostilities between the armies of the sixth European coalition (Russia, Austria, Prussia, Britain, Sweden, Spain and other states) and of Napoleonic France on French territory from the beginning of 1814. Despite a series of defeats, the allies occupied Paris at the end of March 1814, and Napoleon abdicated and was exiled to Elba. His restoration to power in March 1815 led to the formation of the seventh anti-French coalition. There followed his defeat at Waterloo (see Note 30), his second abdication (on June 22, 1815) and his exile to St. Helena.   p. 34

33 Engels mentions the major battles fought during the Greco-Persian wars (500-449 B.C.) in which the Greek city-states managed to uphold their independence and to repulse the Persian state which had undertaken a number

of predatory campaigns in the Balkans. Under the peace treaty of 449 B.C. the King of Persia was compelled to give up his claims to the territories in the Aegean Sea and to recognise the independence of the Greek cities in Asia Minor which had been conquered by the Persians.

At the *battle of Marathon* (a plain in Attica), September 490 B.C., the army of the Athenians and Plataeans under Miltiades defeated the Persians.

In July 480 B.C. a small allied army of Greeks under Leonidas, King of Sparta, blocked the way to Central Greece, through the *Pass of Thermopylae*, for the many-thousand-strong Persian army under Xerxes. However, the Persians managed to outflank the Greeks. Leonidas withdrew his main forces, but three hundred Spartans headed by him continued to defend the passage and fell heroically in an unequal battle.

At the *battle of Plataea* (Central Greece) in the autumn of 479 B.C., the united Greek army under the Spartan Pausanias and the Athenian Aristides defeated the Persians.   p. 35

[34] At the *battle of Crécy* on August 26, 1346 and that of *Poitiers* on September 19, 1356, the English, using a combination of knights and archers, defeated the French army whose main force consisted of cavalry. These battles, like that of *Agincourt* (see Note 25), were fought during the Hundred Years' War (1337-1453) between England and France.   p. 35

[35] In 1812 the English ruling classes began a war against the USA with a view to restoring their domination in North America, lost as a result of the eighteenth-century American bourgeois revolution. At first the war favoured the English but in 1813 the Americans managed to drive them out of the state of Michigan, bordering on Canada. Though the English temporarily seized Washington in 1814, they suffered considerable losses, owing to the successful actions of the American fleet, and were forced to conclude a peace treaty in Ghent in December 1814 on the basis of recognition of the *status quo ante bellum.* Military operations ceased in January 1815.   p. 36

[36] On August 2, 216 B.C., at *Cannae* (Southeastern Italy), the Carthaginian general Hannibal defeated the Romans. This major battle of the Second Punic war between Rome and Carthage (218-01 B.C.) is described in detail by Engels in his article "Cavalry" (see this volume, p. 296).   p. 36

[37] The *battle of Leuctra* (Boeotia) between the Theban and Spartan armies was fought in 371 B.C., during the Boeotian war (378-362 B.C.). In this war Thebes, where democratic elements had come to power, opposed the supremacy of oligarchic Sparta in Greece. The defeat at Leuctra undermined Sparta's might and led to the decline of the Peloponnesian Alliance headed by it.

At *Mantinea* (Peloponnesus) the Thebans and their allies under Epaminondas defeated the Spartan army in 362 B.C. But the Thebans' heavy losses and the death of their general prevented them from consolidating their success. Thus Thebes failed to maintain its supremacy in Greece.   p. 36

[38] At the *battle of Fontenoy* (Belgium) on May 11, 1745, during the War of the Austrian Succession (1740-48), the French army under Maurice of Saxony defeated the allied Anglo-Hanoverian, Dutch and Austrian armies. The war was caused by the claims of some European states, primarily Prussia, to the Austrian Habsburgs' possessions which, after the death of Charles VI, passed to his daughter Maria Theresa, there being no male heir. Prussia's allies were

France, Bavaria (until 1742) and Saxony. England, which strove to weaken France—its commercial and colonial rival—fought on the side of Austria, also supported by the Netherlands, Sardinia and Russia. As a result of the war, Prussia seized and annexed Silesia, but the rest of the Habsburgs' possessions remained in the hands of Maria Theresa.

Chippewa was the site of a battle (July 5, 1814) won by the Americans during the 1812-14 war between England and the United States.   p. 37

39 On August 11, 1857 Marx made in his notebook the following entry concerning the dispatch of this item to New York: "Cyclopaedia. Afghanistan. Abatis." This item seems to belong to the *"militaria"* which Engels (at the time undergoing medical treatment at Liverpool) had promised Marx, in a letter dated July 30, 1857, he would send him as soon as possible (see present edition, Vol. 40). Charles Dana acknowledged receipt of the item in a letter to Marx of September 2, 1857.   p. 39

40 That Engels wanted to write an article on Afghanistan (with emphasis on the Anglo-Afghan war of 1838-42) is evident from the fact that he included this topic in the provisional list of articles for *The New American Cyclopaedia* in his letter to Marx of May 28, 1857. On July 11, 1857, however, Engels informed Marx that the article would not be ready by July 14, as agreed. The work on it apparently took longer than expected. Marx had received it by August 11 and, as can be seen from the entry in his notebook for this date, sent it off to New York. In a letter to Marx of September 2, 1857 Charles Dana acknowledged receipt of "Invasion of Afghanistan".

When working on this article Engels used J. W. Kaye's *History of the War in Afghanistan*, vols. I-II, London, 1851 (see this volume, pp. 379-90).   p. 40

41 Engels uses the term "clan", widespread in Western Europe, to designate *heli* (tribal groups) into which Afghan tribes were divided.   p. 41

42 *Soonees* (*Sunnites*) and *Sheeahs* (*Shiites*)—members of the two main Mohammedan sects which appeared in the seventh century as the result of conflicts between the successors of Mohammed, founder of Islam.   p. 42

43 The *Moguls*—invaders of Turkish descent, who came to India from the east of Central Asia in the early sixteenth century and in 1526 founded the Empire of the Great Moguls (named after the ruling dynasty of the Empire) in Northern India. Contemporaries regarded them as the direct descendants of the Mongol warriors of Genghis Khan, hence the name "Moguls". In the mid-seventeenth century the Mogul Empire included most of India and part of Afghanistan. Later on, however, the Empire began to decline due to peasant rebellions, the growing resistance of the Indian people to the Mohammedan conquerors, and increasing separatist tendencies. In the early half of the eighteenth century the Empire of the Great Moguls virtually ceased to exist.   p. 42

44 The *Mahrattas* (*Marathas*)—an ethnic group who lived in Northwestern Deccan. In the mid-seventeenth century they began an armed struggle against the Empire of the Great Moguls, thus contributing to its decline. In the course of the struggle the Mahrattas formed an independent state of their own, whose rulers soon embarked on wars of conquest. At the close of the seventeenth century their state was weakened by internal feudal strife, but early in the eighteenth century a powerful confederation of Mahratta principalities was formed under a supreme governor, the peshwa. In 1761 they suffered a crushing defeat at the hands of the Afghans in the struggle for supremacy in

India. Weakened by this struggle and internal feudal strife, the Mahratta principalities fell a prey to the East India Company and were subjugated by it as a result of the Anglo-Mahratta war of 1803-05.   p. 42

⁴⁵ The *Sikhs*—a religious sect which appeared in the Punjab (Northwestern India) in the sixteenth century. Their belief in equality became the ideology of the peasants and lower urban strata in their struggle against the Empire of the Great Moguls and the Afghan invaders at the end of the seventeenth century. Subsequently a local aristocracy emerged among the Sikhs and its representatives headed the Sikh principalities. In the early nineteenth century these principalities united under Ranjit Singh whose Sikh state included the Punjab and some neighbouring regions. The British authorities in India provoked an armed conflict with the Sikhs in 1845 and in 1846 succeeded in turning the Sikh state into a vassal. The Sikhs revolted in 1848, but were subjugated in 1849.
                                                                                    p. 43

⁴⁶ The *siege of Herat* by the Persians lasted from November 1837 to August 1838. Intent on increasing Britain's influence in Afghanistan and weakening Russia's in Persia, the British Government declared the Shah's actions to be hostile to Britain and demanded that he should lift the siege. Threatening him with war, it sent a squadron into the Persian Gulf in 1838. The Shah was forced to submit and to agree to a one-sided trade treaty with Britain. Marx described the siege of Herat in his article "The War against Persia" (see present edition, Vol. 15).   p. 44

⁴⁷ During the Anglo-Afghan war the East India Company resorted to threats and violence to obtain the consent of the feudal rulers of Sind, a region in the northwest of India (now in Pakistan) bordering on Afghanistan, to the passage of British troops across their territory. Taking advantage of this, the British demanded in 1843 that the local feudal princes proclaim themselves vassals of the Company. After crushing the rebel Baluchi tribes (natives of Sind), they declared the annexation of the entire region to British India.   p. 44

⁴⁸ *Sepoys*—mercenary troops in the British-Indian army recruited from the Indian population and serving under British officers. They were used by the British to subjugate India and to fight the wars of conquest against Afghanistan, Burma and other neighbouring states. However, the Sepoys shared the general discontent of the Indian people with the colonial regime and took part in the national liberation insurrection in India in 1857-59.   p. 46

⁴⁹ This is one of a number of articles beginning with B for which Marx received a request in the summer of 1857. He forwarded this request to Engels in his letter of August 26, 1857 (see present edition, Vol. 40). The list of articles asked for by Charles Dana has not survived, but later, in connection with an additional request from New York for articles beginning with B, Marx repeated it in his letter to Engels of February 1, 1858, reminding him of the work already done. The list included: "Barbette", "Bastion", "Bayonet", "Barclay de Tolly", "Battery", "Battle", "Bem", "Bennigsen", "Berthier", "Bernadotte", "Bessières", "Bivouac", "Blindage", "Blücher", "Blum", "Bolivar y Ponte", "Bomb", "Bombardier", "Bombardment", "Bomb (-ketch, -proof, -vessel)", "Bonnet", "Bosquet", "Bourrienne", "Bridge (pontoon)", "Brown (Sir George)", "Brune", and "Bugeaud". There is also a list of articles beginning with B (with some of the items crossed out) at the end of Marx's notebook for 1857.

In his letter of August 26, 1857 Marx asked Engels to send articles for the *Cyclopaedia* as soon as possible. By September 15 he had received three articles which, together with the articles "Barclay de Tolly" and "Berthier", he dispatched to New York on that day, as seen from his notebook entry for September 15: "Barclay. Berthier. Bayonet. Barbet. Bastion für die Cyclopaedia". On the same day Marx wrote to Engels that besides these articles he had forwarded to Dana the articles "Blum" and "Bourrienne", but according to his notebook they were dispatched to New York a week later, with other material.   p. 49

50 Engels' letter to Marx of September 10, 1857 and his biographical sketches of Bennigsen and Barclay enclosed in it show that the article "Barclay de Tolly" was a joint work of Marx and Engels, though the final editing was done by Marx. Besides reference books the authors used the following sources when writing this article: Martens' collected treatises and conventions, A. H. Jomini's *Vie politique et militaire de Napoléon* (Vol. 4, Paris, 1827) and Th. von Bernhardi's *Denkwürdigkeiten aus dem Leben des ... Grafen von Toll* (Vol. 2, Leipzig, 1856). In these books Russia's Patriotic War of 1812 against Napoleon's invasion is described tendentiously, which was bound to tell on the elucidation of some of its aspects in the articles written by Marx and Engels, who did not have more objective sources to hand at the time. This article, for example, contains inaccuracies in explaining why Mikhail Kutuzov was appointed commander-in-chief of the Russian army and why he abandoned the position at Gzhatsk (more precisely at Tsarevo-Zaimishche). His role in subsequent Russian military operations is also presented inaccurately. Barclay de Tolly is wrongly opposed to Kutuzov, for the former, though an outstanding Russian military leader and patriot, was far inferior to Kutuzov as regards strategic talent, the understanding of the character of the war, military experience and popularity among the army and the people. These were precisely the reasons why Kutuzov was appointed commander-in-chief under pressure from public opinion and despite Alexander I's dislike for him.

On this article's dispatch to New York see the previous note.   p. 50

51 A reference to the *battle of Preussisch-Eylau* (East Prussia) on February 7-8, 1807 between the French and the Russian army (which also included Prussian units) during the war of the fourth coalition (Britain, Russia, Prussia and Sweden) against France. After the defeat of the Prussian army by Napoleon in 1806 the main theatre of war shifted to East Prussia, where Napoleon came up against stubborn resistance from the allied army of Russia and Prussia. This battle was indecisive (see also Marx and Engels' article "Bennigsen", this volume, pp. 77-78).   p. 50

52 In March 1809 (during the Russo-Swedish war of 1808-09), Russian forces under Barclay de Tolly entered Swedish territory from Finland. This accelerated the carrying out of the Swedish aristocracy's plot against Gustavus Adolphus to limit the King's power in favour of the aristocratic oligarchy. In March 1809 Gustavus Adolphus was deposed and soon after his uncle, the Duke of Zudermanland, was proclaimed king under the name of Charles XIII. In September Sweden was compelled to sign the Frederickshamm Peace Treaty with Tsarist Russia (see Note 9).

A similar operation had earlier been undertaken by the Swedes themselves during the Danish-Swedish war of 1657-58: in January 1658, the Swedish army under Charles X invaded Denmark across the ice-bound straits of the Little and

the Great Belt and forced it to conclude a peace treaty advantageous to
Sweden.   p. 50

53 According to Phull's plan, if Napoleon invaded Russia, the Russian armed
forces were to be divided into three armies. One army was to repulse the
enemy's main blow relying on an entrenched camp in Drissa built for the
purpose in 1811-12, while the other two armies (protecting the southwestern
frontier) were to manoeuvre on the enemy flanks and in his rear. This plan
scattered the Russian forces and doomed them to piecemeal defeat by the
superior enemy forces. However, the Russian command, including Barclay de
Tolly, adopted a timely decision to leave the Drissa camp and withdraw to the
interior so as to unite their armies.   p. 51

54 The *battle of Smolensk* between Napoleon's army and the Russian troops
covering the withdrawal of the main forces of Bagration's and Barclay de
Tolly's armies, which had united on August 3, 1812, took place on August
16-18, 1812. At the cost of heavy losses Napoleon captured the city which had
been abandoned by the Russian rearguard after the withdrawal of the main
Russian forces.   p. 51

55 Russian troops reached *Tsarevo-Zaimishche* (southwest of Gzhatsk) on August
29, 1812. This position was abandoned by the Russian army by decision of
Kutuzov who had been appointed commander-in-chief shortly before. He
intended to give decisive battle to the French when there was a more
favourable alignment of forces, for which it was necessary to win time and
bring up reinforcements. The Russians therefore retreated to Borodino, which
on September 7 became the scene of a great battle, which was to bring about a
turn of the tide in Russia's favour in the Patriotic War of 1812, despite the
forced but expedient abandonment of Moscow.   p. 51

56 Marx and Engels mention a number of battles between the armies of the sixth
European coalition (Britain, Russia, Austria, Prussia, Sweden, Spain and other
states) and Napoleonic France.
     The *siege of Thorn* (Toruń), a Polish fortress on the Vistula held by a
French garrison, was begun by the Russians under Barclay de Tolly in the
middle of February 1813. On April 16 the fortress ceased resistance and on
April 18 an agreement was signed on its capitulation and transfer to Prussia,
Russia's ally.
     At the *battle of Königswartha* (Saxony) on May 19, 1813 the allied
Russo-Prussian forces under Barclay de Tolly defeated the French. Lauriston's
Corps suffered most.
     At the *battle of Bautzen* (Saxony) on May 20-21, 1813 Napoleon's army won
a victory over the allied Russo-Prussian forces, who, however, withdrew in
perfect order, covered by the Russian rearguard under Barclay de Tolly. The
following day a rearguard battle took place at *Görlitz* between the French and
the Russians retreating from Bautzen, who emerged victorious.
     On August 30, 1813, as a result of the *battle at Kulm* (Khlumeč, Bohemia)
between the Austro-Prusso-Russian forces under Barclay de Tolly and the
French army, Vandamme's Corps was cut off from the main body and was
forced to capitulate.
     At the *battle of Leipzig* on October 16-19, 1813 (see Note 31), Barclay de
Tolly commanded the central group of the allied forces.   p. 52

57 See Note 30.   p. 52

[58] At the *battle of the Speyerbach* (Palatinate) on November 15, 1703 the French army won a victory over the German imperial army, the outcome being decided by a French bayonet attack. The battle took place during the War of the Spanish Succession (see Note 16) which was fought in Italy, Spain, Western and Southwestern Germany, and in the Netherlands. p. 55

[59] When writing the article "Berthier" Marx used information on his life and military activity contained in Engels' letter of September 11 or 12, 1857.
p. 56

[60] The American War of Independence (1775-83)—a revolutionary war fought by 13 British colonies in North America. As a result of their victory an independent state was formed, the United States of America. France fought on the side of the Americans. p. 56

[61] On *October 5 and 6, 1789*, during the French Revolution, the masses who had come to Versailles from Paris clashed with the King's guard and forced Louis XVI to return to Paris, thus thwarting a counter-revolutionary plot prepared by the Court against the Constituent Assembly.
On *February 19, 1791* Paris was the scene of popular unrest caused by an attempt of the King's female relatives to flee abroad. p. 56

[62] *Vendée*—a department in Western France; during the French Revolution of 1789-94 the centre of a royalist revolt raised in March 1793 in which the local peasant masses took part. In June 1793 the Vendeans besieged and captured the town of *Saumur* from the republican forces, but later sustained a number of defeats. The revolt was suppressed in 1795 but attempts to revive it were made in 1799 and later. p. 56

[63] The *9th Thermidor* (July 27, 1794)—a coup d'état which led to the overthrow of the Jacobin revolutionary government. p. 56

[64] After the 9th Thermidor Kellermann commanded the Alpine and Italian armies of the French Republic which were to defend the southern borders, including the passes over the Alps, against Austrian and Piedmontese troops threatening invasion. p. 56

[65] Marx lists a number of battles of the 1796-97 campaign in which the French army under General Bonaparte routed the allied Austrian and Piedmontese (Sardinian) armies in Northern Italy. At the *battle of Mondovi* Bonaparte's army defeated the Piedmontese troops, forcing the King of Piedmont to conclude a separate peace treaty with France. The Austrians' defeat at *Lodi* led to Bonaparte's capture of Milan. The *battle of Rivoli* (January 14-15, 1797), also won by Bonaparte, finally determined the outcome of the entire campaign in favour of France. The conclusion of a peace treaty between France and Austria in October 1797 completed the collapse of the first anti-French coalition (1792-97). p. 56

[66] Under the pretext of helping the Italian republicans, Bonaparte sought to establish French rule in Italy by setting up "daughter" republics. In March 1798 a Roman Republic was proclaimed, with the help of the French forces, and Pius VI fled. But in 1799, following the invasion of Italy by the armies of the second anti-French coalition, the Italian republics were abolished and the Pope's power restored in the Roman Papal States. With the restoration of French rule in Italy Napoleon incorporated the Papal States into the French

Empire in 1809, having previously united part of their territory to the vassal
Kingdom of Italy.   p. 57

67 See Note 5.   p. 57

68 The *18th and 19th Brumaire* (November 9-10, 1799)—a coup d'état which led to
the establishment of the military dictatorship of Napoleon Bonaparte, who was
proclaimed Emperor of the French in 1804.   p. 57

69 At the *battle of Marengo* (Northern Italy) on June 14, 1800 the army of
Napoleon, who had received incorrect information on the disposition of the
Austrian forces, was unexpectedly attacked by the Austrians who were
nevertheless defeated. The French victory at Marengo and successful operations on the other fronts led to the collapse of the second anti-French coalition,
formed at the end of 1798 by Britain, Austria, Russia, Spain, Naples and
Turkey. As a result Napoleon's rule was consolidated.   p. 57

70 See Note 28.   p. 57

71 On October 17, 1805, during the war of the third European coalition (Britain,
Austria, Russia and the Kingdom of Naples) against Napoleonic France, the
Austrian army under General Mack, surrounded by the French near Ulm, was
compelled to capitulate.   p. 58

72 Berthier was given the title of Prince of Wagram in honour of the victory of
Napoleon's army over the Austrians at Wagram on July 5-6, 1809, during the
war against the fifth coalition (Austria, Britain, Spain and Portugal). After this
defeat the Austrians were forced to accept a harsh peace treaty with Napoleon
in October 1809.   p. 58

73 A reference to the *provisional government* under Talleyrand set up by the Senate
in April 1814, after the defeat of Napoleon's army and the entry of the Allies
into Paris. It promoted the restoration of the Bourbons.   p. 58

74 As can be seen from the list contained in Engels' letter to Marx of May 28,
1857, Engels intended to write the article "Algeria" together with the first
batch of articles beginning with A. But by the middle of July 1857 it was not
ready, perhaps not even begun (see Engels' letter to Marx of July 11, 1857).
Engels finished it only by the middle of September. On September 18 Marx
made an entry in his notebook on the dispatch of "Algiers, Ammunition" to
New York, and also informed Engels of this on September 21.
    The editors of *The New American Cyclopaedia* made some changes in the
article. As Engels' letter to Marx of September 22, 1857 shows, the no longer
extant original text contained an account of the war of liberation of the
Algerian people under Abd-el-Kader (see Note 80) and a characterisation of
Marshal Bugeaud's colonialist activity. They were probably omitted by the
editors because the *Cyclopaedia* already contained a special item on Abd-el-
Kader and was to include an article on Bugeaud from Marx (see this volume,
pp. 211-14). There are other signs of the editors' interference with the text.
    In his article Engels managed to overcome the tendentious approach to the
history of Algeria in the historical literature and reference books available to
him at the time (in particular he made use of the article "Algeria" in *Wigand's
Conversations-Lexikon,* Vol. I, Leipzig, 1846). Nevertheless, some outdated and
one-sided ideas on particular questions in Engels' sources are reflected in his
article, for example, on the role of Christian countries in fighting Algerian

piracy (these countries themselves engaged in privateering on a large scale), and on the circumstances and motives of the first French occupation of Algeria.

p. 60

[75] *Barbary powers*—a name given by Europeans in the past to the Moslem states along the Mediterranean coast of North Africa.

On the *Knights of Malta* see Note 4.   p. 63

[76] *Janizaries*—the main body of the feudal Turkish footguards, formed of young prisoners of war and Christian subjects of the Sultan converted to Islam. They took part in wars of conquest and performed garrison duties in conquered countries. Forming an isolated body, the janizaries came to play an independent role in political life and participated in feudal strife both at the centre and in the provinces of the Ottoman Empire. The janizaries' corps was abolished in 1826.   p. 63

[77] On April 30, 1827, at a reception in his residence, Hussein, Dey of Algiers, had an argument with the French Consul-General Deval over the French Government's non-payment of a debt to his subjects. In reply to Deval's defiant attitude Hussein slapped him in the face with his fan. This incident served as a pretext for Charles X to blockade the Algerian shores in 1827-29, following which the French colonialists began the conquest of the country in 1830.

p. 64

[78] The government of Charles X intended to transfer the administration of Algeria formally to the Porte under terms which actually established French control over the country and at the same time increased the Ottoman Empire's financial dependence on France. France was to receive four Algerian ports and 20 million francs from the Sultan for "aid" in "returning" Algeria to him. But the negotiations with the Porte were interrupted by the July 1830 revolution in France, which led to the replacement of the Bourbons by the Orleans. The July monarchy began the process of establishing direct French rule in Algeria.

p. 64

[79] In the autumn of 1836 a French expedition under Marshal Clausel against the province of Constantine, which was in the hands of the Algerian insurgents, proved a failure. The following autumn a second expedition was organised under General Damrémont, who had succeeded Clausel as Governor-General of Algeria. This time, at the cost of heavy losses, the French managed to take Constantine by storm.   p. 68

[80] The liberation struggle of the Algerians led by Emir Abd-el-Kader lasted with short intervals from 1832 to 1847. Between 1839 and 1844, the French used their considerable military superiority to conquer Abd-el-Kader's state in Western Algeria. However, he continued guerrilla warfare relying on support from the Sultan of Morocco. When the latter was defeated in the Franco-Moroccan war of 1844, Abd-el-Kader retreated to the Sahara oases. The last stage of this struggle was an insurrection in Western Algeria in 1845-47, which was put down by the French colonialists.

In 1847 Abd-el-Kader was taken prisoner, but even after that the Algerians' anti-colonialist revolts continued both in Western and Eastern Algeria. p. 68

[81] *Marabouts*—Moslim hermits or monks; they took an active part in the liberation struggle of the North African peoples against the European colonialists.

p. 69

[82] *Bureaux Arabes*—French military administrative bodies in Algeria dealing with questions that directly concerned the local population. They were set up in all occupied provinces and had wide powers.   p. 69

[83] Engels intended to write the article "Ammunition" in July 1857, as is evident from his letter to Marx of July 11-12 of that year. But being busy with other articles for *The New American Cyclopaedia* he did not begin writing it until the middle of September. It was dispatched to New York on September 18, 1857, as is shown by an entry in Marx's notebook.   p. 71

[84] In a letter to Marx of September 18, 1857 Engels promised to send him "Battle", "Battery" and, time permitting, other articles beginning with B in accordance with Dana's request (see Note 49). However, by that time only the first of these articles was ready, and Marx sent it off to New York on September 22, 1857, together with the articles "Blum", "Bourrienne" and "Bennigsen". Marx's notebook contains an entry on the dispatch of these articles on that day.   p. 72

[85] At the *battle of Leuthen* (Lutynia), Silesia, on December 5, 1757, during the Seven Years' War, the army of Frederick II of Prussia defeated the Austrians.
   The *Seven Years' War* (1756-63)—a war of Britain and Prussia against Austria, France, Russia, Saxony and Sweden. In 1756 and 1757 the Prussians won a number of victories over Austrian and French troops, but the results achieved were nullified by the Russian successes in Prussia (1757-60). As a result of the war France ceded many of its colonies (including Canada and almost all its possessions in the East Indies) to Britain, while Prussia, Austria and Saxony had largely to recognise the pre-war frontiers.   p. 73

[86] At the *battle of Kolin* (Bohemia) on June 18, 1757, during the Seven Years' War, the army of Frederick II of Prussia was routed by the Austrians.
   At *Kunersdorf* (Prussia, east of Frankfort on the Oder) the Russian and Austrian armies under the general command of Pyotr Saltykov inflicted a heavy defeat on Frederick II's army on August 12, 1759. As the result of their victories, the Russians temporarily occupied Berlin in 1760.   p. 73

[87] The rough draft of this article was made by Engels and enclosed in his letter to Marx of September 10, 1857. It was based largely on A. H. Jomini's book *Vie politique et militaire de Napoléon* (vols. 1-4, Paris, 1827). Marx edited this draft and supplemented it with data from *Biographie universelle (Michaud) ancienne et moderne* (Vol. 3, Paris, 1854), Napoleon's *Mémoires pour servir à l'histoire de France* (Paris, 1823), Fr. Chr. Schlosser's *Zur Beurtheilung Napoléon's und seiner neusten Tadler und Lobredner* (Frankfurt am Main, 1835) and other books. He sent off the final version to New York on September 22, 1857, as can be seen from an entry in his notebook.   p. 76

[88] See Note 85.   p. 76

[89] This refers to the long siege and capture by the Russians in December 1788 of the *fortress of Ochakov*, a stronghold of the Turks in the north of the Black Sea during the Russo-Turkish war of 1787-91.   p. 76

[90] At *Oszmiana* and *Solli* in June 1794, during the Polish national liberation uprising under Kosciusko, Bennigsen's corps inflicted a defeat on Polish troops. In August the Russians broke the resistance of the Polish army defending Vilna (Vilnius) and entered the city.

The suppression of the uprising resulted in the third partition of Poland in 1795 (the first and second partitions took place in 1772 and 1793) among Austria, Prussia and Russia. This partition put an end to the existence of Poland as an independent state.   p. 76

91 The siege and capture by the Russians of the town of *Derbent* (formerly belonging to Persia) in 1796 was a reply to the invasion of Georgia by the Shah of Persia, Aga Mohammed, in 1795, which was accompanied by the mass slaughter and enslavement of many Georgians.   p. 77

92 A reference to the war of the fourth coalition (Britain, Russia, Prussia and Sweden) against Napoleonic France (see Note 51).   p. 77

93 The French began the *siege of Danzig* (Gdańsk) in March 1807. The garrison consisting of Prussian troops and an allied Russian detachment offered stubborn resistance. An attempt to relieve it was made by another Russian detachment. The fortress surrendered to superior enemy forces at the end of May 1807.   p. 78

94 See Note 31.   p. 78

95 On August 26, 1857 Marx wrote to Engels telling him, among other things, that in the list of articles beginning with B requested by Dana for *The New American Cyclopaedia* "there are only two non-military articles"—"Blum" and "Bourrienne"—and on September 15 he informed Engels that he had dispatched them to New York together with other material. However as can be seen from his notebook Marx finished them only a week later and sent them to the United States on September 22, 1857.

When writing his article on Blum Marx made excerpts from the detailed biographical article "Blum" in *Meyer's Conversations-Lexicon* (second Supplement Volume, 1853, pp. 240-46) (see this volume, pp. 391-93), and from Fr. Steger's *Ergänzungs-Conversationslexicon* (Vol. 1, Leipzig, 1846, pp. 153-60), and other sources.   p. 80

96 The Leipzig *Schiller Association* and the *Association of German Authors* in the 1840s united German writers to fight for freedom of the press and spread liberal ideas in Germany.   p. 81

97 *German Catholicism*—a religious movement which arose in a number of German states in 1844. The "German Catholics" did not recognise the supremacy of the Pope, rejected many dogmas and rites of the Roman Catholic Church and sought to adapt Catholicism to the needs of the German bourgeoisie. p. 81

98 The meeting of Leipzig citizens before the riflemen's barracks was held the day after Saxon troops opened fire on a popular demonstration in Leipzig on August 12, 1845. The demonstration took place at the time of the military parade on the occasion of the arrival of Crown Prince John and was in protest against the Saxon Government's persecution of the "German Catholics" movement (see Note 97). Prince John of Saxony was believed to be chiefly responsible for the persecution. Engels described this event in his article "The Late Butchery at Leipzig.—The German Working Men's Movement" (see present edition, Vol. 4, pp. 645-48).   p. 81

99 The *Fatherland's Association* (*Vaterlandsverein*) was a broad democratic organisation founded in Leipzig at the end of March 1848, during the growing revolutionary movement prompted by the February revolution in France and

the March revolution in the German states. It was headed by petty-bourgeois and bourgeois republicans—Blum, Ruge, Jaeckel and others.   p. 81

100 The *Preliminary parliament* or *Preparliament*, which met in Frankfurt am Main from March 31 to April 4, 1848, consisted of representatives of the German states, most of them constitutional monarchists. After the rejection of a proposal to establish a federal republic in Germany and to turn the Preparliament into a constituent organ, a group of republicans headed by Hecker and Struve walked out. A more moderate section of the republican-democratic opposition, headed by Blum, took part in setting up a Committee of Fifty which was proposed by the liberals to secure the convocation of all-German National Assembly by agreement with the Federal Diet (organ of the German Confederation).   p. 82

101 The *Frankfurt Parliament*, or the German National Assembly, which opened on May 18, 1848, in St. Paul's Church in the free city of Frankfurt am Main, was intended to unify the country and draw up a Constitution. The liberal majority turned the Assembly into a mere debating club, and at the decisive moments of the revolution it yielded to the counter-revolutionary forces. In spring 1849, the liberals left the Assembly after the Prussian and other governments rejected the Imperial Constitution they had drawn up. The rest of the Assembly moved to Stuttgart and was dispersed by the Württemberg authorities on June 18, 1849.

Robert Blum was one of the leaders of the Left minority, which consisted of a moderate and a radical faction.   p. 82

102 The *Vienna uprising of October 6-7, 1848* was in response to the Austrian Government's order for the dissolution of the Hungarian Sejm and the dispatch of Austrian troops against Hungary. Headed by petty-bourgeois democrats, the masses prevented the Vienna garrison from marching to Hungary and seized control of the city after a fierce struggle. However, the insurgents did not receive the necessary support from other revolutionary forces in Austria and Germany. On November 1 their resistance was broken by Windischgrätz's counter-revolutionary forces which dealt out harsh treatment to the participants in the uprising.

The students' corps mentioned below in the text or the *Academic Legion*—an armed organisation founded after the March 1848 revolution in Austria—played an active part in the October uprising.   p. 82

103 On Marx's work on the article "Bourrienne" see Note 95 and pp. 394-96 of this volume.   p. 83

104 On *June 20, 1792*, a mass manifestation took place in Paris in front of the Legislative Assembly and the royal palace of the Tuileries. The participants demanded the cancellation of the royal veto on the decree establishing a camp of Marseilles volunteers (*fédérés*) near Paris, and restoration to their ministerial posts of the Girondist leaders (representatives of the moderate republican bourgeoisie) dismissed by the King. The refusal to meet these demands made the atmosphere still more tense. Subsequent events led to a popular uprising on August 10, 1792, which overthrew the monarchy and established a republic in France.   p. 83

105 A reference to Napoleon's campaign in Northern Italy in 1800, during the war against the second anti-French coalition which ended in a victory for the French at Marengo (see Note 69).   p. 83

106 The *Continental System,* or the *Continental Blockade,* proclaimed by Napoleon I in 1806, prohibited trade between the countries of the European Continent and Great Britain.   p. 83

107 See Note 73.   p. 84

108 Marx has in mind *Mémoires de M. de Bourrienne, Ministre d'État, sur Napoléon, le directoire, le consulat, l'empire et la restauration* (vols. I-X, Paris, 1829). Most of these memoirs are assumed to have been written by the former Napoleonic diplomat Villemarest, who specialised in fabrications of this kind.   p. 84

109 The "Army" was listed among the first articles which Dana requested for *The New American Cyclopaedia* and which Engels undertook to write. On May 8, 1857 Dana wrote to Marx: "The principal article is that on *Army.* This should be historical, giving an account of the organization of the antique armies, and of the progressive changes made down to the present day, with notices of peculiarities in the different leading armies of the world. I have marked ten pages as the limit, but if it can be done in less so much the better. This article will not include the statistics of the military force of the different powers, as they will be given under the head of these powers,—Austria for instance. I have marked for you, while the remainder of that article has been given to another." It was all the more difficult to write such a comprehensive article within the time stipulated as Engels was still working on a number of articles beginning with A and had started on those beginning with B. Nevertheless, Engels began collecting the necessary material in July 1857, started writing the article in August and finished it not later than September 24. He kept Marx informed of the course of his work (see his letters of July 11, August 21, and September 8 and 22, 1857, present edition, Vol. 40). Marx did all he could to help Engels collect material for the article: he sent him books and excerpts from reference books and other works (see his letter to Engels of July 16 and Jenny Marx's letter to Engels sent in mid-August 1857).

Engels made use of many sources, beginning with the works of ancient historians and military writers (Herodotus, Xenophon, Sallust, Polybius, Vegetius, and others) and ending with those of nineteenth-century authors (Wilkinson, Clausewitz, Jomini, Rüstow, and others), and consulted various reference books. He mentions some of these sources in the article itself. The following excerpts are extant: from Rüstow's *Heerwesen und Kriegführung C. Julius Cäsars* (Gotha, 1855) and from the article "Army" published in the seventh edition of the *Encyclopaedia Britannica* (1842, Vol. III). Marx, in his turn, also made excerpts on some aspects of the history of war, in particular from Pauly's *Real-Encyclopädie der classischen Alterthumswissenschaft in alphabetischer Ordnung* (vols. 2-6, Stuttgart, 1842-52), *Allgemeine Encyclopädie der Wissenschaften und Künste. Herausgegeben von J. S. Ersch und J. G. Gruber* (published in Leipzig from 1818), from Wilkinson's three-volume *Manners and Customs of the Ancient Egyptians* (London, 1837).

In the article "Army" Engels summarised to a certain extent his long and thorough study of military science and history, and the experience of contemporary wars. Marx praised the article in his letter to Engels of September 25, 1857 and sent it off the same day to New York, as can be seen from an entry in his notebook (Dana acknowledged receipt in a letter of October 9, 1857). Marx also made some critical remarks to Engels concerning the origins of mercenary armies in antiquity (among the Carthaginians), the development of military science in fifteenth- and sixteenth-century Italy, and among the Eastern peoples. Marx thought these questions had not been adequately dealt with in the article. Engels took most of these remarks into consideration later when he wrote the articles "Artillery", "Cavalry", "Fortification" and "Infantry", which supplement his "Army".   p. 85

110 *Testudo* (literally: tortoise)—a shelter used to protect soldiers in siege operations. On the Roman *testudo* see this volume, p. 94.
      Vinea (literally: vineyard)—a wicker shelter covered with moist pelts or turf; used in antiquity by the besiegers of fortresses.   p. 86

111 On the *battles of Marathon, Plataea* and *Thermopylae* see Note 33.
      Greek troops landed on *Mycale* (Asia Minor) in 479 B.C., defeated the Persians and destroyed their ships which had been dragged on shore and used for erecting an entrenched camp. The Greek victories at Plataea and Mycale removed the threat of a Persian invasion of the Balkans.   p. 88

112 See Note 23.   p. 88

113 Solon's reforms (594 B.C.) divided the free citizens of the Athenian Republic into four groups according to the size of their annual income from their land. The first two groups enjoyed considerable political privileges but were liable to military service entailing great expenses (the first had to build warships and the second to supply mounted soldiers). The third group had restricted political rights, but it made up the backbone of the army, its heavy infantry. The fourth or poorest group, that of the "thetes", was for a long time deprived of the right to hold public offices and originally was exempt from military service; later on, however, light infantry was recruited from among it.   p. 89

114 By the *allies of Athens* Engels means the Greek city-states, mainly on the islands in the Aegean Sea and the coast of Asia Minor, which were members of the Athenian Naval Alliance (originally called Delian League) founded in 478 B.C., during the Greco-Persian wars. As Athens grew in power it subdued the allies and made them its tributaries. The Athenian Naval Alliance was dissolved in the late fifth century B.C. Athens managed to restore it partially in 378 B.C. but the new alliance existed only until 355.   p. 90

115 The *Peloponnesian war* (431-04 B.C.)—a war between two groups of Greek states: the Athenian Naval Alliance and the Peloponnesian Alliance headed by Sparta. It was caused by the struggle for hegemony in Greece, commercial rivalry among the Greek city-states and political contradictions between the Athenian slave-owning democracy and the aristocratic oligarchy of Sparta. The war was won by Sparta. Under the treaty of 404 B.C. Athens had to acknowledge Sparta's supremacy and surrender almost all its ships.   p. 90

116 The *Sicilian expedition* was undertaken by the Athenians in 415 B.C. to subdue the Greek city-states of Sicily, above all Syracuse. Athens hoped thus to establish its supremacy in the west of the Mediterranean and to increase its resources in order to deliver a blow at its main rival, Sparta. The military operations in Sicily continued until 413 B.C. and ended in a complete defeat for the Athenian naval and land forces unsuccessfully besieging Syracuse.   p. 91

117 *Ephori*—a body of five Spartan magistrates chosen annually by an assembly of free citizens. They were granted wide powers, including the right to dispose of the treasury, appoint military commanders and control the actions of the kings.
                                                                              p. 91

118 *Periaeci*—a social group in Ancient Sparta. They possessed land and property, and the richest of them had slaves. Personally free, they even enjoyed self-government to some extent but were deprived of many political rights.

p. 92

119 *Helots*—agricultural population of Southern Peloponnesus enslaved by Sparta. Being the property of the Spartan state, the Helots cultivated plots of land granted to individual Spartans to whom they paid rent (usually half of the produce). They frequently raised revolts, which were brutally suppressed by the slave-owners.

p. 92

120 See Note 37.

p. 92

121 See Note 37.

p. 93

122 The town of *Samos* (on the Island of Samos, in the southeast of the Aegean Sea) was besieged by an Athenian naval expedition under Pericles in 440 B.C. The population of the island, which belonged to the Athenian Naval Alliance, had revolted with the intention of seceding from the Alliance. After a siege of many months the town was forced to capitulate, and Athenian rule was restored on the island.

p. 93

123 By the *conquest of Greece* Engels means the subjugation of the Greek city-states by Philip II of Macedon, under whose rule Macedonia greatly increased its influence. An anti-Macedonian coalition headed by Athens was formed in 339 B.C., but its forces were defeated by Philip's army in 338 B.C. The all-Hellenic congress held in Corinth in 337 B.C. proclaimed the King of Macedon commander-in-chief of all the Greek armed forces and confirmed Macedonian rule over the Greek city-states, which continued to be formally regarded as independent.

p. 95

124 The *Achaean League*—a confederation of Peloponnesian city-states formed in 280 B.C. against Macedonia. It had considerable armed forces which were routed by the Romans in 146 B.C. and its territory was incorporated into Macedonia, which became a Roman province in 148 B.C.

p. 96

125 *Tribe* (Rom. Hist.)—a territorial-administrative unit. King Servius Tullius (6th cent. B.C.) introduced reforms under which the city of Rome was divided into four tribes on a territorial basis instead of the earlier division according to the clan or family principle. At the same time several country tribes were formed. All free citizens possessing land within the territory of a given tribe were included in that tribe.

p. 97

126 *Horsemen* (*knights*)—in early Roman history—equites, or rich citizens constituting a privileged class liable for service in the cavalry. Subsequently this name was given to Roman slave-owning merchants and usurers belonging to the class of equites.

p. 97

127 The *First Civil War* (88-82 B.C.)—a struggle for power between two antagonistic groups of Roman slave-owners. One group was headed by Lucius Cornelius Sulla, representing the slave-holding aristocracy (*nobilitas*), and the other by Gaius Marius who relied on merchants and usurers and tried to use the urban and rural plebeians. The war ended in the defeat of Marius' followers and the establishment of Sulla's dictatorship—a step towards the abolition of the Roman Republic and the founding of the empire.

p. 98

[128] A reference to the *battle of the Muthul* (Northern Africa), 109 B.C., in which the Roman army under Quintus Caecilius Metellus defeated the army of King Jugurtha of Numidia. This was the first Roman victory in the Jugurthine war (111-05 B.C.). Rome proved victorious at the end. p. 98

[129] Roman military units of each grade had their own badges. Thus since the time of Gaius Marius a silver eagle attached to the shaft was the badge of a legion. p. 98

[130] The war between Rome and Pyrrhus, King of Epirus (Northwestern Greece), over the Greek towns in the south of Italy took place in 280-75 B.C. At the beginning Rome suffered two major defeats but later, supported by Carthage, it crushed the mercenary army of Pyrrhus and drove him out of the Peninsula. p. 99

[131] A reference to the *battle of Kynoskephalae* (Thessaly) in 197 B.C., during the Second Macedonian war (200-197 B.C.), in which the Roman army under Titus Quinctius Flamininus routed the army of Philip V of Macedon. As a result, the Romans consolidated their influence in Greece, later establishing their rule there. p. 100

[132] The *Social War* (90-88 B.C.)—a war of Rome's Italian allies (*socii*) against the rule of the Roman Republic ("alliance" was a form by which the Roman slave-owners subjugated conquered tribes and peoples). The movement of the Italians who had seceded from Rome was suppressed but in the course of the war Rome was forced to grant them the rights of Roman citizens, initially with certain reservations. p. 100

[133] *Roman Gallia* (corresponding to Provence, a historical region in the south of France)—part of Gallia (Gaul) conquered by the Romans at the end of the second century B.C. p. 100

[134] The *expeditions of the German emperors against Italy* were started by King Otto I who was invested with the crown of the Holy Roman Empire in Rome in 962. These expeditions were especially frequent from the tenth to the thirteenth century and continued until the sixteenth century despite the decline of the Emperor's power and the increasing feudal dismemberment in Germany itself.
On the *crusades* see Note 4. p. 103.

[135] On the *battles of Crécy* and *Poitiers* see Note 34; on the *battle of Agincourt* see Note 25. p. 104

[136] A reference to the wars against the Mongols during their invasion of Central Europe in 1241-42, after their incursions into the Russian lands in 1237-40. Apart from Poland, Moravia, Hungary and Dalmatia were the scene of these wars. The advanced detachments nearly reached Venice, but, weakened by the resistance of the Russian principalities, they were compelled to withdraw to their East-European and Asian territories. p. 105

[137] Engels refers to the liberation wars of the Swiss cantons against the Austrian Habsburgs in the fourteenth and fifteenth centuries, and to the Swiss war of 1474-77 against Charles the Bold, Duke of Burgundy, who tried to seize lands belonging to the Swiss Confederation. The Swiss upheld their independence due to the superiority of their infantry of free peasants and townspeople over the knights. p. 105

138 *Bashi-Bazouks*—soldiers of Turkish irregular cavalry in the eighteenth and nineteenth centuries. p. 106

139 At the *battle of Marignano* (Northern Italy) on September 13-14, 1515 the army of Francis I of France, supported by his Venetian allies, defeated the Swiss mercenary troops of the Duke of Milan. This was one of the major battles in the Italian wars of 1494-1559 (see Note 26). p. 107

140 See Note 26. p. 107

141 This refers to the bourgeois revolution of 1566-1609 (see Note 20). p. 107

142 The *Thirty Years' War* (1618-48)—a general European war in which the Pope, the Spanish and Austrian Habsburgs and the Catholic German princes fought against the Protestant countries: Bohemia, Denmark, Sweden, the Republic of the Netherlands, and a number of German states. The rulers of Catholic France, being rivals of the Habsburgs, supported the Protestants. Germany was the main arena of the struggle, the object of pillage and territorial claims. The treaty of Westphalia (1648) sealed its political dismemberment. p. 109

143 The *battles of Leipzig, Lützen* and *the Lech* were fought in the Thirty Years' War. At the *battles of Leipzig* (or Breitenfeld) on September 17, 1631 and of *the Lech* (Bavaria) on April 15, 1632 Gustavus Adolphus' army routed the Imperial-Catholic troops under Tilly. At *Lützen* (Saxony) Gustavus Adolphus defeated Wallenstein's Imperial army on November 16, 1632. p. 110

144 The *Military Frontier* or the *Military Border Area*—the southern border regions of the Austrian Empire, where military settlements began to be set up in the sixteenth century for protection against Turkish invasions. The inhabitants of these regions—Serbs, Croats, Romanians, Szeklers, Saxons, and others—were allotted plots of land by the state, for which they had to serve in the army, pay taxes and perform certain public duties. The soldiers of these regions were called borderers. p. 110

145 *At Mollwitz* (Malujowice, Silesia) Frederick II's army defeated the Austrians on April 10, 1741, during the War of the Austrian Succession (1740-48) (see Note 38). p. 111

146 This was the first European coalition against revolutionary France. In February 1792, supported by Britain and Russia, Prussia and Austria concluded a military alliance and began intervention in France. After the proclamation of the French Republic and the execution of Louis XVI in January 1793, Britain, the Netherlands, Spain, Naples, Sardinia and several small German and Italian states openly joined the anti-French coalition. France's war against this coalition continued until 1797. p. 113

147 See Note 60. p. 113

148 See Note 85. p. 116

149 At the *battle of Inkerman* on November 5, 1854, during the Crimean war of 1853-56, the Anglo-French forces defeated the Russian army, but the Russians' vigorous action prevented the enemy from storming Sevastopol and instead the city was besieged. Engels described the battle in detail in his article "The Battle of Inkerman" (see present edition, Vol. 13, pp. 528-35). p. 117

[150] *Landwehr*—the army second reserve formed in Prussia during the struggle against Napoleon. In the 1840s it consisted of men under forty who had done three years' active service and had been in the reserve not less than two years. In contrast to the regular army, the Landwehr was called up only in case of extreme necessity (war, or threat of war). p. 120

[151] This paragraph was apparently added by the editors of *The New American Cyclopaedia*. p. 126

[152] "Battery" belongs to a group of articles written in accordance with Dana's first request for articles beginning with B (see Note 49). On September 18, 1857 Engels informed Marx of his intention to send him this article in a few days. But on September 24 he wrote to Marx that he would start writing it, and perhaps some others, the next day, i.e. September 25. Engels finished "Battery" by the end of September. Marx recorded the dispatch of the new material to New York in the following entry in his notebook on September 29, 1857: "Cyclopaedia. Bem. Bessières. Bosquet. Bivouac. Battery. Blindage. Bonnet."

When publishing Engels' article the editors of the *Cyclopaedia* supplemented it with a special section, the article "Floating Batteries" by another author, containing data on the building of warships of this class in the USA. p. 127

[153] The greater part of the article "Bem" was written by Marx. He gave a political characterisation of Bem and did the final editing. At the same time he reproduced, almost textually, the description of Bem's military activity during the Polish insurrection of 1830-31 and the 1848-49 revolutionary war in Transylvania contained in Engels' letters to Marx of September 11 or 12 and 18, 1857 (see present edition, Vol. 40). Marx's excerpts from articles about Bem have been preserved, including those from *The English Cyclopaedia* (Vol. V, London, 1856) and *Meyer's Conversations-Lexicon* (Vol. 4D, Hildburghausen, Amsterdam, Paris and Philadelphia, 1845). p. 130

[154] A reference to the *defence of Danzig* (Gdańsk) in 1813. Held by Napoleonic troops, it was besieged by the Prussians and Russians by land and sea for eleven and a half months. During that time the garrison sustained three regular sieges but finally had to capitulate. The allies entered the city on January 2, 1814. p. 130

[155] The insurrection of units of the St. Petersburg garrison on *December 14, 1825* was headed by a secret society of Russian revolutionary nobles opposed to the autocracy and the feudal-serf system. They are known in history as the Decembrists. The Decembrists sought to prevent the taking of the oath to the new Emperor, Nicholas I, and to secure the introduction of civic liberties and the convocation of a Constituent Assembly to decide the question of a Constitution. The insurrection was suppressed by Tsarist troops and its participants were subjected to severe reprisals. Five of its leaders were hanged and 121 participants were sentenced to hard labour and exile in Siberia. p. 131

[156] By the "Warsaw insurrection of 1830" Marx and Engels mean the *Polish national liberation uprising of November 1830-October 1831*. The majority of its participants were revolutionary gentry (*szlachta*) and its leaders came mainly from the aristocracy. It was suppressed by Russian troops, with the support of Prussia and Austria. The uprising was of major international significance

because it diverted the forces of counter-revolution and thwarted their plans for an offensive against the bourgeois revolutions of 1830 in France and of 1830-31 in Belgium.

At the *battle of Ostrolenka* on May 26, 1831 Tsarist troops under Dibich' defeated the Polish insurgents. The final blow was delivered when the Russians captured Warsaw in September 1831, after storming its suburb Vola on September 6 (see below in the text). The remnants of the insurgent army fled to Prussia and Austria. p. 131

157 Bem planned to take part in the civil war in Portugal (1828-34) between the absolutists (the feudal-clerical party), headed by Dom Miguel who had seized the Portuguese throne in 1828, and the constitutionalists (the liberal-bourgeois party) grouped around Queen Maria da Gloria and her father, Dom Pedro. Bem's plan did not materialise. p. 131

158 The *Viennese Mobile Guard,* consisting mainly of workers and artisans, was formed by Bem during the October 1848 uprising in Vienna (see Note 102) as the most disciplined and efficient part of the insurgent armed forces. p. 131

159 *Honveds* (literally: "defenders of the homeland")—the name of the soldiers of the Hungarian revolutionary army of 1848-49, which was formed by decision of the Hungarian revolutionary government on May 7, 1848. p. 132

160 The *expedition of Bem's army to the Banat* (a region in the Serbian Voivodina, then part of Hungary) was undertaken in the spring of 1849. At the beginning of the 1848 revolution the Voivodina was the scene of the Serbs' growing national movement and of anti-feudal actions by democratic strata in town and country. However, the Serbian movement for autonomy was influenced by the liberal bourgeoisie, the nobility and the clergy and used by the Habsburgs against the Hungarian revolution. Military operations between the Voivodina Serbs and the Hungarians began in May 1848. In the Banat, inhabited by Hungarians, Germans and Romanians as well as Serbs, they were complicated by clashes between the Serbian and non-Serbian population. The struggle against the counter-revolutionary forces in the Serbian Voivodina, Transylvania, and other ethnic regions then included in Hungary, was hampered by the erroneous stand on the nationalities question adopted by the Hungarian bourgeois and aristocratic revolutionaries. Only shortly before the fall of the Hungarian Republic on July 28, 1849 did they officially agree to recognise the equality of all nationalities inhabiting Hungary. p. 133

161 At the *battle of Temesvár* (Timişoara) on August 9, 1849, during the Hungarian national liberation war, the Austrian army under Haynau defeated the Hungarian Southern army which was trying to hold its positions until joining up with the Northern army of the Hungarian Commander-in-Chief Görgey. Four days later the Northern army capitulated to the Russians. The revolution in Hungary was suppressed. p. 133

162 In the autumn of 1850 the Arab population of the city of Aleppo (Haleb) rose against the local Christians and the Turkish authorities. This rising grew into a rebellion against Turkish rule, which was put down by Turkish troops.

  p. 133

163 When working on biographical essays on military leaders, Bessières in particular, Marx wrote to Engels on September 17, 1857 inquiring about their military records and their role in individual battles. Marx took into account

the description of Bessières as a brave cavalry general contained in Engels' letter to him of September 21. Marx's excerpts on Bessières from the following reference books are extant: C. Mullié, *Biographie des célébrités militaires des armées de terre et de mer de 1789 à 1850* (Vol. 1, Paris), *The English Cyclopaedia* (Vol. V, London, 1856), *Meyer's Conversations-Lexicon* (Vol. 4D, 1845), and *Biographie universelle (Michaud) ancienne et moderne* (Vol. 4, Paris, 1854). It seems that Marx also used extracts from A. H. Jomini's book *Vie politique et militaire de Napoléon* (vols. 1-4, Paris, 1827) enclosed by Engels in his letter of September 11 or 12, 1857.

p. 134

164 The *Constitutional Guard* was charged, in accordance with the Constitution adopted in 1791, during the French Revolution, with protecting the King and his palace. It was formed after the disbandment of the Royal Guard. In May 1792 the Legislative Assembly, under pressure from the democratic movement, decreed its dissolution.

p. 134

165 The *guides*—special sub-units in a number of European armies used for guiding troops. In the French army during the Napoleonic wars they protected Napoleon's headquarters and served as his bodyguard.

p. 134

166 The battles mentioned were fought during the wars of France against the first, second, third and fourth European coalitions.

On September 4, 1796, during the campaign in the north of Italy, the French army under Bonaparte defeated the Austrians at *Roveredo.*

On the *battle of Rivoli* in the same campaign see Note 65.

On the siege of the fortress of *St. Jean d'Acre (Acca)* during the French expedition to Egypt see Note 5.

At the *battle of Aboukir* on July 25, 1799, during the same expedition, the French destroyed a Turkish force landed by the Anglo-Turkish fleet on the Egyptian coast.

On the *battle of Marengo* see Note 69.

The *battle of Austerlitz* (Moravia) on December 2, 1805 between the Russo-Austrian and French armies was won by Napoleon I. After this defeat Austria withdrew from the third anti-French coalition and concluded a peace treaty with Napoleon. Russia and Britain formed a new, fourth, coalition in 1806 and continued the war.

At the *battle of Jena* (Thuringia) on October 14, 1806, the French troops under Napoleon routed the Prussians. The same day Marshal Davout's troops defeated the main Prussian forces at *Auerstädt.* The defeat of Prussia—a member of the fourth anti-French coalition—in these two battles (often united in one as the battle of Jena) led to the occupation of most of Prussia by the French.

On the *battle of Preussisch-Eylau* see Note 51.

The *battle of Friedland* between the French and the Russians on June 14, 1807 is described in this volume, pp. 78 and 199.

p. 134

167 A reference to the British naval expedition to the mouth of the Scheldt in July 1809 during the war of the fifth coalition against Napoleonic France. It was undertaken when Napoleon's main forces were engaged against Austria. The British captured Walcheren island, but failed to use it as a base for military operations against Antwerp and other French strong points in Belgium and Holland. They had to evacuate it in December 1809.

p. 134

168 The *battle of Lützen* (Saxony) between Napoleon's army and Russo-Prussian armies took place on May 2, 1813. Napoleon forced the enemy to retreat, but the retreat was orderly.

p. 135

[169] See Note 166.   p. 136

[170] In writing this item Engels made use of Marx's excerpts from Burn's *A Naval and Military Technical Dictionary of the French Language* (London, 1852) which Marx sent him in his letter of September 15, 1857 (see present edition, Vol. 40). These excerpts are extant.   p. 138

[171] The first part of this article was written by Marx, as is seen from the extant excerpts; they are in the main from *The English Cyclopaedia* (Vol. V, London, 1856) and Steger's *Ergänzungs-Conversationslexikon* (Vol. 10, Leipzig and Meissen).
The passage on Bosquet's participation in the Crimean war of 1853-56 belongs to Engels. It reproduces almost word for word part of a letter to Marx of September 22, 1857, in which Engels described Bosquet's role in the major Crimean operations, in compliance with Marx's request in his letters of September 17 and 21, 1857.   p. 139

[172] The *battle of Balaklava* (Crimea) between the Russian army and the allied Anglo-French and Turkish forces took place on October 25, 1854. Units of the Russian army tried to cut off the British and Turkish forces besieging Sevastopol from their base in Balaklava. They succeeded in inflicting serious losses on them, especially on the British cavalry, but failed to achieve the main objective. For a description of this battle see Engels' article "The War in the East" (present edition, Vol. 13, pp. 518-27).   p. 140

[173] See Note 149.   p. 140

[174] A reference to the storming of the Sevastopol fortifications by French and British troops on September 8, 1855, as a result of which the French managed to capture the Malakhov (Malakoff) Hill, the defenders' main strong point. After an eleven months defence the Russian garrison abandoned Sevastopol by order of the command which considered its further defence useless. The storming of Sevastopol on September 8 is described by Engels in his articles "The Fall of Sevastopol" and "The Great Event of the War" (see present edition, Vol. 14, pp. 519-23 and 546-52).   p. 140

[175] The article "Bomb" is the first of a new batch of articles beginning with B which Engels wrote in accordance with Dana's request (see Note 49). Marx made excerpts from reference books in the library of the British Museum, in particular from *The British Cyclopaedia of Arts and Sciences* by Ch. F. Partington and sent them to Engels, presumably on September 16, 1857, together with excerpts on bridges. On October 6 Marx made an entry in his notebook: "*Cyclopaedia*. Bomb. Bombardment. Bomb-Ketch. Bomb-Vessel. Bombardier. Bomb-Proof", which shows that Marx dispatched the articles listed to New York on that day.   p. 141

[176] See Note 21.   p. 141

[177] *Valenciennes composition*—an incendiary mixture of saltpetre, sulphur and powder first used in 1793, during the siege of the French-held town of Valenciennes by Austro-British forces (an episode in the French Republic's war against the first European coalition).   p. 141

[178] *Sveaborg* (Suomenlinna) was a Russian fortress situated on a group of islands at the entrance to the Helsinki harbour in the Gulf of Finland. The bombardment

of Sveaborg by British and French ships took place on August 9 and 10, 1855, during the Crimean war, 1853-56. For more on this event see Marx and Engels' article "The Anglo-French War Against Russia" (present edition, Vol. 14, pp. 484-89).   p. 145

179 See Note 30.   p. 147

180 The *siege of Sevastopol* (during the Crimean war, 1853-56) by the allied forces of France, Britain, Turkey and Sardinia lasted from September 25, 1854 to September 9, 1855.   p. 148

181 On the *bombardment of Sveaborg* see Note 178.   p. 148

182 Engels helped Marx considerably in his work on this article. In his letters to Marx of September 11 or 12, and particularly of September 21 and 23, 1857, he adduced many facts on Bernadotte's military record, especially during Napoleon's campaigns against the third, fourth and fifth European coalitions (1805, 1806-07 and 1809). Engels' account of Bernadotte's role in these campaigns was founded mainly on A. H. Jomini's *Vie politique et militaire de Napoléon* (vols. 1-4, Paris, 1827). It was reproduced by Marx almost word for word.

Marx sought to give a complete picture of Bernadotte, above all as a politician and diplomat. He collected a vast amount of biographical data, as can be seen from his letter to Engels of September 17, 1857 (in which he wrote about the different appraisals of Bernadotte by various historians) and from the extant excerpts from the *Biographie universelle (Michaud) ancienne et moderne, The English Cyclopaedia, Meyer's Conversations-Lexicon* and Fr. Chr. Schlosser's *Zur Beurtheilung Napoleon's und seiner neusten Tadler und Lobredner.*

On October 15, 1857, Marx made the following entry in his notebook: "*Cyclopaedia.* Military Bridges. Brown. Bernadotte", which shows that he sent off these articles to New York on that day. On Dana's request for articles beginning with B see Note 49.   p. 149

183 At *Fleurus* (Belgium) on June 26, 1794, the French under General Jourdan routed the Austrian army of the Prince of Coburg. This victory enabled the French revolutionary army to occupy Belgium and start offensive operations in Holland and on the western bank of the Rhine. Early in October 1794 the French crossed the Ruhr and took possession of the fortress of Jülich, and on November 4 they compelled the fortress of Maestricht to capitulate. p. 149

184 The *Directory* (consisting of five directors of whom one was re-elected every year) was the leading executive body in France set up under the 1795 Constitution, adopted after the fall of the Jacobin revolutionary dictatorship in the summer of 1794. It governed France until Bonaparte's coup d'état of 1799 and expressed the interests of the big bourgeoisie.   p. 149

185 The 1797 invasion of Istria (Balkan province of the Republic of Venice) was undertaken on General Bonaparte's initiative during the campaign against the Austrians in Northern Italy in 1796-97 (see Note 65).   p. 149

186 On the *18th Fructidor* (September 4, 1797), by order of the Directory supported by General Bonaparte, government troops occupied the premises of the Corps législatif and arrested royalist deputies who were preparing a monarchist coup d'état. The Directory itself was renewed. The events of the 18th Fructidor revealed the instability of the Directory's bourgeois regime and its vacillations

either to the left, in face of royalist danger, or to the right, for fear of the democratic movement.   p. 150

187 The *Treaty of Campo Formio* was concluded by General Bonaparte with Austrian representatives on October 17, 1797. It formalised Austria's withdrawal from the first anti-French coalition and sanctioned its relinquishment of its possessions in Northern Italy where the Cisalpine Republic was formed under French protectorate. Belgium, the Ionian Islands and some of Austria's possessions on the Rhine were ceded to France. At the same time a large part of the territory of the abolished Republic of Venice and its possessions in Istria and Dalmatia went to Austria.   p. 150

188 During the *coup d'état of the 30th Prairial* (June 18, 1799) the Corps législatif succeeded in changing the composition of the Directory, from which three outright reactionaries were dismissed. This was done under the influence of growing public discontent over French defeats in Germany and Italy and the republic's worsened economic and financial situation.   p. 150

189 See Note 62.   p. 151

190 See Note 28.   p. 151

191 See Note 166.   p. 151

192 A reference to the *battles of Auerstädt* and *Jena*—see Note 166.   p. 151

193 The *treaties of Tilsit* were signed on July 7 and 9, 1807 by Napoleonic France and Russia and Prussia, members of the fourth anti-French coalition. In an attempt to split the defeated powers, Napoleon made no territorial claims on Russia and even succeeded in transferring some of the Prussian monarchy's eastern lands to Russia. The treaty imposed harsh terms on Prussia, which lost nearly half its territory to the German states dependent on France, was made to pay indemnities, and had its army reduced. However, Russia, like Prussia, had to break its alliance with Britain and, to its disadvantage, join Napoleon's Continental System. Napoleon formed the vassal Duchy of Warsaw on Polish territory seized by Prussia during the partitions of Poland at the end of the eighteenth century, and planned to use it as a springboard in the event of war with Russia.

The military alliance between France and Denmark against Sweden was concluded on October 31, 1807 in Fontainebleau. France's operations against Sweden coincided with the Russo-Swedish war of 1808-09.   p. 152

194 See Note 72.   p. 152

195 See Note 167.   p. 153

196 *Schönbrunn*—the imperial summer residence in Vienna where, in the autumn of 1809, Napoleon I dictated peace terms to Austria after its defeat in the 1809 campaign.   p. 153

197 See Note 9.   p. 154

198 See Note 106.   p. 154

199 The *peace of Bucharest*, concluded on May 28, 1812, ended the Russo-Turkish war of 1806-12. Under this treaty Bessarabia and several Transcaucasian

regions were to go to Russia. Turkey was to grant Serbia autonomy in domestic matters and to seal its former agreements with Russia acknowledging a number of autonomous rights for Moldavia and Wallachia. The peace treaty with Turkey, achieved owing to the victories of the Russian army and the diplomacy of its Commander-in-Chief Mikhail Kutuzov, enabled Russia to free considerable forces for the war against Napoleonic France.   p. 155

200 A reference to the peace treaties and treaties of alliance between Russia and Britain and between Britain and Sweden directed against Napoleonic France.
                                                                                              p. 155

201 This refers to a convention signed by Russia and Sweden in Abo (Turku) on August 30, 1812. It virtually formalised their military alliance against Napoleonic France. The convention also contained a provision obliging Russia to render military assistance to Sweden against Denmark if the latter refused to cede Norway to the King of Sweden. In return, Sweden agreed to support the Tsarist Government's territorial claims, in particular to the Duchy of Warsaw then subject to Napoleon.   p. 156

202 The military treaty of March 3, 1813, signed in Stockholm between Britain and Sweden, provided for the dispatch of Swedish troops to take part in the war against Napoleon's army, and for British subsidies for this purpose. Article 2 of the treaty obliged Britain to support Sweden's claims to Norway.   p. 156

203 The armistice of June 5, 1813 was concluded by Russia and Prussia with Napoleon I until July 20, but later it was prolonged up to August 10. During the armistice Alexander I, Frederick William III and Bernadotte met in the castle of Trachenberg (Silesia) on July 12, 1813 to decide upon further military operations. When the peace negotiations failed Austria officially joined the coalition. Hostilities resumed in August 1813.   p. 156

204 See Note 31.   p. 157

205 See Note 156.   p. 158

206 Under pressure from liberal opposition the Swedish Diet (*Riksdag*) of 1844-45 abrogated the law allowing the government to close down newspapers. It issued a law on the convocation of the Diet every three years, established the equal right of men and women to inherit land, and approved the principles of liberal reforms of the penal code. A parliamentary committee was set up to carry out an electoral reform.   p. 158

207 Engels began to work on this article in the first half of September 1857, but he could not obtain all the necessary source material in Manchester. He therefore wrote to Marx on September 11 or 12 asking him to collect the information he needed in London, including data on pontoons in different armies contained in the third edition of H. Douglas' *An Essay on the Principles and Construction of Military Bridges, and the Passage of Rivers in Military Operations* (London, 1853).
    Marx made extracts from various reference books in the library of the British Museum, in particular from Burn's *A Naval and Military Technical Dictionary of the French Language* (London, 1852), and sent them to Engels. "Many thanks for the thing on bridges. Wholly adequate," Engels wrote to Marx on September 18, 1857. He did not finish the article until the middle of October, as can be seen from the entry in Marx's notebook on its dispatch to New York.
                                                                                              p. 159

208 In 55 B.C., during Caesar's conquest of Gallia (Gaul) (58-51 B.C.), the Romans, pursuing the defeated Teutons, crossed the Middle Rhine and stayed on its right bank for eighteen days. This crossing, undertaken to demonstrate Rome's military power, is described by Caesar in the fourth book of his commentaries on the Gallic war.   p. 159

209 See Note 142.   p. 159

210 A reference to the war of 1846-48 between the United States and Mexico, as a result of which the USA seized almost half of Mexico, including Texas, Upper California and New Mexico.   p. 161

211 See Note 72.   p. 162

212 The article "Brown" was asked for in Dana's first request for articles beginning with B, of which Marx informed Engels on August 26, 1857. On September 17 and 21 he asked Engels for his opinion of Brown and other military leaders, probably intending to begin writing this article. Soon after, Marx made the relevant extracts from *The English Cyclopaedia* (Vol. V, London, p. 948), and edited and used them extensively in his article; he left out the laudatory comments on Brown's role in the Crimean war and added an account of Brown's military qualities that made him popular among the soldiers (probably based on a letter from Engels which has not survived). On October 15, according to the entry in Marx's notebook (see Note 182), the article was dispatched to New York. However, the original was probably lost and, as can be judged from Marx's letter to Engels of February 1, 1858 and from the entry in his notebook on April 17, Marx had to send either a copy or another version, and it was this that the *Cyclopaedia* published.   p. 164

213 The British bombarded Copenhagen in September 1807 to prevent Denmark from joining the Continental Blockade (see Note 106).   p. 164

214 At the *battle of Talavera* (Toledo province, Spain) on July 27-28, 1809, the allied Anglo-Spanish forces under Wellington and Le Cuesta repulsed the attacks of the French, who suffered heavy losses and were compelled to abandon their positions.
      On the *storming of Badajos* on April 6, 1812, see Note 12.   p. 164

215 The events mentioned belong to the final stage of the Anglo-American war of 1812-14 (see Note 35).
      In August 1814, an English detachment 4,000-strong, under Major-General Ross, landed in the Chesapeake Bay. At the village of Bladensburg, six miles from Washington, they routed an American volunteer corps defending the capital and temporarily took possession of it. They set fire to the Capitol, the White House and other government buildings, and returned to their ships.
                                                                        p. 164

216 On the *battle of Inkerman* see Note 149.
      When referring to "the first unsuccessful attack on the Redan" (the 3rd bastion of Sevastopol's defences) Marx has in mind one of the major battles of the Crimean war fought at Sevastopol that ended in defeat for the Allies—their full-scale assault on the southern (Korabelnaya) part of the city on June 18, 1855 launched on the fortieth anniversary of the battle of Waterloo (see Note 30). The assault was repulsed at every point. Marx gave a detailed account of the battle in his report "The Mishap of June 18.—Reinforcements"

and Engels described it in his articles "From Sevastopol" and "The Late Repulse of the Allies" (see present edition, Vol. 14, pp. 297-301, 313-19 and 328-32).   p. 164

217 Engels conceived the idea of writing an essay on the Spanish Armada of 1588 when thinking out subjects for the first articles beginning with A, as we see from his letter to Marx of May 28, 1857. Marx undertook to collect material and began to send it to Engels in July 1857 (see Jenny Marx's letter to Engels of August 12 or 13). But the main portion of the material was evidently prepared later, for Marx himself only mentions it in his letter to Engels of September 21. It consisted of carefully edited excerpts from various sources, including the article "Elizabeth" in *The English Cyclopaedia* (Vol. V, London, 1856, pp.761-64) and works of some contemporaries of the events. The final version of the article mentions only part of the sources originally given by Marx. In particular, it does not contain reference to *Orders Set down by the Dyke of Medina, etc. to Be Observed in the Voyage toward England* (London, 1588) or to the English translation (published in London in 1590) of the work by the Florentine writer Petruccio Ubaldino, *A Discourse, Concerninge the Spanishe Fleete Invadinge Englande in the Yeare 1588, and Overthrowne by Her Majestie's Navy* (Marx used a reprint in *The Harleian Miscellany: A Collection of Scarce, Curious, and Entertaining Pamphlets and Tracts, etc.* (Vol. I, London, 1808). Engels worked on the article between September 21 and October 19: he abridged the material prepared by Marx, edited it again and added some facts. When he sent the manuscript to Marx on October 19, Engels asked him to insert some names which he had been unable to make out in the excerpts. Marx put the finishing touches to the text and, judging by the entry in his notebook, sent it off to New York on October 23, 1857, together with the article "Ayacucho".   p. 166

218 Engels informed Marx of his intention to write an article on Ayacucho on May 28, 1857, but he only began work on it about September 21, when Marx told him about the material he had collected. Extant are Marx's excerpts from the article "Ayacucho" in the *Encyclopédie des Gens du Monde* (Vol. 2, Paris, 1833), from *A View of South America* (New York, 1826), from J. S. Florez' *Espartero. Historia de su vida Militar y Política* (vols. 1-4), and from M. A. Príncipe, R. Giron, R. Satorres, A. Ribot, *Espartero: Su pasado, su presente, su porvenir* (Madrid, 1848).

The battle of Ayacucho was most likely described by Engels. The concluding part belongs to Marx. The portrayal of Espartero and his followers conforms to that contained in Marx's article "Espartero" written in 1854 for the *New-York Daily Tribune* (see present edition, Vol. 13, pp. 340-46). The article was sent off to New York on October 23, together with "Armada".   p. 170

219 At the *battle of Junin* (Peru) on August 6, 1824, Colombian, Chilean and Peruvian troops under Simon Bolivar defeated the Spanish army after a daring crossing of the Andes. The battle took place during the final stage of the Latin American countries' liberation struggle against Spanish colonial rule. The struggle began in 1810 and gained particularly in scope in 1816, when an independent republic was proclaimed on the territory of the former Viceroyalty of La Plata (subsequently the Argentine Republic). With the support of its troops, Chile was proclaimed independent in 1817 and Peru in 1821. The war for the independence resumed by Bolivar, led to the establishment in 1819-22 of the Republic of Greater Colombia. The liberation war of Mexico resumed in 1821. The 1824 campaign of Bolivar's Colombian army in support of the Peruvian republicans dealt the final

blow to Spanish rule in Latin America. In 1826 remnants of the Spanish forces were driven out of Peru. The following independent republics were proclaimed on the territory of the former Spanish possessions: Mexico, the United States of Central America (subsequently split up into five republics—see Note 288), Greater Colombia (later divided into Venezuela, Colombia and Ecuador), Bolivia, Argentina, Paraguay, Peru and Chile.   p. 170

220 Like the previous one, the article "Blücher" was the result of Marx's and Engels' joint work, as is seen in particular from Marx's letters to Engels of September 17 and 21, and Engels' letters to Marx of September 18, 21 and 22, 1857.

The bulk of the biographical material on Blücher was obtained by Marx. Extant are his excerpts from *The English Cyclopaedia* (Vol. V, London, 1856), *Meyer's Conversations-Lexicon* (Vol. 4, 1845) and *Biographie universelle (Michaud) ancienne et moderne* (Vol. 4, Paris, 1854), and from several works, in particular "Der Feldzug von 1813 bis zum Waffenstillstand und der Feldzug von 1814 in Frankreich" (in *Hinterlassene Werke des Generals Carl von Clausewitz über Krieg und Kriegführung* (vols. 7-8, Berlin, 1835-36) and Fr. Müffling's *Passages from My Life: Together with Memoirs of the Campaign of 1813 and 1814* (London, 1853). Marx also did the final editing and polishing up of the text. Marx included in the respective passages extracts from Engels' letter of September 22, 1857 describing Blücher as a military leader and evaluating his activities in the major campaigns. This description, supplemented by factual material collected by Marx, forms the core of the article. Engels' participation in the work on the article is also proved by the inclusion of his extracts from the above-mentioned book by Müffling, which was Marx's main source. Marx's notebook has the following crossed-out entry concerning the dispatch of the article to New York on October 30, 1857: "Blücher (8 $^1/_2$ columns Cyclopaedia) (Campaigns of 1813 and 1814)." Marx informed Engels of the dispatch of the article to Dana in his letter of October 31, 1857 (see present edition, Vol. 40).   p. 172

221 Prussia's intervention in Holland in 1787, supported and subsidised by the British Government, was undertaken to restore the power of the Stadtholder William V of Orange. The latter had been driven out of the country in 1784 as a result of the revolutionary movement directed against the bloc of the nobility and the trading oligarchy, and headed by the bourgeois party of "patriots", advocates of an active struggle against Britain, their colonial rival. The armed forces of the Dutch bourgeoisie were unable to offer any serious resistance to the Prussian army, which restored the power of the Stadtholder and the oligarchic system.

p. 172

222 Under the *peace of Basle* concluded separately by Prussia and the French Republic on April 5, 1795, Prussia acknowledged the cession of the left bank of the Rhine to France. The treaty was not only the result of the French victories but also of the deepening contradictions among members of the anti-French coalition, Prussia and Austria above all. Peace with Prussia meant the beginning of the coalition's disintegration; on July 22, 1795 a separate peace with France was also signed in Basle by Spain.   p. 173

223 See Note 166.   p. 173

224 On the *battles of Auerstädt* and *Jena*, mentioned below, see Note 166. p. 173

225 The *Tugendbund* ("Union of Virtue")—one of the patriotic societies founded in Prussia after the defeat by Napoleonic France in 1806-07. It united

representatives of the liberal nobility and the bourgeois intelligentsia and aimed at spreading the idea of an anti-Napoleonic liberation war and supporting moderate liberal reforms. The Tugendbund was banned on Napoleon's demand on December 31, 1809 by Frederick William III, who also feared its activities. However, it continued to exist secretly until the end of the Napoleonic wars.

On the *peace of Tilsit* see Note 193.   p. 174

226 On these two battles see notes 168 and 56 respectively.   p. 174

227 See Note 203.   p. 174

228 At the *battle of Dresden* on August 26-27, 1813 Napoleon's army routed the allied forces of Austria, Prussia and Russia (the Bohemian or chief army), commanded by the Austrian Field Marshal Schwarzenberg.   p. 176

229 On the *battle of Leipzig* and its influence on the outcome of the 1813 campaign, see Note 31. The events that led up to the battle are described below in the text.
                                                                           p. 176

230 The *Confederation of the Rhine* (*Rheinbund*)—a union of sixteen states in Southern and Western Germany (Bavaria, Württemberg, Baden and others) established in July 1806 under the protection of Napoleon I, after he had defeated Austria in 1805. Later on twenty other states in Western, Central and Northern Germany joined the Confederation. It fell apart in 1813 after the defeat of Napoleon's army.   p. 179

231 The peace negotiations at Châtillon (on the Seine) between representatives of the allied powers, members of the sixth anti-French coalition, and Napoleon I's representative took place from February 4 to March 19, 1814. The Allies' main condition for concluding peace was Napoleon's renunciation of all conquered territories and France's return to the 1792 borders. The negotiations were broken off because of Napoleon's categorical rejection of this condition.   p. 180

232 The *Young Guard*—the name given to regiments of Napoleon's Imperial Guard formed in 1807 and later, as distinct from earlier formed regiments, which were called the Old Guard. Conditions of admission of officers and men to the Young Guard were not so strict as for the Old Guard, for which it provided reinforcements.   p. 180

233 The first *peace of Paris* was concluded on May 30, 1814 between the main members of the sixth anti-French coalition (Russia, Austria, Britain and Prussia) and France after Napoleon's defeat. Under this treaty France was deprived of all territories conquered since 1792, except for several border fortresses and Western Savoy, which were taken away by the second peace of Paris. This was signed between the same countries on November 20, 1815, after the short-lived restoration of Napoleon's rule and his second deposition. The second peace treaty of Paris restored France to its frontiers as of January 1, 1790.   p. 186

234 At the *battle of Ligny* (Belgium) on June 16, 1815 the Prussian army under Blücher, marching to join up with the Anglo-Dutch army of Wellington, was defeated by Napoleon. But Blücher's troops escaped from their pursuers commanded by Marshal Grouchy and reached the battlefield of Waterloo at the decisive moment on June 18 (see Note 30), thereby determining the outcome of the battle in favour of the Allies.   p. 186

235 When ordering this article for *The New American Cyclopaedia* Charles Dana wrote
to Marx on May 8, 1857: "*Artillery* should give the whole science and practice of
that arm, and everything relating to it, with the single exception of what relates to
the casting of guns, which will come under another head."

As we see from Engels' letter to Marx of July 11, 1857, he was going to start
writing the article "Artillery", as well as the article "Army", immediately after
finishing smaller articles beginning with A from Dana's first requested batch. But
busy with the "Army" and articles beginning with B, he did not begin "Artillery"
till after October 19. On that day he wrote to Marx: "Now I set to writing 'The
History of Cannon'." In subsequent letters (Engels to Marx, October 29 and
November 15 and 17, and Marx to Engels, October 31, November 13, 1857 and
January 23, 1858) the article in question was also called "The History of Cannon"
or simply "Cannon". Marx and Engels apparently did not expect that it could still
be inserted in the respective volume of articles beginning with A. However, it
was finished by the end of November and sent to New York on the 27th of that
month, as can be seen from Marx's notebook, and was therefore in time for
inclusion in Volume II of the *Cyclopaedia* under its original title "Artillery".

Some of the sources Engels used when writing the article are mentioned in the
text. The article "Artillery" in *Encyclopaedia Britannica* (Vol. III, Edinburgh,
1853) and German encyclopaedic publications were of great help to him. Engels'
notes on the calibres of guns used in the Prussian artillery, presumably compiled
from a military reference book, are extant.   p. 188

236 A reference to the seventh-century Arab conquest of Mesopotamia, Persia, Syria,
Palestine, Egypt and other countries, and the formation of the Arabian Caliphate.
                                                                              p. 189

237 This refers to *Epistolae fratris Rogerii Baconis, de secretis operibus artis et naturae et de
nullitate magiae*. The date of its writing has not yet been exactly established, though
in nineteenth-century literature on the history of the art of war it is often dated
1216 (Engels also gives this date). In later researches, however, this work is
believed to date to the 1240s. The first edition of the book was published in Paris
in 1542.   p. 189

238 In 1118 the army of Alfonso I of Aragon besieged the city of *Saragossa* (Aragon),
held by the Mohammedans from 712, and captured it. This was a stage in the
reconquest of the territories on the Iberian Peninsula seized by the Arabs and
African Berbers (Moors) during the Arab conquests in the early eighth century.
The main role in this reconquest, which began in the eighth to ninth centuries,
belonged to the Spanish kingdoms of Castile and Aragon, and to Portugal. In the
second half of the twelfth century it was interrupted by the invasion of the
peninsula by the Almohads, a Mohammedan sect that had united around itself
mountain Berber tribes and subdued Algeria, Tunisia, Morocco and Mohammedan Southern Spain under its first Imam, Caliph Abd-el-Mumen. Early in the
thirteenth century, Castile and Aragon, supported by the crusaders, defeated the
Almohads and resumed the reconquest. In 1236 the Castilians captured Cordova,
capital of the former Cordovan Caliphate (which had disintegrated in 1031), and
by the end of the thirteenth century only the Emirate of Granada in the south
remained in the possession of the Mohammedans. In 1492 it was conquered by the
Spaniards. Later in the text Engels mentions some episodes from the history of the
reconquest.   p. 189

[239] The siege of the Puy Guillaume castle (Western France) by the English took place at the beginning of the Hundred Years' War (1337-1453) between England and France (see Note 25).

The *German knights in Prussia*—knights of the Teutonic Order founded in 1190, during the third crusade. In the thirteenth century it conquered Eastern Prussia by subjugating and annihilating the local Lithuanian population and this land became the Order's base for aggression against Poland, Lithuania and Russian principalities. In 1237 the Teutonic Order united with the Livonian Order, another German Order, that had settled in the Baltic area. After the battle of Chudskoye Lake (Ice Battle) in 1242 and still more after that of Grünwald in 1410, the Order declined and subsequently retained only a small part of its possessions.   p. 190

[240] At the *battle of Fornovo* (Northern Italy) on July 6, 1495 the forces of the feudal states of Northern Italy attacked the army of Charles VIII of France returning from its expedition to Italy. The battle, which was won by the French, belongs to the initial stage of the Italian wars of 1494-1559 (see Note 26).   p. 191

[241] See Note 139.   p. 191

[242] The *battle of Renty* (Flanders) took place on August 13, 1554, during the war of Henry II of France, in alliance with the German Protestant princes, against Charles V, Holy Roman Emperor and King of Spain. The Spanish army forced the French to raise the siege of Renty and retreat to their frontiers. p. 192

[243] See Note 20.   p. 193

[244] See Note 142.   p. 194

[245] The battles mentioned were fought between the army of Gustavus Adolphus of Sweden and the German imperial army during the Thirty Years' War (see Note 142). In December 1630 Gustavus Adolphus' army approached the fortress of *Greifenhagen an der Oder* and after storming it twice compelled its garrison to leave it. In April 1631 Gustavus Adolphus' troops took Frankfort on the Oder by storm.
                                                                                   p. 195

[246] At the *battle of Malplaquet* on September 11, 1709—one of the major battles in the War of the Spanish Succession (see Note 16)—the allied armies of Britain, Austria and the Netherlands under Prince Eugène of Savoy and the Duke of Marlborough defeated the French army under Marshal Villars.   p. 195

[247] See Note 85.   p. 196

[248] See Note 86.   p. 197

[249] On the *battle of Friedland* between the French and Russian armies on June 14, 1807, see this volume, p. 78.
On the *battle of Wagram* see Note 72.   p. 199

[250] At the *battle of Pirmasens* (Rhenish Palatinate) on September 14, 1793, during the war of the first European coalition against the French Republic, the Prussians defeated the French Moselle army.   p. 199

[251] On the *bombardment of Sveaborg* see Note 178.   p. 206

[252] Having undertaken to write about some military leaders and politicians in accordance with Dana's request for articles beginning with B (see Note 49), Marx

asked Engels' opinion of them, including Bugeaud (see his letters to Engels of September 17 and 21, 1857). In his letter of September 22, 1857 Engels described Bugeaud's military activities in Algeria. Marx took this into account when working on the article later, probably in November. The article was finished by the end of that month and sent off to New York on the 27th, together with Engels' "Artillery", as is seen from the entry in Marx's notebook.

Extant excerpts show that Marx used the following sources: M. Wagner, *The Tricolor on the Atlas; or, Algeria and the French Conquest* (London, Edinburgh and New York, 1854) and D. Stern, *Histoire de la révolution de 1848* (Vol. I, Paris, 1850). Marx possibly also used the data on Bugeaud's activities in Algeria contained in Engels' first version of the article "Algeria" and left out by the *Cyclopaedia* editors (see Note 74).   p. 211

253 The *sieges* and *battle of Ordal* took place during the Peninsular war of 1808-14 (see Note 12).   p. 211

254 The *Hundred Days*—the period of the short-lived restoration of Napoleon's empire, which lasted from the moment of his arrival in Paris from Elba on March 20, 1815 to his second deposition on June 22 following his defeat at Waterloo.
                                                                        p. 211

255 The French invasion of Spain was undertaken by decision of the Verona Congress of the Holy Alliance (an alliance of European monarchs founded in 1815 by Russia, Austria and Prussia) for the purpose of suppressing the second bourgeois revolution in Spain, 1820-23. French troops under the Duke of Angoulême entered Spain in 1823 and restored the absolutist regime of Ferdinand VII. They remained in the country until 1828.   p. 211

256 In the official report of the debates in the Chamber of Deputies on January 25, 1834, published in *Le Moniteur universel* (No. 26, January 26, 1834), the editors omitted Dulong's remark on Bugeaud's statement. But on January 30 (Issue No. 30) they had to explain references made by other newspapers to the incident between the two generals and reports on the duel between them.   p. 212

257 The Paris republican uprising against the July monarchy on April 13-14, 1834, like the revolutionary actions in some other French towns, was in response to the powerful proletarian uprising that had begun in Lyons. As in Lyons, the uprising in Paris was directed by the secret republican-democratic Society of the Friends of the Rights of Man and the Citizen. For two days the Paris workers, the main participants in the uprising, carried on bitter barricade fighting against government troops.   p. 212

258 The *treaty of Tafna* between Bugeaud and Abd-el-Kader was signed on May 30, 1837, after the French resumed military operations against Abd-el-Kader in 1835, in violation of the peace treaty concluded a year earlier. The French were forced to conclude the new peace (the treaty of Tafna) since they had failed to achieve substantial results and required military forces to subdue the insurgent regions of Eastern Algeria. Under the treaty of Tafna France again recognised the independence of Abd-el-Kader's state in Western Algeria, except for Algiers, Oran, Arzew and other coastal towns. In 1839 the peace was again violated by the French, and the Algerian liberation struggle under Abd-el-Kader (see Note 80) was resumed.   p. 212

259 By 1844 Bugeaud and other French generals had subdued Western Algeria by bribing the local feudal lords and terrorising the Algerian tribes. Taking

advantage of the Sultan of Morocco's refusal to extradite Abd-el-Kader who had crossed into Morocco, Bugeaud invaded that country. On August 14, 1844 he defeated the Moroccans in the battle of the Isly. Under the Tangiers treaty of September 10, 1844, Bugeaud made the Sultan drive Abd-el-Kader out of Morocco and disband the frontier detachments. But the threat of interference by Britain, worried by the prospect of French expansion in North Africa, prompted Bugeaud to withdraw his troops from Morocco.   p. 213

260 The differences between Bugeaud and Guizot were caused by the former's intention to use the suppression of the Algerian revolt of 1845-47 for further conquests in North Africa (his expedition of May 1847 to Kabylia also served this purpose), and for a new invasion of Morocco. Though a supporter of an active colonial policy in general, on this occasion Guizot feared that Bugeaud's actions would aggravate the already sharp Anglo-French contradictions.

p. 213

261 The posts in the Provisional Government of the French Republic set up on February 24, 1848 were held mainly by moderate republicans (Lamartine, Dupont de l'Eure and others). There were also three representatives of the *Réforme* social-democratic party—Ledru-Rollin, Flocon and Louis Blanc, and a worker, Albert (real name Martin).   p. 213

262 Marx informed Engels of his intention to write an essay on Brune in his letter of September 17, 1857. But he apparently did not begin working on it before the end of November. There is no entry in Marx's notebook about its dispatch to New York. One can only assume that the word "etc." in the entry of January 8, 1858 about the dispatch to Dana of Marx's "Bolivar" and Engels' "Campaign", "Cannonade" and "Captain" refers to this essay. On February 1, 1858, in a letter to Engels, Marx mentioned it among the articles beginning with B already written and sent off to the United States.

Marx's excerpts on the subject from Fr. Chr. Schlosser's book *Zur Beurtheilung Napoleon's und seiner neusten Tadler und Lobredner*, Frankfurt am Main, 1835 (probably made long before Marx started writing the essay), and a rough draft (more detailed than the final version) of the essay based mainly on Schlosser's book and on relevant articles in the *Biographie universelle (Michaud) ancienne et moderne* (Vol. 6, Paris, 1854) and *The English Cyclopaedia* (Vol. V, London, 1856) are extant (see this volume, pp. 397-401).   p. 215

263 The *Club of the Cordeliers*—a popular club founded in Paris in July 1790, during the French Revolution. It derived its name from the former convent of Franciscan Cordeliers where its members met. Its official name was the *Société des amis des droits de l'homme et du citoyen* (Society of the Friends of the Rights of Man and the Citizen). With the Jacobin Club it played an important part in France's political life. Originally it united representatives of various trends which later on made up the Right (Dantonist) and the Left (Hébertist) wing of the Jacobins. With the growth of the revolution the Left elements prevailed. During the revolutionary-democratic Jacobin dictatorship the club was the stronghold of the Hébertists, existing until March 1794.   p. 215

264 The anti-monarchist demonstration of Paris artisans and workers in the *Champ de Mars* took place on July 17, 1791. It was directed by the leaders of the Club of the Cordeliers who drew up a petition to the Constituent Assembly demanding the abdication of the King. The demonstration was fired on by government troops and the National Guard of the city's bourgeois districts

commanded by La Fayette with the support of big bourgeois constitutional-monarchist circles.   p. 215

265 On September 2-5, 1792 Paris was the scene of popular unrest caused by foreign intervention and internal counter-revolution. The people seized prisons and staged improvised trials of imprisoned counter-revolutionaries, many of whom were executed. This Red Terror was an act of revolutionary self-defence.   p. 215

266 At the *battle of Hondschoote* on September 6-8, 1793, during the war of revolutionary France against the first European coalition, the French defeated the allied armies of Britain, Hanover, the Netherlands and Austria.   p. 215

267 Counter-revolutionary insurrections in the Gironde, Calvados and many other departments of Western, Southwestern and Southeastern France were raised in the summer of 1793 by the Girondists (the party of the big commercial and industrial bourgeoisie) allied with the royalists. The Girondists revolted against the Jacobin government and the revolutionary masses on the pretext of defending the rights of the departments to autonomy and federation. In the autumn of 1793 the counter-revolutionary "federalist" movement was suppressed by troops of the French Republic.

The *Committee of Public Safety* (*Le Comité de salut public*) — the leading body of the revolutionary government of France, established in April 1793. During the Jacobin dictatorship (from June 2, 1793 to July 27, 1794) it headed the struggle against home and foreign counter-revolution and supervised the carrying out of revolutionary measures.   p. 215

268 A reference to Dantonists who survived after the execution of Danton and his comrades-in-arms and who expressed the interests of the so-called new bourgeoisie which emerged during the revolution. With other counter-revolutionary forces they took an active part in the coup d'état of the 9th Thermidor (see Note 63).   p. 216

269 On the 12th and 13th Vendémiaire (October 4-5), 1795 government troops under General Bonaparte suppressed a royalist revolt in Paris.   p. 216

270 In May 1796 Babeuf and his closest associates, who sought to overthrow the existing regime by revolution and to establish the community of goods, were arrested. In the autumn of that year, the Babouvists made an attempt to release them and to raise a revolt in the Grenelle military camp under the slogan of overthrowing the Directory (see Note 184) and restoring the Jacobin Constitution of 1793. The revolt was put down by government troops.
                                                                    p. 216

271 See Note 65.   p. 216

272 See Note 187.   p. 216

273 At the end of August 1799, during the war of the French Republic against the second anti-French coalition, an Anglo-Russian corps under the Duke of York landed at Helder (Northern Holland) for the purpose of abolishing the Batavian Republic which was dependent on France, restoring the pre-revolutionary regime and seizing the Dutch fleet. But in October the allied troops were routed by the Franco-Dutch army commanded by Brune. On October 18 the Duke had to sign the Alkmar capitulation which, besides the return of French

and Dutch prisoners-of-war, provided for the withdrawal of the anti-French coalition troops from Holland.   p. 216

274 See Note 68.   p. 216

275 The *camp at Boulogne* was set up by Napoleon I in 1803-05 as a base for invading England across the Channel. Napoleon was compelled to abandon his plan by the defeat of the French fleet in the war with Britain and the formation in Europe of a new, third, anti-French coalition including Britain, Russia and Austria.   p. 217

276 See Note 28.   p. 217

277 A reference to the act of the French Senate deposing Napoleon and restoring the Bourbon dynasty. It was passed after the entry of the armies of the sixth anti-French coalition into Paris on March 31, 1814.   p. 217

278 See Note 254.   p. 217

279 See Note 30.   p. 217

280 Marx wrote the article on Bolivar at a time when the history of the Latin American countries' war for independence (1810-26) had not yet been adequately studied. Books and memoirs by European adventurers who had taken part in the war out of mercenary motives were widely read at the time. Many of these authors, having failed to achieve their aims in Latin America, gave a distorted idea of the war of independence. Examples of such books are *Memoirs of Simon Bolivar* by Ducoudray Holstein, a Frenchman who was at one time Bolivar's chief of staff and had become his personal enemy, *A Narrative of the Expedition to the Rivers Orinoco and Apuré* by G. Hippisley, an English deserter from Bolivar's army, and *Memoirs of General Miller* by John Miller, which dealt unscrupulously with the notes of William Miller (John Miller's brother) who fought for the independence of Peru. Marx's excerpts from the first two books are extant. The third is mentioned in Marx's preparatory materials for the article and in the article itself. The authors of these books attributed numerous imaginary vices to Bolivar (perfidy, arrogance, cowardice) and greatly exaggerated his actual shortcomings (love of the spectacular and ambition). Bolivar's struggle against federalist and separatist elements and for the unification of Latin American republics was presented as a striving for dictatorship. There were also downright factual inaccuracies, such as Ducoudray Holstein's statement that in 1810 Bolivar refused to take part in the struggle for the independence of Venezuela, or the allegation that his participation in Miranda's arrest was motivated by personal considerations (in fact he was convinced of the latter's presumed betrayal).

In reality, as later objective researches confirmed, Simon Bolivar played an outstanding role in Latin America's struggle for independence, rallying for a time the patriotic elements among the landowning creoles (Latin Americans of Spanish descent), the bourgeoisie and the masses, including Indians and Negroes. His activity, contradictory though it was, helped to liberate several Latin American countries from the Spanish yoke, to establish republican forms of government, and to carry out progressive bourgeois reforms.

Marx had only the above-mentioned sources at his disposal. Hence his one-sided view of Bolivar's personality in this article, in his letter to Engels of February 14, 1858, and in *Herr Vogt* written later (see present edition, Vol. 17, pp. 219, 328). His attitude to Bolivar was to a certain extent determined by the fact that the sources he used exaggerated Bolivar's striving for personal power, and over-emphasised the Bonapartist features of his policy, against which Marx and Engels waged a relentless struggle. Nevertheless, Marx pointed out the progressive aspects of Bolivar's activity, such as his liberation of Negro slaves, and on the whole appreciated the revolutionary anti-colonial struggle for national liberation in Latin America.

There is an entry in Marx's notebook on the dispatch of "Bolivar" to New York on January 8, 1858, together with some articles beginning with C by Engels. In his letter to Marx of January 25, Charles Dana acknowledged receipt of the article. At Dana's request Marx had also enclosed a list of sources used.

p. 219

281 Emperor Napoleon I was proclaimed King of the Kingdom of Italy formed in Northern Italy in 1805 in place of the Italian Republic. His stepson Eugène Beauharnais was appointed Viceroy.

p. 219

282 On April 19, 1810, the colonial regime was overthrown in the city of Caracas and a new government set up consisting of creole landowners, merchants and intellectuals. Under the influence of the radical Patriotic Society headed by Miranda and Bolivar, an independent Venezuelan Republic was proclaimed at a congress in Caracas on July 5, 1811. The Caracas events served as a signal for uprisings against the Spanish colonial authorities in other Latin American countries (on the general course of this struggle see Note 219). In New Granada, bordering on Venezuela, Spanish rule was overthrown in the capital city of Bogota, in the seaport city of Cartagena and in Quito, the main city of the province of Quito (now Ecuador). In this last, however, it was soon restored. When the Venezuelan Republic fell in July 1812, Cartagena became one of the strongholds of struggle for its restoration. The further struggle, in which the establishment of a second Venezuelan Republic (August 1813-July 1814) was a remarkable episode, ended in a temporary restoration of Spanish rule in the former colonies except La Plata. At this stage the liberation struggle was hampered by the narrow class policy of the creole landowners who would not satisfy the peasants' demands and preserved Negro slavery and the inequality of Indians.

p. 219

283 The federal *Republic of New Granada* was established in 1813 as a result of anti-Spanish uprisings in various towns and provinces of the New Granada viceroyalty. It united the insurgent regions which were bound by a federal treaty and acknowledged the supremacy of the Congress of New Granada. The Republic fell in 1816 owing to superior Spanish forces and discord among the autonomous governments of the different regions.

p. 223

284 A reference to the *Republic of Haiti* (Hayti) established as a result of the uprising of Negro slaves and mulattos on the island of Hispaniola (the western part belonged to France and the eastern part to Spain, which was obliged to cede it to France in 1795) and their liberation struggle against the French, British and Spanish colonialists which had lasted since 1790. In 1804 the island was proclaimed independent and its old Indian name—Haiti—restored.

p. 224

285 A reference to the battles between the Venezuelan insurgent army and Spanish forces in New Granada. In the summer of 1819 Bolivar's army marched over the Andes to liberate New Granada. The Spaniards were defeated in a decisive

battle on the river Boyaca on August 7. Bolivar's victories led to the liberation of the most of New Granada and to the establishment in December 1819 of a united republic of Greater Colombia, which included Venezuela and New Granada and was joined by Quito (Ecuador) in 1822, after the Spaniards had been driven out. p. 228

286 The *revolution on the Isle of Leon*—an uprising against the absolutist regime in Spain, raised in January 1820 by army officers headed by Colonels Riego and Quiroga. Its aim was to restore the 1812 Constitution abrogated by the government of Ferdinand VII in 1814. The leaders of the uprising made use of the discontent among the soldiers of the expeditionary army concentrated in Cadiz (seaport on the Isle of Leon) to be sent against the Latin American patriots. These events sparked off a second bourgeois revolution in Spain (1820-23) which thwarted the government's plans to send large military contingents to suppress the liberation movement in its Latin American colonies. The revolution was put down by the forces of internal reaction and by French intervention (see Note 255). p. 228

287 *Llaneros*—inhabitants of the llanos, vast grassy plains in the north of South America, mostly free mestizo cattle-breeders. Boves, a Spanish agent, exploited their hostile attitude to the creole landowners to recruit mestizo troops to fight against the patriots of Venezuela and New Granada in 1813-14. But in 1816 the llaneros, under their new, mestizo leader Joseph Antonio Paez, joined the liberation army of Bolivar who promised to give them land. The llanero horsemen took part in many of Bolivar's operations, including the victorious battle of Carabobo mentioned in the text (June 24, 1821), which led to the almost complete expulsion of the Spaniards from Venezuela. p. 229

288 In 1821, a number of countries of Central America overthrew the rule of the Spanish colonialists, proclaimed their independence and were for a short time incorporated in Mexico, but in 1823 formed a federation—the United States of Central America. In 1839 the federation split into five republics—Guatemala, Honduras, Salvador, Nicaragua and Costa Rica. Panama, which was part of the New Granada viceroyalty, was incorporated in the Republic of Greater Colombia as a consequence of the 1821 uprising. p. 230

289 The *"Bolivian Code"*—a reference to the Constitution of the Republic of Bolivia adopted by the Bolivian inaugural congress on November 6, 1826.
The *Code Napoléon*—the code of French civil law promulgated in 1804— exerted a great influence on legislation in many European and a number of Latin American countries. p. 230.

290 The Pan-American congress in Panama met from June 22 to July 25, 1826. It adopted a resolution on the "perpetual confederation" of Latin American republics, a mutual defence treaty and a military convention. But not one of the republics ratified the congress decisions. The plan for establishing a Latin American Confederation, as well as Bolivar's later, less extensive plan for an Andes Federation (comprising three republics governed by him—Peru, Bolivia and Greater Colombia), fell through because they lacked an economic basis, and because of divisions between and among the ruling landowners and bourgeoisie of the various states. The sharpening of these contradictions resulted in the overthrow of Bolivar's rule in Peru in 1827 and in Bolivia in 1828, and in the disintegration of Greater Colombia, from which Venezuela separated in 1829 and Ecuador in 1830. p. 231

291 These are the basic terms of the peace treaty between Peru and Colombia concluded in Guayaquil in September 1829. p. 231

292 The list of the sources attached by Marx to this article at Dana's request (see Note 280) contains the 1831 French edition of Ducoudray Holstein's book, whereas Marx's excerpts show that he used the two-volume English edition published in London in 1830. There is also an inaccuracy as regards the second book (published in two volumes in London in 1828-29). Its author is John Miller, but it was not he but his brother General William Miller who was in the service of the Republic of Peru and who is supposed to be telling the story. p. 233

293 Having finished his share of Dana's first request for articles beginning with B and the essay "Artillery", Engels began writing articles beginning with C, the first of which is "Campaign". Dana's C list has not come down to us. From Engels' letter to Marx of January 28, 1858 one can see that this list did not satisfy Engels, who asked his friend to send Dana the C list he himself had drawn up (see present edition, Vol. 40). By that time Engels had already written several articles beginning with C and begun collecting material for others, "Cavalry" in particular. On January 7, 1858 he sent Marx, in London, the three articles "Campaign", "Cannonade" and "Captain", which, according to Marx's entry in his notebook, were dispatched to New York on January 8, together with the article "Bolivar". A fortnight later, Engels sent some more articles beginning with C to Marx, who forwarded them to the United Sates on January 22. Meanwhile a new request for articles beginning with B had arrived from Dana and as it was urgent Engels had to put off his articles beginning with C.

In writing the article "Campaign" Engels made use of Clausewitz's *Vom Kriege*, which he told Marx he was studying in his letter of January 7, 1858. p. 234

294 On the *battle of Marengo* see Note 69.

At the *battle of Hohenlinden* (Bavaria) on December 3, 1800 the French army under Moreau defeated the army of Archduke John of Austria. The outcome of these two battles was of great importance for France's victory over the forces of the second European coalition. p. 234

295 On September 20, 1792 *at Valmy* (Northeastern France), the French revolutionary forces under Dumouriez and Kellermann halted the Austro-Prussian interventionists, under the Duke of Brunswick, and a detachment of French émigré nobles accompanying him. The interventionists were compelled to retreat and on October 5 were thrown back over the French border. p. 236

296 The "Carabine" belongs to the second group of short articles beginning with C Engels sent to Marx after the dispatch of the first three articles of this group on January 7, 1858 (see Note 293). On January 22 Marx made an entry in his notebook about the dispatch of the following seven articles he had received from Engels by then: "Carabine", "Carabineers", "Carcass", "Carronade", "Cartouch", "Cartridge" and "Case Shot". The second article was not published in *The New American Cyclopaedia* and the manuscript is not extant.

In *The New American Cyclopaedia* the article "Carabine" ends with the sentence: "Several improvements in breech-loading carabines have recently been made in the United States, and submitted for trial to an ordnance board at West

Point (July, 1858)." The date quoted shows that this was added by the editors.
                                                                          p. 238

[297] A reference to the American War of Independence (see Note 60).   p. 241

[298] See Note 35.   p. 242.

[299] The article "Berme" was written by Engels in compliance with Dana's second
request for articles beginning with B contained in his letter of January 8, 1858.
On January 23, Marx forwarded Dana's letter to Engels and asked him to
return it. Reproducing the list of articles beginning with B in his letter to
Engels of February 1, 1858, Marx wrote: "New B's are: 'Bidassoa' (battle of),
'Blenheim' (ditto), 'Burmah' (war in), 'Bomarsund' (siege), 'Borodino' (battle),
'Brescia' (assault), 'Bridge-Head', 'Bülow', 'Buda' (siege of), 'Beresford', 'Berme'.
When Dana says, 'most of them I asked you before', he is mistaken, and is
confusing *your* list of B's with *his* own" (see present edition, Vol. 40). Dana also
requested for an article on Bengal Rebellion (i. e. on the Indian national
liberation uprising of 1857), but Engels found it impossible to do it within the
time stipulated (see his letter to Marx of January 25, 1858. The description of
this uprising was included in the article "Hindoostan" published in *The New
American Cyclopaedia* later). Engels started the other articles beginning with B
and by January 29 he had three—"Berme", "Blenheim" and "Borodino"—
ready. Marx sent them off to New York the same day, as can be seen from his
notebook. In February and March Engels continued to fulfil this order and at
the same time resumed work on the articles beginning with C which he had
been forced to interrupt.   p. 248

[300] For this item Engels made excerpts from the article "Höchstädt" in Brockhaus'
Allgemeine Encyclopädie der Wissenschaften und Künste edited by I. S. Ersch and
I. G. Gruber. These excerpts are extant.   p. 249

[301] At the *battle of Höchstädt* on September 20, 1703 the allied French and Bavarian
troops under Villars, Marshal of France, defeated the Austrian army. This
battle and that of Blenheim were fought in the War of the Spanish Succession
(see Note 16).   p. 250

[302] In the article on the battle of Borodino (1812), which was a major event in
Russia's Patriotic War against Napoleon's invasion, Engels gave an idea of the
scale of the battle and of the stubbornness and staunchness displayed by the
two belligerent armies, and presented a more objective picture than the authors
of many West European works on military history, but he did not avoid
inaccuracies in elucidating some of its aspects. Engels was influenced to a
certain extent by the German historian Bernhardi's book about General Toll,
which he mentions at the end of the article and which contains a number of
tendentious assertions emanating from Toll himself and from his biographer
(Th. von Bernhardi, *Denkwürdigkeiten aus dem Leben des ... Grafen von Toll*, vols.
1-4, Leipzig, 1856. Engels' notes from the second volume are extant). In the
main the inaccuracies concern the evaluation of the results of the battle, which
Engels was inclined to consider a victory for Napoleon's army, according to the
tradition in the West, and the role of Mikhail Kutuzov, Commander-in-Chief of
the Russian army. Kutuzov was not passive during the battle but constantly
influenced its course by countering and thwarting Napoleon's plans. In
particular, it was on his orders that the Russian cavalry made a successful raid
into the rear of the French left wing. The outcome of the battle was highly

unfavourable for Napoleon: he failed to destroy the main forces of the Russian army and himself sustained heavy losses. This led to a turn in the course of the war in favour of Russia and to the defeat of Napoleon's army, despite the fact that the Russians had temporarily to leave Moscow.

Later researches led to substantial corrections concerning the correlation of forces and the losses sustained by the two armies. They showed that at the time of the battle the French had 135,000 men and 587 guns, and the Russians 120,000 men and 640 guns. French losses amounted to 58,000 killed and wounded, while the Russians lost about 44,000 men.

There is an entry in Marx's notebook on the dispatch of this article to New York on January 29, 1858.   p. 251

303 See Note 55.   p. 251

304 A reference to the raid of Uvarov's cavalry corps and Platov's Cossack corps sent by Kutuzov to outflank the advancing French troops. Their appearance on the flank and in the rear of the French made Napoleon hold back the attacks in the centre, thus enabling Kutuzov to regroup the Russian forces to repulse subsequent attacks.   p. 253

305 The "Bridge-Head", "Buda" and other articles beginning with B were written by Engels in fulfilment of Dana's second request for B articles (see Note 299). The time of writing of these two articles can be established only approximately. On February 12, 1858 Marx wrote in his notebook: "French bank, etc. Buda, Bidassoa, Bridge-Head." This presumably means that, according to the accepted form of settling accounts with the editorial board of the *New-York Daily Tribune* (including accounts for the articles for *The New American Cyclopaedia* published under its aegis), Marx had drawn a bill on it on account of the fee for these articles, although it is known from other sources that the article "Bidassoa" was still not finished by the last week in February. However, we may assume that the other two articles were either ready or nearing completion by that time.   p. 256

306 In this article Engels gives a short account of some results of his study of the 1848-49 revolutionary war in Hungary. He had already written about the course of this war in the *Neue Rheinische Zeitung* (see present edition, vols. 8 and 9) and in the early 1850s intended to devote a special work to it and to the military events of the Italian revolution. The sources Engels used—memoirs of the Hungarian generals Görgey and Klapka—are mentioned in the article itself. On when it was written see Note 305.   p. 258

307 The printing establishment of the University of Pest was accommodated in the observatory building from 1810 to 1927.   p. 258

308 A reference to the *Itinerarium Antonini* compiled about 300 B.C. and showing the most important routes of the Roman Empire, populated points along them, and the distance between them.   p. 259

309 See Note 159.   p. 261

310 Engels planned to write the articles "Camp" and "Catapult" in January 1858 but at first he did not have the necessary sources. On January 7 and 14 he asked Marx to go to the British Museum and collect the necessary material. Marx's letter to Engels of February 1 shows that Marx complied with this request a little later. No direct information is available about the progress of

work on these articles, nor is there any entry in Marx's notebook on their dispatch to New York. In a letter to Marx of February 18, 1858 Engels wrote that he had enclosed "a few small pieces for Dana". It can be assumed that this refers to the articles in question and probably to the article "Coehorn" on which Engels was working about the same time, as can be seen from the Marx-Engels correspondence.   p. 262

311 *Levites*—members of the tribe of Levi who assisted the priests of the Hebrew temple.
Tabernacle—a tent used as a temple.   p. 263

312 *Augurs*—Roman religious officials who foretold the future by observing the flight, cries and entrails of birds, etc., before all important state acts.
Gnomon—an ancient astronomical instrument.   p. 264

313 A reference to the *battle of Vercellae* (Northern Italy) in 101 B.C., at which the Roman general Marius defeated the Germanic Cimbri tribe. This victory ended Rome's war against the Cimbri and Teutons (113-101 B.C.), who had invaded South Gaul and Italy several times.   p. 265

314 The *siege of Jerusalem* by the Roman general Vespasian and later, after he became Emperor, by his son Titus, took place in A.D. 68-70, during the Judaean war (A.D. 66-73) caused by the Jewish uprising against Roman domination. After the capture of the city walls the besieged inhabitants continued fighting for a long time in the Temple of Jerusalem and in the streets.   p. 266

315 Letters exchanged by Marx and Engels on January 14, 1858 show that originally it was Marx who intended to write this article. But owing to lack of time he could not obtain the necessary sources, whereas Engels had comprehensive material on Coehorn collected when studying problems of military history. Engels therefore undertook to write the article. No precise data is available when he wrote it. It might have been written with "Camp" and "Catapult" and finished by February 18 (see Note 310).   p. 267

316 The unsuccessful siege of the French-held fortress of *Maestricht* in the Netherlands by the Dutch under William III of Orange in July and August 1676 and the *battles of Senef, Cassel, St. Denis* and *Fleurus* took place during the war of 1672-79 waged by France, in alliance with Britain (who withdrew in 1674) and Sweden, against the Netherlands and the Spanish and Austrian Habsburgs. The war, caused by commercial rivalry between France and the Netherlands, and by Louis XIV's desire to seize the South (Spanish) and North Netherlands, led to the territorial expansion of the French monarchy but failed to achieve its main purpose—the conquest of Holland.   p. 267

317 The *peace of Nimeguen,* concluded by Louis XIV's government with Holland and Spain in 1678 and with the Austrian Habsburgs in 1679, ended the war between them and France started in 1672. By this peace France received the Franche Comté and several towns in the Spanish Netherlands. Holland recovered the fortress of Maestricht and the hereditary lands of the House of Orange but in return acknowledged the French colonial conquests in Guiana and Senegal.   p. 267

318 The French captured the fortress of *Bergen-op-Zoom* in 1747, during the War of the Austrian Succession (see Note 38).

The campaigns from 1688 to 1691 took place during the war of 1688-97 between France and the so-called Augsburg League comprising Holland, Britain, Spain, the German Empire under the Austrian Habsburgs, Savoy, Sweden and a number of German and Italian princes. The war ended with the Treaty of Ryswijk (1697), which confirmed the prewar boundaries with a few alterations. France had to acknowledge the revolution of 1688 in England which brought the Dutch Stadtholder William III of Orange to the throne.

p. 268

319 See Note 16.   p. 268

320 In a letter to Marx dated January 25, 1858 Engels wrote that he had "to do some preliminary research on 'Bidassoa'". On February 12 Marx drew a bill on the editorial board of the *New-York Daily Tribune* on account of the fee for a few articles beginning with B, including "Bidassoa" (see Note 305). At that time Engels was still working on the article, and it was not received by Marx in London till about February 22-23 (see his letter to Engels of March 2, 1858, present edition, Vol. 40). There is no entry in Marx's notebook on the dispatch of the article to New York.

The main source used by Engels when writing "Bidassoa" was Napier's *History of the War in the Peninsula and in the South of France, from the Year 1807 to the Year 1814* (vols. I-VI, London, 1828-40).   p. 269

321 At the *battle of Vittoria* on June 21, 1813, during the Peninsular war (1808-14), the allied British, Spanish and Portuguese army under Wellington defeated the army of Joseph Bonaparte, who then had to hand over the command to Marshal Soult.   p. 269

322 This sketch was drawn by Engels on the basis of the description and the plans of the battles of the Bidassoa of August 31 and October 7, 1813 given in Napier's *History of the War in the Peninsula and in the South of France* (Vol. VI, London, 1840, "Explanatory Sketch No. 5"). The following names are written on it: "Urogne, Rhune, Sans Cullotes, Puerto, Bayonnette, Hogsback, Comissari, Croix de Bouquets, Biriatu, Bildox, Mandale, Vera, Salinas, Irun, San Marcial, Lesaca, Peña de Haya." In the bottom right-hand corner is the inscription: "Battle-field on the Bidassoa."   p. 275

323 Engels enclosed the article "Brescia" in his letter to Marx dated February 24, 1858. But it was not sent to New York until March 9 together with his article "Burmah". On that date Marx's notebook has the entry: "Burman War. Brescia (battle of)."   p. 277

324 The *Guelphs* and the *Ghibellines*—political parties in Italy in the twelfth-fifteenth centuries, in the period of struggle between the Roman Popes and the German Emperors. The Guelphs, supporters of the Pope, belonged to the top urban merchants and artisans. The Ghibellines, supporters of the Emperor, represented mainly the feudal aristocracy.   p. 278

325 The Republic of Venice existed from the fifth century and was abolished as a result of its occupation by General Bonaparte in 1797 and the division of its territory between France and Austria under the Treaty of Campo Formio (see Note 187).   p. 279

326 In his letters of February 11, 18 and 24, 1858 Engels informed Marx of his work on "Burmah" and his difficulties in obtaining material on the history of

that country and particularly the Anglo-Burmese war of 1852. On March 4 he wrote telling Marx that he had almost finished the article but was compelled to make "sundry necessary additions from another source". An entry in Marx's notebook shows that "Burmah" was sent to New York on March 9 (see Note 323) though Marx did not inform Engels that he had received it until March 15.
                                                                              p. 280

327 Burma became a victim of Britain's colonial policy in the first decades of the nineteenth century. In the first Anglo-Burmese war (1824-26) troops of the East India Company seized the Province of Assam bordering on Bengal, and the coastal districts of Aracan and Tenasserim which were ceded by Burma under the Yandabo peace treaty of February 24, 1826 imposed upon it by the British. Besides, Burma was forced to pay an indemnity of £1,000,000. The second Anglo-Burmese war (1852) resulted in the British capture of the Province of Pegu, where the guerrilla movement against the invaders lasted until 1860. In the 1860s Britain imposed a number of unequal treaties on Burma and in 1885, at the end of the third Anglo-Burmese war, it annexed the whole of the country.
                                                                              p. 280

328 Engels informed Marx of his work on "Bomarsund" on February 24 and March 4, 11, 16 and 17, 1858. In Marx's notebook there is an entry on the dispatch of this article to New York on March 19, 1858.
                                                                              p. 287

329 As can be seen from Marx's letter to Engels of February 22 and Engels' letters to Marx of February 24 and March 4, 11, 16 and 17, 1858, they intended to write the article "Bülow" together. Engels, who as usual had undertaken to elucidate the military aspect of the biography, looked through several works on the history of the Napoleonic wars (including those of A.H. Jomini, G. Cathcart and W. Siborne) but did not find enough information there. On March 19 Marx told Engels to cease collecting material for the article, informing him that he would write it himself since he had sufficient material about the man for a brief biography. Marx's excerpts from *Meyer's Conversations-Lexicon* (Vol. 6, Hildburghausen, Amsterdam, Paris and Philadelphia, 1843) are extant (see this volume, pp. 402-03).
                                                                              p. 288

330 See Note 30.   p. 288

331 Marx and Engels had agreed that Engels would write about Beresford's military activity while Marx was to elucidate other aspects of his life (see Marx's letter to Engels of February 22, 1858). On March 11 Engels sent his version of the article to London, telling Marx that he could not find anything about Beresford's expedition to Buenos Aires in 1806 and other important aspects of his career.
    Engels' version was substantially supplemented by Marx and dispatched to New York on April 9, 1858, according to an entry in Marx's notebook. For this article Engels mainly used Napier's *History of the War in the Peninsula,* and Marx used reference books and encyclopaedias (in particular, he made excerpts from the article "Beresford" in *The English Cyclopaedia,* London, Vol. V). p. 289

332 Here Marx and Engels mention some colonial expeditions in which Beresford took part.
    In 1806 the British took advantage of the uprising of the Boer colonists against the Dutch colonial authorities and seized South African lands around the Cape of Good Hope (Cape Colony) under the pretext that Holland, being a

vassal of Napoleon, was taking part in his wars against Britain. Officially the Cape Colony was annexed to Britain after the end of the Napoleonic wars.

In the same year a British expedition was sent to take possession of Buenos Aires, which belonged to Spain, then an ally of Napoleonic France. Meeting with no serious resistance from the Spanish colonial authorities, Beresford's detachment seized Buenos Aires but was surrounded and compelled to surrender by the Argentine patriots. A new British expedition to the Rio de la Plata in 1807 also failed.

The Portuguese island of Madeira was seized by Beresford's troops at the end of 1807 under the pretext of defending it against the French. It remained in the hands of the British until 1814.   p. 289

333 The *Convention of Cintra* (Portugal) was signed on August 30, 1808 by Dalrymple and Junot, commanders-in-chief of the British and French armies in Portugal. It was the result of the defeat of French troops by the Anglo-Portuguese army, and of the popular uprising in the Peninsula against Napoleon's rule. The French agreed to evacuate Portugal (where they had been since autumn 1807), and the British undertook to ship Junot's troops to France where they were included by Napoleon in the 200,000-strong army with which he invaded the Peninsula for the second time in November 1808.

At the *battle of Coruña* (Spain) on January 16, 1809, the retreating British army of General Sir John Moore repulsed attacks by Marshal Soult's French army and on January 17 and 18, covered by Beresford's division, it embarked at Coruña for Britain.   p. 289

334 At the *battle of Salamanca* on July 22, 1812, the allied armies of Britain, Spain and Portugal under Wellington repulsed the French army of Marshal Marmont, which suffered heavy losses. As the result of the *battle of Vittoria* on June 21, 1813 (see Note 321) the main French forces were pushed back to the Pyrenees and by the end of 1813 the war had been carried onto French territory. At *Bayonne* (Southwestern France), on December 9-13, 1813, Wellington's troops mounted an offensive against the entrenched camp of Marshal Soult's army and pressed it hard.

In 1814, during a general offensive of the armies of the sixth anti-French coalition in France, Wellington's advancing army won victories over Soult's army (on February 27 at *Orthes* and on April 10 at *Toulouse*). On April 18, after Napoleon's abdication, Soult concluded an armistice with Wellington.

p. 290

335 A reference to Beresford's participation in suppressing the national liberation uprising against the Portuguese colonialists that began in 1817 in the Northeastern Brazilian province of Pernambuco under the slogan of the struggle for an independent republic. The movement for separation from Portugal was subsequently led by local landowners and aristocrats, who succeeded in proclaiming Brazil an empire in 1822.   p. 290

336 Beresford supported the feudal-clerical party of absolutists, headed by Prince Dom Miguel, which crushed the Portuguese bourgeois revolution of 1820-23 and restored absolutism. But Dom Miguel did not succeed in holding power and was forced to emigrate in 1824. In 1828 he seized the Portuguese throne, and this led to the resumption of the civil war, which lasted until 1834 (see Note 157).   p. 290

337 Engels began working on "Cavalry" in January 1858 (see his letter to Marx of January 14). But the need to write articles beginning with B (see notes 293 and 299) constantly compelled him to interrupt this work. From Engels' letters to Marx of March 26 and April 22, we see that he prepared more intensively for the article on "Cavalry" at the end of March. Besides the sources he had used for the "Army" (see Note 109), Engels collected a large amount of new material, in particular from Theodor Mommsen's *Römische Geschichte* (about the actions of Hannibal's cavalry in the second Punic war), from documents and works on military history reflecting the role of cavalry in modern wars (the Seven Years' War, the Peninsular and other Napoleonic wars). Engels mentions some of the sources in the text.

The article was ready by June 22, 1858, when it was sent to New York, as is seen from an entry in Marx's notebook.   p. 291

338 The Carthaginian general Hannibal turned Italy into the main theatre of the second Punic war (218-201 B.C.). In 218 B.C. Hannibal made an expedition with his mercenary army from Spain to Northern Italy, across the Alps. At the *battle of the Ticino* in October 218 B.C. he defeated the advance guard of one of the two Consular armies sent against him, and in December he routed them both on the *Trebia*. Having penetrated into Central Italy, Hannibal completely defeated the Romans at *Cannae* in Apulia in August 216 B.C. (Engels describes these battles in detail later in the text). His successes, however, were brought to naught by Roman victories in Spain and Sicily and a landing of Roman troops in North Africa, which prompted the Carthaginian Senate to recall Hannibal from Italy. In 202 B.C. he was defeated at Zama. The war ended with the conclusion of a peace treaty which imposed harsh terms on Carthage.
                                                                          p. 294

339 The *Punic wars* (264-241, 218-201 and 149-146 B.C.)—wars between Rome and Carthage, the two largest slave-owning states of antiquity, for domination in the Western Mediterranean and the conquest of new territories and slaves. As a result of the first Punic war Carthage was compelled to cede Sicily and the adjoining islands to Rome; in the second it lost its fleet and all its other non-African territories including Spain and the Balearic Islands, and had to pay an enormous indemnity to Rome. Having broken the might of the Carthaginian state, the Romans put an end to it by the third war; the city of Carthage was destroyed.   p. 297

340 A reference to the *battle of the Casilinum* (near the city of Capua, Southwestern Italy) in A.D. 554, in which the Byzantine general Narses defeated the Germanic tribes of the Franks and the Alemanni. Having repulsed the invasion of the Franks and Alemanni and destroyed the remnants of the Italian Kingdom of the Ostrogoths (493-554), whose main forces had already been smashed before in an encounter with the Franks, Narses' army established the rule of the Eastern Roman Empire (Byzantium) for a short time in Italy.
                                                                          p. 297

341 At the *battles of Merseburg* (933) and *Lech* (955) the armies of the German kings Henry I the Fowler and Otto I, his successor, defeated the Hungarians who had invaded Germany.   p. 297

342 See Note 4.
                                                                          p. 297

343 On April 9, 1241, at the *battle of Wahlstatt* near Liegnitz (Legnica) the allied forces of Polish and German feudal lords were defeated by the Mongol invaders (see Note 136).   p. 298

344 At the *battle of Novara* (Northern Italy) on June 6, 1513, Swiss mercenary troops in the service of the Duke of Milan defeated the French army whose main force consisted of mounted knights. This led to the failure of Louis XII's Italian campaign in 1513, one of the numerous invasions of Italy during the Italian wars of 1494-1559 (see Note 26).   p. 299

345 See Note 20.   P. 299

346 See Note 142.   p. 300

347 On the *Civil War in England* see Note 27.
     At the end of the paragraph Engels mentions two major battles of this war—at *Marston Moor* (Yorkshire) on July 2, 1644 and *Naseby* (Northampton-shire) on June 14, 1645—where the parliamentary army defeated the army of Charles I. Cromwell's cavalry, the core of which consisted of detachments recruited from among the yeomen and artisans, played a decisive role in these battles. Their outcome, particularly of the battle of Naseby, decided the final victory of the parliamentary forces.   p. 300

348 On the *battle of Mollwitz* see Note 145.
     Silesian wars—part of the War of the Austrian Succession (see Note 38). The first Silesian war embraced military operations between Prussia and Austria in 1740-42, beginning with the invasion of Silesia by Frederick II and ending with the conclusion of the first separate peace treaty between him and Austrians. The second Silesian war was fought by Prussia against Austria allied with Saxony in 1744-45, from the resumption of the war in August 1744 to the conclusion of a new separate peace treaty by Frederick II.   p. 301

349 See Note 85.   P. 302

350 Engels mentions a number of battles fought during the War of the Austrian Succession (1740-48) and the Seven Years' War (1756-63), in which cavalry played an important role.
     At the *battle of Hohenfriedberg* in Silesia (sometimes called the *battle of Striegau*) on June 4, 1745, the troops of Frederick II of Prussia defeated the allied armies of Austria and Saxony. At *Kesselsdorf* (Saxony) on December 15, 1745 the Prussians defeated the Saxons, which made it possible for Frederick II to sign the peace treaty with Austria and Saxony which put an end to the second Silesian war (see Note 348).
     At the *battle of Rossbach* (Prussia) on November 5, 1757, Frederick II defeated the combined forces of the French and the German states hostile to Prussia.
     On the *battle of Leuthen* (December 5, 1757) see Note 85.
     At *Zorndorf* (Sarbinovo) on August 25, 1758, Frederick II gave battle to the Russian army, as a result of which both sides sustained heavy losses. The battle was not decisive, however, and did not prevent a new Russian offensive the following year.   p. 302

351 At the *battle of Würzburg* (Bavaria) on September 3, 1796, during the war of the French Republic against the first European coalition, Austrian troops under

Archduke Charles defeated the French army of General Jourdan and forced it
to retreat beyond the Rhine.   p. 302

[352] See Note 275.   p. 302

[353] The *Grand Duchy of Warsaw*—a vassal state set up by Napoleon I in 1807 under
the peace treaty of Tilsit (see Note 193) and comprising some of the Polish
lands earlier annexed to Prussia. In 1809, after Austria's defeat, some of the
Polish lands under its rule were also incorporated into the duchy. By decision
of the Congress of Vienna (1814-15) the duchy was divided among Prussia,
Austria and Russia.
    On the *Confederation of the Rhine* see Note 230.   p. 302

[354] At *Dannigkow* (Möckern), in Saxony, on April 5, 1813 the Russo-Prussian
troops under the Russian general Wittgenstein defeated a French army under
the Viceroy of Italy, Prince Eugène Beauharnais. On the participation of the
Prussian general Bülow in this battle see this volume, pp. 402-03.   p. 303

[355] See Note 168.   p. 304

[356] See Note 30.   p. 304

[357] See Note 150.   p. 305

[358] See Note 172.   p. 309

[359] In 451, on the *Catalaunian Plains,* near the site of the chief town of the
Catalauni, now occupied by Châlons-sur-Marne, the army of Huns, conquerors
of Turk descent under Attila (and also men from many tributary tribes), was
defeated by the army of the West Roman general Aetius, consisting of soldiers
of different nationalities: Germans, Romans, Gauls, etc. Dissension among the
victors prevented the utter defeat of the Huns.
    The *Sepoy mutiny*—the Indian national liberation uprising of 1857-59
against British rule. It started in the spring of 1857 among the Sepoy units (see
Note 48) of the Bengal army and spread to vast regions of Northern and
Central India. Peasants and poor artisans from the towns took an active part
in the uprising, but the leaders were, as a rule, local feudal lords. The uprising
was defeated because of India's lack of unity and its religious and caste
differences and the military and technical superiority of the British. p. 311

[360] *Mamelukes*—Turkish, Georgian, Circassian and some other Caucasian slaves
from among whom the ruling dynasty in Egypt began recruiting its guard in
the twelfth century. In 1250 the Mameluke top commanders seized power and
set up their own state supported by a strong army. Early in the sixteenth
century the state was subjugated by the Ottoman Empire and incorporated in
it. But with the decay of the Empire at the end of the seventeenth century, the
Mameluke feudal aristocracy in fact restored its domination in Egypt and was
only under the nominal control of the Turkish Sultan. Irregular horsemen
made up the bulk of the Mameluke army.
    On *Napoleon's expedition to Egypt* see Note 5.   p. 311

[361] See Note 31.   p. 312

[362] See Note 3.   p. 313

[363] See Note 72.   p. 313

364 At the *battle of Waterloo* on June 18, 1815 General d'Erlon's corps was ordered by Napoleon to attack the left wing of Wellington's allied army with his four divisions each formed in column. In the very first attack the corps suffered heavy losses. p. 314

365 At *Garcia Hernandez* on July 23, 1812, during the Peninsular war (1808-14), dragoons of the German legion in Wellington's army attacked the rearguard of the French, retreating after the defeat at Salamanca (see Note 334), and broke and dispersed the infantry square. p. 315

366 On the *battle of Ligny* see Note 234. p. 315

367 After Engels had written his articles beginning with C, his work for *The New American Cyclopaedia* was interrupted. But on March 15, 1859, Charles Dana asked Marx to write articles "Fortification" and "Infantry". They were in fact written by Engels.

On June 10, 1859 Marx acknowledged receipt of Engels' "Fortification", which he described as "splendid". He wrote: "I must say I feel some twinges of conscience about having made such demands on the little spare time you have." Dana acknowledged receipt of the article in a letter to Marx of July 30.

Engels' excerpts from the article "Fortification" in the *Encyclopaedia Britannica* (Vol. IX, Edinburgh, 1855) survive. This was however far from Engels' only source for his article (some of them are mentioned in the text).

"Fortification" was published in 1859 in Vol. VII of the *Cyclopaedia*. The editors added, with an explanatory note, a table of US fortifications. p. 317

368 See Note 20. p. 327

369 During the *War of the Spanish Succession* (1701-14) (see Note 16) the French-held fortress of *Landau* (Palatinate) was recaptured by German imperial troops in 1702. In the following year the French retook it but in 1704 the Germans again laid siege to it and forced its capitulation after three months. In 1713 the French recaptured it. p. 330

370 On the military operations at Danzig in 1807 see Note 93. p. 331

371 The defence of Vienna against the Turkish army that besieged it in July 1683 ended in the rout of the Turks on September 12 by Austro-German-Polish forces. The Poles under John Sobieski, who came to the relief of Vienna, played a decisive role in this rout. p. 332

372 See Note 180. p. 334

373 The *Maximilian towers*—32 towers of special construction by Archduke Maximilian d'Este of Austria, erected around Lintz in 1826-36. They were to serve as independent forts in defensive operations. p. 334

374 The entrenched *camp at Bunzelwitz* (Boleslawice)—a system of field-type fortifications whose construction was begun by order of Frederick II of Prussia in 1760, during the Seven Years' War (1756-63). In 1760-62 his army took up defensive positions several times in this camp against the Austrian and Russian armies.

The *lines at Torres Vedras* (near Lisbon) were built by order of Wellington in 1810 to protect the Anglo-Portuguese army against the French. Consisting of three rows of powerful fortifications, these lines played an important role in the Peninsular war (1808-14). In 1810-11 they helped to halt the offensive of Marshal Masséna's army on Lisbon.

The French *lines of Weissenburg* (Alsace) were fortifications built in 1706, during the War of the Spanish Succession (1701-14), by the army of Marshal Villars as a defensive position against the German imperial forces. Subsequently the lines were improved by Louis de Cormontaigne. A particularly fierce battle for these fortifications developed between the French and the Austrians during the war of the French Republic against the first European coalition (1792-97).

On the *Austrian entrenchments before Verona* and their role in the military operations of the counter-revolutionary Austrian army against Piedmontese troops in 1848, see Engels' work *Po and Rhine* and his article "The Austrian Hold on Italy" (present edition, Vol. 16, pp. 211-55 and 183-89).   p. 339

375 In late 1848 and early 1849, during an Austrian offensive, the entrenched camp and fortress of Komorn (Komárom), Northwestern Hungary, remained in the hands of the Hungarians in the rear of the Austrians. From January to April 1849 the fortress withstood a siege by the Austrians. After the siege was lifted on April 19, as a result of a successful Hungarian offensive and the restoration of the entrenched camp at Komorn, the Hungarians twice resisted superior Austrian forces—on July 2 and 11, 1849. Though in the end the Austrian enemy managed to take only part of the Komorn fieldworks, the general war situation prompted the Hungarian army to retreat from the fortress, whose defence was entrusted to General Klapka's corps. The garrison held out until September 27, 1849.   p. 339

376 Marx received Dana's request for the "Infantry" and "Fortification" articles in the spring of 1859 (see Note 367). Engels undertook to write both. However, he could not begin work on "Infantry" until the end of August, after finishing "Fortification" and writing articles for the London *Das Volk* and the *New-York Daily Tribune,* as well as a review of Marx's book *A Contribution to the Critique of Political Economy* (see present edition, Vol. 16). In his letters to Marx of September 23-27 and of October 3 he informed him of the progress of work on "Infantry". Marx acknowledged receipt of the article on October 10, 1859.

In writing the article Engels made extensive use of W. Rüstow's *Geschichte der Infanterie* (vols. I-II, Gotha, 1857-58) and other sources, including a work by the Prussian Major Trotha on the influence of improved rifles on infantry tactics, etc.   p. 340

377 The *Dorians*—one of the main groups of ancient Greek tribes which moved from the North to the Peloponnese and the southern islands of the Aegean Sea in the twelfth and eleventh centuries B.C. As compared to tribes which settled in Greece earlier (Achaeans, Ionians and Aeolians), the Dorians preserved more of the archaic patriarchal characteristics. But the break-up of the primitive communal system led to the emergence of a hereditary aristocracy among the Dorians too, and to the formation in the eighth-sixth centuries B.C. of slave-owning states, among which Sparta was the most powerful.   p. 340

378 See Note 118.   p. 340

379 See Note 33.   p. 341

380 See Note 119.   p. 341

381 See Note 115.   p. 341

³⁸² See Note 114.   p. 342

³⁸³ *Condottieri*—leaders of mercenary troops in the service of various sovereigns and Popes in Italy in the fourteenth-sixteenth centuries.   p. 342

³⁸⁴ The *Samnite wars* (343-341, c. 327-304 and 298-290 B.C.)—wars between the Romans and the Samnites (a group of Italic tribes in the Central Apennines) during Rome's struggle for domination over Central Italy. The victory over the Samnites was an important stage in uniting the various Italic tribes under Rome.
On the *Punic wars* see Note 339.   p. 345

³⁸⁵ See Note 132.   p. 347

³⁸⁶ At the *battle of Laupen* (near Berne) on June 21, 1339, Swiss infantry defeated an allied army of Austrian, German and Italian feudal lords. This was an important stage in the Swiss cantons' struggle for independence (see Note 137).
                                                                                 p. 350

³⁸⁷ At the *battle of Pavia* on February 24, 1525 (see Note 26) the German Landsknechts in the service of Emperor Charles V and the Spanish infantry successfully fought the French mounted knights and Swiss mercenaries of Francis I of France.   p. 351

³⁸⁸ A reference to the war of 1481-92 waged between the united Kingdom of Castile and Aragon (Spanish monarchy) and the Emirate of Granada, the final stage in the reconquest of the Peninsula from the Moors (see Note 238). The war ended with the Spaniards' capture of Granada.   p. 351

³⁸⁹ See Note 20.   p. 353

³⁹⁰ See Note 142.   p. 354

³⁹¹ See Note 16.   p. 356

³⁹² See Note 246.   p. 357

³⁹³ See Note 166.   p. 359

³⁹⁴ See Note 144.   p. 359

³⁹⁵ See Note 60.   p. 359

³⁹⁶ At *Lexington* and *Concord* (Massachusetts) on April 19, 1775, British regular forces were defeated by American insurgent skirmishers. These battles marked the beginning of the war of the British North-American colonies for independence.   p. 359

³⁹⁷ See Note 275.   p. 361

³⁹⁸ The war of France and the Kingdom of Sardinia (Piedmont) against Austria lasted from April 29 to July 8, 1859. It was unleashed by Napoleon III who, under the pretext of "liberating" Italy, sought to acquire new territories and strengthen his regime at home. The Italian big bourgeoisie and liberal nobility, on the other hand, hoped in the course of the war to unify Italy under the Savoy dynasty ruling in Piedmont. Napoleon III, however, was worried by the scope of the Italian national liberation movement against the Austrian oppressors and, after several victories won by Franco-Piedmontese forces,

concluded a separate peace treaty with Austria in Villafranca on July 11, behind Sardinia's back. France received Savoy and Nice, Lombardy was annexed to Sardinia, and the Venetian Republic remained under Austrian rule.

p. 363

399 During preliminary discussions Marx asked Dana to place the order for the article "Navy" with another author. Nevertheless, in his letter of September 8, 1860 Dana asked Marx to send him the article urgently. Marx passed the letter on to Engels on September 25, requesting him to write the article if at all possible. Engels began working on it early in October, as can be seen from his letter to Marx of October 1. On November 23 Marx acknowledged receipt of the draft copy (see present edition, Vol. 41).

Engels made use of various sources, including Howard Douglas' *Treatise on Naval Gunnery* (4th ed., London, 1855); the article "Navy" in the *Encyclopaedia Britannica* (Vol. XVI, 8th ed.); Prince de Joinville's works on the condition of France's steam fleet (see Note 402); W. James' *The Naval History of Great Britain, from the Declaration of War by France in 1793, to the Accession of George IV* (1st edition, 1822-24), and Zweytinger's *Die Seemacht Englands und Frankreichs militärisch-statistisch* (Leipzig, 1854).

p. 364

400 During the first Punic war, 264-241 B.C. (see Note 339), the Romans, who initially had had no means for fighting the Carthaginian navy, built a comparatively large fleet which inflicted a number of defeats on the Carthaginian navy.

p. 364

401 A reference to Napoleon's *camp at Boulogne* (see Note 275).

p. 368

402 In 1844 Prince de Joinville published an article entitled "Notes sur l'état des forces navales de la France" in the *Revue des deux Mondes*. It came out the same year as a separate pamphlet on the same subject. The article evoked a lively response. It developed the idea that, by improving its steam fleet, France could attain the same naval might as Britain. In 1859 the *Revue* printed Joinville's article "Le marine à vapeur dans les guerres continentales", in which he argued that if France possessed a powerful steam fleet the impregnability of the British Isles in the event of an Anglo-French war would be called in question. Both articles were included in Joinville's book *Etudes sur la marine*, which appeared the same year. It is probable that Engels had this book in mind.

p. 370

403 On the *bombardment of Sveaborg* see Note 178.

p. 371

404 On October 17, 1855, during the Crimean war (1853-56), the small Russian fortress of *Kinburn*, defending the entrance to the Dnieper-Bug estuaries, was bombarded by the Anglo-French fleet. Three French iron-clad floating batteries took part in the bombardment.

p. 371

405 Engels changed this viewpoint when studying the naval battles of the American Civil War (1861-65). In the articles "The American Civil War and Armoured and Ram Vessels" and "Artillery News from America" (see present edition, Vol. 19) he pointed to the use of armoured vessels with turret armament as a most important trend in the future development of navies and naval warfare.

p. 372

406 See Note 35.

p. 374

407 At this point *The New American Cyclopaedia* has a passage, added by the editors, containing information on the history of the US navy and its condition in 1861, when Volume XII of the *Cyclopaedia* was published.   p. 375

408 A whole group of preparatory materials by Marx and Engels for their articles in *The New American Cyclopaedia* survives. These manuscripts are either summaries of or extracts from various sources, or preliminary rough drafts of articles which contain details omitted in the final version. This volume includes a selection of different types of such material showing the various stages in the work of Marx and Engels on their articles. By comparing them with the final text, the reader can obtain an idea of how Marx and Engels used the sources and prepared for writing the articles.   p. 377

409 The summary of John W. Kaye's *History of the War in Afghanistan* (vols. I-II, London, 1851) was made by Engels as a basis for his article "Afghanistan" (see this volume, pp. 40-48 and Note 40). Engels managed to summarise the contents of a two-volume work abounding in quotations from various sources and with the documents appended totalling 1,346 pages. As a rule, he presented a selection of the facts in very concise German, generally following the chronological order of the book. Only on rare occasions did he reproduce passages, phrases or words from Kaye's book in English, French or other languages. (In the present edition the use of the English expressions is mentioned in footnotes while the French and other foreign words are given as in the original.) Since on the whole the text of the original summary is neither a translation into German nor a version of passages from Kaye's book, but is largely an original work, it is given in ordinary and not small type, as is usually the case. Words abridged by Engels are printed in full; explanations by the editors are given in square brackets.   p. 379

410 *Blue Books*—a series of parliamentary and foreign-policy documents. Here the reference is to the *Correspondence Relating to Persia and Afghanistan* (London, 1839), comprising the reports submitted to Parliament on the negotiations between Alexander Burnes, the British representative in Kabul, and the Emir of Afghanistan, Dost Mohammed. As a result of the negotiations the British Government, at Palmerston's insistence, declared war on Afghanistan in 1838. The reports were submitted to Parliament in 1839 but, as subsequently transpired, the most important papers were not produced, which made it possible to claim that Dost Mohammed was the initiator of the Anglo-Afghan conflict. Marx wrote about the falsifications contained in this publication in the *New-York Daily Tribune* (see present edition, Vol. 12, pp. 606-07).   p. 379

411 *Gurkhas*—general name given to a number of peoples in Nepal from whom the British colonial authorities in India recruited soldiers for special regiments in their army.   p. 382

412 The Russian expedition to the Khanate of Khiva in November 1839 was undertaken under V. A. Perovsky, Military Governor of Orenburg. His 5,000-strong detachment, with artillery and a food convoy, proved unprepared for a winter march through the barren steppes and lost half its men through mass disease. Failing to reach Khiva, Perovsky was forced to return to Orenburg.   p. 382

413 These excerpts were made by Marx when working on the article "Blum" for *The New American Cyclopaedia* (see this volume, pp. 80-82 and Note 95). They

are from the article of the same title published in *Meyer's Conversations-Lexicon,* second Supplement Volume, Hildburghausen, 1853, pp. 240-46. As can be seen from Marx's notes he compared the text of this article with that of "Robert Blum" in Fr. Steger's *Ergänzungs-Conversationslexicon,* Vol. 1, Leipzig, 1846, pp. 153-60. In the latter source Blum's biography, up to 1845, is set forth in greater detail, but in the main the texts of the two articles coincide. This gives grounds for assuming either that both articles were written by the same author or that Robert Blum's own autobiographical material was used in both cases. Marx chose *Meyer's Conversations-Lexicon,* where Blum's biography is given up to his death, as the main source for his own article on this revolutionary leader.

Direct quotations and summaries of the text from *Meyer's Conversations-Lexicon* are given in this volume in small type, in the case of direct quotations the text is printed in editorial quotation marks. Marx's own notes are in ordinary type. p. 391

414 These excerpts for the article "Bourrienne" (see this volume, pp. 83-84 and notes 95 and 103) are the result of Marx's primary work on three sources. The bulk of them were made from "Bourrienne" in the *Biographie universelle (Michaud) ancienne et moderne* (Vol. 5, Paris, 1854) and from the article bearing the same title in *The English Cyclopaedia* (Vol. V, Biography, London, 1856). Marx remarked that the two articles closely resembled each other textually. Marx made some additions and notes based on Fr. Chr. Schlosser's *Zur Beurtheilung Napoleon's und seiner neusten Tadler und Lobredner* (Frankfurt am Main, 1835).

Excerpts from the *Biographie universelle* are made mostly in French and those from *The English Cyclopaedia* in English, with German words inserted here and there. Marx's own remarks and the summary of some of Schlosser's propositions are written in German. They are given in ordinary type in this volume. The rest of the text is published in small type and in cases of direct quotations in editorial quotation marks. The use of English quotations and expressions is mentioned in footnotes. p. 394

415 See Note 269. p. 395

416 The *preliminaries of Léoben* (Styria) were signed by Napoleon Bonaparte and Austria's representative in April 1797 following the defeats of the Austrians by the French army of Italy. Their signing preceded the conclusion of the peace treaty of Campo Formio (see Note 187) mentioned later in the text. p. 395

417 See Note 69. p. 395

418 See Note 73. p. 396

419 The *Chambre introuvable*—a nickname given by Louis XVIII to the Chamber of Deputies in 1815-16, the majority of whose members were ultra-royalists. p. 396

420 The rough draft of the article "Brune" is written in English, with some French and German words inserted here and there and a few French quotations at the end. Some aspects of Brune's activity are given in more detail than in the final version. In the manuscript there is hardly any division into paragraphs, and in the present publication this has been done mostly by the editors. p. 397

421 The *10th of August 1792* is the day when the monarchy in France was overthrown as a result of a popular uprising in Paris. p. 397

422 Marx presumably refers to the following excerpt from Fr. Chr. Schlosser's *Zur Beurtheilung Napoleon's und seiner neusten Tadler und Lobredner* (Frankfurt am Main, 1835):

"*Brune*. In the campaign of 1796-97 Napoleon fetters him to himself for political reasons.

"Lavallette says of this: 'Brune was one of the heads of the *Cordeliers*, he was, it was said, the man who had led the popular movement on the Champ de Mars (in 1791 after the flight of the King), which Bailli later dispersed by having martial law proclaimed. He was arrested, thrown into gaol, and the rumour spread that the supporters of the Court had attempted to get rid of him by odious means. At the beginning of the war Brune was employed in fairly insignificant posts, and, either because the Directory feared a man of his immense daring, or because he felt that his courage would be better employed in the army, he received a recommendation for an appointment in Italy. General Bonaparte, who *foresaw* that one day he would have a lot of trouble with the Jacobins, attributed to General Brune a share of the honour for the victory of Rivoli ("*he did honour to General Brune for part of the success of the battle of Rivoli*"), either because he had discovered talents in him, which he moreover displayed on several occasions, or because he wanted to tie to his person the heads of [...] a party to which belonged men of merit who had distinguished themselves by their energy. [...] He made Brune general of a division and a few years [later] [...] commander-in-chief of an army of whose generals he had been one of the least distinguished' (*Lavallette in Schlosser*)". Marx used here passages from *Mémoires et Souvenirs du Comte Lavallette* (Vol. 1, Paris, London, 1831, p. 196) quoted by Schlosser on pp. 58-59 of the first part of his book.

p. 398

423 A reference to the buildings of the Dutch East India Company founded in 1602. The Company had a monopoly of trade with the eastern countries and played an important role in Holland's colonial expansion, particularly in the area of the Indian Ocean. It carried on a bitter competitive struggle against the British East India Company. In 1798 the Dutch East India Company was abolished and the whole of its property went over to the Batavian Republic, which was virtually a French protectorate.

p. 399

424 These excerpts from the article "Bülow" in *Das Grosse Conversations-Lexicon für die gebildeten Stände, herausgegeben von J. Meyer* (Vol. 6, Hildburghausen, 1843, pp. 732-33) served as preparatory material for Marx's short article on Bülow for *The New American Cyclopaedia* (see this volume, p. 288 and Note 329). In the present edition the text quoted or summarised from the *Conversations-Lexicon* is in small type, with direct quotations in editorial quotation marks. Marx's own remarks and generalisations are in ordinary type (in some cases they contain information taken from other sources to supplement the text of the article).

p. 402

425 *La Belle Alliance*—a village in Belgium about two and a half miles south of Waterloo which served as Napoleon's headquarters during the battle of Waterloo on June 18, 1815 (see Note 30). In German literature this battle is sometimes called the battle of Belle Alliance.

On the *battle of Ligny*, which preceded the battle of Waterloo, see Note 234.

p. 403

426 The *Battle of the Nations*—the name given to the battle of Leipzig on October 16-19, 1813 (see Note 31).

p. 403

⁴²⁷ This letter to the editor of the Darmstadt *Allgemeine Militär-Zeitung* obtained for Engels the opportunity to publish his military articles in this weekly.

The editor's reply survives, dated October 11, 1860, making it clear that Engels was allowed to contribute provided he abstained from a political appraisal of military events. It reads as follows:

"Darmstadt, October 11, 1860
"Dear Sir,—Immediately upon our return from a long journey to Berlin, Danzig, etc., we found your kind letter of August 24 of this year, to which we hasten to reply.

"It would be very desirable for us and the *Allgemeine Militär-Zeitung* to receive literary contributions from you from time to time, but we would ask you above all to include in your accounts only facts (not mere political observations, etc.). To this end we beg to suggest that you should send us informal 'Letters from and about Great Britain' (say, one every six weeks) and to deal with one or several definite themes in each. Especially welcome would be accurate accounts of the results of shooting exercises, military establishments (*Woolwich Arsenal*, for example), military schools, etc., similar to those we published about France last year and the year before.

"It would be also desirable for us to know exactly your conditions as regards payments.

"With the highest regard

"Yours faithfully

"The Editorial Board of the *Allgemeine Militär-Zeitung*"

Engels contributed to this weekly from 1860 to 1864, during which time several military items were published, beginning with the one suggested in the above letter. Some of his reports for the *Allgemeine Militär-Zeitung* were not published and have come down to us in manuscript form. This volume contains Engels' articles published in the newspaper in 1860-62. His articles for 1863 and 1864 are included in Volume 19. p. 407

⁴²⁸ The review, in particular, appreciated Engels' view on the unsoundness of the theory according to which Germany should be master of Northern Italy in order to protect its own security. p. 407

⁴²⁹ Engels did not carry out this intention. He had described the Whitworth gun shortly before in a series of articles, "On Rifled Cannon", published in April and May 1860 in the *New-York Daily Tribune* (see present edition, Vol. 17).
p. 407

⁴³⁰ On Engels' participation in the campaign of the revolutionary Baden-Palatinate army in the summer of 1849 see his work *The Campaign for the German Imperial Constitution* (present edition, Vol. 10, pp. 147-239) and his letter to Jenny Marx of July 25, 1849 (Vol. 38, pp. 202-04). p. 407

⁴³¹ This article was written for the *Allgemeine Militär-Zeitung* and was first published there under the heading "Eine Musterung englischer freiwilliger Jäger (Correspondenz aus Manchester)". Engels translated it into English and it was published with some changes in *The Volunteer Journal, for Lancashire and Cheshire* as "A German Account of the Newton Review" and with an introductory note by the author himself. In the spring of 1861 it was included in the collection of Engels' articles *Essays Addressed to Volunteers* under the title given in this volume. An editorial note to it said: "Translated for *The Volunteer*

Journal by the author of the original article, which appeared in the *Allgemeine Militär-Zeitung,* September, 8th, 1860."

Besides *The Volunteer Journal* Engels sent the translated article, with the introductory note, to other periodicals, many of which published it in abridged versions. On September 21, 1860 it appeared in *The Morning Herald, The Standard, The Sun* and *The Manchester Guardian,* and the next day in *The Morning Advertiser.* Extracts from the article were published in *The Times,* which described it as of "very high standing" and "very accurate" (September 24, 1860). Other newspapers also printed excerpts from it. In his letter to Ferdinand Lassalle of October 2, 1860 Marx wrote that the "entire London press" had reprinted and discussed the article (see present edition, Vol. 41). Its popularity made a strong impression on Marx's and Engels' friends and acquaintances. Sigismund Borkheim wrote to Marx on September 27, 1860: "Let's promote Engels to 'General'! Moreover, no longer ago than last week I read a lengthy note about this, either in the *Observer* or the *London Review,* not knowing, of course, that Engels was the author of the article in the *Militär-Zeitung.*"

With the printing of the article in *The Volunteer Journal* (No. 2, September 14, 1860) Engels became a constant contributor to this progressive Manchester periodical. He had been invited to write for the journal already in August 1860, when it was being prepared for publication.

On August 11, 1860, Nodal, one of the editors, addressed the following request to Engels: "My dear Sir. If you see the volunteer parade today, I should be glad of a *few words* from your pen on their military appearance, possible efficiency, etc." A few days later Engels received a letter from another editor, Isaac Hall: "Dear Engels, Sam Moore tells me that you don't intend to write in the review because if you do you will have to *pitch into them.*—Never mind that—all the better—it will do us all good to be severely criticized. Yours truly *Isaac Hall.*"

Engels regularly published in it articles and essays on various military subjects. He also revised for it some articles written for the *New-York Daily Tribune.* In all, 18 works by Engels, including several series of articles, were printed in the journal during the time of its existence (August 1860-March 1862).

Engels' first article published in *The Volunteer Journal* was unsigned, but beginning with the second article ("The French Light Infantry") his articles were usually preceded by the editorial remarks: "By the Author of 'A German Account of the Newton Review'", and later: "By the Author of 'The History of the Rifle'" or "By the Author of 'Essays Addressed to Volunteers'." Some of the articles were published anonymously. From the beginning of April 1862 ("Brighton and Wimbledon") they were signed "F.E.", except for the article "The War in America", which was again preceded by the editorial: "By the Author of 'Essays Addressed to Volunteers'."   p. 409

432 In *The Volunteer Journal* this article, with the introductory note, was published under the general title "A German Account of the Newton Review".

p. 409

433 The *adjutant* in a volunteer unit was a military instructor; he was a regular officer and was appointed by the General Staff on the recommendation of the district command.   p. 410

434 The *civic guard* or *civic militia,* formed in Prussia after the March 1848 revolution, consisted of members of the bourgeoisie. Its main function was to

preserve order, and it was poorly organised and trained. It was disbanded during the offensive of the counter-revolutionary forces in November 1848.

p. 410

435 In *The Volunteer Journal* the words "By the Author of 'A German Account of the Newton Review'" were added to the headings of sections II and III published in Nos. 5 and 7 for 1860. In 1861 the article was included with some changes in the collection of Engels' works *Essays Addressed to Volunteers*. In this volume the changes are mentioned in footnotes. The sections, merely numbered in Roman figures in *The Volunteer Journal*, were called chapters in the *Essays*.

The editors and many readers of the journal valued the essay highly. In September 1860, after the publication of the first section, Isaac Hall wrote to Engels: "My dear Engels, I have never had an opportunity of thanking you for your very good and very instructive article on French Light Infantry. It is highly appreciated by the proprietors and has been most favourably spoken of by many people. As we are all here this week will you kindly send the next contribution to Mr. Nodal at Jackson 62 Corporation Street. Won't you come and have a look at us. Yours faithfully (in haste). *Isaac Hall*."

p. 417

436 *Brown Bess*—the flintlock, smooth-bore musket used in the British army in the eighteenth and early nineteenth centuries. The name derived from the brown walnut stock.

p. 418

437 On the Algerian war of liberation under Abd-el-Kader see Note 80.

p. 419

438 The substitution system was for a long time practised in the French army. It was a privilege of the propertied classes allowing their members to buy themselves free from military service by hiring substitutes. During the French Revolution this practice was banned but Napoleon I legalised it again. Under the 1853 law, substitutes were selected in the main by government bodies and the payment for them contributed to a special "army donation" fund. The substitution system was abolished in 1872.

p. 419

439 The Crimean war of 1853-56, a war between Russia and a coalition of Britain, France, Turkey and the Kingdom of Sardinia (Piedmont), is dealt with in this volume in the articles "Bosquet" by Marx and Engels, "Brown" by Marx and "Bomarsund" by Engels. Some episodes are also mentioned in other articles written for *The New American Cyclopaedia*.

On the *Italian war of 1859* between France and the Kingdom of Sardinia (Piedmont) on the one hand and Austria on the other see Note 398.

p. 420

440 On the *siege of Sevastopol* see Note 180.

p. 423

441 At the *battle of Palestro* (May 20-31, 1859), *Magenta* (June 4) and *Solferino* (June 24), between the Franco-Sardinian and the Austrian troops during the Italian war of 1859 (see Note 398), the Austrian army was defeated. Engels made a thorough analysis of the course of these battles in his military essays "Strategy of the War", "A Chapter of History", "The Battle at Solferino", and others (see present edition, Vol. 16, pp. 349-53, 372-79, 392-95).

p. 423

442 Engels wrote this article at the request of Alfred Walmsley, one of the editors of *The Volunteer Journal*. His letter to Engels survives, as follows: "My dear Engels,—I enclose you a few remarks, I think from the *Times*, in reference to

Volunteer Artillery.—We very much desire a few lines on the subject, and as I find the Volunteer Artillery officers in Manchester have no very great literary abilities, I shall have to venture to ask you to give us a paragraph on the subject. As you are aware the Artillery in Manchester is progressing but slowly. And an article on the subject may do great good; though my opinion is that inland artillery corps are not so very much required. I am, dear Sir, Yours truly, Alfred Walmsley."

Engels included the article in the collection *Essays Addressed to Volunteers,* abridging and changing the first paragraph.   p. 429

443 Engels conceived the idea of a work on the history of the rifle in the summer of 1860. Originally, he intended to publish it in the *New-York Daily Tribune* (see his letter to Marx of August 1, 1860, present edition, Vol. 41). When he began contributing to *The Volunteer Journal* he carried out his intention by printing his "History of the Rifle" in a series of eight articles. Each article was marked: "By the Author of 'A German Account of the Newton Review'." In the spring of 1861 the series was reproduced in the collection *Essays Addressed to Volunteers.* Engels made slight changes in the text.

On December 20, 1860 Nodal, one of the editors of *The Volunteer Journal,* wrote to Engels telling him of the impression his articles had produced on Major Preston, a large manufacturer of rifles. Nodal wrote: "I have seen Major Preston today. He is an immense admirer of your 'History of the Rifle'".

Part of the seventh article was published in *The Army and Navy Gazette,* No. LVI, January 26, 1861, under the title "The Whitworth Rifle, from the *Volunteer Journal*". (Nodal sent this issue to Engels together with his letter of January 28, 1861.)   p. 433

444 A reference to the American War of Independence, 1775-83 (see Note 60), and the war of the French Republic against the counter-revolutionary European coalition begun in 1792 (see Note 146).   p. 434

445 See Note 436.   p. 434

446 See Note 439.   p. 441

447 See Note 398.   p. 446

448 See Note 150.   p. 450

449 This article was written at the request of Nodal who wrote to Engels on November 19, 1860: "I should feel much obliged, at some future time, if you could let us have a paper on *Volunteer Engineers,* a subject which is just now attracting much attention. Yours very faithfully. J. H. Nodal."

The article was published in *The Volunteer Journal* under the title "Volunteer Engineers", with no indication of Engels' authorship. In the *Essays Addressed to Volunteers* the words: "Their Value and Sphere of Action" were added to the title. The title in this volume is the same as in the *Essays.*
                                                                                p. 460

450 The *Horse Guards*—the headquarters of the Royal Horse Guards, thus called ever since it began to be used to accommodate commanders of a number of cavalry regiments of the Guards.   p. 463

451 This article was first intended for the *New-York Daily Tribune,* but when Nodal asked Engels to write an article for *The Volunteer Journal* Engels revised it for

that periodical. It was preceded by the editorial remark: "By the Author of 'The History of the Rifle'."
p. 465

452 See Note 398.
p. 466

453 Besides the substitution system (see Note 438), it was a practice in the French army at regular call-ups to transfer some of the conscripts to the reserve by drawing lots. When the number of conscripts reached the necessary figure, transfer to the reserve by lots was virtually equal to being freed from military service.
p. 467

454 Engels selected passages from Marshal Bugeaud's book *Aperçus sur quelques détails de la guerre* (Paris, 1832), translated them into English, and supplied them with a short introduction. The work was published in *The Volunteer Journal* without any indication of the compiler or author of the introduction. Engels' authorship is clear from his reference to this publication in the article "Waldersee on the French Army" published later (see this volume, pp. 508-17).

On Marshal Bugeaud as a military leader and politician see Marx's article "Bugeaud" (this volume, pp. 211-14).
p. 469

455 See Note 166.
p. 474

456 The initiative of publishing Engels' articles from *The Volunteer Journal* as a separate book belongs to the editors of that periodical. On December 20, 1860 Nodal wrote to Engels: "Has Mr. Hall informed you of our intention of republishing 4 of your essays, contributed to *V. Journal*? I send you the proofs of all but the German Zeitung article, which I will forward hereafter. If there is any alteration you would wish making, please mark, and return proofs at convenience. I propose altering the title page to Essays Addressed to Volunteers, etc. Would you like your name attached or any *nom de plume*, or will you give the credit entirely to the Journal, and publish anonymously? The Essays will be sold throughout England. Of course we will append an advertisement of the *V. Journal*, so as to make our little paper more widely known."

Engels accepted the proposal and included five of his articles in the *Essays Addressed to Volunteers*. But he did not arrange them in chronological order. The collection contained "The History of the Rifle", "The French Light Infantry", "Volunteer Artillery", "Volunteer Engineers: Their Value and Sphere of Action" and "A Review of English Volunteer Riflemen". Some editorial alterations were made in the text. The short preface was signed "F: E." The collection was published in March 1861.

On March 23, 1861, the London *United Service Gazette* carried a review of the *Essays*. Having examined the contents of some of the articles and emphasised in particular the merits of such works as "The History of the Rifle" and "Volunteer Artillery", the reviewer concluded: "We may say of the whole brochure that it is modestly and carefully written, with evident zeal and interest in the subject matter, and will be a most acceptable offering to every intelligent and thinking Volunteer."
p. 476

457 In *The Volunteer Journal* this article was marked: "By the Author of 'Essays Addressed to Volunteers'."
p. 479

458 See Note 433. p. 482

459 *The Volunteer Journal* gives the following editorial footnote to the heading: "By the Author of 'Essays Addressed to Volunteers', whose contributions to the *Journal* in future will be distinguished by the initials placed at the end of the present article." p. 484

460 See Note 450. p. 485

461 A reference to the Indian national liberation uprising of 1857-59 (the Sepoy mutiny) brutally suppressed by British troops (see Note 359). p. 496

462 *Aldershot*—a town some 40 miles southwest of London; site of a large military training camp established in 1855, during the Crimean war. p. 500

463 See Note 450. p. 504

464 This work was published in instalments in four issues of *The Volunteer Journal* for 1861 (Nos. 42, 44, 46 and 62). The final instalment appeared with the following editorial footnote: "The conclusion of this paper has been unavoidably delayed." The delays in publication were presumably due to Engels' delay in supplying the translations of passages from Waldersee's book, and his comments on them, and because he was busy writing another article for *The Volunteer Journal*, "A Military Criticism of the Newton Review". p. 508

465 See Note 398. p. 508

466 On the *battles of Magenta* and *Solferino* see Note 441. p. 514

467 The Newton review described by Engels took place on August 3, 1861.
    Though the article was signed "F. E.", the editors of *The Volunteer Journal* inserted "By the Author of 'A German Account of the Newton Review', 1860" after the heading. p. 518

468 Engels refers to the military operations between the armies of the Union (the North) and the Confederacy (the South) during the first eight months of the American Civil War, started in April 1861 by the open revolt of the slave-owning South against the American Union. The main cause of the war was the struggle between two social systems—the capitalist system of wage labour in the North and the slave system in the South. The war, which had the character of a bourgeois-democratic revolution, passed through two stages: constitutional war for the preservation of the Union and revolutionary war for the abolition of slavery. The emancipation of Negro slaves proclaimed by the Lincoln Administration in September 1862 was a turning point in the war. Workers, farmers and the Negro population played a decisive role in the defeat of the slave-owners of the South and the termination of the war in April 1865 in favour of the North. The causes and nature of the events in America are analysed in articles published in the Vienna newspaper *Die Presse* (see present edition, Vol. 19). p. 521

[469] See previous note.   p. 525

[470] At the beginning of the Civil War, Kentucky—one of the frontier states (those adjoining the 38th parallel separating the slave-owning South from the North)—declared its neutrality. The state itself was the scene of a bitter struggle between the supporters of the Union and of the Confederacy, whose troops invaded Kentucky in violation of its "neutrality". In September 1861 the state's legislative assembly declared its adhesion to the Union despite the Governor's resistance.   p. 525

[471] The *Federals* or *Unionists* in the American Civil War were supporters of the North, opposed to the Secessionists or Confederates, supporters of the Confederacy of the Southern States.   p. 527

[472] A reference to the wars between Britain and the USA in 1812-14 and between the USA and Mexico in 1846-48 (see notes 35 and 210).   p. 527

[473] See Note 433.   p. 528

[474] This is an abridged version of the series of articles about the American Civil War (see Note 468) which Engels wrote in the first half of March 1862 for the *New-York Daily Tribune.* For an idea of Engels' work on the series, see his letter to Marx of March 8, 1862 and Marx's reply of March 15 (present edition, Vol. 41). Engels, however, did not manage to publish the articles in the *Tribune* (by that time a break had occurred between Marx and its editors, among whom supporters of a compromise with the Southern plantation owners increased influence). Marx translated Engels' work into German, supplemented it with his own text, and sent it to the Vienna newspaper *Die Presse* where it was printed on March 26 and 27, 1862 under the heading "The Civil War in America" (see present edition, Vol. 19). The text of *The Volunteer Journal* version in this volume and that of *Die Presse* therefore largely coincide, though the latter is naturally more complete and informative, in particular as regards details of the capture of Nashville by the Northerners, news of which was received after the article for *The Volunteer Journal* had been written.

In *The Volunteer Journal* the article was published unsigned, but with the editorial remark: "By the Author of 'Essays Addressed to Volunteers'."
                                                                            p. 530

[475] On the *Secessionists* and *Federals* (the latter term is used later in the text) see Note 471.   p. 530

[476] The *Bull Run,* a river near Manassas (southwest of Washington), was the scene of the first major battle in the Civil War. At this battle, on July 21, 1861, the Southerners defeated the Northerners, who were numerically superior but badly trained. However, the Southerners did not pursue the defeated enemy and thus failed to consolidate their victory.   p. 531

[477] At the *battle of Balls Bluff* (northwest of Washington) on October 21, 1861, the Southerners routed several regiments of General Stone's army which had crossed to the right bank of the Potomac and were left without reinforcements.
                                                                            p. 531

478 This article was most probably written by Engels immediately after the military review of Lancashire volunteers at Heaton Park on August 2, 1862. Judging by the text, Engels must have been present. It was presumably in this content that he informed Marx on August 8 of his resumed contact with the *Allgemeine Militär-Zeitung* editorial board after a two-year interval (see present edition, Vol. 41). The article was printed in two issues, with the comment "Correspondenz aus Manchester". Engels' initials were placed at the beginning of the text in square brackets, as was the practice of the newspaper.

A letter survives dated November 14, 1862, from the editorial board of the *Allgemeine Militär-Zeitung* to Engels, informing him of the dispatch of the issues containing his article and requesting him to send more contributions.

p. 535

479 See Note 47.   p. 536

NAME INDEX

A

sion in the Crimea in 1854, nicknamed Plon-Plon and the Red
Prince.— 17

Borosdin, Nikolai Mikhailovich (1777-
1830)—Russian general, fought
against Napoleon.— 253

*Bosquet, Pierre Jean François Marie
Joseph* (1810-1861)—Marshal of
France; took part in the conquest of
Algeria in the 1830s-1850s, com-
manded a division and then a corps
in the Crimea (1854-55).— 17, 139-40

Bourbons—royal dynasty in France
(1589-1792, 1814-15 and 1815-30).—
157, 211

Bourmont, Louis Auguste Victor de
(1773-1846)—French general, Marshal of France from 1830, commanded
the French expeditionary corps in
Algeria in 1830.— 64, 67

Bourrienne—wife of Louis Antoine
Fauvelet de Bourrienne.— 395

Bourrienne, Louis Antoine Fauvelet de
(1769-1834)—French diplomat and
politician, personal secretary of
Napoleon Bonaparte (1797-1802),
chargé d'affaires in Hamburg (1804-
13), went over to the side of the
Bourbons.— 83, 84, 157, 217, 394-96,
400

Bousmard, Henri Jean Baptiste de (1749-
1807)—French military engineer;
emigrated in 1792, served in the
Prussian army, in charge of the
defence of Danzig against Napoleonic
troops (1807).— 331

Boves, José Tomas (c. 1770-1814)—
Spanish army officer; leader of llanero detachments which fought
against the Creole landowners and
were used (up to 1814) by Spain to
suppress the national liberation movement in South America.— 222

Brancas, Countess—Belgian aristocrat.—
84, 396

Brion, Louis (1782-1821)—participant
in the war of independence of the
Spanish colonies in South America,

supporter of Bolivar, admiral of the
Colombian navy; Dutch by birth.—
224-26

Broussier, Jean Baptiste, comte (1766-
1814)—French general, fought in
Napoleonic wars.— 253

Brown, Sir George (1790-1865)—British
lieutenant-general, commanded a division on the Danube and in the
Crimea (1854-55).— 17, 164-65

Brune, Étienne—French lawyer, father
of Marshal Brune.— 397

Brune, Guillaume Marie Anne (1763-
1815)—Marshal of France, fought
in wars of the French Republic
and Napoleonic France.— 215-18,
397-401

Brydon, William (1811-1873)—English
army doctor, took part in the Afghan
campaign of 1838-42.— 47

Bubna Littić, Ferdinand, Count of (1768-
1825)—Austrian general and later
field marshal, Czech by birth; fought
against Napoleon.— 183

Buell, Don Carlos (1818-1898)—
American general, fought in the Civil
War on the side of the Union.— 533

Bugeaud, Jean Ambroise—father of
Marshal Bugeaud.— 211

*Bugeaud de la Piconnerie, Thomas Robert,
duc d'Isly* (1784-1849)—Marshal of
France, Orleanist; an organiser of the
wars of conquest in Algeria and
Morocco; Governor-General of
Algeria in 1841-47.— 211-14, 469,
470, 472, 514

Buggenhagen (18th cent.)—German
military engineer, colonel in Mecklenburg.— 333

*Bülow, Friedrich Wilhelm, Baron von,
Count of Dennewitz* (1755-1816)—
Prussian general, fought against
Napoleon.— 156, 176, 179, 183, 184,
288, 402-03

Bureau, Gaspard (d. 1469)—French
military engineer.— 191

land, Scotland and Ireland (1660-85).—268

Charles V (1500-1558)—Holy Roman Emperor (1519-56) and King of Spain under the name of Charles I (1516-56).—62, 192, 325

Charles V, Duke of Lorraine (1643-1690)—Austrian field marshal, in 1683-88 fought in the Austro-Turkish war of 1683-99.—259

Charles VII (1403-1461)—King of France (1422-61).—106, 191

Charles VIII (1470-1498)—King of France (1483-98).—107, 191

Charles X (*Gustavus*) (1622-1660)—King of Sweden (1654-60).—50

Charles X (1757-1836)—King of France (1824-30).—64

Charles XII (1682-1718)—King of Sweden (1697-1718).—111, 301

Charles XIII (1748-1818)—King of Sweden (from 1809) and of Sweden and Norway (1814-18).—153, 154, 157

Charles XIV—see *Bernadotte, Jean Baptiste Jules*

Charles Emmanuel II (1751-1819)—King of Sardinia (1796-1802).—216, 398

Charles Louis (*Karl Ludwig*) (1771-1847)—Archduke of Austria, field marshal, fought in wars against the French Republic and Napoleonic France, War Minister (1805-09).—27, 28, 32, 58, 149

Charles Martel (c. 688-741)—Frankish mayor of the palace, in 715 became the virtual ruler of the Frankish state.—297

Charlotte, princesse (1796-1865)—daughter of Lucien Bonaparte.—153

Chased—Indian poet of the early 13th cent.—189

Christian Frederick (1786-1848)—Danish prince, Viceroy (1813-14) and King of Norway (1814), King of Denmark under the name of Christian VIII (1839-48).—157

Clary, Eugenie Bernardine Désirée (1777-1860)—wife of Jean Baptiste Jules Bernadotte.—150

Clausel, Bertrand, comte (1772-1842)—French general, Marshal of France from 1831, fought in the Peninsular war (1809-14), Governor of Algeria (1830-31 and 1835-37).—67, 68, 269, 270, 273

Clausewitz, Karl von (1780-1831)—Prussian general and military theorist.—234

Cleombrotus I—King of Sparta (380-371 B.C.).—93

Cleomenes III (255-219 B.C.)—King of Sparta (235-221 B.C.).—92

Cleopatra VII (69-30 B.C.)—last Queen of Egypt of the Ptolemy dynasty.—5

Clerfayt, Karl, Count (1733-1798)—Austrian field marshal, fought in the Austro-Turkish war (1788-89) and the war against the French Republic (1792-97).—36, 149

Coburg-Saalfeld, Friedrich Josias, Prince (1737-1815)—Austrian field marshal, fought in the Seven Years' War (1756-63) and in the war against the French Republic (1792-97).—12

Coehorn (*Cohorn* or *Coehoorn*), *Magdalena van Scheltinga*—wife of Menno Coehorn.—267

Coehorn (*Cohorn* or *Coehoorn*), *Menno van, Baron* (1641-1704)—Dutch general and military engineer.—54, 267-68, 332

Collado, Luis (16th cent.)—Spanish military engineer.—192

Colt, Samuel (1814-1862)—American manufacturer and military inventor.—449

Columbus, Christopher (1451-1506)—Genoese-born navigator, discoverer of America.—365

(1867-68), President of the United States (1869-77).— 532, 533

Grey and Ripon, George Frederick Samuel Robinson, Count of (1827-1909)— British liberal statesman, Under-Secretary for War (1859-January 1861 and July 1861-63), Secretary for War (1863-66).— 505

Grey de Wilton, Charles William, Earl (1804-1870)— British general, participant in the Volunteer movement.— 536

Gribeauval, Jean Baptiste Vaquette de (1715-1789)— French general, inspector of the French artillery from 1764 to 1789 (with an interval).— 116, 194, 198-99, 200

Griffiths, Frederick Augustus (d. 1869)— British army officer and military writer.— 432

Gritti, Andrea (c. 1455-1538)— Venetian military leader and statesman, Doge of Venice (1523-38).— 278

Grosvenor, Hugh Lupus, Count (1825-1899)— British liberal politician, took part in the Volunteer movement.— 488

Grouchy, Emmanuel, marquis de (1766-1847)— French general, Marshal of France from 1815, fought in Napoleonic wars.— 253

Guizot, François Pierre Guillaume (1787-1874)— French historian and statesman; virtually directed France's home and foreign policy from 1840 to the February 1848 revolution.— 213

Gustavus II Adolphus (1594-1632)— King of Sweden (1611-32), general and military reformer.— 109-11, 194, 195, 300, 354, 355, 358, 400

Gustavus IV Adolphus (1778-1837)— King of Sweden (1792-1809), deposed in 1809 by a military coup.— 50, 152, 155, 217

Gyulay, Ferenc, Count (1798-1868)— Austrian general, War Minister (1849-50), commander-in-chief of the Austrian army in the war against France and Piedmont (1859).— 180

Gyulay, Ignatius, Count (1763-1831)— Austrian general, fought against Napoleon.— 514

H

Hall, or Halle, Edward (c. 1498-1547)— English chronicler and lawyer.— 24

Halleck, Henry Wager (1815-1872)— American general, fought in the Civil War on the side of the Union, commander-in-chief (July 1862-March 1864).— 532, 533

Hamilcar Barca (Barcas) (c. 270-c. 228 B.C.)— Carthaginian general and statesman, father of Hannibal.— 294

Hamilton, James (d. 1580)— Scottish nobleman, supporter of Mary Stuart.— 25

Hannibal (c. 247-183 B.C.)— Carthaginian general.— 35, 96, 294-96

Hardinge, Sir Henry, Viscount (1785-1856)— British general, field marshal from 1855; fought in the Peninsular war (1808-14), Secretary at War (1828-30 and 1841-44), commander-in-chief of the British army (1852-56).— 10, 290

Hartmann, Georg (1489-1564)— German physicist and expert in mechanics.— 192

Hartmann, Moritz (1821-1872)— Austrian writer; deputy to the Frankfurt National Assembly (Left wing) in 1848-49.— 393

Hasdrubal (Asdrubal)—Carthaginian general, fought in the second Punic war (218-201 B.C.).— 296

Haynau, Julius Jakob, Baron von (1786-1853)— Austrian field marshal, brutally suppressed the 1848-49 revolutionary movement in Italy and Hungary.— 279, 304

Marggraff, Hermann (1809-1864)—
German author and journalist.—392

Mariño, Santiago (1788-1854)—
Venezuelan general, a leader in the
war of independence of the Spanish
colonies in South America.—221-22,
224, 226, 227

Marius (*Gaius Marius*) (c. 156-86
B.C.)—Roman general and statesman.—98, 344, 346, 347

Marlborough, John Churchill, Duke of
(1650-1722)—British general, in
1702-11 commander-in-chief of the
British forces in the War of the
Spanish Succession.—249, 250, 268

*Marmont, Auguste Fréderic Louis Viesse,
duc de* (1774-1852)—Marshal of
France, fought in Napoleonic wars.—
178, 179, 181-85

Marolois, Samuel—French mathematician in the Netherlands in the first
half of the 17th cent.—328

Marsin (*Marchin*), *Ferdinand, comte de*
(1656-1706)—Marshal of France and
diplomat, fought in the War of the
Spanish Succession.—249

Martens, Georg Friedrich (1756-1821)—
German lawyer and diplomat; from
1776 published collections of international treaties.—217, 400

Martinez de Ricalde, Juan (d. 1588)—
Spanish admiral, second in command
of the Spanish Armada in 1588.—
167, 168

*Masséna, André, duc de Rivoli, prince de
Essling* (1756-1817)—Marshal of
France, fought in wars of the French
Republic and Napoleonic France.—
19, 28, 57, 58, 153, 216, 217, 398,
399, 401, 473

Matthias Corvinus (*Matthias I*) (1443-
1490)—King of Hungary (1458-
90).—259

Maudin (17th cent.)—French military
engineer.—323

Maurice (*Moritz*) *of Nassau, Prince of
Orange and Count of Nassau* (1567-
1625)—Stadtholder of the Netherlands (1585-1625); military leader in
the war of independence.—108, 195,
299

Maximilian, Josef von Österreich-Este
(1782-1863)—Archduke of Austria,
general, invented a special type of
fortification.—334

Maximilian I Joseph (1756-1825)—
Elector (from 1799) and King of
Bavaria (1806-25); fought in
Napoleonic wars, joined the
anti-French coalition in 1813.—58

Maximilian II (*Maximilian II Maria
Emanuel*) (1662-1726)—Elector of
Bavaria (1679-1726), fought in the
War of the Spanish Succession.—249

Mayne, Sir Richard (1796-1868)—Chief
Police Commissioner in London
(from 1850).—505

Mecklenburg, Friedrich Ludwig, Duke of
(1778-1819)—German prince, married to the sister of Alexander I of
Russia.—83, 396

*Medina Sidonia, Alonso Pérez de Guzmán,
Duke of* (1550-1615)—Spanish aristocrat, commanded the Spanish Armada in 1588.—167

Meer Musjedee—chief of an Afghan
tribe.—389

Mehemet Ali (or *Mohammed Ali*) (1769-
1849)—Egyptian ruler (1805-49),
waged wars against the Sultan of
Turkey (1831-33 and 1839-40).—4,
64

Mehrab Khan—chief of a tribe in South
Afghanistan (Baluchistan).—381, 382

Melas, Michael, Baron von (1729-
1806)—Austrian general, fought in
wars against the French Republic,
commander-in-chief of the Austrian
troops in Italy.—57

Melder, Gerard (b. 1693)—Dutch military engineer.—328

Melville, Robert (1723-1809)—British
general and military inventor.—367

1801), an organiser of the plot against Emperor Paul I.—77

Paixhans, Henri Joseph (1783-1854)— French general, military engineer and inventor.—205, 368

Palmerston, Henry John Temple, 3rd Viscount (1784-1865)—British statesman; at first Tory and from 1830 Whig; Foreign Secretary (1830-34, 1835-41 and 1846-51), Home Secretary (1852-55), and Prime Minister (1855-58 and 1859-65).—158

Papacino d'Antoni, Alessandro Vittorio (1714-1786)—Sardinian military engineer.—196

Paravey, Charles Hippolyte de (1787-1871)—French engineer and orientalist.—188

Parma, Prince of—see *Farnese, Alexander*

Parseval-Deschênes, Alexandre Ferdinand (1790-1860)—French admiral, a squadron commander in the Baltic in 1854.—287

Partouneau—French general, fought in the war waged by France and Piedmont against Austria.—512

Paskiewitch (*Paskevich*), *Ivan Fyodorovich, Prince* (1782-1856)—Russian general, later field marshal-general; fought against Napoleon; took part in suppressing the Polish insurrection of 1830-31 and the Hungarian revolution (1849).—253

Paul I (1754-1801)—Emperor of Russia (1796-1801).—77

Pax (*Paz*) *Salas, Pedro de* (16th cent.)— author of a report on the Spanish Armada.—166

Pedro I (1798-1834)—Emperor of Brazil (1822-31), King of Portugal under the name of Pedro IV (1826); abdicated in favour of his daughter, Maria II da Gloria.—131

Pélissier, Aimable Jean Jacques, duc de Malakoff (1794-1864)—French general, Marshal of France from 1855; took part in the conquest of Algeria

in the 1830s-1850s; commander-in-chief in the Crimea (May 1855-July 1856).—69

Pelletier, Jean Baptiste (1777-1862)— French general, head of a number of artillery schools in France.—130

Peña, Miguel (1781-1833)—Venezuelan lawyer, fought in the war of independence of the Spanish colonies in South America.—220

Pericles (c. 490-429 B.C.)—Athenian statesman and military leader.—90, 93

Pétion, Alexandre Sabès (1770-1818)— West-Indian politician and general; President of the Republic of Haiti (1807-18).—224, 225

Philip II (1527-1598)—King of Spain (1556-98).—166

Philip II of Macedon (c. 382-336 B.C.)— King of Macedon (359-336 B. C.); father of Alexander the Great.—94, 95, 292

Philip V (c. 237-179 B.C.)—King of Macedon (221-179 B.C.).—100

Philostratus (c. 170-245)—Greek rhetorician, sophist philosopher and writer.—189

Phull, Karl Ludwig August, Baron (1757-1826)—Prussian general, chief of the general staff of the Prussian army in 1806; served in the Russian army in 1806-12.—51

Piar, Manuel Carlos (1782-1817)— Venezuelan and Colombian general, fought in the war of independence of the Spanish colonies in South America.—225-26

Piccinino, Niccolo (1386-1444)—Italian condottiere, commanded the Milan forces in wars between Italian city-states in 1426-43.—278

Pichon, Louis André, baron (1771-1850)—French politician, civilian commissary in Algiers in the early 1830s.—68

Pius VI (Giovanni Angelo Braschi)
(1717-1799)—Pope (1775-99).—57

Plönnies, Wilhelm von (1828-1871)—
Hessian army officer and military
inventor.—443

Podewils, Philipp, Baron (1809-1885)—
Bavarian army officer and military
inventor.—443

Pollock, Sir George (1786-1872)—British
general, subsequently field marshal,
fought in the Afghan campaign of
1838-42.—47, 48

Polybius (c. 201-c. 120 B.C.)—Greek
historian.—345

*Poncharra, Charles Louis César du Port,
marquis de* (1787-1860)—French
army officer and military inventor.—
362, 419

Poniatowski, Joseph Anthony, Prince
(1763-1813)—Polish politician and
general, fought in Napoleonic wars
in 1809-13.—252

Poniatowski, Stanislaus Augustus II
(1732-1798)—King of Poland under
the name of Stanislaus II Augustus
(1764-95).—83, 394

Potemkin, Grigory Alexandrovich, Prince
(1739-1791)—Russian statesman,
field marshal-general, commander-in-
chief in the Russo-Turkish war of
1787-91.—76

Pottinger, Eldred—British army officer,
fought in the Afghan campaign of
1838-42.—388, 390

Prélat, Joseph (b. 1819)—Swiss gun-
smith, modernised the Minié rifle in
1854.—441

Príncipe y Vidaud, Miguel Agustín
(1811-1866)—Spanish liberal writer
and historian.—171

Psammetichus I—Egyptian Pharaoh
(663-610 B.C.), military leader.—86

Ptolemy (Claudius Ptolemaeus) (2nd
cent.)—Greek mathematician, as-
tronomer and geographer.—60

Ptolemy Lagi (Ptolemy I) (c. 360-283
B.C.)—general under Alexander of
Macedon, ruler (from 323) and
then King of Hellenistic Egypt (305-
285 B.C.).—88, 293

Puchner, Anton, Baron (1779-1852)—
Austrian general, fought against revolutionary Hungary in 1848-49.—
132

*Pugatcheff (Pugachov), Yemelian Iva-
novich* (c. 1742-1775)—leader of an
anti-feudal peasant and Cossack
uprising in Russia in 1773-75.—76

Puisaye, Joseph Geneviève, comte de
(1755-1827)—French general, royalist, a leader of the counter-revolutionary Chouan revolt (1793-97).—
215, 397

Pyrrhus (319-272 B.C.)—King of Epirus (307-302 and 296-272 B.C.), military leader.—99

Q

Quirini, Angelo Maria (1680-1755)—
Italian cardinal and writer.—278

R

*Raglan, Lord Fitzroy James Henry Somer-
set, Baron* (1788-1855)—British field
marshal, commander-in-chief of the
British army in the Crimea (1854-
55).—7, 17

Ramses II (Sesostris)—Egyptian Pharaoh (1317-1251 B.C.), military leader.—85

*Randon, Jacques Louis César Alexandre,
comte de* (1795-1871)—French general, Marshal of France from 1856;
Governor-General of Algeria (1851-
58).—69

Ranelagh, Thomas Heron John, Viscount
(b. 1812)—British army officer, took
part in the Volunteer movement.—
484-87, 505

Raphael Sanzio (Raffaello Santi) (1483-
1520)—Italian painter.—278

S

Sacken—see Osten-Sacken, Fabian Wilhelm von, Prince

Saint-Arnaud, Armand Jacques Leroy de Achille (1801-1854)—French general, Marshal of France from 1852, Bonapartist; took part in the conquest of Algeria in 1836-51; commander-in-chief of the French army in the Crimea in 1854.—17, 69, 213

Saint-Hilaire, Louis Vincent Joseph le Blond, comte de (1766-1809)—French general, fought in Napoleonic wars.—33

Saint-Priest, Guillaume Emmanuel Guignard, comte de (1776-1814)—French-born general in the service of Russia, fought against Napoleon.—183, 185

Saint Remy, Pierre Surirey de (c. 1650-1716)—French general, second in command of the French artillery from 1703.—195

Saladin (full name Salah-al-Din Yusuf ibn-Ayyub) (1138-1193)—Sultan of Egypt (1171-93), founder of the Ayyubid dynasty.—4

Sale, Sir Robert Henry (1782-1845)—British colonel, fought in the Afghan campaign of 1838-42.—47, 381, 384, 386, 388

Salles, Charles Marie, comte de (c. 1804-1858)—French general, took part in the conquest of Algeria in the 1830s-1850s.—213

Sallust (Gaius Sallustius Crispus) (86-c. 35 B.C.)—Roman historian.—98

Sands—British colonel, fought in the war of independence of the Spanish colonies in South America.—230

San Michele (Sanmicheli), Michele (1484-1559)—Italian architect and military engineer.—322, 324

Santa Cruz, Don Alvarez de Bassano, Marquis de (1526-1588)—Spanish admiral, commanded the Spanish navy in 1576-88.—167

Santander, Francisco de Paula (1792-1840)—Colombian general, fought in the war of independence of the Spanish colonies in South America, Vice-President of the United States of Colombia (1821-28), participant in the conspiracy against Bolivar.—227, 228, 229, 231

Savary, Anne Jean Marie René, duc de Rovigo (1774-1833)—French general and politician, Minister of Police (1810-14), Governor-General of Algeria (1831-33).—68

Saxe, Hermann Maurice, comte de (1696-1750)—Marshal of France and military writer.—20

Saxe-Coburg, Duke of—see Ernest III (Ernest Anton Karl Ludwig)

Scarlett, Sir James Yorke (1799-1871)—British general, took part in the Crimean war, adjutant-general in 1860.—486

Scharnhorst, Gerhard Johann David von (1755-1813)—Prussian general, War Minister (1807-10) and Chief of Staff (1807-13); reorganised the Prussian army; an organiser of the liberation struggle against Napoleonic rule.—174, 197

Scheither, Johann Bernhard (17th cent.)—German military engineer.—328

Schilder, Kaspar Gd.—lighterman, Robert Blum's stepfather.—391

Schiller, Johann Christoph Friedrich von (1759-1805)—German poet, dramatist, historian and philosopher.—81

Schlosser, Friedrich Christoph (1776-1861)—German historian, democrat.—394, 398

British army officer, served in the engineers in the 1850s.—498

Soojah Shah (d. 1842)—Shah of Afghanistan (1803-09 and 1839-41); henchman of the British.—43-45, 46, 48, 380-84, 385-87, 389-90

Sorbier, Jean Barthélemy (1762-1827)—French general, commander of the guards artillery in 1810-12.—254

Soult, Nicolas Jean de Dieu, duc de Dalmatie (1769-1851)—Marshal of France and statesman; commanded the French forces in Spain in 1808-14; War Minister (1830-34 and 1840-45), Minister of Foreign Affairs (1839-40) and Prime Minister (1832-34, 1839-40 and 1840-47).—10-11, 151, 152, 173, 211, 269, 270, 273

Spearman—British army officer, reorganised British field artillery in the early 19th cent.—199, 201

Speckle (Specklin), Daniel (1536-1589)—German military engineer, a founder of bastion fortification.—318, 325-28, 329-32, 333

Steger, Friedrich (1811-1874)—German writer, historian and publisher.—391, 392

Steinberg—see *Bennigsen, Amalie Luise*

Steinberg, Baron—Hanoverian ambassador to Vienna, father of Bennigsen's first wife.—76

Stewart, Charles William, Marquis (1778-1854)—British general and diplomat.—156

Stoddart, Charles (1806-1842)—British army officer and diplomat; in 1838 was appointed envoy to Bukhara where he was killed.—382

Stone, Charles Pomeroy (1824-1887)—American general, commanded the Union troops in Virginia in 1861, convicted of high treason after their defeat at Bols Bluff in October 1861; released at the end of 1862.—531

Struensee, Karl August von (1735-1804)—Prussian mathematician, economist and statesman.—197

Suchet, Louis Gabriel, duc d'Albufera da Valencia (1770-1826)—Marshal of France, fought in the Peninsular war (1808-14).—470

Suchtelen, Pyotr Kornilovich (1751-1836)—Russian general and diplomat, Dutch by birth; commanded the siege of the Sveaborg fortress in 1808; ambassador to Stockholm from 1809.—155

Sucre, Antonio Josè de (1795-1830)—leader in the war of independence of the Spanish colonies in South America, supporter of Bolivar, President of Bolivia (1826-28).—170, 230

Suwaroff (Suvorov), Alexander Vasilyevich, Count Suvorov Rimniksky, Prince Italiisky (1729 or 1730-1800)—Russian field marshal and military theorist.—76

T

Tallard, Camille d'Hostun, duc de (1652-1728)—Marshal of France, fought in the war of the Spanish Succession.—249, 250

Talleyrand-Périgord, Charles Maurice de (1754-1838)—French diplomat; Foreign Minister (1797-99, 1799-1807 and 1814-15); France's representative at the Vienna Congress (1814-15).—150, 157, 396

Tamerlane (or Timur) (1336-1405)—Central Asian military leader and conqueror, founder of a vast state in Asia with Samarkand as its capital.—42

Tamisier, François Laurent Alphonse (1809-1880)—French army officer and military inventor.—440

Tartaglia (Tartalea), Nicolò (c. 1499-

manded the forces that attacked the rear of Napoleon I's retreating army.—51, 155

Tshen-byoo-Myayen—see Bayinnaung

Tuam, Archbishop of—see Beresford, William

Tutchkoff (Tuchkov), Nikolai Alexeyevich (1761-1812)—Russian general, fought against Napoleon.—252, 253

U

Ufano, Diego de (16th-early 17th cent.)—Spanish military engineer.—192

Urban, Karl, Baron von (1802-1877)—Rumanian colonel, later lieutenant field marshal in the service of Austria; Right-wing leader of the national movement in Transylvania; fought against revolutionary Hungary in 1848-49.—132

V

Vallière, Jean Florent de (1667-1759)—French general, artillery commander in 1720-47.—197

Vandamme, Dominique René, comte d'Unebourg (1770-1830)—French general, fought in Napoleonic wars.—51

Vasiltchikoff, Larion Vasilyevich (c. 1777-1847)—Russian general, fought against Napoleon.—253

Vauban, Sébastien Le Prêtre (Prestre) de (1633-1707)—Marshal of France, military engineer, economist; worked out a method of fortification and siege.—54, 192, 267, 268, 319, 326, 328-31, 335, 337, 338

Vécsey, Károly, Count (1807-1849)—Hungarian general, fought in the revolutionary war of 1848-49.—133

Vega, Georg, Baron von (1756-1802)—Austrian army officer and mathematician.—197

Vegetius (Flavius Vegetius Renatus) (late 4th cent.)—Roman military writer.—103

Victor (Victor-Perrin), Claude Victor Perrin (1764-1841)—French general, Marshal of France from 1807; fought in Napoleonic wars.—174, 181, 183, 184

Victoria (1819-1901)—Queen of Great Britain and Ireland (1837-1901).—523

Villemarest, Charles Maxime de (1785-1852)—French man of letters.—84, 396

Vitkievicz (Vitkevich), Ivan Viktorovich (c. 1810-1839)—Russian army officer, diplomatic representative in Afghanistan (1837-38).—379

Voirol, Théophile, baron (1781-1853)—French general; Governor-General of Algeria (1833-34).—68

Völker (17th cent.)—Dutch military engineer.—328

W

Wade, Sir Claude Martine (1794-1861)—British army officer, served in India, fought in colonial wars.—381

Waldersee, Friedrich Gustav, Count (1795-1864)—Prussian general and military writer, War Minister (1854-58).—508-10, 513-14, 516

Wallenstein, Albrecht Wenzel Eusebius von, Duke (1583-1634)—general in the Thirty Years' War, commanded the forces of the German Emperor in 1618-30 and 1632-34; born in Bohemia.—110

Wallinger—British army officer.—495

Wellesley, Richard, Colley, Marquis (1760-1842)—British statesman, Governor-General of India (1798-1805), Foreign Secretary (1809-12), Lord Lieutenant of Ireland (1821-28 and 1833-34).—219

INDEX OF LITERARY AND MYTHOLOGICAL NAMES

INDEX OF QUOTED AND MENTIONED LITERATURE

WORKS BY FREDERICK ENGELS

Army (this volume). In: *The New American Cyclopaedia,* Vol. II, 1858.—340

Brighton and Wimbledon (this volume). In: *The Volunteer Journal, for Lancashire and Cheshire,* No. 31, April 6, 1861.—490, 505

Fortification (this volume). In: *The New American Cyclopaedia,* Vol. VII, 1859.—206

The French Light Infantry (this volume). In: *The Volunteer Journal, for Lancashire and Cheshire,* Nos. 3, 5, 7, September 21, October 5 and 20, 1860; *Essays Addressed to Volunteers,* London-Manchester, 1861.—476

The History of the Rifle (this volume). In: *The Volunteer Journal, for Lancashire and Cheshire,* Nos. 9, 11, 14, 15, 17, 19, 20, November 3, 17, December 8, 15, 29, 1860, January 12, 19, 1861; *Essays Addressed to Volunteers,* London-Manchester, 1861.—436, 439, 442, 476

On the Moral Element in Fighting. By Marshal Bugeaud (this volume). In: *The Volunteer Journal, for Lancashire and Cheshire,* Nos. 23, 24, 26, February 9, 16, March 2, 1861.—514

Po and Rhine (present edition, Vol. 16)
— (anon.) *Po und Rhine,* Berlin, 1859.—407

A Review of English Volunteer Riflemen (this volume). In: *The Volunteer Journal, for Lancashire and Cheshire,* No. 2, September 14, 1860; *Essays Addressed to Volunteers,* London-Manchester, 1861.—409, 476
— *Eine Musterung englischer freiwilliger Jäger (Correspondenz aus Manchester).* In: *Allgemeine Militär-Zeitung,* No. 36, September 8, 1860.—407, 409

Savoy, Nice and the Rhine (present edition, Vol. 16)
— *Savoyen, Nizza und der Rhein, Vom Verfasser von "Po und Rhine",* Berlin, 1860.—408

Volunteer Artillery (this volume). In: *The Volunteer Journal, for Lancashire and Cheshire,* No. 6, October 13, 1860; *Essays Addressed to Volunteers,* London-Manchester, 1861.—476

Volunteer Engineers: Their Value and Sphere of Action (this volume). In: *The Volunteer Journal, for Lancashire and Cheshire,* Nos. 12 and 13, November 24 and December 1, 1860; *Essays Addressed to Volunteers,* London-Manchester, 1861.—476

Volunteer Generals (this volume). In: *The Volunteer Journal, for Lancashire and Cheshire*, No. 28, March 16, 1861.—484, 485, 505

WORKS BY DIFFERENT AUTHORS

[Alghisi, G.] *Delle fortificationi di M. Galasso Alghisi da Carpi, architetto dell' eccellentiss. Signor duca di Ferrara. Libri tre, All' inuittissimo Imperatore Massimiliano Secondo, Cesare Augusto,* [Venetia,] 1570.—324

Allgemeines Theater-Lexikon oder Encyklopädie alles Wissenswerthen für Bühnenkünstler, Dilettanten und Theaterfreunde unter Mitwirkung der sachkundigsten Schriftsteller Deutschlands herausgegeben von R. Blum, K. Herlossohn, H. Marggraff, Bd. 1-7, Altenburg und Leipzig, 1839-42.—81, 392

Antoninus. *Itinerarum.*—259

Arrianus, Flavius. *The Anabasis, or Ascent of Alexander.*—159

[Aumale.] *Les Zouaves.* In: *Revue des deux Mondes,* t. IX, 15 Mars 1855, Paris. Signed V. de Mars.—427

[Bacon, R.] *Epistolae fratris Rogerii Baconis, de secretis operibus artis et naturae et de nullitate magiae,* Paris, 1542.—189

[Bem, J.] *Erfahrungen über die Congrevschen Brand-Raketen bis zum Jahre 1819 in der Königl. Polnischen Artillerie gesammelt und an Seine Kaiserliche Hoheit den Grossfürst Constantin, General en Chef aller Königl. Polnischen Truppen, berichtet von Joseph Bem, Hauptmann in der Königl. Polnischen reitenden Artillerie,* Weimar, 1820.—130
— *O machinach parowych,* Tom I, Lwów, 1829.—131

Bernhardi, Th. von. *Denkwürdigkeiten aus dem Leben des kaiserl. russ. Generals von der Infanterie Carl Friedrich Grafen von Toll,* Zweiter Band, Leipzig, 1856.—255

[Berthier, L. A.] *Mémoires du Maréchal Berthier, prince de Neuchatel et de Wagram, Major-Général des Armées Françaises. Campagne d'Égypte,* Ire Partie, Paris, 1827.—59

Bible
The Old Testament
Numbers.—263
Ezekiel.—87

Biographie des célébrités militaires des armées de terre et de mer de 1789 à 1850, par M. C. Mullié, membre de l'université, de la société nationale de Lille, de la commission du Département du Nord, de l'institut historique, et auteur des fastes de la France, etc., Tome Premier, Paris—"Brune".—217, 401

Biographie universelle (Michaud) ancienne et moderne, ou histoire, par ordre alphabétique, de la vie publique et privée de tous les hommes qui se sont fait remarquer par leurs écrits, leurs actions, leurs talents, leurs vertus ou leurs crimes. Nouvelle édition, publiée sous la direction de M. Michaud. Paris, 1854, t. 5, 6
— t. 5—"Bourrienne".—394, 396
— t. 6—"Brune".—217, 400, 401

Biringoccio, V. *Pirotechnia,* Venetia, 1540.—192

[Blücher, G. L. von.] *Kampagne-Journal der Jahre 1793 und 1794, angefertiget von G. L. von Blücher,* [Berlin,] 1796.—173

Blum, R. *Staatslexikon für das deutsche Volk*, Leipzig, 1848.—392
— *Weihnachtsbaum.*—392

[Böckh, A.] *Die Staatshaushaltung der Athener, vier Bücher von August Böckh.* Mit einundzwanzig Inschriften. Erster Band, Berlin, 1817.—91

Boniface, L. *Paris, 29 janvier.* In: *Le Constitutionnel*, No. 30, January 30, 1859.—466

[Bourrienne, L. A. F. de.] *Mémoires de M. de Bourrienne, Ministre d'État, sur Napoléon, le directoire, le consulat, l'empire et la restauration*, t. I-X, Paris, 1829.—84, 157, 394, 396

Brune, G. M. A. *Voyage pittoresque et sentimental dans plusieurs provinces occidentales de la France*, Paris, 1788.—397

[Bugeaud de la Piconnerie, Th. R.] *L'Algérie. Des moyens de conserver et d'utiliser cette conquête, par le Général Bugeaud, Gouverneur-Général de l'Algérie*, Paris, 1842.—214
— *Aperçus sur quelques détails de la guerre, avec des planches explicatives; par M. Bugeaud, Marechal-de-Camp*, Paris, 1832.—469-75, 514
— *De la colonisation de l'Algérie*, Paris, 1847. Signed Duc d'Isly.—214
— *De l'établissement de légions de colons militaires dans les possessions françaises du nord de l'Afrique, suivi d'un projet d'ordonnance adressé au gouvernement et aux chambres; par M. Bugeaud, Lieutenant-Général*, Paris, 1838.—214
— *Mémoire sur notre établissement dans la province d'Oran, par suite de la paix; par M. le Lieutenant-Général Bugeaud (Juillet 1837)*, Paris, 1838.—214
— [Remark in the Chamber of Deputies on January 25, 1834.] In: *Le Moniteur universel*, No. 26 (first supplement), January 26, 1834.—212

[Busca, G.] *Della architettura militare di Gabriello Busca milanese*, Primo libro, Con privilegio, Milano, 1601.—324
— *Della espugnatione, et difesa delle fortezze. Di Gabriello Busca milanese*, Libri Due, Turino, 1585.—324

Cambridge, Duke of. [Speech at the regimental dinner of London Rifle Brigade in St. James's Hall, April 13, 1861.] In: *The Times*, No. 23907, April 15, 1861.—500

Certaine Advertisements out of Ireland, concerning the losses and distresses happened to the Spanish Navie, upon the west coastes of Ireland, in their voyage intended from the Northerne Isles beyond Scotland, towards Spaine, London, 1588.—168

[Clausewitz, C. von.] *Vom Kriege.* In: *Hinterlassene Werke des Generals Carl von Clausewitz über Krieg und Kriegführung*, Zweiter Band, Berlin, 1833.—234

Coehorn, M. *Nieuwe Vestingbouw*, Leeuwarden, 1685.—268

Conde, J. A. *Historia de la dominacion de los Arabes en España, sacada de varios manuscritos y memorias arabigas*, t. I-III, Madrid, 1820-21.—189

[Cormontaigne, Louis de.] *Architecture militaire, ou l'art de fortifier*, Première Partie, La Haye, 1741.—54

Ctesias. *Indian History.*—189

Details of the English Force Assembled to Oppose the Spanish Armada, MS.—167

[Ducoudray Holstein.] *Histoire de Bolivar, par le Général Ducoudray Holstein; continuée jusqu'à sa mort par Alphonse Viollet*, t. 1-2, Paris, 1831.—233
— *Memoirs of Simon Bolivar, President Liberator of the Republic of Colombia; and of His Principal Generals; comprising a Secret History of the Revolution, and the*

— Bd. 4, 1845: "Blücher".—172, 174
— Bd. 6, 1843: "Bülow".—402-03
— Zweiter Supplement-Band, 1853: "Blum".—391-93

Miller, J. *Memoirs of General Miller, in the Service of the Republic of Peru*, Vols. I-II, London, 1828-29.—220, 233

[Montalembert, M. R.] *La fortification perpendiculaire, ou essai sur plusieurs manières de fortifier la ligne droite, le triangle, le quarré, & tous les polygônes, de quelqu'étendue qu'en soient les côtés, en donnant à leur défense une direction perpendiculaire.* Tome premier, Paris, 1776.—333

Morla, T. de. *Tratado de artillería.* T. 1-3, Segovia, 1784-86.—197

Müffling, Fr. F. K. *Passages from My Life; Together with Memoirs of the Campaign of 1813 and 1814.* Edited, with Notes, by Colonel Philip Yorke, F. R. S. Second edition, revised, London, 1853.—174, 176, 180

M'Murdo. [Address to volunteers at Wimbledon on April 1, 1861.] In: *The Times*, No. 23896, April 2, 1861.—488-89, 490

Napier, W. F. P. *History of the War in the Peninsula and in the South of France, from the Year 1807 to the Year 1814* (in 6 vols), Vol. III, London, 1831.—304, 526

Napoleon I. *Mémoires pour servir à l'histoire de France, sous Napoléon, écrits à Sainte-Hélène, par les généraux qui ont partagé sa captivité, et publiés sur les manuscrits entièrement corrigés de la main de Napoléon*, Paris, 1823.—51, 78, 311, 510

[Neubauer.] *Discursus et verae architecturae militaris praxis, durch Neubauer, Oberstlieutenant der Artillerie- und Ingenieur-Kunst*, Stargard, 1679.—328

[Niebuhr, C.] *C. Niebuhrs Reisebeschreibung nach arabien und andern umliegenden Ländern*, Zweyter Band, Kopenhagen, 1778.—23

[Paravey, Ch. H. de.] *Mémoire sur la découverte très-ancienne en Asie et dans l'Indo-Perse de la poudre à canon et des armes à feu, par M. le Chevalier de Paravey, ancien inspecteur de l'École Polytechnique*, Paris, 1850.—188

Paz Salas, P. de. *La felicissima armada*, Lisboa, 1588.—166

Polybius. *Histories.*—345

[Príncipe, M. A., Giron, R., Satorres, R., Ribot, A.] *Espartero: Su pasado, su presente, su porvenir*, Madrid, 1848.—171

Ronge, J. [The open letter to Bishop Arnoldi, dated October 16, 1844.]—392

Rosetti, D. *Fortificatione a rovescio*, Torino, 1678.—324

Rouvroy, F. G. *Dynamische Vorstudien zu einer Theorie der gezogenen Feuerwaffen von W. H. Rouvroy, Generalleutnant und Commandant der königlich sächsischen Artillerie*, Dresden, 1858.—197
— *Handbuch des Batteriebaues oder die Anlegung und Erbauung der Batterien beim Angriff fester Plätze*, Leipzig, 1809.—197

— *Vorlesungen über die Artillerie zum Gebrauch der königlich sächsischen Artillerie-Akademie von F. G. Rouvroy, Directeur der Artillerie-Akademie und Major im Königl. Artillerie-Korps*, Th. 1-3, Dresden, 1811-14.—197

[Saint-Rémy, P. S. de.] *Mémoires d'artillerie, Recueillis par le Sr Surirey de Saint Remy, Commissaire Provincial de l'Artillerie, et l'un des Cent et un Officiers Privilégiez de ce Corps*, t. 1-2, Paris, 1697.—195

Sallust, Gaius Sallustius Crispus. *Jugurthine War.*—98

Scharnhorst, G. von. *Handbuch der Artillerie*, Bd. 1-3, Hannover, 1804-14.—197
— *Handbuch für Officiere, in den anwendbaren Theilen der Krieges-Wissenschaften*, Hannover, 1787.—197

Scheither, J. B. *Novissima praxis militaris*, Braunschweig, 1672.—328

Schlosser, Fr. Chr. *Zur Beurtheilung Napoleon's und seiner neusten Tadler und Lobredner, besonders in Beziehung auf die Zeit von 1800-1813*, Frankfurt am Main, 1835.—394

Schmerling, A. [Speech in the German National Assembly on November 17, 1848.] In: *Stenographischer Bericht über die Verhandlungen der deutschen constituirenden Nationalversammlung zu Frankfurt am Main*, Fünfter Band, Frankfurt am Main, 1848.—393

Speckle, D. *Architectura von Vestungen*, Strassburg, 1589.—318

Steger, Fr. *Ergänzungs-Conversationslexikon*, Erster Band, Leipzig, 1846
— "Robert Blum".—391-92

Stern, D. *Histoire de la révolution de 1848*, Paris, 1850.—213

Struensee, K. A. *Anfangsgründe der Artillerie*, Liegnitz, 1760.—197

[Tartalea, N.] *Quesiti, et inventioni di verse de Nicolò Tartalea Brisciano*, Venezia, 1554.—323

[Tempelhof, G. F. von.] *Le bombardier prussien ou du mouvement des projettiles en supposant la résistance de l'air proportionelle au quarré des vitesses par Mr. Tempelhof, Capitaine d'Artillerie au service de sa Majesté le Roi de Prusse*, Berlin, 1781.—197

Trotha, von. *Beitrag zur Erörterung der Frage: Welchen nothwendigen Einfluss haben die jetzt gebräuchlichen weittragenden Handfeuerwaffen auf das Gefecht der Infanterie?* Wittenberg, 1857.—363

Vega, G. *Praktische Anweisung zum Bombenwerfen mittelst dazu eingerichteter Hilfstafeln*, Wien, 1787.—197

Vegetius, Flavius Renatus. *Epitome Institutorum Rei Militaris.*—103

[Waldersee, F. G.] *Die französische Armee auf dem Exercirplatze und im Felde. Mit einem Rückblick auf den Feldzug in Italien im Jahre 1859. Von einem alten Offizier*, Berlin, 1861.—508-16

Wigand's Conversations-Lexikon. Für alle Stände. Von einer Gesellschaft deutscher Gelehrten bearbeitet, Erster Band, Leipzig, 1846.
— *"Algier".*—68

Wilkinson, J. G. *Manners and Customs of the Ancient Egyptians, Including Their Private Life, Government, Laws, Arts, Manufactures, Religion, and Early History; Derived from a Comparison of the Paintings, Sculptures, and Monuments Still Existing, with the Accounts of Ancient Authors.* In three volumes, Vol. I, London, 1837.—86

Yule, H. *A Narrative of the Mission Sent by the Governor-General of India to the Court of Ava in 1855, with Notices of the Country, Government, and People,* London, 1858.—280, 284, 286

Zastrow, A. von. *Geschichte der beständigen Befestigung oder Handbuch der vorzüglichsten Systeme und Manieren der Befestigungskunst,* Leipzig, 1854.—330

DOCUMENTS

Actes relatifs à l'évacuation de la Hollande par les troupes sous le commandement de S. A. R. le duc d'York, et capitulation conclue en son nom, par le général Knox, avec le général Brune, le 18 octobre 1799. In: G. F. Martens, *Recueil des principaux Traités d'Alliance, de Paix, de Trêve, de Neutralité...,* t. VI, 1795-1799, Gottingue, 1829.—216, 399

Almanach de Gotha. Annuaire diplomatique et statistique pour l'année 1861: "Armée française en 1860-1861".—465-66

Armistice conclu entre les puissances belligérantes, à Pleiswitz le 5 juin 1813. In: G. F. Martens, *Nouveau Recueil de Traités d'Alliance, de Paix, de Trêve, de Neutralité...,* t. I, 1808-1814, Gottingue, 1817, pp. 582-83.—156

Armistice entre les troupes françaises et suédoises conclu à Schlatkow, le 18 avr. 1807. In: G. F. Martens, *Recueil des principaux Traités d'Alliance, de Paix, de Trêve, de Neutralité...,* t. VIII, 1803-1808, Goettingue, 1835, pp. 694-95.—217, 400

[Airey, R.] *Opening Address of Major-General Sir Richard Airey, K. C. B., Quartermaster-General of the Forces. Before the Board of General Officers Assembled at the Royal Hospital, Chelsea. Together with His Summing-up Address, and a Written Memorandum Handed into the Board on Supplies of Camp Equipage,* London, 1856.—7

Allen, *Report on the Northern Frontier of Pegu,* dated 18th July, 1854. In: H. Yule, *A Narrative of the Mission Sent by the Governor-General of India to the Court of Ava in 1855, with Notices of the Country, Government, and People,* London, 1858.—284

An die Wiener [an address of the Left wing of the Frankfurt National Assembly]. In: *Wiener Zeitung,* No. 290, October 22, 1848.—82, 393

[Bernadotte.] *Adresse des citoyens composant la troisième division, commandée par le général Bernadotte, au directoire exécutif.* In: *Gazette nationale ou le moniteur universel,* No. 325, August 12, 1797.—150

— [The order of the day, July 7, 1809.] In: *Mémoires de M. de Bourrienne*, t. VIII, Paris, 1829.—153

Bolivar, S. *Decree by which Simon Bolivar assumed the dictatorial power... en Bogotá à 23 de noviembre de 1826.* In: Ducoudray Holstein, *Memoirs of Simon Bolivar, President Liberator of the Republic of Colombia...*, Vol. II, London, 1830, pp. 277-78. —231

— *Decree for the Provisional Government of Colombia. 27th August, 1828.* In: *British and Foreign State Papers. 1827-1828*, London, 1829, pp. 1196-1200.—231

— *Message of the Liberator President, on the Installation of the Constituent Congress of Colombia.—20th January, 1830.* In: *British and Foreign State Papers. 1829-1830*, London, 1832, pp. 1226-32.—232

— *Simon Bolivar, libérateur, président de la république, général en chef de l'armée, etc., etc., au très excellent seigneur don Miguel de la Torre, etc., etc.* In: *Mémoires du Général Morillo...*, Paris, 1826, pp. 441-43; Ducoudray Holstein, *Memoirs of Simon Bolivar*, Vol. II, London, 1830, pp. 164-68.—229

— [Proclamation of May 9, 1815.] In: Ducoudray Holstein, *Memoirs of Simon Bolivar...*, Vol. I, London, 1830, pp. 238-39.—224

— *Simon Bolivar, Supreme Chief, &c. &c. to the Inhabitants of Venezuela. Head-quarters, at Ocumare, July 6th, 1816.* In: Ducoudray Holstein, *Memoirs of Simon Bolivar...*, Vol. II, London, 1830, p. 6.—225

— *To the Inhabitants of the Plains. Head-quarters at Sombrero, 7th of February, 1818.* In: Ducoudray Holstein, *Memoirs of Simon Bolivar*, Vol. II, London, 1830, pp. 74-75.—226

[Bolivar, S. and Marinno, S.] *Arrival of Generals Bolivar and Marinno, and Exposition of the Motives which obliged them to leave Venezuela, and to seek a Refuge in New Granada, the 30th of September, 1814.* In: Ducoudray Holstein, *Memoirs of Simon Bolivar*, Vol. I, London, 1830, pp. 188-93.—223

Buonaparte, génerál en chef de l'armée d'Italie. In: *Gazette nationale ou le moniteur universel*, No. 305, July 23, 1797.—150

Capitulation de l'isle de Rugen, en date du 7 Sept. 1807. In: G. F. Martens, *Recueil des principaux Traités d'Alliance, de Paix, de Trêve, de Neutralité...*, t. VIII, 1803-1808, Goettingue, 1835, pp. 695-96.—217, 400

Capitulation de Ratkau, pour le corps du général Blucher; du 7 novembre 1806. In: G. F. Martens, *Recueil des principaux Traités d'Alliance, de Paix, de Trêve, de Neutralité..*, t. VIII, 1803-1808, Goettingue, 1835, pp. 545-46.—173

Constitution norvégienne, décretée par la Diète Extraordinaire.—Christiania, le 4 novembre 1814. In: *British and Foreign State Papers. 1812-1814*, Vol. I, Part II, London, 1841, pp. 926-42.—157

Constitution of the Republick of Colombia. Rosario de Cucuta, 30th August, 1821. In: *British and Foreign State Papers. 1821-1822*, London, 1829, pp. 698-723.—229

Convention arrêtée entre le citoyen Alex. Berthier, général en chef de l'armée françoise en Italie, et S. Excellence le baron de Mélas, général en chef de l'armée impériale en Italie, après la bataille de Marengo. In: G. F. Martens, *Recueil des principaux Traités d'Alliance, de Paix, de Trêve, de Neutralité*..., t. VII, 1800-1803, Gottingue, 1831, pp. 71-72.—57

Convention définitive entre les armées Anglaise et Française pour l'evacuation du Portugal par l'armée Française, signée à Lisbonne le 30. Août 1808. In: G. F. Martens, *Nouveau Recueil de Traités d'Alliance, de Paix, de Trêve, de Neutralité*..., t. I, 1808-1814, Gottingue, 1817, pp. 96-100.—289

Convention pour la prolongation de l'armistice du 5 Juin 1813 jusqu'au 10 Août, signée à Neumark en Silésie le 26/14 Juillet 1813. In: G. F. Martens, *Nouveau Recueil de Traités d'Alliance, de Paix, de Trêve, de Neutralité*..., t. I, 1808-1814, Gottingue, 1817, pp. 587-88.—156, 174

Correspondence relating to Persia and Affghanistan, London, 1839.—379

Elphinstone, G. W. K. [Letter to Macnaghten, dated November 6, 1841.] In: J. W. Kaye, *History of the War in Afghanistan,* London, 1851, Vol. II, p. 39.—387

Extrait des registres du Sénat-Conservateur.—Séance du dimanche 3 avril 1814, présidée par M. le sénateur comte Barthélemy. In: *Le Moniteur universel,* No. 94, April 4, 1814.—58, 217, 401

— *Séance du mercredi 6 avril 1814.* In: *Le Moniteur universel,* No. 98, April 8, 1814.—217, 401

Federative Act of the United Provinces of New Granada.—Santa Fé de Bogotà, 27th November, 1814. In: *British and Foreign State Papers. 1812-1814,* Vol. I, Part II, London, 1841, pp. 1069-89.—223

Frederick William II. *Disposition, wie sich die Officiere von der Cavallerie in einem Treffen gegen den Feind zu verhalten haben,* July 25, 1744.—301
— *Instruction für die Cavallerie im Falle eines Gefechts,* March 17, 1742.—301
— *Instruction für die Obersten und sämmtliche Officiere von Regimentern der Husaren,* March 21, 1742.—301

Frederic Guillaume III. *Proclamation du Roi de Prusse, de Guerre contre la France.—Breslau, le 17 mars 1813.* In: *British and Foreign State Papers. 1812-1814,* Vol. I, Part II, London, 1841, pp. 1042-43.—174

The Harleian Miscellany: A Collection of Scarce, Curious, and Entertaining Pamphlets and Tracts, etc. Vol. I, London, 1808.—168

[Letters to Bonaparte] In: *Gazette nationale ou le moniteur universel,* No. 325, August 12, 1797.—150

Macnaghten, W. H. [Letter to Major Rawlinson, dated April 20, 1841.] In: J. W. Kaye, *History of the War in Afghanistan,* Vol. I, London, 1851, pp. 620-21.—386

— [Letter to Robertson, dated August 20, 1841.] In: J. W. Kaye, *History of the War in Afghanistan*, Vol. I, London, 1851, pp. 602-03.—385

Napoleon I. *A Lyon, le 13 mars 1815* [a decree]. In: *Le Moniteur universel*, No. 80, March 21, 1815.—84, 396

Napoleon III. *Décret impérial concernant l'infanterie légère. 23 Novembre 1854.* In: *Collection complète des lois, décrets, règlements et avis du Conseil d'État, etc...* Par J. B. Duvergier, t. 54, année 1854, Paris [1856], pp. 547-48.—418
— [Speech in Bordeaux on October 9, 1852.]—466

Ordonnances sur l'Exercice et les Manoeuvres de l'Infanterie du 4 Mars 1831.—419

Seconde convention Additionnelle d'Alliance entre la Suède et la Russie.—Segnée à Abo, le 30 Août, 1812. In: *British and Foreign State Papers. 1812-1814*, Vol. I, Part I, London, 1841, pp. 346-49.—156

Traité d'alliance entre S. M. le Roi de Prusse et S. M. l'Empereur des Français Roi d'Italie; signé à Paris le 24 févr. 1812. In: G. F. Martens, *Nouveau Recueil de Traités d'Alliance, de Paix, de Trêve, de Neutralité...*, t. I, 1808-1814, Gottingue, 1817, pp. 414-24.—174

Traité d'alliance offensive et défensive entre la Suède et la Russie.—Signé à St. Pétersbourg, le 5 avril 1812. In: *British and Foreign State Papers. 1812-1814*, Vol. I, Part I, London, 1841, pp. 306-13.—155

Traité d'armistice conclu entre les Chefs de l'armée royale espagnole et ceux de l'armée républicaine de Columbia, signé à Truxillo, le 25 novembre 1820. In: G. F. Martens, *Nouveau Recueil de Traités d'Alliance, de Paix, de Trêve, de Neutralité...*, t. V, 1808-1822, Gottingue, 1824, pp. 535-39.—229

Traité de concert et de subside entre S. M. Britannique et le Roi de Suède, signé à Stockholm le 3 mars 1813. In: G. F. Martens, *Nouveau Recueil de Traités d'Alliance, de Paix, de Trêve, de Neutralité...*, t. I, 1808-1814, Gottingue, 1817, pp. 558-63.—156

Traité entre le Général français Bugeaud et l'Emir Abd-el-Kader, conclu à Tafna dans la province d'Oran en Algérie, le 30 mai 1837 et ratifié par la France. In: G. F. Martens, *Nouveau Recueil de Traités d'Alliance, de Paix, de Trêve, de Neutralité...*, t. XV, 1830-1838, Goettingue, 1840, pp. 154-56.—212

Traité de paix entre Sa Majesté le Roi de Prusse et la République française, conclu et signé à Bâle, le 5 d'avril 1795. In: G. F. Martens, *Recueil des principaux Traités d'Alliance, de Paix, de Trêve, de Neutralité...*, t. VI, 1795-1799, Gottingue, 1829, pp. 45-48.—173

Traité de paix conclu à Campo-Formio, le 26 vendemiaire an 6 (17 oct. 1797) entre la République française et l'empereur, roi de Hongrie et de Bohême. In: G. F. Martens, *Recueil des principaux Traités d'Alliance, de Paix, de Trêve, de Neutralité...*, t. VI, 1795-1799, Gottingue, 1829, pp. 420-37.—150, 216

INDEX OF PERIODICALS

SUBJECT INDEX

A

GLOSSARY OF GEOGRAPHICAL NAMES [a]

Abo	Turku	Chuquisaca	Sucre
Aboukir	Bukyr	Coleah	Koléa
Åland	Ahvenanmaa	Comorn	Komárno
Alba Julia	Karlsburg,		(Komárom)
	Tepenec	Constantine	Konstantyna,
Aleppo (Haleb)	Aleppo or		Kasr Tina
	Halebes-Shabba	Constantinople	Istanbul
Alle	Lyna	Culm	Chlumec
Aquincum,		Dantzic (Danzig)	Gdansk, Gdańsk
Ofen	Budapest	Deichsel, Schnelle	
Arbela	Erbil	Deichsel	Skora
Arzew	Árzevna, Arzaw	Farsistan	Fars
Aufidus	Ofanto	Fischau	Fiszewo
Austerlitz	Slavkov	Frederikshamm	Hamina
Balch	Balkh	Friedland	Pravdinsk
Beni Sillem	Beni Sliman	Goldberg	Zlotoryje
Bidassoa	Baztán	Gorkum	Gorinchem
Bona	Annaba	Greifenhagen	Gryfino
Bougiah	Buddzsája, Bid-	Gzhatsk	Gagarin
	jaya, Bejaia		
Brescia	Brixia	Haynay, Haynau	Chojnów
Brünn	Brno	Heilsberg	Lidybark War-
Bunzelwitz	Boleslawice		miński
Carlsbad	Karlovy Vary	Hellespont	Dardanelles
Carniola	Kraina	Hermannstadt	Sibiu
Christiania	Oslo	Hohenfriedberg	Dobromierz

[a] This glossary includes geographical names occuring in Marx's and Engels' articles in the form customary in the press of the time but differing from the national names or from those given on modern maps. The left column gives geographical names as used in the original (when they differ from the national names of the time, the latter are given in brackets); the right column gives corresponding names as used on modern maps and in modern literature.— Ed.

Iglau	Jihlava	Oxys	Amu Darya
Insterburg	Csernyahovzk	Persia	Iran
Jaxartes	Syr Darya	Placentia	Piacenza
Julia Caesarea	Cherchell,	Prausnitz	Pruśnica
	Szerczel	Preussisch-Eylau	Bagrationovsk
Kandia	Iraclion	Ratisbona	Regensburg
Katzbach	Kocaba,	Reichenbach	Dzierzoniów
	Kaczawa	St. Jean d'Acre	Acca
Kock	Kozk	Schässburg	
Königsberg	Kaliningrad	(Segesvar)	Sighişoara
Krieblowitz	Krobielowice	Schweidnitz	Swidnica
Kroitsch	Krotoszyce,	Siam	Thailand
	Krotoszyn	Sommepuis	Sommepuits
Kunersdorf	Kunowice	Stettin	Szczecin
Kunzendorf	Drogoslaw,	Striegau	Strzegom
	Mokrzeszów	Sund	Oeresund
Küstrin	Kostrzyn	Sweaborg	
Laibach	Ljubljana	(Sveaborg)	Suomenlinna
Lemberg, Lvow,		Temesvár	Timişoarä,
Lwów	Lvov		Timişoara
Leuthen	Lutynia	Thorn	Torún
Lycus	Gt Zab	Ticinus	Tessin
Marienwerder	Kwidzyn	Tilsit	Sovetsk
Marignano	Melegnano	Tirlemon	Tienen
Mohrungen	Morag	Tlemcen, Tlem-	
Mollwitz	Malujowice	sen	Talmacan
Mostaganem	Musztagánem	Trachenberg	Zmigród
Mykale	Samsan Dagh	Urogne	Urrugne
Napoli di Roma-		Vahlstadt, Wahl-	
nia	Nauplia	statt	Legnickie Pole
Neisse	Nysa	Vilna, Wilna	Vilnius
Niedercrayn	Krain, Krajów	Wartenburg	Gartenberg
Nimeguen, Nim-		Zaab	Saab, Zab
megen	Nijmegen	Zarrah	Gaud-i Zirreh
Ofen, Buda	Budapest	Zorndorf	Sarbinowo

The English-language edition of the *Collected Works* of Marx and Engels, which is a joint publication of Lawrence & Wishart Ltd., London, International Publishers Co. Inc., New York, and Progress Publishers and the Institute of Marxism-Leninism, Moscow, will include all the works of Karl Marx and Frederick Engels published in their lifetime and a considerable part of their legacy of manuscripts as well as their letters.

The whole edition is planned to comprise fifty volumes, organised into three main groups: (1) philosophical, historical, political, economic and other works, in chronological order; (2) Marx's *Capital,* with his preliminary versions and works directly connected with it, particularly the Economic Manuscripts of 1857-58, better known under the editorial heading *Grundrisse der Kritik der Politischen Ökonomie;* (3) letters of Marx and Engels after they began to work together (August 1844).

The earlier volumes will appear in numerical order. Thereafter the sequence of publication of volumes will not necessarily follow the numerical order in the series.

Previously published translations of works of Marx and Engels will be checked and revised for this edition. Many works are, however, being translated into English for the first time. Articles by Marx and Engels written in English for the British and American press of their day will in many cases be republished in English for the first time.